The Crisis of the Negro Intellectual

The Crisis of the Negro Intellectual

BY

Harold Cruse

Quill
New York 1984

Copyright 1967 by Harold Cruse
First and expanded 1984 by James McPherson and Frederic Watson

All rights reserved. No part of this book may be reproduced or utilized in any form or by any means, electronic or mechanical, including photocopying, recording, or by any information storage and retrieval system, without permission in writing from the Publisher. Inquiries should be addressed to William Morrow and Company, Inc., 105 Madison Avenue, New York, N.Y. 10016.

Library of Congress Cataloging in Publication

ISBN 0-688-03886-9
ISBN 0-688-03886-9 (pbk.)

Printed in the United States of America

First Quill Edition

1 2 3 4 5 6 7 8 9 10

Library of Congress Catalog Card Number: 84-60206

ISBN: 0-688-01390-2
ISBN: 0-688-03886-7(pbk)

Printed in the United States of America

First Quill Edition

1 2 3 4 5 6 7 8 9 10

Contents

I

II

III

IV

V

VI

Foreword

The Crisis of the Negro Intellectual, Harold Cruse's strikingly original analysis of twentieth-century black intellectuals, is as directly relevant to understanding the black condition today as it was to the late 1960s when first published. Indeed, reread today it continues to clarify the unfinished intellectual and political agendas still before the Afro-American community.

In the decade and a half since its first appearance, the *Crisis* has established itself as one of the most intellectually provocative and authoritative works of American social criticism published during the tumultuous decade of the 1960s. Unlike so many other controversial books of that politically charged period—expressions of the times rather than analyses of them—Cruse's work provided a model of what could be achieved by black scholars. It attacked the extreme present-mindedness of the period, and was itself rooted in the historical antecedents of the black movement, while simultaneously providing a penetrating sociological analysis of contemporary groups and personalities. As a consequence, it still speaks to the issues and audiences of the 1980s and 1990s with the same acuity that it showed for earlier readers, while other works have faded into obscurity. Historian Christopher Lasch wrote in a prescient evaluation of the book that "when all the manifestos and polemics of the Sixties are forgotten, this book will survive as a monument of historical analysis."

The lasting impact of the book derives in large measure from the interaction of its unusual structure, the originality of its arguments, and the needs it answers in its readers. The structure of the book is simultaneously social commentary, biography, historical essays, and political analysis. This has helped ensure its appeal to a wide audience. Many of its chapters, such as those on Lorraine Hansberry and on *Freedomways Magazine* for example,

i

can profitably be read as freestanding essays in their own right.

The critical, iconoclastic stance of the book is informed by an intelligence writing from a unique perspective—not only one independent of the familiar camps of traditional mainstream Negro organizations like the NAACP or the Urban League, but also apart from the organized critics of orthodox Marxism or radical black nationalism. Cruse stood apart, and few were spared as he took on established positions across the political spectrum.

Also, the original audience of the book was the informed lay reader, particularly the black intellectual. It was especially directed to those "creative intellectuals" (journalists, novelists, editors, critics, etc.) whom Cruse identified as bearing the historic communal responsibility for the cultural and intellectual leadership of black Americans. In the 1960s, a time in the United States that was even more anti-intellectual than usual, this critical independence seemed especially audacious, because among other tasks the author forcefully insisted on the imperatives of careful if committed reflection.

Even through today's more quiescent optic the book seems special, written as it was before the unfortunate overprofessionalization and bureaucratization of so much of intellectual life. One fears that the nonacademic "free-floating" intellectual, like Cruse in the 1960s, is destined to disappear altogether. Yet Cruse was not trying to score points with his counterparts in academia. He deliberately chose as his audience the actual and aspiring progressive black intellectuals who might heed his warnings and avoid the pitfalls of the past. For what he attempted was simultaneously a critique and synthesis of prevailing intellectual practices, and a call to arms around a new approach to resolve the important unfinished business of black intellectuals.

These features of structure, audience, and argument alone would have given the book lasting historical interest. Since so much of the social reality that Cruse described remains with us today, however, the *Crisis* can also be read as a guide for cultural politics in the 1980s. Its contemporary relevance has been ensured by the continuing crisis of the black race in America. While one cannot deny that there have been impressive and in many ways profound changes in race relations over the past twenty years, neither can one deny the equally massive continuities. Many of the old problems of economy and culture are still with us, and new ones have come to the surface that are, in many ways, even more perplexing and difficult to resolve.

For, unseen at the time, in tandem with the long-sought gains of the Civil Rights Movement there also came a sense of loss of community. This was as true for the black intellectual (indeed, perhaps even more true in some respects) as it was for the community as a whole. Ironically perhaps, but with exactly the kind of irony that Cruse so masterfully dissects for us, as the *number* of professionally trained black intellectuals has grown, there has been a parallel lessening of a collective sense of common experience, common purpose, and perhaps even common commitment. Larger numbers have proven no automatic guarantee of more wisdom or better analysis. And unfortunately this dissipation occurs exactly when the intellectual tasks ahead are enormous, precipitated by the badly deteriorating economic standing and social fabric of working-class black communities, and worsened by the apparent failures of conventional political remedies.

Where does the *Crisis* fit in the intellectual and cultural history of black America? Should the book be read, as some commentators have suggested, as no more than a hypercritical outpouring of bitterness because its author was considered, as Cruse himself has written elsewhere, a "glaring intellectual misfit—an incomprehensible gadfly to some, and a pretentious neophyte to others . . . "? While there is widespread agreement over the book's importance, there also has been criticism of particular aspects that affect one's overall evaluation of the book. For, as with any truly original work, the *Crisis* engendered sharp reactions when it first appeared. Indeed, serious students of black America will want to take note, as Cruse himself did after the book's publication, of the points raised by early critics of the *Crisis*. Writers like Julian Mayfield and Robert Chrisman, for instance, were pointed in their criticism of key aspects of the work. Such challenges did not detract from the book's genuine merit, however, as both Mayfield and Chrisman conceded. Indeed, the critiques ensured that this book, like its historical predecessors, would be the center of long-lasting political and cultural debates.

We believe that the book rightfully stands in a long and honorable succession of intellectual landmarks in Afro-American social thought. Many of these landmark works share with the *Crisis* its spirit of independent analysis, its iconoclastic disregard for the popular pieties of the time, and its debunking of the self-legitimations of the dominant personalities, institutions, and practices of a period. We can find expressions of this "iconoclastic tradition" in the contributions to modern Afro-American intellectual history made by W.E.B. Du Bois's cogent and lyrical *The Souls of Black Folk*, published in the third year of this century; by the collective manifesto of the Harlem Renaissance, *The New Negro*, edited by Alain Locke and published in the mid-twenties; by Carter G. Woodson's biting historical critique of educational practices, *The Mis-Education of the Negro*, in the early 1930s; by the innovative literary works and cultural essays of Richard Wright in the forties and fifties, of Ralph Ellison in the fifties and the sixties, of James Baldwin and LeRoi Jones—Amiri Baraka in the sixties; or by central works of sociological criticism like E. Franklin Frazier's *Black Bourgeoisie*. Subsequent works by William J. Wilson and even Thomas Sowell continue this tradition of black iconoclastic inquiry. The *Crisis* in its structure and tone shares something of each of these works.

For Cruse, too, worked with perennial themes of black life in America. One such theme was the tension between radical and conservative wings of the intelligentsia. Generally speaking, disputes among black intellectuals in the post-Reconstruction era have revolved about ideological conflicts over the alternative survival strategies of protest and accommodation. As Cruse convincingly shows throughout the *Crisis*, these two positions are not fixed to any particular political orientation that can be permanently characterized as radical or conservative. Thus, for example, in the so-called Age of Booker T. Washington in the early twentieth century, Du Bois's protest orientation may be set over against Washington's accommodationist orientation as a struggle between radicalism and conservatism, respectively. Later in this century, however, as in the late 1960s when Cruse was writing the *Crisis*, protest on behalf of integration had become "conservative" while accommodation to existing arrangements on behalf of internal communal development had become "radical."

This historical lesson, that we look beneath the surface of what is ostensibly radical and what conservative, should be a useful lesson for today's intellectuals. Cruse writes that "American Negro history is basically a history of the conflict between integrationist and nationalist forces in politics, economics, and culture, no matter what leaders are involved and what slogans used" (p. 564).

In fact, Cruse urges us to move beyond the simple dichotomies of popular debate. The book can indeed be viewed as setting out an impressive list of intellectual tasks for those who would contribute to the ongoing enterprise that is black scholarship and racial advancement. The central tasks that Cruse sets out for would-be intellectuals are:

1. to familiarize themselves with their own intellectual antecedents and with previous political and cultural movements;

2. to analyze critically the bases for the pendulum swings between the two poles of integration and black nationalism, and try to synthesize them into a single and consistent analysis;

3. to identify clearly the political, economic, and cultural requisites for black advancement in order to meld them into a single politics of progressive black culture. This process requires greater attention both to Afro-American popular culture and to the macroeconomic, structural context of modern capitalism in which group culture either flourishes or atrophies;

4. to recognize the uniqueness of American conditions, and to insist that one incorporate this uniquenesss when studying numbers 1 through 3 above. Black intellectuals must at all costs avoid slavish borrowings or uncritical importations of ideologies and strategies from other continents or cultures, from other times, or even from other ethnic groups in the United States. The Afro-American experience is unique, and the irrevocable imperative of cultural self-definition demands that it be treated as such.

Yet who is to carry out these difficult tasks? A key question raised but not systematically explored by Cruse is, who are to be the new standard-bearers for the difficult tasks ahead? Will it be black youth in general? This is the question Robert Allen asked of Cruse in his own work, *Black Awakening in Capitalist America.* Which segment of the politically ambivalent and economically weak middle class, or the small intelligentsia, is most likely to serve progressive black causes?

This question is exceedingly important today, with a new half-generation, now sixteen years old, that was not yet born when the book was first published. These youths have directly experienced neither the indignities and the solidarities of enforced racial segregation, nor the searing emotional imperatives and political commitments of the racial rebellions of the 1960s. This fact of demographics and history may make this rising generation of black intellectuals quite unlike its predecessors. As a consequence, perhaps, *The Crisis of the Negro Intellectual* needs to be read now more than ever.

Harold Cruse closes his book with the words of philosopher George Santayana, the teacher of Du Bois: "Those who cannot remember the past are condemned to repeat it." In this decade and a half of nearly unprecedented social change and its attendant historical discontinuities, the message of this book remains painfully apt today. We ignore its lessons at our peril. The crisis of the Afro-American intellectual has yet to be resolved.

BAZEL E. ALLEN   ERNEST J. WILSON III
Program in American Culture   Political Science Department

University of Michigan
Ann Arbor
January, 1984

The Crisis of the Negro Intellectual

I

Individualism and the "Open Society"

In 1940, as one of my first acts in the pursuit of becoming a more "social" being, I joined a YMCA amateur drama group in Harlem. I wanted to learn about theater so I became a stage technician —meaning a handyman for all backstage chores. But the first thing about this drama group that struck me as highly curious was the fact that all the members were overwhelmingly in favor of doing white plays with Negro casts. I wondered why and very naïvely expressed my sentiments about it. The replies that I got clearly indicated that these amateur actors were not very favorable to the play about Negro life, although they would not plainly say so. Despite the fact that this question of identity was first presented to me within the context of the program of a small, insignificant amateur drama group, its implications ranged far beyond. A theater group, no matter how small, must have an audience. What did the audience at the Harlem YMCA really think about the group's productions?

Although I continued to work with this group, my preoccupation with its aesthetic values inevitably led me toward a consideration of other, related, social issues peculiar to Harlem. Thus began my first steps toward a long process of social enlightenment. Life was quite complicated and there were no simple answers for anything.

Harlem in 1940 was just beginning to emerge from the depths of the Great Depression and it seethed with the currents of many conflicting beliefs and ideologies. It was the year in which Richard Wright reached the high point of his literary fame, with *Native Son,* and was often seen in Harlem at lectures. The American Negro Theater, a professional experimental group, was preparing to make its 1941 debut as a permanent Harlem institution. The Federal Theater Project had been abolished in 1939 and the echoes of that disaster were still being heard in Harlem's cultural

3

circles. Everything in Harlem seemed to be in a state of flux for reasons I was not then able to fully appreciate. But soon came the war and I was caught up in the army for four-and-a-half years. I returned with a radically altered vision to find that although Harlem had the same old problems, it had a new community consciousness. Hence, I could see these old problems from a new point of view. Indeed, what I have learned about Harlem since 1946 is pretty much summed up in this book.

I have attempted to define what a considerable body of Negroes have thought and expressed on a less analytic and articulate level. I do not claim to represent the thinking of *all* the people in America who are called Negroes, for Negroes are certainly divided into classes—a fact white liberals and radicals often overlook when they speak of "the Negro." There is, however, a broad strain of Negro social opinion in America that is strikingly cogent and cuts through class lines. This social outlook cannot be and never has been encompassed by the program of an organization such as the NAACP, whose implied definition of racial integration offers no answers to the questions that agitate the collective minds of those Negroes who reject such a philosophy. And yet, since it could never be said that such Negroes do not want social progress, what are they looking for that the NAACP does not offer?

To put the question in another way, and in better focus—although until recent years the NAACP has had the prestige of being the major civil rights organization—its membership, usually hovering somewhere between three hundred and fifty thousand and four hundred thousand—it can hardly be said to reflect the pervasive sentiment of an ethnic group as large and as hardpressed as the American Negro. In other words, there is a definite strain of thought within the Negro group that encompasses all the ingredients of "nationality" and strikes few sympathetic chords with the NAACP.

Historically, this "rejected strain," as Theodore Draper describes it, emerged simultaneously with its opposite—the racial integration strain—although the word "integration" was not then in the Negro vocabulary as a synonym for civil rights or freedom. The prototype leader of the latter strain was Frederick Douglass, the great Negro Abolitionist, and there is almost a direct line of development from him to the NAACP and the modern civil rights movement. However, the rejected, or nationality strain that exists today can be traced back to certain Negro spokesmen who were Douglass' contemporaries but who are now barely remembered—Martin R. Delany, Edward Blyden, Alexander Crummell, Henry M. Turner and George Washington Williams. Douglass, Booker T. Washington, Marcus Garvey and W.E.B. DuBois, on the other hand, are well known to the average Negro as historical personalities.

It is important to note that just prior to the Civil War there was conflict among Negroes over what would be the best course of action for the soon-to-be emancipated slaves. Should they return to Africa or emigrate to Latin America; or should they remain and struggle for racial equality in the United States (or seek to accomplish both at the same time)? As one historian has described this conflict:

> Some Negroes in America showed an interest in Africa before the 1860's—usually in the face of the criticism of the black abolitionists such as Frederick Douglass who considered the African dream a dangerous diversification of energies which were needed in the fight for emancipation and civil rights at home.[1]

This historian goes on to point out that "one of the major pre-Civil War Negro-American exponents of the 'Back-to-Africa' dream [was] Martin R. Delany, Harvard-trained physician and the first Negro to be commissioned with field rank by President Lincoln. . . . He visited Liberia in July, 1859, and saw in the proposed Liberian College 'a grand stride in the march of African Regeneration and Negro Nationality.' "[2] It was also in 1859 that Delany originated and used the phrase "Africa for the Africans." However, even most contemporary Black Nationalists believe that Marcus Garvey of the 1920's invented that slogan.

Thus it can be seen that the present-day conflict within the Negro ethnic group, between integrationist and separatists ten-

[1] George Shepperson, "Notes on Negro American Influences on the Emergence of African Nationalism," *Journal of African History.* 1. No. 2. 1960. p. 301.
[2] *Ibid.*, p. 301.

dencies, has its origins in the historical arguments between personalities such as Frederick Douglass and as Martin R. Delany.* Although the peculiar social conditions and race relations in America have made it possible for the Frederick Douglass trend to be the more articulate and dominant up to now, this has not always been so; and it does not mean, moreover, that the opposite strain has become nonexistent. On the contrary, the emergence of the Malcolm X brand of nationalism proves its persistence, despite the fact that both strains have undergone considerable change and qualification. In fact, with W.E.B. DuBois they nearly merged into a new synthesis, for DuBois, in addition to being a founder of the NAACP integrationist trend, was also a leading exponent of the Pan-Africanism that had its origins with Martin R. Delany.

Throughout my adult life I have observed that the ideas of one particular stratum of Negroes on such questions as race, color, politics, economics, art, Africa, minorities or interracial relations are pretty uniform. These ideas are expressed in many different ways but, because of the fact that the American Negro exists under the dominating persuasion of the Great American Ideal, the philosophy of these Negroes has not been allowed the dignity of acceptance as an ethnic conception of reality. Nonetheless, this stratum persists in its own inarticulate way as the residuum of what might be called the Afro-American ethnic group consciousness in a society whose legal Constitution recognizes the rights, privileges and aspirations of the individual, but whose political institutions recognize the reality of ethnic groups only during election contests. Every four years the great fiction of the assimilated American (white and/or Protestant) ideal is put aside to deal with the pluralistic reality of the hyphenated-American vote,

---

* Martin Robison Delany, born May 6, 1812, Charleston, Virginia, died January, 1885. Delany should be considered the historical prototype of the "Afro-American Nationalist." As co-editor with Frederick Douglass of the leading Abolitionist organ *The North Star* founded in 1847, Delany's presence reflected the nationalist element of the embryonic Nationality vs. Integrationist conflict within the Abolitionist movement (which also had its white faction). For a short biographical sketch of Delany see Jessie Fauset's "Rank Imposes Obligations," *Crisis* magazine, November, 1926, p. 9. Important works by Delany are: *The Condition, Elevation, Emigration of the Colored People of the United States, Politically Considered,* published by the author in Philadelphia in 1852; and *The Official Report of the Niger Valley Exploring Party,* New York, T. Hamilton, 1861.

of which the largest is the Negro-American. But since the Supreme Court decision of 1954 on public school integration, the Negro-American has been catapulted into the role of being the mover and shaker of modern America while putting the Great American Ideal to the most crucial test of its last hundred years.

And what precisely is this Great American Ideal? The superficial answer is that, in practice, it is the living expression of that body of concepts sanctified in the American Constitution. For the Negro, the Fourteenth and Fifteenth Amendments are of special relevance. But this is true because these Amendments, especially, have an historical relationship to the way in which the Negro has influenced the evolution of the American Ideal. They will have a pertinency just as long as the Negro's lot falls short of the egalitarian ideal as set down. But does not the fact that a new Civil Rights Act of 1964 was required in pursuance of the enforcement of these Amendments, indicate that something more is implied than what is stated in them? Is it true that what this Negro stratum of which I speak wants from America is merely this enforcement? Or does the American default on these Amendments indicate that there is something conceptually or legally deficient about the scope of the Constitution itself? Does it indicate perhaps that the real scope of the social implications of the Negro's demands on American society today is not fully spelled out or conceptualized by the Negro himself—or at least that body of Negroes who are today most vocal on the civil rights front?

Whatever the case, it has to be noted that the most vocal opponents of the Civil Rights Act of 1964 *cite* the American Constitution and object to measures aimed at enforcing the Fourteenth and Fifteenth Amendments as violations of the rights of individuals and private property—privileges which are guaranteed by the same Constitution. This emotional and legal conflict over the interpretation of the Constitution, in the slow and painfully bitter struggle towards the enforcement of constitutional guarantees of racial equality, points up a very real dilemma inherent in the Negro's position in America.

On the face of it, this dilemma rests on the fact that America, which idealizes the rights of the individual above everything else, is in reality, a nation dominated by the social power of groups, classes, in-groups and cliques—both ethnic and religious. The individual in America has few rights that are not backed up by the political, economic and social power of one group or another. Hence, the individual Negro has, proportionately, very few rights indeed because his ethnic group (whether or not he actually identifies with it) has very little political, economic or social power (beyond moral grounds) to wield. Thus it can be seen that those Negroes, and there are very many of them, who have accepted the full essence of the Great American Ideal of individualism are in serious trouble trying to function in America.

Very understandably, these people want to be full-fledged Americans, without regard to race, creed, or color. They do not stop to realize that this social animal is a figment of the American imagination and has never really existed except in rare instances. They cite the American Constitution as the legal and moral authority in their quest for fully integrated status (whichever interpretation out of several they lend to this idea) and find it necessary to shy away from that stratum I mentioned before, which forms the residuum of the Negro ethnic group consciousness.

However, each individual American is a member of a group. The white Anglo-Saxon Protestants, the white Catholics, and the white Jews are the three main power groups in America, under the political and economic leadership of the WASPs. The American Constitution was conceived and written by white Anglo-Saxon Protestants for a white Anglo-Saxon society. The fact that what is called American Society, or American Culture, did not subsequently develop into a nation made up totally of WASPs—because of Negro slavery and immigration—did not prevent the white Protestants from perpetuating the group attitudes that would maintain the image of the whole American nation in terms of WASP cultural tradition. These attitudes, as sociologist Milton M. Gordon points out, "all have as a central assumption the desirability of maintaining English institutions (as modified by the American Revolution), the English language, and English-oriented cultural patterns as dominant and standard in American life."[3] Naturally, the historical priorities and prerogatives established by the English settlers early in the seventeenth century have been expanded through all the succeeding generations of white

[3] Milton M. Gordon, *Assimilation in American Life* (New York: Oxford University Press, 1964), p. 88.

Protestants into a well-entrenched social position, characterized by a predominance in economic and political power, buttressed with a strong, cohesive, group solidarity.

> Thus, what is usually referred to as 'general American society' turns out in reality, insofar as communal institutions and primary group relations are concerned, to be a white Protestant social world, colored and infused with the implicit assumptions of this particular ethnic group. To be sure, it is the largest ethnic group in the United States, and like other ethnic groups it is divided in major fashion by social class.[4]

Although the three main power groups—Protestants, Catholics and Jews—neither want nor need to become integrated with each other, the existence of a great body of homogenized, inter-assimilated white Americans is the premise for racial integration. Thus the Negro integrationist runs afoul of reality in the pursuit of an illusion, the "open society"—a false front that hides several doors to several different worlds of hyphenated-Americans. Which group or subgroup leaves its door wide open for the outsider? None, really. But Gordon does point out one subsocietal exception to this state of affairs between groups which, for our purposes, it is important to note very attentively: "The only substantial exception to this picture of ethnic separation is the compartment marked intellectuals and artists.' "[5]

Gordon goes on to explain this stratum, ". . . suffice it here to point out that in the situation of men and women coming together because of an overriding common interest in ideas, the creative arts, and mutual professional concerns, we find the classic sociological enemy of ethnic parochialism."[6] In other words, in the detached social world of the intellectuals, a considerable amount of racial integration and ethnic intermingling does take place on a social level. While the Negro intellectual is not fully integrated into the intellectual class stratum, he is, in the main, socially detached from his own Negro ethnic world. Gordon points out that there is evidence that the "outflow of intellectuals from the religioethnic groups of America, their subsequent estrangement from the

[4] *Ibid.*, p. 221.
[5] *Ibid.*, p. 111.
[6] *Ibid.*, p. 58.

life of these groups, and the resultant block in communication between the ethnic subsociety and the intellectual [might] have dys-
functional consequences."[7]

In the face of these sociological findings, then, how do Negro
intellectuals measure up to the complex problem of being spokesmen on behalf of their ethnic group, the Negro masses? This has
to be examined on two levels: First, as creative artists, how can
their creative output be assessed? Second, as Negro spokesmen, to
what extent do their analyses of the Negro situation get to the
bottom of things? Also, is there any correlation between these two
intellectual levels of performance, any value judgments to be
derived?

For several years the chief spokesman for the Negro among the
intellectual class was James Baldwin, who, it might be said, has
signalized a new level of involvement. Following Baldwin there
have been other literary voices, such as John O. Killens, the late
Lorraine Hansberry, Ossie Davis, Paule Marshall and LeRoi
Jones. However, if one closely examines the ideas, the social status,
the literary content or even the class background of these writers
and intellectuals, it is found that they are not at all in agreement
on what general course the Negro should follow towards racial
equality.

Thus, today, the Negro civil rights-integration movement calls
into play two aspects of Negro reality which now demand closer
examination and analysis than heretofore—the residual stratum of
Negro ethnic group consciousness, of which I have spoken, and the
"new" Negro intellectual class that has emerged as of the late
1950's and 1960's.

[7] *Ibid.*, p. 256.

Harlem Background—
The Rise of Economic Nationalism
and Origins of Cultural Revolution

In liberal and radical circles it is often said that New York City is not truly representative of what America is, deep in its hinterlands. It has been said that it is a mistake to confuse the cosmopolitanism of New York with the outlook of the Midwest, the Deep South, the North and Far West, the state of Texas or even Maine. This would seem to raise the question: Where is the "real" America to be found? Or, who is the "typical" American and from what region in the United States does he come?

On the other hand, the idea suggests that the United States does not represent a truly uniform nation of peoples. One could explain this lack of uniformity by pointing out that America is a nation that is still in the process of formation, that it is too young to have achieved the kind of advanced cultural fusion found in certain European nations. Yet, with all the long centuries of national development typical of European nations, Paris is not like Normandy or Brittany, London is not the British Midlands and Rome is most unlike Italy south of Naples. It seems, then, that even when nations mature in age it is merely the maturation of variety underneath a uniform surface.

By the same token, American Negroes under the impress of American development have their regional variations. Harlem is not Birmingham, New Orleans or Los Angeles. Yet, these same American conditions have resulted, today, in a degree of cultural affinity among Negroes of all regions that is neither compelled nor needed among the whites. The black world of America is unlike the white in more ways than mere color. Thus to say that Harlem is not Birmingham would call for much qualification. The truth of the matter is that Harlem has, in this century, become the most strategically important community of black America. Harlem is still the pivot of the black world's quest for identity and salvation. The way Harlem goes (or does not go) so goes all black America.

Harlem is the black world's key community for historical, political, economic, cultural and/or ethnic reasons. The trouble is that Harlem has never been adequately analyzed in such terms. The demand often heard—"Break up the Harlem ghetto!" (as a hated symbol of segregation)—represents nothing but the romantic and empty wail of politically insolvent integrationists, who fear ghetto riots only *more* than they fear the responsibilities of political and economic power that lie in the Harlem potential. Caring little or nothing for the ethnic solvency of the Negro group, the integrationists maintain that since Harlem was created by segregation the only solution is to desegregate it by abolishing it. But this is fallacious logic that refuses to admit the class nature of the American social dynamic that permits social mobility only upwards into the middle class. On the other hand, a forced abolition of a ghetto composed primarily of unemployed and unskilled non-whites would be tantamount to resettlement by decree with all its "undemocratic" implications. Thus, it has not been understood that with all the evils and deprivations of the Harlem ghetto, this community still represents the Negro's strongest bastion in America from which to launch whatever group effort he is able to mobilize for political power, economic rehabilitation and cultural reidentification. Hence, for the Negro to lose his population control of the Harlem area means an uprooting from his strongest base in the American social structure. It is these considerations which reveal the incompetence of much Northern integrationist philosophy, which when carried to its characteristic extremes, sees integration as solving everything. Since integrationists see very little in group economic power, or black political power, to say nothing of cultural identity, they ultimately mislead many Negroes on the bottom of the social scale whose fundamental ethnic group problems the integrationists evade and cannot solve. It must be said that these are the causes behind ghetto uprisings. These glaring defects in the social analysis of Negro ghettoes are what lend that quality of unreality to much of what integrationists say and do.

As long as the Negro's cultural identity is in question, or open to self-doubts, then there can be no positive identification with the real demands of his political and economic existence. Further than that, without a cultural identity that adequately defines *himself*, the Negro cannot even identify with the American nation as a whole. He is left in the limbo of social marginality, alienated and directionless on the landscape of America, in a variegated nation of whites who have not yet decided on their own identity. The fact of the matter is that American whites, as a whole, are just as much in doubt about their nationality, their cultural identity, as are Negroes. Thus the problem of Negro cultural identity is an un-solved problem within the context of an American nation that is still in process of formation.

It is the Negro movement's impact that brings such historical questions to the fore. It forces the whole nation to look into itself—which it has never wanted to do. Historically, the American psy-chology has been conditioned by the overriding economic motiva-tion of plundering the continent for the wealth of its natural re-sources. Every aspect of America's national morality is predicated on that materialistic ethos. With no traditional love for the land he adopted, the American has remained to this day a stranger in the land of his birth: ill-at-ease with his power, uncertain about his nationality, an extroverted pragmatist for whom every exposure of the social immorality of his inner life becomes a scandal. A racial integration movement that does not care to look first into the internal disorder of its own house, is also blind to the fact that ghetto pathologies cannot be treated by attacking them from the other side of the racial fence, by way of integration. A social cri-tique of the Negro's position in America that does not perceive the pivotal characteristics of Harlem as a community, fails as a positive critique and throws the entire Negro movement into a disordered melee of conflicting, and often directionless, methods. These prag-matic protest methods, as a result, become so institutionalized that they can no longer be guided, altered, and channeled away from the pursuit of the integrationist mirage, which in the North, re-cedes farther away after every protest demonstration. The result has been that the northern civil rights movement, in recent years, has created a legion of zealots for whom integration has been hypostatized into a religion rather than a socially scientific method based on clearly understood principles. It is perhaps cruel to have to say so, but we have to face many truths: In the North, the civil rights movement has produced a crackpot trend marked by a zealous commitment without understanding that borders on anarchism; there has in fact been considerable verbal exposition of the desire for the "revolution of chaos," rather than what could be called "mainstream social change." This anarchistic development has its roots in the accumulated history of incompetent methods.

In Negro life the cultural spheres appear to many as being rather remote, intangible and hardly related to what is called the more practical aspect of race relations. However, the truth is that the more practical sides of the Negro problem in America are bogged down organizationally and methodologically precisely because of cultural confusion and disorientation on the part of most Negroes. *Thus it is only through a cultural analysis of the Negro approach to group "politics" that the errors, weaknesses and goal-failures can cogently be analyzed and positively worked out.*

The years between the day I entered the army, and the war's end in 1945, marked the end of an era for Harlem. For myself, at that time, it merely meant the disappearance of that special adolescent flavor that attaches to a certain locale. Beyond that, it took awhile to understand that World War II represented a very abrupt break, a switchover in the continuity of Harlem traditions. New migrations from the South (as in World War I), the creation of a new middle-class stratum on the crest of the war boom, the war veteran's psychology, etc., all served to hide prewar Harlem behind the mask of a transitional kind of postwar personality. If one tried to be nostalgic about the Harlem flavor that was gone forever, such sentiments were quickly dissipated in the urgencies of adjustment to postwar problems—and they were many.

But after a few years, it became apparent that the very abruptness of that break in the continuity of Harlem traditions served to confound and aggravate the community's postwar problems. Harlem was trying to push forward, it seemed, by cutting itself off from every vestige of its past in that strangely distant time before the war. Intellectually, this attitude proved, in time, to be unworkable. Eventually, one had to go back into the 1930's, the 1920's and even before World War I, in order to understand the Harlem saga—where it had come from, where it had been, and where it might be going.

For myself, the real necessity for seeing Harlem in a retrospective context came slowly. The American ethos is impatient with history and cares deeply only about today, and possibly about tomorrow. History is valid for the American only when it can be used as a facile justification for what is half-heartedly pursued today in defense of pragmatic "Americanism." Negroes are no different in this respect; thus even those who glory in certain black antecedents learn very little from their past.

The profound ineffectiveness of social action in Harlem did not strike me forcibly until around 1950-1951, when Harlem's political leftwing initiated a protest action against the Apollo Theater on 125th Street—the business thoroughfare of white economic control of the Harlem community. A picket line was ordered to protest the showing of the film satirizing Russia, *Ninotchka*, starring Greta Garbo. Without a doubt, this interracial picket line had been ordered by the Communist hierarchy downtown and agreed upon by the captive Negro leadership in Harlem. But from a Harlem point of view, the picketing was as ludicrous as it was meaningless, as few Harlemites who frequented the Apollo really cared about the movie. (They go, first and foremost, to see and hear variety stars in performance. Movies are usually a timing device added to fill in the gaps between stage shows, during which time the theater is practically empty.)

For a native, unassimilated Harlemite, nurtured in Harlem's idiosyncrasies, to be forced to walk in such a picket line represented the height of embarrassment and the depths of ignominy. For it pointed up all too graphically how far removed was the Communist-oriented leftwing from the facts of life and the native psychology of the Harlem mass mind. This protest action met with the open hostility of Harlemites, especially those employed by the Apollo Theater. And the action itself revealed the damning fact that the Harlem leftwing, during this period, took no interest at all in the long-standing grievances of the performers, musicians, stagehands, etc., against the Apollo management. There were no picket lines protesting these issues.

The Negro radical leftwing leadership of Harlem had always shown a snobbish and intolerant attitude towards the type of stage fare featured weekly at the Apollo. The "cultural" tastes of the masses never sullied the aesthetic sensibilities of the Communist elite. Knowing this, we soon realized that it was *not* the picket line that was wrong but that it was being staged for *the wrong issue.* In a flash the idea dawned that the Russian-baiting film, although a cultural issue being made political, was not the *right* cultural issue at stake here. The *real* cultural issue for Harlem was the Apollo Theater itself: its role as an institution, its ownership, its influence and its history. None of the picketers were old enough to know that their action was simply the most recent of a long list of actions, both open and closed, carried out against the Apollo management since the 1920's. No one was kept out of the Apollo Theater by the picket line, of course, but larger implications became clear.

During the same period, the Apollo Theater became an issue in the Harlem press over a controversy inspired by a stage joke that was interpreted as a slur against Negro women, specifically the prostitutes who frequented the neighborhood near the Apollo. The incident took place at the very time certain members of the Harlem theater movement were trying to convince the Apollo management to permit the presentation of some legitimate drama. The Apollo had responded by presenting Negro versions of *Rain* and *Detective Story,* both of which were box-office failures. The Apollo went back to its usual variety entertainment, and then came the stage joke: A white ventriloquist had his dummy say that he was having a hard time with women lately, whereupon the ventriloquist replied that "just around the corner, women are a dime a dozen." A Harlem Women's Group protested and the Apollo management was chastised in the press which was still smarting over being rebuffed by the Apollo on "legitimate drama."

The owners of the Apollo had been known as people who believed they knew best what Harlemites wanted in the way of entertainment, and said so. Thus Jack Schiffman, one of the managers, was forced to answer with a statement of policy which appeared in the *Amsterdam News,* for the week of September 22, 1951:

> The Apollo Theater launched an experiment which it then considered noble and worthwhile. . . . that of putting on fine legitimate stage plays with an all-Negro cast. The experiment proved to be a rather disastrous failure. . . . And so, it's back to the vaudeville policy for us with an occassional flyer in the legitimate field to be anticipated. And, the vaudeville policy is

good enough for us because there is a great deal of satisfaction, in varying degrees, in putting on our weekly shows. . . . Then too, there is the talented youth to be considered. There are many youngsters who are trying to crash into show business and we at the Apollo like to feel that we're playing an important part in supplying the opportunity for these young folk. . . .

From the point of view of the Apollo management, this settled the issue most conveniently; but for the community, it answered none of the larger questions that had hovered about the heads of the Apollo management since the 1920's. One of the members of the pioneer Harlem Writers Club wrote the first of an intended series of articles answering the Apollo management, and tried to get Paul Robeson's *Freedom* newspaper to publish them. Robeson's chief editor, a Communist bureaucrat, sidestepped the issue and refused for reasons of "policy" and "space." Thus, the most fundamental cultural institutional issue in the Harlem community was never aired by the Harlem leftwing.

The Apollo Theater episode was only one of several issues that further widened the breach between certain members of the Harlem Writers' Club and the leftwing cultural inner circle of *Freedom* newspaper. The Apollo Theater issue was rife with many related challenges. The legitimate dramas that failed on the Apollo stage were not representative of Negro Theater despite the all-Negro casts, for the question of the Negro dramatist's role was not considered. *Rain* and *Detective Story,* both white plays, answered only the actor's plea—for integrated casting, for instance serving the short-term interests of such actors as Sidney Poitier, on his way "up" from the defunct American Negro Theater.

The implication of the junior Schiffman's claim that the Apollo management's interest in helping Negro youth crash show business was all altruism was never publicly examined in Harlem. What were the real inside relationships between the Apollo management and the variety, musicians' and theatrical craft unions? How did Negro youth entering show business fare with these unions? Why did the Apollo management close up theater and movie houses in Harlem and sell out only to churches? This prevented rival and competing theater interests from gaining a foothold in Harlem that has worked to the detriment of Harlem cultural life. But the Harlem leftwing evaded these problems, and the official Communist Party leadership could look at the Apollo and see only one thing to attack—an "anti"-Soviet propaganda film!

The crowning irony in these 1951 events was that right in the midst of the Apollo episode, the Communist Party of the United States saw fit to move its national headquarters onto Harlem's 125th Street in order to escape the pressures of political and press harassment growing out of McCarthyite hysteria. Under a headline—"Communists Woo Harlem—Open Big Drive in Local Area" —the *Amsterdam News* of September 29, 1951, said that the Communists had retreated to Harlem because "this belabored, belittled community is considered to be America's weakest line of resistance against the movement." Yet, with all the seven Communist front groups listed and functioning in Harlem, the Communist Party had no program that could deal with the fundamentals of Harlem reality.

However, for this writer at least, the Apollo picket line started another train of thought, and established a method and a line of historical investigation into the complex origins of Harlem's problems. There were too many tall tales and glamorous legends in the folklore about Harlem's good old days that refused to die. Wise old men would talk of events of forty years ago as if they happened last year, and conjure up the image of personalities long dead whose great fame was unrecorded except in crumbling newspaper clippings. When, how, and why did they all appear?

The pioneer history of Harlem, James Weldon Johnson's *Black Manhattan*, was, essentially, a cultural history. From a sociological point of view, Johnson was correct in his choice of cultural analysis as a method. Yet the cultural aspects of Harlem developments had economic determinants and political consequences. In economic terms, the origins of Harlem's black community are to be found in the rise of *black economic nationalism*. At the turn of this century Harlem was a predominantly white community that had been "overbuilt with new apartment houses. It was far uptown, and the only rapid transportation was the elevated running up Eighth Avenue—the Lenox Avenue Subway had not yet been built. . . . So landlords were finding it hard to fill their houses."[1]

---

[1] *Black Manhattan* (New York: Alfred Knopf, 1930), p. 148. (Used by permission of Mrs. James Weldon Johnson.)

However, the Harlem whites organized to use all means—legal, persuasive, and conspiratorial—to stem the Negro influx which assumed mass proportions around 1905.

The spirit behind this influx was economic nationalism. The economic organization behind this nationalism was the Afro-American Realty Company, a group of Negro leaders, business men, and politicians of whom the leading voices were Philip A. Payton, a real estate man, and Charles W. Anderson, a Republican Party stalwart who, in 1905, was appointed collector of internal revenue in New York by Theodore Roosevelt.* Behind these men stood T. Thomas Fortune, editor of the *New York Age,* the oldest and most influential Negro newspaper in New York. But behind them all stood the guiding mind of Booker T. Washington and his National Negro Business League founded in 1900. All of the personalities in or around the Afro-American Realty Company were proteges of Washington and members of his business league. They were, thus, representatives of Washington's Tuskegee Machine, a power in Negro affairs, and the bane of the civil rights radicals led by W.E.B. DuBois in his Niagara Movement of 1905. By this time nationalism had become aggressive and assertive in economics but conservative in civil rights politics, hence the clash over "program" between Washington and DuBois's new civil rights "radicalism."

The operations of the Afro-American Realty Company spearheaded the growth of black Harlem by either leasing or buying apartment dwellings that could not be rented and renting them to Negroes. In many cases whites voluntarily abandoned houses, in other cases whites were evicted and replaced by Negroes.

The whole movement, in the eyes of the whites, took on the aspect of an "invasion"; they became panic-stricken, and began fleeing as from a plague. The presence of one colored family in a block, no matter how well bred and orderly, was sufficient to

* Other associates of the Afro-American Realty Company were: Fred R. Moore, Emmet J. Scott, Joseph H. Bruce, Sandy P. Jones, Henry C. Parker, John B. Nail, William Ten Eyck, James E. Garner, Edward S. Payton, Stephen A. Bennett. James Weldon Johnson married Grace Nail, sister to John B. Nail. At this writing, Mrs. James Weldon Johnson still resides in Harlem. Note also that Emmett J. Scott, who was secretary to Booker T. Washington at Tuskegee, also worked closely with Marcus Garvey, personifying the link between Washington's economic nationalism and Garvey's "Back to Africa" nationalism.

precipitate a flight. House after house and block after block was actually deserted.[2]

Philip A. Payton organized the Afro-American Realty Company to counter the thrust of the Hudson Realty Company, a white group, formed to stop and turn back the black influx after it had begun to spread west of the Lenox Avenue "line" of demarcation. Payton's group then attempted to incorporate with a capitalization of $500,000 at ten dollars per share with the aim of expanding operations to include building apartments. For a long period the *New York Age* carried an ad appealing for buyers of shares. From 1905 to the beginning of World War I, a legal and financial struggle went on in Harlem between black and white realty interests, during which time Negroes gained a solid foothold.

The dominant thinking of the times was reflected in the remarks of several of the leading minds behind the organization of the Afro-American Realty Company. Speaking to an audience of farmers at the fourteenth annual session of the Tuskegee Negro Conference, Washington was quoted by the *New York Age* as saying "When Race gets Bank Book, its Troubles will Cease."[3] He further advised Negroes "Get some property . . . Get a home of your own." W.E.B. DuBois was unhappy over the way Washington emphasized his gospel of "Work and Money." Speaking at a celebration of Lincoln's birthday to the "Professional and Business Men's" group, Philip A. Payton discussed the Afro-American Realty Company's operations and aims, stating "There is strength in financial combination". In pleading for more race support, he declared: "How often do we see because of (this) lack of race confidence a competent Afro-American lawyer or doctor hardly able to exist from want of patronage from his race."[4]

The Afro-American Realty Company lasted about five years. It collapsed, Johnson wrote, because of "lack of the large amount of capital essential . . . but several individual colored men carried on. Philip A. Payton and J.C. Thomas bought two five-story apartments. . . . John B. Nail bought a row of five apartments . . . St.

[2] James Weldon Johnson, "Harlem: the Cultural Capitol," in Alain Locke (editor), *The New Negro*, 1925, Albert and Charles Boni, p. 304.
[3] *New York Age*, February 23, 1905, p. 1.
[4] *Ibid.*, p. 2.

Philips Episcopal Church, one of the oldest and richest colored congregations in New York bought a row of thirteen apartments on One Hundred and Thirty-fifth Street between Lenox and Seventh Avenues."[5] The Afro-American Realty Company initiated a wave of real estate buying among Harlem's new Negro arrivals. Despite much bitter feeling during a fifteen year struggle of Negroes to gain a foothold, Harlem was won without serious violence.

The social role of economic nationalism in the rise of black Harlem and similar movements has been either ignored or poorly understood by most professional Negro historians. Even writers such as John Hope Franklin and E. Franklin Frazier fail to mention either Payton, his realty company or the men around him. More than that, the important influence of Booker T. Washington's philosophy on the rise of black economic nationalism has not been generally acknowledged. This omission of the role of nationalism leaves much of the analysis common to Negro historiography open to question. Philip A. Payton was a disciple of Booker T. Washington, thus the affinity of Washington's economic ideas to the founding of black Harlem is historically factual. Johnson wrote:

> The move to Harlem, in the beginning and for a long time, was fathered and engineered by Philip A. Payton. . . . But this was more than a matter of mere business with Mr. Payton; the matter of better and still better housing for colored people in New York became the dominating idea of his life, and he worked on it as long as he lived. When Negro New Yorkers evaluate their benefactors in their own race, they must find that not many have done more than Phil Payton; for much of what has made Harlem the intellectual and artistic capital of the Negro world is in good part due to this fundamental advantage.[6]

Harlem became what the historian, James Weldon Johnson, called "the intellectual and artistic capital of the Negro world" for a very good reason—because New York City was the intellectual and cultural capital of the white world in America. This is of historical and cultural importance in more ways than one. By

[5] *Black Manhattan, op. cit.,* p. 149.
[6] *Ibid.,* p. 147.

understanding this, it is then possible to see that the emergence and growth of Negro Harlem took place within the framework of Negro-white relations, both in New York and elsewhere. Manhattan real estate interests, the relations of various national groups, southern Negro migrations, war economics, etc., made Harlem a new Promised Land for the black worker and former "peasant" from both the South and the West Indies. But Harlem also fostered something else which has not been adequately dealt with in the history books—a cultural movement and a creative   intelligentsia. That this occurred was not at all strange in terms of the Negro's native artistic gifts. What *was* unique, however, was that this Negro cultural movement ran almost parallel to, and in interaction with, a white American cultural resurgence. Again the historical motif of the Negro dynamic, acting and reacting within the context of Negro-white relations, was demonstrated—but on the cultural plane. Thus it is more than coincidence that Negro Harlem, which began as a trickle of black settlers quickly grew into a city within a city, and the fact that in 1912, a group of white creative intellectuals came together in the "salon" of Mabel Dodge in Greenwich Village to launch the American literary and cultural renaissance that reached its zenith in the 1920's.

In 1930, James Weldon Johnson wrote:

> In the history of New York the name Harlem has changed from Dutch to Irish to Jewish to Negro; but it is through this last change that it has gained its most widespread fame. Throughout coloured America Harlem is the recognized Negro capital. Indeed, it is Mecca for the sightseer, the pleasure seeker, the curious, the adventurous, the enterprising, the ambitious, and the talented of the entire Negro world; for the lure of it has reached down to every island of the Carib Sea and penetrated even into Africa. It is almost as well known to the white world, for it has been much talked and written about.[7]

Here, Johnson was describing the Harlem of the 1920's, the age of the Negro renaissance (often called the Harlem Renaissance). A list of its most outstanding personalities would include Langston Hughes, Claude McKay, Countee Cullen, Walter White, George S. Schuyler, E. Franklin Frazier, J.A. Rogers,

7 *Ibid.*, p. 1.

Charles Gilpin, Alain Locke, Gwendolyn Bennett, W.E.B. Du-Bois, Paul Robeson, Abbie Mitchell, Noble Sissle, Eubie Blake, Josephine Baker, Florence Mills, Roland Hayes, Louis Armstrong, Bill Robinson, Duke Ellington, A. Philip Randolph, Jean Toomer, and Ethel Waters, to mention only those who would be known or remembered today. But there were many others whose creative contributions were important. Note that the majority of this creative generation were not New Yorkers, but hailed from places as distant as Joplin, Missouri (Hughes), and the British West Indies (McKay). Harlem was the Mecca for the intelligentsia.

Out of the Greenwich Village literary and cultural movement, centered around Mabel Dodge's famous "23 Fifth Avenue" salon near Washington Square, came the following: Carl Van Vechten; George Cram Cook, the discoverer and mentor of Eugene O'Neill; Emilie Hapgood; Ridgely Torrence; Paul Green; John Reed, the first American Communist martyr-hero; Louise Bryant, Reed's wife; Max Eastman, editor of the original *Masses* magazine of the radical Left; Walter Lippmann, then a Socialist (still a leading journalist); Lincoln Steffens; Elizabeth Gurley Flynn*, a ranking Communist leader; William English Walling, a leading Socialist, and the first Chairman of the Executive Committee of the NAACP, organized in 1910; Sinclair Lewis; Michael Gold; Dorothy and DuBose Heyward—to name the more prominent. These white artists and intellectuals are listed not only to reveal something of the character and quality of this early Village renaissance, but also because most of them are to be remembered for their close personal relationships with certain Negro individuals from the Harlem Renaissance. Historically, there was an ethnic or aesthetic interaction between these two "racial" movements. It was a relationship that helps not only to explain these parallel movements, but reveals much about the nature of the American nationality problem in its evolutionary process.

This 1912 salon coterie later expanded from its first, bohemian

---

* Elizabeth Gurley Flynn was not an artist but a radical member of IWW (International Workers of the World). Mabel Dodge's group played host not only to artists, but to many of the leading labor radicals of the day such as anarchists Emma Goldman and Alexander Berkman, and William "Big Bill" Haywood, the leading figure in the IWW.

stage (the Harlem movement also had its bohemian element) to include such figures as Floyd Dell, V.F. Calverton, H.L. Mencken and Frank Harris—more solid intellectuals, who lent stability to a movement with a pronounced madcap fringe. Both movements had a much greater social potential than they ever realized, and a brief analysis of why, is of useful interest even now. In fact, Harlem's cultural history cannot be fully appreciated without such an evaluation.

The Harlem Renaissance differed from the Greenwich Village renaissance first, in racial content, and also in the respective social levels of the participants and their creative standards, in terms of content and form. Moreover, the Village movement began under the rare guidance and sponsorship of a patroness with a very broad and cultivated background, in the person of Mabel Dodge. The Harlem Renaissance had at its helm no such comparable personality, and thus was rather directionless. C. Wright Mills, our greatest sociologist of late, wrote of the significance of Mabel Dodge:

> The type of woman known as the Salon Lady—who passes before us in the pages of Proust—has never been known in America. . . .
>
> Apart from stray figures like Mabel Dodge of lower Fifth Avenue and Taos, New Mexico, there have not been women who ran genuine salons in the sense that salons were run as artistic and intellectual centers in Europe. . . .[8]

The nearest approach to the "Salon Lady" produced by the Harlem Renaissance was not an heiress of old, upper-class white prominence. She was the famous A'Lelia Walker, the daughter of the equally famous Madame C.J. Walker, one of the leading Negro business pioneers who, early in this century, had accumulated a million-dollar fortune from the manufacture of hair and skin preparations.

Madame Walker exemplified the emergence of a new economic class—the black bourgeoisie. This class, of course, was never to achieve any substantial stake in American high finance, and was limited to serving certain special needs of the Negro market. Being late, limited, and marginal, the black bourgeoisie as a class, did not achieve the kind of cultural and intellectual maturity that would

---

[8] *Power Elite* (New York: Oxford University Press, 1959), pp. 78-79.

have produced a Mabel Dodge for the Harlem Renaissance. But it produced most of that movement's creative artists.* These Negro developments, taking place around 1898 to 1910, were symptomatic of the quality of rapid change in the economics of the American social dynamic—a dynamic that creates new middle-class layers. But each new black middle-class trend with new aspirations, gets checked by the color line, and is unable to solve, fully, the tasks set before it. This was the problem of the emergent Negro business class—it could not expand beyond those consumer needs of the Negro community that white businesses passed up. Thus, E. Franklin Frazier was to write of Madame Walker: "It was in the manufacture of cosmetics that Negroes—women—first achieved a spectacular success. . . . The numerous beauty shops, which constitute a large proportion of Negro business undertakings, have provided outlets for these products."[9] It is interesting that twenty years earlier James Weldon Johnson had admonished: "Notwithstanding, it is idle to expect the Negro in Harlem or anywhere else to build business in general upon a strictly racial foundation or to develop it to any considerable proportions strictly within the limits of the patronage, credit, and financial resources of the race."[10]

This was, of course, an old NAACP "integration" type of argument, and became the interracial rationalization for evading the issue of nationalism and its economic imperatives for the Negro community. The logic of this argument has been retarding and detrimental to the Negroes' ghetto welfare. The real reason Negro businessmen have not been able to gain "patronage [and] credit" *outside* the "financial resources of the race" is because they failed, precisely, to "build business upon a strictly racial foundation." In

---

* Another Negro business pioneer with artistic offspring was Dr. W.A. Attaway, a Mississippi physician, who in 1909 organized the first Negro legal reserve insurance company in his state. Two of his children are William and Ruth Attaway, the former well known in the 1940's for his novels, *Let Me Breathe Thunder* and *Blood on the Forge*. Actress Ruth Attaway started her career in the original cast of *You Can't Take It With You* on Broadway, and has recently been cast in two of the Lincoln Center Repertory Theater company's productions—*After the Fall*, and *Danton's Death*. See E. Franklin Frazier, *The Negro In The United States* (New York: Macmillan Co., 1949), pp. 408-409.

[9] Frazier, *loc. cit.*

[10] Johnson, *op. cit.*, p. 283.

other words, Negroes of Harlem have never achieved economic control inside Harlem, or inside any other major black community. Failing this, the black bourgeoisie has been condemned to remain forever marginal in relation to its own innate potential within American capitalism. It has also remained politically subservient, intellectually unfulfilled and provincial. Thus, the black bourgeoisie was unprepared and unconditioned to play any leading sponsorship role in the Harlem Renaissance—this class was and still is culturally imitative and unimaginative.

Obviously the famous A'Lelia Walker made an effort, but could not adequately fill the role of Salon Lady—her new class lacked a broad cultural conditioning. Langston Hughes aptly assessed her:

> A'Lelia Walker was the then great Harlem party giver. . . . [She] however, big-hearted, night-dark, hair straightening heiress, made no pretense at being intellectual or exclusive. At her "at homes" Negro poets and Negro number bankers mingled with downtown poets and seat-on-the-stock-exchange racketeers. Countee Cullen would be there and Witter Bynner, Muriel Draper and Nora Holt, Andy Razaf and Taylor Gordon. And a good time was had by all. . . . A'Lelia Walker was the joy-goddess of Harlem's 1920's.[11]

Carl Van Vechten, a music critic, novelist, photographer and art patron, was one of the most important figures in Mabel Dodge's salon. He was the first to establish a link between the Harlem and Greenwich Village artistic movements. He subsequently became the leading white patron of Negro art and artists during the heyday of the Harlem movement in the 1920's. In his first autobiography, Langston Hughes speaks of Van Vechten:

> He never talks grandiloquently about democracy or Americanism. Nor makes a fetish of those qualities. But he lives them with sincerity—and humor.[12]

> What Carl Van Vechten did for me was to submit my first book of poems to Alfred A. Knopf, put me in contact with the editors of *Vanity Fair*, who bought my first poems sold to a magazine, caused me to meet many editors and writers who were friendly and helpful to me, encouraged me in my efforts to help publicize the Scottsboro case, cheered me on in the writing of my first short

[11] Langston Hughes, *The Big Sea* (New York: Alfred A. Knopf, 1945), p. 244.
[12] *Ibid.*, p. 255.

stories. . . . Many others of the Negroes in the arts, from Paul
Robeson to Ethel Waters, Walter White to Richmond Barthe
[sculptor], will offer the same testimony as to the interest Van
Vechten has displayed toward Negro creators in the fields of writing, plastic arts, and popular entertainment. To say that Carl
Van Vechten has harmed Negro creative activities is sheer poppycock.[13]

Van Vechten had come under fire from Negro newspaper critics
for his choice of the title *Nigger Heaven* for his novel on Harlem
life, published in 1926. However in 1912-1913, Van Vechten had
convinced a rather unwilling Mabel Dodge to permit the first
Negroes to attend one of her famous artists' soirees. She had been
consulting with Van Vechten, Walter Lippmann and Lincoln
Steffens, and Hutchins Hapgood, on how to add special attractions
to her "evenings." She wrote in her memoirs:

> The first evening I can remember was engineered by Carl [Van
> Vechten], who wanted to bring a pair of Negro entertainers he
> had seen somewhere who, he said, were marvelous. Carl's interest
> in Negroes began as far back as that. . . .
> So as readily as I let Carl bring Negroes [once], I let Steff [Lin-
> coln Steffens] suggest another pattern.

She related—"I didn't betray my feelings"—as she watched the
"unrestrained Negroes":

> While an appalling Negress danced before us in white stock-
> ings and black buttoned boots, the man strummed a banjo and
> sang an embarrassing song. They both leered and rolled their
> suggestive eyes and made me feel first hot and then cold, for I had
> never been so near this kind of thing before; but Carl rocked
> with laughter and little shrieks escaped him as he clapped his
> pretty hands. His big teeth became wickedly prominent and his
> eyes rolled in his darkening face, until he grew to somewhat
> resemble the clattering Negroes before him.

But after discussing this kind of experience with Lippmann and
Steffens, she decided: "One must just let life express itself in whatever form it will.[14]

Mabel Dodge's salon did not represent the first contacts between

13 *Ibid.*, p. 272.
14 Mabel Dodge Luhan, "Movers and Shakers," *Intimate Memories* (New York:
Harcourt, Brace, 1936), Vol. III, pp. 79-80. Used by permission.

Negro and white in the artistic fields. This had already taken place in the theatre as far back as 1898-1900—before Negro Harlem was created—when the talented pioneer Bob Cole wrote music and sketches for white vaudeville shows. But the Mabel Dodge group represented a new American intellectual and creative movement on another level. It was the first white intellectual revolt against the deadening materialistic pall that a triumphant industrialism had spread over the American landscape, choking up the spiritual pores of the nation and threatening to smother its creative potential. "America is all machinery and money making and factories," Mabel Dodge had said after ten years of cultural rejuvenation in Europe. "It is ugly, ugly, ugly."[15]

The new trend of creative intellectuals who gathered around her all felt the same way. They were deeply disturbed and agitated over the way America was developing into a nation without soul. In coming to Greenwich Village from the hinterlands or from universities, they were escaping the real America they had grown up in, in order to find ways of making themselves capable of changing America into what they thought it ought to be. Negro creative artists, on the other hand, came to Harlem seeking creative fulfillment on whatever terms offered to them.

Many of the white creative intellectuals in the new Village movement were inclined towards radical social thought and were not, by any means, ivory tower aesthetes remote from the living issues of the day. Thus several of them, like Van Vechten, looked the facts square in the face and admitted that the racial factor in American thinking was inseparable from the problems of culture and art. And, that in order to deal positively and creatively with cultural and artistic problems, one had also to deal with race. Mabel Dodge was loath to accept this reality at first, but she later changed her mind in a typically American way—salving her conscience on the race question by going over to the side of the Indians, and eventually even marrying one. Interestingly enough, her marriage to an Indian named Luhan was not unconnected with the fact that her good friend, D.H. Lawrence, although British by birth and upbringing, was able to write so cogently on the problems and psychology of Indian-white relations in the United

[15] Mabel Dodge Luhan, *op. cit.*, "European Experiences," Vol. II, p. 453.

States, in his 1923 collection of essays, *Studies in Classic American Literature*. These essays were completed in 1922, in New Mexico, where Mabel Dodge had retired from Greenwich Village.

That the new creative intellectual movement around Mabel Dodge's salon had individuals who immediately concerned themselves with the implications of Negroes and Indians in American society—from an ethnic and cultural point of view—was neither accidental nor surprising. It was all in the nature of things American and/or cultural. These intellectuals could not avoid dealing with these obvious factors in the unsolved American nationality problem. Then, as now, the gnawing question was—who and what is an American? Although it appears that none of Mabel Dodge's intellectuals said so in so many words, the complex and perplexing questions of American cultural revival could not be answered until this nationality question was dealt with, if not settled philosophically.

As an outsider, D.H. Lawrence saw into the heart of one side of the problem in his study of Fenimore Cooper's novels:

> The American landscape has never been at one with the white man. Never. And white men have probably never felt so bitter anywhere, as here in America, where the very landscape, in its very beauty, seems a bit devilish and grinning, opposed to us.
>
> The desire to extirpate the Indian. And the contradictory desire to glorify him. Both are rampant still, to-day.
>
> The minority of whites intellectualize the Red Man and laud him to the skies. But this minority of whites is mostly a high-brow minority with a big grouch against its own whiteness. So there you are.
>
> But you have there the myth of the essential white America. All the other stuff, the love, the democracy . . . is a sort of by-play. The essential American soul is hard, isolate, stoic, and a killer. It has never yet melted.[16]

Lawrence was able to ignore Negroes in the American democratic equation but Mabel Dodge's American companions in culture could not. Historically, a three-way ethnic component was involved in the original basic ingredients of the formative American nation—white Englishmen, black Africans, and red Indians.

[16] *Studies in Classic American Literature* (Anchor ed.; New York: Doubleday & Co., 1951), pp. 43-73.

By the time the twentieth century came around, it was axiomatic that the future of the American nation would depend on how it could reconcile, democratically, the presence of these three groups. The fact that nineteenth-century immigration added millions of white Europeans who were not of prime English stock, does not essentially alter the qualities of the original ethnic triad. In twentieth-century America, English orientation of the white Anglo-Saxon Protestant group has remained the dominant factor.

Within the Mabel Dodge following, the white intellectuals and artists developed both a pro-Indian and a pro-Negro trend in their cultural approaches. There was another ethnic minority question involved in the Village movement that was not played up—the Jewish question—due to the fact that quite a number of the leading intellectuals in the movement were Jews. Mabel Dodge never discussed the Jewish "group" issue in her memoirs despite the apparent Jewishness of many of her artistic acquaintances. In view of the ever-present issue of anti-Semitism, it is interesting to see that Jews have never been debarred from full and equal participation in American cultural fields. The new Village movement of 1912 was an example of this fact. However the Negro issue was approached with care, and in the face of certain doubts. Mabel Dodge's first and only evening with Negroes present, at 23 Fifth Avenue, was by invitation only. Her regular weekly gatherings had usually been "open."

The following excerpt from a letter to Mabel Dodge from Maurice Sterne (with whom she had had a tempestuous affair), foreshadows her departure for Taos, New Mexico. There, as the wife of an Indian, she was to set up a new artists' colony and begin her memoirs.

> Do you want an object in life? Save the Indians, their art-culture—reveal it to the world! I hear astonishing things here about the insensitiveness of our Indian Office.
>
> That which Emilie Hapgood and others are doing for the Negroes, you could, if you wanted to, do for the Indians—You'll say it is different with the Negroes—They are scattered all over the U.S. so it is easier to bring them before the public. This isn't at all an advantage, for we have become too familiar with them, and our antagonism towards them was deep-rooted, whereas, as far as the public is concerned, no prejudices exist against the Indians,

only a patronizing attitude which to my mind is worse as far as the Indian is concerned. And it would be the easiest thing in the world to get a number of Indians from different parts of the country to perform at N.Y., and above all at Washington, to make the American people realize that there are such things as other forms of civilizations besides ours. . . .[17]

The Emilie Hapgood mentioned in Sterne's letter belonged to the pro-Negro segment among the new Village intellectuals (as opposed to Mabel Dodge, and others, who were pro-Indian). She had made a patron's splurge in a forbidden area of the race question—the Negro creative world of Harlem. She initiated the swing to the Negro "image theme" in the theater three years before Eugene O'Neill revolutionized dramatic art with *The Emperor Jones:*

April 5, 1917 is the date of the most important single event in the entire history of the Negro in the American theatre; for it marks the beginning of a new era. On that date a performance of three dramatic plays was given by the Coloured Players at the Garden Theatre in Madison Square Garden, New York, and the stereotyped traditions regarding the Negro's histrionic limitations were smashed. It was the first time anywhere in the United States for Negro actors in the dramatic theatre to command the serious attention of the critics and of the general press and public.

The plays were three one-act plays written by Ridgely Torrence;* they were produced by Mrs. Emilie Hapgood; the settings and costumes were designed by Robert Edmond Jones, and the staging was under his direction.[18]

What was it that motivated the involvement of the white creative intellectuals of this period with Negro culture? Was it merely what Hutchins Hapgood,† in writing about Emilie Hapgood's theatrical venture, called "pure mental interest"? Why did white intellectuals take such conflicting, but seemingly principled, positions on matters of art, culture and race? Was it a kind of ideal-

[17] Luhan, . . . *Memories, op. cit.,* Vol. III, pp. 534.
* Ridgely Torrence was a close friend of Mabel Dodge's. The plays were: *The Rider of Dreams, Granny Maumee* and *Simon the Cyrenian.*
[18] Johnson, *op. cit.,* pp. 175-179.
† Hutchins Hapgood was the brother-in-law of Emilie Hapgood whose husband, Norman Hapgood, was a pioneer journalist in the field of pure foods, conservation of natural resources and other reforms, from 1900 to the 1920's.

ism peculiar to that era? Was it purely white guilt? Was it white Anglo-Saxon racial and cultural ego? Was it a duty assumed under the obligation of cultural uplift? Did these white intellectuals fully understand the implications of what they were doing? Did they have a definitive cultural goal or were they instinctively groping? Or were their motivations, taken collectively, a confused, spontaneous eclectic mixture?

In any event, during Mabel Dodge's salon period the Village movement had roughly eight years' start over the Harlem movement, which reached its zenith in the 1920's. By then Mabel Dodge's salon was dispersed; the intellectuals who had clustered around her were now playing diverse personal roles both in art and politics. It was post-World War I: Newer and broader challenges and a new, younger, intellectual wave appeared, with a new spokesman—Harold Stearns—who voiced the pessimistic spirit of the Lost Generation. Mabel Dodge was to write in her memoirs: "When a man or a race has to make a new adaption, it is sometimes unsuccessfully hurried like an apple that is rotted before it is ripe, as are many Negroes of Harlem."[19]

Mabel Dodge wanted an American cultural renaissance, but shrank from the implications of a black American renaissance as a socially-necessary, historically-determined, parallel movement. Because of her racially-limited view she could not, or would not, see the black cultural renaissance in its more definable role as a cultural catalyst for the reordering of the disordered and disparate ethnic ingredients of American nationality.

Ironically, the view of the Negro intellectuals involved in the Harlem Renaissance was also limited. Only one man saw deeply into the social implications of the movement: W.E.B. DuBois. He outlined his insights in "The Criteria of Negro Art," which was published in *Crisis* in 1926, but he did not carry his analysis far enough. One reason was that DuBois was not functioning as a creative artist (although he has since assumed this role), but as a voice in the politics and economics of civil rights organizations.

The three writers who wrote specifically about the Harlem Renaissance, and were also representatives of it—Langston Hughes, James Weldon Johnson, and Claude McKay—all failed to render

[19] Luhan, . . . *Memories, op. cit.,* Vol. III, p. 363.

the kind of analysis the movement demanded. A fourth, Wallace Thurman, wrote a sardonic, satirical novel based on the renaissance—*Infants of the Spring*. The situation in Harlem and the world beyond was indeed conducive to criticism. As Langston Hughes later described the era:

> I was there. I had a swell time while it lasted. But I thought it wouldn't last long. . . . For how could a large and enthusiastic number of people be crazy about Negroes forever? They thought the race problem had at last been solved through Art plus Gladys Bentley. . . .
>
> I don't know what made many Negroes think that—except that they were mostly intellectuals doing the thinking. The ordinary Negroes hadn't heard of the Negro Renaissance. And if they had, it hadn't raised their wages any.[20]

Yet, Langston Hughes was created by, and helped to create, this Negro Renaissance. A movement that he never truly understood made him what he is today. In a recent critical study of Langston Hughes, François Dodat wrote that Hughes "integrated himself with the Negro Renaissance," and added; "This poet is not a thinker, but nobody would dream of reproaching him for it, because, on the contrary, he possesses an extraordinary faculty for defining the confused sensations that constitute the collective conscience of simple minds." On the Harlem Renaissance Dodat asserts: "Although it seemed to have such a brilliant future assured, in reality it was the work of a handful of artists and intellectuals who made illusions by their rapid ascent after the total failure of the old ideals, which in any case would not have survived the First World War."[21]

James Weldon Johnson, older than most of the Harlem Renaissance intellectuals, and with more insight into Negro cultural forms, also saw the renaissance somewhat more clearly. Born in 1871, Johnson was in his fifties during the Harlem movement and published *Black Manhattan* at fifty-nine. In 1912, he had published his first novel, *Autobiography of an Ex-Coloured Man*, anonymously. The novel caused a great stir but he did not publish it

---

[20] *The Big Sea, op. cit.*, p. 228.
[21] François Dodat, "Langston Hughes," *Presence Africaine* (Paris, Second Quarter, 1965), Vol. XXVI, No. 54 (English edition), pp. 283-285.

under his own name until 1927. He was the first Negro to be admitted to the Florida Bar and later became American Consul first in Venezuela and then Nicaragua (1903-1912). He was also one of the early lawyer-leaders of the NAACP. Johnson's main literary contribution was in poetry, yet today, when everything about the American Negro must be seen in its historical perspective, Johnson's descriptive history, *Black Manhattan,* and his autobiography, *Along This Way* (1933), emerge as his most important writing. These two works give us practically the entire panorama of Negro cultural history in America by a man who participated in that history from the 1890's—the decade that marked the actual beginning of the modern Negro cultural movement—until his death in 1938.

In *Black Manhattan,* Johnson traces the history of the Negro in New York City from 1626, when there were eleven Negroes in Dutch "New Amsterdam," down to the establishment of black Harlem, and ends the book in 1929 with a description of the Harlem Renaissance. Johnson's great emphasis was on achievement with very little, if any, analysis. Yet he had a long-range vision of the Harlem movement, if not a deep one. His conclusions, unsatisfactory as they were, vaguely indicated where the Harlem movement might have led:

> Harlem is still in the process of making. It is still new and mixed; so mixed that one may get many different views—which is all right so long as one view is not taken to be the whole picture. This many-sided aspect, however, makes it one of the most interesting communities in America. *But Harlem is more than a community; it is a large-scale laboratory experiment in the race problem, and from it a good many facts have been found.* . . .
>
> Through his artistic efforts the Negro is smashing [an] immemorial stereotype faster than he has ever done through any method he has been able to use. . . . He is impressing upon the national mind the conviction that he is an active and important force in American life; that he is a creator as well as a creature; that he has given as well as received; *that his gifts have been not only obvious and material, but also spiritual and aesthetic; that he is a contributor to the nation's common cultural store; in fine, he is helping to form American civilization* [italics added].[22]

[22] *Black Manhattan, op. cit.,* pp. 281-284.

If Johnson had said "American nationality" rather than "American civilization," or if he had said "the American Negro nationality within the American nation," he would have made a definite theoretical contribution and things would have been clearer, perhaps, for Langston Hughes. But Johnson could transcend neither the limits of his times nor his own class background. As a ranking exponent of the NAACP interracial philosophy, he instinctively suppressed (as Robeson did later) whatever feelings of cultural nationalism were within him. Thus he ignored the obvious fact that the Harlem Renaissance, in its creative form, content, and essence, was paying a high price for being allowed, now, to contribute "to the nation's common cultural store" and "to form American civilization." The price was that in exchange for the patronage gained from Carl Van Vechten and others among the downtown white creative intellectual movement, the Negro's "spiritual and aesthetic" materials were taken over by many white artists, who used them allegedly to advance the Negro artistically but actually more for their own self-glorification. As a result, a most intense (and unfair) competition was engendered between white and Negro writers; the whites, from their vantage point of superior social and economic advantages, naturally won out.

A tradition of white cultural paternalism swiftly became entrenched in the Harlem movement. From 1917 to 1930, no less than fifteen white playwrights presented works on Broadway dealing with Negro themes. During the same period, five plays by Negroes were produced, of which four were serious. The one that was fairly successful—*Appearances,* by Garland Anderson—was not about Negroes, nor even whites, as such, but about the Christian Science doctrine. There were two box-office failures: *The Chipwoman's Fortune,* by Willis Richardson, produced by Mrs. Sherwood Anderson, and *Meek Mose,* by Frank Wilson, which was produced by Negroes. Only one play, *Harlem* by Wallace Thurman, was actually produced in Harlem.

It is interesting to note that it was not until after World War I that serious Negro playwrights emerged. Prior to the war, the Negro's forte had always been the stage musical. *Shuffle Along,* a musical by Sissle and Blake that was produced in 1921, was the most outstanding Negro achievement in the theater since the Negro broke with the old minstrel form in the 1890's. In fact, it has not yet been equalled or surpassed, and in terms of book, lyrics and music, it established a new criterion for the American stage musical.

White critics of the theater have all refused to admit the impact of *Shuffle Along* on the evolution of the American musical comedy form. Gilbert Seldes, however, admits to its "vitality" while declining to call it art."[23] The Negro writer, Claude McKay, saw it differently: "The metropolitan critics dismissed it casually at first. There were faults. . . . *Shuffle Along* was conceived, composed and directed by Negroes. There had been nothing comparable to it since the Williams and Walker Negro shows. It definitely showed the Negro groping, fumbling and emerging in artistic group expression."[24]

All in all, in this period, the rather lopsided interracial collaboration in the theater did not project the Negro playwright, but it did open the doors for the Negro actor-performer who progressed unaided by the playwright. Every Negro dramatic star, including Paul Robeson, Charles Gilpin, and others who emerged out of the Harlem Renaissance, rose to stardom in the plays of white dramatists. Robeson was launched by the plays of Mary Hoyt Wiborg, Nan Bagby Stevens, Eugene O'Neill, James Tully, Edna Ferber, Oscar Hammerstein, and Jerome Kern. (*Taboo, Roseanne, All God's Chillun Got Wings, Black Boy*, and *Show Boat*, respectively). The novelists and poets of the Harlem Renaissance fared better than the dramatists, but the actors and performers fared best of all.

James Weldon Johnson did not truly grasp the crucial nature of the Negro writer's role in the Harlem Renaissance, especially the dramatist's role in the theater as an institution that combines nearly all the other art forms. He was not certain that it was necessary to develop Negro playwrights:

> The Negro as a writer for the theatre has not kept pace; he has, in fact, lost ground, even in the special field where he was once prominent, the field of Negro musical shows. In the serious drama three attempts have been made in the professional theatre, only one of which was successful. Coloured people often complain about the sort of light that is shed upon the race in most Negro

[23] *The Seven Lively Arts* (New York: Sagamore Press, 1924), p. 147.
[24] *A Long Way from Home* (New York: Lee Furman, 1937), p. 141.

plays. It may be—*there is no certainty*—that their remedy lies in the development of Negro playwrights. Some good reasons can be assigned for this discrepancy between the status of the actor and of the playwright, but they do not alter the fact [italics added].[25]

Notwithstanding Johnson's lack of "certainty"—*without Negro playwrights there can be no true Negro ethnic theater* (provided that one really wants such a thing).* And without an ethnic theater how can there be a cultural renaissance? Or better—what is the cultural renaissance for? If it is for the enhancement of the Negro's cultural autonomy, his artistic and creative development or his nationality, or his group consciousness, or his identity in white America, then he must develop Negro creative writers of every type—*but especially for the theater.* But if the cultural renaissance is merely for cultural integration, then it does not really matter who writes plays or books about certain people who "just happen to have a dark skin" in white America. In that case the Negro renaissance is a misnomer, a fad, a socially assertive movement in art that disappears and leaves no imprint. A cultural renaissance that engenders barriers to the emergence of the creative writer is a contradiction in terms, an emasculated movement. For the creative edge of the movement has been dulled, the ability of the movement to foment revolutionary ideas about culture and society has been smothered. The black creative writer as interpreter of reality or as social critic must wed his ideas to institutional forms. Undermine the concept of the institutional form (such as denying the institution of the Negro ethnic theater in America) and the renaissance must fail, as the Harlem movement of the 1920's failed.

The analytical flaws in James Weldon Johnson's treatment of the Harlem Renaissance developments, reflected the lack of a definitive cultural philosophy characteristic of the other Harlem intellectuals. Langston Hughes' attitudes were merely an extreme expression of the movement's inspired aimlessness. His grateful but uncritical acceptance of white patronage was the other side of the coin of Johnson's grateful but uncritical acceptance that a white

[25] *Black Manhattan, op. cit.*, p. 225.

* And without an ethnic theater, the Negro playwright is hampered in his development. Thus the seeds of the American Negro Theater's collapse in the 1940's were planted in the 1920's.

playwright (Ridgely Torrence) and a white producer (Emilie Hapgood) were responsible for projecting Negro actors onto a white stage for a white audience so that they commanded "the serious attention of the critics . . . for the first time anywhere in the United States." There was nothing morally or ethically wrong in accepting this patronage at the very outset. The problem was, the pattern was adopted as a permanent *modus operandi* in interracial cultural' affairs, without any critical reflections on its outcome for the future of the movement. Thus, the Harlem Renaissance became partially smothered in the guilty, idealistic, or egotistical interventions of cultural paternalism. But this was typical NAACP "interracialism," extended by Johnson from the politics of civil rights to the politics of culture.

What really lay behind James Weldon Johnson's weak neutrality on the question of Negro vs. white creative competition, and his reluctance to come to critical grips with such obvious failures as the Harlem Renaissance, was the class factor in the Negro movement of the 1920's; for the Negro bourgeois-middle-class stratum did not support the Harlem Renaissance movement morally, aesthetically, or financially The Negro middle class, being politically, socially, and economically marginal, was both unwilling and unable to play any commanding role in the politics and economics of culture and art, *as either patrons or entrepreneurs.* Thus the Harlem Renaissance was an insolvent movement in ways other than in the lack of a cultural philosophy . . . which amounts to the same thing.* A real analysis on the cultural plane of Negro affairs brings one face to face with the hard economic and political facts of American society. Culture and art are spiritual, intellectual, ethical, aesthetic, revolutionary, political, etc.—but they are also a business aspect of private enterprise or of the state. Yet, a truly radical approach to the problems of culture and art cannot be inhibited by the realities of the economic and class barriers against cultural freedom.

* There was some support from the NAACP for the writers of the Harlem Renaissance, despite the fact that the NAACP was, and is, a bourgeois organization. No doubt the influence of leaders such as DuBois and Johnson were responsible for this. Certain wealthy whites, influential in the NAACP leadership, offered literary prizes through the Association's *Crisis* magazine, of which DuBois was then the editor. These prizes were established in 1924. *Opportunity*, the Urban League's publication, followed suit.

W.E.B. DuBois, of the same generation as James Weldon Johnson, was truly groping for the kind of cultural philosophy the Harlem Renaissance needed. This was revealed by Hutchins Hapgood, who had known DuBois at Harvard in the 1890's, and described visiting him sometime around 1912 or 1913:

> One of my disappointments as a journalist was my failure to persuade W.E.B. Dubois to help me to get in touch with the Negroes. I liked the fact that the class of 1890 at Harvard had elected DuBois class orator. Then later, when I was studying in Berlin, I met him, apparently having a good time in the way young men do. So when I was working on the *Globe,* and he was the editor of an important paper devoted to the interests of the Negroes, I felt I could approach him. I saw myself writing a series of attractive articles on Negroes. But when I told DuBois with great enthusiasm of what I intended to do and asked him to give me introductions to some of the more expressive of the race, he declined absolutely. "The Negroes," he said, "do not wish to be written about by white men, even when they know they will be treated sympathetically. Perhaps especially then, they do not desire it." DuBois, as he said this, seemed to me proud and truthful, so much so that I gave up the idea.[26]

During the Chicago conference of the NAACP in 1926, DuBois made the following remarks to a Negro audience:

> It is not the positive propaganda of people who believe white blood divine, infallible and holy to which I object. It is the denial of a similar right of propaganda to those who believe black blood human, lovable and inspired with new ideals for the world. White artists themselves suffer from this narrowing of their field. They cry for freedom in dealing with Negroes because they have so little freedom in dealing with whites. DuBose Heyward writes "Porgy" and writes beautifully of the black Charleston underworld. But why does he do this? Because he cannot do a similar thing for the white people of Charleston, or they would drum him out of town. The only chance he had to tell the truth of pitiful human degradation was to tell it of colored people. . . . In other words, the white public today demands from its artists, literary and pictorial, racial pre-judgment which deliberately dis-

[26] *A Victorian in the Modern World* (New York: Harcourt, Brace & World, 1939), pp. 344-345.

torts Truth and Justice, as far as colored races are concerned, and it will pay for no other.[27]

With DuBois' incisive cultural criticisms it was no wonder that the NAACP eventually ousted him in 1934.

From within Harlem itself there was another indigenous trend that bears consideration in relation to the Harlem Renaissance: the group of Negro writers and radicals functioning around A. Philip Randolph's *Messenger* magazine. Randolph was then a Socialist and his group was allied with the official white American Socialist Party. The most prominent of the very few Negro Socialists, or sympathizers, of the time were Chandler Owen (Randolph's co-editor of the *Messenger*), Lovett Fort-Whiteman, W.A. Domingo, Hubert H. Harrison, Richard B. Moore, Otto Huiswoud, W.E.B. DuBois, Grace Campbell, Cyril V. Briggs and Frank Crosswaith. When the great split struck the Socialist Party in 1919 over whether to support the Russian Revolution's Bolsheviks, Randolph and Owen did not go over to the pro-Communist, leftwing Socialist faction. Those who did were Fort-Whiteman, Campbell, Moore, Huiswoud and Briggs. In subsequent years, this split among the Negro Socialists was the root cause of more destructive rivalry in Harlem's civil rights and labor politics than the records reveal. Randolph went on to organize the Brotherhood of Sleeping Car Porters and Owen turned conservative.

The *Messenger** was founded in 1917 and prided itself on being "the only Radical Negro Magazine in America," militantly espousing a program for "the Negro and the New Social Order." This "new social order" was to be frankly socialistic: The early editions of the *Messenger* meticulously described its political, economic and civil rights platforms for the Negro, and openly preached social revolution. However, the *Messenger* did not have much rapport with the cultural affairs relating to the Harlem Renaissance. It declared bluntly that its socialistic "economics and politics" took precedence over culture and art. The magazine's real attitudes on such questions were revealed in an editorial remark on W.E.B DuBois and the way he handled his column, "Horizon," in the NAACP magazine, *Crisis:*

[27] "Criteria of Negro Art," *Crisis* magazine. [NAACP] (October, 1926), pp. 290-297.
* It was formerly *The Hotel Messenger*, a worker's union paper, started in 1916.

The leading column of the "Horizon" is always "music and art." Then "meetings" which signify the gathering of literateurs. Next "The War," which inspires pictures and scenes for literary descriptions and word painting. "Industry" and "Politics" sections follow. This is no coincidence, but a logical product of DuBois's cerebration. [The *Messenger* carries as its first column, after editorials "Economics and Politics."] This is natural for us because with us economics and politics take precedence to "Music and Art."[28]

This column on DuBois was unsigned but the writing resembled that of Chandler Owen. In that crucial year of 1919, the *Messenger* Socialists were making their positions clear with regard to all other trends and leaders, especially Negro leaders. In its December, 1922 issue it conducted a broad symposium on the Garvey movement. The *Messenger* admitted that DuBois was "the most distinguished Negro in the United States today. For the last twenty years he has been known as a radical among Negroes." But it disputed the claim that DuBois really deserved the title of sociologist "as we understand it," because none of his sociological studies were strictly scientific, but more historical and descriptive. The *Messenger* attributed this to the fact that: DuBois was educated at a time and place where political science was not in great favor and where political science was little taught. Greek, Latin and classicism were stressed at Harvard. Few of the older Negro leaders have had the modern education.[29]

Thus as far back as 1919, DuBois was considered to be—at the age of fifty-one—an "old leader" by the new wave Socialists of the *Messenger:*

> DuBois's conception of politics is strictly opportunist. Within the last six years he has been Democrat, Socialist, and Republican. . . .
> He opposes unionism instead of opposing a prejudiced union. He must make way for the new radicalism of the New Negroes.

But:

> Radicalism is a relative term and three decades hence may

---

[28] *Messenger,* March, 1919, p. 22. N.B. It was admitted, however, that DuBois was "courageous and honest."
[29] *Ibid.*

pronounce the radicals of today as the reactionaries of tomorrow.[30]

The *Messenger*'s critique of W.E.B. DuBois reveals, today, the
early vanity of the then youthful Socialist Party, in thinking that it
had mastered a version of the Marxian "scientific socialism." Came
the NAACP, the Garvey movement, the Russian Revolution, the
American Communist Left, the Harlem Renaissance plus the
aftermath of World War I, and the Negro Socialists, particularly, had to demonstrate their socially scientific prowess even
more strongly to avoid being inundated by someone else's new
trend. But the *Messenger* unwittingly revealed that, in American
Negro terms, it was further behind the times than it charged Du-
Bois with being. For it could not deal with the implications of the
Harlem Renaissance. It had adopted the old European version of
Socialist programming wherein economics and politics took precedence over culture and art. As pioneering Negro Socialists, the
Messenger intellectuals were just as unoriginal as the Negro Communists were to become during the 1920's. They took their political schemes from the whites, and thus did not grasp the fact that
from the native American Negro point of view, neither politics,
economics nor culture took precedence over each other but were
inseparable and had to function together.

DuBois, however, grasped this fact. In his speech on the "Criteria of Negro Art," he said in part:

> I do not doubt but there are some in this audience who are a
> little disturbed at the subject of this meeting, and particularly at
> the subject I have chosen. Such people are thinking something
> like this: "How is it that an organization like this, a group of
> radicals, trying to bring new things into the world, a fighting
> organization . . . how is it that an organization of this kind can
> turn aside to talk about Art? After all, what have we who are
> slaves and black to do with Art?
>
> Or perhaps there are others who feel a certain relief and are
> saying, "After all it is rather satisfactory after all this talk about
> rights and fighting to sit and dream of something which leaves a
> nice taste in the mouth."
>
> Let me tell you that neither of these groups is right. The thing
> we are talking about tonight is part of the great fight we are

[30] *Ibid.*

carrying on and it represents a forward and an upward look—a pushing forward. . . .

What do we want? What is the thing we are after? As it was phrased last night it had a certain truth: We want to be Americans, full-fledged Americans, with all the rights of other American citizens. But is that all? Do we simply want to be Americans? Once in a while through all of us there flashes some clairvoyance, some clear idea, of what America really is. We who are dark can see America in a way that white Americans can not. And seeing our country thus, are we satisfied with its present goals and ideals? . . .[31]

In this speech, W.E.B. DuBois went on to describe Negro art in its functional relationship to the civil rights movement, and its aims as Negro cultural expression within the context of the American nationality idea. It was a brief exposition, but it was, undoubtedly, the very first time the theme was ever voiced by a ranking Negro leader, and the decade of the Harlem Renaissance was the proper historical moment for it to be expressed. But the *Messenger* intellectuals did not see this. As the 1920's progressed toward the fateful 1930's, their early radicalism softened, until by 1928, the only vestige of the *Messenger's* 1919 revolutionary initiation was the magazine's cover. Langston Hughes* was to write:

The summer of 1926, I lived in a rooming house on 137th Street, where Wallace Thurman . . . also lived. Thurman was then managing editor of the *Messenger,* a Negro magazine that had a curious career. It began by being very radical, racial, and socialistic, just after the war. I believe it received a grant from the Garland Fund in its early days. Then it later became a kind of Negro society magazine and a plugger for Negro business, with photographs of prominent colored ladies and their nice homes in it. A. Philip Randolph, now President of the Brotherhood of Sleeping Car Porters, Chandler Owen, and George S. Schuyler were connected with it. Schuyler's editorials, à la Mencken, were the most interesting things in the magazine, verbal brickbats that said sometimes one thing, sometimes another, but always vigorously. I asked Thurman what kind of magazine the *Messenger*

[31] DuBois, *op. cit.,* p. 290.
* In 1926, Hughes, Thurman, Zora Neale Hurston, Gwendolyn Bennet, and others attempted the publication of a magazine called *"Fire*—a Negro quarterly of the arts." Its first and only issue was attacked by the older Negro intellectuals, said Hughes; "Dr. DuBois in the *Crisis* roasted it." See *The Big Sea,* p. 235.

was, and he said it reflected the policy of whoever paid off best at the time.[32]

If Langston Hughes explained the Harlem Renaissance mostly in terms of himself and his limited perceptions, and James Weldon Johnson wrote an admirable and informative essay on the renaissance as an important movement with a history and a future, Claude McKay, a West Indian, could view the Harlem Renaissance both as a participant and as an objective, but interested, outsider. In so doing he unwittingly revealed important aspects of the Harlem Renaissance that Hughes wouldn't have told if he could, and Johnson couldn't have told if he wanted to. For McKay, in his autobiography, sheds important light on two trends that directly or indirectly influenced the Harlem Renaissance: the Garvey movement and the Communist-oriented leftwing of the 1920's.

Claude McKay was more than a decade older than the young group of creative intellectuals who made up the main wave of the Harlem Renaissance. Born in 1890,* he came to the United States from the West Indies at the age of twenty-one, or just about the time Mabel Dodge was establishing her Greenwich Village salon. By 1914 he had been introduced into the circles of the white creative intellectuals in the Village—the new trend growing out of the Dodge salon and Max Eastman's *Masses* magazine. Among McKay's first literary contacts was the international literary bohemian, Frank Harris, editor of *Pearson's Magazine,* who published a few of McKay's early poems. By 1921 McKay had become an associate editor of the *Liberator* (a continuation of the earlier *Masses* magazine, which had been suppressed by the Federal authorities in 1917). Here McKay met the radical wing of the Village movement, centered around the personality of Max Eastman, the *Liberator's* editor.† Thus McKay started his literary career not as a part of the Harlem Renaissance, but as an associate of the white radical leftwing of the Village movement.

[32] Hughes, *op. cit.,* pp. 233-234.
* Some sources say 1889 or 1891.
† This group consisted of Crystal Eastman, the editor's sister; Floyd Dell, novelist; Art Young and Hugo Gellert, artists; Genevieve Taggard, poet; William Gropper, cartoonist; Michael „Gold, writer; Louis Untermeyer, poet; Arturo Giovanitti, anarchist-poet, and the previously mentioned Maurice Sterne of Mabel Dodge's salon.

As an editor of the white radicals' main publication in New York, McKay was placed in a position of having to introduce the *Liberator* radicals to Harlem radicals, although he himself was not very well acquainted with the Harlem group.* In 1921, Hubert Harrison, Richard B. Moore, W.A. Domingo, Cyril V. Briggs, Otto Huiswoud, and Grace Campbell came to visit the *Liberator* offices to discuss Harlem radical problems. Most of these Negroes were members of what was called the African Blood Brotherhood, founded by Cyril V. Briggs in 1919. They were predominantly West Indians and represented two or three simultaneous aspects of Harlem radical developments of the 1920's. In the first place, the ABB marked the split within Randolph's *Messenger* group over definitions of radicalism. The predominant West Indian composition of the ABB signified a conflict between American and West Indian Negroes over radical policies, inasmuch as Randolph and his coeditor Owens considered themselves the leaders of the "new Negro" trend, a strictly American Negro development. More than that, the ABB represented a momentary break with radical socialism in favor of a radical nationalism that Randolph eschewed. However, the West Indian ABB soon dropped its radical nationalism; won over by the new Communist movement, its top leaders became the "core of the first American Negro Communist cadre."[33] It was from the ABB that the white Communists got their first outstanding Negro Communists—there is no record of any Negroes participating in the 1919 founding rites of the Communist movement. Thus the overall split in the American Socialist Party over whether to support or reject the Russian Revolution was reflected in Harlem in the split between Randolph's *Messenger* and the ABB leaders.

However, because of its crypto-nationalism, the African Blood Brotherhood soon got caught in the middle of the clash between

---

* James Weldon Johnson's article, "What the Negro Is Doing for Himself," appeared in the *Liberator*, June, 1918, pp. 29-31, describing the work of the NAACP. In the prior issue of April, 1918, p. 40, Johnson took issue with Floyd Dell's review of his book "Fifty Years and Other Poems" in the *Liberator*, March, 1918.

[33] Theodore Draper, *American Communism and Soviet Russia* (New York: Viking Press, Compass Edition, 1963), p. 326.

the Garvey movement and the Communist movement. The already troublesome conflict that existed between American and West Indian Negroes, over the implications of the Garvey movement, pitted West Indians against West Indians over the issue of Communism. Early in the 1920's Marcus Garvey came out against the Communist movement as follows: "I am advising the Negro working man and laborer against the present brand of Communism . . . as taught in America, and to be careful of the traps and pitfalls of white trade unionism in affiliation with the American Federation of white workers or laborers."[34]

This leader of "Back-to-Africa" Black Nationalism said much more on the Communist issue, and his attitudes effectively blocked the determined efforts of the Communists to influence, collaborate with, or undermine his movement. This situation greatly frustrated the Communists in their effort to capitalize on the current Negro discontent—as indeed had Garvey. As a result the Communists began to assail Garvey's program as reactionary, escapist and utopian. At the same time, they attempted to infiltrate Garvey's movement. Mrs. A. Jacques Garvey, the leader's second wife, later described Communist tactics: "The Communists now conceived a plan how they could play Garvey against the Klan, then worm their way into his organization. . . . They infiltrated in some of the branches, and secretly sent delegates to the [1924] convention, who moved a motion that the Organization, in the interest of its members, should declare war on the Klan.[35]

It was very apparent that these infiltrators used by the Communists were none other than the West Indian members of the African Blood Brotherhood. In this regard it is ironic that in the legend built up around the personality of Garvey, the notion has come down that his worst enemies and detractors were all American Negroes who did not appreciate the man's nationalist genius. However, the truth of the matter was that while Garvey's most inspired followers were West Indians, so were his most vitriolic and effective enemies—both in the United States (Briggs) and in the West Indies (the supporters of the "West Indian Protective Society of America," an anti-Garveyite organization headquar-

---

[34] *Garvey and Garveyism*, A. J. Garvey, 1963 (Published by the author, 1963), p. 87.
[35] *Ibid.*, p. 138.

tered in Harlem). The real difference was that none of Garvey's West Indian critics were prominent leaders like DuBois, Randolph and others.

West Indians are never so "revolutionary" as when they are away from the Islands. Thus what weakened the whole Garveyite criticism of the American Negro scene was that, without an economic power base, the Garvey movement could not be launched in Jamaica; this very same flaw created difficulties for him in the United States. Mrs. A. Jacques Garvey wrote that "the subtle economic thralldom of Colonial Powers in the Caribbean fools many West Indians."[36] This was so true that Garvey's initial organizational efforts in Jamaica were defeated, forcing him to come to the "greener pastures" of the United States for success.

In addition to the West Indian's traditional political apathy at home, there was less liberty and elbowroom for political agitation than there was in the United States. Thus it was difficult for the Garveyites to swallow the fact that much of the criticism coming from American Negro leadership was justified; because the West Indians wanted American Negroes to achieve the kind of nationalist unity as a minority, that the West Indians could not achieve as a majority at home, and never have to this day.

As a Jamaican, Claude McKay was also caught in the middle of the multisided American Negro vs. West Indian vs. Garvey vs. Communist controversy. It appears that during this early stage of the conflict McKay assumed a reticent neutrality. Later, McKay openly rejected Marcus Garvey, and much later than that, the Communist Party, also.

After the *Liberator* conference of black and white radicals, McKay made his first contacts with the Harlem intelligentsia. He met W.E.B. DuBois and was surprised at his "cold, acid hauteur of spirit."[37] He also met Walter White, the novelist Jessie Fauset, and James Weldon Johnson (who was his favorite among the NAACP officialdom). From this point on, it was apparent that McKay's relationship to everyone and everything connected with the Harlem Renaissance was very tentative. He was not really at home in the United States or with Negro movements. Always apparent was a vague, undefined barrier between him—as a West Indian—and the American Negroes. He maintained much better rapport with the whites, if only because they seemed to have more to offer him personally and literarily. He goes into great detail in his autobiography about his relations with whites, both in the United States and in Europe. Through it all he was a wanderer, seeking something "a long way from home"—as indeed, he named his book. As such, he was free not to commit himself fully to the Harlem Renaissance and its radical offshoots. Thus he remained, at all times, the critical outsider looking·in, the objective traveler passing through on his way to the next adventure or attraction.

McKay undoubtedly saw, better than most, that despite the positive creative features of the Harlem Renaissance, the whole drama was being acted out in a setting of extreme aimlessness, conflict and confusion. In the upheaval of the postwar period, too many diverse trends from different directions met head on, both in Harlem and the Village. Harlem was full of new migrants and veterans. The NAACP had swung into action on a new level of protest against the rise in anti-Negro terror all over the country. It also clashed bitterly, through DuBois, with the wave of Garvey nationalism that was appealing to the lower classes. On the political front, the Russian Revolution had split white American socialism into pro- and anti-Bolshevik factions, the former of which was trying to woo the Negro plus the Garveyite. The radical split was reflected in the ranks of the white intellectuals with whom McKay was allied in the Village. McKay himself, wary of wholehearted commitment to anything but his own art, was blandly attempting to "play ball" with white radicals, the NAACP, the Harlem Renaissance *literati* and all the rich white patrons he could locate.

Thus uncommitted, he made the most of the literary and social aspects of both the Village movement and the Harlem Renaissance. In McKay's autobiography, as in Langston Hughes', there is much description of parties and celebrities. In his discussions of Hemingway and Joyce he revealed that he was very much interested in establishing his own literary worth among his European "peers." But he seldom discussed critically any of the work coming from the Harlem Renaissance. His own novel, *Home to Harlem*, he compared with Van Vechten's *Nigger Heaven*, both of which

had been roundly denounced and rejected by the Negro bourgeoisie.

It was not long before McKay clashed with the *Liberator*'s editorial board. Obviously, the Communists' "line" on politics, culture and art, Negroes, etc., was "hardening" too much for the
romantic poet McKay essentially was.* Michael Gold, who had
been appointed executive editor in Max Eastman's absence in
Russia, perfectly personified this new line. Gold thought the *Liberator* "should become a popular proletarian magazine, printing
doggerels from lumberjacks and stevedores and true revelations
of chambermaids."[38] He had come into the ranks of the radical
writers through the Provincetown Playhouse of O'Neill and
George Cram Cook, Susan Glaspell, and Edna St. Vincent Millay.
But, "he was still intellectually battling up from the depths of
proletarian starvation and misery," McKay pointed out, and his
"social revolutionary passion was electrified with personal feeling
that was sometimes as acid as lime-juice. When he attacked it was
with rabbinical zeal, and often his attacks were spiteful and bitter."[39]

McKay and Gold could not make it on the same editorial board,
so McKay resigned. It was revealed that Gold was either envious or
fearful of McKay, a fact which posed, probably for the first time,
the touchy question of the relationship of Jews and Negroes
within the Communist Left during the Harlem Renaissance. Indeed on one occasion, Gold challenged McKay to box outside a
Village restaurant.

Without a doubt, Michael Gold was not sympathetic to McKay's
literary work or anything coming out of the Harlem Renaissance.
After 1926, when the *Liberator* ceased publication and *New
Masses* appeared (with the same writers), McKay's famous poem
"If We Must Die" was severely criticized by the Communists and
Gold with the assertion that McKay had "written an indignant
poem, attacking lynching, wholly lacking in working-class con-
tent."[40] Four years later Gold wrote:

---

* For McKay's early views on white radicalism and race, see his review of T.S.
Stribling's novel *Birthright, Liberator*, August, 1922, pp. 15-16.
[38] Claude McKay, *op. cit.*, p. 139.
[39] *Ibid.*, p. 140.
[40] *Ibid.*, p. 226.

We believe Carl Van Vechten the worst friend the Negro ever had. This night club rounder and white literary sophisticate was one of the first to take an interest in Negro writers in this country. He has thus influenced many of them. He has been the most evil influence—Gin, jazz, and sex—this is all that stirs him in our world, and he has imparted his tastes to the young Negro literateurs. He is a white literary bum, who has created a brood of Negro literary bums. So many of them are wasting their splendid talents on the gutter-life side of Harlem.[41]

Note that this example of Communist puritanical puerility was written in 1930, the same year Johnson's *Black Manhattan* appeared—as if to say that the Village literary movement from which Gold himself had emerged, was *not* highly activated by "gin, jazz, and sex" on its Bohemian fringes. As if to say that when the Village whites invaded Harlem "discovering" Negroes, "gin, jazz and sex" would not be required to soften the initial shock of cultural confrontation. At any rate, Gold's critical bomb revealed that the coming of the economic crash had not stilled the ideological uproar, settled no issues, clarified no problems, nor resolved a single cultural question in Negro-white relations first posed in the 1920's.

The critical zeal and political bias that McKay attributed to Michael Gold was a trademark that he carried into the 1930's, and ignited the bitter literary wars between the Communists' *New Masses* and the *Partisan Review*. Started in 1934 as the organ of the John Reed (Writers') Club, *Partisan Review* was something of a literary opposition front to *New Masses*. An angry dialogue was launched in *Partisan Review* in February, 1936, when James T. Farrell attacked Clifford Odets' play, *Paradise Lost,* as "loaded with dull speeches and swaggering platitudes."[42] The same month, Michael Gold defended Odets by attacking Farrell in *New Masses,*[43] but was himself in turn rebuked three weeks later, by Josephine Herbst, for being as "subjective" as Farrell. She wrote, again in *New Masses:* "If we are to compel our writers on the Left to chant the same song our ranks will thin, not gain recruits, that is certain, and in the process we shall have bankrupted the

[41] "Notes of the Month," *New Masses* [Negro Literature], February, 1930, p. 1.
[42] Farrell, *Partisan Review,* February, 1936, pp. 28-29.
[43] Gold, *New Masses,* February 18, 1936, pp. 22-23.

intellectual integrity of the cultural movement. . . . You seem to have made yourself a watchdog for strictly workingclass writing. . . . Your anti-intellectualism has bothered me for a long time."[44] To which Gold replied in the same issue: "It seems to me truer to say that Farrell left the path of authentic criticism . . . to make an unforgiveable personal attack on Odets before saying a word about the play itself."[45] During this period, Max Eastman, who was Michael Gold's first mentor on the *Liberator,* had become an anti-Communist and was attacking the writers and artists around *New Masses* as not being representative of the cultural revolution. Later, a Samuel Sillen of the *New Masses* staff could accuse John Dos Passos, in the July 4, 1939, issue, of hating Jewish Communists in his review of Dos Passos' *Adventures of a Young Man.* In the midst of all this literary and cultural polemics on the Left, were both Langston Hughes and Claude McKay—lined up on the side of Michael Gold. They were soon joined by Richard Wright and Ralph Ellison whose articles and book reviews began to appear in *New Masses* during the late 1930's. But neither Hughes' Renaissance writers nor the newcomers of the 1930's ever achieved among themselves the level and intensity of literary polemics that occurred on the white Left.

The retreat of Claude McKay from his strategic post on the *Liberator* in 1922 was an indication that the trends of the 1920's had thrown the Negro intelligentsia onto the cultural stage in an intuitive and romantic outpouring of "soul," but without the depth of philosophical insight that would have enabled them to grasp the implications of their movement. It should have been the Hugheses, the Johnsons and the McKays, who created the critical terms to be laid down on this movement—*not* the Michael Golds. Gold and company on the Communist Left made no great original contribution to either the Harlem Renaissance or the white movement. All the Michael Golds accomplished was to inject a foreign cultural and political ideology into a basically American cultural phenomenon, and engender confusion upon confusion. The essentially original and native creative element of the 1920's was the Negro ingredient—as all the whites who were running to Harlem

[44] Herbst, *New Masses,* March 10, 1936, p. 18.
[45] Gold, *op. cit.,* p. 20.

actually knew. But the Harlem intellectuals were so overwhelmed at being "discovered" and courted, that they allowed a *bona fide* cultural movement, which issued from the social system as naturally as a gushing spring, to degenerate into a pampered and paternalized vogue.

The Negro intellectuals represented the crucial American "minority" group in this situation. They were on the ascendant, yet they were placed in a position wherein representatives of another minority could dictate cultural standards to them. This was historically unwarranted. It was as if to say that a Michael Gold came from the Jewish minority in America with a *bona fide* gripe against the system for having been culturally deprived. However, even in the early 1900's, culture thrived in New York's Jewish ghetto. Why did a Michael Gold desert this world in 1917? If it was because he desired to "Americanize" himself out of the Jewish ghetto, by way of the radical Left, then it should have been that his critical polemics on cultural affairs be directed to the Jews who did not follow him into the Communist Party, *not* with the views of the representatives of another ghetto minority*— of whom he knew next to nothing and understood less. On Michael Gold and Negroes in the first great Harlem uprising of 1935, Ernest Kaiser commented: "Oversimplification and sanguineness on the Negro question led Communists during the war to blame all anti-Negro riots and the like on fifth column agents in this country. The Harlem riot, a different kind of a riot, became, in the words of Michael Gold, a hoodlum-led Negro pogrom against the Jewish shopkeepers of Harlem! Even liberals had better understanding of the different types of riots."[46]

In the 1920's the Communists were not telling Jewish writers in the ghetto how to write. If the Negro creative intellectuals had taken a strong position on critical standards during the 1920's, there could have been a lot more constructive criticism within the Harlem Renaissance, which would have benefited the development of the movement.

---

* Jewish Communists seek to work politically with Negroes on the basis of being white Americans in the labor movement. But ironically, when ghetto Negroes attack Jewish business exploitation in ghettoes (because they are white Americans), it is then termed anti-Semitism.

[46] Kaiser, "Racial Dialectics, The Aptheker-Myrdal School Controversy," Atlanta University, *Phylon* magazine, Vol. 9, No. 4, 1948, p. 299.

McKay's retreat revealed the weak-kneed, nonpolitical, noncommittal naïveté which was characteristic of many of the Negro intellectuals. Yet, seeing the 1920's in perspective, this default is understandable. The Harlem Renaissance had too much to contend with in the new Communist leftwing and the new Garvey nationalism. On the other hand, the new Communist Left, due to its own foreign inspiration, was rendered unable to cope with the native literary and cultural movement on the American scene. V.F. Calverton* used the book review pages of *New Masses* to complain: "The revolt of the artist has switched from the neuroticism of the nineties to the eroticism of the twenties!" Calverton expanded his critique to include "the American intellectual [who] thus has become ingrown rather than expansive. He has been as afraid of adventurousness in the intellectual life as the pioneer was unafraid of adventurousness in the practical life."[47]

Prior to this, John Dos Passos had clashed with Michael Gold over leftwing policy in literature and art, again in *New Masses*. Said Dos Passos: "I don't think there should be any more phrases, badges, opinions, banners, imported from Russia or anywhere else. Ever since Columbus, imported systems have been the curse of this country. Why not develop our own. The *New Masses* must at all times avoid the great future that lies behind it."[48]

---

* Calverton was the founder and editor of *Modern Quarterly*, an independent radical magazine in 1923. Calverton, though himself white, wrote an article, "The Advance of Negro Literature," for *Opportunity* magazine, February, 1926; edited an *Anthology of Negro Literature* for Modern Library (Random House, 1929); and wrote *The Liberation of American Literature* (Charles Scribner's Sons, 1932).

In 1937, Calverton edited *The Making of Society—An Outline of Sociology* for Modern Library. The aim of this outline was to assist in "Americanizing the Marxian approach." In the introduction, he said American Marxists "have done little to reconcile Marxian propositions with American facts," and "Marxism has contributed little to American sociology." Yet Calverton's compilation of the thought of nearly sixty social thinkers, both ancient and modern, did not include a single Negro sociologist despite the fact that at least three—W.E.B. DuBois, E. Franklin Frazier, and Abram L. Harris—wrote for *Modern Quarterly* during the 1920's. However in 1932, Calverton made an original criticism of Marxist practice in America through his theory of "Cultural Compulsives" (*q.v.*), a conception that had direct relation to the Negro in American culture; but no Negro thinkers took up the question in support of Calverton, who was defeated by the Communists. This controversy over "Cultural Compulsives" showed that neither blacks nor whites were prepared to make any form of radicalism conform with American facts.
[47] V.F. Calverton, "Intellectuals and Revolution" (review of Floyd Dell's *Love in Greenwich Village*), *New Masses*, October, 1926, p. 28.
[48] Dos Passos, *New Masses*, June, 1926, p. 20.

What Dos Passos meant was that the *New Masses,* under the cultural and political leadership of Michael Gold, had come under solid Communist control. He was trying to say that the New Masses should forget the entire period of its predecessors—*Masses* and *Liberator*—and seek a new course that had nothing to do with the Russian enchantment with which Gold was so obsessed. So were many others, including Claude McKay, who after resigning from the *Liberator,* had gone to "see for himself" what was happening in Russia.

He arrived in time to attend the 1922 Fourth Congress of the Communist International in Moscow. There he was selected as a "special delegate" representing American Negroes—merely because he was the only Negro in Moscow at that moment:

> I went to Russia. Some thought I was invited by the Soviet Government; others that I was sent by the Communist Party. . . . I was not one of the radicals abroad important to the Soviet government; and I was not a member of the Communist Party. All I had was the dominant urge to go. . . . Millions of ordinary human beings and thousands of writers were stirred by the Russian thunder rolling around the world.[49]

The fact that the Russians took up McKay so readily revealed that they were much more eager to receive Negroes and learn about them than the American Communists were to send them over. When the official American Communist Party delegation arrived, they were opposed to McKay's presence and tried to have him sent back to the States. The Americans had brought along their own handpicked Negro representative (whom McKay described as being so fairskinned in pigmentation that the average Russian refused to accept him as genuine, preferring McKay because he *was* black). Oddly enough, McKay got help not from the American Communist Whites in Moscow, but from a veteran Japanese Communist named Sen Katayama, one of the earliest Japanese revolutionaries, born in 1858. Katayama was well known in the United States among Socialists, and was a power in Moscow. McKay went to Katayama seeking protection from harassment by the Americans; the Japanese took up his case with Lenin, Trotsky, Zinoviev, and Radek—the Big Four. From that point on McKay had the keys to the city, with the official title of "unofficial observer." He attended all the sessions of the Congress on the American situation.

McKay wrote, "I listened to the American delegates deliberately telling lies about conditions in America, and I was disgusted." He reported that not only Communist delegates but radical American intellectuals were deceiving the Russians with false pictures of the American situation. McKay heard the chairman of the American delegation say—"In five years we will have the American revolution." McKay, himself, was expected to corroborate this forecast, but refused. He wrote: "Truly, I could not speak such lies. I knew that the American workers in 1922 were generally better off than at the beginning of the World War in 1914. . . . How, then, could I stand before the gigantic achievement of the Russian Revolution and lie?"[50]

The Americans misled the Russians about an incipient social revolution in the United States and the Russians believed them because that was what they wanted to hear. In attempting to satisfy the Russian curiosity and thirst for knowledge about American Negroes, the white American Communists revealed their own confusion, ignorance and prejudice. McKay related:

> The Negro question came under the division of the Eastern Bureau, of which Sen Katayama was an active official. Because of his American experience and his education among Negroes, Sen Katayama was important as a kind of arbiter between black and white on the Negro question. He was like a little brown bulldog with his jaws clamped on an object that he wouldn't let go. He apparently forgot all about nice human relationships in conferences. Sen Katayama had no regard for the feelings of the white American comrades, when the Negro question came up, and boldly told them so. He said that though they called themselves Communists, many of them were unconsciously prejudiced against Negroes because of their background. He told them that really to understand Negroes they needed to be educated about and among Negroes as he had been.[51]

Karl Radek, one of the big men in the Politbureau, invited

---

[50] *Ibid.*, p. 175.
[51] *Ibid.*, p. 180.

McKay and the official Negro delegate* to discuss with him some essentials of the American Negro situation:

> Radek wanted to know if I had a practical policy for the organization of American Negroes. I said that I had no policy other than the suggestion of a Negro *Bund,* that I was not an organizer or an agitator and could not undertake or guarantee any practical work or organization.[52]

The Negro delegate told Radek that McKay "was a poet and a romantic"—this—despite the fact that before their meeting with Radek, McKay and this delegate had had a private talk about the Negro issue at the conference. McKay had compared the powerless situation of the Negroes within the American Communist Party to the strong position of the Finnish and the Russian federations.

> The Finnish and Russian federations were not only the most highly organized units of the American party, but, so I was informed, they contributed more than any other to the party chest. They controlled because they had the proper organization and the cash.
>
> I told the [Negro] delegate: "That's what Negroes need in American politics—a highly organized all-Negro group. When you have that—a Negro group voting together like these Finns and Russians—you will be getting somewhere. We may feel inflated as individual Negroes sitting in on the councils of whites, but it means very little if our people are not organized. Otherwise the whites will want to tell us what is right for our people even against our better thinking. The Republicans and the Democrats do the same thing. . . . But we remain politically unorganized. What we need is our own group, organized and officered entirely by Negroes, something similar to the Finnish Federation. Then when you have your own group, your own voting strength, you can make demands on the whites; they will have more respect for your united strength than for your potential strength. Every other racial group in America is organized as a group except Negroes. I am not an organizer or an agitator, but I can see what is lacking in the Negro group."[53]

---

* McKay never names this delegate, but Theodore Draper claims he was Otto Huiswoud. See *American Communism and Soviet Russia* (New York: Viking Press, Compass Edition, 1963), p. 327.

[52] McKay, *op. cit.,* p. 182.

[53] *Ibid.,* pp. 177-178.

McKay saw the problem clearly enough, but he did not tell the Russians his views. Despite the fact that the Russians had accepted him as a *bona fide* representative of American Negroes, he kept insisting that he was not qualified to represent the American Negro group.

McKay should have enlightened the Russians while he was in a position to do so. He should have told them that the Communists in America were about to make serious blunders in handling the national group question. He should have told them that the American Party was not a party of the American workers, as such, but an organization in which leftwing political power was exercised and predicated on national groups; not only on the Finnish and Russian groups, but particularly the Jewish group that later came to dominate leftwing affairs in a degree all out of proportion to its numbers. Jews were also able to play a three-way game inside the Communist leftwing: as "Americanized" Jews, à la Gold; as Jewish Jews; and as pro-Zionist, nationalistic Jews. Leftwing Jews were able to drop their Jewishness and pick it up whenever it suited them. They were able to function as American whites without prejudice, especially in the cultural fields. They were able, as Jews, to wield power through the Jewish Federation. Later they were able to function as pro-Zionist nationalists inside the Left. At the very time McKay was in Moscow seeking audiences with Lenin and Trotsky, the pro-Russian Jewish leftwing in New York had gotten Communist support in putting out a pro-Communist Jewish newspaper, *Freiheit* (*Freedom*), "two years before the American Communists were able to put out a daily organ in English."[54]

American Negroes never achieved, or were not allowed to, what other organized national groups achieved within the Communist Left, and never fought for the right to do so. But they allowed Jewish leaders who came out of the Jewish Federation to become experts on the Negro problem in America. Here was the great default of the Negro intellectuals of the period. McKay, for example, could tell the Negro delegate that the Negro needed the group power of the Finns and the Russians, but he himself was

[54] Draper, *The Roots of American Communism* (New York: Viking Press, Compass Edition, 1957), p. 341.

not about to take any responsibility as an artist to educate the Negro masses in Harlem along such lines. This, he felt, was the responsibility of the Negro Left politicians, whose failings on this score he criticized. But it was also the responsibility of the intellectuals, who did not have to play the opportunistic politics of the leftwing machine as Negro politicians were forced to, in order to stay in favor with white hierarchies. Instead the intellectuals of the Harlem Renaissance shuttled back and forth between the NAACP officialdom and the Communists, from the Village radical intellectuals to rich white patrons seeking artistic support. If one wants to claim that the prominence of interracial partying on a high cultural level was, in fact, a "social revolution," then perhaps something *was* actually achieved. But it all went down the drain with the coming of the 1929 Crash, and the Negro intellectual class has been badly disoriented ever since.

The Garvey movement was one trend in existence in the twenties that appealed to the group solidarity of the Negro. Yet, like other Negro intellectuals of the period, McKay* steered away from any association with it. He referred to Marcus Garvey as "a West Indian charlatan [who] came to this country, full of antiquated social ideas. . . ."[55] A more positive attitude might have dealt with some of the obvious flaws in Garveyism.

After his pilgrimage to Moscow, which McKay considered the highpoint of his career, he traveled about Europe, ending up finally in Paris—a destination that was, in a sense, preordained. Paris had become the last resort of many other literary and artistic Americans, black as well as white. "It was interesting in Paris," McKay wrote, "among the cosmopolitan expatriates. The milieu was sympathetic. It was broader than the radical milieu of Greenwich Village." Then he added: "Frankly to say, I never considered myself identical with the white expatriates. I was a kind of sympathetic fellow-traveler in the expatriate caravan. The majority of them were sympathetic toward me. But their problems were not my problems. They were all-white with problems in white which were different from problems in black."[56]

---

* See also: Claude McKay. "Garvey as a Negro Moses." *Liberator*, April. 1922. pp. 8-9.
[55] Claude McKay, *op. cit.*, p. 354.
[56] *Ibid.*, p. 243.

Yet, McKay showed himself to be very much preoccupied with these "white" problems. He was an internationalist in spite of himself, and told all about his personal relationships in Paris with such people as Sinclair Lewis, Gertrude Stein, Eugen Boissevain and his wife, Edna St. Vincent Millay. He met up again with Max Eastman, and with his first literary contact in America—Frank Harris. In Paris, among the expatriates, McKay was able to be a literary man among the literary greats and discuss creative values with his "peers." However his most significant encounter in Paris was with Louise Bryant, the wife of the martyred John Reed.

Paris was symbolic of the fate of the Village movement, and Claude McKay and Louise Bryant made it all the more so. They came from opposite sides of the color line of the 1912 Village movement and both came up in the first wave, before the war. Louise Bryant was in Mabel Dodge's group during this period. She was in love first with Eugene O'Neill (who married Agnes Boulton*), then she fell in love with John Reed and won him away from Mabel Dodge. She had accompanied Reed on his mission to Moscow and was with the Communist hero when he contracted fever and died. For all intents and purposes this ended Louise Bryant's career in the radical movement. For her, as for McKay, Paris became the turning point. Louise Bryant was another one of those rare women who defy conventional categories—much like Mabel Dodge and Emilie Hapgood. McKay described her: "Externally her tastes were bourgeois enough. She liked luxurious surroundings and elegant and expensive clothes and looked splendid in them. But her fine tastes had not softened her will or weakened her rebel spirit."[57]

This "bourgeois" gloss made it certain that Louise Bryant was not destined to travel the long road from Mabel Dodge's group into the Communist Party. Her husband did, but what Reed's actual attitude was toward the Communist cause when he died has remained an unsolved mystery. Theodore Draper, in his remarks about Reed,[58] presented evidence to the effect that the American Communist Party made a founding martyr-hero out of a

* See Agnes Boulton's *Part of a Long Story*, on Louise Bryant, O'Neill, and Harlem (New York: Doubleday, 1958).
[57] McKay, *op. cit.*, p. 291.
[58] Draper, *The Roots . . .* , *op. cit.*, p. 291.

man who was "probably as disillusioned as it was possible to be and still remain in the movement." "Reed lived and died an undomesticated American radical," wrote Draper. "He did not fit into the established order before he became a Communist, and he did not fit into the order established by Communism."[59] Claude McKay himself never became a full-fledged Communist. But unlike Reed, he never became a flamboyant independent radical in his own right.

At the time McKay first met Louise Bryant, she was doing what he called "a brilliant set of articles about Russia for a Hearst paper."[60] (These articles came out in book form in 1923 under the title *Mirrors of Moscow—Portrait of Eleven Russian Leaders.*) However, in 1918, she had already published *Six Months in Revolutionary Russia*, probably the very *first* book by an American on what was happening in what was then a strange, faraway land. Both of these books make extremely interesting reading even today. And it is to be noted that one was published the year before the 1919 appearance of John Reed's famous *Ten Days that Shook the World*, the book that is credited with first informing American opinion on the Russian enigma.

As writers, John Reed, Louise Bryant and Claude McKay were in conflict with Communist politics; as politicians, they were in conflict with their consciences as writers:

> Louise Bryant thought, as I did, that there was no bourgeois writing or proletarian writing as such; there was only good writing and bad writing. I told her of my great desire to do some Negro stories, straight and unpolished, but that Max Eastman had discouraged me and said I should write my stories in verse. . . . John Reed had written some early stories about ordinary people with no radical propaganda in them, she said, and suggested that I should do the same about my Negro stories—just write plain tales.[61]

The Communist Party's literary authoritarians, such as Michael Gold, did not agree with this sort of thinking. Yet McKay and Louise Bryant were actually much closer to Leon Trotsky's views

[59] *Ibid.*, p. 282.
[60] McKay. *op. cit.*, p. 254.
[61] *Ibid.*

on the literature than the Communists, who in the early 1920's were praising Trotsky's great genius in everything. Trotsky had written in *Literature and Revolution:* "It would be monstrous to conclude that the technique of bourgeois art is not necessary to the worker. Yet there are many who fall into this error. 'Give us', they say, 'something even pock-marked, but our own.' . . . Those who believe in a 'pock-marked' art are imbued with contempt for the masses."[62]

This excruciating dilemma perhaps helped to kill Reed, as it was said he had lost his will to live. It destroyed Louise Bryant, in the end, because she had committed herself so deeply to the politics of the revolution. McKay endured, no doubt, because he refused to commit himself, and because he was black, and in that blackness had learned to endure so much in order to survive. We cannot but admire these three early intellectuals for what they did achieve under such trying and complex circumstances. In the America of the early twentieth century, they confronted unique philosophical and theoretical problems. Reed is to be admired for his daring and, above all, his unfailing independence of thought, his radical romanticism that refused to conform to the foreign authoritarians. McKay is to be credited with his stubborn refusal to give up the search for answers other than those the authoritarians tried to impose on him (although it is remarkable that he accepted so much tutelage from whites on how he, a black writer, should write about Negroes). Louise Bryant is to be admired for her ordeal and her achievements, although few. Women like her, and like Mabel Dodge and Emilie Hapgood, have no place of honor in American cultural history—which says much about the intellectual sickness of this society. Whatever flaws they had in the eyes of the conventional, they were *bona fide* pioneers of a kind. In their restless personalities there was mirrored the growing problem of the modern American woman—an endemic lack of sexual fulfillment. The road from Greenwich Village to Moscow to Paris was tragic for Louise Bryant. Samuel Putnam, another expatriate, gives us a glimpse of her deterioration:

> As John Reed's wife, Louise Bryant had been not only a spectator but, for America, one of the chief chroniclers of the Russian

[62] *Literature and Revolution* (London: George Allen and Unwin, Ltd., 1925), p. 204.

Revolution, and along with her husband had become a heroic figure and something of a legend for our leftward looking intelligentsia. . . . At the time I knew Louise she was drifting from cafe to cafe and was famous for the daring studio parties that she gave in the early hours of the morning. She no longer seemed to care; yet . . . she was invariably warm, friendly, altogether likeable, and never once did she speak of the past, nor would anyone have thought of questioning her about it.[63]

Questioning her about it would have been useless. Louise Bryant was of the first wave of 1912, most of whom played a certain initiating role and either passed off the scene or handed the mantle to the next wave. They could do no more. This was true also of Claude McKay, although he lived until 1948.

Putnam made other observations about the Lost Generation that are worth noting:

The story of this generation is not Europe's alone; it forms a part of America's annals both social and cultural. Never before in history had there been such a mass migration of writers and artists from any land to a foreign shore. . . .

All these were signs that indicated a deepening discontent with American cultural and spiritual values. The revolt was of a mixed character, being marked on the one hand by a popular-democratic trend as in Anderson, Sandburg, and Lindsay, and on the other hand by a certain tendency to esotericism and a contempt for the arts of the people that with Mencken and his followers became a contempt for the people themselves.[64]

This interpretation has its value, but it is not nearly the whole story. The *real* "popular-democratic trend" was not Sherwood Anderson, *et al.*, but the Negro renaissance trend. The problem was that Claude McKay and his co-aspirationists in culture did not get around to articulating it. For Langston Hughes's superficial and subordinated consciousness, it was merely a period of parties and patrons "when the Negro was in vogue." If the white creative intellectual's discontent was an extension of the crisis in Western European cultural and spiritual values, then the Harlem Renais-

[63] Samuel Putnam, *Paris Was Our Mistress—Memoirs of a Lost and Found Generation* (New York: Viking Press, 1947), pp. 87-88.
[64] *Ibid.*, p. 21.

sance intellectuals should have pointed out, at least in broad terms, that the American Negro intellectual's cultural awakening was not only a countertrend to white discontent, but a twentieth-century harbinger of the African awakening in political and cultural terms. Such an intellectual premise fully established in the 1920's, cultivated from 1930 to the 1950's, would not have permitted the growth of the "identity vacuum" that the Negro movement of the 1960's has encountered. Unable to arrive at any philosophical conclusions of their own as a *black intelligentsia,* the leading literary lights of the 1920's substituted the Communist left-wing philosophy of the 1930's, and thus were intellectually sidetracked for the remainder of their productive years.

Mass Media and Cultural Democracy

During the 1920's, the development in America of mass cultural communications media—radio, films, recording industry, and ultimately, television—drastically altered the classic character of capitalism as described by Karl Marx. This new feature very obviously presented new problems (as well as opportunities) for all the anti-capitalistic radicals; problems which they apparently have never appreciated. The capitalist class, according to the Marxists, have the political and economic power through class ownership of all the industrial and technological means of production, to exploit the working class and control opinions through the press. If that be so, then consider the added range and persuasiveness, the augmented class power, the enhanced political control and prerogatives of decision making that result from the new mass communications industry. What happens to the scope of popular democracy when this new technological-electronic apparatus spreads throughout the land, bombarding the collective mind with controlled images?

But it was almost historically inevitable that the appearance of the mass communications media would coincide with the era of the American cultural renaissance. For, if the growth of capitalism creates its opposite—the working-class (the Marxian source of class-struggle revolution)—then it is possible to say that the growth of the mass communications media coincided with the appearance of an opposing class-force of radical creative intellectuals. Unfortunately, the radical intellectuals of the 1920's did not complete—or better, follow through on—the revolution they instinctively started out to make: an American cultural revolution* for which all the necessary conditions either existed or were coming into existence. This was the revolution that imported Russian politics confounded.

* Another dimension in social revolution.

64

It took ten years—the 1930's decade of economic collapse—before the failure of the 1920's could be properly assessed. By then it was too late, for the government-sponsored New Deal became the legally constituted proxy for carrying out the platforms of social progress demanded by the radical strata below. Thus, social change became controlled from the top down. It goes without saying that the Negro intellectuals of the Harlem Renaissance could not see the implications of cultural revolution as a *political demand* growing out of the advent of mass communication media. Having no cultural philosophy of their own, they remained under the tutelage of irrelevant white radical ideas. Thus they failed to grasp the radical potential of their own movement.

The serious consequences of the introduction of the mass media into American capitalism have not been matched in any other country in the Western world. They were consequences not taken into account by the Marxist theories about capitalism and the class struggle. The mass communications media have, over the past forty years, changed America into a mass society:

> In a mass society, the dominant type of communication is the formal media, and the publics become mere *media markets.* . . .
>
> In this view, the public is merely the collectivity of individuals each rather passively exposed to the mass media and rather help-lessly opened up to the suggestions and manipulations that flow from these media.
>
> The top of modern American society is increasingly unified, and often seems willfully co-ordinated: at the top there has emerged an elite of power. The middle levels are a drifting set of stalemated, balancing forces: the middle does not link the bottom with the top. The bottom of this society is politically fragmented, and even as a passive fact, increasingly powerless: at the bottom there is emerging a mass society.[1]

And on the bottom where this mass society emerges stands the Negro, not quite passive as of now, but still subject to manipulation and still politically fragmented, if not more so than ever. The Negro is, today, the victim of the incompetence of radical social theory and the forty-year default of the Negro intelligentsia. The "crisis in black and white" is also a crisis in social theory wherein American capitalism, the racial exploiter, has, by its own inner

[1] C. Wright Mills, *Power Elite, op. cit.*, pp. 299-344, *passim.*

dynamic, swept everything before it by its power of rapid development and ability to recover, adjust, and absorb and institutionalize *even anti-capitalistic features.* But if American capitalism with its mass media continues to propagate the myth of the Great American Dream, its politics has not solved poverty, war, corruption, waste, or the race question. The issues of the 1920's, qualitatively enlarged, are still here.

In 1963, the Rockefeller Brothers Fund, Inc. brought together a group of learned citizens from all parts of the country and varying walks in life, "to join in a study of the future development and support of the performing arts in the United States." This study, completed and published in 1965, comes over fifty years after Mabel Dodge's first-wave salon group recoiled in the face of the American cultural void and attempted to stage a renaissance. The opening section, entitled "The Arts in America," includes the following statement:

> Observers of American society, since the establishment of the Republic, have proclaimed the incompatability of democracy with the attainment of high standards of excellence in the arts. A significant minority, however, has never accepted this judgment. . . . Indeed, there have long been thoughtful people among us who believe that the ultimate test of democracy lies in the quality of the artistic and intellectual life it creates and supports.
>
> It has, however, taken a long time for this view to receive wide currency. "In the eighteenth century," as Eric Larabee has noted, "the question that preoccupied thoughtful people was the achieving of political democracy—and in the main we answered it. In the nineteenth century, the question was one of achieving economic democracy—and we answered that too, at least in theory and potentiality. *In the twentieth century, the main challenge to the United States is the achieving of cultural democracy—but that still remains very far indeed from being answered.*" [italics added][2]

The term "cultural democracy" was used only once. The study group preferred the term "the arts," and approached the whole problem most tentatively by declaring:

---

[2] *The Performing Arts—Problems and Prospects* (Rockefeller Brothers Fund, Inc. [New York: McGraw-Hill, 1965]), pp. v-12, *passim.*

This report on the state of the performing arts in the United States is intended as a challenge, not an answer.

Further:

Our study is limited to the *live performing* arts, and we concentrate on the *professional organizations* that sponsor and present opera, drama, instrumental and choral music, and dance. . . .

Our choice of focus on the live performing arts is not due to any lack of appreciation of the importance of the performing arts presented electronically. On the contrary, we fully recognize that electronic devices—movies, television, radio, and recording—have a tremendous role to play in the development of the performing arts. But it is a role of such magnitude and complexity, so different in form, that it can be treated adequately only by a separate study, differently conceived and executed.[3]

Oddly enough, the report avoids discussion of the "Roaring Twenties," *i.e.*, the age of the advent of the mass communications media. Although there is a reference to the need for a "general re-evaluation of the role of the arts in society," there is no attempt to evaluate the mass media which, as C. Wright Mills points out, "have not only filtered into our experience of external realities, they have also entered into our very experience of our own selves."[4] Thus the main source of the corruption and banalization of the culture is left untouched. The power elite cannot tamper with an arm of its own elite power.

The survey makes the point that "many social and political forces have combined, at this moment of history, both to compel interest in the arts and justify that interest in practical terms."[5] But these "social and political forces" are never identified. However, the Negro civil rights movement is surely one such social force on the current scene. If the Negro intelligentsia of the 1920's had created a cultural philosophy and institutionalized a lasting cultural movement when the Village and the Harlem Renaissance movements (emerging from the vortex of Negro-White experience in America) met and interacted, the Rockefeller survey

[3] *Ibid.*, pp. v-12, *passim.*
[4] Mills, *op. cit.*, p. 314.
[5] Rockefeller report, *op. cit.*, p. 8.

would have been compelled to probe much more deeply into the problems and prospects of the American performing arts.*

The Rockefeller report reveals the lost and isolated position of the Negro creative intelligentsia today. Relegated as they are to the lowest social rungs of mass society—the Negro community— Negro intellectuals are less able than any other intellectuals to command a stake, or a position of decision or control, in the mass communications media. On the other hand, the report makes no attempt to deal with the problems of the American performing arts in terms of race, ethnic group, class, community—or within the context of the "crisis in black and white." Thus discussion of the essential elements—historical, cultural, and aesthetic of the native American tradition—was also evaded. The American performing arts are socially predicted on a *culturally pluralistic tradition.* Any report that discusses the "future of theater, dance, music in America" must also discuss the race question, for it is precisely the race factor in American history that created American theater, dance and music.

The Harlem of the 1960's presents a serious problem for the new-wave, creative intelligentsia. They are far removed from first- and even second-hand knowledge of the Harlem cultural past. Now that it is possible to assess the post-World War II era of the integration of the Negro in the arts, it is sobering to conclude that what the Negro truly achieved artistically in Harlem (even before the 1920's) was far superior in scope and energy to what has been achieved today (Ossie Davis, John Killens, Lorraine Hansberry, Ruby Dee, etc., notwithstanding). It is true that these contemporary artists, as a small coterie, might lay claim to more of what might be called modern sophistication, but rela-

---

* Lerone Bennett writes: "Having fought off one challenge in the Garvey movement of the twenties, the [black] Establishment found itself face to face with another mass-based black nationalist movement, the Nation of Islam. In this same period, there was a complete *revolution in mass communication,* a revolution that bewildered the Establishment and almost isolated it" [italics added]. Elsewhere, Bennett says: "The Negro rebellion, then, is a cultural as well as a social upheaval."

Bennett, however, is unable to interpret all of this historically: He does not understand the 1920's and mistakes the 1930's as a "key" decade for the Negro movement, which actually created its basic ingredients in the 1920's when the revolution in mass communication was in its first stages. See Lerone Bennett, *The Negro Mood* (Chicago, Johnson Publications, 1946), pp. 43-47. *passim.*

tively speaking, I am not so sure that even that is true. For with all their prattle about "integration," vital Negro theater, "The Negro writer and his roots," their confusion about "I *am* but I am *not* a Negro writer," or "My play about Negroes was not really a Negro play," their intellectual premise on the cultural arts is built on shifting sands that have been slipping from under them ever since the Harlem Renaissance and its radical allies missed the implications of cultural revolution in the 1920's.

It is true that the coming of Wright and Ellison marked new achievements in the novel, and Baldwin, after a fashion, did prevent that trend from losing its luster. But in *quality* the Negro has retrogressed in every creative field except jazz. The Negro has turned his back on his own native American dance forms and refused to cultivate them—he, the creator of all American popular dance forms from the fox-trot to the twist. What passes for new drama is but glorified soap opera about domestic conformity—the "best-face forward" evasion of the crucial facts about Negro inner-group class conflict—or else, the 1930's protest message revamped for the 1960's. LeRoi Jones managed to break new ground in *Dutchman,* but even there a question remains about the meaning of the play's shock-symbolism. In the musical theater genre, in which Negro composers, librettists, and lyricists were once so inventive, there has not been a worthwhile Negro production *since 1921.*

The precarious position in our culture of the Negro composer exemplifies in particular the cultural defacement of the Negro tradition in America. It calls into serious question many of the claims of the achievement of cultural integration and also calls into question the way that integration is being pursued.

The Rockefeller survey, predictably, devoted much space to the condition of the symphony orchestra in America. But symphonic music is not really an American product. The native American music is Negro jazz. Why, with the Negro folk-music tradition forming the basis of almost all American popular music, has America never produced a *black* Gershwin? To even begin to answer this complex creative question, one must start by declaring that the music publishing field in America is saturated with prejudice and corruption from top to bottom. The Rockefeller survey group knew what it was doing in staying clear of certain commercial areas of our performing arts, although "they obviously play a big role in the field as a whole and particularly in the theater."[6] Commercialism is bad enough, but the fraud, exploitation, banality, plagiarism, corruption and race bias in the American popular music field have degraded the cultural values of the entire nation. Since the very beginning of popular music publishing in America, around 1900, publishers have used and exploited the Negro composer unmercifully. This pattern has continued up to the present. It has even been carried over into the classical and symphonic music fields where the European creative tradition holds sway. The serious white composer in America is victimized by the American genuflection before European musical standards, but the serious Negro composer is practically a nonentity, with all his native musical heritage. When the Rockefeller survey dealt with music as a performing art in America, it could not even begin to examine the commercial, ideological and institutional barriers against native American originality. Whatever cultural patriotism Americans have is predicated mainly on the financial exploitation of America's undeveloped cultural resources.

But sad to admit, if many of our Negro creative luminaries studied this Rockefeller survey (which is highly doubtful), it is certain that their washed-out brains reacted with not a modicum of critical assessment. This is especially true of that clique of writers and critics hatched out of the cultural henhouse of the old leftwing in Harlem. For their collective mentalities are obsessed with little else but the folklore of integrationism, transposed from the civil rights front to the cultural front. Their simple, uncultivated outlooks, which have been nurtured by the American myth-makers, are socially conditioned *against* original thought, even in their own behalf. So insensate are the Negro intelligentsia to the mortal illness of American creative culture, they are not even embarrassed by their ludicrous attempt to integrate something that is withering away. Lacking even the fundamentals of a cultural critique of their own, they adopt every shibboleth of the white cultural standard as practiced.

The Negro creative intelligentsia cannot truly interpret the Negro's position in the United States beyond "Civil Rights." Thus

---

[6] *Ibid.*, p. 16.

when legal redress in civil rights reaches the point of saturation *de jure,* the civil righters are disarmed and naked in the spotlight of adverse power. They babble about "social change," "revolution," "movements," etc., but they understand nothing about "a movement of scientific thought on a national scale"[7] as one great revolutionary once described such phenomena. In such a movement in America, whatever the organizational formula, the basic ingredients must be a synthesis of politics, economics and culture, and from the Negro point of view it is the cultural side of the problem that puts politics and economics into their proper focus within a movement. The Negro intelligentsia does not understand this. But the truth of this social proposition was foreshadowed in the events within Harlem forty years ago. These experiences were recorded but not interpreted in the interests of later generations, and the Negro, like most Americans, too easily forgets his own history.

The 1920's renaissance was actually the culminating phase of a previous renaissance that had emerged with the initial growth of black Harlem around 1910. James Weldon Johnson refers to it as the "third theatrical period." The second or middle period had begun in 1890 when Negroes broke with the minstrel show form, the slave creation of the plantation era, which was the only original American contribution to theater.[8] The first period had begun after the Civil War. when Negroes first entered the professional stage.

During the period from 1914-1930, when the Negro population in Harlem was less than half of what it is today,* the community experienced what amounted to a broad theatrical revival. In fact, from 1910-1930, there was infinitely more theatrical activity in Harlem than occurred between 1945 and 1960. The Apollo Theater, in terms of the kind of variety entertainment seen on its stage,

---

[7] Trotsky, *op. cit.,* p. 9. N.B. It should be added that great as foreign revolutionary leaders were in their own societies, none of them really understood the United States or the Negro in it. Even Marx understood the Negro only within the context of slavery and the Civil War. Thereafter, America and the Negro went through such expansive changes that Marx's collaborator, Engels, clearly saw the ineffectualness of Marxist practice in America, during his visit here in 1888.

[8] *Black Manhattan, op. cit.,* p. 87.

* In 1914, the Negro population of Harlem was estimated at just under 50,000; by 1920 it approached 80,000, and by 1930, over 200,000.

is the last of a long line of theaters institutionalized in those early years. It can be said that the modern Negro artistic movement that produced the music, dance and theatrical innovations that have left their ineradicable mark on America, began with the second period in 1890. Before the Harlem settlement took place, in the first decade of this century, Negroes had lived in various sections of New York City. In 1880, most of New York's Negro population were living in Greenwich Village—on Sullivan, Bleeker, Thompson, Carmine, and Grove Streets and Minetta Lane. By 1890, however, the main center of Negro population had moved up to the Twenties and Thirties near Sixth Avenue, *i.e.*, the Tenderloin district. Later there was a movement to West Fifty-third Street, and another to the San Juan Hill district in the West Sixties. During all these years however, the majority of upper-class Negroes lived in Brooklyn, where the first Negro settlers had migrated to escape the New York Civil War Draft riots.

The cultural significance of the migration uptown to Harlem has been vividly described by Johnson:

> So, with the establishment of the Negro theatre in Harlem, coloured performers in New York experienced for the first time release from the restraining fears of what a white audience would stand for; for the first time they felt free to do on stage whatever they were able to do.
>
> This sense of freedom manifested itself in efforts covering a wide range; efforts that ran all the way from crude Negro burlesque to Broadway drama. This intermediate and experimental theatrical period developed mainly in two Harlem theatres, the Lafayette and the Lincoln. Within several years both these houses had good stock-companies, and for quite a while their repertories consisted chiefly of downtown successes. The Lafayette Players developed into a very proficient organization that gave adequate presentations . . . These melodramatic plays made a great appeal to Harlem audiences. To most people that crowded the Lafayette and the Lincoln the thrill received from these pieces was an entirely new experience; and it was all the closer and more moving because it was expressed in terms of their own race. For a time, Negro sketches and musical shows were swept off the stage, but they are now back again.[9]

[9] *Ibid.*, pp. 171-172.

Thirty-two years later, the playwright Loften Mitchell, writing on "The Negro Theatre" in the special Harlem issue of *Freedom-ways*, tells a little story about Jesse Shipp, one of the early Negro directors who flourished during the early 1900's in the days of the great Negro comedy team, Williams and Walker. Shipp told a friend that he was moving: "Uptown. 100,000 Negroes in New York now. Lots of them moving to Harlem. I'll go there. Maybe they'll be needing a theatre." Mitchell goes on to quote a contemporary Negro actor-director named Ed Cambridge, who commented very wryly and bitterly about Shipp's statement—made over fifty years earlier. "It's a good thing Jesse Shipp didn't go up there this year [1962] looking to work in theatre. He'd have been hungry as hell!"[10] Very true, only Cambridge and Mitchell did not explain that this is the price *all* Negroes in the theater are paying for the precarious integration of a *few*.

Since the time described by Johnson when the first Negro theatrical companies established themselves in early Harlem, *four* major live entertainment theaters have disappeared—the Lafayette and Lincoln theaters Johnson mentions, as well as the Alhambra and the Harlem Opera House, which became Negro stages somewhat later. Countless amateur and semi-professional groups have disappeared as well. Repertory and stock companies have gone out of existence; nightclubs which gave employment to thousands of people are closed; performers, musicians, composers, singers are scattered downtown or gone overseas. And, in the 1940's, the American Negro Theater, which was at the time Harlem's new hope for cultural revival, collapsed.

But let us recreate a Harlem episode of forty years ago, which will reveal some of the intimate facts that have gone into the making of Harlem's rise and decline. At Seventh Avenue and One Hundred and Thirty-second Street stands an edifice that was once the famous Lafayette Theater. Today it is a church, and the utter drabness of the area in 1967 makes it hard to believe what glamor and glitter once strutted on Harlem's Seventh Avenue from World War I to World War II.

In September, 1926, a bitter struggle cropped out in Harlem

[10] Loften Mitchell, "The Negro Theatre," *Freedomways*, Summer, 1963, Vol. 3, No. 3, p. 384.

between labor and the Lafayette Theater management. Soon after, several spokesmen from other levels of Harlem life joined in what was to become one of the most significant controversies ever to arise in this community. It began when eleven Negro motion picture projection operators accused the Lafayette management of racial discrimination, both in hiring policies and in pay scales. The action against the Lafayette management was highlighted by the fact that Local 306 of the American Federation of Labor had admitted the Negro operators into the union only shortly before. The Negroes had forced the union to accept them by threatening to set up a school to train more Negro operators—of whom only a handful existed at the time. Thus the union opened its doors to Negroes for the first time, in order to protect its craft exclusiveness.

The action brought out the fact that due to seniority, most of the chief projectionists in all the Harlem movie houses were white and drawing the top union wage scale. Most Negro operators who worked were "assistants" who were paid below scale. However, the Lafayette house situation was complicated by the fact that this theater was also the leading Negro vaudeville center of Harlem, a status it shared with the popular Lincoln Theater on West One Hundred and Thirty-fifth Street (today also a church). Since the full houses drawn by the Lafayette and the Lincoln were in response *not* to movies but to vaudeville shows with famous Negro stars, the strike of the operators found little sympathetic reactions from the populace, who would have filled the Lafayette even if the movies were discontinued. That rather bitter fact weakened the whole fight.

The Lafayette Theater operators' action developed into a community issue that projected for the first time all of the following problems into one composite issue: unions; skilled Negro labor vs. skilled white labor; the impact of the film as mass media and its relation to the Negro community; the role of the Negro in drama and live entertainment, both inside and outside the Negro community; the economics of labor; the economics of the Negro community as mass consumer; and the economics of management and property control. Then, that November, Harlem voted in a gubernatorial election right in the midst of the conflict; it was the classic representation of the three elements that underlie the social fate of Harlem—*economics, politics* and *culture*—projected within the scope of one issue at the height of the Harlem Renaissance. The outcome of the brief struggle revealed that Harlem as a community was not in the least prepared to rise to the seizure of its own economic, political and cultural autonomy. The Negro projectionists eventually won their rights, but the failure on the larger community issues which their fight illuminated, doomed Harlem to the agonizing decline it suffered from the 1929 Crash down to the 1960's.

The Lafayette episode glaringly revealed the inexperience, the incompetence, the backwardness—but at the same time the eagerness and the militancy—of the young Harlem Communist leftwing. On the heels of the revolt of the operators came the new Communist stalwarts who had split with Randolph's *Messenger* Socialists in 1919. Chief among these were Richard B. Moore and Cyril V. Briggs. They were soon joined by Hubert H. Harrison, who had not gone over to the Communists but assisted them in their support of the strike. Moore was arrested for making militant speeches in front of the Lafayette, and given a suspended sentence. Thus the Lafayette issue immediately became a "free speech" test for the Communists. But the real motive behind Moore's free speech case was the Communist Left's trade union policy for Negro workers. Beyond this, there is no evidence that these pioneer Negro Communists saw the Lafayette episode from any other but this narrow viewpoint.

Cyril V. Briggs, who was then functioning as a "strike publicity director" (for the ill-fated Passaic, New Jersey, Textile Strike of 1926), wrote a letter to the *Amsterdam News* in support of the Negro projectionists, in which he said: "The Negro workers must organize along economic lines. The labor unions are increasingly opening up to us as the American labor movement gains knowledge and experience and goes about rectifying its mistakes, organized labor is beginning to realize that the interests of all workers— black and white—are inextricably interwoven and can never be separated."[11]

In his philosophy on Negro economic organization, Briggs had made the complete cycle from the nationalist separatism of the

[11] *Amsterdam News*, September 25, 1926, p. 10.

African Blood Brotherhood to black and white labor unity along class lines. In 1919, as editor of the *Crusader,* Briggs advocated the creation of a Negro state in Africa, South America, or the Caribbean, in preference to fighting for equality in the United States where the rights of the black minority "would always be dependent upon the state of mind of the majority."[12] Richard B. Moore, Briggs' closest collaborator, went through the same metamorphosis. But neither their separate-state philosophy nor their Communist leftwing program for the organization of Negroes along economic lines were at all adequate to cope with the complex issues raised by the revolt of the Negro operators against the Lafayette Theater owners. Much more was involved than mere trade-union politics.

For one thing, Briggs was far more optimistic about black and white labor possibilities than the facts of the Passaic Textile Strike revealed. An authoritative study on Negro labor of the 1920's stated:

> In Passaic, New Jersey, during the strike of 1926-1927, but one mill, the United Piece Dye Works in the suburb of Lodi, employed colored workers. They numbered about 300 in a total force of about 3000. About half of these 300 Negroes answered the strike call, while the rest remained at work. . . . The company was careful to avoid the race issue. It imported about one hundred Negro strike breakers but used them only to take the place of Negro strikers.[13]

But the Passaic Textile Strike was the first big labor action the Communist leftwing initiated in the 1920's; thus Briggs' newly found labor enthusiasm was predicated on a political strategy that had been directed from Moscow, that was remote from Harlem economic realities. A few months later the Communists, on orders from Moscow's decisions of the Sixth Comintern Meeting of 1926, disowned their own strike, pulled out and turned the whole business over to the American Federation of Labor's United Textile Workers.[14] In Harlem, the AFL Motion Picture Operators' local, after accepting the Negro operators under pressure, put them into separate Harlem locals.

[12] *Crusader,* September, 1919, pp. 11-12; April, 1921, p. 8.
[13] Sterling D. Spero and Abram L. Harris, *The Black Worker* (New York: Columbia University Press, 1931), p. 348.
[14] Draper, *American Communism and Soviet Russia,* pp. 223-233.

As the Lafayette Theater struggle in Harlem progressed, Hubert H. Harrison took up the cudgels for the Negro operators, but in a different way. He wanted to assist the operators in getting a fair and better deal with the Harlem theaters but he was *against* their joining an AFL local because of the union's long-standing, anti-Negro bias. When he learned that the operators had been required to pay the two hundred dollar initiating fee, but had been barred from attending regular union meetings downtown, he backed off with the statement: "Unlike Abraham Lincoln, my prime objective was not to save the union but to free the slaves."[15] The AFL took advantage of the Negro operators' case to initiate a strike by white operators against the movie houses for other wage advantages. This strike action also spilled over into the AFL's Local 802—the Musicians' Union—which also began to affect the Lafayette's vaudeville shows, and brought Negro and white musicians into conflict, inasmuch as Negro musicians considered Negro vaudeville shows their special province. Hubert Harrison concluded that the Negro operators had been used by the AFL. Note here the sharp division within the Harlem radicals over how the Negro should organize along economic lines.

The white owners of the Harlem vaudeville and movie houses, led by Frank Schiffman (who still operates the famous Apollo Theater in 1967), reacted to the Lafayette Theater strike with much pain, anger and remorse. By November, 1926, the Leo Brecher theater interests, represented by Schiffman, had come under bitter attack from all articulate segments of Harlem opinion. Not only was Schiffman's Lafayette house affected, but so were other Negro vaudeville theaters in other cities. Schiffman complained to the Harlem press of his agonized disappointment over the way he was being treated after "five years of my labor in Harlem." He cited the fact that "The Lafayette Theater is an institution," and added: "We must not forget that the present management has improved and dignified the Lafayette Theater and that it brings to the colored people of Harlem motion picture and musical comedy entertainment which is not equalled elsewhere in the city."[16]

By now, however, representatives of Harlem's new, aspiring

---

[15] *Amsterdam News*, October 6, 1926, p. 11.
[16] *Ibid.*, November 17, 1926, p. 11.

black bourgeoisie joined the attack on Schiffman as the middle-
class intelligentsia began to assail the Lafayette management on
issues other than those of the leftwing radicals—Briggs, Moore, and
Harrison. In the cultural pages of the *Amsterdam News*, the social
critics spoke, through the pen of one Edgar M. Grey, a leading
journalist:

> What advancement has been gained to the colored motion pic-
> ture industry?
> What benefits have come to the community?
> What encouragement has come to the individuals of the groups
> who might aspire to the profession of screen actor?
> What pecuniary benefits have reached the group which were
> not of an individual character? Which affected the group as a
> social unit? None whatever. For the only beneficiaries were the
> owners of the playhouses which employed Mr. Schiffman to man-
> age them.

Grey broadened his criticism to include all white businessmen
in Harlem:

> Their first act is to discredit all of the social and educational in-
> struments among us which refuse to do their will.[17]

This was in reference to the fact that Schiffman had retaliated
against the Harlem press by removing all of his theater advertising. Grey advised Schiffman that he could not pretend to be serious about benefiting Harlem until he agreed *to share his profits.*
But this was an aspect of community economic organization that
neither Schiffman nor the Communist leftwing of Briggs and
Moore would ever touch. Then, the assault in the *Amsterdam
News* on Schiffman shifted from economics to cultural criticism
when questions were raised about the quality of the vaudeville. A
"Professor S.R. Williams, Director of the National Negro Centre,
Political Party" charged that: "Mr. Schiffman has found the kind
of shows which carry a strong appeal to a certain class of people,
but it was at the expense of that high class kind of patronage
which used to pack the Lafayette when the drama held sway."[18]
Around 1910 began a period when the Lafayette presented legitimate drama of quality, which highly pleased the old Harlem

[17] *Idem.*
[18] *Amsterdam News*, November 10, 1926, p. 10.

uppercrust who were quite sensitive and proud of their cultural standards. As James Weldon Johnson said later: "All through this intermediate period there were times when polite comedy and high-tension melodrama gave way to black-face farce, hilarious musical comedy, and bills of specialties. The black Harlem audience enjoyed being thrilled, but they also wanted to laugh."[19]

But this was not the *whole* story: Those quality stage pieces just didn't accrue enough profit to the management—thus the Lafayette fare was mixed and spiced with vaudeville for financial reasons. Came the Leo Brecher-Frank Schiffman administration in the 1920's, and legitimate drama was ruled out altogether in order to appeal to "a certain class of people" who guaranteed full houses. Moreover, few of those "quality" plays had been original, but rather "white" plays with Negro casts.* As pointed out, the first successful and original dramas on Negro life were written and produced by whites—Ridgely Torrence and Emilie Hapgood in 1917—and not in Harlem, but downtown on Broadway. This had served to fragment Harlem's creative forces by dividing their loyalties between uptown and downtown. The Lafayette Theater conflict impelled some of the older, established intelligentsia (who had never really sponsored or desired original Negro theater or original Negro playwrights) to come forward and attack the Lafayette management on its lack of quality drama. It was ironic that what these conservative Negroes criticized as stage fare was the one aspect of theater in which the Negro creator was truly original— Negro musical comedy. It was in fact this unique originality in musical comedy that had made the Lafayette Theater famous years before Brecher and Schiffman came to Harlem: Indeed, the famous *Darktown Follies* of 1913 brought none other than Florenz Zeigfeld to the Lafayette, whereupon he actually bought the rights to about half of the show for his own *Ziegfeld Follies*. Just such predatory and discriminatory practices by Broadway producers angered Negroes in the theater and engendered mixed emotions about Broadway. Thus one of the cries that went up in Harlem during the Lafayette Theater controversy was: "We should not

---

[19] Johnson, *op. cit.*, p. 173. N.B. Johnson did not write about the Lafayette strike in his book, however.

* *Madame X, The Love of Choo Chin, Within the Law*, et al.

allow Harlem to become a battleground for Broadway!"

By December, 1926, the Lafayette Theater crisis subsided with hardly anything achieved but a thorough airing of a fundamental social problem, in all of its aspects. But aired and debated it was, in a fashion that was never to be duplicated in all of Harlem's subsequent history. It can be fairly said that the way this 1926 community debate was handled (or mishandled) actually settled the fate of Harlem until now. Then the dominant Harlem classes bared their aspirations and their souls; they also bared their weaknesses, their narrowness, their helplessness—their utter *class impotence.* What they desperately wanted to be able to do was to assume absolute control of Harlem affairs in economics, politics and culture, but they could not. The underlying reason was the very question they dared not, and did not, openly debate—property relations in Harlem between black and white. The Communist leftwing discussed property relations, but in ultra-remote terms involving capital and labor, which did not touch the wellspring of Harlem realities. In 1926 the essence of the clash was between black bourgeois, and white class, ownership. And in part, so it remains today, if under changed conditions.

But added to the class disabilities of the Harlem bourgeoisie in terms of property ownership was the cultural alienation of this class from their Negro mass ideology. It was this flaw that specifically weakened their struggle against the white property owners. Edgar M. Grey, the *Amsterdam News* spokesman, was fully aware of the class ownership factor that effectively blocked Negro economic aspirations when he suggested that the Lafayette management "share their profits." He did not specify with whom, but the meaning was clear even if it did reveal the essential naïveté of the black bourgeoisie, who believes that equality in the economic sphere can be won through a voluntary sharing of the wealth (or a sharing through integration, as it became in the 1950's).

But in addition to the stumbling block of legal property rights, the Harlem bourgeoisie forfeited the one privilege they had—that of affording the kind of leadership philosophy that could have boycotted the Lafayette management into submission. Lacking such a philosophy, they were caught between the persuasive demands and imperatives of two aspects of native American cultural developments: the growth of the mass media of the film, and the spontaneous developments of their own ethnic theatrical movement, one exceedingly rich in ideas, energy, potential and creativity. They did not fully appreciate the implications of these developments and, therefore, could not grasp their potential for group benefit. During the entire period when the Lafayette conflict raged, not a single scheduled vaudeville or musical comedy show failed to play to full houses. The operators struck, the Communist leftwing agitated, the bourgeois intellectuals raved and ranted, but the "show went on." And no one grasped the implications of the fact that this profound conflict, that touched on practically every aspect of community life and its relationships to white society, was the result of a controversy that started *on the cultural plane*. It was not police brutality, or high rents, or bad schools—but *the impact of the developing American cultural apparatus* on the economics, the politics, the creative and social development of the black community—that sparked this conflict. The issues were joined, fought out, debated and lost in such an impassioned way, that in subsequent years, no public protest or demonstration of any kind has succeeded in developing such an all-embracing debate on Harlem affairs.

These events caused several Harlem spokesmen to go through agonizing reappraisals concerning their community—such as Edgar M. Grey, who began a long series of articles in the *Amsterdam News,* dissecting the social ills of the Negro in an article called "The Sleeping Giant—The Harlem Negro."[20] He pointed out that Harlem had a population of two hundred twenty-five thousand with a registered voter count of twenty-two thousand, but only seventy-two percent of this number actually voted in 1926. The responsible leaders were aghast at this stark evidence of political apathy. Forty years later, the political situation in Harlem is not very much improved, because the successive generations of leaders in Harlem have not created the kind of community issues that cause the average man to become excited politically. If these same leaders were told they should establish an *independent* black political party, they would be even more aghast then at grassroots disinterest in political machines.

Even sharper insight into the leadership deficiencies of Harlem

---

[20] *Op. cit.,* November 10, 1926, p. 15.

during the Lafayette Theater episode, can be gleaned from an examination of how the Garvey Nationalists reacted to the issue. Their strictly hands-off position (and not only because Marcus Garvey, their leader, was in jail) revealed that this predominantly West Indian movement was not really attuned to the internal peculiarities of the Negro-white situation in the United States. They saw the solution to the problem outside the system—namely, in Africa. But not a single Garveyite settlement, either from America or the West Indies, exists in Africa today. In 1926, the highly inspirational, but also romantic and escapist, character of the Garvey movement served to hide the fact that the movement was not facing the hard realities in a scientific way—either at home or in Africa. For example, during the Lafayette Theater strike none other than Garvey's first wife, Mrs. Amy Ashwood-Garvey, brought her own musical comedy on to the Lafayette stage (on November 1, 1926), for a limited engagement. Coolly received by the critics, the musical was titled "Hey, Hey!," and was composed of African, West Indian and American Negro folk elements, blended together (the author believed) in aesthetic, as well as historical, unity. But the timing of the appearance of this musical by a leading nationalist, showed that as far as the Lafayette strike was concerned, the nationalists were sorely lacking in the virtues of political unity concerning issues closer at hand than the distant shores of Africa.

Of course the enmity between the Garveyites and the Communist leftwing had a lot to do with this: Briggs and Moore, the leftwing critics of Garvey, had already taken over agitational priorities in the Lafayette strike. But the differences between their politics in the strike, and that of their colleague, Hubert H. Harrison over the AFL unions, further complicated matters. More than that, it was soon revealed that Harrison was in Mrs. Amy Ashwood-Garvey's corner. For during December, 1926, the sensational divorce case involving Garvey and his first wife hit the front pages of the Harlem press.[21] The lurid details of adultery charges against each other by Marcus and Amy Garvey reached the eyes of eager Harlemites. Involved was Amy *Jacques*-Garvey, Garvey's second wife, whom he had married three years after his first marriage in

[21] *Amsterdam News*, December 8, 1926, p. 1.

1919. During the court proceedings it was revealed that Hubert Harrison was ghostwriting Mrs. Amy *Ashwood*-Garvey's story of her life with Marcus Garvey, to be titled *The Rise and Fall of Marcus Garvey*. This book was never published, however, and it is not generally known what happened to the manuscript. Yet the scandal strengthened the anti-Garveyites cabal among the radical West Indians against Garvey's West Indian movement. It was a group struggle within a larger group struggle, a vexatious and complicated racial brew further confounded by foreign politics and domestic social unrest.

These Harlem developments of the 1920's form the essential historical backdrop to the problems of Harlem from 1929 to the contemporary scene. The precise nature and form of the original issues in dispute have been buried in the archives, so beclouded by the passage of time that they are now but vaguely remembered, if at all. However, these issues reveal that what was really at stake in the 1920's was what is today called Black Power—a slogan whose meaning is as vague to the people who use it, as it is a generalization of aspirations for those who believe they understand it. But the specifics of what this slogan implies were better understood by Harlem leaders in the 1920's because their struggle was precisely over those areas of community power they did not possess. Their failures, moreover, left a dismal heritage for the current generation and a monumental problem to solve in the future.

What were the causes of this disintegration of the "intellectual and artistic capital of the Negro world"? In terms of the peculiarities of American interracial relations in the world of art and culture, this becomes a highly intricate and delicate question. It was complex even before the racial integration mania became rampant in the North, but since, it has become even more so. However there are several underlying factors discernible in Harlem's cultural disintegration. If these are clearly grasped, the entire range of secondary ramifications of Negro-white cultural relations in the creative fields can be understood:

1. Middle-class Negroes have rejected the basic art expressions of the Negro folk in music, dance, literature and theater. This was first noticeable during the 1920's at the height of the Negro literary and artistic renaissance.

2. The Negro intelligentsia must cope with cultural arts diffusion and thematic acculturation on the creative level. White writers, dramatists and musicians, etc., assume the dominant role in the use of Negro thematic material in music, literature and theater.

3. Negro creative intellectuals, if not already of middle-class origins, adopt middle-class values.

4. Negro creative intellectuals as a stratum tend toward total acceptance of racial integrationist premises.

5. The status of Harlem as a community vis-à-vis the white community (Protestant, Catholic, Jewish), expressed in economic terms, renders Harlem a community of tenants, consumers, employees, and unemployed—*but not owners.* In purely cultural terms, cultural arts expressions in Harlem are controlled, discouraged, negated or otherwise stifled: the direct result of white ownership of properties and sites suitable for the housing, cultivation and encouragement of cultural expressions (*i.e.*, theaters, clubs, halls and film houses).

6. An economic factor in Harlem's cultural situation, growing out of basic Negro-white property relations, is that the Negro middle-class strata do not sponsor Negro cultural arts expressions either as businessmen or patrons. This factor is related to the basic attitude of the Negro middle class toward Negro art generally.

7. The objective of integration of the Negro in the arts leads to the participation of Negro artists in the cultural arts either on the basis of white middle-class standards, or as stepping stones to middle-class status using Negro art expressions.

8. As integration in the arts proceeds to the saturation point, each successive wave of young, creative intellectuals approaches the stage where diminishing returns leave them in a crisis, without the basis of a cultural philosophy with which to deal with that crisis.

One could list other factors, such as the social role of the "mixed-blood Negro," sometimes called the mulatto, and the special racial role he plays as intermediary in interracial cultural affairs (especially in relation to white liberals who favor this Negro type). However, this skin-color factor is no longer as decisive as it once was, and it is already evident that the integration process itself will tend to reveal what special role skin color will play in the future.

Integration will inevitably intensify class conflict within the Negro ethnic group, especially in the North, where integration goals become less and less tangible, and the middle classes will have to contend with the rising expectations of the Negro lower classes. We have not seen the last Harlem riots yet.

However, it is important to emphasize here that racial integration is not being criticized as a social philosophy on purely moral or ethical grounds as a human condition. It is being criticized on sociological grounds, because its *methodology* is open to question, in terms of *means* to achieve an *end*. It is the means that are under attack here; because the ends that are sought could very well be defeated by faulty means. Nowhere is this overall possibility more evident than in what has already occurred in the cultural areas of Negro life, in the very center of its highest population: Harlem, once the artistic and cultural mecca of the Negro world, has been almost completely deracinated culturally; this deracination happens to coincide with the Northern Negroes' highest gains in integration. Integration is thus leading to cultural negation.

Practically every Negro innovation in music, dance and theater has come out of Harlem to water and fertilize the arid, materialistic and anti-cultural way of American life. All of these innovations have been barred from classical cultivation (except in the hands of the white cultural elite like the Gershwins, etc.), but on the other hand, have been glorified by absorption into the American popular idiom and thoroughly "whitened." The Negro carriers of these popular art idioms have passed through the decades into cultural oblivion. Their names are legion and they were spawned by the thousands in the theaters, nightclubs, dens and dives, churches and halls of Harlem. They came from the South, the East and the West but they became Harlemites. They were singers, dancers, comedians, composers, writers, librettists, lyricists, poets, choreographers, musicians, arrangers, teachers, pupils, innovators, and imitators. They were courted, applauded, used, cheated, exploited, controlled, limited, deprived, starved—lionized too early or too late, and often never. Many whites praised them but at the same time feared them, and were jealous of their native originality. The Negro audience loved them and gloried in their prowess, but never fully understood the implications of their artistic role in American culture.

These artistic legions have left their imprint on the memories of peoples of every cosmopolitan capital in the world but there was never a cultural base, established in the byways of Harlem, to give them birth. White ownership of property rights conspired to control and restrict the growth, range, and emergence of talent, the avenues for its cultivation within as well as without Harlem. White theater-owners, both inside and outside Harlem, exploited Negro talent, profiting by the millions while, at the same time, eliminating the Negroes' cultural base by closing their theaters. Other property sites were prohibited from use by exorbitant rentals or controlled tenancy.

Harlem is a victim of cynical and premeditated cultural devegetation. Harlem is an impoverished and superexploited economic dependency, tied to a real estate, banking, business-commercial combine of absentee whites who suck the community dry every payday. In short, Harlem exists for the benefit of others and has no cultural, political or economic autonomy. Hence, no social movement of a protest nature in Harlem can be successful or have any positive meaning unless it is at one and the same time *a political, economic and cultural movement*. A Harlem movement that is *only* political, or *only* economic, or *only* cultural, or *merely* a protest movement—has to fail. It must be a *combined* movement, yet the characteristic disunity of purpose, peculiar to Harlem movements, prevents such united efforts. The unique problem facing a combined Harlem social movement is that if the cultural aspects and implications of Harlem are left out of the equation, the movement collapses. Hence, a political protest that is not economic and cultural as well, cannot get off the ground. The Harlem tenant's strike of 1963, for example, had to fail because it did not include economic and cultural goals; thus it could not take on broader political connotations. However, such a three-pronged movement cannot be properly launched without utilizing, understanding, and applying cultural analysis. But this analysis has to be historical, and it must explore all the reasons why Harlem has undergone cultural disintegration. A proper cultural analysis of Harlem's decline must lead logically to the conception of cultural reform measures—and ultimately to the fuller conception of cultural revolution.

A social movement of combined forces in Harlem must press

relentlessly for *Harlem autonomy in politics, economics and culture.* The first step towards economic autonomy must be in the nature of a Harlem-wide boycott that will wrest ownership of all cultural institutions (theaters, halls, club sites, and movie houses) out of the hands of private, outside concerns, for the key idea is cultural institutions (theaters, halls, club sites, and movie houses) *owned and administered* by the people of Harlem; they must become nationalized, operated and administered for the educational and cultural benefit of the Harlem community, under the control of Harlem community-wide citizens' planning commissions.

Ultimately, the role and function of such commissions must be extended to include all businesses and commercial institutions within Harlem that are now owned by absentee white private interests. The present outcome of Harlem Negro-white economic relations demands that Harlem Negroes can no longer defend or uphold the old economic concept of individual rights inherent in the idea of private property. The Harlem community as a whole must adopt for itself the concepts of cooperative and collective economic organization and administration of its inner community life, or else the Negroes' chances for survival in the U.S. are very slim. It is in Harlem where the first launching of this combined political, economic and cultural social movement must take place, for as Harlem goes, so goes all black America. All of black America has to take Harlem's social lead because virtually no other Negro community in America has the combined political, economic and cultural features that are characteristic of Harlem. This uniqueness of Harlem has never been fully grasped in terms of the overall characteristics, goals and methods of the Negro movement as a whole.

It happened that the growth and expansion of Harlem as a black community coincided with the period of the Negroes' highest cultural renaissance, in both the serious and popular idioms. In this process there was, of course, a pronounced duality, for along with a flowering of ethnic expression in art, there was also a strong imitative trend, evidenced for example, in the staging of white Broadway hit shows (for lack of Negro playwrights) with Negro casts. One can also maintain that if the social expansion of the Harlem community did not result ultimately in a parallel achievement of economic and political autonomy, (*i.e.,* self-sufficiency, or home rule, in economics and political development), it was because of poor leadership with a faulty social orientation. Whatever case can be made for or against Harlem's leadership, however, Harlem's only social compensation in terms of spiritual morale and racial pride was as the spawning ground for the American nation's popular cultural idiom in music, dance and song. (It was not for nothing that the Gershwins, *et al.,* spent so much of their time up in Harlem.) But the price Harlem paid for its cultural gifts to America was a cultural scorched-earth policy, directed against the community by outside economic and political forces. Harlem's cultural decline was but a prolonged prelude to its ultimate degradation: social disintegration, hopelessness, political backwardness, poverty and economic slavery. The Harlem riots are nothing but the belated outbursts of popular resentment and bitterness over a degrading social condition that has been in force for decades.

The following are some of the basic organizational objectives that must be immediately pursued in Harlem:

1. Formation of community-wide citizens' planning groups for a complete overhaul and reorganization of Harlem's political, economic and cultural life. The programs of such planning groups must aim *beyond* the goals of mere anti-poverty welfare state programs such as *HARYOU-ACT*.

2. Negroes with business experience should come together into business cooperatives which will take over completely the buying, distributing, and selling of all basic commodities used and consumed in Harlem, such as food, clothing, luxuries, services, etc.

3. There are too many small, privately-owned businesses in Harlem, all selling the same commodities. Negro business cooperatives would eliminate this overlapping, lower prices, and improve quality. Cooperatives would also create jobs. Many of the excess stores could be transformed into nurseries, supplementary classrooms, medical dispensaries for drug addicts, etc.

4. Harlem needs citizens' committees to combat crime and drug peddling. These committees should seek legal permission to be armed to fight the dangerous network of drug-selling.

5. Harlem needs to form a new, all-Negro, community-wide political party to add bargaining force to social, cultural and economic reforms.

6. Extensive federal and state aid will be necessary to finance complete economic, political and cultural reforms in Harlem. Without political power these social changes cannot be won.

7. Tenants' groups can no longer hope to improve housing conditions or to eradicate the economic evil of rent-gouging, as long as Harlem housing is *privately owned*. The fact must be driven home that marching to City Hall to force landlords to act decent is futile. Harlem's only salvation besides new housing is the abolition of private landlordism, to be replaced by tenants' cooperative ownership, or, at least, municipally controlled, housing.

8. Citizens' planning groups on the reorganization of Harlem's political, economic and cultural life should aim to establish *direct* lines of communication from the community to appropriate de-ı .rtments and agencies of the Federal government in Washington, D.C. Whenever it is deemed necessary and politically apropos, and in the interests of expediting community decisions, municipal and state echelons should be by-passed.

9. Citizens' planning groups must devise a new school of economics based on class and community organization. Such a school should be predicated on the need to create a *new black middle class* organized on the principle of cooperative economic ownership and technical administration. Such a class would be more responsible to the community in social, political and cultural affairs than middle classes based on free enterprise and laissez-faire economics. Such a class development along cooperative lines must be, in part, federally financed.

10. Citizens' planning groups should petition the Federal Communications Commission on the social need to allocate television and radio facilities to community group corporations rather than only to private interests.

More could be added to the above, but such elaboration can, and should, come about only in the course of implementing the essential, practical steps of such a radical program. But the hour for Harlem is late, insofar as autonomous, self-directed social change from the *bottom up* is concerned. Under capitalism, the dynamics of time and tide wait for no one. Ghetto uprisings have alerted the power structure that ghettoes need change, redevelopment, planned community rehabilitation, and so forth. Quietly, and with a minimum of fanfare, the city fathers and their big-business offspring have moved into planned action. *They* will change Harlem from the *top down*. And since the Harlem-based, black bourgeoisie is tied to the chariot of the power structure by a thousand political, economic, and cultural strands, the question arises: *For whom and for whose class interests will the power structure redevelop Harlem?*

The middle classes of Harlem that furnish community leadership are neither sovereign nor solvent; neither independent nor autonomous. They thrive on the crumbs granted them by the power structure for keeping the unruly masses mollified. They are the recipients of those few well-paying jobs from white businesses —both inside Harlem and beyond. Others have gained possession of a few parcels of real estate property, or have opened up a successful business. They are the lawyers, doctors, accountants, public relations experts, etc., who are of the same stamp as others who have made their mark in Democratic or Republican politics. Here in this class-stratum of ghetto aristocrats, the ministers of churches vie with professional social workers and police chiefs over which brand of community uplift is best for soothing the tortured ghetto soul 'twixt Hell on earth and Heavenly hereafter. Taken together, they are not bad people (some of my best friends are middle-class Negroes); they are simply inconsequential. Many of them "mean well" toward the "masses" but they are frightened to death of power—others' *and their own.* Hence they can be depended upon to rubber-stamp every design the power structure projects to "redevelop" Harlem, to wit: "Integration of Harlem by 1975 Is Aim of Area Planning Group," ran a *New York Times* subhead in a front-page story for April 5, 1965. To further this integration, "the shifting of large blocs of Negroes and Puerto Ricans both within the area under study and to outside communities has been suggested." And in addition, "the planning board has created its own councils of volunteers on *economic and cultural problems* [italics added]."

The planners, of course, left out "political" problems and for good reasons. The integration of Harlem will not only reduce what little political power Harlem has in fact, but if successful, will undermine the political potential, lying fallow, that the Negro middle class has never dared use. The economics of this plan are assuredly not meant to enrich Harlem's black bourgeoisie or render them more financially solvent. They will be offered a few more lower-five figure jobs with titles, and they will bargain away the most important black community power base in the whole United States under the banner of Integration, in reverse. It has already happened on paper, and the black bourgeoisie, as a result of its own self-administered impotence, has been suckered into an integration swindle they simply begged for. The cultural side of this redevelopment plan' is merely a decoy issue—supposed to divert attention away from the fact that this plan involves the aim of racial or ethnic dispersal for reasons *other* than those of relieving ghetto congestion. If the Harlem bourgeoisie were capable of giving real cultural leadership, then redevelopment would *not* be for integration in reverse. But, to repeat, the black bourgeoisie cannot give economic and political leadership because it cannot give *cultural leadership*—the three sides of the question go hand in hand. The tragedy of the black bourgeoisie in America is not that it simply "sells out," since all bourgeois classes are prone to compromise their sovereignty in a crisis. It is rather that no class the world over sells out so cheaply as the American black bourgeoisie, whose nation, the richest in the world, wastes billions overseas buying the fickle friendship of unworthy allies.

Thus, when *The New York Times* of December 7, 1966, announced that Governor Rockefeller was on hand in Harlem to announce his magnanimous contribution of a twelve-million-dollar State office building to Harlem's "rebirth," the political kinship of this gesture to that of the Rockefeller Brothers' survey on the performing arts, struck home with clarity. A rebirth of Harlem on the political, economic and cultural planes will never be achieved by community redevelopment administered solely from the top down. Neither will the "cultural democracy" vaguely hinted at in the Rockefeller Brothers' survey be created in America from the top down. The programmatic affinity of these concepts of redevelopment are closer than the incompetent Harlem middle-class leadership ever imagined. Hence, the cultural aspects of Harlem's redevelopment will have to be fought for by the younger generation of Harlem intellectuals, artists and writers. One can be certain that long before Harlem is integrated ("by 1975"), the impoverished corridors of American culture will reverberate with the din of fateful happenings now unforeseen.

The Rockefeller survey hardly even scratches the surface of the question of American cultural backwardness. Submerged in the report is the burning issue of who owns and controls the mass media, and for whose ends; also lurking is the unspoken, unresolved nationality question—the cultural image of the nation, especially abroad:

> When the arts go abroad, as they are in increasing degree through cultural exchanges, they can disclose the vital and creative aspects of the countries originating them. . . . Also, the overseas tours of our artists help to counter the widespread view that the United States is interested in little except material values. . . .
>
> As important as this activity is, there is a more significant political aspect to the arts than "image-building for the state." Art, in short, reminds us of our better nature in a world that too easily forgets and places the crises and torments of the moment in a larger perspective.[22]

In other words, culture is first a problem of a nation's image of itself before it can become the problem of what kind of cultural face the nation puts up for foreigners to view. But, even so, culture has more than a political aspect; it also has its economic side. From the Negro side of the black-white cultural equation in America, American capitalism comes up for serious criticism by the Negro intellectual of today, but *not* the Marxists, for they have confounded the issue of anticapitalism by oversimplification. Their mechanical and incompetent analysis of American capitalism makes them most "un-American" because it is non-cultural.

From the black point of view, the Negro intelligentsia does not comprehend the strategic importance of the cultural front in relation to the political and economic fronts. Like A. Philip Randolph's *Messenger* intellectuals of 1919, they parrot the belief that economics and politics take precedence over culture. This "practical" approach, though typically American, lacks an economic and political foundation. They do not see that a truly pragmatic economic and political program *cannot* be put into motion in the United States unless it is simultaneously linked to the cultural front. Like most Americans, Negroes are profoundly antitheoretical. Deeply committed to an activist tradition, they clamor

[22] Rockefeller report, *op. cit.*, p. 8.

—"We Want Action!" (or Freedom Now or Instant Integration or Immediate Liberation)—but it is all impatient action without much plan or deep reflection. All of the militant action that has gone down the drain since the various movements began would not be a waste had the leaders learned something in the process besides that "direct action" has its limitations. Then comes a moratorium, in the retreat behind the slogan of Black Power (in reality, merely another name for a certain raft of issues fought out and defeated forty years ago). But the leaders either care little for, or fail to understand the issues of, history.

The activist tradition of the Negro movement is, from an economic and political point of view, implicitly procapitalistic. But being also anti-theoretical, it lacks a leadership able to assess the compatibility of its own economic methods with its professed social aims of racial equality. Any movement committed to social change under American capitalism cannot be anti-theoretical, else how then can it determine which school of economic organization to be guided by? What practical economic steps will the movement take towards racial equality? What brand of politics will it practice to complement or legitimize these economic aims?

The black ghettoes today, especially Harlem, subsist on two kinds of economics: laissez-faire, free-enterprise capitalism, and welfare state, anti-poverty economics. Are either of these schools of economic method compatible with racial equality? They are not. Therefore, logic demands that a movement for social change must be motivated by some other school of economic thought, or else it is fooling itself and wasting the people's time. This is especially true in view of the fact that both free-enterprise capitalism and welfare state economics are administered and controlled from the top down. It means that every person pushed off the platforms of the labor and commercial markets theoretically comes under the ministrations of the benign and bureaucratic anti-poverty programs. But anti-poverty only soothes the wounds of poverty; it does not cure. As long as this situation prevails, the poor are trapped, and countertrends like Black Power are nullified. Anti-poverty administration is like a lightning rod that draws off the potential energy of the poor—energy that could be galvanized into a meaningful political and economic resistance against capitalistic poverty. For poverty among Negroes in the Harlem ghetto, in this instance, is far beyond the purview of piecemeal handouts and spoon-fed reform panaceas. It is a problem of lifting the ghettoes wholesale out of the stagnant mire of being captive consumers and cheap labor reserves, maintained for the extraction of profits and exploited by outside economic and political interests. Anti-poverty blocks the development of such politics by institutionalizing poverty and absorbing potentially independent political leadership in the ghettoes. Even the architects of antipoverty programs realize this:

> The coexistence in New York of enormous wealth and abject poverty is unparalleled in America. . . . This condition represents nothing less than a massive breakdown in the functioning of both *local government and the private enterprise system.* An enormous, if clumsy, public welfare program keeps the poorest of the poor badly housed and modestly fed and clothed. Starvation is thus avoided, even if normal family life is not positively encouraged. Welfare keeps the poverty problem from explosively demanding more adequate solutions than the handout [italics added].[23]

But the leaders of Negro movements do not understand the implications of this breakdown "in the functioning of . . . the private enterprise system," else they would be "demanding more adequate solutions than the handout," and would determine how to create programs toward that end. Caught up in the maze and vagaries of American materialistic values and the middle-class ethos, Negro leaders of all persuasions are just as trapped by the system as the poor. They cannot chart a course by finding their own political bearings because they do not grasp what ingredients must go into the making of a program.

History has placed Negro leadership in the favorable position of not having to beg the question of free enterprise, for it is free enterprise that must prove itself. American capitalism must prove that political democracy, economic democracy and cultural democracy are possible under free enterprise. It means that free enterprise must lay the economic basis for all three objectives by

[23] "Let There Be Commitment—A Housing, Planning Development Program for New York City"; Institute of Public Administration, September, 1966, Introduction, p. 1.

direct financing of new parallel institutions within the ghetto of an economic, cultural and class-ownership nature. If the traditional morality of free enterprise, private property considerations obstructs the democratization of economic relations between the white power and the black ghettoes, then the "rights" of private property must yield to other forms of economic organization or practice, by legal coercion.

The present leadership of Negro movements, of whatever faction, is unable to fashion suitable programs for the ghettoes of the United States because they fail to grasp the key nature of the Harlem ghetto, and also because they inherit the leadership failures of the black bourgeoisie of previous generations. The new generation leadership may condemn the incompetence of their fathers but they find it extremely difficult to shake off their legacy. Movements rise and fall, organizational efforts collapse for lack of proper orientation. In Negro life, economics, politics, and culture are the inseparable elements of social change.

None of these conclusions could have been clearly reached during the Harlem Renaissance of the 1920's, but the issues that force one to such conclusions today were germinated at that time. It becomes necessary, then, to digress, and explore many related aspects of the American phenomenon to show that "the more things change, the more they remain the same."

Cultural Leadership and Cultural Democracy

Racial democracy is, at the same time, cultural democracy; and the question of cultural democracy in America is posed in a way never before seen or considered in other societies. This uniqueness results historically from the manner in which American cultural developments have been influenced by the Negro presence. Since a cultural philosophy has been cultivated to deny this truth, it remains for the Negro intellectual to create his own philosophy and to bring the facts of cultural history in focus with the cultural practices of the present. In advanced societies it is not the race politicians or the "rights" leaders who create the new ideas and the new images of life and man. That role belongs to the artists and the intellectuals of each generation. Let the race politicians, if they will, create political, economic or organizational forms of leadership; but it is the artists and the creative minds who will, and must, furnish the all important content. And in this role, they must not be subordinated to the whims and desires of politicians, race leaders and civil rights entrepreneurs whether they come from the Left, Right, or Center, or whether they are peaceful, reform, violent, non-violent or laissez-faire. Which means to say, in advanced societies the cultural front is a special one that requires special techniques not perceived, understood, or appreciated by political philistines. There are those among the latter who give lip-service to the idea that Culture and Art belong to the People, but what they actually give to the people (not to speak of what is given to Negroes as people) is not worthy of examination. It is the Negro creative intellectual who must take seriously the idea that culture and art belong to the people—with all the revolutionary implications of that idea.

To bring this idea into proper focus, and into the context of our peculiar American cultural ideology, let us quote from Gilbert Seldes' book, *The Public Arts,* written in 1956:

"This country, with its institutions, belongs to the people who inhabit it," said Abraham Lincoln, and as he was then facing the possible dissolution of the United States, he added, "Whenever they (the people) shall grow weary of the existing government, they can exercise their Constitutional right of amending it or their revolutionary right to dismember or overthrow it."

, I am suggesting that the cultural institutions of a country also belong to its inhabitants, and, not having the courage of Lincoln's radicalism, I do not insist upon the revolutionary right of the people to destroy whatever wearies them. Moderately, I propose the idea that the people have valid rights over those cultural institutions which can be properly called "the public arts."[1]

Seldes had come a long way from 1924 when he wrote *The Seven Lively Arts*. He pointed out, in 1956, that a revolution had taken place in American cultural arts communication, which had transformed what he had called in the 1920's the "seven lively arts," into what are now the "public arts": "For convenience, the beginning of that revolution can be placed in the late summer of 1929, when millions of Americans, with more money to spend on recreation than they had ever had before, spent nothing because they were staying home to be entertained by the Amos 'n' Andy radio program."[2]

The fact, of course, that "Amos 'n' Andy" was a modernized version of the old-time minstrel show—in which whites blackened their faces in order to imitate the original plantation minstrels created by Negroes—probably did not strike Seldes as being highly significant in a cultural way because of "content." But the fact that the program was an imitation Negro comic show *is* significant. The Negro-white cultural symbolism involved here was expressed and given significance by Gilbert Seldes himself, during the 1920's when his critiques of American art forms damned the Negro with faint praise, condemning him forever to the back alleys of American culture. Seldes claimed then that Negro music and musicians could not hope to rise to "classic" stature. He implied also that Negro theater ought not to be looked upon as art in the sense that the devotees of Western culture think of art. "The one claim never made for the Negro shows is that they are artistic,"

---

[1] *The Public Arts* (New York: Simon and Schuster, 1956), p. 207.
[2] *Ibid.*, p. 1.

Seldes wrote. He was then talking about such hit shows as Sissle and Blake's *Shuffle Along*:

> Set beside them [Negro shows], then, a professedly artistic revue, the *Pinwheel* [a white show], compounded of native and exotic effects. It had two or three interesting or exciting numbers; but the whole effect was one of dreariness. The pall of art was upon it; it died nightly. And *Shuffle Along, without art*, but with tremendous vitality, not only lived through the night, but dragged provincial New Yorkers to a midnight show as well.[3]

Yet, according to Seldes, Negro shows were not art. And what, pray tell, *is* art? The peculiar and perverse tradition of cultural criticism, practiced by Gilbert Seldes and others, has severely distorted native American artistic standards by over-glorifying obsolete European standards. Seldes debased Negro creative artists by refusing to accept their native originality as truly American. He rejected what was truly American because it was not European, but Afro-American. Thus by downgrading Negro musical originality, he helped to undermine the only artistic base in the American culture in which the Negro could hold his own as an original artist. And, from this base, he could eventually, by dint of creative discipline, raise his own level of sophistication and finesse in all other American art forms. Thus, in the 1920's, Seldes' criticisms encouraged undemocratic ethnic tendencies in American culture. Yet contradictorily, in 1956 Gilbert Seldes wants the "public arts" of America democratized by returning them to the people. But which people? Seldes, of course, knows that the "seven lively arts" did not belong to the people in the 1920's. Because if they had, America would not have witnessed that un-cultural spectacle of Hemingway, Harold Stearns, Sinclair Lewis, T.S. Eliot, Ezra Pound—the lost generation refugees—hotfooting it to Paris and Madrid to escape American cultural suffocation. While all of these white intellectuals were escaping because they could not be real artists in America, the Negroes were trying to create new art in their own native American way. And, as things have turned out "culturally" in America, there is now *only one* group of American creative intellectuals who have the motivation (or at least the potential) for democratizing American culture and forcing the

---

[3] *The Seven Lively Arts, op. cit.,* p. 147.

return of the public arts to the people. These are the new young generation of Negro intellectuals—the cultural and ethnic progeny of those very Negroes whom Seldes critically downgraded in the 1920's as being mostly primitive and non-intellectual as creative artists. These young people, however, will have to go far beyond Seldes' proposed "moderation" in techniques and will have to search for the "revolutionary rights" of confrontation that Seldes disavows.

This new young generation must first clear the way to cultural revolution by a critical assault on the methods and ideology of the old-guard Negro intellectual elite. The failures and ideological shortcomings of this group have meant that no new directions, or insights have been imparted to the Negro masses. This absence of positive orientation has created a cultural void that has spawned all the present-day tendencies towards nihilism and anarchism, evident in the ideology of the young. This new generation of Negro poets, artists, writers, critics and playwrights bursts onto the scene; fed and inspired by the currents flowing out of movements at home and abroad, they are full of zeal but have no well-charted direction. They encounter the established old guard (even some lingering representatives of the 1920's) and the results are confusion and a clash of aims. The old guard attempts to absorb some of the new guard. This process has been seen at work in the Harlem Writers Guild, the Artists for Freedom group, *Freedomways* and *Liberator* magazine and in the recent proliferation of Negro Writers' Conferences. The young wave attempts to criticize *and* emulate the old guard at one and the same time, which creates more ideological confusion. The young wave cannot completely break from the old order of things cultural, because the old guard stands pat and blocks the path to new cultural frontiers. This state of interference has existed rather consistently since 1961. Out of this process a number of provocative issues have emerged and been debated, but nothing resembling a real critique has come out of it. The old guard gives no leadership, clarifies nothing and confuses everything.

How would one define cultural leadership? How would it be differentiated qualitatively from ordinary civil rights leadership, or the overworked "civil writism" of the old guard, or the emulation of the new? This has to be clarified because American Negroes are, after all, Americans who pattern their social reasoning on white American standards of social logic. White Anglo-Saxon Protestants are fundamentally anti-theoretical, anti-aesthetic, anti-cultural, anti-intellectual. They often try hard not to be that way, but have a deep-seated suspicion of art, culture, and intellect nonetheless. They prefer the practical, by which they mean the application of practical values in the pursuit of materialistic ends. They actually look upon the enjoyment of art and culture as a materialistic end, especially if it is "entertaining." But they are not overly concerned about the cultivation of creativity. Creative values are usually subordinated to materialistic values. This outlook permeates everything in the United States, including the outlook of American Negroes. The philosophy of the civil rights movement is predominantly materialistic, aiming at the achievement of a bigger share of American materialistic abundance. But whereas most American whites see the enjoyment of art and culture as one of the acceptable ends of materialistic achievement, Negroes (who might imitate these values, socially) rarely participate as cultural or artistic personalities for any purpose other than materialistic ends. In either case there is no creative cultural philosophy involved.

The civil rights movement cannot really give cultural leadership in any effective way—it is too suffused with the compulsion to legitimize its social aims with American standards. The leaders of the civil rights movement, along with all the "civil writers," subordinate themselves to the very cultural values of the white world that are used either to negate, or deny the Negro cultural equality, and to exploit his cultural ingredients and use them *against* him. This is one of the great traps of racial integrationism —one must accept all the values (positive or negative) of the dominant society into which one struggles to integrate. Let us examine two very prominent cultural questions out of the American twentieth-century past and see how they were handled. Both of these are issues of the 1920's that have become institutionalized in today's Americana. One is exemplified by the folk-opera *Porgy and Bess,* a cultural product, the other by Duke Ellington, a cultural personality.

In May, 1959, following the successful opening of *A Raisin in the Sun,* its author Lorraine Hansberry debated Otto Preminger on a television program in Chicago, over what she labeled the deplorable "stereotypes" of *Porgy and Bess*. The film version of the folk-opera, directed by Preminger, had just been released and it starred none other than Sidney Poitier, who also headlined Miss Hansberry's play on Broadway. This was, of course, not the first time *Porgy and Bess* had been criticized by Negroes. Ever since its premiere in 1935, it has been under attack from certain Negro quarters because it reveals southern Negroes in an unfavorable light. Hence Miss Hansberry's criticisms were nothing very new or original. What *was* new, however, were the times and the circumstances. Miss Hansberry objected to *Porgy* because stereotypes "constitute bad art" when "the artist hasn't tried hard enough to understand his characters." She claimed that although Gershwin had written a great musical score, he had fallen for what she called the exotic in American culture: "We, over a period of time, have apparently decided that within American life we have one great repository where we're going to focus and imagine sensuality and exaggerated sensuality, all very removed and earthy things—and this great image is the American Negro."

When Preminger asked Miss Hansberry if she suspected the motives of those who had written and produced *Porgy,* she replied: "We cannot afford the luxuries of mistakes of other peoples. So it isn't a matter of being hostile to you, but on the other hand it's also a matter of never ceasing to try to get you to understand that your mistakes can be painful, even those which come from excellent intentions. We've had great wounds from great intentions."[4]

During this debate there was also injected a discussion of *Carmen Jones*—a white-created, Negro version of the Bizet opera, *Carmen*. Miss Hansberry did not like *Carmen Jones* either; but oddly enough (and also characteristically), she weakened her argument on the subject of artistic integrity by wanting to know why no whites had been cast in this caricature of *Carmen,* as if to imply that interracial casting would have made it more acceptable as art. Behind this query there lurked, of course, the whole muddled question of integration in the arts. Also implicit was the Negro integrationist's main peeve in the theater—the "all-Negro play"

⁴ *Variety,* May 27, 1959, p. 16.

(or musical), which they deplore as a symbol of segregation, and the "all-white play," which it is their bounden duty to "integrate" even if the author never had Negroes in mind. Needless to point out, the film *Porgy and Bess* had its Broadway and neighborhood run, and hundreds of working-class Negroes (whom Miss Hansberry claimed she wrote about in *Raisin*), lined up at the box offices to see this colorful film "stereotype" of their people.

This whole episode revealed some glaring facts to substantiate my claim that the Negro creative intellectual does not even approach possession of a positive literary and cultural critique—either of his own art, or that other art created for him by whites. In the first place, Lorraine Hansberry revealed that she knew little about the history of this folk-opera, or how or why it was written. She was only concerned with the fact that it was a stereotype. This already precluded the possibility of Miss Hansberry or anyone rendering the kind of critique *Porgy and Bess* deserves from the Negro point of view. Hence, the whole debate was worthless and a waste of time except from the point of view of making some more noisy, but superficial, integrationist propaganda.

The real cultural issues surrounding *Porgy and Bess*. as it relates to the American Negro presence, have never been confronted by the Negro intelligentsia—inside or outside the theater. The two most obvious points a Negro critic should make are: 1.) that a folk-opera of this genre *should have been written* by Negroes themselves and has not; 2.) that such a folk-opera, even if it *had been written* by Negroes, would never have been supported, glorified and acclaimed, as *Porgy* has, by the white cultural elite of America.

Lorraine Hansberry, taking to the television rostrum on art and culture *à la Negre,* was like a solitary defender, armed with a dull sword, rushing out on a charger to meet a regiment. But once having met an opposing general she immediately capitulates—"My intentions are not really hostile but you all have wounded *us.*" For Miss Hansberry to have criticized *Porgy* merely on content was, of course, her unmitigated privilege; but on this basis, her own play was wide open for some criticism on art and the image of the American Negro, which it never got. To criticize any play today involving Negroes, purely on content, is not enough. Most Negro criticism of *Porgy* has been of middle-class origin, although the

Negro middle class has never been at all sympathetic to the realities of southern Negro folk characteristics in any way, shape or form. Hence, a generically class-oriented non-identification was inherent in Miss Hansberry's views.[5]

Porgy and Bess has successfully weathered all such criticisms on its content and has been enshrined in America's rather empty cultural hall of fame as the great American musical classic. It has been shipped all around the world and proudly displayed as America's greatest artistic achievement. How can one really attack America's "greatest artistic achievement," especially when it is about Negroes? *Porgy* is surely the most contradictory cultural symbol ever created in the Western world.

To attack it, one must see it in terms of something more than mere content. It must be criticized from the Negro point of view as the most perfect symbol of the Negro creative artist's cultural denial, degradation, exclusion, exploitation and acceptance of white paternalism. *Porgy and Bess* exemplifies this peculiarly American cultural pathology, most vividly, most historically, and most completely. It combines the problems of Negro theater, music, acting, writing, and even dancing, all in one artistic package, for the Negro has expressed whatever creative originality he can lay claim to, in each of these aspects of art. However, Negroes had no part in writing, directing, producing, or staging this folk-opera about Negroes (unless it was in a strictly subordinate role). In fact, the first recording of *Porgy* used the voices of Lawrence Tibbett and other white singers, because it was not at first believed that Negroes were "good" enough. As a symbol of that deeply-ingrained, American cultural paternalism practiced on Negroes ever since the first Southern white man blacked his face, the folk-opera *Porgy and Bess* should be forever banned by all Negro performers in the United States. No Negro singer, actor, or performer should ever submit to a role in this vehicle again. If white producers want to stage this folk-opera it should be performed by white performers made up in blackface, because it is distorted imitation all the way through. Musically, it is a rather pedestrian blend of imitation-Puccini and imitation-South Carolina-Negro folk music that

[5] See also "Why Negroes Don't Like *Porgy and Bess,*" *Ebony,* October, 1959, pp. 50-54.

Gershwin culled.* In theme, it presents the "simple black people"
just the way white liberal paternalists love to see them. The fact
that such Negro types *did* exist is beside the point. Culturally, it
is a product of American developments that were intended to
shunt Negroes off into a tight box of subcultural, artistic dependence, stunted growth, caricature, aesthetic self-mimicry imposed by others, and creative insolvency.

But the superficial Negro creative intelligentsia, who have become so removed from their meaningful traditions, cannot see
things this way, so blindly obsessed are they with the modern
mania for instant integration. They do not understand the cultural history of America and where they fit in that historical
scheme. They understand next to nothing about the 1920's and
how the rather fluid, contending cultural trends among blacks and
whites were frozen in that decade, once white control of cultural
and creative power patterns was established to the supreme detriment of blacks. They are not aware that the white critics of that
time were saying that Negro creative artists were, for the most
part, primitives; and that Gilbert Seldes, for example, asserted
that Negro musicians and composers were creatively and artistically backward. They are not aware that for critics like Seldes, the
Negroes were the anti-intellectual, uninhibited, unsophisticated,
intuitive children of jazz music who functioned with aesthetic
"emotions" rather than with the disciplined "mind" of white
jazzmen. For such critics, the real artists of Negro folk expression
were the George Gershwins, the Paul Whitemans and the Cole
Porters. Seldes asserted in 1924:

> Nowhere is the failure of the Negro to exploit his gifts more
> obvious than in the use he had made of the jazz orchestra; for
> although nearly every Negro jazz band is better than nearly every
> white band, no Negro band has yet come up to the level of the
> best white ones, and the leader of the best of all, by a little joke,
> is called [Paul] Whiteman.[6]

---

* Seldes said, "It seemed to me that the style of the opera had been imposed on
the materials, it did not grow out of them." *The Seven Lively Arts*, p. 94.
    See also Hall Johnson's critique of *Porgy and Bess* in *Opportunity*, January,
1936, pp. 24-28. Probably the best professional criticism on record.
[6] *The Seven Lively Arts*, p. 100.

This was a personal opinion, but whether true or false, it typified the white cultural attitudes toward all forms and practices of Negro art: Compared to the Western intellectual standards of art and culture, the Negro does not measure up. Thus every Negro artist, writer, dramatist, poet, composer, musician, *et al*, comes under the guillotine of this cultural judgment. What this judgment really means is that the Negro is artistically, creatively, and culturally inferior; and therefore, all the established social power wielded by the white cultural elite will be used to keep the Negro creative artist in his place. But the historical catch in all this is that the white Protestant Anglo-Saxon in America has nothing in his native American tradition that is aesthetically and culturally original, except that which derives from the Negro presence.

Seldes' mixed feelings and critical ambivalence concerning Negro music stemmed from his awareness that jazz would have to become America's national music, or at least form its basic ingredients. This grievously worried many white critics then, and it explains why they still maintain the artistic superiority of the European symphonic music tradition, refuting that jazz is the basis of the American classical music tradition. From these attitudes on the cultural arts, based on racial values, whites have cultivated their own literary and cultural critique. But it has been a critique predicated on the cultural ideals of a group whose English-North European antecedents have been too culturally ego-ridden, unoriginal, ultra-conservative and desiccated to generate a flourishing national culture. Hence historically, there has been on the cultural front in America a tense ideological war for ethnic identity and ascendancy. This competition has taken on strange and unique patterns. Often it is between WASPs and Jews, but more often than not, it is a collaboration between WASPs and Jews, on high levels, against the Negro. Since it is less possible for the Negro to "pass" for a WASP, than for a member of any other ethnic group, it is the Negro minority who is the most vulnerable and defenseless on the cultural front. In this war of indentity over cultural arts standards, the Negro functions under a double or triple jeopardy: Without a literary and cultural critique of his own, the Negro cannot fight for and maintain a position in the cultural world.

Thus the Hansberry attack on *Porgy and Bess* was almost totally meaningless. Even a total Negro boycott of this film which (theoretically) should have been called, could not have been—for the same reason that Negro actors and performers, led by Sidney Poitier, did not refuse to act in this film in the first place. If the Negro creative intellectuals actually had any real aesthetic standards of their own, Hollywood could not have made this film at all. Since the 1957 boycott by the Montgomery Negroes, showing what kind of sacrifices are necessary when it comes to a principle, every Negro—high or low, rich or poor—has the moral obligation at all times to give up immediate comforts and privileges for long-range objectives.

The *Porgy and Bess* controversy had another important angle. In December, 1955, the State Department sent a company to perform it in the Soviet Union. The folk-opera was well received by the Russians and given a tumultuous ovation. Truman Capote, the American novelist and playwright, reported on this cultural exchange in his book, *The Muses Are Heard*. One of the Leningrad critics said, in part, of *Porgy and Bess*: "We are not used to the naturalistic details in the dance, to the excessive jazz sound of the symphony orchestra, etc. Nevertheless the performance broadens our concept of the art of contemporary America, and familiarizes us with thus far unknown facets of the musical and theatrical life of the United States."[7]

Of course, this is an enthusiastic overstatement of the facts of life, inasmuch as the opera was written in the 1930's, based on a novel written in 1925. But the fact that the Russians praised the work revealed the awkward, false, and highly irrelevant position of the American Communist leftwing on the Negro in culture. From the leftwings's cultural thesis on art, we get the aesthetics of Soviet socialist realism that was imposed on leftwing Negro writers. This thesis agrees with those non-Left Negroes who call the folk-opera a stereotype. But, if Soviet-loving Paul Robeson, for example, ever publicly set the Russians right on how to assess this work of art, I am ignorant of when or how.[8] The Russian reaction proved that it

[7] New York: Random House, 1956, p. 180.
[8] See "Porgy and Bess Wins Ovation in Moscow," *Daily Worker*, January 12, 1956, p. 2. See also, David Platt, "Letters from Prague Reveal Divided Opinions on Porgy and Bess," *Daily Worker*, March 22, 1956, p. 6.

is impossible to attack *Porgy and Bess* on content alone, for the Russians could not possibly have grasped the real and actual "facets of the musical and theatrical life of the United States" simply by seeing this work performed in Leningrad.

In 1965, Duke Ellington, America's greatest exponent of orchestrated jazz music and composition, was turned down for the Pulitzer Prize citation for "long-term achievement" in American music. In *The New York Times* story, the Pulitzer Prize advisory board gave no reason for refusing the citation to Ellington. For just about forty years, he has been, by general popular and professional acclaim, the foremost jazz orchestra leader and composer in America. This turn-down indicates that the same old, ethnic-group war for cultural supremacy in American music is still being waged.* Ellington was quoted as saying: "Fate's being kind to me. Fate doesn't want me to be too famous too young."[9]

Ellington could be denied this kind of recognition only because of the undemocratic way the cultural machine in America is run. Here was an affront to the entire musical and cultural heritage of every Negro in America. If the Negro creative intellectuals were really educating their people—every jazz musician, singer, and actor would have understood the meaning of this contemptuous attitude. They would have walked off their jobs and demonstrated collectively in a march down Broadway. Every movie house in Negro neighborhoods would have been boycotted, in a sympathy strike against the racist views that have for decades permeated American culture, poisoned its creative bloodstreams, corrupted its ideology, and retarded the national potential. But the incident passed with only a momentary response to its cultural implications, so blind, benumbed, amoral, crass and corrupted have we become, so aesthetically untutored are our collective sensibilities. The Negro creative intellectuals, the literary and cultural civil righters, supposedly understand and appreciate jazz music. But even LeRoi Jones, whose *Blues People* is an important critical landmark in the analysis and interpretation of jazz in terms of a social art, almost completely passed over the 1920's. He did not

---

* Seldes, in 1957, still did not consider Ellington's impact on American music comparable to Whiteman's, *et al.*

[9] *The New York Times*, May 5, 1965, p. 49.

deal at all with those first attacks on Negro jazz and the "damning-with-faint-press" criticisms of Seldes and others. Jones deals adequately with the evolution of jazz styles (*i.e.*, the *content* of jazz and blues modes of expression), but not enough with the social structure (the nature of the cultural apparatus to which Negro jazz and its artists are subordinated). Afro-American folk music became the aesthetic ingredient, the cultural material, the wealth exploited by white American cultural imperialism. This kind of appropriation can be explained only by an analysis of the cultural apparatus in all its economic, class, political and institutional ramifications. Without it, one cannot explain how or why an Ellington does not achieve his due recognition today, while the Gershwin-type musicians achieved status and recognition in the 1920's for music that they literally stole outright from Harlem nightclubs. The impact of Negro jazz was powerful enough to arouse the concern of white critics about the idiomatic direction of American music. But it was a concern that critics like Seldes could not afford to extend to its logical conclusion. The critics would talk all around this question while evading it, as Seldes did, when he wrote: "Of the music itself—of jazz and the use of spirituals and the whole question of our national music—this is not the place to write."[10]

This same attitude crops out in the 1965 Pulitzer Prize issue; one could almost paraphrase: "Of the music itself—of jazz and the use of spirituals and the whole question of [Duke Ellington]—this is not the [time to give prizes]."

Negro creative intellectuals, however, are neither equipped nor willing to contribute cultural leadership on a question like this. They are most adept when it comes to sentimentalizing in public about their preoccupation with the indigenous qualities of the "Folk." But somewhere deep in their consciousness is the same attitude, borrowed from whites, that jazz music does not edify but merely entertains. A jazz artist is, therefore, merely an entertainer who, in certain cases, makes a lot of money—or at least a lot more than the average Negro earns. Such artists are successful, at least in quasi-middle-class terms. Therefore, in their practical minds, jazz entertainment is rated according to what degree its Negro practi-

[10] *The Seven Lively Arts, op. cit.,* p. 150.

tioners earn money enough to achieve middle-class status. When this earning power reaches a level that permits one to purchase a Life Membership in the NAACP, an entertainer has "arrived." Sammy Davis, Jr. even went one better, for he was recently elected Chairman of the Association's Life-Membership Drive. This is an entertainer who has *truly* arrived! *The New York Times* described the occasion this way: "This is the serious side of the entertainer, a man whose public image is that of a perpetual-motion, rapid fire showbusiness factotum."[11]

Every NAACP bigwig feels exactly the same way about entertainers of color: Just as long as they do not stereotype the Negro and offend middle-class sensibilities in such vehicles as *Porgy and Bess,* they are appreciated, but not taken too seriously. Thus the real impact of the Negro entertainer on race politics in American culture does not penetrate the minds of these colored, middle-class philistines.

These people do not want to comprehend the fact that the role of the Negro, as entertainer, has not changed since the 1920's. In 1967 the Negro entertainer is still being used, manipulated, and exploited by whites (predominantly Jewish whites). Negro entertainment talent is more original than that of any other ethnic group, more creative ("soulful" as they say), spontaneous, colorful, and also more plentiful. It is so plentiful, that in the marketplace of popular culture, white brokers and controllers buy Negro entertainment cheaply (sometimes for nothing) and sell it high— as in the case of Sammy Davis. But there is only *one* Sammy Davis. In the shadows, a multitude of lesser colored lights are plugging away, hoping against hope to make the Big Time, for the white culture brokers only permit a few to break through—thus creating an artificial scarcity of a cultural product. This system was established by the wily Broadway entrepreneurs in the 1920's. Negro entertainment posed such an ominous threat to the white cultural ego, the staid Western standards of art, cultural values and aesthetic integrity, that the entire source had to be stringently controlled.

Forty years after the 1920 era, Duke Ellington has outplayed, outcreated and outlasted all the Benny Goodmans and

[11] April 13, 1966, p. 24.

Paul Whitemans—yet the situation has not changed very much. A Sammy Davis goes on Broadway in a musical, *Golden Boy*, which was fashioned as a theatrical vehicle using the same cultural rule of thumb as *Porgy and Bess*, with a few minor variations. The story was not originally about Negro life, but was adapted. The creative functions—writing, composing and lyric versifying—were all done by whites. The music was purely routine. Although it is well known that it is a rare white composer, indeed, who can write Negro music, the Broadway entrepreneurs did not employ any of the several gifted ,Negro composers available who have never been commissioned to write music for the theater. Yet the public, Negro and white, are propagandized to believe that *Golden Boy* was a landmark in theatrical and symbolic racial democracy, simply because it was "integrated" on stage. This is tantamount to saying that if *Porgy and Bess* were to be staged with an integrated cast, that would make it more acceptable to the audience as an achievement in democratic casting. But all of this amounts to nothing but a dishonest illusion. Theatrical practices in America that exclude the participation of Negro creative artists —the writer, dramatist, poet, composer, designer, *et al.*—are not democratic practices at all. No amount of integrated casting can cover up this fact.

But the Negro creative intellectuals cannot exert themselves to deal with the *roots* of these problems, because they permit too many of the surface issues to pass without dealing with *them.* The question of Ellington and the Pulitzer Prize is a surface issue. The prize itself is not really that important, but what lies behind the denial of the prize, *is:* a whole history of organized duplicity and exploitation of the Negro jazz artist—the complicated tie-in between booking agencies, the musicians' unions, the recording companies, the music publishers, the managers, the agents, the theater owners, the nightclub owners, the crooks, shysters, and racketeers. The Negro creative intellectuals have to look into the question of how it is possible for a Negro jazz musician to walk the streets of large cities, jobless and starving, while a record that he cut with a music company is selling well, both in the United States and in Europe. They have to examine why a Negro jazz musician can be forced to pay dues to unions that get him no work, and that operate with the same discriminatory practices as clubs, halls and theaters. The impact of the cultural tradition of Afro-American folk music demands that the racially-corrupt practices of the music-publishing field be investigated.

The Negro creative intellectuals must also take action against the film-producing conspiracy in the United States, where a "one-star" system has been manufactured around Sidney Poitier. He is supposed to represent the cultural presence, the aspirations, and the social psychology of the largest minority in the United States, a minority whose population is considerably larger than many independent nations in the world. The Negro creative intellectuals cannot make peace with a cultural apparatus that will not take *Invisible Man,* or any other representative novel, and film it. Whether such works are good, bad or excellent is academic, in view of the millions of dollars wasted annually in filming trash for the movie market. There are those who will object to this criticism of the cultural apparatus—allegedly in the interests of a cultural laissez-faire policy. However, any advanced nation that has allowed its inner cultural expressions to be so debased and corrupted, deserves nothing less than governmental investigation, correction, and control.

But the Negro intelligentsia cannot give cultural leadership on these questions because they have sold out their own birthright for an illusion called Racial Integration. Having given up their strict claim to an ethnic identity in politics, economics and culture, they haven't a leg to stand on. They can make no legitimate claims for their group integrity in cultural affairs. They take the *illusion* of the integrated world of the creative intellectuals as the social *reality,* and do not know how to function within its cultural apparatus.

What lurks behind the disabilities and inhibitions of the Negro creative intellectuals is the handicap of the black bourgeoisie. Unless this class is brought into the cultural situation and forced to carry out its responsibilities on a community, organizational, and financial level, the cultural side of the black revolution will be retarded. The snail's pace of bourgeois civil rights reform, and white power-structure manipulation, will combine to stall it indefinitely. The problem of cultural leadership, then, is not only a problem of the faulty orientation of the Negro creative intellectuals; it is also a problem of the reeducation of the black bourgeoisie, especially its new, younger strata.

II

1920's-1930's—West Indian Influence

The 1929 Crash brought the expatriate members of the Harlem Renaissance back to their native haunts to face a bleak decade, with the Negro no longer in vogue as artistic creator. Claude McKay, for example, spent his final months abroad in Morocco finishing his collection of stories, *Gingertown*, published in 1932. He mentioned in his autobiography that "the cream of Harlem was in Paris" during those last days of the 1920's; among them were the Robesons, Countee Cullen, Alain Locke and Adelaide Hall.

From this point on, not much is known here about McKay's literary relationship with the Communist leftwing. Wilson Record's study, *The Negro and the Communist Party*, mentions McKay only once, but not in connection with any specific organizational activity: "The party undoubtedly influenced a great many Negro intellectuals, particularly such writers as Claude McKay, Langston Hughes, and Richard Wright. It affected them not only as men of letters but also as men of political action."[1]

Claude McKay, however, was not the type to be embroiled in any action involving the American Negro problem in the United States. He remained the outsider, critically looking in upon a unique situation. He was attuned to a different psychology about the whole matter. He wrote about a letter he had received from James Weldon Johnson "inviting me to return to America to participate in the Negro renaissance movement," but explained: "But the resentment of the Negro intelligentsia against [my book] *Home to Harlem* was so general, bitter, and violent that I was hesitant about returning to the great Black Belt. I had learned very little about the ways of the Harlem elite during the years I lived there."[2]

[1] Record, *The Negro and the Communist Party* (Chapel Hill: The University of North Carolina Press, 1951), p. 305.
[2] McKay, *op. cit.*, p. 306.

As an Afro-Britisher, McKay devoted his short spell of active political involvement to working with Sylvia Pankhurst's labor causes in England in 1920. In 1937, his autobiography was reviewed by Alain Locke under the title "Spiritual Truancy." There, Locke called McKay the "playboy of the Negro Renaissance" and accused him of "chronic and perverse truancy" and a "lack of common loyalty"[3] for his stand-offish attitude towards the American Negro situation. Yet, McKay's conclusions about the American Negro situation were (and still are) important. In his autobiography, he summed them up in the last chapter aptly titled, "On Belonging to a Minority Group":

> I might say that I too have suffered a lot for my knowledge of, and contact with, the white race. . . .
>
> It is hell to belong to a suppressed minority and outcast group. For to most members of the powerful majority, you are not a person; you are a problem. . . . As a member of a weak minority, you are not supposed to criticize your friends of the strong majority. You will be damned mean and ungrateful. Therefore you and your group must be content with lower critical standards. . . .
>
> Well, whatever the white folks do and say, the Negro race will finally have to face the need to save itself. The whites have done the blacks some great wrongs, but also they have done some good. They have brought to them the benefits of modern civilization . . . but one thing they cannot do, they cannot give Negroes the gift of a soul—a group soul.
>
> But there is very little group spirit among Negroes. The American Negro group is the most advanced in the world. It possesses unique advantages for development and expansion and for assuming the world leadership of the Negro race. But it sadly lacks a group soul. And the greatest hindrance to the growth of a group soul is the wrong idea held about segregation. Negroes do not understand the difference between group segregation and group aggregation. And their leaders do not enlighten them, because they too do not choose to understand. . . .
>
> Yet it is a plain fact that the entire world of humanity is more or less segregated in groups. . . .
>
> But Negro institutions in general are developed only perfunctorily and by compulsion, because Negroes have no abiding faith in them. Negroes wisely are not wasting thought on the chimera

of a separate Negro state or a separate Negro economy within the
United States, but there are a thousand things within the Negro
community which only Negroes can do. . . .

The Negro intelligentsia cannot hope to get very far if the
Negro masses are despised and neglected. . . .

Anyway, it seems to me that if Negroes were organized as a
group and as workers, whatever work they are doing (with or
without the whites) and were getting a practical education in the
nature and meaning of the labor movement, it might even be
more important and worthwhile than for them to become members of radical parties. . . .

Such is my opinion for all that it may be worth. . . . And all I
offer here is the distilled poetry of my experience.[4]

Here was Claude McKay's clear insight as the outside observer—
mixed with the unavoidable confusions of the times. Intellectually, he was stranded at some undefinable point on the interracial
spectrum between integration and "group identity." He was ad-
vocating cultural pluralism, without naming it. On the other
hand, typical of most West Indians (and later the Africans), he
was complaining about the lack of a "group soul" among American Negroes. Although he was correct in criticizing Negro leaders,
he failed to emphasize that these leaders invariably come from the
educated upper-class Negro stratum—it is usually with these same
upper-class Negroes that most West Indians (and Africans) inden-
tify when they arrive in the United States—hardly ever with the
"masses." Further, McKay's vague assessment of the Negro's relationship with labor and radical parties was more a reflection of his
own dubious experiences—less than objective, really, since he was
neither a worker nor a *bona fide* member of a radical party. It
seems not to have occurred to him that such a party did not *have* to
be "white"; or indeed, that it *might* have to be "black." But the
ascendant Communist leftwing in the 1920's or 1930's would have
found such an idea even more heretical than Trotskyism came to
be.

As far back as 1919, one of the problems of the first Negroes to
enter the newly emerging Communist leftwing was the ideological split between American and West Indian Negroes. This split

4 McKay, *op. cit.*, pp. 342-354, *passim.*

was exacerbated by the rise of Garvey Nationalism. It was also influenced by the fact that the 1919 split within the Socialist movement, proper—over the Russian Revolution—also reflected itself among Negro Socialists. Among these early Socialists were W.E.B. DuBois (who had joined the movement in 1911), Hubert Harrison, and Frank Crosswaith. Later came A. Philip Randolph, Lovett Fort-Whiteman, Chandler Owen, Richard B. Moore, W.A. Domingo, Otto Huiswoud and Cyril V. Briggs. After 1919, when the Communist factions were formed, the split among Negro Socialists tended to take on a more or less American Negro vs. West Indian Negro character: The Americans, led by Randolph, refused to join the Communists, while the West Indians—Moore, Briggs and Huiswoud—did. One exception, Fort-Whiteman, an American, did join the Communists. He also migrated to Russia later on and stayed there. Harrison and Domingo apparently remained independent radical Socialists. Another exception, W.E.B. DuBois, was to take forty-odd years to make up his mind to join the Communist Party. Under the leadership of Briggs, the West Indian Communists had formed themselves into the African Blood Brotherhood. Although the official organ of the Brotherhood became the *Crusader,* with Briggs as editor, various other members of this radical trend also published their own magazines. Hubert Harrison conducted the *Voice* of the "Liberty League of Afro-Americans." There was also the *Challenge,* by one William Bridges whose radical identity is cloudy. Richard B. Moore joined up with W.A. Domingo on *The Emancipator,* which, as Moore was to write later, "Warned against the weaknesses of the Garvey movement, while striving for an end to colonialist subjugation and all forms of oppression."[5]

This is, of course, an understatement of what went on, for the critical onslaught against Marcus Garvey by the African Blood Brotherhood was one of vituperation, rancor and bitter accusations of deceit, dishonesty, fraud, lunacy, racial disloyalty, charlatanism and ignorance. These early American Negro vs. West Indian, Socialist vs. Communist, nationalist vs. liberal and Left interracialist controversies can only become clear if one separates Negroes, proper, from Marxist politics, and examine their move-

[5] "Africa-Conscious Harlem," *Freedomways,* Summer, 1963, Vol. 3, No. 3, p. 320.

ments purely within the context of nationalist vs. integrationist trends. However the West Indian question, projected into the American Negro context, serves to complicate matters, inasmuch as we are dealing with two different ethnic group psychologies, usually serving different motivations.

West Indians are essentially conservatives fashioned in the British mold. Thus it has been observed that West Indian radicalism and militancy, especially in the United States, has been an outlet for a lack of "revolutionary" elbow room in the black West Indies, where slow reform rather than radical social change has been the tradition. The Garvey movement was a prime example. Due to the apathy in Jamaica, Garvey could not initiate his movement in the West Indies until it had been established in New York; and even then, examination of his policies at home and abroad revealed a marked duality—Garvey's nationalism in the United States took on a revolutionary character but his Jamaican policies were strictly reformist. Garvey's ultimate undoing was his blindness to many facts about America, particularly the differences in the psychologies of West Indian and American Negroes. His markedly pro-British bias left him wide open to charges by W.E.B. DuBois that he was "trying to solve the West Indies' problems with Britain in the United States." Richard B. Moore wrote:

> It is difficult and still perhaps somewhat hazardous to attempt an objective estimate of the Garvey movement. . . . Unfortunately, Marcus Garvey veered evermore toward the more extreme forms of empire building, unlimited individual control, and unrestrained racism. . . .
>
> Besides, the constant attacks which Marcus Garvey made upon people of both African and European ancestry, whom he derisively called "the hybrids of the Negro race," did not conduce to the unifying of all people of African descent. . . .
>
> Nevertheless, the Garvey movement did heighten and spread the consciousness of African descent on a wider scale than ever before.[6]

Moore's 1963 criticism of Garvey was most considered and subdued, compared to the vitriol his African Blood Brotherhood poured into their attacks on Garvey back in the 1920's. In 1921,

---

[6] *Freedomways, op. cit.*, p. 323.

Cyril V. Briggs published a criticism calling Garvey a "Judas Iscariot" who was "the Moses that was to have been." Briggs had sent Garvey a confidential letter, part of which is quoted below, seeking cooperation between the African Blood Brotherhood and Garvey's Universal Negro Improvement Association (UNIA):

> For your information I may state that the ABB is essentially a secret organization, though at present engaged in open recruiting in the Northern States [U.S.]. We are organized for immediate protection purposes and eventual revolutionary liberation in Africa and other countries where Negroes constitute a majority of the population.[7]

In a case involving Briggs and Garvey heard before a Justice Renard in New York's twelfth District Magistrate's Court on October 20, 1921, Garvey had shown this letter to the Judge. Briggs was outraged at Garvey's breach of confidence, and accused him of "racial disloyalty." He utilized the pages of his *Crusader* with an article headed, "Garvey Turns Informer." The text below read: "Garvey tells white magistrate that Briggs sent him an invitation to cooperate in the overthrow of white governments to free Africa."[8]

This Briggs-Garvey fight represented an inner-group West Indian conflict between integrationist and nationalist trends, which was more related to the position of the West Indians in the United States than to Briggs' avowed interest in Africa. Later on, Briggs' essential integrationism would come out in his theoretical position on American Negroes in the official Marxist publication of the Communist Party.

Among the American Negro Socialists, the criticisms levelled at Garvey were also indirect criticisms of West Indians generally. At that time the West Indian influx to New York coincided with the great migration of Southern Negroes, northward. The majority of both Southern and West Indian Negroes were of agrarian peasant origins—but not all. However, native New York Negroes frowned on the West Indians mainly because the islanders presented a threat of competition for jobs available to blacks. There were other reasons, but an undercurrent of bias on the part of both groups persists to this day.

[7] *Crusader*, November 1921, p. 1.
[8] *Idem*.

An anti-West Indian bias was implicit in some of the relentless editorial assaults in Randolph's *Messenger* against the Garvey movement, as part of the "Garvey Must Go!" campaign carried on by the American leadership. This campaign reached a high pitch in 1923. The previous October 25, Garvey had made a speech before an audience at the State Fair in Raleigh, North Carolina. Randolph and his group were enraged by Garvey's words and answered him in the *Messenger* under the editorial heading, "A Supreme Negro Jamaican Jackass":

> In his role of unquestioned fool and ignoramus, Marcus Garvey proceeded:
> "When I came down here I had to get on a white man's train, on a white man's railroad. I landed in a white man's town, came out here on a white man's car, and am now speaking from a white man's platform. Where do you Negroes come in? If I had depended on getting here on anything that you have furnished I would have been walking six months."

This speech was replete with typical Garveyite pomposity and arrogance—as if to say that when Garvey, himself, left Jamaica for greener pastures he did not sail on a white ship on a white steamship line owned by his British colonial masters, not to speak of other means of transportation in Jamaica. The *Messenger* editorial replied:

> Before proceeding to analyze this statement we would have the reader note that this is the same Negro who pitched over a million dollars of Negroes' money into the Black Star sea, after collecting it under the pretense that he was going to establish a ship line. . . .
>
> This same rascally renegade and scoundrelly traitor had the unmitigated effrontery to [complain of white-owned transportation]. . . . Is that so? We doubt it. In fact we know those very dupes to whom Marcus Garvey was talking, along with other poor ignorant wretches, supplied the funds with which he was able to secure his passage on the railroads. . . . Owning the price of a ticket is the chief factor in transportation. Whoever heard, anyway, of a person's going to a station window for his ticket and being asked—"Do you own any stock in this railroad?" Such logic could only emanate from the diseased brain of this supreme Jackass from Jamaica.[9]

[9] *Messenger*, January, 1923, p. 561.

The Garvey controversy raged on through the following months. In March, 1923, the *Messenger* ran an Open Forum on the problem. There was one article, "Madness of Marcus Garvey," by a Robert W. Bagnall, who described Garvey as "gifted at self-advertisement, without shame in self-laudation, promising ever but never fulfilling, without regard for veracity, a lover of pomp and tawdry finery and garish display, a bully with his own folk but servile in the presence of the Klan, a sheer opportunist and a demagogic charlatan."[10]

Although the West Indians themselves were sorely divided over Garveyism, they had to stick together in defense of their image, which was under attack by the "Americans"—their distantly-separated and often snobbish "cousins." Thus, the touchy and emotionally-charged question of West Indian and American Negroes was discussed in the magazine under the heading of "The Policy of the *Messenger* on West Indian and American Negroes." Chandler Owen, Randolph's co-editor, took up the American case, and W.A. Domingo, also on the staff, presented the West Indian side. Note that, as a West Indian radical Socialist, Domingo also had fraternal ties with Briggs' African Blood Brotherhood's nationalist leanings, but his exact status with the ABB is not clear. McKay intimates that Domingo was a member of the ABB, but Draper does not. Moreover, Domingo did not follow Briggs, Huiswoud and Moore into the Communist movement as a result of their split with Randolph but stayed on with the *Messenger*—only to split over the West Indian question. Domingo wrote:

> Since the Messenger began its belated fight to rid the race of the disgrace of Garveyism, I have noticed that many of the articles dealing with the subject have stressed Mr. Garvey's nationality.
>
> I am a West Indian. I am so through no act of mine, and am neither proud nor ashamed of what is purely an accident.

Chandler Owen replied:

> Apparently, however, Mr. Domingo [does place] some emphasis upon nationality, as shown in his utterance. . . . Again, while difference of opinion may be purely a mental quality from the

[10] *Ibid.*, March, 1923, p. 638.

point of view of effect, national influences are frequently the causes of those differences. And Garvey's case is just about as good a citation as could be summoned. For instance, Garvey is from Jamaica, British West Indies. The British are the leading shipping and maritime nation; hence the natural suggestion of some form of shipping by a British subject, namely, the Black Star Line. The British Empire has a royal court, so Garvey imitates with his royal black court. The British Potentate, as it were, creates Knights, Dukes, Peers, Counts, and Ladies, so Garvey makes black k(nights), dukes, peers, counts, and ladies. In his cabinet Garvey again mimics the British. To illustrate, America has a Secretary of the Treasury, but Great Britain has a Chancellor of the Exchequer; so Garvey creates a chancellor of the U.N.I.A. exchequer. Even the so-called "Provisional President of Africa" is a British counterfeit. It grew out of the existence of De Valera, then provisional president of Ireland. De Valera represented the president of a British possession who was not in the country over which he was supposed to preside. Hence, Garvey decided that he, also a British subject, and also desirous of claiming control over territory held largely by Great Britain, would copy the title of De Valera. Sir Ferris, Sir Bruce, and Sir Poston are British "Sirs" and there is no other way by which to explain the Garvey schemes without a resort to nationality.

Since Domingo was not defending Garveyism but West Indians, he went on to point out the large number of West Indians who had achieved status and success in the United States and had "contributed" to the American Negroes' "progress." Owen continued:

Mr. Domingo also shows that he is strongly nationalistic in pointing out the large number of West Indians who have achieved. This is perfectly correct. The only trouble with Domingo is that he would hail the West Indians when they hit, but not mention them when they miss.

The subjects imitate their rulers which means the West Indians think English [British]. Finally, Domingo to the contrary notwithstanding, the Garvey movement is a British West Indian Association. It does not have a large following even of ignorant American Negroes. This is not an indictment of the West Indian Negro. It is simply an explanation of their psychology which grows out of nationalistic conditions.[11]

[11] *Ibid.*, pp. 639-645, *passim.*

It was never really known how much of a following Garvey actually had. Like all nationalistic, charismatic or inspirational leaders of movements for redemption, Garvey had, no doubt, his hardcore members surrounded by an unknown number of "fellowtravellers." His membership, however, was predominantly West Indian and whatever the number of American Negroes attracted to Garveyism, it was *not* an Afro-American Nationalist movement engaged in an historical confrontation with the realities of the American situation out of which it sprung. Garveyism was Afro-British nationalism functioning outside its historical British empire context, hence avoiding British confrontation. Estimates of Garvey's membership have ranged from eighty thousand in the United States, alone, to "several million in the United States, the West Indies, Central America, and Africa." But the Garvey movement touched on the potential depths of sentiments so emotionally profound that Garvey had to be either supported or rejected with equal vehemence. Even W.A. Domingo once supported Garveyism and then tried to outdo Garvey's American Negro opponents in his rejection of the Jamaican. In his letter of protest to the *Messenger* on the West Indian question, he went so far as to say:

> Who are the bitterest and most persistent opponents of Garvey? Aren't they West Indians like Cyril V. Briggs, R. B. Moore,* Frank R. Crosswaith, Thomas Potter and myself—who caused his arrest and his indictments? West Indians: Grey, Warner, Briggs, and Orr! Who conducts the Crusader-Service, Garvey's veritable nemesis? Briggs assisted by this writer. . . .[12]

Domingo's admission that West Indians comprised Garvey's most "persistent opponents" is very crucial in any attempt to assess the Garvey movement in terms of yesterday and today. The *Messenger* wanted to have Garvey deported as an undesirable alien, but the West Indian antagonists wanted him in jail for fraud. However, this is not what the followers of Garveyism will have you believe today. They blame Garvey's failures solely on the opposition and "treason" of American Negroes. But here West Indians are misled by the notion that their *own* nationalism, oper-

* Richard B. Moore
[12] *Ibid.,* p. 640.

ating outside of the West Indies proper, transcends that of American Negroes and of Africans as well. In Harlem today, one hears stories about the mysterious "Eight," meaning the Committee of Eight Negro leaders banded together to destroy Marcus Garvey. According to the legend it was this Committee of Eight, inspired mainly by the NAACP and W.E.B. DuBois, who were responsible for Garvey's arrest and prosecution. Five were businessmen and newspaper editors, not civil rights leaders. But neither Randolph nor DuBois belonged to the "Eight." In fact, as critics of Garvey's African program, both Randolph and DuBois were the most perceptive, objective, and positive. Both saw the glaring impracticalities of Garvey's African plan. Randolph wrote in connection with Garvey's colonization schemes:

> I think that we are justified in asking the question that if Mr. Garvey is seriously interested in establishing a Negro Nation why doesn't he begin with Jamaica, West Indies (not Jamaica, Long Island).[13]

Certain African spokesmen from Liberia, Senegal, and Nigeria voiced opposition to Garvey's colonization plans. (Blaise Diagne, Senegalese member of the French Chamber of Deputies, was one, President C.D.B. King of Liberia was another.) Garvey's plans ended in fiasco because of opposition in Africa, his own egoism and financial incompetence.

To many Garveyites today, Garvey is the Father of African independence, although he never set foot in Africa. Certain Garveyites even believe that they are *more* "African" than certain natives of Africa who reside in the United States, and have said as much. What has not been clearly understood is that what is involved in Garveyism are two different kinds of nationalism—Afro-American and Afro-British—reflecting two different traditions. As one writer has said: "Garveyism failed largely because it was unable to come up with a suitable alternative to the unsatisfactory conditions of American life as they affect the Negro. Escape, either emotional or physical, was neither realistic nor a lasting answer."[14] But none of the protagonists in this fateful and bitter 1920's drama realized

---

[13] *Ibid.*, January, 1923, p. 569.
[14] Edmund David Cronon, *Black Moses—The Story of Marcus Garvey* (Madison: University of Wisconsin Press, 1964), p. 224.

this. The twentieth-century revolution had churned up too many ingredients from the depths of society for any one movement to successfully contend with. A post-World War period that could give rise to the ideologies of colonial unrest, migrations, nationalism, socialism, communism, unionism, racism, reformism, and all forms of radicalism and federal repression could hardly be comprehensively grasped by the participants. W.E.B. DuBois described the situation most profoundly when he wrote:

> My thoughts, the thoughts of Washington . . . and others [Garvey, etc.] were the expression of social forces more than of our own. These forces or ideologies embraced more than our reasoned acts. They included physical, biological, and psychological forces; habits, conventions and enactments. . . . the total result was the history of our day. That history may be epitomized in one word— Empire; the domination of white Europe over black Africa and yellow Asia, through political power built on the economic control of labor, income, and ideas.[15]

For all the antagonists and protagonists of this or that trend, the 1920's must have been a terrific emotional, intellectual, and physical ordeal. What Theodore Draper describes as the molding of Communist Party leaders must have also applied to the leaders of Negro movements: "This molding process of both the movement and its leaders consumed an entire decade. . . . For this molding process to have penetrated so deeply and persisted so tenaciously, it must have been . . . savage in its intensity and brutal in its thoroughness."[16]

Once the Negro Socialists split to form the African Blood Brotherhood (only to encounter the onrush of militant Black Nationalism and militant Communism), the radical Negro Socialist who stood alone was due to be caught in the middle of an ideological crossfire in which only the stoutest could survive. Add to this the American Negro vs. West Indian split and one sees, for example, the cruel quandary of W.A. Domingo: He went from West Indian Nationalism to Socialism (and possibly the quasi-Socialist-crypto-Nationalist ABB), flirted with Communism—but backed off only to embrace Garveyism and then reject it—finally to

---

[15] DuBois, *Dusk of Dawn* (New York: Harcourt, Brace, 1940), p. 96.
[16] Draper, *American Communism and Soviet Russia, op. cit.,* p. 5.

split with the *Messenger* Socialists over the West Indian question.

As a radical Socialist Afro-Britisher, Domingo personified more than others a deepseated ambivalence toward the American Negro. As one of Richard B. Moore's closet collaborators, it is difficult to discover what prevented Domingo from following Moore into the Communist Party. At any rate, four years before he had aired his sentiments on the West Indian question in his debate with Chandler Owen in the *Messenger,* Domingo had confidentially revealed his attitudes towards the American Negro. In a long document addressed to the Socialist Party leaders (white) of Rand School, the Socialists' educational institute, Domingo expressed opinions which, had they been submitted to the *Messenger,* would have increased the bitterness already spewed forth. This document was meant to be confidential, and it came to light only because of the investigation by the New York State Lusk Committee into "revolutionary" and "seditious" activities. Domingo's document was captured in a raid on the Rand School on June 21, 1919. Containing roughly eight thousand to nine thousand words, the document was titled "Socialism Imperilled, or the Negro—A Potential Menace to American Radicalism."[17]

In the text Domingo warned the Socialist leaders that the Negro (meaning the American Negro) was not only unready to embrace socialism, but might even be used by the ruling classes *against* any move by the Socialists to take power in the United States. Therefore, the Negro was a potential menace to the American white revolutionary movement. Why Domingo, a West Indian, took this seemingly illogical and racially unpatriotic position, is easily explainable. But what was more curious, and also revealing, about the early 1919 revolutionary Socialists was that none other than the famous John Reed, the Communist martyr-hero, had said the exact same thing about the average *white worker* in the American Labor movement.[18] It was absolutely correct that neither whites nor blacks were ready for Socialist ideas. Why, however, did

---

[17] *New York State—Seditious Activities,* Joint Legislative Committee—Revolutionary Radicalism, Vol. II, Part I (1920), pp. 1489-1511.

[18] "The American workingclass is politically and economically the most uneducated workingclass in the world. It believes what it reads in the capitalist press. . . . It believes that Labor laws mean what they say. It is more prejudiced against Socialism." See Draper, *The Roots . . . , op. cit.,* p. 135.

Domingo believe that white workers would become ready very soon, while having serious misgivings about Negroes? The answer is to be found in the West Indian Nationalist psychology which was reflected also in Moore, Briggs, and Huiswoud. Garvey had some of the same psychology, but expressed it in another way.

The British West Indies offered no fertile ground or local encouragement for open revolutionary activity against British colonial rule. But in transferring to the United States, the West Indian revolutionary found himself championing not West Indian, but American, Socialism. Racially, this Socialism had to be based on the predominantly American Negro presence—whose social implications vis-à-vis the American whites the West Indian has never accepted nor felt at home with, as his psychological conditioning has never been as a *minority*. His majority status in the Caribbean softened the fact that he was still a colonial slave. The West Indian has always been loath to admit that he was ever a chattel who had to be emancipated.

However, once in the United States, the West Indian revolutionary had to adopt a philosophy created not by him, but by European whites. Like W.A. Domingo, the West Indian took up European Marxism as "his very own." But he adopted it as a West Indian—*not* as an American Negro. This residual West Indian nationalism colored his Marxist thinking to such an extent that he refused to, was in fact unable to, accept or even reject Marxist ideas as an American Negro would. This dichotomy of approach accounts more for the split among the *Messenger* Socialists than anything else. Once the split took place, it became mandatory for the West Indian revolutionary Socialist, such as Domingo, to maintain that it was the American Negro leaders and people who were anti-socialist, not the West Indian. And in the general conflict within the Communist-Socialist leftwing of 1919, between the Americans and the Foreign Language Federations, Domingo sided with the "foreigners" against the American Negro. In speaking of the Negro, Domingo never referred to the West Indian either in New York or back home. Describing Negroes to the white Socialists, he wrote: "Their circumscription tends to narrow their outlook which rarely reaches beyond their own racial concern. The few Negroes who have become radicals have been in many cases foreigners, and, if native, have been led to their way of thinking through mental curiosity stimulated by white radicals."[19]

In "many cases" this was certainly true, but not all. The acceptance by any non-white, of white radical ideas in 1919, was rather late in history (inasmuch as Marxist ideas had been in America at least since 1869, when Marx's First International was set up). White Marxists had even tried to woo Frederick Douglass and the Abolitionists before the Civil War. Moreover, not a single innovation that Briggs, *et al.* formulated in the African Blood Brotherhood was actually new. Every "Back to Africa," "separate state," "emigration" program that Briggs experimented with had been anticipated back in the nineteenth century beginning with Martin R. Delany's work. In 1879 Moses Singleton's migration crusade out of the South towards the West *mobilized as many, if not more, American Negroes* than the Garvey movement. Every Pan-Africanist trend of the twentieth century, including Garvey's, had its roots in nineteenth-century American Negro trends. The radical elements in these nineteenth-century trends were not Marxian, but native American, in essence. The Reconstruction Period was replete with radical imperatives, but they were not the kind of ideas Domingo was obsessed with when he criticized the Negro's lack of radical perspective.

Concerning the Negro of the 1920's, Domingo told the Socialists that they should not place "any reliance . . . upon a purely theoretical and dogmatic assumption that groups of the population can be depended upon, because of their suffering and oppression, to arrive at an instinctive understanding of where their support should be cast when the crucial moment arrives."[20] If they did, Domingo warned of a "disaster which may set back economic radicalism in America for an indefinite period." For Domingo, this "crucial moment" for economic radicalism was at hand. He had fallen for the Russian-inspired notion that the "revolution" was imminent. Yet he believed that Americans "his color" weren't ready, because "every medium of Negro thought functions in the interest of capital." Moreover: "With the exception of the few who work in the garment industry in New York and come in contact with the wholesome radicalism of Russian Jews, the major-

[19] *New York State—Seditious Activities, op. cit.,* p. 1508.
[20] *Ibid.,* p. 1489.

ity of Negro men and women are deprived of the stimulating influences of advanced political thought."[21]

This advanced political thought was, of course, Menshevik and Bolshevik Marxism. However, these Russian Jews knew exactly how to use this advanced political thought for themselves as Jews *first* and Marxists second. By his very act of toadying and genuflecting before the revolutionary superiority of white Socialist philosophy, Domingo revealed that he preferred to be a revolutionary Marxist first, a West Indian second, and a Negro last. Of course, in this analysis Domingo could not account for his West Indian compatriots, since those who were not following Garvey were sedulously scheming to get rich as fast as possible, using every "medium of [American] thought [that] functions in the interest of capital."

In clarifying the Socialists on Negro traits, Domingo continued:

> Occupational traits are also developed to a marked degree. Being of slave origins and depending on tips to a large degree. . . . tips take on magnified importance in the eyes of the tip receiver. . . .
> All of [the] foregoing influences exerted upon Negroes have tended to make the race docile and full of respect for wealth and authority, while creating an immense gulf between the white and black workers. . . .[22]

But, what about his own West Indian countrymen? Were they not of slave origins? Did they not come to the United States and take jobs with tips, and were not most of them glad to get the tips? Were they not just as docile in the West Indies and full of respect for British wealth and authority—especially the upper- and lower-middle-class West Indians, and even the "peasants"? If the West Indian was not exactly "docile," he must have been exceedingly accommodating to foreigners; for despite the fact that blacks were in the West Indian majority, the local economy of small and medium-size businesses fell into the hands of Syrians, Arabs, Jews, East Indians and others. But Domingo was most indignant about American Negroes, because "servants unconsciously imbibe their

[21] *Ibid.,* p. 1494.
[22] *Ibid.*

master's psychology and so do Negroes. Nobody is more intolerant against foreigners than Negroes."[23]

In this instance, Domingo failed to grasp the difference between an Afro-American and an Afro-Britisher: They both were imbued with the psychologies of two different masters—American whites and British whites. The American white Protestants were anti-foreign in America, so the American Negro followed suit; especially since the WASPs were using foreigners against Negroes. In the British West Indies the British whites were *not* against non-black foreigners coming in to better themselves at the expense of the black West Indians, hence the blacks were accommodating. Said Mrs. A. Jacques Garvey years later, describing Jamaica in 1929:

> The birth-rate increased with unemployment, as idleness encourages child production. . . . The grocery trade—wholesale and retail—were in the hands of Chinese, whose ancestors came to the Island as indentured labourers. Now their offspring were the Traders. The Syrians and Lebanese practically monopolized the clothing and shoe trades. Thus money that had to be spent to buy the barest necessities of life went into the pockets of alien traders.[24]

And this in a land of a solid black majority! But once a West Indian gets to the United States he becomes critical of Negroes being exploited because they "don't understand business." To get out from under the double yoke of British colonialism and alien traders, the West Indian emigrates. Socialist revolutionaries such as Domingo did not fight British colonialism in the islands. It was necessary first to go to America and learn such advanced thought from the Russian Jews. After learning it, it took on the nature of something philosophically transcendent. It was right because it was white; it was essentially pure because it was Western and thus advanced. For Domingo it was so pure, wholesome, and inviolate it had to be defended against American black subversion and desecration. When the revolution came to America, Domingo warned that the big bourgeoisie would "quickly turn to the white south and the Negros of the nation as the most likely defenders of the old order.

[23] *Ibid.*
[24] *Garvey and Garveyism, op. cit.,* p. 195.

They would play upon the ignorance of both and seek to use them against *the class-conscious Northern proletariat* [italics added]."[25]

In Domingo's eyes this class-conscious proletariat was both Northern and white. He analyzed the revolutionary events in Russia and Finland where the counter-revolutionary White Guard armies were used against the revolutionary forces in these countries. He compared the Negro to these reactionary forces as a potential counter-revolutionary threat: "Thus can the Negro be the black White Guards of America."[26]

Domingo further warned the Socialists not to depend too much on the American Negroes helping to "encompass their own salvation." Rather, the Socialists must understand that "upon white radicals devolves the duty, out of consideration for their own self-preservation, the success of their cause, to aid to the limit of their greater ability to enlighten this most benighted section of the American proletariat."[27]

Here we get deeper into the motivational roots of the American Negro vs. West Indian conflict. Domingo's document serves as a key to the understanding of what motivates the West Indian on every level of Negro-white relations—social, economic, political or cultural. It sheds light on the many mysteries of the early American radical trends of 1919 between Negro and white. It reveals the causes behind the American Negro vs. West Indian split in the Communist movement: the jockeying for power; the duplicity; the subservience to whites camouflaged by super-revolutionary militant phraseology; the ambivalent loyalties; the venal group jealousies; the egotistical lust for status and acceptance by the white revolutionary powers both at home and abroad; even the self-hatred hidden behind nationalism that had to turn to alien philosophies for recognition. Here was a man, a self-styled Socialist revolutionary who could boast that he had aided in the prosecution, indictment, and jailing of a nationalist leader through capitalist justice, warning Socialist leaders to watch out for a "White Guardist" threat coming from Negroes.

As a convinced Socialist with nationalist sentiments, Domingo was impatient with capitalist ideology. Garvey was openly pro-

[25] *New York State—Seditious Activities, op. cit.,* p. 1497.
[26] *Ibid.,* p. 1506.
[27] *Ibid.,* p. 1508.

capitalistic—as are most West Indians. "Capitalism is necessary to the progress of the world," said Garvey, "and those who unreasonably and wantonly oppose or fight against it are enemies of human advancement."[28] Of course, Garvey's capitalistic business methods of handling his Black Star Line were wasteful and atrocious. Hence, Domingo could not sanction Garveyism despite its West Indian nationalism. He conspired against Garvey. As the American Negro was also procapitalistic, Domingo had no faith in him either. He was a man without a (Socialist) country.

But the African Blood Brotherhood represented a handful of West Indian revolutionaries who *did* believe in Socialism. They also believed in a kind of nationalism, but not enough to prevent them from attempting to fuse nationalism and Socialism. As it turns out in Africa today, it can be seen that this was to be a difficult fusion to attempt. But in 1919 this was too far into the future for the ABB to see, and W.A. Domingo wanted "Socialism—Now!" He went so far in his capitulation and fealty to the Socialist cause that he wandered farther away from American realities than anyone else during that tumultuous transitional period of black radicalism and nationalism.

The African Blood Brotherhood period of transition from nationalist-socialism to socialist-nationalism to Communism demonstrated, fundamentally, that the West Indians involved did not really believe that the American Negro *was* or *could be* genuinely nationalistic, as *all* West Indians are alleged to be. Once a complete transition was made to Communism, as in the case of Briggs and Huiswoud, both men refused to accept the idea of American Negroes being included in the category of oppressed colonial nations, such as West Indians and Africans. Domingo went further: The American Negro was not even of acceptable Socialist human material. *Theoretically* then, for Briggs, Huiswoud, Domingo, and Moore, American Negroes could not be in any way revolutionary unless influenced accordingly by West Indian ideology, whether nationalistic or Socialistic. But these were theoretical errors which confounded them all.

Why had the African Blood Brotherhood sought cooperation

[28] Marcus Garvey, *Philosophy and Opinions* (New York: Universal Publishing House, 1923-1925), Vol. II, p. 72.

with Garvey in 1921, only to switch and plot against him in 1923? How could these West Indian opponents of Garvey maintain that his policies on African liberation were utopian or fraudulent when their own African policies were practically the same—with merely a difference in method? Was this only an inner-group West Indian leadership power struggle? Was it also a power struggle between American Negro and West Indian revolutionaries for leadership? It was all these things and indeed, more. For behind it all there loomed another power center—the newly formed Communist movement. (Recall now that Claude McKay mentioned the visits made to the *Liberator* magazine offices in 1922 by Harlem radicals—Harrison, Moore, Domingo, Briggs and Huiswoud, et al.)

Inevitably, the ABB adopted Russian Marxism, which divided their loyalties between Russia and "Free Africa." This happened in 1921 when the Russians told the ABB how to solve the American Negro problem in the United States (not in the West Indies). It was acceptable, as in no way did it threaten the West Indian's sentimental ties to the British Crown.

What really motivated the African Blood Brotherhood from the start was the Communist illusion that world revolution was just around the corner. All the original Communists believed this, though most of the Socialists did not. Men like Cyril V. Briggs and Richard B. Moore were obviously convinced that the Garveyites had to go the way of the Communists or fail, for in their eyes, the "scientific" persuasion of Russian Marxist doctrine had to supersede the naïve machinations of a Garvey. For them international Marxist Communism took precedence over international revolutionary nationalism; but here they misread the signals and fell into a trap set by history—Garvey, too, misread the signals and grandiosely overplayed his hand. But in doing so he achieved an actual mass movement among Negroes—one the Communists sought to capture in 1921 through the coöperation of a Negro radical group. Garvey's exposure of Cyril V. Briggs in court, and his repudiation of the Communist movement (known then as the Workers Party), was his retaliation against the African Blood Brotherhood.

From the Communist point of view, the theoretical work of the African Blood Brotherhood was carried on by Briggs and Huiswoud, who ran into difficulties in the broad area of the American

Negro question. These West Indian theoreticians inserted their own "psychology" into the picture, much as Garvey did but for different reasons. From the West Indian point of view, America (rather than England) was the land of opportunity. Therefore, as immigrants, they were in America to "make good," whether in pursuit of a more affluent or bourgeois status, or as revolutionaries. Neither status could be fully achieved in the West Indies. One of the reasons that the British West Indies have remained statically conservative, impoverished and without a revolutionary movement is that all such radicals leave home, like other ambitious locals, and go off to make revolutions somewhere else.

Ironically, in 1925 Moscow ordered the African Blood Brotherhood to be replaced by the American Negro Labor Congress (ANLC) at the head of which was put an American Negro, Lovett Fort-Whiteman. Politically, this nullified the ABB's West Indian nationalism and "Free Africa" orientation, subordinating this ideology to what the Communists saw as American Negro imperatives. As good Communists, Briggs, Moore and Huiswoud could accept the integrationist implications of this new "line," insofar as American society was concerned. But as Huiswoud later showed, the West Indians could not accept the Afro-American nationalist implications: For them, the American Negro was not representative of the national colonial character (as were the Africans and West Indians), and therefore did not need "self-determination."

There was a lengthy stretch during the early 1920's when the newly-formed Communist factions were so busy trying to cash in on Garvey's movement that little, if any, theoretical work was done on the broad Negro question. But after the Communists failed either to win Garvey over or undermine him, they tried to win Negro support through the Labor movement. This was done through the American Negro Labor Congress, touching off a prolonged theoretical debate on the Negro question in the official organ of the Communist movement. This organ was variously known as *The Labor Herald, The Workers Monthly, The Communist,* and *Political Affairs.*

In *The Workers Monthly* of March and April, 1925, a two-part article on Negroes in labor was published—"Negroes in American

Industries," by William F. Dunne.[29] Then, in the 1925 December issue, Robert Minor, another of the leading white Anglo-Saxon mentors of the Party, presented an article on the ANLC entitled the "First Negro Worker's Congress." Minor, of course, praised this ANLC congress, but at the same time revealed the tactical motivations of the Workers Party and referred to the Garvey movement and the Negro community as follows:

> The case of the Universal Negro Improvement Association [Garvey's UNIA] in 1920 made a demand for the Negro's right in the trade unions, but has since entirely forgotten the demand under the influence of a reactionary "Zionism". . . .

Then he added:

> With the exception of the African Blood Brotherhood which had and still has a splendid theoretical program, but which never attained mass influence, all movements among Negroes have ignored the class basis of the Negro's problems.[30]

But Minor admitted that with the Communists' new "class basis" approach to Negro labor, the ANLC delegates represented only a few thousand organized Negro workers, and no farmers. Yet to the Communists, it augured well for the eventual undermining of Garvey's influence. In another article in *The Workers Monthly*, Robert Minor obliquely criticized Cyril Briggs, Richard B. Moore, *et al.*, for the ABB's failure to win mass influence. But neither did the ANLC, as Wilson Record was to write much later: "The ANLC in fact never amounted to much more than a paper organization, though it continued a more or less formal existence until 1930, at which time it was "transformed" into the League of Struggle for Negro Rights [LSNR]."[31]

The theoretical debate on the tormenting question of the position of the Negro in white society raged through the 1920's into the 1930's and beyond.* Therefore an examination of the quality

---

[29] *The Workers Monthly*, March, p. 206, and April, p. 257 (1925).
[30] *Ibid.*, December, 1925, p. 68.
[31] Wilson Record, *op. cit.*, p. 33.
* When the Communists began their theoretical discussion on Negroes in the labor movement, A. Philip Randolph had already begun organizing his Brotherhood of Sleeping Car Porters (1925). The jealousy of the Communists towards Randolph's effort was revealed in the fact that, during this period, not a single

and the issues of this debate reveals for all to see (who *will* see) exactly how tragically and inevitably wrong the Communists were, both black and white. Negro Communists had the elements within their reach for creating an independent black radical program for the true benefit of the black masses, but were led astray because their eyes were on what Moscow was saying and their minds, subordinate to white Marxist leadership and thinking, were not attuned to what Negroes actually needed in America.

They might have learned something, for example, from an article in *The Workers Monthly* for January, 1926, entitled "The Cooperative Movement in America." The writer was a white Communist named George Halonen, who, as his name indicated, came from one of the Socialist federations of foreign language national groups (Finnish, Latvian, etc.) that made up the early Communist movement. As Claude McKay pointed out in his book,[32] these Socialist federations were able to wield enormous political and financial power both in the Communist Party and in Moscow precisely because they were based on the cooperative method of economic group development. It was the only way these foreign language ethnic groups were able to survive and flourish in America in the face of the privileges and encroachments of Anglo-Saxon economic prerogatives. George Halonen wrote: "Membership in the cooperatives must be increased [because] cooperative work is a part of Communist activity."[33]

Of course it was, but the Communists did not pursue this question and no extensive treatment of the cooperative movement such as this ever appeared again. For the Negro, however, and especially "Negro labor," this was actually the most crucial of all

---

article was devoted to the Negro Pullman Porters in *The Workers Monthly* (or *The Communist*). Otto Huiswoud, Randolph's former *Messenger* colleague, wrote an article in *The Communist* of December, 1928, on "The Negro and the Trade Unions." He pointed out the number of porters and dining car waiters then organized in the Brotherhood of Sleeping Car Porters. Huiswoud said not a word about how they were organized nor did he even mention Randolph's name in the article.

[32] McKay, *op. cit.* "What we need is our own group, organized and officered entirely by Negroes, something similar to the Finnish Federation. . . . I am not an organizer or an agitator, but I can see what is lacking in the Negro group." Pp. 177-178.

[33] *The Workers Monthly*, January, 1926, p. 129.

economic questions, as here was the very ethnic minority in America *most* in need of education along economic cooperative lines.

Halonen's article was probably written as a defense against the attempts of the Communists to reduce and annihilate the prestige of the foreign language groups who had first dominated the affairs of the newly formed movement. In the early 1920's the white Anglo-Saxons in the new movement were a distinct minority—in great demand as spokesmen or fronts for a Party that was not only radical and revolutionary but also predominantly foreign and, thus, most "un-American." At the same time, there were a good many factional struggles between the native Americans and the foreign-born over who would run the Communist movement in the United States. Over the years of internal Party conflict, the foreign language federations became severely disrupted and fragmented as the native American leadership succeeded, finally, in cutting them down to size.[34] As an indirect result of this leftwing Americanization program, native-born black Americans were denied the important indoctrination along economic cooperative lines which, in the long run, would have proven more beneficial in the struggle against exploitation than the formation of trade unions. But both Negro and white Communists made trade-union struggles primary, and thus wasted much energy in their attempts to force organizational black and white unity in the labor movement—a unity that the white workers did not want and refused to accept.

Here in the conflict between nationalist and interracialist ideas the bald opportunism of the Communists on the Negro question begins to show. Communists are opposed to black nationalist tendencies as a matter of principle because they seek, or pretend to seek, international solidarity of all laboring classes without regard for race and ethnic differences. But Garvey nationalism was a living, organizational fact even if it was distrustful of white labor. Thus the new Communists were forced to do something about this black movement whether they liked it or not. When they failed to

[34] "Another step toward 'Bolshevization' was the decision to do away with the federations. They were officially named sections of the party, and their branches were dissolved. . . . This drastically reduced the sphere of activity and authority of the language groups." See Melech Epstein, *The Jew and Communism, 1919-1941* (New York: H. Wolf, 1959), p. 120, on the reorganization of the Workers (Communist) Party in 1923.

influence Garvey, the Communists turned to Negro labor proper, with the idea of teaching Negro workers not nationalism but internationalism (with white workers). Once the Communists took this path it became patently awkward for them, if not impossible, to take up Halonen's plea for economic cooperatives, much less to apply such group techniques to Negro communities both urban and rural. To do the latter would have been tantamount to appealing to Negro group identity in economics, which is the same thing as appealing to group nationalism. Although the early Communists had tried to capture a nationalist movement, it went against their Marxist grain to encourage another one. The great error of Marx, himself, was to underestimate the role nationalism was destined to play in working-class ideology of all countries the world over, especially in the twentieth century. In America, his ideas about working-class "international solidarity" so bedazzled his Communist progeny, both black and white, that they could look at the Garvey movement and do everything but understand its implications in terms of the United States and the West Indies proper.

Although Marx erred in terms of twentieth-century developments he could not have foreseen, he did leave behind him the dialectic method that the twentieth-century Communists never understood how to use. Thus, the American Communists, who were never original thinkers, could not see that George Halonen was right when he wrote:

> To ignore the class struggle in the cooperative movement is to ignore its whole purpose. The cooperative movement was created by the workers as a result of capitalist exploitation; therefore this movement must be a workingclass movement against capitalism.
>
> The Communists should be the real pioneers, the ones who put life and energy into this movement, and at the same time exhibit an intelligent understanding of its possibilities and limitations.[35]

Halonen's plea was for cooperatives *plus* trade unionism; and it was here that dialectical thinking should certainly have been applied, but was not.

George Halonen's clear thinking on labor economics had no

---

[35] Halonen, *op. cit.*, p. 130.

counterpart in the views of such notoriously militant Negro Communists as Otto Huiswoud, Cyril V. Briggs and Richard B. Moore. These men loudly took to the rostrum on behalf of the black masses, in support of the Communists' "Negro-white" unity campaign in the labor movement. In blindly echoing the Communist Party line on trade unions, Negro Communist leaders of the 1920's revealed what was, more often than not, a characteristic of Negro Marxists. They were essentially integrationists; thus the emphasis the Communists placed on the alleged necessity of integrated trade unions fitted in with their own social outlook in all areas of race relations. This was clearly demonstrated when the trade union issue brought forth the first theoretical polemic between the American Negro and West Indian factions within the Communist Party over the "correct" interpretation of the Negro question.

In June, 1929, during a textile strike in North Carolina, the Communist-sponsored National Textile Workers' Union attempted to organize Negro and white workers of Gastonia, Charlotte, and Bessemer City, into the same union on a Negro-white unity basis of local membership. The organizers ran into strong opposition from white workers on this issue of social equality, nor could they get the Negro workers to support it. Some of the Communist organizers thought it best to yield to local mores and tended to accept the principle of separate locals. This provoked a serious controversy and scandal in New York Party headquarters—one result of which was an article by Cyril Briggs: "It is not only necessary to fight the chauvinism of the white workers but the *segregation tendencies* of the Negro workers themselves [italics added]."

To back up this position, Briggs cited the then recent Moscow Comintern decision on Negro trade union work in America: "It must be borne in mind that the Negro masses will not be won for the revolutionary struggles until such time as the most conscious sections of the white workers show by action that they are fighting with the Negroes against all racial discrimination and persecution."[36]

---

[36] *The Communist*, June, 1929, pp. 324-328. In 1919, Briggs did not consider his nationalist-separate state ideas to be self-segregation. When he turned Communist, he switched to integration for Negro workers.

In Bessemer, Negro workers had come out on strike with the white workers. Briggs accused Otto Hall, one of the Negro Communists active there, of previously retreating on the question of fighting for interracial locals. Hall corrected Briggs in the July issue of *The Communist,* stating that he had proposed that the Negro textile workers be organized into the American Negro Labor Congress, (a separate group, organized by the Communists themselves in 1925 for the purpose of bringing Negroes into the labor movement). From any practical point of view, including that of the Communists, Otto Hall's tactic was more intelligent than Briggs'.

Some background is needed to explain how Briggs, who lacked any native knowledge of the South, was able to take this strong stand on trade-union interracialism. Prior to 1928 the Communists' policy had been to build revolutionary Negro labor organizations, on a *separate* basis, into a broad organization such as the ANLC wherein the Communists could form a strong party base. But Moscow had seen the crucial nature of the relationship of the Negro to its policies. After the Sixth World Congress of the Comintern in 1928, there was a new line that called for the "self-determination of the Negroes in the Black Belt" of the South, and the development of "a solid Communist Party and a revolutionary trade union movement among workers, Negro and white, in the South." There were several contradictory proposals here, inasmuch as it could not be definitely established whether or not "self-determination" and interracial unions were compatible ideas, or whether separatist trends would be acceptable as "self-determination." At any rate, this abrupt change in line ordered by Moscow had serious consequences for the Party even before it was put into motion. It split the 1928 Party leadership, and caused so much resistance that, in 1929, a large segment of the membership under the Lovestone-Gitlow-Wolfe leadership was expelled on orders from Moscow.* It was an organizational and political disaster that historians maintain actually wrecked the Communist Party, leaving it in a condition from which it never really recovered, despite its later achievements.

---

* Otto Huiswoud's disagreements with this new line eventually drove him out of the Party, back to his native Dutch Guiana.

The implementation of this line on Negroes in the South created almost insuperable difficulties for the Communist field-
workers; for it brought them up against the hard racial barriers
deeply rooted in the American fabric, barriers which could not
be breached by moral and ethical exhortations to rid white workers of race prejudice. But the Briggs-type theoreticians from the
North carried on a relentless assault on the Communist whites for
their chauvinism, and blamed Negro Communists for not fighting
it within the Party. This was a well-nigh impossible approach,
rigidly doctrinaire and self-defeating. The Comintern officials,
with their unreal picture of American conditions, were actually
forcing their followers to depart from many true Marxist tenets of
dealing with human beings. Such ideas as race prejudice cannot be
outlawed by decree. Marx himself had maintained that the consciousness of man does not determine his material condition, but
rather, the reverse. It requires much insight to apply this truth.

In January, 1930, the Cyril Briggs article was followed by a
piece by James W. Ford, an up-and-coming Negro leader who, in
1932, was to be the Communists' Vice-Presidential candidate. Ford
cited the Comintern's resolution on the Negro question and called
for a "national revolutionary movement."[37] The next month, the
West Indian, Otto Huiswoud, followed with an article maintaining that the Africans and Caribbeans were semi-colonials who
suffered from colonial exploitation, but that American Negroes
were merely a racial minority, subject only to racial persecution.[38] Six months later, an article appeared by Harry Haywood,*
who criticized Huiswoud's conclusion as a direct violation of the
resolutions of the Comintern's Sixth World Congress. He accused
Huiswoud of accepting the race theories of the white bourgeois
liberals, who used such ideas to play down the "imperialistic economic exploitation of Negroes in the Southern states"[39] and to hide

[37] Ford, "The Negro and the Struggle Against Imperialism." *The Communist*,
January, 1930, pp. 22-34.
[38] Huiswoud, "World Aspects of the Negro Question," *The Communist*, February,
1930, pp. 132-147.
* Haywood and Otto Hall are brothers. Haywood was to become the leading
Negro theoretician of the 1930's and 1940's and is credited with having personally
brought back the official Moscow line on the Negro, in 1928.
[39] Haywood, "Against Bourgeois Liberal Distortion of Leninism on the Negro
Question in the United States," *The Communist*, August, 1930, p. 694.

the semi-colonial nature of the problem. In short, Haywood said that what Huiswoud really sought in American race relations were liberal remedies behind left-radical talk. In many ways Haywood had Huiswoud over a barrel, from a theoretical point of view. If the American Negro question is purely a "race" question, then it cannot have truly revolutionary potentialities. The only possible solutions must wait on time, education, integration and liberal reforms. But if so, then revolutionary social philosophies are irrelevant for the Negro, and Marxist philosophy in particular does not apply, because American white workers are not revolutionary as a class. However, by the 1930's, white workers had not wholly revealed their pro-capitalistic sentiments.

After the Haywood-Huiswoud polemic, Haywood returned to the fray in April, 1931, with an analysis of the fading Garvey movement:

> Jim-crow nationalism is towards building up a sort of segregated group economy among Negro masses in the cities with the Negro bourgeoisie as intermediary between the Negro masses and the ruling imperial bourgeoisie. It is clear that social equality in their sense means equal communities of Negro and white peoples living side by side in the cities but separated.[40]

This was, roughly, what the ABB desired before Briggs, Moore, and Huiswoud turned Communist.

In Haywood's view this was opposed to the "revolutionary solution of the question by a fighting alliance of the Negro masses and white workers."[41] This *had* to be the official Communist line on Garvey, since the Party's mechanical refusal to investigate the question of economic cooperatives from the Negro group point of view allowed no other conclusion.

In the same year, Richard B. Moore was involved in a very special function on the Communist Party's "national group" front, as a member of the Negro department of the International Labor Defense (ILD). The ILD had been established by the Communists in 1925, as a defense organization on behalf of class-

---

[40] Haywood, "The Crisis of Jim-Crow Nationalism of the Negro Bourgeoisie," *The Communist*, April, 1931, pp. 330-338.
[41] Haywood, *op. cit.*, p. 338.

war prisoners, persecuted labor leaders, *et al.* The most famous of the ILD's cases was its defense of the nine Scottsboro Boys in the early 1930's. However, during the very month that these boys were arrested in Alabama on a rape charge, Richard B. Moore was playing a prominent role as defense counsel in the public trial of a foreign-born Communist named August Yokinen, charged with race prejudice against Negroes in the Party. Specifically: "Yokinen, charged with practicing social discrimination aganst Negroes, was given an open hearing, at which were present 211 delegates from 133 mass organizations, as well as 1500 spectators. Found guilty by the workers' jury, he was expelled, but promised to change his course thereafter."[42]

For a long time afterward, the Communists played up the significance of this trial as demonstrating the Party's zeal in eradicating white chauvinism from its ranks. As defense counsel for Yokinen, Moore went all-out, in his characteristic oratorical style, in administering Party justice to the Finn for his transgression of Party law in Negro-white relations. But on closer examination of Moore's summation of the case, and the Party's position on Negro-white unity, clearly Moore was simply defending the Communist Party line in a situation where its policies were seriously open to question. Actually, the prime transgressor in this case was the Communist Party itself. Yokinen's "crime" was a secondary consideration. For involved here was the reality of the "national group" question as opposed to the Party's "class" interpretation of that question.

Yokinen, who apparently did not speak English well, belonged to a Finnish cooperative group within the Communist Party (or at least allied with the Party through the membership of certain Finns). At a social affair given by this Finnish group, Yokinen was accused of objecting to the presence of three Negro Communists from the neighboring Harlem black community, who considered the social a "Party affair"; on the other hand, Yokinen apparently considered it a "Finnish group affair." But even if his attitude were a clear example of race prejudice, the Communists handled the matter somewhat questionably; Communist policy, remem-

---

[42] William Z. Foster, *History of the Communist Party of the United States* (New York: International Publishers, 1952), p. 288.

ber, was aimed at the eradication of ethnic group units within the membership structure—in the pursuit of working-class unity—even when it was detrimental to the interests of the workers involved. So fanatic was the Communist Party on this subject, that its leaders could almost be accused of willful sabotage of the Party's self-elected role in society, if their ambivalent motivations were not understood. In "defending" Yokinen, Richard B. Moore's words reveal the Negro Marxist-integrationist, Party-line defender of the 1930's at his impassioned best:

> American imperialism uses this artificial separation of the workers into groups to further split them from each other. . . . We must unite all the workers white and Negro, native and foreign born to fight against the white chauvinist, fascist lynchers and terrorists. Together we must also combat the opportunist Negro bourgeois-nationalist misleaders, the De Priests, [W.E.B.] Du-Boises, [Marcus] Garveys, [A. Philip] Randolphs etc., who are doing the dirty work of the bosses by attempting to stir up the Negro masses against the white workers, and are attacking *the foreign born workers, Negro as well as white* [italics added].[43]

Note the demagogic irresponsibility of these declarations. Note the obsession with Garvey, who had already departed from the scene, and the irrelevant references to DuBois and Randolph, leaders whose policies had no direct bearing on the issues of the Yokinen case. Moore's references to the conflict between the Negro masses and white workers, and also the "foreign born workers, Negro as well as white" reveal, again, the malfunction of the West Indian psychology in matters of a social reality it has never accepted, and misinterprets in the heat of personal passions. From Moore's point of view it was American Negro workers *against* foreign-born white workers *and* foreign-born West Indian workers. Thus American Negro workers, who until 1931 had been excluded from the trade unions and privileges of white workers and who had also been pushed aside and undercut in favor of foreign-born workers in many areas of labor, had to bear *both* the cross of exclusion and the burden of "unity" for Richard B. Moore. At any rate, Moore's vengeful courtroom rhetoric typified Communist

---

[43] *Race Hatred on Trial* (A. Yokinen), a pamphlet issued by the Communist Party, New York, 1931, p. 37.

distortion and fanaticism. Yokinen was, of course, expelled from the Party, with a probationary period of good behavior for readmittance. The axe of expulsion, the worst fate ever to befall a "good Communist," had already been sharpened even before the trial. But Moore, in the manner of one begging for immortality in the Communist priesthood, drove home to the sinner, Yokinen, the gravity of his fate and his hope for redemption. Moore would pray for Yokinen's white soul during his dark period of explusion in the cold, capitalistic world. Said Moore: "As for myself, I would rather have my head severed from my body by the capitalist lynchers than to be expelled from the Communist International."[44]

This was a religious ritual—not the deliberations of a movement committed to "scientific" politics. There were several such spectacles and it is small wonder that an embittered ex-Communist once referred to them, contemptuously, as "White Bias Show Trials." Yokinen was persecuted not because he was racially prejudiced but because he was unsophisticated enough to express it openly in a situation where he thought his group interests were being threatened. But these "show trials" only served to cover up the more subtle, and damaging, prejudice of group power politics against the Negro, which were sanctioned by official internal Communist policy.

[44] *Ibid.*, p. 32.

Jews and Negroes in the Communist Party

During the Communist Party's "Anglo-Saxon" period of Dunne, Minor, William and Earl Browder, etc., there was more open inquiry into the precise nature of the Negro question than there was to be later on. Right or wrong, there was a certain flexibility and a willingness to survey and debate. But this open-minded freshness went out of the Communist Party very rapidly. By 1929, when the West Indian-American Negro era of debate began, an unyielding, narrow-minded rigidity permeated the Party's thought on all questions. What should have been the Negro theoreticians' period of pioneering achievements and creative originality became, by default, a period of cheap militancy, imitative posturing, and a blind evasion of Negro realities. The West Indian-American Negro braintrust could not utter a single theoretical idea about themselves unless they first invoked the precedent of the Moscow "line," so that everybody would know in advance they had not the slightest intention of disagreeing with it.

This situation led inexorably to the period of Jewish dominance in the Communist Party. It culminated in the emergence of Herbert Aptheker and other assimilated Jewish Communists, who assumed the mantle of spokesmanship on Negro affairs, thus burying the Negro radical potential deeper and deeper in the slough of white intellectual paternalism. The new inner group was composed of Old Guard, first-generation Communists from the Jewish Socialist Federation and the trade unions, plus a young wave that was to emerge as the Communists' intellectual and theoretical corps of the 1930's and 1940's. This younger group, who took command of *The Daily Worker, New Masses* and *The Communist,* assumed various roles. Some remained Communist Jews, others became assimilated Jewish-American Communists, a few became triple-threat experts on Jews, Negroes, and Gentile labor organizations, with foreign affairs thrown in for good measure.

There were even some who became more Negro than the Negroes, never mentioning their Jewish background. These Jewish Communists were often more arrogant and paternalistic than the Anglo-Saxons, more self-righteous and intellectually supercilious about their Marxist line on America, than any other minority group striving for an ideal standard of radical Americanism. One wonders how it was possible for Negroes (both Americans and West Indians) to remain in the Party and accept such demeaning subordination. Nothing could account for this but the mesmerizing appeal of the Marxist doctrine which had seduced away the ability of their minds to think independently.

From 1935 to 1937, James W. Ford, the leading Negro of the Party, wrote article after article on the subject of the Negro and the Democratic (or People's) Front. From 1932 onward, of course, the Communists had their biggest propaganda windfall in the infamous Scottsboro Case; the importance of this episode goes far beyond its organizational and propaganda aspects. For, as Quentin Reynolds once pointed out, it coincided with the exact period in which *The Daily Worker* was able to purchase its own printing presses.[1] This was the Communist Party's "heroic" era. However, as a true indication of which of the ethnic groups was getting the most mileage out of the People's Democratic Front, *The Communist* of September, 1938, came out with an article by V.J. Jerome honoring "A Year of Jewish Life." It reported that *Jewish Life,* a monthly cultural magazine in English, had been started in June, 1937, by the Jewish Bureau of the New York State Communist Party. In other words, while assimilated Jewish-American Communists were leading on the broad fronts in the Communist Party, the unassimilated Communist Jews were upholding the historical purity of Jewish cultural identity in the *same* Communist Party. Of course it goes without saying that the Communist Party assumed that neither the American Negro at large, nor his Negro brethren in the ranks of the Party, had any real cultural identity to defend, especially in cultural publications supported

---

[1] Quentin Reynolds, *Courtroom—The Story of Samuel S. Leibowitz* (New York: Farrar and Straus, 1950). "When the New York *Daily Worker* installed magnificent new presses in its plant . . . more than one Harlem leader hinted broadly that the presses had been paid for by Negro donations intended to help the Scottsboro defense." P. 311.

by Party funds. With the Negro in the People's Front, everything went under the heading of Negro-white working-class unity. During this unity process there would be little time for Negro Communists with ideas about self-determination to get together to put out a Party-sponsored publication called, for example, *Black Life*. The very proposal of such a publication would have raised the horrible nationalist spectre of a Garveyite inner-party plot.* Thus, any radical Negro writers or poets of the time who had anything to say had as media either *The Daily Worker* or *New Masses*—in effect, two more white publications with editorial policies like any other white publications.

In that same issue of *The Communist* (September, 1938), there was an article by Irene Browder, in which she wrote:

> In the United States a national group is not a nation or even a national minority as understood in European countries. A tendency exists to identify the problems of the national groups with the general problems of oppressed nations. On the other hand some of our comrades regard the Negro people as a national group. . . . [People] belonging to various nationalities [in America] look back to their native country or to the countries of their ancestors and cannot be indifferent to the conditions they see there. . . .[2]

It was as if to say that the Garvey movement in the preceding decade had *not* demonstrated that many blacks in America looked back to the country of their ancestors and could not be indifferent to it. But the Communists and all the Negro leaders felt such sentiments (for Negroes) were utopian and let the matter drop. This article graphically reveals the basis of the Communist Party's dereliction on the problem of the national group, especially the Negro national group. There was, in fact, some very deep decep-

---

* From 1925 to 1935, the Community Party published two separate newspapers on Negro labor affairs—the *Negro Champion* and the *Negro Liberator*—as the official organs of the American Negro Labor Congress (ANLC) and the League of Struggle for Negro Rights (LSNR), both of which went out of existence in the 'thirties. Until 1932, when the *Negro Liberator* ceased publication, these organs came out irregularly. The *Negro Liberator* was revived again as the *Harlem Liberator* from 1933 to 1935, during which time it appeared semi-monthly or irregularly. Copies of these publications are difficult to locate today.

[2] "For a Correct Approach to the Problems of the National Groups," *The Communist*, September, 1930, pp. 797-810, *passim*.

tion involved, for it does not matter what a group is called—minority, nation, or nationality—fundamentally it all amounts to the same thing. Peculiarities such as race, color, culture, religion, economic status, geographical location, etc., may differ, as will the relationship and status of smaller groups to larger and more powerful ones. Nevertheless, all groups come under one political heading—the national question, whether in Marxist terminology or in the language of the science of international relations.* The hairsplitting over terms shown in the above article—revealed more than mere confusion—it was *willful* confusion that was openly permitted to persist as a way of avoiding conflict with the official Party line on the Negro.

Unable or unwilling to accept the reality that America is a group society, that next to the Anglo-Saxon Protestant group, the American Negro is the largest national minority in America, the Communists clung to the "oppressed nation in the Black Belt" concept of Moscow theoreticians, a concept that separated the entire Negro national group into two artificial sections—North and South. It was meant to leave the non-Southern Negro the option of assimilation (in theory)—which logically ruled out nationalistic movements as utopian, reactionary and anti-unity, etc. This approach also ruled out (again, in theory) all pure cultural group expressions such as economic cooperatives, special publications, literary and artistic groups.

This unwillingness or inability of the Communists to come to grips with Negro national group realities was displayed on both sides of the racial fence among the Party leaders and theoreticians. It was the white Communist leaders who actually laid down the line, but the Negro leaders followed it without deviation. The whites, for the most part confused themselves, were forced to raise many questions and doubts on the Negro issue—questions only Negroes themselves could have answered. Negro leaders, however, consistently failed to answer them. In 1921, when the white leaders were courting the reality of organized black nationalism, the Negroes in the ABB were trying to subordinate nationalism to

---

* For example, what the Marxists call the "national question," in theory, International Law of Western States must deal with in terms of "nationalism" insofar as international relations involve nations, nation-states, national minorities within nation-states, etc.

communism. Later, when the Communists turned their backs on black nationalism, the same Negro leaders followed suit.

The Negro intellectuals and radical theorists of the 1920's and 1930's did not, themselves, fight for intellectual clarity. They were unable to create a new black revolutionary synthesis of what was applicable from Garveyism (especially economic nationalism), and what they had learned from Marxism that was valid. Yet with such a theoretical synthesis, Negroes would not really have needed the Communist Party. They could have laid down the foundation for a new school of revolutionary ideas, which, if developed, could have maintained a programmatic continuity between the issues and events of the 1920's and the Negro movements of the 1950's and 1960's. And the young Negro intellectuals of today would probably not be facing a theoretical and intellectual vacuum.

All through the late 1920's and into the 1930's, there were several factions of white intellectual radicals who kept up a steady barrage of criticism—very valid criticism—about the program and tactics of the Communist Party. There was, in fact, a violent literary war going on, but waged only among the whites. Negro intellectuals, representing the newest of social trends, were not involved in this war to the slightest degree. By the 1930's, the Negro still had not learned that for him, economics, politics and culture are inseparable.

The economic panic brought on by the 1929 Crash also caused cultural panic among the white intellectuals; from the point of view of their own class and creative status, they saw in these events the beginning of the terrible disintegration of Western civilization. Where was American culture going as a result of all this? It was the conflict among different schools of white intellectuals on how to save Anglo-Saxon and European cultural values, that caused the literary war. It never really occurred to most of these people that the only way to preserve the limited achievements of American culture and to extend its creative range was to take all possible steps to democratize it, racially and ethnically. Most of the white intellectuals, including the assimilated Jews in the Communist leftwing, were bowing and scraping before the creative altars of literary and cultural Anglo-Saxonism. They would not deal with America as a "nation of nations." They talked about social revolution, but it was a revolution of cultural Americanization in accordance with the dominant American image (if such a thing is conceivable). The only ones who talked Americanization but did not fall for it "culturally" were the Communist Jews who never overlooked a single stratagem for the preservation of Jewish cultural identity.

One of the main fronts of the literary war was the conflict between the literary and cultural pundits of the Communist Party and the non-Communist but pro-leftwing, pro-revolutionary writers and critics. From the 1920's into the 1930's, this literary Left opposition was centered mainly around the magazine *Modern Quarterly*, edited by V.F. Calverton and S.D. Schmalhausen. From this source came some of the most intelligent and trenchant criticisms of the whole Communist Party approach to literary and cultural affairs. Many of the arguments raised in this publication had direct bearing on the Negro struggle in economics, politics and, above all, culture. But since the Communists were feuding with V.F. Calverton, not a single idea on the Negro raised in the *Modern Quarterly*, was ever discussed in *The Communist*. All literary and cultural questions on the Negro were left to Michael Gold's sectarian care—in *New Masses*—the "united front" publication, although *New Masses* would never print a single line of criticism that the commissars of *The Communist* could quarrel with. As a result, the Negro radical intellectuals and the Harlem Negro Communist theoreticians either learned nothing at all from the wealth of critical material printed in the *Modern Quarterly*, or else were so subordinate to the ideas and influence of the Communist whites that they dared not express a single idea themselves that was independently critical.

In the October-December, 1925, issue of *Modern Quarterly*, W.E.B. DuBois opened up a discussion on the effects of the Harlem Renaissance, which represented a new cultural challenge to accepted American creative standards:

> There is without a doubt a certain group expression of art which can be called American Negro. . . . Whence did this art come? . . . If allowed enough of intellectual freedom and economic wealth [Negroes] will in time almost inevitably found a school of art and will in this way contribute to the great artistic wealth of the world. . . . Already this art expression is showing its

peculiarities, its unique content. . . . The American who wants to serve the world has unusual opportunity here.[3]

In the May-June, 1926, issue, appeared an article by Alain Locke on "The American Literary Tradition and the Negro." In the winter issue of January, 1927, Clarence Cameron White, a Negro composer, wrote on "The Labor Motif in Negro Music." A stunning article by Carl E. Gehring, called the "Western Dance of Death," appeared in the winter issue of 1930-31. Gehring wrote:

> Lending weight to the belief that the civilization of the west is receding, the aspects of musical art point to decline.

But for America:

> Jazz is this country's individual contribution to musical composition. . . .
> To sum up jazz more conclusively in terms of western music and its relation to the future of Occidental civilization, as against American music and its bearing on a mulatto United States to come, it has made little impression on the music of the west. . . .
> At home, it is more immediately momentous in being the united musical expression of two races, living side by side and ultimately commingling; away, its significance assumes broader impact in that jazz's rhythmic propensities have duplicated Russian musical tendencies. . . . The significance of jazz is further reaching. Jazz is hybrid, the mulatto of musical composition, offering the union of aboriginal rhythms with the Caucasian scheme of music. . . . To sum up the American situation, musicologists of perspective are honest enough to grant that the Negro race has given this country its only pure folk music. In this material is good material for a national music, but not for the Caucasian race to exploit as white men's music. This is also of Black and tan concern. . . .[4]

Although the author mentions a score of ranking composers from Beethoven to Gershwin to Wagner, not a single Negro was cited. However, the important question of America's national music was honestly raised; it was rare in those days when jazz became the rage in New York, and is even rarer today. As I pointed out previously, the exploitative racial factors involved in

[3] *Modern Quarterly*, October-December, 1925, pp. 53-55.
[4] *Ibid.*, Winter issue, 1930-31, pp. 492-503, *passim*.

jazz music posed a serious and complex socio-economic, plus cultural, challenge. It was, in fact, the truly *native* American touchstone on which the whole concept of cultural revolution could have hinged—had the creative intellectuals, both black and white, seen the implications and faced up to them in a political fashion. But the Negro intellectuals did not take up this issue, develop it, and fight it out as *their* issue, *their* stake, *their* main platform, and *their* specific demand for cultural revolution. In fact, there is little evidence that they ever saw the material basis of this revolution appearing in the form of radio, films and electronic recording—a technological revolution in the field of education, entertainment and the arts. They did not understand the more profound reasons behind the fears and concerns of certain perceptive people of the 1920's, that mass communications media might fall entirely into private ownership. The Negro radical intellectuals did not see the implications of this threat for the simple reason that cultural revolution was not the revolution the Communists were talking about. How could they have caught up with the realities of culture when they had not even caught up with their own group realities in economics and politics? With this failure of the Negro intellectuals, the perceptive cultural whites had no political point of departure on which to base *their* criticisms of the official Communist stand on social revolution in the United States.

In 1929, E. Franklin Frazier was already marshalling sociological arguments that would emerge full-blown, twenty-eight years later, in *Black Bourgeoisie—The Rise of a New Middleclass*. In his *Modern Quarterly* article that year, Frazier elected to use the French title, "La Bourgeoisie Noire" (no doubt, to camouflage his Negro self-criticism, even less popular then, than in 1957). In this article Frazier effectively demolished several shibboleths about the Negro movement in Harlem of the 1920's. He cut the ground from under much of what later became Communist-Party dogma about the Negro working class, and also analyzed the reasons why Negro intellectuals as a class could not be original radical thinkers:

> Many of those who criticize the Negro for selecting certain values out of American life overlook the fact that the primary struggle on his part has been to acquire a culture. In spite of the efforts of those who would have him dig up his African past, the Negro is a stranger to African culture. The manner in which he

has taken over the American culture has never been studied in intimate enough detail to make it comprehensible. The educated class among Negroes has been the forerunner in this process.

In other words, Frazier saw that the American Negro question was, and is, also a cultural one, which has never been examined closely enough by all concerned.

Frazier implied, then, that Garvey's Back-to-Africa movement, for example, was utopian only because it was escapist; because it abstracted the Negro, ideologically, out of the American context and identified him with an African culture to which he was a stranger. The educated Negro classes in America did not accept Garvey's nationalism because of their ready adoption of American white values. Garvey, however, like other educated West Indians, was demonstratively pro-British in his values. Frazier continued:

> Except perhaps through the church, the economic basis of civil-ized classes among Negroes has not been within the group. Al-though today the growing professional and business classes are finding support among Negroes, the upper-classes are subsidized chiefly from without. To some outsiders such a situation makes the Negro intellectual appear as an employee of the White group. At times the emasculating effect of Negro men appearing in the role of mere entertainers for the whites has appeared in all its tragic reality. . . .

Note that three, clearly discernible social strata are defined here: the old, established, educated upper-class Negroes subsidized by whites; a new rising professional and business class; and the Har-lem Renaissance creative intellectuals and allied performing art-ists, entertainers, etc.

Only the new black bourgeois class tends to be based economi-cally in the Negro community. Although all of these strata tend to conform to bourgeois class values, if not white values, they are not uniform in the nature of their ties and/or loyalties to the Negro lower-class group. How, then, would one deal with these class fac-tors, especially from a revolutionary point of view?

> But the creation of this educated class of Negroes had made possible the civilization of the Negro. It may seem conceivable to some that the Negro could have contended on the ground of abstract right for unlimited participation in American life on the basis of individual efficiency; but the Negro had to deal with

realities. It is strange that today one expects this very class which represents the most civilized group to be in revolt against the system by which it was created, rather than the group of leaders who have sprung from the soil of Negro culture.

Frazier did not specify who these leaders were who had "sprung from the soil of Negro culture"; but he was grappling with Negro class realities in a way that would have enlightened some of the more flaming revolutionaries of the time, had they not been forced to follow Moscow's dictates. Frazier went on to point out that:

> There has come upon the stage a group which represents a nationalistic movement. This movement is divorced from any program of economic reconstruction.

> It is unlike the Garvey movement in that the Garvey movement through schemes—fantastic to be sure—united his nationalistic aims with an economic program. This new movement differs from the program of Booker T. Washington which sought to place the culture of the Negro upon a sound basis by making him an industrial worker. Nor does it openly ally itself with those leaders who condemn the organization of the pullman car porters [Randolph] and pursue an opportunistic course with capitalism. It looks askance at the new rising class of black capitalism, while it basks in the sun of white capitalism. It enjoys the congenial company of white radicals while shunning association with black radicals. The new Negro movement functions in the third dimension of culture; but so far it knows nothing of the other two dimensions—Work and Wealth.

Referring to the Harlem Renaissance in the same article, Frazier had said:

> The new Negro group which has shown a new orientation towards Negro life and the values which are supposed to spring from Negro life has restricted itself to the purely cultural in a narrow sense.

The unique literary and cultural revival of the 1920's turned out to be a directionless movement, Frazier explained, because it was divorced from the politics and economics of Negro culture as a group concept. It represented a cultural nationalism that looked down on black capitalists, while getting patronage and support from white ones. This movement was also courted, with favors from white radicals, while having no original radical philosophy of its own. Hence, it shunned association with black radicals because it had no radical ideas to offer. This fact, however, worked both ways—*the political black radicals were not interested in cultural problems.* Thus the Negro movement was economically insolvent as well as ideologically confused:

> Here we are brought face to face with a fundamental dilemma of Negro life. Dean [Kelly] Miller at Howard University once expressed this dilemma aphoristically, namely, that the Negro pays for what he wants and begs for what he needs. The Negro pays, on the whole, for his church, his lodge, and fraternities, and his automobile, but he begs for his education. Even the radical movement a few years back was subsidized by the white radical group. It did not spring out of any general movement among Negroes toward radical doctrines. Moreover black radicals theorized about the small number of Negroes who had entered industry from the security of New York City, but none ever undertook to enter the South and teach the landless peasants any type of self-help.

The traditional distrust Negroes had for trade unions, or the anti-Negro sentiments prevalent in established trade unions, could not be overcome by a mechanical, frontal attack, but only by a dialectical attack. There were other economic sides of the problem that required work and attention. In capitalistic society, Negro workers, just like white workers, adopt the individualistic ideas of free enterprise and accept its values. Frazier corroborated Halonen:

> For example, a group isolated to the extent of the Negro in America could have developed cooperative enterprises. There has been no attempt in schools or otherwise to teach or encourage this type of economic organization. The ideal of the rich man has been held up to him. More than one Negro business has been wrecked because of this predatory view of economic activity.[5]*

Neither white radicals nor black, of course, paid any attention to such an analysis as this, appearing in the pages of *Modern*

---

[5] E. Franklin Frazier, "La Bourgeoisie Noire," *Modern Quarterly*, Vol. V (1928-1930), pp. 78-84, *passim*.

* This "predatory view of economic activity" was a basic flaw in the strategy of Garvey's nationalist economic methods. Garvey's economic methods were capitalistic throughout. Twentieth-century nationalism, however, unlike nineteenth-century nationalism, could not be predicated on purely capitalistic economics.

Quarterly. The Communist Party continued with its notion that revolutionary, interracial trade union organizations alone were sufficient to deal with the Negro's economic disabilities under capitalism; and Negro Communist leadership unreservedly supported this doctrine.

As a white oppositional publication of the Left, *Modern Quarterly* permitted much more uncensored comment from Negroes than either *The Communist* or *New Masses,* and its topical range was broader. Calverton's following realized that European Marxism did not fit American conditions, thus American Negroes could not implement it. For Negroes, however, Marxism was a great new thing, a social science, a revolutionary social philosophy which, like all such grand intellectual systems of thought, was contemplated with great awe and the "proper" respect. Thus independent white radicals like Calverton never did get the kind of intellectual support from Negroes they deserved.

It evidently never occurred to Negro revolutionaries that there was no one in America who possessed the remotest potential for Americanizing Marxism but themselves. Certainly the Jews could not with their nationalistic aggressiveness, emerging out of Eastside ghettoes to demonstrate through Marxism their intellectual superiority over the Anglo-Saxon *goyim.* The Jews failed to make Marxism applicable to anything in America but their *own* national-group social ambitions or individual self-elevation. As a result, the great brainwashing of Negro radical intellectuals was not achieved by capitalism, or the capitalistic bourgeoisie, but by Jewish intellectuals in the American Communist Party. Beginning with the appearance of James S. Allen, who at the age of twenty-six, published two official Communist Party pamphlets ("The American Negro" and "Negro Liberation") over the heads of Haywood, Briggs, Huiswoud, Moore, Ford, etc., the Jewish Communist intelligentsia established theoretical dominance over the Negroes in the interpretation of the Negro question in the United States. This development was predicated on the conviction that Marxism was a white- (if not a Jewish-) created social science; thus it had to be "taught" to Negroes in the manner in which one teaches backward peoples Western Democracy.* One of the graphic

* In Harlem, during the 1949-1951 Negro-white inner-party conflict over white leadership, several white Communists indignantly replied that "it was white people who brought the ideas of Marxism to Harlem in the first place!"

results of all this was that later in 1946, during a Communist Party rehash of the Negro question, James S. Allen was able to refute the views of Doxey Wilkerson who, Allen said, ". . . confuses the basic theoretical principles of Marxism in relation to the national [Negro] question, and therefore, also fails to apply the necessary tactical positions and programs of action in the present situation."[6]

Wilkerson, a Negro, had written: "Marxist theory recognized that the problem of each nation might call for a unique solution. . . . The prospects were that the American Negroes would not disintegrate as a people . . . but develop further as a *national minority* and as a "distinct" and increasingly self-conscious community of Negro Americans."[7]*

Note that now the Negro had become a "national minority." But what was this "unique solution"? Wilkerson, assuredly, did not know but at least he *was* groping for an answer. The ingredients of this solution, however, lay in theoretical limbo, buried beneath the forgotten issues of one of V.F. Calverton's controversial essays on Marxism. In 1931, Calverton had projected in his theory of "cultural compulsives" what should rank today as possibly the only valid attempt at an original contribution to Marxism by an avowed American Marxist. Calverton had been leading up to his grand concept in the pages of the *Modern Quarterly*, but it was finally elaborated in an essay published in the *American Journal of Sociology:*

> The science of Anthropology is closely bound up with the doctrine of evolution. Both grew out of the same milieu. Nineteenth-

---

[6] James S. Allen, "The Negro Question," *Political Affairs*, November, 1946, p. 1046.
[7] Doxey A. Wilkerson, "The Negro and the American Nation," *Political Affairs*, July, 1946, pp. 652-658, *passim*.
* During this post-World War II Marxist debate on the Negro question, Harry Haywood published his first extended theoretical study of the question—*Negro Liberation* (New York: International Publishers, 1948). At least fifteen years late to be of any definitive value, *Negro Liberation* presented nothing that resolved the dispute between Wilkerson and Allen, etc. The entire debate revealed the Negro Marxists to be hopelessly confused, sidetracked, defeated and subordinate to white Marxists of other minorities. In his summary chapter, "The Negro Liberation Movement" (pp. 168-218), Haywood completely muddled the entire question: "The inherent fallacy in the [Booker T.] Washington doctrine was its counterpoising of the Negro's participation in politics to his economic rehabilitation" (p. 172). For Haywood it was not fallacious for the Marxists to counterpoise the Negro's economic rehabilitation to his participation in Communist politics that was remote to group economic survival. Haywood dismissed all group economic ideas as "ghetto nationalism of Negro urban bourgeoisie" (p. 197).

century anthropologists were interested primarily in finding universal evolutionary laws which would explain the rise of man from primitive to nineteenth-century civilization. . . .

The best way to explain the attitude and convictions at work in this controversy—and all similar controversies—is by means of the theory proposed here, namely, the theory of cultural compulsives. The existence of cultural compulsives make objectivity in the social sciences impossible.[8]

Expanding on his theory, in a later *Modern Quarterly* discussion Calverton argued against Henry Hazlitt's views on literary criticism, as follows:

Objectivity, thus, in critical matters as well as in others—is a myth. The critic, at best, can make his judgments only in terms of a class objective—and not as an absolute objective. One makes judgments in terms of one's culture and in keeping with the cultural values which are a part of his personal and immediate heritage. These cultural values depend for their duration upon the survival of the classes which created them.[9]

Hazlitt had written that "the critic is to express a judgment regarding the value of the work of art before him, but as a free agent."[10] Calverton's rebuttal was: "True enough—but a judgment for whom?"

Literary values, for example, which are but one form of cultural value, are not the product of individual taste any more than moral values are. They are the creation of group facts and are not individual ones. They arise out of the cultural tendencies of groups and not the personal predilection of individuals.

Mr. Hazlitt refuses to admit that art, like morality, politics, education, and economics, is a product and an expression of class ideology; that while within this ideology conflicts may exist and actually thrive, the social philosophy underlying them remains basically the same.

The Cultural Compulsives at work in such sociological experiences make it impossible for individual logic to solve them.[11]

[8] V.F. Calverton, *American Journal of Sociology*, Vol. XXXVI (March, 1931), No. 5, pp. 689-720, *passim.*
[9] Hazlitt and Calverton, "Art and Social Change," *Modern Quarterly*, Winter, 1932, Vol. XI, No. 1, pp. 16-27, *passim.*
[10] *Ibid.*, p. 16.
[11] *Ibid.*, p. 21.

In the meantime, the Communist theoreticians fired back at Calverton with a two-part article in the October and November, 1931, issues of *The Communist:*

> The latest attack on the theory of revolutionary Marxism comes from the so-called "Cultural Communists" in the person of V.F. Calverton.
>
> Behind Calverton's public avowal of adherence to Communism there looms a fundamental criticism of its philosophy which reveals him as a person utterly alien to the theory of revolutionary Marxism.[12]

A little reflection will reveal that there was nothing essentially anti-Marxian in Calverton's views. His thesis was, in fact, an attempt to bring nineteenth-century Marxism more into line with certain twentieth-century sociological and psychological realities in the United States. These were fundamentally cultural realities which, for example, were exemplified particularly in the social existence of Negroes and Jews, but more cogently in terms of groups than in what the Marxist called class alignments. But, theoretically, the Marxists could *not* deal with groups or the cultural compulsives of groups. They wanted to eradicate, in practice, the vertical ordering of group structure and contention, and align these elements horizontally into class formations within the labor movement. But the two most prominent groups involved in Communist Party politics—Negroes and Jews—simply refused to respond to such a reordering.

Actually, Calverton was offering a theoretical method that would have enabled the Communists to stop saying one thing and doing another—or rather, to get more in line with American cultural group realities. The Communists, however, had to reject all ideas which went counter to Moscow's wishes in politics.

In presenting a germinal theoretical departure for cultural revolution in the United States, V.F. Calverton anticipated by some thirty years the ideas of C. Wright Mills. In groping for the same thing, Mills began to study the intellectuals in their relation to the cultural apparatus as an agency of social change. Calverton's limitation, however, was that although he saw the reality of cultural

[12] A. Landy, "Cultural Compulsives or Calverton's Latest Caricature of Marxism," *The Communist,* October and November, 1931, pp. 851-864, *passim.*

compulsives in theory, he could not transform it into a praxis. In America only a non-white group could have transformed the concept into a functional social theory—specifically the Negro group, through its creative intellectuals—since *this* was the group that needed it most. White groups, whether Anglo-Saxon, Jewish or whatever, could not objectively accept the validity of the theory; for it would be tantamount to admitting that *their* social dominance (or else the striving for such dominance and prestige, as in the case of Jews), could neither be maintained nor motivated except in terms of their own group cultural compulsives. Since Marxism explicitly made no provisions for such a theory, Marxists did not have to support it even though the same Marxists were proving it, in terms of their own groups. Cultural compulsives had confirmed the Anglo-Saxon group in social power in America, and now formed the basis of the new Jewish bid for social power and prestige. But neither group could be objective enough to admit the truth of this, especially when they had to contend with Negroes—a "non-white" group. To admit it meant permitting Negroes the use of their own cultural compulsives in the struggle for cultural and political power in life—or for theoretical leadership plus political power inside the Communist Party. Hence, the very rejection of Calverton's ideas* bore out the truth of his theory: *"The actual claim to objectivity in the social sciences has been largely a defense mechanism, an attempt unconsciously to cover up the presence of compulsive factors and compulsions. . . . Interpretation necessitates a mind set, a purpose, an end."*[13]

How else explain the fact that a Party with the professed purpose of creating a society with complete *racial equality* could allow such rank internal inequalities among contending ethnic groups? The group dominance and privileges of Jewish Communists could only be explained by Calverton's theory, since this dominance was all out of proportion to their group population. In order to preserve an "American" image, the very top leadership of the Communist Party was denied the Jewish theoreticians; there-

---

* For a fuller account of the V.F. Calverton vs. Communist Party controversy, see Daniel Aaron, *Writers on the Left—1912-World War Two* (New York: Harcourt Brace, 1961). Reprinted in Avon Books (1965) pp. 335-346.
[13] V.F. Calverton, *American Journal of Sociology*, Vol. XXXVI, No. 5, March, 1931, p. 719.

fore, the Jewish sense of inferiority, or pride, or envy mixed with a challenging claim of counter-superiority, spurred Jewish Communists to capture as many second-level posts of command as possible. The great threat to this goal was no longer the Anglo-Saxon in the Party, but the Negro. Thus, in order to ensure political and ideological power over Negroes, Jewish intellectuals had to master not only the cultural compulsives of their own group politics, but those of the oncoming Negro group as well. In the same way that white playwrights, during the 1920's, were able to compete against the Negro playwright in the theater by using the Negro's own thematic material, Jewish Communists, during the 1930's and 1940's, were able to compete with the Negro Marxist theoretician in the interpretation of the Negro question. As late as the late 1930's the top Communist leader—the section organizer—in the Harlem Communist Party was Jewish. Needless to say, no one in the Communist Party spoke theoretically for Jews but other Jews.

Between 1932 and 1937, James S. Allen was commissioned to write four books and pamphlets on Negro affairs. The last one was *Reconstruction—The Battle for Democracy*. What inspired this hurriedly-written Marxist study was the appearance, in 1935, of W.E.B. DuBois' classic work on the same period in American history, *Black Reconstruction*—the most definitive study ever to be written on Reconstruction from the Negro point of view. A good part of the foreword to Allen's book is given over to a Marxist criticism of "DuBois in his praiseworthy *Black Reconstruction*" and his "errors."[14]

In the late 1940's and early 1950's, the Communist Party, through the researches of Herbert Aptheker, brazenly attempted to establish scholarly and theoretical dominance over Negro studies. The Party even bypassed Carter G. Woodson who, as far back as 1915, had established the Association for the Study of Negro Life and History (ASNLH). Communists tried to take over the political control of certain branches of this association, especially in New York, and openly competed with the official ASNLH groups in the preparation and celebration of their yearly com-

[14] J. S. Allen, *Reconstruction—The Battle for Democracy* (New York: International Publishers, 1937), p. 11.

memoration of Negro History Week—an institution created by
Woodson. For many years after World War II, many white
Communists were under the impression that the Party had
founded this celebration, so adroit and dishonest was its propaganda on the subject.

Following the publication in August, 1949, of an article by
Doxey Wilkerson on "Negro Culture," Morris U. Schappes, a Jewish cultural spokesman, published an article in March, 1950, on
"problems of Jewish Culture."[15] Note the close coincidence of
these expressions of Negro-Jewish competition and the way they
crop out—as if to say that in 1950 American Jews were having great
cultural problems. But there was only one Jewish group in America that was having real problems—the Zionists. Yet for them the
only cultural problem was that all Jews were not Zionist enough
to suit them, despite the fact that within the 1948 establishment of
Israel, Jewish Communists in America managed officially to blend
Zionist ideas with Marxism.*

In 1959, Melech Epstein, by then an ex-Communist, gave a
frank assessment of the attitude of Jews in the Party toward Negroes in the 1930's:

> The number of Negro party organizers and officers was out of
> all proportion to the small number of Negro members. It became
> an unwritten rule [in the 1930's] that every committee must
> include a certain proportion of Negroes. More Negroes were sent
> to Party schools in Moscow and here. Harlem and the Southside
> in Chicago were "concentration" points, with special headquar-
> ters. The South where the party was practically nonexistent, was
> dotted with Negro organizers. . . .
>
> Negroes were coddled in the party, which did neither them nor
> the party any good. It created an unhealthy atmosphere and led
> to demoralization. Parenthetically, few Negro women joined the
> party.[16]

The author admitted that this "emphasis orginated in Moscow."
Although he still did not like to admit that Moscow felt Jews less

[15] *Masses and Mainstream*, March, 1950. Reissued as a pamphlet May, 1950, under
the auspices of the School for Jewish Studies.
* "Back to Israel" Zionism, unlike "Back to Africa" Garveyism, was neither
escapist nor Utopian.
[16] Melech Epstein, *The Jew and Communism: 1919-1941* (New York: H. Wolf,
1959), p. 246.

important than Negroes to the Comintern line,* he pointed out that:

> Throughout the 1920's, Jewish Communism had more links with its environment than the party had. It exploited to the utmost the rising prestige of the Soviet Union and its own concern for the Jewish group. Jewish Communists were forging positions of strength on several fronts, confidently looking ahead to further expansion. However, their stand on the Palestinian outbreaks alienated them from the community.[17]

Epstein explained how during the middle of the 1930's Jewish Communism was to experience more expansion during the Communist Party's united front periods of inner democracy:

> Unity and democracy led to a changed attitude in the party to Jewish work. Belittling and sneering was replaced by an awareness of the vital part that Jewish Communism had in the party's ambitious schemes. . . .
> The Jewish Bureau was given the green light to approach the American-born on Jewish issues. . . . The monthly *Jewish Life,* published by the Jewish Bureau of New York State, August 1937, was the immediate consequence.[18]

Melech Epstein described this period as one of "Judaizing Communism." His candidness is enlightening because it meant that no "Negroizing" of Communism had a modicum of a chance, despite Party "coddling." In approaching the "American-born on Jewish issues," an ideological process was put in motion that also led into Jewish liberal circles and ultimately into "American-born" Christian liberal circles. In fact, Jewish and Christian liberals were allies not only in solving Jewish issues but in the liberal analysis and solving of Negro issues. Lerone Bennett, in *The Negro Mood,* has

---

* The ratio of Negroes to whites in the Communist Party was related to questions raised by Joseph Stalin in 1925 before American Negro delegates in Moscow: "The Negroes represented the most oppressed section of the American working class. Therefore, the American party should have more Negroes than whites. Why weren't there more Negroes in the American party? . . . The whole approach of the American party to the Negro question is wrong. You are a national minority with some characteristics of a nation." Draper, *American Communism and Soviet Russia, op. cit.,* p. 334. Author's note—White Communists, including Jews, would not have tolerated a black majority even if it were possible.

[17] Epstein, *op. cit.,* p. 252.
[18] *Ibid.,* pp. 318-319.

cited the outcome of this trend in civil rights organizations.[19] All of this is of crucial importance today in Negro-Jewish relations. But what is of even more historical importance is the fact that, in the 1930's, the Negro creative intellectuals and Marxist theoreticians missed their main and timely calling. With the new materio-economic factor of the mass communications media emerging, Moscow's "line" was a dead issue as far as Negroes were concerned.

The emergence of the mass media depersonalized the cultural arts and, as far as the mass public was concerned, separated the creative artists from their audience and transformed them into a new kind of a class, with different problems, demanding new approaches in politics. If this was the case with the whites, it was all the more so with the Negro creative intellectuals. The mass media would seriously distort the Negro cultural image; make the Negro style banal and trivial, thus ripe for low-level entertainment values; ban originality; and intensify the cultural exploitation already at work, especially in music. With the coming of mass media, the Negro's problems were now *cultural* to such a degree that no social revolution in the United States was possible unless all factors—economic, political, social and racial—were encompassed within the scope of cultural revolution and projected within the scope of that social idea. All the elements were there—*a nationalist movement, revolutionary political theories, a cultural arts renaissance, a new consciousness of Africa, a capitalistic crisis, masses in motion, a new, young intellectual class, a literary war on the aesthetic and cultural fronts, and the emergence of the mass cultural media.* But the one factor that was not brought to bear was the Negro group cultural compulsive—as the one vehicle for a new social theory that could have, and would have, transcended Moscow's Communist Marxism.

[19] "The family of power includes not only Negro organizations but white organizations. Racial policy is subtly shaped and diluted by the expectations, priorities and fears of liberal, labor, religious, and minority groups. From this white liberal nexus, the [Black] Establishment seeks allies and donations. . . . Among the leading organizations in this shadow cabinet of the shadow cabinet are the UAW and other liberal unions, the American Civil Liberties Union, the American Jewish Committee and the American Jewish Congress, the race relations departments (under various names) of the YMCA, the National Council of Churches, the Roman Catholic Church and the American Friends Service Committee." Lerone Bennett, *The Negro Mood* (Chicago: Johnson Publications, 1964), cited, p. 30.

On another level this is what the Jewish Communist intellectuals had accomplished when they "Judaized" Communism from the late 1930's onward. Melech Epstein described the process under the heading "The Passion for Jewish Culture":

> Once Jewish Communism became "anxious for Jewish life and rights," a surging concern for Jewish culture was inevitable. . . . building a cultural position does not necessarily require being accepted by rival groups; initiative and hard work are sufficient. . . .
>
> The National Conference of Jewish Communists, September 25-27, 1936, heard professions of loyalty to the Jewish people and love for their culture. . . . But this new concern was negated by the old devotion to proletarian culture. . . . However, Jewish Communists did not have to wait long for a full-scale drive on the cultural front. A Committee for a World Cultural Congress appeared in Paris in September, 1936.[20]

As a direct result of this development, Epstein could write:

> In the field of literature and art the [Communist] party extended its influence through the Writer's League, the Artist's League, the Screen Actor's Guild, the Script Writer's Union, and the Theater Arts Committee. The stirrings on the campus were channelled through the American Students Union, launched by the YCL [Young Communist League] and, later, through the American Youth Congress, for all practical purposes an auxiliary body of the CP [Communist Party].[21]

It should be pointed out that the developments Epstein describes show that Jewish Nationalism was winning out *within* the context of the Communist Party. Up to then, it had banned all ethnic group nationalisms as being antipathetic to working class unity, and had criticized all Jewish group institutions, such as *shules,* as "nests of nationalism." Negro Communists, however, who developed the same kind of resurgent group nationalism inside the Party, soon found themselves expelled for "bourgeois nationalist deviations" or "anti-white" tendencies. As a result, when the Party's cultural front expanded from New York's Eastside to Hollywood, many Jewish Communist intellectuals went along to

[20] Epstein, *op. cit.,* p. 324.
[21] *Ibid.,* p. 276.

those lush Western pastures, but very few—if indeed any—Negroes. Of the Party's Hollywood phase, Epstein wrote: "The most useful was the Hollywood Anti-Nazi League, comprising middle-class elements and a sizable display of Hollywood talent. A statement in support of a cause, or in protest, bearing the names of Hollywood stars had a wide resonance here and even abroad."[22]

Under Jewish Communist prodding, the Communist Party took up the anti-Hitler crusade in the late 1930's. Negro Communists and Negro Nationalists had been completely powerless, however, in 1935. During the Italian-Ethiopian war not even millions of Negroes could mount a movement on the political Left, in support of the African cause, remotely matching the Jewish crusade on the Left against Hitler. Black radicals and Black Nationalists had failed to remold the implications of Garveyism and to re-adapt it to the demands of the 1930's. However, a very large corps of Negro volunteers went to Spain during the Spanish Civil War of 1936-1939 to fight and die for Spanish democracy. Not only had these Negro volunteers known no democracy in the United States, they also experienced no "group democracy" inside the Communist Left. Of these black volunteers, whose number is not generally known, Langston Hughes was to say, thirty years later: "With so many unsolved problems in America, I wondered why would a Negro come way over to Spain to help solve Spain's problems— perhaps with his very life. I don't know. I wondered then. I wonder still."[23] Yet in 1959, Melech Epstein was still sulking because the Communist Party of the 1930's had "coddled" Negroes. Which national group was really being coddled? In America, Jews (whether radical, liberal, conservative, orthodox, reform, or Zionist) have no real problems, political, economic or cultural. And they have no honest cause for complaints about anti-Semitism, inasmuch as they, as a group, are by no means themselves immune to race prejudice. They are a group capable of becoming bankers, financiers, and merchant capitalists who hire Christians at high salaries; yet their absence on the .executive boards of Christian capitalist firms is to the Jews a sign of anti-Semitism. One might just as easily say that having become the

[22] *Ibid.,* pp. 276-277.
[23] Hughes, *I Wonder as I Wander* (New York: Rinehart, 1956), p. 354.

most affluent group in America in per capita income and wealth, *despite anti-Semitism,* is too much of a cross for American Jews to bear under "democratic" capitalism! Karl Marx, an "emancipated" Jew, was unfortunately right: "When the Jew demands emancipation from the Christian state, he asks that the Christian state give up its religious prejudices. Does he, the Jew, give up *his* religious prejudice? What right, therefore, has he to demand of others the abdication of their religion?"[24]

In Negro-Jewish relations in the Communist Left there has been an intense undercurrent of jealousy, enmity and competition over the prizes of group political power and intellectual prestige. In this struggle, the Jewish intellectuals—because of superior organization, drive, intellectual discipline, money and the motive power of their cultural compulsives—have been able to win out. In the name of Negro-white unity (the Party's main interracial slogan), the Jewish Communists acted out the role of political surrogates for the "white" working class, and thereby gained the political whip of intellectual and theoretical domination of the Negro question. At the same time there was put forth a subsidiary slogan, a gesture to the group reality of things—a plea for Negro-Jewish unity—but unity against what? Morris U. Schappes, one of the leading Jewish Communist intellectuals around the *Freiheit-Jewish Life* group wrote:

> Outstanding in the fight to prove the absence of scientific basis for white supremacy was the work of such Jewish scholars as Franz Boas, Melville J. Herskovits, Otto Klineberg, Ruth Benedict and their many academic disciples. James S. Allen, Philip S. Foner, and Herbert Aptheker began to make their significant contributions to the study of the history of the Negro people. Bonds of solidarity between Negro and Jew in the fight against racism were being forged which were to expand tremendously in the forties and fifties.[25]

Schappes was speaking of "bonds of solidarity" between certain Negro and Jewish leaders inside the Communist Party and beyond. This solidarity was never a real fact down below among the

---

[24] Karl Marx, *A World Without Jews,* ed. D.D. Runes (New York: Philosophical Library, 1959), p. 1.
[25] *The Jews in the United States* (New York: Citadel Press, 1958), p. 233.

black or Jewish masses, and it is misleading nonsense to claim that it was ever so. The relationships of Negroes to Jews, and vice versa, have always been rather ambiguous, due to the nature of things, and are growing more so every day. The expansion in scope and quality of the Negro civil rights movement has brought to the surface the residual anti-Semitism that has always existed among Negroes, a group attitude which the Jews themselves are at least partially responsible for fostering. At the same time, many Jews today are frightened by the implications of the civil rights movement, especially ghetto uprisings with anti-Semitic overtones. Yet there was a great deal of Jewish idealism that spawned some of the very Negro tactics (many of which were highly questionable) which now have unsettled other Jews who fear a radical rightwing reaction. It cannot be said, as Schappes also asserted, that the Communist Party's Negro-Jewish politics has helped in the present problem of settling Negro-Jewish group conflict. Hence, today one must bear with the accusations of anti-Semitism, in order even to discuss the validity of these longstanding but unrealistic policies in group relations. But such problems are ones that the Negro intellectual of today has inherited, unsolved, from the previous forty-five years or so. His crises in social thought, critical analysis and creative originality, are rooted in the history of these problems.

The National Negro Congress

In the mid-1930's, the Communist Party experienced a changed attitude towards the Negro middle class, which is described by Wilson Record:

> The new Negro program contained a different version of the black social structure and the role of its component groups. The Negro middle class, the hated "black bourgeoisie," was now viewed as a progressive element in the struggle for Negro rights. It was not the "natural" enemy of colored workers or the national liberation movement, as the Party had previously insisted. It was a potential ally. It was the most articulate of the Negro strata and could play a focal role in building the united front among the American blacks.[1]

This change of line by the Communists coincided with a movement inspired by Ralph J. Bunche and John P. Davis and others, who led a conference that "reviewed a wide range of Negro problems." Out of this conference came the idea of the National Negro Congress, a "national agency embracing all Negro unions, together with religious, fraternal and civic groups." As the Negro "united front" organization, the NNC brought into the leftwing a new type of Negro—the middle-class professional intellectual for whom the NAACP was much too moderate. With the enthusiastic backing of A. Philip Randolph and James W. Ford, plus many other ranking Negro reform leaders like Lester Granger and Alain Locke, the first organizing conference of the NNC was held in Chicago, February 14-15, 1936. There were 817 delegates from 585 Negro organizations of various types. Randolph was elected president, John P. Davis, national secretary; several Negro Communists and pro-Communists were elected to posts on the NNC's national level. At the outset many conservative Negroes were

---

[1] Wilson Record, *op. cit.*, p. 134.

scared away from the NNC by the open participation of high-level Negro Communists. Ralph Bunche at that time, however, was not one of those who feared the radical tinge. By April, 1940, when the NNC held its third conference, "the [Communist] Party was in complete control; it dominated the meeting from the outset and alienated most of the non-party delegates by forcing through a series of anti-Roosevelt and "anti-war" resolutions. (The Russo-German pact had been signed in August, 1939) . . ."[2]

During this month A. Philip Randolph quit as president of the NNC, over the issue of Communist Party control of its policies and funds. He said that "the National Negro Congress should be dependent on resources supplied by Negro people alone. The grounds for my belief is that history shows that where you get your money you also get your ideas and control."[3]

In A. Philip Randolph's keynote speech at the 1936 organizing conference, the following statement was made: "the New Deal is no remedy. It does not seek to change the profit system. It does not place human rights above property rights, but gives the business interests the support of the state."[4]

In the midst of the most catastrophic economic depression America has ever experienced, Randolph was accusing the Roosevelt New Dealers of saving the capitalistic system for the capitalists. Randolph was quite correct but he did not add, however, that once Roosevelt had salvaged American capitalism it would never be quite the same. For various socialistic, or rather welfare-state, innovations which had not previously existed, became institutionalized within it (the Tennessee Valley Authority, Social Security and Wages and Hours administrative reform legislation). While attacking Roosevelt's policies from the standpoint of Marxist theory, Randolph and the other NNC leaders failed to see, then, that what was actually at work was Keynesian economic theory. In fact, it was not until the post-World-War-Two period, after

---

[2] *Ibid.*, p. 161.
[3] *The New York Times*, April 29, 1940, p. 17.
[4] See "Official Proceedings of the National Negro Congress," 1936, 1937. Also Ralph J. Bunche, "The Programs, Ideologies, Tactics and Achievements of Negro Betterment and Interracial Organizations," New York, Carnegie—Myrdal Study, Vol. 2, *The Negro in America*, 1940.

Keynesism had done its work, that Marxist-Communists began to warn the working class against the dangerous influence of the Keynesian doctrine (while defending, at the same time, all the New Deal reforms that came out of it).[5]

At any rate these New Deal reforms, Keynesian or otherwise, were inadequate for both the NNC and the Communist Party. For the NNC there was the special problem of the economically hard-hit Negro communities, handicapped even in prosperity years, but now doubly ravaged by joblessness, deeper poverty, and intensified exploitation. The NNC leaders had to propose something in terms of economic theory that was more effective than the New Deal policies. They constituted no remedy, and what was needed, said Randolph, was "mass consumers' movements to protect housewives against price manipulation."

> There should be built up great consumer's cooperatives which while less fundamental, they none the less provide the base for mass collective action on the part of the workers and lower middleclass.
>
> We recommend that the Negroes everywhere give thoughtful and studious consideration to the organization and development of consumers and producers cooperative organizations, because of the great benefit to be derived therefrom.[6]

This economics resolution was on behalf of the Negro workers mainly, but since the NNC was actually a broad united front movement of the Negro bourgeois classes, Randolph had to incorporate also into this resolution a plea for the development and support for Negro business, a bourgeois demand. Note that this important question of economic cooperatives for the workers was the same as that raised by George Halonen back in the 1920's. Things were so bad in 1936 that it was raised again—this time by a newly emerging Negro organization—but, again, the Communists did not go out of their way to back up this resolution and the Negroes in the NNC did little to implement it themselves.

A profound combination of ideological confusion and disorientation was at work here. Emanating from both sides of the racial fence, from the Negro leadership and the Communist Party

[5] See William Z. Foster, *op. cit.*, pp. 241, 425, 481-484.
[6] Official Proceedings of the National Negro Congress," 1936, *op. cit.*

policies, it was leading Negroes and whites away from a vital confrontation with the economic group essentials of American society.
From a theoretical point of view, Randolph the Socialist was not
prepared to define in what way, and just how far, forms of economic cooperation among Negroes were removed from the fundamental remedies he felt the New Deal failed to provide. Yet, if
Randolph and company were serious in demanding more far-reach-
ing economic changes how could the NNC make a plea for support
for Negro business at a time when businesses were failing all over
the country? This was not a working-class demand, to be sure. *But
were the class aims of the NNC really that contradictory?* Is the
development of Negro business a progressive step for Negroes generally in the American economy?

In the view of the overwhelming majority of Negroes of whatever class, Negro business development is most desirable. But it is
precisely the Marxist-Communist whites (as well as some Negro
Marxists) who disagree. Marxists never have and never will support the idea of developing Negro business. Obsessed with the
naïve aim of "radicalizing" Negroes—both working-class and
bourgeois—Marxist-Communists have completely overlooked the
fact that, in the long run, economic and political policies *must*
cater to the inner-group Negro needs in order to win and hold the
Negro working class. The Negro question, contrary to Marxist
dogma, is more a group problem than a class one, simply because
Negro businessmen must depend on the Negro group for their
support, regardless of class differentiation. But note how the
white Marxist Left treated the NNC resolution on Negro business:
"as for Negro business, which exists as a highly reactionary influence in Negro life, in strictly Negro questions as well as in relation
to the white world, the [NNC] congress resolution runs as follows":

> Whereas the development of sound and thriving business is
> most indispensable to the general elevation of the Negro's social
> and economic security, therefore be it resolved that all Negroes
> consider it their inescapable duty to support Negro business.

> The Left supporters of the [NNC] congress maintain that the
> Negro masses must be reached—for that very reason the endorse-
> ment of the Negro church and Negro business is, to say the least,
> most unfortunate. . . . It will bind the Negro worker more firmly

to the most reactionary institutions in his heritage, and tend to cut him off even more completely from his natural allies—the workingclass.

Hence:

[The National Negro Congress] passed two resolutions (church and business) which can only add to the general confusion already existing in many Negroes.[7]

This was typical white Marxist-Communist thinking on Negro problems in those days, and even today; and one need not wonder why the already alien Marxist-Communist ideology *remained* so. Note also that his statement against the NNC's resolutions on church and business did not appear in an official Communist Party publication but in an editorial in *The Nation,* a white liberal magazine. It indicates just how far Communist Party infiltration and propaganda had spread beyond the limits of the Marxist movement proper.

As far back as 1900, Booker T. Washington counseled the Negro to seek economic self-sufficiency; to soft-pedal civil rights and social equality until he was on the road to achieving his own "economic" base for survival. Although the ordinary Negro has always understood the fundamental wisdom of this advice, his middle-class civil rights leadership (both Left and Reform) has chosen not to. Said Washington:

Brains, property, and character for the Negro will settle the question of civil rights. The best course to pursue in regard to a civil rights bill in the South is to let it alone; let it alone and it will settle itself. Good school teachers and plenty of money to pay them will be more potent in settling the race question than many civil rights bills and investigation committees.

In response to this, W.E.B. DuBois, Washington's critic, wrote: "The question then comes: Is it impossible, and probable, that nine millions of men can make effective progress in economic lines if they are deprived of political rights . . .?"[8]

DuBois answered emphatically—*No!*—and spent twenty years, from the NAACP's inception in 1909, in furthering this organiza-

---

[7] "Toward Negro Unity," *The Nation,* March 11, 1936, p. 302.
[8] W.E.B. DuBois, *Souls of Black Folk* (Chicago: A.C. McLurg, 1907), p. 51.

tion's social equality platforms. Then, around 1940, DuBois changed his mind about the effectiveness of NAACP methods. "There are, however, manifest difficulties about such a program," he wrote. "First of all it is not a program that envisages any direct action of Negroes themselves for the uplift of their socially depressed masses."[9] The venerable scholar-intellectual went even further than that, implying, in 1940, that the racial segregation practiced against the Negro, "despite anything he can do will persist for many decades."[10] Without ever admitting that Booker T. Washington had indeed been closer to the truth in 1900, DuBois switched his attention to the problem of economic self-sufficiency.

Now one can see more clearly into the roots of the Negro's economic debacle. Negro leadership has usually been caught up in the unresolved conflict between group needs and individual needs, economic nationalism and economic integration. On the social level it comes out as nationalism vs. integration, separatism vs. interracialism, black vs. white, etc. Within this context, we also discern the curious line of development, the twists and turns, of the great leader—W.E.B. DuBois—and the phases of his ideological development. This example by itself reveals that uncritical deification of leaders is not a good thing, especially as it is implicit in today's crisis in ideas among Negro intellectuals.

Ever since the 1930's, both radical and reform Negro intellectuals have refused to admit that despite DuBois's brilliance and scholarly achievements, he has, several times, been grievously wrong; either too far ahead or too far behind, but out of step with mass thinking. For how else does one explain the incongruity of this learned man's actions? Inexplicably, he joined, in 1961, the decimated ranks of the American Communist Party—a violent about-face from a man who spent the 1920's and the 1930's rejecting Communism, and wrote in 1940: "The split between white and black workers was greater than that between white workers and capitalists; and this split depended not simply on economic exploitation but on racial folklore grounded on centuries of in-

[9] W.E.B. DuBois, *Dusk of Dawn, op. cit.,* p. 193.
[10] *Ibid.,* p. 199.

stinct, habit and thought. . . . This flat incontrovertible fact, imported Russian Communism ignored, would not discuss."[11]

Even DuBois, himself, in 1940, called on Negroes to establish their economic cooperative commonwealth in America. But by then DuBois was already seventy-two years old! Economic organization had to be undertaken by younger men. However, the younger spirits of the National Negro Congress had other ideas about social equality.

It was easy during the 1930's to give lip service to group economic needs without the least intentions of carrying out such resolutions. Every single middle-class Negro who entered the Communist leftwing through the NNC was a consummate economic integrationist. Thus the NNC was actually the training ground for the new Negro leftwing integrationist elite that was to emerge full-blown in the Harlem leftwing movement of the late 1940's. This NNC elite furnished leadership in all the Harlem front organizations, such as the Committee for the Negro in the Arts, *Freedom* newspaper, the Civil Rights Congress, the Council on African Affairs, etc. If the roots of the Negro creative intellectual's crisis lie in the 1920's, the roots of the economic and political aspect of the Negro intellectual's debacle lie in the 1930's. And deep beneath the ideological frosting of Communist Party-National Negro Congress politics lay the submerged reality of nationalism and the nationality group. The Communists distorted and then smothered this issue, and the NNC integrationists backed off from espousing it. The tragic irony was that without a revival of the nationalist spirit in the politics of the Depression era, there could be no impetus for any program of cooperative economics for the Negro community. Here was the culmination of the working-class sellout of the black ghettoes—by the Negro left.

Negro intellectuals as a class have never explained the cold, raw economic facts of life to the Negro wage earner. Negro leaders (both Left and Reform) only discuss economics in terms of exhorting Negroes to man the picket lines for integrated jobs. When it came to initiating economic struggles on the home front—*inside* Harlem—during the Depression, in order to get white business-

[11] *Ibid.*, pp. 204-206, *passim.*

men to hire Negro personnel, it was *not* done by the NAACP, the NNC, or the Communist Party, but by Harlem Black Nationalist groups. During the same period, Communist Party ideological influence within Harlem movements insinuated the idea that it was useless for black radicals to study the intimate and fine details of capitalistic enterprise, or to master the techniques of conducting small businesses. This, the Communists called "bourgeois." Negroes instead were to learn from the Communists how to overthrow the capitalistic system once and for all. I clearly recall that in Harlem radical circles after the war, anyone found studying the contents of *The Wall Street Journal* or *The Journal of Commerce* was looked upon with deep distrust. Anyone who showed an interest in starting a small business was accused of falling prey to capitalistic ideology or political deterioration, etc. This, in effect, was what the Communist Party told Randolph, *et al.* in the NNC regarding the organization's economic resolutions. The NNC did not answer the Communists by resolutely waging a determined campaign for a realistic economic program for the Harlem ghetto. As a result, the ghetto conditions got worse and worse; and, ironically, when the NNC and the rest of the Communist front organizations collapsed during the late 1940's and the 1950's, the great majority of the elite Negro leadership of the NNC ventured to seek the best jobs they could find in the free enterprise business world.

The economic philosophy of the black bourgeoisie, whether radical or reform, reflects a kind of social opportunism that has been forced on this class by the American system. The black bourgeoisie is self-seeking but in a shortsighted, unsophisticated, unpolitical and cowardly fashion. It is one of the rare bourgeois classes of color that will sell itself out to white power without a principled struggle for its economic rights.

It is the historical prerogative of every bourgeois class to be as successful in capitalistic entrepreneuring as it can manage to be, under prevailing conditions. It is up to other classes to delimit the economic ambitions of the bourgeoisie, even though the bourgeoisie may claim that what is good for its profits is good for its nation. However, the mentality of the black bourgeoisie in America is conditioned by the fact that it has never shared in the fruits of the abundant capitalistic developments in America. Denied the privilege of achieving anything to its own profit, it could not even pretend to do very much on behalf of its nation or group, in terms of economic development. Because this class does nothing for the economic development of its group, the masses in its group neither respect nor support it. Concomitantly, because the masses do not support the black bourgeoisie, the latter is powerless as a class. Because the Negro is a minority, internal group economic growth becomes a two-way street, in terms of class collaboration.

But the economic philosophy of the black bourgeoisie itself rules out economic class collaboration of a positive sort. The black bourgeoisie fails to organize its group against the ravages of economic exploitation in a *political* fashion. The middle-class Negro would much prefer to accept a job from the white profiteer, and if he does anything at all for the masses, it is to help get them on public welfare (or else on anti-poverty programs—and thus more plush political jobs for members of the black bourgeoisie). This explains E. Franklin Frazier's characterization of the Negro middleclass as a "lumpen-bourgeoisie." Actually, a better term would be the native American non-white *comprador* class, for the black bourgeoisie sells not cheap labor, but skills and abilities, the products of education. But even within the ranks of the black bourgeoisie there are class contradictions. For it is the younger generation, middle-class elements who become politically radicalized.

This radicalization takes different political directions. During the 1930's it veered toward New Deal-leftwing political and economic integration. The black bourgeoisie can be radicalized only if the politics of radicalism coincide with its class aims and immediate social needs. If they require economic integration, then group-oriented economics go by the board. The question of Negro business becomes hypothetical, because it is easier and more politically acceptable to fight for integrated jobs inside the white economic structure, than to fight the control of the economic structure over the black community. In fact, the white leftwing radicals will furnish political rationalizations for abandoning the group economic interests of the black community, by calling Negro business a reactionary institution.

Yet the political expediency that colored many of the economic

approaches to the plight of the hard-pressed Negro communities
during the Depression, did not satisfy *all* the articulate middle-
class leaders. One of the younger thinkers was moved to write that
what was needed "is an intelligent relation of our problem to the
total American economic scene, the relentless fight against caste in
labor unions, the organization of Negro labor when necessary for
bargaining with white labor, and the organization of the Negro as
producers and consumers."[12]

In 1967, this is still unfinished business.

[12] J.G. St. Clair Drake, Jr., "Economics for James, Jr. . . . Revised," *Opportunity*,
December, 1935, p. 374.

Richard Wright

It appears now that the late Richard Wright, the emerging novelist of the late 1930's, made the last outstanding attempt to clear up the Negro intellectual's severe confusion of the 1920's and 1930's. Even before the appearance of *Native Son* during the Communist Party's Democratic Front heyday (when Jewish nationalism à la Marx was dominating leftwing affairs), Wright was trying to work out the deep problem of how Negro creative intellectuals should cope with the realities of Negro nationalism. The considered results of his thoughts on this problem appeared in an article in the Negro magazine *New Challenge*.[1] Here is what Wright said:

> Generally speaking, Negro writing in the past has been confined to humble novels, poems, and plays, prim and decorous ambassadors who went a-begging to White America. They entered the court of American public opinion dressed in the knee pants of servility, curtsying to show that the Negro was not inferior, that he was human, and that he had a life comparable to other people. For the most part these artistic ambassadors were received as though they were French poodles who do clever tricks.

It can truthfully be added that, despite the modern literary school of conscience-pleading civil writism (Baldwin and Hansberry, *et al.*), Negro writing has not advanced very far since 1937. Wright continued: "White America never offered these Negro writers any serious criticism. The mere fact that a Negro could write was astonishing. Nor was there any deep concern on the part of the White America with the role Negro writing should play in American culture."

Although Wright objectively saw the formal gist of the problem, he viewed it upside down. He perhaps did not recognize that

[1] Wright, "Blueprint for Negro Writing," *New Challenge*, Fall, 1937, pp. 53-64, *passim*.

criticism of Negro writing is mainly the Negro's responsibility, in this instance, not the white's. For the white, criticism is merely a prerogative which, in any case, would be governed by an Anglo-Saxon or Jewish cultural compulsive thus negating any possible objectivity of a positive nature from the black point of view. Wright should have read V.F. Calverton more closely. But at this time, as we shall see, he took his Marxism very seriously, and was so ideologically blinded by the smog of Jewish-Marxist nationalism that he was unable to see his *own* clearly: "Shall Negro writing be for the Negro masses, moulding the lives and consciousness of the masses toward new goals, or shall it continue to go begging the question of Negroes' humanity?"

Here, Wright reveals how he had swallowed whole the Communist Party's dogma about proletarian literature, a bastard literary form of dubious class validity. Wright, a Southerner, should have known that the Holy Bible was the most popular literary work among Negroes not just because it was proletarian literature, and that the classics of Marx and Engels were written not for the proletariat but for the intelligentsia (at least that was the class who interpreted Marx to the proletariat). Wright confused the role of Negro literature (a cultural problem) with the role of the Party line on Negro-White labor unity. Thus, he did not see that the Negro writer's first and main task had to be that of "moulding the lives and consciousness" of the black intelligentsia, not the masses, "toward new goals." It was the Negro intelligentsia who had no goals, hence how could they impart any to the Negro masses? Wright's faulty, if penetrating, critique of Negro writing led him into a quandary when he attempted to face up to the reality of nationalism:

> No attempt is being made here to propagate a specious and blatant nationalism. Yet the nationalist character of the Negro people is unmistakable. Psychologically this nationalism is reflected in the whole of Negro culture, and especially in folklore. Let those who shy at the nationalist implications of Negro life look at this body of folklore, living and powerful, which rose out of a unified sense of common life and a common fate.

Wright came on the scene after the ideological shock of Garveyism had subsided, but he was still feeling the tremors. Pure Garveyism, however, was no longer the answer. Its role had been similar to that of a holy baptism in which the black soul was purged in preparation for the more refined and complex nationalist problems to come. They came in the 1930's, but by then, Communist Party dialectics had done its disorienting work too thoroughly. Yet, Wright admonished:

> Negro writers must accept the nationalist implications of their lives, *not in order to encourage them,* but in order to change and transcend them. . . .
> They must accept the concept of nationalism because, in order to transcend it, they must possess and understand it. And a nationalist spirit in Negro writing means a nationalism carrying the highest possible pitch of social consciousness. It means a nationalism that knows its origins, its limitations; that is aware of the dangers of its position, that knows its ultimate aims are unrealizable within the framework of capitalist America. A nationalism whose reason for being lies in the simple fact of self-possession and in the consciousness of the interdependence of people in modern society. . . .
> For purposes of creative expression it means that the Negro writer must realize within the area of his own personal experience those impulses which, when prefigured in terms of broad social movements, constitute the stuff of nationalism.

"Nationalist implications" were for Wright a great unknown quantity, even though he tried to face up to them. How can one accept the implications of something, understand them, and carry them to the "highest possible pitch of social consciousness" without encouraging them? No one can really transcend goals which are, in the first place, ultimately unrealizable, unless one spells out what indeed was unrealizable in the first place. Wright did not do this and was apparently referring, obliquely, to the unrealizable goals of Garveyism, or quasi-Garveyistic trends, still around in 1937. However, at least Wright realized that he was in a quandary, although his view of the problem was upside down:

> For Negro writers even more so than for Negro politicians, nationalism is a bewildering and vexing question, the full ramifications of which cannot be dealt with here. But among Negro workers and the Negro middleclass the spirit of nationalism is rife in a hundred devious forms; and a simple literary realism which

seeks to depict the lives of these people devoid of wider connotations, devoid of revolutionary significance of these nationalist tendencies, must of necessity do a rank injustice to the Negro people and alienate their possible allies in the struggle for freedom.

On the contrary, it was precisely these same allies Wright mentions, whose influence was the very thing that prevented Negro writers and the Negro middle-class intelligentsia from seeing, using, and developing, the "revolutionary significance of nationalist tendencies." Richard Wright and his Negro intellectual colleagues never realized the plain truth that no one in the United States understood the revolutionary potential of the Negro better than the Negro's white radical allies. They understood it *instinctively*, and revolutionary theory had little to do with it. What Wright could not see was that what the Negro's allies feared most of all was that this sleeping, dream-walking black giant might wake up and direct the revolution all by himself, relegating his white allies to a humiliating, second-class status. The Negro's allies were not about to tell the Negro any thing that might place him on the path to greater power and independence in the revolutionary movement than they themselves had. The rules of the power game meant that unless the American Negro taught himself the profound implications of his own revolutionary significance in America, it would never be taught to him by anybody else. Unless the Negro intellectuals understood that in pursuit of this self-understanding, they would have to make their own rules, by and for themselves, nationalism would forever remain—as it was for Wright—"a bewildering and vexing question." In a near frenzy, distilled from his crucial sense of the Negro writer's supreme destiny in America, Wright exhorted others to understand what he could only explain in terms of broad generalities:

> The Negro writer who seeks to function within his race as a purposeful agent has a serious responsibility. In order to do justice to his subject matter, in order to depict Negro life in all of its manifold and intricate relationships, a deep, informed, and complex consciousness is necessary; a consciousness which draws for its strength upon the fluid lore of a great people, and moulds this lore with the concepts that move and direct the forces of history today. With the gradual decline of the moral authority of the

Negro church, and with the increasing irresolution which is paralyzing the Negro middleclass leadership, a new role is devolving upon the Negro writer. He is being called upon to do no less than create values by which his race is to struggle, live and die. . . .

By his ability to fuse and make articulate the experiences of men, because his writing possesses the potential cunning to steal into the utmost recesses of the human heart, because he can create the myths and symbols that inspire a faith in life, he may expect either to be consigned to oblivion, or to be recognized for the valued agent that he is.

Note that Wright could not specify *what* "forces of history today" the Negro writer could possibly move and direct. Yet he insisted that the Negro writer prepare himself for this world-shaking assignment:

This raises the question of the personality of the writer. It means that in the lives of Negro writers must be found those materials and experiences which will create a meaningful picture of the world today. Many young writers have grown to believe that a Marxist analysis of society presents such a picture. It creates a picture which, when placed before the eyes of the writer, should unify his personality, organize his emotions, buttress him with a tense and obdurate will to change the world. And, in turn, this changed world will dialectically change the writer. Hence, it is through a Marxian conception of reality and society that the maximum degree of freedom in thought and feeling can be gained for the Negro writer. Further, this dramatic Marxist vision, when consciously grasped, endows the writer with a sense of dignity which no other vision can give. Ultimately, it restores to the writer his lost heritage, that is, his role as a creator of the world in which he lives, as a creator of himself. . . . Yet, for the Negro writer, Marxism is but the starting point. No theory of life can take the place of life. After Marxism has laid bare the skeleton of society, there remains the task of the writer to plant flesh upon those bones out of his will to live.

The magazine, *New Challenge,* in which Wright's article appeared, was started in the spring of 1934 as a Negro literary monthly, sponsored by a Negro newspaper, *The Boston Chronicle.* After its first issue in 1934 it became a quarterly, and lasted until 1937. All together it published seven issues, the last one, containing Wright's analysis. The previous six issues were very undistinguished, and revealed the growing lack of ability of Negro writers to come to grips with the critical demands and potentialities of their own social facts of life. None of the fiery polemic raging around *New Challenge* in the literary and cultural world of the white leftwing was reflected in the pages of this magazine. The writers (such as Langston Hughes, James Weldon Johnson, Arna Bontemps, Frank Yerby, Ralph Ellison, Claude McKay, Eslande G. Robeson, Margaret Walker, William Attaway, Alain Locke, *et al.*) appeared to be off in a quiet, contemplative cultural eddy watching the fireworks elsewhere. In these fateful years of the 1930's, the literati of the Harlem Renaissance appear to have been subdued and beaten into such a state of perplexity, they could not speak loudly even to each other. The new arrivals, such as Ellison, Attaway and Yerby, seemed possessed with problems of "craft," but tongue-tied in terms of ideas. It was significant, then, that right after Richard Wright's tormented bout with nationalist ideas, the magazine folded. The Negro writers of that day walked off the stage as if anticipating 1939 and 1940, whose events brought down the curtain on a fateful decade, but one that had settled no pertinent issues for the Negro in America. Yet another Negro publication had failed to sustain itself . . . and its only bequest to the next young generation, its ideological poverty.

The failure of *New Challenge* indicated that the Negro intellectuals of the period were unable to fashion for themselves an independent social philosophy predicated on politics, economics, cultural arts and Wright's "nationalist implications." But their failure was, to a great degree, an anti-climactic failure—a rather feeble and half-hearted attempt to recoup lost ground given up in the 1920's without a principled struggle. *New Challenge* was a belated effort to rally the tattered and defeated forces of the Harlem Renaissance for a new stand on a new line of defense on the cultural battlefield. For this task there were new forces—Ellison, Wright, Attaway, Yerby, *et al.*—but little that was new in the realm of ideas. Moreover, the *New Challenge* effort was nullified in advance by the inexorable persuasions of the social dynamic in the guise of New Deal capitalistic reforms. This dynamic swept everything before it and absorbed every progressive political, economic and cultural trend. Furthermore, the New Deal and its wavering alliance with the Communist leftwing ushered in another kind of alliance: Communists and Left-oriented Negro middle-class elements in the National Negro Congress. Here were planted the seeds of the new, oncoming leftwing middle-class integrationism; an integrationism that could talk radicalism and practice reformism better than the NAACP—and with more stylistic dynamism and international connections. This New-Deal-nurtured breed and their Communist reinforcements made certain that nothing tainted with Richard Wright's "nationalist implications" would ever see daylight in their Harlem circles. They nurtured conditions for the rise and fall of the American Negro Theater, later the Committee for the Negro in the Arts, *Freedom* newspaper and other Harlem front groups of this typical leftwing genus. Thus it was not surprising that five years after the demise of *New Challenge* the new left trend of the 1930's came out with a new magazine—*The Negro Quarterly: A Review of Negro Life and Culture,* edited by Angelo Herndon and Ralph Ellison and published, it said on the masthead, by the "Negro Publication Society of America, Inc."

The editors managed to get out four issues, beginning with Spring, 1942, and ending with Winter-Spring, 1943—and this effort is mentioned here only for the purpose of historical accuracy. Angelo Herndon was an early 1930's Negro Communist *cause célèbre,* railroaded to jail in Georgia for his activities on behalf of the Scottsboro boys. Sentenced to eighteen to twenty years, he was freed in 1937. There was nothing at all distinguished about this publication beyond its unabashed Communist Negro-white unity editorial slant. Literally swamped as it was with white writers, it serves as an example of how Communist influence and Left literary values smother and choke black cultural expression. The fear of black cultural assertion is so strong in the white Left that every precaution must be taken to influence even the most feeble rise of cultural self-evaluation among Negroes. This was a fact that a Richard Wright could not deal with even when he confronted it. *The Negro Quarterly* died after four issues because Communist Left literary and critical values cannot sustain a "Review of Negro Life and Culture" even when these values emerge from the Negro Left. The "cultural compulsives" are not strong enough.

It was interesting to note that *after* the victorious ascendancy of Jewish nationalism in Communist Party affairs of the 1930's, *The*

Negro Quarterly was induced to take up the question of Negro-Jewish relations in its Summer, 1942, issue. Featured were the articles "Anti-Negroism Among Jews" by Louis Harap, and "Anti-Semitism Among Negroes" by L.D. Reddick. These articles were reissued in 1943 under the title "Should Jews and Negroes Unite?" The questions "Unite against whom?" or "Who would unite with or against Negro-Jewish unity?" were not answered. However, the fact that 1930's radicalism had propelled American Jewry with an added boost towards the status of a power factor among the "have" groups revealed that the Negro intellectuals of the period had been grossly deceived with a false bill of goods in ethnic and cultural dialectics. Richard Wright's blueprint message to Negro writers fell on deaf ears.

Poor Richard Wright! He sincerely tried, but he never got much beyond that starting point that Marxism represented for him. Less than eight years after his article was written, he resigned from the Communist Party and went into exile, never to return. He could not gather into himself all the ingredients of nationalism; to create values and mould concepts by which his race was to "struggle, live and die."

It will never be known whether or not Wright ever grasped the extent to which vulgar Marxism had rendered him incapable of seeing unique developments of American capitalism. Uncharted paths existed for the Negro creative intellectuals to explore, if only they could avoid being blinded by Communist Party propaganda. The path to the ethnic democratization of American society is through its culture, that is to say through its cultural apparatus, which comprises the eyes, the ears, and the "mind" of capitalism and its twentieth-century voice to the world. Thus to democratize the cultural apparatus is tantamount to revolutionizing American society itself into the living realization of its professed ideas. Seeing the problem in another way, to revolutionize the cultural apparatus is to deal fundamentally with the unsolved American question of nationality—Which group speaks for America and for the glorification of which ethnic image? Either all group images speak for themselves and for the nation, or American nationality will never be determined. In America, the materio-economic conditions relate to a societal, multi-group existence in a

way never before known in world history. American Negro nationalism can never create its own values, find its revolutionary
significance, define its political and economic goals, until Negro
intellectuals take up the cudgels against the cultural imperialism
practiced in all of its manifold ramifications on the Negro within
American culture. But this kind of revolution would have to be
predicated on the recognition that the cultural and artistic originality of the American nation is founded, historically, on the
ingredients of a black aesthetic and artistic base.

III

Artists for Freedom Inc.—
Dialogue Off-key

During the month of June, 1964, members of the Association of Artists for Freedom* debated some leading white liberals† at New York's Town Hall on the theme: "The Black Revolution and the White Backlash." This debate revealed that the Artists for Freedom, as a representative group of Negro intellectuals, were agreed among themselves on only one cogent idea—an almost unanimous derogation of white liberals. Of course many Negroes had, long before then, been severely critical of white liberals. Indeed, James Baldwin, the leading literary spokesman, had previously complained that they are "our affliction."

Baldwin, who was associated with this artists' group, did not participate in the Town Hall discussion. Some months before, he and Dr. Kenneth Clark, the Negro psychologist, had joined in a round-table debate with a group of white liberals associated with *Commentary*,[1] published and sponsored by the American Jewish Committee. In this debate Baldwin was pitted against such leading liberal social scientists as Gunnar Myrdal and Sidney Hook.

In Marvin Elkoff's article on Baldwin, it is reported that just before going to this discussion, Baldwin asked "What the hell [was he] supposed to say to them in there about all this sociology and economics jazz?" Elkoff attributed this to Baldwin's "intellectual uneasiness" over having to cross ideological swords with members of the white intellectual establishment who are also part of the

---

* John O. Killens, novelist; Lorraine Hansberry, playwright; James Baldwin, novelist-essayist; Ossie Davis, actor-playwright; Ruby Dee, actress; LeRoi Jones, playwright-poet; Paule Marshall, novelist; Louis Lomax, journalist.

† Charles E. Silberman, editor, *Fortune;* James A. Wechsler, editor, *The New York Post;* David Susskind, television commentator.

[1] See "Liberalism and the Negro—A Round-table Discussion." *Commentary,* March, 1964, pp. 25-42. Used by permission.

"liberal affliction." Instead of discussing "sociology and economics jazz," Baldwin, according to Elkoff, was bent on making those liberals "accept his black reality before they talked of ethics and the future of society and housing programs."[2] As a result, he was put on the defensive and kept there by pointed questions such as that asked by Charles Silberman:* "Mr. Baldwin, since you said that there is no role for the liberal, could I ask you how this radical reconstruction of American society that you insist is necessary can take place? Are the White conservatives going to do it?"

Baldwin failed to answer this question at all. He could not because in order to do so one *must* indulge in precisely that "sociology and economics jazz" that Baldwin eschews. This failure to discuss the racial conflicts either in terms of possible practical solutions, or in terms of American economic and sociological realities, made Baldwin's assault on white liberals a futile rhetorical exercise; it was further weakened by the intellectual inconsistencies, incoherence and emotionalism of his line of argument.

Norman Podhoretz, editor of *Commentary* and moderator of the discussion, was quoted by Elkoff in the *Esquire* article as saying: "I purposely got Jimmy [Baldwin] to the seminar to get him off that personal kick and make him talk about solutions and programs. It didn't work."

One would have expected more of Dr. Kenneth Clark† in this debate. But all that Clark had to contribute to the general understanding of things social, economic, cultural, and class-conscious, was to agree with Baldwin's estimation of the liberal. In other words, Clark was defending Baldwin in his predicament, but had not a single original idea to contribute to the problem at hand. Said Clark: "I'm glad that James Baldwin is around because he's helping some of the rest of us cope with this difficult problem of facing the American liberal with the fact that in relation to the Negro he has never been as liberal as he likes to profess."

This line of polemic against the white liberal establishment,

---

[2] Elkoff, "Everybody Knows His Name", *Esquire*, August, 1964, pp. 59-64, 120-123; quote, p. 121.

* Author of *Crisis in Black and White* (New York: Random House, 1964).

† Kenneth Clark is Professor of Psychology at City College of New York and one of the leading architects of Harlem Youth Rehabilitation Program—Harlem Youth Unlimited (HARYOU).

that has become the radical pose of the emergent Negro intellectual stratum, is significant in that it helps clear away many of the
shibboleths of white liberalism that have beclouded and confused
the whole issue of integration. For, if it is true as Kenneth Clark
charges, that "the ethical aspect of American liberalism or the
American creed" (*i.e.* the American Ideal) "is primarily verbal,"
and is therefore now exposed for all Negroes to see as a sham that
cannot overcome "an equally persistent illiberalism of action,"
then a question is posed of crucial validity: Whom can the Negro
look to for an effective alliance in this age of resurgent conservatism? Not the conservatives, to be sure. On the face of it, this
epidemic of white liberal-baiting, aside from being childish and
futile, is also an unsophisticated display of desperation.

Time and mass movements are bringing race issues to a head in
America and the time-honored crutch of liberalism has been
snatched away just as that other crutch—the white radicalism of
the Communists—collapsed during the 1950's. On the face of it, it
would appear that now would be the time for Negro intellectuals
to start thinking for themselves as truly independent and original
radicals. This is what the entire Negro movement demands today,
not the radical-gadfly pose of flailing liberals.

One need only be a part-time reader of *Commentary* to know
that the white liberals have been long aware of their own diminishing vitality, their inability to play any dynamic role in America.
But Baldwin and Clark talked as if all they read about American
race problems and liberalism is what they themselves published.
Otherwise, we would get from these Negro intellectuals critiques
of American liberalism as a creed that would be more enlightening
than the complaint that the race issue is the white liberals' responsibility and nobody else's—"So you liberals solve it!" This is what
Baldwin and Clark were actually implying.

Baldwin, while desiring only to be accepted as a writer (and not
necessarily a Negro writer at that), takes himself seriously as a
Negro spokesman. But a Negro writer cannot, today, make declarations about the need for a "radical reconstruction" of American
society while, at the same time, scoffing at "sociology and economics jazz" as not being worth the time of serious study by writers such as himself. Debates on morals and ethics, emotional appeals to conscience, the literary explorations of the American

psychic malaise, the cult of chic belles-lettres fortified with the current phraseology of the protest movement, sprinkled with personal ironies and social witticisms, make fascinating reading for aesthetes. But *that*—by itself—becomes a rather superficial literary mode of involvement when pitted against the ideas of the ranking exponents of social reform, liberal, radical or otherwise.

The Association of Artists for Freedom did a little better than Baldwin, but not much. Unlike Baldwin, several of this group have backgrounds in radical politics. Hence they are pretty well versed in the language of radicalism, if not the action.

Interestingly enough, the most vehement voice of anti-liberal bias was that of LeRoi Jones. Jones was the youngest of the group and represented a literary departure among Negroes, in being a devotee of avant-garde expression in poetry and drama. Not being able to boast of much of a political background, but having proven himself (by dint of his radical play, *Dutchman*) to be very "far out," Jones, in keeping with his literary reputation as one of the "angry young men," went one up on the rest with his anti-liberal tirades. The Town Hall debate was advertised, according to James Wechsler of *The New York Post*, "as an effort to conduct a dialogue between 'white liberals' and Negro 'militants' about where men go from here in the civil rights battle." But LeRoi Jones considered a dialogue with such liberals as Charles Silberman a waste of time, and said as much. He seized on the fact that Silberman is an editor of *Fortune* magazine as typical of a white liberal parading under false colors, of running with the hounds while pretending friendship for the hares.

The frenetic bitterness of Jones' attacks—not only against Silberman, *Fortune,* and *The New York Times* but also against the daily voice of New York liberalism, *The New York Post*—so pained and startled James Wechsler that he devoted two whole columns to this debate in his newspaper. He called the meeting "bewildering," "a sad failure," and deplored "the estrangement between 'white liberals' and self-proclaimed 'black radical' intellectuals."[3] But Wechsler's very casting of doubt on the validity of these writers' opinions goes far in proving just the point they were making—about the obdurate, and often obtuse, white liberal, so

[3] *The New York Post.* June 22, 1964. p. 26; June 23, 1964, p. 26.

steeped in the do-gooder's complex as to become laden with paternalism. Heretofore, any and every self-proclaimed white liberal has enjoyed the option of sounding off authoritatively on The Negro. But when these particular liberals were stung in public with criticism from "self-proclaimed Black radical intellectuals," the tense rejoinder was: "Which Negroes, now, are you people speaking for?" It was, to be sure, a good question but its tone and taste were very bad.

What was the gist of what the Artists for Freedom had to say to Wechsler, Silberman and Susskind? And what does it signify for our times? First, John Killens, in his opening remarks, asserted that the role of the Negro artists and intellectuals in the civil rights struggle was *not* in conflict with the official civil rights organizations. However, the intensification of this struggle was causing white backlash, which called for a new dialogue between Negroes and liberals. Later on, Killens warned that this white backlash amounted to a counter-struggle against the Negro revolution—before the latter had even begun. By which, he implied that what was being *called* the Negro revolution did not really fulfill this definition at all. Ruby Dee, the actress-wife of playwright Ossie Davis, asserted that the Negro revolution did not have to be violent. But Killens cited the CORE "stall-in" non-violent tactics, pointing out, in his contradictory way, that revolutionaries blow up, rather than stall in, bridges, which is as close as non-violent methods come to violence.

Paule Marshall, a novelist, charged that the Civil Rights Act then being debated in Congress "was being amended to death" and would be rather useless if passed. She called for a "new organization" among Negroes based in the South and in the black communities of the North, which would be "truly independent." She gave, however, no precise definition of how this new organization could possibly be any different in program and structure from any other civil rights institutions, past or present. Finally after suggesting intensified "economic boycotts," (which was nothing new) she called for closing the gap between Negro intellectuals and the masses. How much there is, positive, or simply rhetorical, in Miss Marshall's proposal on the intellectuals we shall see later. However, her plea for new organization indicated how severely throttled the Negro civil rights movement is, as a whole, if all the

Negro groups involved in the struggle could be put down as unsatisfactory and insufficient in scope.

Ossie Davis dug deeper than the rest into what might be called the peculiar pathology of the now-diseased relations between white liberals and the Negro civil rights movement. According to him, the institutionalizing of Negro-white liberal interracialism in all the Negro civil rights groups, especially the NAACP and the Urban League, has actually functioned as a very deceptive façade for what has always been white liberal domination and policy control. In other words, Negroes are not the decisive policy makers in these organizations.

Whites, including liberals, Paule Marshall had pointed out, are really opposed to change that is not "gradual." In effect they actually retard and restrict the range of civil rights organizations through their control of Negro leaders. Like other whites, liberals also stand to lose certain accustomed privileges as the price of Negro social advance. Ossie Davis substantiated this by pointing out that some white liberals even own property in Harlem, for example, and, in effect, profit from the misery of Negro ghetto existence.

The history of the radical leftwing movement, especially in New York City over the last fifteen years or so, made it inevitable that many of its slogans, dogmas, and issues involving Negroes would crop up again in this debate. Thus there was Lorraine Hansberry's echo of the old leftwing plea for "some kind of socialism," as a final, all-embracing solution. This talk of socialism was, of course, rather old hat and nobody cared to debate the exact meaning or potential of that disputed state of human and interracial bliss. It was not surprising that Ossie Davis, in addition to criticizing today's liberals, also dug up their sins of yesterday—their failure to wage a principled fight against McCarthy and his persecution of the Communists. Although his reiteration of the McCarthy-Communist-liberal fracas of the early 1950's was a separate issue from that in debate at Town Hall, it was used as a ploy to nail down the indictment of white liberals on the Negro issue even more stringently. James Wechsler observed:

> To compound the bewildering aspects of the meeting, more than three-fourths of the audience was white, and it was from white throats that one heard the most passionate, sometimes semi-

hysterical, responses to the more feverish assaults on the white liberal corrupters. From the reactions to some peripheral foreign-policy exchanges, one gathered that there was a solid segment of readers of the pro-Peking *National Guardian* (in which the meeting had been heavily promoted) on hand.[4]

The peculiar political coloration of the majority of whites at this meeting was of course related to the intimate political, literary and artistic background of the Artists for Freedom, especially in the case of Killens, Hansberry, Davis and Dee. These four members of the Artists for Freedom, because of their apparent social and professional exclusiveness, as well as their associations with Harlem leftwing cultural organizations, were considered to be a clique by people involved in Harlem cultural life. However, if it is true that white liberals have exercised a pernicious, corrupting effect on Negro organizations, the role of white leftwingers, specifically the Communist whites, whether old-Stalinists or neo-anti-Khrushchev dissidents, has definitely been no better. The Artists for Freedom assault on the white liberals must lead one to assume that in view of the presence at Town Hall of a predominantly white audience (obviously loaded against the white liberals, with a voluble anti-liberal leftwing claque), the theme of the so-called black revolution was not the *only* issue present. Smuggled in through the side door were some old feuds between the now dried-up and burnt-out Communist Party and the white liberals, going back to the days of the McCarthy inquisition (about which younger Negro militants know very little, and care less).

What was the gist of the white liberals' reply to this assault* by Negro intellectuals? While all the liberals on the dock at Town Hall agreed that a new dialogue was the order of the day, they also felt it should be a two-way proposition, an objective exchange of positive ideas, regardless of what one might think of the liberal philosophy. Conceding that American liberalism needs a "new theory of politics," Charles Silberman asked his tormentors how to go about establishing a dialogue. He also let it be known that he considered Baldwin's vision of the white liberal to be decidedly

---

[4] *Ibid.*, June 22, 1964, p. 26.
* A writer for *The Village Voice*, New York's Greenwich Village weekly, called it a mugging.

stereotyped, a fact which is revealed in Baldwin's play, *Blues for Mr. Charlie.** The tormented inconsistency that runs through much of Baldwin's work was very much in evidence in the approach of the Negro intellectuals at Town Hall. It left them wide open, for instance, for Charles Silberman to put to them the sixty-four thousand dollar question—much as, earlier, he had put it to Baldwin: *What exactly do you intellectuals propose should be done?* We white liberals agree that we need "a new theory of politics"; can you intellectuals provide it? Do you want us white liberals as equal allies or do you want us in the backseat? (Wechsler characterized this role as, liberals, playing the part of waterboys.) It was pointed out that an authentic dialogue, after all, means equality between black and white in the Negro movement.

The very fact that the Artists for Freedom group asked the white liberals to appear, seemed to imply "equals," participating across the board on relevant issues. But Paule Marshall's call for a "new independent Negro organization" implied that the white liberals would be bringing up the rear, if indeed they were not banished altogether, or relegated to the netherworld of the arch-conservatives and reactionaries. For such a course of action as this, however, why was it necessary for anybody (Negro intellectuals *or* white liberals) to show up at Town Hall at all?

It is apparent that, through the pointed interrogation of Charles Silberman, the Negro intellectuals' severe dilemma was revealed. They had no definitive answers for the crucial questions. They adopted a radical-sounding pose, trying to place the onus of their social predicament on white liberals—the real patrons and sponsors of their privileged position as Negro intellectuals. They attacked by implication the white liberal program agreed upon by liberals and Negro integrationists; but as intellectual spokesmen for the Negro, they were unable even to hint at the outlines of another kind of program. All in all, their Town Hall spectacle was just another Northern protest demonstration—in the expensive interior of Town Hall rather than the streets around City Hall. Intellectual grandstanding! They were accusing white liberals of not

* Here, the white liberal character, Parnell James, comes across more as a rather naïvely-drawn human prop for the action, than a character in depth; so sympathetically portrayed as to border on the maudlin, despite the author's professed view of white liberals.

being radicals when they themselves did not compose a group with a radical Negro philosophy of any kind. Even those in the Artists for Freedom who once *professed* political radicalism have been retreating towards middle-class moderation for the last fifteen years, in line with their retreat from the black community. Thus, they cannot admit that the locus for the attack on the problem lies in the black community itself, not in Town Hall debates.

Ossie Davis prophesied a revolutionary "movement of masses" among Negroes in the future, but could not refute the contention of one liberal that a recent poll showed the majority of Negroes supported Martin L. King and Lyndon B. Johnson—hardly an indication of revolutionary things to come. Another white liberal was of the opinion that these Negro intellectuals were really speaking only for themselves: *Which Negroes are you speaking for?*

The same question had been put very sharply, to Baldwin, by Norman Podhoretz of *Commentary:*

> *Podhoretz:* Mr. Baldwin, is it conceivable to you that the Negroes will within the next five or ten or twenty years take their rightful place as one of the competing groups in the American pluralistic pattern? Or is something more radical—or perhaps less radical—more likely to happen the way things are going now?
>
> *Baldwin:* In the first place—I want to say this particularly to Mr. Hook—I don't feel at all hopeless. . . . That's why when you ask about the Negroes in the next five or ten or fifteen years taking their place as a competing group and getting their share of the pie, I can't answer directly. I can't put it that way to myself. What pie are you talking about? From my own point of view, my personal point of view, there is much in that American pie that isn't worth eating.
>
> *Podhoretz:* O.K., that's you, but what about your fellow Negroes? Wouldn't they be perfectly happy to eat everything in that pie? You said in *The Fire Next Time* that Negroes wonder whether they want to be integrated into a burning house, and at that point—as someone observed—you were speaking as an American social critic rather than as a Negro. Now the question is, is it the Negroes who feel that the house is burning and that the pie is rotten, or is it only James Baldwin?[5]

If Baldwin was defeated at *Commentary,* his literary peers of the

[5] *Commentary, op. cit.,* p. 35.

Artists for Freedom group managed to bring off a heated deadlock with the liberals. Silberman, at the end, admonished all and sundry that the Negro radicals and the white liberals are all in the same boat. Whether these intellectuals liked it or no, Silberman spoke the truth when he pointed out that building a "new Negro organization" of the type vaguely hinted at by Paule Marshall would be a long, rough, hard job (in which, and this is a personal opinion, most of the Artists for Freedom group will never be involved).

Nothing that was said at Town Hall by these writers and artists indicated that they really grasped the economic, political and cultural fundamentals implicit in the faltering drive for racial equality, or even the real nature of the white liberal default. What they revealed, mainly, were their own deep confusions and conflicting individual points of view. Some lean to the Martin L. King passive resistance or non-violent methods, while condemning the very liberals who support non-violence; eschewing violence, they demand more militancy. They call for Negro leadership unfettered by white liberal control somewhat as the nationalists do, but are careful to avoid nationalism or separatism. They have taken on a radical veneer without radical substance, yet have no comprehensive radical philosophy to replace either the liberalism they denounce or the radicalism of the past that bred them. They are representative of the Negro intellectual's quandary in America. And the social root of their problem is directly traceable to their class separation from the ethnic-group consciousness level of Negro thought (that resides mostly in the lower mass of disinherited ghetto Negroes, for whom the American middle-class liberal establishment offers no way out). For ghetto Negroes, the liberal panaceas never have had any meaning, and they have been powerless and inarticulate *just* as long as the NAACP-integrationist type of leadership has been viable and official. Even the radicalism of the Communist Party never struck deeply sympathetic chords in the consciousness of these forgotten people.

Overall, the Negro movement is guided by the integrationist* forces: the philosophy of the NAACP, Urban League, CORE, Martin L. King in the Northern states and (chiefly) the Students'

---

* More aptly called, *assimilationist* forces.

Non-Violent Coordinating Committee in the Southern states (SNCC). However, the North and the South present the racial situation on two different levels. Despite organizational overlapping, integration in the South does not mean the same thing as integration in the North. This is why Northern integrationist forces at this present moment, actually have none of the clearly defined goals that are abundantly provided by the social structure of the South. This is also why it appears to many that the South is the crucial area where the fate of the entire Negro movement in America will be settled. But it is in the Northern cities, where the tangible goals toward which the Southern forces have been working have already been achieved after a fashion, that the real, decisive struggles must take place. Programmatically then, the Northern integrationist movement has little to offer save moral and financial support for the Southern movement.

The Association of Artists for Freedom came into existence in 1964 as a result of the Birmingham Church bombing and killing of six children; but *not* through any prior intellectual comprehension that Negro writers, artists, and creative individuals had a political role to fulfill in the Negro movement, in any event. Now having assumed this rather belated militant political stance, and attempting to palm it off as super-radicalism, these intellectuals, straining at the leash, find themselves the tactical and programmatic prisoners of their Northern roles. They are integrationists, active or implied, with no tangibly visible worlds to conquer in the North, beyond furthering their own individual careers as creative artists.

What truly lay behind their militant-sounding assault on the white liberals was the mounting sense of frustration and desperation that is shared by all Northern integrationist forces of whatever faction. The structure of American society can easily defeat, check, negate, balance out and control integration on any level; but it can at the same time permit whatever amount of token integration is necessary either to let off steam as it were, or to satisfy the gradualists, Negro or white, that progress is indeed being made—against terrific odds. What the super-militants and the radicals cannot stomach is that integration *cannot* proceed in any other way or at any other pace in America, given the present interplay of social forces at work, and the rules of battle agreed upon by the integrationists themselves. As I have pointed out, the integrationists act as if they are about to make into an open society a white world that was never homogeneous to begin with, and never open to all *whites,* let alone Negroes. They have not even been perceptive enough, as yet, to recognize which power group in America it is possible (or most profitable) to crack open.

The integrationists' lack of perception does not prevent terrific pressure boiling up from the Negro masses below. When this occurs in the North especially, it really puts the spokesmen in a predicament: Where do we go from here—and how? becomes the burning question. Perceiving no clear path ahead, the Negro integrationists decide in desperation that they themselves are the *last* people to blame for this lack of decisive direction; the nearest whipping-boys available, of course, are their erstwhile allies, the white liberals. The fact that the liberals are in just as dark a quandary only proves that the black intellects have not been thinking on an original level as an emergent, representative class. But do these intellectuals, as they allege, really represent the aims and aspirations of the Negro masses? Or, more specifically, do they really represent the point of view of that Negro "residual stratum of ethnic consciousness" that is so inarticulate? Since everything these intellectuals have said or done over the last ten to fifteen years (and more), proves that they are not nationalists or separatists, but integrationists, why do they attack obliquely the official integrationist organizations (NAACP, Urban League, CORE, etc.) by openly attacking the very white liberals whom these organizations support? After the Town Hall debate, James Wechsler was prompted to write in his column:

> What was the argument about? Each participant may have a different view. In my own, this was not primarily a quarrel between "white liberals" and Negro crusaders; it was actually a dispute between the emerging cult of firebrand Negro intellectuals and several men who weren't there—Martin Luther King, Jim Farmer, Roy Wilkins and A. Philip Randolph.[6]

This was no doubt true, but there is more to it than that. How this Artists for Freedom group came to take this radical stance at

[6] *The New York Post,* June 22, 1964, p. 26.

Town Hall has a history. LeRoi Jones, the new arrival, was more candid than the others when he implied the whole argument was a waste of time. But it was a waste of time only because these intellectuals came to Town Hall empty-handed. Their polemic represented merely another symptom of America's endemic sociological ailment—the race question in the crisis of transition. Not only did they fail to point the way to a possible cure in an empirical sense, they did not even render a diagnosis.

Origins of the Dialogue

When James Wechsler of *The New York Post* observed that the Association of Artists for Freedom was ambushing captive white liberals in order to carry on an interior dispute with Martin Luther King, James Farmer, Roy Wilkins and A. Philip Randolph "who weren't there," he was only partially correct. This charge could apply to Killens, Hansberry, Davis and Dee, but not necessarily to Marshall and Jones. The Artists for Freedom actually represented a group within a group, the former consisting of Killens, Hansberry, Davis and Dee. It was this Killens group that set the tone for this Association. A group whose outlook was shaped by a special kind of literary and political conditioning, its literary, artistic, and political origins are to be found in the radical leftwing movement in the Harlem of the late 1940's and early 1950's. The brand of social and literary criticism of the Killens group is, in fact, so much influenced by the early Harlem leftwing philosophy that its members have remained intellectual prisoners of that tradition, to date.

In Town Hall, by their radical, grandstand assault on white liberals, the Killens group would have had the public believe that the Association of Artists for Freedom was a group of intellectuals prepared to play a unique role in the new Negro movement. They intimated that the Town Hall debate represented their debut—merely a preview of more important and provocative things to come. But since the legacy of the past, with its irresponsibilities, defects and incompetencies could not be repudiated, it was predictable at the very outset that the Association would accomplish absolutely nothing of importance. It would produce or initiate nothing original, unique, creative or positive insofar as the new Negro movement is concerned.

As a group, Artists for Freedom was much too eclectic; it was loaded internally with opposing loyalties. Lomax has nothing much in common with the Killens group, and Baldwin—the biggest literary name—was, in effect, subordinated to it. Because she was younger than most of the members and a West Indian of traditionally "divided" loyalties, Paule Marshall's exact position and sentiments vis-à-vis the Killens group were not very clear. LeRoi Jones, the youngest member of all, was the only one in the Artists for Freedom group who really deserved the title of Literary Radical. But the literary radicalism of a Jones is a far cry from what passed for radicalism in the Harlem leftwing and ultimately produced the middle-class, Left-tinged conformity of Killens, Hansberry, Davis and Dee.

The Artists for Freedom practiced the old leftwing organizational tactic of presenting a united front in the literary field, with sponsorship by "name" writers who were not previously leftwing. By the 1960's, however, this tactic had lost both its meaning and effectiveness, inasmuch as the political leftwing has lost its old power to persuade and control. More than that, the Killens group, once established, was faced with an entirely new situation in the Negro movement which demanded more creative ideas from intellectuals than the Artists for Freedom were capable of contributing.

Back in the early 1950's it had been the custom of the Harlem leftwing to denounce the NAACP, the Urban League, and A. Philip Randolph for their slow-footed reformism. But in 1959 the Communist Party switched its position to the support of the NAACP, *et al.*, on racial integration. Thus when new, younger civil rights forces came into play, accusing the NAACP of conservatism and challenging its divine right to official leadership, the Communist-oriented leftwing found itself in a rather uncomfortable predicament. Entirely apparent in the Artists for Freedom Town Hall debate, this predicament was compounded by the presence of an issue, felt if not heard, that has plagued the radical leftwing ever since the 1920's and has not yet been solved: What should be the relationship of art to politics, and vice versa? For many reasons this question did not become crucially pertinent to the Negro movement until the post-World War II period.

In the late 1940's, the Committee for the Negro in the Arts,*

---

* A forerunner of the CNA was the Negro Playwrights Company, founded in 1940 by Theodore Ward, the leading Negro leftwing playwright. According to Harlem gossip at that time, this group represented a rival movement to ANT. Ward's group

(popularly known as CNA) was organized as the cultural arm of the Harlem political leftwing. At first CNA was located downtown on lower Fifth Avenue; then, under pressure of criticism for being too far away from the Negro community, it moved its offices to Harlem. This organization had as its overall cultural objective, the integration of the Negro into the American cultural arts. Thus, CNA could not have been called, for example, the American Negro Committee *on* the Arts.

From the very outset the Committee was interracial and included white Communists, white leftwing sympathizers and Left-liberals. Although the Committee's most influential and thriving activity was in theater, it was not simply a theatrical group but rather a cultural organization with a theater section. It was this theater section, however, that accomplished the most in Harlem, when there. Moreover, this section differed from all the rest in that it was actually political (although politically-oriented in a fashion that retarded its growth and influence). The other departments of CNA did not achieve very much.

When the CNA was formed, a number of writers, journalists and fledgling social critics (including myself) joined it. Some of us, however, were critical of its implicit aims. Our ideas on the matter were nor too clear-cut or definitive. We were certainly not against integration of the Negro in the arts; but at the time, it struck us that since Negroes had no flourishing ethnic cultural arts institutions in their own community, pursuing this integration theme was like launching a campaign with no thought of building a starting base.

America's entry into World War II had marked the beginning of the end of Negro ethnic group insularity; an entirely new phase of American Negro life was underway. Until 1940, the word integration had not appeared, even in the language of the NAACP; the war inspired the first articles in *Crisis*, NAACP's official publi-

---

produced his *Big White Fog*, which, according to *Freedomways*, was "the first play to deal with the Garvey movement," but it did not have a successful run in Harlem. Loften Mitchell writes that not long afterward, "Financial difficulties brought this organization to an untimely end." In 1947, Ward's play, *Our Lan'*, about the Reconstruction South, failed on Broadway after a successful off-Broadway debut—raising the question as to whether the Negro writer's values are congenial to Broadway's.

cation, demanding the "integration of the armed forces." (Prior to that, the organization's theme had been civil rights.) But the spirit of the Negro intellectuals was already one step ahead of the NAACP's legal considerations of *de facto* segregation. For example, during the 1940's, articles of social and cultural criticism appeared in magazines like *Phylon, the Atlanta University Review of Race and Culture,* originally founded by the Negro scholar, W.E.B. DuBois. Such articles showed the first tendency of Negro intellectuals to argue against the racial tag in art, literature, education, and so forth.

When the Committee for the Negro in the Arts came into the field in 1947, it took a position that corroborated and legitimized the trend that had shortly before undermined the idea of the purely Negro ethnic theater (*i.e.,* the then defunct American Negro Theater).

The ANT, which had been the main training ground and creative hope of the Negro in the theater, had collapsed during the last half of the 1940's amidst ugly rumors, scandal and accusations of all manner of malfeasance, including misappropriation of funds. Up to the end of World War II, however, this organization had an excellent record of achievement, despite the fact that it had to be launched in Harlem under very unfavorable physical and financial circumstances. By 1945 the American Negro Theater had been able to boast a list of 264 patrons and subscribers, including many substantial citizens, Negro and white, both inside and outside Harlem. That year the directors were able to state:

> The A.N.T. is a tax exempt organization. Your subscriptions and contributions are deductible for your Federal Income Tax. Very early in the post-war period, the A.N.T. expects to start building its playhouse. Construction of this building with modern producing facilities will cost approximately $250,000. Many of our patrons have already made donations to this fund. Won't you be among those who are helping us to build this playhouse?

The following note from an ANT theater program for the 1944-45 season expressed the organization's artistic aims:

> The American Negro Theater is a permanent cooperative acting company co-ordinating and perfecting the related arts of the theater; eventually deriving its own theater craft and acting style

by combining all standard forms and putting to artful use the
fluency and rhythm that lies in the Negro's special gifts. The
group, professionally trained for the past 4 years, has presented
several notable productions. Arthur Pollack, one of New York's
major critics, said in reviewing one of its productions:

"The American Negro Theater looks like it could amount to
something very important in the theatrical life of New York. It is
a city long in need of a first rate Negro theater. . . . And this
perhaps is that Negro theater. . . . The group will have a world
beating a path to its door if it continues as it has begun."

Yet despite this auspicious beginning, the ANT collapsed, and
ever since, the question keeps recurring among Negroes in the
theater—Why? Frank Fields, one of the original members of the
ANT, and a gifted musician and theatrical composer, expressed
to me his opinion—"*The people in the ANT didn't really believe
in a Negro theater.*" He was, without a doubt, correct: A separate
Negro Theater simply was not wanted. But if this was so, why was
it launched in the first place? For one thing, opportunities for
Negroes in the white theater were non-existent for the many, and
scarce for the few; moreover, those few who worked occasionally,
did not care at all for their stereotyped roles.

A conflict over aims was implicit in the ANT's institutional
structure. In other words, characteristic of all Negro movements
and groups, especially in the cultural field, there existed ideological conflicts over integration versus ethnic group identity. This
was clearly demonstrated in the conflicting motivations of the
playwrights involved—for whom a Negro theater was mandatory,
and those of the actors—for whom *any theater* that provided work
was acceptable. Generally speaking, in Negro theater it is the
actors rather than the playwrights who dominate the thinking;
therefore, the ANT was essentially an actors' institution, despite
the fact that its founder and director was the playwright, Abram
Hill.* It followed then, that once the greener-looking fields of
"integration in the theater" downtown beckoned to the actors,
ANT's all-Negro theater idea would be undermined. The same
ethnic-identity vs. integration conflict within ANT was carried

* Hill was the author of ANT's first real hit, *On Strivers Row*, a satire on Negro
middle-class values. His assistant director at ANT was Frederick O'Neal, an actor,
now the president of Actor's Equity.

over into CNA: the only difference was that CNA *openly* stated its integrationist aims—thus further discouraging and preventing the founding of an institutional cultural base within the ethnic community.

At the time of the ANT's collapse, about one hundred professional or student Negro actors, writers and technicians were listed on its membership roster. Of this impressive number of hopefuls, only a small handful are around today to boast of some success in the theater—Ruby Dee, Ossie Davis, Sidney Poitier, Alice Childress, Maxwell Glanville, Harry Belafonte and Frederick O'Neal. Interestingly enough, with the exception of O'Neal, all these survivors found their pathway to later prominence in the integrated theater—through the Harlem political leftwings, especially through the Committee for the Negro in the Arts.* It should be pointed out, however, that participation in the Harlem radical leftwing does not imply actual Communist Party membership.

While the CNA was being organized, efforts were still being made to revive the collapsed ANT. *Freight,* one of the short, original plays produced in this connection, featured Sidney Poitier. These revival efforts failed, however, and the American Negro Theater passed from the scene. The leftwing cultural forces had moved into postwar prominence. Sidney Poitier was soon to be seen on the stages of a theater operated by CNA. He was also featured off-Broadway in *Longitude 49,* written by a white leftwing playwright. Some ten years later, Poitier along with Ruby Dee (and later Ossie Davis) were the stars of Lorraine Hansberry's initial Broadway success, *A Raisin in the Sun.* It is hardly coincidence that to this day the names of Poitier, Davis and Dee (and others) repeatedly turn up in juxtaposition. After all, these artists have in common the same literary, artistic and political interests, and have functioned as an in-group since CNA's founding. In fact, even in 1950, before the CNA's theater section presented its first serious productions, the exclusive nature of this organization caused people in Harlem's cultural circles to refer to it derisively as "The Committee for *Some* Negroes in the Arts." Since the cultural problems of Harlem demanded a broad demo-

---

* Poitier, Childress, Belafonte and Glanville were members of CNA. Davis and Dee came through the leftwing via other routes.

cratic approach in community institutions, the early demise of CNA was foredoomed. The ANT, for all its subsequent failures, had at least been more intrinsically democratic.

The anti-white liberal outburst at Town Hall in 1964 was completely out of character for Negro artists who had maintained a strictly pro-white policy in cultural and political affairs all the way from the 1950's through the 1960's. In Harlem, back in the early 1950's, the Killens group had always been in strong, silent favor of interracial unity, in line with the Negro-white unity ("Black and White Unite and Fight") theme of the radical leftwing. White Communists and leftwingers, unlike white liberals later on, could do no wrong. Back then, the reasons were quite clear: At the time of CNA's founding these aspiring novelists, dramatists, poets, actors and performers could not afford to be attacking the downtown whites—radical or liberal—with whom they were in league. The writers all had hopes of getting their novels published, their dramas produced (whether in Harlem or beyond), their poetry and articles published in *Masses and Mainstream;** the actors needed work wherever possible. Thus, in those days, neither Ossie Davis and Lorraine Hansberry, nor John Killens, ever spoke out against white radical control in the Harlem leftwing, as they were to, against white liberal control in civil rights organizations in 1964. They were not then so sensitive to the glaring truth—Negro radicals did not have an independent organization, *even inside their black community.*

Negro intellectuals may rail against the whites when it suits their purpose, but they know their own middle class does not support, and rarely understands or appreciates, art and culture. Hence, the radical revolt against white liberal influence in the civil rights movement came at a time of crisis to be sure, but too late. Members of Artists for Freedom had by then achieved varying levels of fame and success—and only the naïve could take their newfound yen for independent organization seriously. The proper time for such a grand show of "black independence" should have been around 1950.

However, while the CNA inner-circle was being courted and pampered by the white leftwing hierarchy, there *was* a revolt

---

* Formerly the Communists' main cultural publication, now defunct.

among one group of leftwing Negro writers against the white paternalism of the Communist-influenced political and cultural apparatus in Harlem. These writers were largely journalists, part-time critics, and novices struggling with ideas and craft problems. A few of them, snubbed by CNA, had formed themselves into a group that, by implication, was opposed to much of what comprised CNA's cultural policy. These writers felt the need to break away from enforced interracialism and attempt to deal with Negro reality as they, *as Negroes,* saw it. They realized that a leftwing, interracial organization such as CNA, could *never* take root in Harlem as a representative ethnic cultural institution. Yet, what even they did not fully grasp at the time, was that CNA *was never meant to.**

This dissident group formed the Harlem Writers Club, and as such, manifested the first ideological split within the Harlem leftwing movement. The issues at stake were several: the political, ethnic, and cultural implications of integration; interracialism; the role of whites in the political and cultural affairs of Harlem; interracial marriage; nationalism; Marxist Communism; Negro leadership philosophy; form and content in literature and art from the Negro's point of view; the Communist Party creed of socialist realism in aesthetics, and all such related problems. In postwar Harlem, the social climate, within and without, was inexorably forcing all of these issues to the fore. To this extent, the younger radical generation was forced to voice them as political issues. But since none of these issues was ever rationally or intelligently thought through, by the Harlem leftwing, much conflict, confusion, bitterness and rivalry developed. The resulting ideological split was profound, and it could not be resolved because there was no one able to deal with its implications. Merely to voice doubts about these real problems brought one into collision with the leadership hierarchy of the left, which interpreted all such personal critical feeling as being in opposition to the official line of the Communist Party on Negroes. Inevitably, this suppression of independent views resulted in the buildup of deep resentments, which finally in 1950 exploded in a bitter attack by members of the Harlem Writers Club on the role of whites. The late Benja-

* Another echo of ANT's problems.

min J. Davis, the ranking Negro Communist leader, was then forced to step in and dispatch scores of whites out of Harlem—against the will of the top Communist leaders downtown.

Although this episode and its implications were never recorded, and the revolt was not broad enough to be known outside the Harlem leftwing, or Communist headquarters downtown, it had distinct repercussions. It was, in effect, the first indication that the postwar radical leftwing was politically doomed to extinction in the Negro community. The Negro movement, as a whole, was maturing: Now open to debate were more new issues and new complexities than the mechanical, over-simplistic, unreal political line of the Communists could ever hope to deal with. At the bottom of it all was the historical reality of the nationality question, a new resurgence of the "rejected strain." This time, however, the militants formed a literary front against the aesthetics implicit in cultural integration. Even then, the rebels, not fully aware of where they were heading, also had to direct their attack on Communist politics. Thus Harlem had its revolt against Stalinism six years before Hungary. As it turned out, this early literary revolt presaged a new wave of Negro writers. They were to take more than a decade to mature, yet they posed pertinent, creative questions not fully answered to this day.

The political leaders of the Harlem Left, under whose forbearance CNA functioned, tolerated artistic and cultural ideas only insofar as they could be used for their own political ends. Their aesthetic judgment of art, literature, drama, poetry, music and dance was guided by what is called in the Soviet Union, "socialist realism":

> The Communist Party is a bureaucratically controlled power center . . . it must necessarily politicize all aspects of life. Negro art, literature, theatre, or sports can claim no pluralistic values in themselves. They are judged in terms of their contribution to the realization of immediate—and vaguely ultimate—Party goals. A Negro painter who does not depict Negro suffering may be considered a slave of "bastard modernism." A Negro novelist who does not take Negro struggle as a theme may be dismissed as an opportunist seeking acceptance by the white elite and concerning himself only with the large royalty checks that might come his way. The colored dramatist is not worth his salt if his plays do

not portray revolt against existing patterns. (Of course, during the war period these dramas were expected to tone down the protest angle.) The race historian who fails to provide a radical past for the Negro is judged to be a conscious betrayer of the race—if the Party line at the time demands a radical past. The same for the Negro composer.[1]

In American terms, socialist realism means several vague but related attitudes about the role of art as a mirror of human beings functioning in class society. However, to the crude mentalities of the political Left, socialist realism, in Negro terms, means the portrayal of the Negro struggle against jimcrow in pure, uncomplicated, black and white terms. (Even better would be the depiction of Negroes and white workers struggling together against jimcrow, or better yet, a triumvirate of Negroes, white workers and white Communists joined in this struggle.) Broadly speaking, any civil rights theme can fall within the aesthetic range of socialist realism, and if such a theme just happens to coincide with a current or past issue prominent in radical politics, that is all the better. The political leftwing will then support it with dutiful critical observations about this or that aspect of artistic interpretation of class truth. In the artistic treatment of Negro history, slave heroes come in for special consideration, with John Brown and Frederick Douglass leading the list of the acceptable. It goes without saying that the Negro artist must hew to the line of naturalism or realism—anything else is suspected of being decadent or formalistic. In this way the favored Negro is given political and organizational backing but kept "in line," while others who attempt to seek other forms or themes in their creative efforts are weeded out and pushed aside by "natural selection."*

An undercurrent of critical rejection of the restrictions of socialist realism loomed behind the split between the Harlem Writers Club and the CNA. However, this rejection was never made ex-

---

[1] Wilson Record, *op. cit.,* p. 292.

* On socialist realism, see Langston Hughes, *I Wonder as I Wander, op. cit.,* p. 121: "I did not believe political directives could be successfully applied to creative writing. They might apply to the preparation of tracts and pamphlets, yes, but not to poetry or fiction, which had to be valid, I felt, had to express as truthfully as possible the individual emotions and reactions of the writer . . ." Hughes, however, never made an issue of this in the political Left during the 1930's.

plicit. Since the dissidents themselves were not prepared to deal with the problem in an articulate fashion, an open debate within the Harlem leftwing over this particular aesthetic question never developed. Nonetheless, the conflict served to wean those writers who were instinctively anti-socialist realist further and further away from the political leftwing. Most of them instinctively knew that in order to influence a broad audience, a Harlem literary and cultural movement had to use forms that were steeped in the popular idiom and images, yet as free as possible of alien political propaganda. In other words, the thematic material and ideas expressed had to be purely ethnic, no matter how the artist preferred to mold or experiment with them. In this regard, the writer was all-important and *all* writers had to be brought together whether they were realists, naturalists, symbolists, avant-gardists, existentialists, satirists, or whatever. No political divisions could be allowed among Negro writers and artists over these different intellectual approaches.

There is nothing wrong with the art of protest* or political agitprop *in its place;* but it was a foregone conclusion and an unavoidable fact, that the CNA, with its white leftwing patronage and control and its myopic leadership, would favor *only* the socialist realist writers of civil rights or protest material. Scores of talented Negroes at first embraced the CNA, and then backed off at the first intimation that it was to represent an exclusive, leftwing elite. Though it was not clearly understood by the critics of the CNA at that time, the vital question was: *What would be the precise nature of the role of the Negro creative intellectual without the context of the new Negro movement and in the broad politics of American culture as a whole?* By stressing the integration of the Negro in the arts, the CNA had put the cart before the horse; in effect, the ends were established before the means were in view.

In the fall of 1949, the Harlem Writers Club demanded (and they were the first to do so) that the Harlem political leftwing establish a Harlem cultural commission to oversee the complicated and aggravated situation in the community. This brought the dissident group into open conflict with both the leftwing political

---

* James Baldwin deplores this literary conceit in his essay "Everybody's Protest Novel," but had to use it in his play, *Blues for Mr. Charlie.*

leaders in Harlem and the inner circle of CNA. The political leaders, however, could not at that time avoid taking up the question of the commission, for cultural ideas were very much in the air.

It so happened that in the August, 1949, issue of *Masses and Mainstream*, Doxey Wilkerson, one of the leading Negro intellectuals in the Communist Party, had published an article, "Negro Culture: Heritage and Weapon," which had caused quite a stir in cultural circles uptown and downtown. The Harlem Writers Club cited this article in making their demands. Under pressure, the political leaders agreed to form a cultural commission but immediately took steps to handpick its hierarchy from the CNA's inner circle. Members of the Harlem Writers Club protested against such exclusion, since they were the first to project the idea, and the gap between them and CNA widened. The rejected strain of nationality consciousness was in conflict with the integrationist trend over community cultural policies (backed to the hilt by the Party line). This heated battle was carried into the Communist Party's Harlem headquarters by the Chairman of the Club (myself) and the Co-Chairman. The wrangle that ensued was extremely caustic because the political leaders knew the real motivations behind the Club's militant confrontation. The idea behind the formation of a Harlem Cultural Commission was to establish not only cultural but political autonomy in Harlem's leftwing, in order to break the control and domination that whites exerted through their grip on CNA. It was a bold stroke that could not possibly have succeeded, in view of the way power in the Communist Party was exerted from the top down. This very open demand for autonomy only brought the wrath of the ruling-party whites down upon the members of the Harlem Writers Club, who had always been regarded with deep suspicion and distrust. Against their will, however, the political leaders were forced to call what was probably the first cultural conference on Negro problems that the Communist Party ever held. It took place downtown in the Jefferson School of Social Science (the Marxist Institute of the period), and the leading participants were, of course, the CNA leaders—who had merely to persist in defending their party line. The conference, in effect, was loaded and stacked against the Harlem Writers Club. Among those present were V.J. Jerome, the Party's top cultural commissar, and the Negro writer Lloyd Brown, associate editor of *Masses and Mainstream*.*

The *cause célèbre* of this conference turned out to be Ernest Kaiser, then a member of the Harlem Writers Club. In the course of making some critical sallies upon the white Marxists during the debate, Kaiser made the fatal mistake of referring to (the then heretical) Leon Trotsky. He was merely illustrating how, by certain policies, Communists had played into the hands of their political enemies; he was by no means pro-Trotskyist. But certain Marxist-Communists, including Jerome and Brown, were already gunning for Kaiser's scalp for an article he had published in 1948. In this article, which Kaiser called "Racial Dialectics," he had reviewed some of the ideological issues at stake in the controversy between Herbert Aptheker, the white Marxist-historian, and Gunnar Myrdal, sociologist and author-editor of the well-known study of American Negro-White relations, *American Dilemma*. Kaiser had referred to Aptheker disparagingly as a "near-Marxist," and his critique of Aptheker's reply to Myrdal, "The Negro People in America," amply revealed that the man whom the Communists had installed as *the* authoritative historian and spokesman on the Negro in America was decidedly a second-rate thinker. Kaiser had written: "Historically, Aptheker is also superficial and liberalistic when he states that Negro slaves revolted merely because they were human beings with 'developed reasoning facilities' and 'the glorious urge to improve themselves and their environment.' This is un-Marxian and liberal in tone."[2]

This theoretical blast, leveled at one of the most hallowed sacred cows in the white Left hierarchy, caused irate tremors in the Party that were a long time dying out. In this essay Kaiser had also taken two other Communist luminaries to task—Lloyd Brown and Doxey Wilkerson—who had written the introduction to Aptheker's reply to Myrdal. Kaiser had criticized Wilkerson and Brown for revealing "their middle-class hangovers" and for refusing "to admit that Negro psychology is unique and different from that of the whites."

At the cultural conference, once Kaiser had left himself open to

<hr>

* In 1951, Lloyd Brown published a novel, *Iron City*, that became the shining example of literary socialist realism.

[2] Ernest Kaiser, "Racial Dialectics—The Aptheker—Myrdal School Controversy," *Phylon*, Atlanta University, Georgia, Fourth Quarter, 1948, p. 298.

counterattack, Lloyd Brown seized the opportunity to bury the rebel Harlem Writers Club for all time. He delivered a strident political attack on Kaiser for smuggling Trotskyite propaganda into the conference, an attack that impugned all the intentions of the Harlem Writers Club and nullified its efforts. The group had always been suspected of harboring a cell of anti-leadership critics and disrupters, and Brown's political assault was also a demonstrative act of personal disassociation. All of this affords a modicum of insight into the seriousness and complexity of the Harlem situation as it redounded on these idealistic, militant, but inexperienced Negro writers. It was an impossible task for them to establish a positive orientation within the ideological and cultural confusion that was Harlem in those days.

Aside from the fact that the Harlem Cultural Commission never came into being, this conference caused the Harlem Writers Club to come under direct investigation by the Party's cultural commission for its political deviations. Under threat of forcible disbandment and excommunication from the Harlem leftwing movement, the writers were placed on a kind of probationary "good behavior," during which period they had to tone down their rebellious criticism of cultural policies.

By playing a waiting game, the group resisted efforts to bring it under CNA authority, and managed to keep intact until 1951, when Paul Robeson's *Freedom* newspaper was established. Nonetheless, the ill-fated cultural conference had divided all the potential writers into factions; because of this factionalism, the Harlem cultural movement of the postwar period lacked the organizational viability that would have enabled it to cope with all the new issues and challenges that were to arise. There were not even any independent Negro magazines devoted to cultural problems published until the 1960's, although there was a dire need for same. When Benjamin Brown, one of the members of the Harlem Writers Club, did attempt to launch *The Harlem Quarterly* in 1949, it failed, for lack of financial support, after a few issues. The writers who were won over to the policies of the CNA were not helpful. Having accepted CNA's policies of integration in the arts, they also accepted the leftwing's socialist realist indoctrination, all of which ultimately had to lead to the abandonment of the Harlem community as a cultural base.

For a long time, Communist whites and their sympathizers on

both the political and cultural fronts had much of a free hand in Harlem and did as they pleased. This is what Lorraine Hansberry saw when she first arrived, giving her the impression that "white people were always welcomed in Harlem," as she said thirteen years later.[3] But Miss Hansberry never had to work politically or culturally around Harlem's grass roots. Her frame of reference in Harlem was the leftwing interracial set, which had little to do with broad Harlem sentiments—especially that segment represented by the nationalists. By 1950, even within the Harlem leftwing, the anti-white sentiment was steadily mounting: Communist whites became more and more overbearing and arrogant and began to overplay their hand.

From 1949-51, the Communist Party's cultural apparatus downtown stepped up its white "colonization" tactics in Harlem. The CNA, of course, was strenuously promoted as the dominant cultural organization on the Harlem scene. Toward other independent theater groups, such as the Elks Community Theater—an all Negro group seriously attempting to cultivate an ethnic style— CNA's superior attitude was: You work with *us;* we don't have to work with *you.** White Communists appeared in the audience of plays staged by playwright Loften Mitchell's Harlem Showcase and openly criticized the plays because the content was not socialist realist or "protest." Mitchell† once co-produced a play with music that was purely entertainment, and was forced to reprimand leftwing whites who wanted to know why such a play was even being produced in Harlem and why certain people were working in it. Negroes with leftwing political affiliations were criticized for working in these productions as actors or even as technicians. Therefore, the interracial Harlem theater audience that developed as a result of CNA's programs, served only the organizational and publicity interests of CNA, for it was CNA's taste that dictated the artistic tone.

---

[3] *Village Voice,* June 6, 1963, interview, p. 3.
* To bring the Elks into the CNA fold, the Communists sent uptown a number of young white theater people. Their assignment was to "interracialize" the Elks out of character, and cause internal frictions and resentments. The Communist dictum on the Negro, after all, was that there would be no ethnic togetherness.
† Guggenheim Fellowship winner of 1956-1957 for his play, *A Land Beyond the River.*

Since Harlem is the key community in American Negro cultural affairs, the postwar failure in Harlem is the root cause of the entire Negro cultural situation today. Sadly, the integration mirage hides the fact that Negroes are losing ground in practically every artistic field. Theater seasons have come and gone with Negro playwrights unrepresented. Negroes produce no films, not even documentaries. Negro novels are few and unexceptional in literary scope and critical literature is practically non-existent. Leaving out the special area of jazz, the same low level of creativity is the case in all fields. The basic impulse behind all creativity is national or ethnic-group identity, but in the process of racial integration the Negro creative intelligentsia sheds this identity day by day.

However, the cultural integration trend as pronounced by the Harlem cultural leftwing has had to run a natural course. Its inner circle had to evolve over the years into the Association of Artists for Freedom, before the innate fallacies and illusions of this trend could become demonstrable. Only a few Negro writers comprehended in the 1950's that the political leftwing in New York was entering into a decline coincident with yet another one of those periodic cycles of Harlem's recurring urge for cultural revival. In this regard, it has to be seen that previous cultural revivals (e.g., the so-called Negro renaissance of the 1920's) were social phenomena native to Negro life, but always occurring within the context of Negro-white relations. It was always a question of either a reaction against white aesthetic values and accommodating the tastes of white audiences, *or* whether Negro creative energies were to be directed toward ethnic self-expression. In the 1920's, white audiences discovered the Negro and ran to Harlem to enjoy his art. In the late 1940's and 1950's, the white political leftwing ran to Harlem in order to establish a political hegemony over Negro art and artists—for the purposes of distorting and wielding both into pragmatic weapons. Art, of course, is always a weapon—depending on who uses it and for what purposes.

In a country such as the United States, with its unique and peculiar history of race relations, the question of the content of national artforms takes on a sociological character and impact unduplicated elsewhere in the world. The cultural arts are the mirror of the spiritual condition of a nation, and the use of a nation's social ingredients in its art reveals a great deal about how a nation looks at itself. Thus, the way in which the social relations in the United States between black and white are reflected in the artforms, represents an open book of the American psyche. The impact of the Negro presence on American artforms has been tremendous, and also historically conditioned; but this fact the American psyche is loath to admit in its established critical schools of thought. As Americans, white people in America are also Westerners, and American white values are shaped by Western cultural values. Americans possess no critical standards for the cultural arts that have not been derived from the European experience. On the other hand, the basic ingredients for native (non-European) American originality in artforms derive from American Negroes who came to America from a non-Western background. We need only point to American music to prove the point. Thus in American art a peculiar kind of cultural duality exists, which is an ideological reflection of the basic attitudes of blacks and whites toward each other. One can begin to understand how this aesthetic acculturation functions in the American ideology, by studying the ideas of a Western philosopher-aesthetician like the late Bernard Berenson: "But even the arts of China and of India, remarkable and deeply human as they are and with histories of their own worthy of every attention, are not history for us Europeans. Only to the extent that we influenced and affected them, and they influenced and affected our arts, should they find a place in our history."[4] What Berenson said elsewhere, about *African* art, was even less appreciative; for in a mind such as his, what is seen as exotic can never share the same pedestal with what is classic. What critical status, then, can Americans allow Afro-American artforms, if American culture is merely an extension of the Western cultural tradition?

Western artforms have long enjoyed the beneficent patronage and material support of the bourgeois classes, even if many an artist died before his contemporary bourgeois countrymen realized that he had actually once been alive. Thus, despite the fact that upper-class tastes were often scandalized by plebeian aesthetics and

---

[4] Bernard Berenson, *Aesthetics and History* (New York: Doubleday, Anchor Edition, 1948), p. 257.

artistic revolts in the creative ranks of class deserters among the intellectuals, the politics of art in the Western world have, generally speaking, been more democratic than the politics of class warfare over property rights, and class privilege. In the United States, however, the Negro creative artist has never been given any substantial degree of patronage or material support from *any* section of the American upper, middle or lower bourgeois classes. More than that, the Negro creative artist has not even enjoyed the support, patronage or acclaim of members of his *own* Negro bourgeois classes. They, for the most part, are either uneducated or disinterested philistines when it comes to cultural matters; or at worst, only lukewarm, if not thoroughly opposed, to what passes for Negro or Afro-American art expressions. In other words, the Negro bourgeoisie, as a class, espouses no cultural philosophy with regard to Negroes as an ethnic group, that is not integrationist. Thus, the Negro creative intellectuals who emerge do not have the sponsorship of their own upper classes, and must seek the feeble, parsimonious and grudging support of the whites in order to survive. They further compound their own naked uncelebrated position by fighting for integration, in order to approximate the white standard—which has become more and more untenable, decadent and unfulfilling, even for white Americans.

Western culture, in terms of the vitality of its artforms, has long been in a state of aesthetic decline, and this degeneration has been most glaring in the United States.

What, then, does integration in the arts really mean for the Negro creative intellectual?

The Negro community must always be the last refuge and the ultimate hope of the American leftwing, when it is on the downgrade. And Negro efforts in the cultural fields will always be fair game for the leftwing, because the Negro has been forced to exist in a perpetual state of cultural and artistic unfulfillment. That he should be the ethnic source of America's only native and original artistic ingredients, and yet remain, at the same time, this country's most culturally deprived minority, represents a profound paradox that must soon be resolved. It is a crucial problem, more crucial and also more unique than most Americans, even most Negroes, realize. For the question of whether or not America will ever arrive at her potential of becoming a first-rate nation in cultural attainments (which she never has been), depends on its solution. But this Negro cultural problem cannot be solved through the social eventualities of what is called integration, initiated *outside* the Negro communities. It must be tackled and its solution pursued, from inside Harlem. For the key Negro community *is* Harlem, and Harlem's cultural defeat is but another side of its overall problems of economic degradation and political subserviency to all parties, whether leftwing or conventional.

There was yet another event that was to affect the Harlem cultural scene. All these white leftwing luminaries—actors, directors, writers, producers and hangers-on—had come East after being expelled from Hollywood as a result of the McCarthy hearings. They were still being harassed in, or banned from, the cultural media (radio, television, and Broadway theater), and began to flock to Harlem in the 1950's and pay homage to the in-group of the Committee for the Negro in the Arts. The stage was thus set, and the road paved, for the exodus of creative talent out of Harlem. It led to the collapse of CNA, *Freedom* newspaper and all the other cultural groups of the time, leaving a cultural desert in the wake. Integration in the arts, à la leftwing, was off and running. The Supreme Court Decision on School Integration, handed down in 1954, only seemed the legal and moral sanctioning of the mood of Harlem's leftwing elite to integrate the white world of art and culture—"one at a time"—as Ossie Davis was to remark nine years later.

Freedom Newspaper

In 1949-50, prior to the time Paul Robeson's *Freedom* newspaper was established, the Communist-oriented leftwing movement was undergoing its worst siege of Federal prosecution since the Palmer Raids of the early 1920's. I refrain from using the word "persecution" (which would be more appropriate) only because there are no more vindictive persecutors of "enemies" and "renegades" than Communists, when *they* have that kind of power in their hands. But it was an ironic fact that the decline and fall of the Communist leftwing should occur precisely in that decade, the 1950's, that was to see the American Negro assume his most militant drive for civil rights and/or integration. More pointedly, the Montgomery bus boycott, which electrified the nation in 1955, came right on the heels of the collapse of *Freedom* newspaper and just before the resounding revelations of Soviet Communist immorality disclosed at the 20th Congress of the Russian Party in Moscow. These revelations wreaked factional havoc within the American Communist Party and just about finished the movement as a political force of real consequence in America.

The truth of the matter was that the American Communist leftwing met a fate it richly deserved, and the effects of the Moscow Congress of 1956 only corroborated what many dissident leftist Negroes had been saying about the influence of the Communist leftwing in the Negro community. Communist practice, effective in the 1930's, had remained a powerful determinant behind the political philosophy of a great number of white radical intellectuals. But it was hardly relevant to the new period that followed World War II and to the greatly changed Negro situation in particular. The new Negro radicals who emerged after World War II, however, were not able to create a radical philosophy of their own persuasive enough to counter the militant dogmatism of the Communist Party.

White radical social theory (*i.e.,* Marxism), as practiced in the United States, has only been truly applicable as it concerns the history of white people and white classes. When it comes to Negro history, Marxism invariably departs from truth. Marxism could not deal with the fact that just prior to the Civil War, two opposing trends were firmly established in Negro leadership thought, and have persisted to this very day. As pointed out earlier, this conflict was between the integrationist (Douglass) and the nationality (Delany) strains. It can be shown that Marxist-Communism has been able to wield political influence in Negro life only during those periods when the integrationist trend was predominant. Thus the Communist Party's influence on Negroes was extremely limited during the 1920's heyday of Garvey nationalism. The Communists made inroads into Negro life beginning with the 1930's and maintained a degree of influence well into the 1940's, until a new nationalistic undercurrent began to be noticeable among Negroes in the ghettoes.

Marxist-Communist historians have never been able to square their social theory with the very real nationalist-integrationist duality inherent in Negro life. They have continuously evaded the implications of this duality by their overt and consistent apotheosis of the Frederick Douglass integration trend.[1] Inside the Negro urban communities, the false historical analysis of the Communists has led to ludicrously inept and blundering methods which have kept clashing against the persistent ideology of the "rejected strain." It is a curious fact that many Negroes did not become nationalistic or anti-white until *after* they had had a taste of Communist politics. This is why nationalism cropped out inside the Communist Party on the part of Negroes who had never been active nationalists before. However, the nationality strain had already been dormant within them. As a result of this, Harlem in the late 1940's and early 1950's became a seething battleground over the issues of white leadership prerogatives. The political motivation behind Communist Party influence, beamed into Harlem, was the enforcing of "Negro-white unity" both from above and without. Thus Communist influence became a retard-

[1] See Herbert Aptheker's one-sided treatment of "The Developing Negro Liberation Movement," in *A Documentary History of Negro People in the United States* (New York: Citadel Press, 1951), pp. 827-928.

ing, divisive, and destructive political force. The privileges and prerogatives of even the lowest rank and file white outweighed those of the highest Negro Communist leader; yet those among the rank and file Negroes who resisted white influence were subjected to all kinds of "disciplinary" measures, including expulsions. As a result of these practices, although there was no community that allowed the Communist Party the freedoms of speech, assembly and movement as did the Harlem community, the Party's influence in Harlem was nonetheless destroyed.

The waning and gradual weakening of Communist Party influence in Harlem leftwing affairs presented the opportunity for all the dissident Negro radicals to seize control of the organizational, political and cultural apparatus and form a self-determining movement in the *real* interests of the community, free from outside political manipulation. Thus the emergence of Paul Robeson's *Freedom* newspaper in January, 1951, appeared to be a manifestation of that rising hope; and for many radical dissidents, Paul Robeson became the very symbol of black independence. How terribly naïve many of us were in that hope! *Freedom* newspaper all too clearly demonstrated the innate inability of the Negro radical intelligentsia to create an independent political and cultural philosophy. Or it is more correct to say that this intelligentsia could not create a new philosophy that would encompass the "nationality" strain. Their own radical philosophy was nothing more than integration, couched in leftwing phraseology, which came to mean less and less to the Negro ghetto masses.

The members of the Harlem Writers Club, the rebel group, were among those who looked to Paul Robeson for their salvation. He was especially attractive to them as a cultural personality in a movement whose cultural approaches were exceedingly narrow and provincial. Robeson, however, turned out to be neither very independent nor much of a leader, in terms of political astuteness and imagination. This may sound paradoxical to many in view of Robeson's great personal magnetism. But a close examination of his views shows that he was not at all an original thinker. His effectiveness was hampered by a considerable idealistic naïveté about racial politics in America. Although the inside gossip had it that the Communists were having considerable difficulty controlling him, the number of articles appearing in *Freedom* by and about

Communists, revealed that he was in fact pretty much under their control.

As a result of this situation, *Freedom* newspaper became the end of the road for the short-lived but pioneering existence of the Harlem Writers Club. The literary rebels soon discovered that they were not really wanted on *Freedom* as long as they remained a separate entity. The club had voted to lend its support to the building of this newspaper as the authentic voice of Harlem radicalism (as they saw it), but its members were very subtly discouraged and eliminated by the ruling Communist faction. In other words, they were not considered to be a part of the literary and cultural in-group already established as the ruling elite in the Committee for the Negro in the Arts. Having rebelled against CNA's "party line," they were a club of marked men. In 1951, the group disbanded. Only two of its members eventually made peace and went back into the *Freedom* fold. As for the rest, they departed one by one from the Harlem leftwing movement, eventually ending their political careers to become independent writers of one kind or another. The Harlem Writers Club, itself, had suffered internally all the strains, ambivalences and conflicts over political loyalties that were characteristic of the Harlem postwar period, when the first indications of a new Negro movement appeared. Yet, half-unconsciously it had initiated a trend that was not to bear fruit until more than a decade later.

Under the symbolic leadership of Paul Robeson, *Freedom* lasted almost five years (1951-1955). During that time, despite Robeson's doubtless sincere intentions of reaching the masses, there was very little printed in his newspaper that could have appealed to them. And nothing Robeson has ever written indicates that he grasped the implications of why his message fell short. In the 1950's, the mass Harlem mind represented the resurgence of the ideology of nationalism.

The very tenor of thinking of the people on *Freedom*'s staff—the inbred and often snobbish self-righteousness, the Negro middle-class bias—clearly showed that although one can get middle-class Negroes into the radical movement (especially on a pro-integrationist basis), they will not easily shed their middle-class prejudices. Only their verbiage changes. Thus, *Freedom* newspaper, despite all its hopped-up journalistic fever over trade-union conventions, the Fair Employment Practices Committee, Africa, the "role of Negro workers," etc., presented nothing more than the same Communist Party line of the white radicals parroted by their colored imitators. Here was no more than a Negro version of the Communist *Daily Worker*. Such a political and journalistic approach could never have a mass appeal among Negroes, even with Robeson's magnetism. That Robeson himself never seemed to understand this was a source of bitter torment to many of his rebel supporters.

However, if we critically examine the real outlook on life of the Negro intellectual stratum as represented, in this instance, by those intellectuals who gathered around *Freedom,* we can see what actually motivates this class as a whole. In this regard, *Freedom* newspaper represented two developments: First, the power group that the Committee for the Negro in the Arts had established in the Harlem leftwing cultural movement broadened their base of operational control by moving into the *Freedom* inner family. Walter Christmas, one of the top CNA leaders, became a regular contributor to *Freedom*. (Christmas, like all of the writers of the CNA-*Freedom* inner circle, also had access to the pages of *Masses and Mainstream*.) The second development centered around the personality of John O. Killens, the novelist. Not long after Killens appeared on *Freedom,* a new group, the Harlem Writers Guild, emerged under his leadership. Whether the Guild was planned before or after the establishment of *Freedom* cannot be ascertained, but it seems certain that it was projected as a countermove against the Harlem Writers Club, which disbanded at the same time the Killens group began functioning. Thus the early members of the Harlem Writers Guild took over that function on *Freedom* newspaper first proposed by the Harlem Writers Club. The latter was further discouraged from functioning on *Freedom* through the efforts of Robeson's chief editors, Louis E. Burnham and George B. Murphy, neither of whom were accomplished writers, but rather, ranking Communist politicians.

Thus the practicing journalists of the Harlem Writers Club were banned from a newspaper for political reasons by leftwing Negroes whose main integration plea was the right of Negroes to be employed on the basis of willingness and ability! By "ability" was really meant the ability to foist middle-class social aims upon so-called working-class movements. Here, middle-class radicalism and middle-class integrationism became synonomous, in an age when the mass psychology begins to turn to nationality or identity. In this context Negro middle-class radicalism, for all its militancy, can have no mass appeal. The radicalism of Negro Left intellectuals has a militant verbiage but a middle-class orientation.

What the Negro intellectuals truly want is integration and equal acceptance by their own peers among the white liberals and radicals. Hence, Negro intellectuals have developed as a stratum that expresses not the needs of the Negro masses but its own needs as an articulate class. But such needs, such acceptance, such integrated status within the integrated intellectual world, are not among the *immediate* social, political or cultural needs of the Negro masses for whom these intellectuals presume to speak. Immediately there is a very crucial contradiction at work here, but it is a contradiction that most Negro intellectuals refuse to, or are unable to, face. They find it intellectually and psychologically impossible to separate Negro *individual* needs from Negro *group* needs and hence, are forever projecting them as one and the same thing. In American society, where the democratic cult of Individualism reigns supreme, this has become a deep-rooted class rationale among Negroes.

The philosophy of integration makes the Negro intellectual "outer-directed" rather than "inner-directed"—toward basic ethnic community factors. Today it is crucially important that the implications of the integrationist philosophy be thoroughly understood, because every Negro intellectual somewhere, somehow, will succumb to its persuasions without due consideration of both its positive practicalities and utopian realities. Thus, if the Negro intellectual comes to believe that *his* aspirations lie along the integrated "outer-directed" path of social endeavor, then all of his political and cultural ideas are nothing but rationalizations for that direction. Hence white radical philosophies have been embraced by Negro intellectuals, not so much because of their *intrinsic* worth, but because of their application as militant reinforcements to integrationist aims. The Negro masses to whom the white radical philosophies are allegedly geared have rejected these philosophies for the same reasons. The superficial and opportunistic accommodation of Negro intellectuals to the Marxist philosophy as a whole is shown by the fact that, in an effort to make the ideology amenable to Negro mass psychology, they have added not a single original conception to American Marxism. Yet when Negro intellectuals embrace Marxist-Communism, they are capable of producing some of the most inflexible of Party-line bureaucrats. If they are, on the other hand, creative intellectuals, they embrace socialist realism like obedient sycophants and dutifully apply a muzzle to their own free imaginations.

Paul Robeson's *Freedom* newspaper, the last hope of Harlem radical independence, never got off the ground because of the political and creative default of the Negro leftwing intellectuals. The stance of the Association of Artists for Freedom at Town Hall was nothing but a reenactment of the role its original in-group played on *Freedom* newspaper. They spoke in radical terms on behalf of the Negro masses in the same way they spoke for the Harlem masses on *Freedom*—without ever reaching them. And these intellectuals were even further away from the Negro masses in Town Hall then they were in 1951-1955, when at least they were functioning in the ghetto. In Town Hall, however, they beat the drums much louder for independent political organization for Negroes in the ghetto than when they, themselves, were ghetto radicals "toeing-the-line." This bears examination, for it was the political and creative failures of their own past that haunted these people, more than any white liberal default on the Negro civil rights movement. Behind them lie the failures of the American Negro Theater, the Committee for the Negro in the Arts, *Freedom* newspaper—the whole gamut of wasted talents of the radical generation of postwar Harlem. Behind them looms the tragic demise of Paul Robeson—the artistic Pride of the Negro in America—who went into exile after the collapse of *Freedom* newspaper in 1955. No matter what these intellectuals, this leftwing cultural elite achieve, Robeson's political failure is also *their* failure. As representative radicals of a past era, they flunked out. The futile quarrel of the Artists for Freedom with white liberals was but a continuation of the social method (or lack of it) that had been projected on *Freedom* newspaper.

The editorial board of *Freedom* newspaper consisted of certain individuals whose names are important for the purposes of this study: Shirley Graham, Louis E. Burnham (Editor) and the previously mentioned George B. Murphy, Jr. (General Manager). Others are of no political importance today inasmuch as the *Freedom* board contained both Communists and pro-Communists, a lineup arranged to give the newspaper what was called a united front façade. Although there is no indication that Robeson, himself, was a *bona fide* member of the Party, one must remember that the Party was never willingly involved in any united front it did not control. Such narrow-minded control, exerted to keep the coalition in existence, always defeated the very objectives of that coalition. But the cultural and literary nucleus of the Harlem leftwing never understood why.

This tragic lack of social perception and political originality on the part of this Negro leftwing intellectual elite was the root cause of the disillusionment and dispersal of a whole postwar generation of new Harlem radicals. Many of them were young veterans of the war who entered the postwar scene in New York avidly seeking a political orientation that had relevance to their situation and their times.* But in turning to the leftwing (or being led there), many were cruelly humiliated by being caught in the toils of a movement already in a state of political disintegration. Lacking an alternative leadership, the potential of this generation was lost and they drifted into cynicism and apathy. Consequently, very few radicals of World War II vintage are to be seen in the current Negro movement.

Postwar Harlem was prepared to receive and debate new ideas, but the politically advanced intellectual elements had no new ideas to contribute to *Freedom* newspaper. They did not really constitute an avant-garde and showed little conception of what the new Harlem situation demanded of them. The complexities of Harlem could brook none of the mechanical oversimplifications that are common to vulgar leftwing thought. Answers could be arrived at only through entirely new organization for specific purposes, and a new analysis of every social question of vital concern to the people themselves.

A truly concerted intellectual effort along these lines would

---

* The United Negro and Allied Veterans of America (UNAVA) was a case in point. UNAVA was formed in Chicago, April, 1946, with George B. Murphy, Jr. as acting adjutant. It dissolved after a couple of years of failure.

have resulted in the kinds of programs Harlem (or all ghettoes, for that matter) require. Instead, that 1950's period only revealed how utterly divorced was the point of view of the Negro intellectual stratum from the real gist of ghetto realities. What ghettoes need is not social integration, since ecological dispersement solves very little, but social reorganization from the inside.

The basic fallacy in *Freedom* orientation was that it was a Harlem publication whose policies were outer-directed—and in an incurably leftwing fashion—as if to imply that Left ideology possessed a magic appeal for untutored minds. Its political point of view was a Negro-white blend of diluted reform Marxism that Harlem people found totally irrelevant.

It was within this political and cultural framework that the Harlem leftwing literary and cultural elite functioned. Thus, whatever they discussed on *Freedom* newspaper was hardly ever posed in connection with local issues.

When novelist Julian Mayfield interviewed actress Ruby Dee, for example, in the September, 1952, issue of *Freedom,* the controversy that had cropped up in the American Negro Theater in 1946, when Miss Dee had left to go to Broadway in *Jeb,* was never even mentioned. However, Mayfield did quote her strong opinions about the future of the Negro in the theater: "I think the next few years will see us develop a great theater because the Negro people are at that point in their history which inevitably produces real works of art. . . . I think the vital theater in America will come from the Negro people."[2]

In other words, this new vital theater had nothing to do with Harlem's cultural life and development, despite the then recent, tragic demise of ANT.* What, then, did Ruby Dee mean by "vital" theater in 1952? The great assimilated American ideal has so warped the sense of reality of the Negro cultural integrationists that they lose sight of the fact that vital theater must be based on national or ethnic identity.

Like Miss Dee, none of the other presently prominent personal-

---

[2] *Freedom,* September, 1952, p. 7.

* The ANT, the only new vital theater Negroes had, had collapsed after being exploited by downtown theater whites. They had made a fortune from the hit production of *Anna Lucasta;* ANT, where the production had originated, made mere pennies.

ities of this CNA-*Freedom* group ever discussed theater or film in the pages of *Freedom* in connection with Harlem (which had neither a theater of any consequence nor a film movement). It is a fact that several people from CNA and other facets of the Harlem movement went to school for film techniques. But they all used their knowledge for the sole purpose of getting integrated employment in the downtown film industry. As a result, not a single documentary film on Harlem was ever made for the film market of the caliber of *The Quiet One,* which was made in 1949 by white people. The only film planned in the 1950's that I heard about was one that was to deal with leftwing propaganda about unions in Harlem. There was no talk of recording aspects of life as people live it in the ghetto. Thus many old neighborhoods, institutions, and landmarks have disappeared over the last fifteen years with no film record of their existence.

Lack of interest in ethnic culture goes hand in hand with a lack of real sympathy for the social problems of people in ghettoes and how such problems can best be tackled. Integrationism, with or without radicalism, is still only integrationism, and the dynamics of integration are its social aims. In fact, integration does not really need the Marxist movement at all—the marriage is a demonstrable mismatch of convenience. The integrationist philosophy sees Negro ghettoes as products of racial segregation that should not even exist. Hence, nothing in the traditions of ghettoes are worth preserving even when ghettoes *do* exist in actuality. This is typical integrationist logic on all things social.

In the 1950's the community of Harlem cried for social analysis, with a whole raft of unresolved issues. Who runs Harlem "two-party" politics? Who owns Harlem? How do racketeers function in Harlem? What are the problems of the Negro business class in Harlem? What are the cultural problems of Harlem? How does migration of Negroes into ghettoes affect social stability? How do American-born and Caribbean-born Negroes relate? What are the facts behind organized prostitution and the Harlem woman—both inside and outside Harlem? Is it or is it not possible to abolish ghettoes? What is integration? What is assimilation? What is separatism? What is nationalism? Is Harlem divided into castes and classes? If so—define them. Who is in them and where are they located? How do classes function and relate in Harlem? Of this mere random sample of topics that could have been explored profitably, practically nothing appeared in *Freedom*. The tight *Freedom* in-group seemed concerned mainly with the status and fortunes of its own membership and had a strong antipathy toward "outsiders." How they loved to "interview" one another! When they were not fawning over Robeson as if he were a god, they were bowing and scraping before the influential white cultural left-wingers downtown. But never was a single Harlem individual from the masses interviewed on what he or she might think about Harlem problems, cultural or otherwise.

In *Freedom*'s pages in 1952 John O. Killens* revealed his abject conversion to the political leftwing's literary religion of socialist realism by denouncing Ralph Ellison's *Invisible Man*. Killens seemed like nothing so much as the convert who adopts the "true faith" not in repentance, but only because he had already been born steeped in aesthetic grace:

> Mix a heavy portion of sex and a heavy, heavy portion of violence, a bit of sadism and a dose of redbaiting (Blame the Communists for everything bad) and you have the making of a bestseller today.
>
> Add to this a decadent mixture of a Negro theme with Negro characters as Uncle Toms, pimps, sex perverts, guilt-ridden traitors—and you have a publisher's dream.
>
> But how does Ellison present the Negro people? The thousands of exploited farmers in the South are represented by a sharecropper who has made both wife and daughter pregnant. The main character of the book is a young Uncle Tom who is obsessed with getting to the "top" by pleasing the Big, Rich White folks. A million Negro veterans who fought against fascism in World War II are rewarded with a maddening chapter [of] crazy Vets running hogwild in a down home tavern. The Negro ministry is depicted by an Ellison character who is a Harlem pastor and at the same time a pimp and a numbers racketeer.
>
> The Negro people need Ralph Ellison's *Invisible Man* like we need a hole in the head or a stab in the back.
>
> It is a vicious distortion of Negro life.[3]

Well, there you have it! The socially restrictive covenant of radical Left socialist realism, establishing the inviolable range of social theme for the Negro writer, was never better stated.

---

* Author of the novel *Youngblood* (New York: Dial Press, 1954).

[3] *Freedom*, June, 1952, p. 7.

The Negro people are a beautiful, pure people who are unsullied by the social and psychological ravages of American capitalism. To be sure, we certainly have among us, crooks, pimps, whores, perverts, shysters, sadists, addicts, numbers hustlers, careerists and Uncle Toms who might also be incestuous—but we should not honor their presence in life by treating such characters in novels. Such human dregs should be banned from literature just as surely as Black Nationalists are banned from leftwing politics.

For the Communists, an approved Negro working-class literature can only be a literature *about* the working class written by middle-class Negro writers who were never really *of* it. This dull fusion of black bourgeois sentiments and leftwing ideology usually gives off a very prissy, neo-Victorian, pseudo-revolutionary social ethos. For example, the Negro workers depicted for the most part are those whose social behavior, values and mores would actually admit them to middle-class social status, given the appropriate income. (One of the most significant examples of this use of Negro "workers" in drama to reflect middle-class values was Lorraine Hansberry's *A Raisin in the Sun,* of which more, later.)

The sharp contrast between the literary visions of a Killens and an Ellison merely reflects the greater gulf that separates them on more fundamental issues: the main body of Negro reality in all its ecological and psychological variations. What Killens, Robeson and their middle-class-leftwing ethos truly idealized were nice, upright Negro workers; who, even if they did go to church and worship God and not Russia, at least tilled the Southern soil as solid citizen sharecroppers; or worked in factories or service industries but were never, never anti-union; who always knew which American wars were progressive and just and which were "imperialist"; who instinctively loved all foreign-born whites and were never, never anti-Semitic; and (God forbid!) who never, but never, had a single nationalistic sentiment in their naïve revolutionary souls!*

* True to the idealized worker image, there were actual Negro worker-types in the Communist leftwing who were conditioned to approach and reflect these behavioral standards. These workers were so far removed from the mass psychology of the Negro that they were ludicrous to contemplate. And they were rarely the class types that rose to leadership power in the leftwing. To achieve that status one had to be middle-class with a college education, middle-class with a distinctly puritanical streak—outside the boundaries of the bedroom, of course, but puritanical.

In this regard, Ernest Kaiser, who boldly criticized Communist literary pretensions in his article "Racial Dialectics," had this to say:

> Some Negro leftist and Communist writers ignore and refuse to deal with Negro psychology thus revealing their middle-class hangovers. W.E.B. DuBois, in his *New York Herald Tribune* review of [Richard] Wright's *Black Boy* and in his newspaper columns and magazine articles reprimanding ill-mannered, drunken Negroes, Doxey Wilkerson in his introduction to Aptheker's *The Negro People in America* and Lloyd Brown, a Negro editor of *Masses and Mainstream,* in his lecture on the Negro character in American literature to Contemporary Writers are all examples of this failure to deal with Negro psychology.[4]

This blind spot on Negro psychology was a hallmark of the Communists' socialist realist approach to literature. Carried over into practical politics, this literary middle-class ethos had also blocked the natural evolution of the Harlem social and political movement. For a literary point of view such as Killens' is the kind of middle-class puritanism that rejects the human dregs in the real *social* world of pimps, whores, perverts, Uncle Toms, number runners and race traitors from the purview of its practical politics: *Come psychologically balanced, socially upright, and morally clean, before you are worthy to be anointed with the holy water of our revolutionary religion!*

Between 1951 and 1955, before the big blow struck the international leftwing, the *Freedom* staff discussed and wrote about practically everything save what was basic to Harlem problems. There was an occasional piece, merely reportorial, about Harlem schools and housing, but *Freedom* newspaper originated no movement of any kind. Instead, its writers blasted the U.S. Congress on poll taxes, FEPC, and the anti-lynch bills which were the NAACP's meat (and Robeson also blasted the NAACP); *Freedom* roamed all over the world—to China, Africa, British Guiana elections, the war in Korea—and Walter Christmas, of CNA, wrote a meaningless article on refugee writers from Europe.

In the May, 1951, issue of *Freedom* there was an article on the Willie McGee case. McGee had been sentenced to death in Missis-

[4] Kaiser, *op. cit.,* p. 299.

sippi on a trumped-up rape charge involving a white woman. Shortly after the sentencing, there was a protest march staged by the white leftwing in Harlem in McGee's defense. It was a sad fact that Negroes in Harlem did *not* join this march, but stood on the sidelines watching a ninety-nine per cent *white* line of people shouting slogans. It was a very embarrassing situation for the handful of Negroes in that line (one of whom was myself), to realize what little influence *Freedom* newspaper had in Harlem.

The last time I visited the offices of *Freedom,* in 1952, I left with a feeling of desolation and angry disgust at the cliquish remoteness from changing reality that pervaded this newspaper. One could plainly discern that its writers were intellectual prisoners of the dying leftwing movement, dutifully and blindly obeying the mandate to "hang on"; but at the same time, they were preparing for their own grand exit into the integrated cultural world.

And what in fact could one expect the sentiments of Killens, Hansberry, Dee, Mayfield, Clarke and company to be—when the great intellectual scholar, Dr. W.E.B. DuBois, had given his official sanction to *Freedom* newspaper's philosophy? All his life, DuBois had periodically swung back and forth between the ideological poles of integration and nationalism. Although he was never an out-and-out nationalist, in his 1940 autobiography, *Dusk of Dawn,* he had abandoned what was in effect an integrationist position, in favor of the economic, political and cultural rehabilitation of the Negro community. He even went so far as to uphold the separate black economy idea, long the chief platform of the nationalists. DuBois had said, apropos of the NAACP's civil rights program: "There are, however, manifest difficulties about such a program. First of all it is not a program that envisages any direct action of Negroes themselves for the uplift of their socially depressed masses; in the very conception of the program, such work is to be attended to by the nation and Negroes are to be the subjects of uplift forces." On American racial prejudice, DuBois recognized that "attitudes and habits thus built up cannot be changed by sudden assault." As a result, DuBois asserted that for the Negro, "His present racial segregation [will] persist for many decades."[5]

Sociologist E. Franklin Frazier felt similarly: "The Negro com-

---

[5] DuBois, *Dusk of Dawn, op. cit.,* pp. 193-194.

munity will only wither away slowly and will not only form a refuge for the Negro masses but for those middle-class Negroes who continue to be identified with Negro institutions within the Negro community."[6]

However, by 1953, W.E.B. DuBois had changed his mind again on the question of integration, and wrote in *Freedom:* "When we compare American Negroes with other groups, we are not comparing nations, nor even cultural groups; since American Negroes do not form a nation, and are not likely to if their present fight for political integration succeeds."[7]

But no one on *Freedom* cared to discuss what happens if the Negroes (or Harlems) are *not* integrated out of existence. If one wants to understand the factors that lie at the roots of Negro ghetto explosions of the 1960's, one must examine the class policies of the racial integrationists of the 1940's and 1950's, especially the unrealistic outlook of the radical leftwing.

[6] Frazier, "The Negro Middle Class and Desegregation," *Crosscurrents*, Summer, 1957, pp. 213-224.

[7] DuBois, *Freedom*, January 1, 1953, p. 7.

From *Freedom* to *Freedomways*

In 1955, the year of its collapse, Paul Robeson's *Freedom* newspaper claimed it had twenty-five thousand readers. Its April issue stated that if the readership did not respond to its plea for funds the May issue might not appear. In the combined July-August issue for 1955 (which appears to have been its last), there was a suggestion from the editors that *Freedom* be changed from a newspaper to a pocket-size monthly magazine. Here was a newspaper—hardly emergent from the Negro Left-labor mentality of the 1930's—aspiring to enter the Johnson Publication *Jet*-Age! Assuming *Freedom*'s circulation claim to be true, one wonders that twenty-five thousand devoted readers could not keep it alive.

Perhaps the most important factor in *Freedom*'s demise, aside from its blatant lack of originality, was the electrifying effect of the 1954 Supreme Court decision on school integration, upon both Left and Reform integrationists. This decision later motivated various intellectuals to quit the Communist Party. For after 1954, of what value was the Communist leftwing, *Freedom* newspaper, etc., to the cause of integrated freedom? The highest court in the land had rendered its verdict on a cause dear to the hearts of most Negro middle-class constituents. The long legal campaign of the NAACP and the Black Establishment had paid off. If the judicial branch of our heretofore maligned federal government is going to sponsor social revolution—who needs the Communists? If partnership with the government makes it all legal, then agitation, unless it is carried on by lawyers, becomes superfluous. Thus, one can well understand why Lorraine Hansberry could find nothing in Harlem to write on for *Freedom*'s last issue save: "YWCA—Integration Major Theme at 20th National Convention." Aside from Miss Hansberry's contribution, this last issue had not a single article on Harlem problems. It talked about terror in the South, about Congress, South Africa, and about the Smith Act persecution of Negro Communist leaders. John Henrik Clarke reviewed West Indian George Lamming's book, *The Emigrants.*

The big front-page story was "Paul Robeson Pushes Passport Fight; Support Needed." The State Department had denied Robeson a passport on the grounds that he had refused to sign a non-Communist affidavit. Robeson wrote: "If enough people write Washington I'll get my passport in a hurry." He complained further: "It has been five years since the State Department arrogantly and arbitrarily refused to let me travel abroad to practice my craft as a singer and actor, to earn my living wherever people wanted to hear me."[1]

In the twilight hours of his civil rights leadership Paul Robeson, deep in his soul, remained what he had always been—an actor-performer who, come what may, had to practice his craft and earn his living; but who nonetheless had "renounced a socially safe, financially profitable career on the concert stage for a program of agitation and action in behalf of oppressed peoples of the world."[2] Thus, in the end, he wound up neither fish nor fowl. He got his passport and went into exile in England in 1958, three years after the passing of *Freedom* newspaper.

Whether Robeson stayed in the United States or not was no longer important by 1957, because by then his leadership was passé. Such events as the Montgomery, Alabama, bus strike and the Little Rock, Arkansas, school desegregation battle had signaled the entry of the new wave—a new era that would call for new tactics and reevaluations. The old Communist leftwing was dead—after a long sickness within, plus a cruel battering from without. The emergence of the new civil rights trends in 1960 posed serious threats to all the old guard leadership, whether in the NAACP or the shattered Communist Left. Members and supporters of the latter, who were also high up in the ruling hierarchy of the former Harlem cultural and literary inner circle, had to do something to meet these new challenges. Their incompetent policies had lost them their last Harlem propaganda base—*Freedom* newspaper. Even Killens' Harlem Writers Guild had quit the Harlem scene

---

[1] *Freedom,* July-August, 1955, p. 2.
[2] Ira De A. Reid, "Negro Movements and Messiahs, 1900-1949," *Phylon,* Atlanta University, Georgia, Fourth Quarter, 1949, p. 368.

and was meeting in Brooklyn (though still calling themselves a "Harlem" group). For the first time since the 1920's and the 1930's, Harlem was completely devoid of active Communist influence. But, now, a new force had accumulated in Harlem—the Muslims of the Nation of Islam and their dynamic leader, Malcolm X. It was something like the 1920's again when the new Communist movement ran up against the influence of Garvey. For the old guard, it was like beginning all over again after forty years. Concessions had to be made, and they had to be concessions made to realities. Thus, in 1961, the Communist-oriented leftwing did something it had never done before: It allowed the publication of a magazine for the express purpose of exploring issues pertaining to the Negro movement and the *hidden* purpose of reestablishing the leftwing hegemony over the new wave. With Paul Robeson in exile, the remainder of the ruling clique from *Freedom* newspaper launched the independent magazine, *Freedomways*, subtitled "A Quarterly Review of the Negro Freedom Movement." Now, after more than forty years, the political trend that had always insisted that it had all the answers admitted in print that the Negro question had to be explored.

Before dealing with this new publication, it is best to point out two facts. First, in terms of the personnel involved, *Freedomways* of 1961 was essentially a continuation of *Freedom* of 1951-55, but with some subtle differences. Under Robeson's leadership, *Freedom* initially had the real possibility of being a completely independent publication with a Harlem base, since Robeson was *not* a Communist Party member. Second, *Freedomways*, however, although it was able to put up an "independent" face, has *never* been independent since its inception. This is because its founders, with or without Communist Party ties, have no independent political and cultural philosophy of their own and no real black community base.

In the spring of 1961, exactly ten years after the founding of Robeson's *Freedom*, *Freedomways* appeared with Shirley Graham as Editor; W. Alphaeus Hunton, Associate Editor; Margaret Burroughs, Art Editor; and Esther Jackson, Managing Editor. The lineup here is important: Graham and Hunton had been on the controlling editorial board of *Freedom;* Esther Jackson is the wife of James E. Jackson, now the leading Negro theoretician in the

Communist Party; in 1951 Shirley Graham had married W.E.B.
DuBois, who was still the leading American Negro intellectual,
and the "most distinguished Negro in the United States," as
A. Philip Randolph's *Messenger* had said in 1922. It is enlightening to note very carefully what *Freedomways'* editors had to say
in their statement of aims:

> Now, we come to a national crossroad. *Which way will we go?*
> All who are deeply concerned know that this is a time for much
> serious thought, for careful balancing of ways and means. *There
> is a need for much discussion on every level.*
>
> FREEDOMWAYS is born of the necessity for a vehicle of communi-
> cation which will mirror developments in the diversified and
> many-sided struggles of the Negro people. It will provide a public
> forum for the review, examination, and debate of all problems
> confronting Negroes in the United States.
>
> FREEDOMWAYS offers a means of examining experiences and
> strengthening the relationship among peoples of African descent
> in this country, in Latin America, and wherever there are com-
> munities of such people anywhere in the world. It will furnish
> accurate information on the liberation movements in Africa it-
> self.
>
> FREEDOMWAYS *will explore, without prejudice or gag,* and from
> the viewpoint of the special interests of American Negroes, as well
> as the general interest of the nation, the new forms of economic,
> political and social systems now existing or emerging in the
> world.
>
> FREEDOMWAYS provides a medium of expression for serious
> and talented writers—for those with established reputations as
> well as beginners seeking a reading audience for the first time.
>
> "Ye shall know the Truth—and the Truth shall set you free!"
> This is our precept. We invite historians, sociologists, economists,
> workers, students—all who have something constructive to con-
> tribute in this search for TRUTH—to use this open channel of
> communication that we might unite and mobilize our efforts for
> worthy and lasting results.
>
> FREEDOMWAYS *has no special interests to serve save those al-
> ready clearly stated—no political, organizational or institutional
> ties.* Those who commit themselves to its support become patrons
> only of a publication and an editorial policy designed to provide
> an open forum *for the free expression of ideas.* Sponsors of the
> publication will assume no responsibility for the particular views

of any of its contributors; nor will contributors be constrained to abide by any editorial preference or bias of the publishers or editors.

FREEDOMWAYS offers all of us the opportunity to speak for ourselves.

Lift every voice and sing—of Freedom!

THE EDITORS

[N.B. All italics added.]

I have copied this prospectus in its entirety to point out that this new orientation on Negro affairs was precisely what the dissident Harlem Writers Club had insisted on, back in the late 1940's and early 1950's. In 1949-1950, there had also been "a need for much discussion on every level" concerning the complex and conflicting currents even then present in Harlem. That was why the Harlem Writers Club had been formed in the first place.

By 1961, Miss Graham and others of her political persuasion had to admit, implicitly, that earlier they had *not* permitted open discussion "without prejudice or gag." Now they had become perfervid seekers of the "Truth." Now they had become solicitous for the care of "serious and talented writers," much concerned about "the free expression of ideas." They were constrained to point out for the benefit of the wary, and for those once-bitten-twice-shy cynics from the old days, that *"Freedomways* has no special interest to serve save those already clearly stated—no political, organizational or institutional ties." For everyone knowledgeable in the ways of the Communist leftwing, these were earthshaking intellectual concessions, evidently forced by the temper of the times. Every bank management knows when it is bankrupt but it must put up a business-as-usual front, even to the extent of offering higher interest rates for anyone naïve enough to believe that the bank is still solvent. Now there was a rich harvest of new customers on the scene—eager for direct action, full of verve, spirit and open minds. *Freedomways* was established to cash in on this promising young market. One cannot doubt for a moment that there was a mood of sincerity behind this new look in Negro Left journalism. But there was also a profound, unseen catch in the whole affair. *Freedomways* had inherited a problem in Negro intellectual creativity that went all the way back to the 1920's. And who, pray tell, on *Freedomways* was about to open up a discussion of that past decade?

There was only one man alive who even remotely understood the 1920's, and that was W.E.B. DuBois. But by 1961 he was too old and weary to be effective with yet another project of the wayward and incompetent black intellectual generation of the 1940's and early 1950's. During the 1920's, when DuBois had been in his intellectual prime, he had advanced many revolutionary ideas which Negro intellectuals have never developed. His "criteria of Negro art" were never elaborated, nor were his original insights into the limitations of Marxism on the Negro question (every Negro that sided with the Communists swallowed European Marxism whole, and added not a single new concept that the Russians had not thought of beforehand).

The people who had gathered around *Freedomways* were even emptier in thought than their predecessors of the 1920's, who had been at least exciting, even if superficial. What, precisely, were these people prepared to submit for "discussion on every level"? Where would they begin? On which level—politics? Economics? Culture? Integration? Nationalism? Interracialism? Civil rights? Marxism? Communism? Socialism? Trotskyism? Liberalism? Africa? As was subsequently shown, the truth was that the *Freedomways* staff was unable, unwilling and also intellectually unequipped to initiate and sustain a full analytical discussion on *a single crucial issue involving the new Negro civil rights movement of the 1960's.* To initiate such a discussion would require a complete break from the context of the white radical leftwing. They would have to sever their forty-year-old ties to the Marxist movement, and in turn subject the entire Marxist-Communist philosophy in America to the most rigorous, uncompromising and exacting criticism of which black intellectualism is capable. Not only were they *in*capable, neither would they dare. And in the absence of such thorough "housecleaning," there was no possibility, at all, of a "full discussion" on anything else. How could they speak of seeking the "Truth" that would "set you free" when there was no obstacle blocking the path to this glorious "Truth" but themselves? But *Freedomways* gave its own game away from the very outset, when it subtitled itself "A Quarterly Review of the Negro Freedom Movement": For *that* is all it has been doing since 1961— reviewing the movement as it passes by. Like all of its journalistic predecessors, it reflects the emptiness of Negro intellectuals in the field of social analysis. Afraid of nationalism, and even more afraid to criticize Marxism, *Freedomways* has remained critically paralyzed. It has developed into a publication that does not even embarrass the NAACP on the occasions when Roy Wilkins graces its pages.

The first issue carried articles on Frederick Douglass (one of his 1847 editorials); on Guinea, by Alphaeus Hunton; on Cuba, by John Henrik Clarke; on Nkrumah in the United Nations; on aid to Africa by socialist states, by John Pittman; on China, by Shirley Graham; on African women, by an African; and a review-article on J.C. Furnas' *Good-bye to Uncle Tom*, by Ernest Kaiser. Of these, only Kaiser's piece elevated this first issue beyond *Freedom* newspaper's fare of 1955. There was an historical sketch by W.E.B. DuBois, "The Negro People in the United States," which was obviously dragged out of him in order to give the issue prestige. Another article, "The Negro People and American Art," by Elizabeth Catlett Mora, hinted at something new—but was never followed up in subsequent issues. It echoed rather faintly what DuBois had said in his "Criteria of Negro Art" speech in 1926 (a fact of which the author was apparently not aware). Beyond this, the first *Freedomways* issue posed not one provocative question nor one stimulating analysis on any aspect of the Negro movement.

Freedomways' question "Which way will we go?" was a plea from intellectuals in a quandary: intellectuals who were jumping on the new integration bandwagon while protesting that they did not trust its direction; intellectuals who wanted to influence this new movement to go in some other direction but were not certain where. For when the Left launched *Freedomways*, the pertinent racial question was immediately raised—*Is it a Negro magazine—or an interracial magazine?* If intended as the former, then it would have had to incline toward a nationalist position. As neither one, however, *Freedomways* has become a superfluous trimming for the integration movement (which needs it only as a mirror of its own achievements).

The very premise of racial integration negates the idea of Negro ethnic identity. It means the shedding of the race tag. It means, insofar as ideological creativity is concerned, that a James Baldwin will constantly demur against being classified as a Negro writer, that a Lorraine Hansberry will deny her play was a Negro play. Why does even a LeRoi Jones write on "The Myth of Negro

Literature"?[3] If there is no such thing as a Negro writer or a body of Negro Literature, then, it follows, there is or can be no such thing as a Negro psychology or a distinctly Negro sociology, or a Negro political theory or a particular kind of Negro cultural theory that has relevance to American society as regards the Negro situation in America. But if all this is true, then there should be no such thing as a *Freedomways* magazine edited by Negro writers concerned with the Negro Freedom Movement; no such thing as a collection of Negro artists and writers calling themselves the Association of Artists for Freedom. The very existence and emergence of these Negro group expressions runs counter to practically every premise of integration—the alleged objective of the very Negroes who form these groups. But in fact the groups are self-defeating: Stirred by integration, they first run after the white Leftists and Liberals who toss them leftover crumbs; then they reverse themselves and splinter off into an independent identity group, during which time the white Leftists and liberals chase after them offering bigger crumbs. In recent years, as at Town Hall, they even bite the hand that feeds them the crumbs, protesting all the while that what they want in America is Freedom—a blessed state of existence they have not defined. They start magazines such as *Freedomways* and put out the call for new Negro writers (who should not exist), since only Negro writers can make such a magazine meaningful in terms of the Negro freedom movement (which does rightly exist).

It is this tension between opposing alternatives, this dual racial-intellectual motivation, that immobilizes the Negro intelligentsia. Once beguiled into the leftwing camp, they are further trapped and confounded. As writers, the well-springs of their creativity are already so saturated with the old Party-line myths they cannot muster up enough originality to write articles that enlighten and inspire. *Freedomways* pretended to call for "serious and talented writers," those who were "established as well as beginners." *Freedom* newspaper was the special province of John O. Killens' Harlem Writers Guild; every other new writer was a menace to the establishment, and as such, regarded with deep suspicion. But ten years later the Harlem Writers Guild members were still the hard core of *Freedomways*. John Henrik Clarke, the associate editor of

[3] *Saturday Review,* April 20, 1963, pp. 20-21.

Freedomways, came into the *Freedom* newspaper family by way of the Harlem Writers Guild back in Harlem. Although the Guild had acquired a considerable number of new writers, very few articles from these new people have so far been seen in the pages of *Freedomways.* The Harlem Writers Guild, in fact, has been wracked internally by a split between the original founders of the Guild (such as Killens and Clarke), and those same new writers who came in after the collapse of Robeson's newspaper. These younger writers, the nationalistic wing of the Harlem Writers Guild, are in opposition to the founding faction over the role of the Guild as a writer's organization, and the role of the Negro writer as creative intellectual and social critic. In view of *Freedomways'* stated aims, it is curious that this conflict has never been aired in the pages of *Freedomways.* Articles by the Killens-Clarke faction, however, have been most prominently featured in this magazine from issue to issue. In the meantime, the ideological control of *Freedomways* has remained solidly entrenched in the old-guard Negro Left.

In clamping censorship on the wrangle within the writers' organization closest to it, *Freedomways* has evaded its social and journalistic responsibilities. For if the Negro writer's function is merely reportorial, a mere documenting of the civil rights movement, then of what special value is *Freedomways?*

Since its founding in 1961, *Freedomways* has published in its pages samples of the social thought of a larger number of Negro intellects from various levels of status and achievement. This material represents a rather broad consensus of what is actually being thought about the Negro-white situation in America, as of now. Therefore it is not just the old guard leftwing nucleus that is here but the social perceptions expressed by the articulate Negro intelligentsia as a whole. There is no mistaking it, the entire Negro integrationist elite speaks through *Freedomways'* pages. Twenty-two of them were represented in the special *Freedomways* Harlem issue (Summer, 1963) and what they said is today the credo of their counterparts in every big city in the United States. Thus the fact that the controlling group behind *Freedomways* is leftwing-oriented is of little consequence in viewing the Negro movement as a whole.

Take away the labels of parties, organizations, factions, and movements and all these Negroes see eye to eye on racial integration. Many of them are new people, others have been around the leftwing since the 1920's, or are the products of the 1930's and 1940's. Kenneth B. Clark, the psychologist, for example, is one of the politically unaffiliated integrationists who once wrote for Robeson's newspaper side by side with Negro Communists on their way to jail, without fear of guilt by association. The very disturbing thing about what *Freedomways* prints is that it is all so frighteningly superficial, routine and unoriginal, when stacked against the complexity of the Negro situation today in a steadily worsening crisis. It is not that many of *Freedomways'* articles are not interesting or informative, for a number of them are. However, for the most part, *Freedomways'* writers take the premises of the integration movement for granted and draw no conclusions other than what the official civil rights movement implies. The marriage of leftwing ideology with integrationism reveals the superfluity of the former; it battens on the integration movement because there is nothing else happening to justify its functional existence.

In 1961, the leftwing literary clique graced the pages of another new magazine, mercifully shortlived, called *The Urbanite: Images of the American Negro.* What images! No more *Freedom* newspaper-Robeson radicalism to stir the Harlem heartbeat; no more "youngblood" and socialist realist aesthetics and leftwing critical attacks on the literary renegade of a Ralph Ellison; in fact, no more pretexts of expounding colored middle-class values with working-class Negroes à la *Raisin*—all that was a thing of the past. For *The Urbanite* had only one salient departure from *Ebony* magazine—the fact that it was a notch or two above the straight, unadorned magazine journalism style. But whereas *Ebony* (and its infant, *Jet*) aimed for mass circulation, *Urbanite* made it quite plain, editorially, to whom it was intended to appeal:

HAVE YOU SEEN YOURSELF IN PRINT?

* * * * * * * * * *

Almost exclusively the Negro is fictionally cast in low life— often in the most unauthentic symbols—to the complete refutation of his existence as a businessman, a professional, or just an ordinary Joe making it in the world as the world befalls a colored man.

When has the Negro been presented as the guy in the gray flannel suits (policeman or fireman blue; or deliveryman khaki either, for that matter) whose wife, if not contentedly raising her children in a comfortable neighborhood in suburbia, is the urbanite teacher, salesgirl or secretary that caught your eye yesterday?[4]

One would have thought that *Ebony* had, long ago, taken care of this problem of class appeal. The *Urbanite,* however, was out to prove that Negro writers and creative intellectuals also "belong"— if not by birth, at least by the creative achievement that had rescued them from the slums; that, therefore, writers and such were not to be classified along with other déclassé "beats" and nonconformists. For *Ebony, any* achievement conferred status and respectability; for the *Urbanite,* only literary achievement. Hence, for the latter, there was an important educational job to do on whites to correct certain erroneous "Images of the American Negro." *Urbanite* editorialized, "It is up to the writer who is Negro to do it," because "for some Negroes, increasing social mobility means the 'right' house, the 'right' school, the 'right' set, the writer who is white cannot detail why. The writer who is Negro must."[5]

Answering the *Urbanite*'s "literary" call to arms to expound this new image of class, caste, and status were Hansberry, Killens, Baldwin, LeRoi Jones, Langston Hughes, Loften Mitchell— among the choice Negro literati—with the integration motif supplied by the addition of some glittering whites. The *Urbanite* lasted just long enough to clearly reveal where the post-radicalism of the Hansberry-Killens literary syndrome was headed, if, indeed, where it had not already arrived. These new images in the *Urbanite* were beguiling enough to make the most sectarian and fundamentalist Negro radical from the Harlem slums give up his revolutionary religion. Some of the most delicious-looking, brown-skinned sex kittens of our age beamed alluringly from the *Urbanite* covers. They beckoned the reader to enter pages chock-full

[4] April, 1961, p. 2.
[5] *Ibid., idem.*

of all the symbols of chic affluence, and the rising expectations of a new class stratum—the colored literary and creative elite of the Jet-Set Age.

Although the *Urbanite*'s subtitle was "Images of the American Negro," there was also a definite West Indian streak evident in its content which, I suppose, indicates that the Caribbean brethren did not so much mind being classified along with those lowly American Negroes, if it were clearly understood which *class* image was being pushed. There was a small item in the March, 1961, issue of the *Urbanite* to the effect that the "most IN publication around town is the *West Indian American,* a monthly newspaper which, after only 2 years of publication, is way out in front with a circulation of 10,000 here and throughout the West Indies." It said further that "this powerful, peripatetic 12-page paper was founded for the purpose of providing the large West Indian colony in the U.S. with reliable news from home and home-bound Islanders with up-to-the-minute news of their fellows abroad." This newspaper did not last much longer than the *Urbanite*. Quite possibly its failure has to do with the fact that West Indian Americans and West Indian Britishers are forever boasting about their origins in front of American whites and American Negroes, but they are always "from there" or "leaving there" for greener pastures elsewhere. Obviously, there is nothing happening in the West Indies that makes for any exceptional interest beyond what was already known by those who left. Thus this very "IN" newspaper soon went out.*

Another interesting item in the *Urbanite* told that "the most IN Africans, financially, are the members of the Gold Coast Marketing Board. The Board, an All-African enterprise, is a public corporation with reserves of $280 million. Names you'll be hearing in the future are Kwame Poku . . . etc."[6]

By 1961, the African had made it possible to be black and also "in" at one and the same time in the eyes of the colored intelligentsia in the U.S. Prior to that it was not so, especially if it involved the skin-color snobbery of British West Indians in America. But what made black Africa most "in" is money—African de-

---

* An earlier *West-Indian American* was started in 1927 but folded in 1928.
[6] March, 1961, p. 21.

velopment financiering. Hence all this new-found interest in Africa is not the pride of heritage. It is also class-oriented because places like the former Gold Coast now have a new African bourgeosie, who, like the *Urbanite* writers, are equally interested in the social mobility of the "right" house, the "right" school, and the "right" set. Said an *Urbanite* editorial: "In an era in which many changes are taking place throughout the world, the American Negro and the African are finally being accorded a long overdue basic recognition: the recognition of the dignity of man, regardless of color, race, or creed."[7]

What the above implied, reflects the real state of mind of the new class here and in Africa. *We have now arrived, so let us proceed onwards and upwards peacefully and gradually, with our arms locked firmly in integrated partnership with white liberals and all ex-imperialists of goodwill.*

The *Urbanite*'s intentions, clearly stated, were never to speak to the Negro masses or to educate *them;* the publication was beamed to a "right" set. Thus the ease with which Hansberry and Killens, in particular, moved into this journalistic frame of reference called into question everything they claimed to have stood for from their early days on *Freedom* newspaper. However, it was not that Hansberry and Killens had changed; it only meant that their leftwing radicalism, their Robesonite idolatry, was thoroughly middle-class to begin with. Even *Freedom* newspaper was beamed to the "right" set, which explains again why it could never reach the masses. It was not intended for them any more than was the shortlived *Urbanite*. The difference was that the *Urbanite* editors were direct about it. The *Urbanite* represented the long-deferred dream taking distinct shape, coincident with the arrival of the Negro at the threshold of status. From the *Urbanite* social stance, Negro writers had the role of fashioning the image of an affluent class of Negro sophisticates who could discuss every topic, every aspect, of their "Negroness" that appeared in the *Urbanite* pages—over cocktails in the plushest of integrated salons.

[7] March, 1961, p. 2.

Richard B. Moore

Freedomways' inability to deal concretely with Negro-white realities is characteristic of the peculiar backwardness of the other black publications that have appeared since 1961. Since they cannot deal adequately with the past, they cannot deal perceptively with present social complexities. But what can be expected of the young writers when the old writers, such as Richard B. Moore, write articles that do not reveal the issues of their own political history?

Richard B. Moore is one of the few active links between Harlem of the 1920's and *Freedomways* of the 1960's. His career begins at least as far back as 1917 when he joined the old Socialist Party, which he "left again when Algernon Lee, in a lecture to Harlem Socialists, declared that Negroes were sharecroppers, not industrial workers, and could not be organized."[1] Between that moment and the summer of 1963 when Moore's article "Africa Conscious Harlem" appeared in the special Harlem issue of *Freedomways*—forty-six years—he became a living, active repository of the history of the first three generations of American Negro Communists. Moore participated in the founding events of the American Communist movement in 1919, the formative years of the 1920's, the crisis of American Communism in 1929 when Moscow expelled the Lovestone-Wolfe-Gitlow-Cannon groups (a purge that left the American Party in a state of wreckage from which it never really recovered), and the 1930's—the high water mark of the Communist appeal. According to Wilson Record,[2] Moore was still a member of the party in 1939. But somewhere between 1939 and 1946 when I first met Moore, he had either quit or been expelled. At

[1] Oakley C. Johnson, "Marxism and the Negro Freedom Struggle (1876-1917)," *Journal of Human Relations*, Central State College, Wilberforce, Ohio, Vol. XIII, No. 1 (First Quarter, 1965), p. 35.
[2] Wilson Record, *op. cit.*, p. 181.

that time, much to my surprise and curiosity, Moore was very critical and bitter against the Communists, although he remained a steadfast Marxist in his point of view on Negro affairs. Interestingly enough, Moore later joined the Harlem Writers Guild.

In his article, elder statesman Moore did a good job of tracing the historical American Negro-African ties, but passed very lightly over the role of the militant socialists, beginning with the *Messenger* group in Harlem. He discussed Marcus Garvey, devoting a whole page to an "estimate" of the Jamaican Nationalist. After that Moore briefly described the Harlem literary renaissance and moved quickly into a discussion of the Harlem reaction to Mussolini's aggression in Ethiopia in the 1930's. Naturally, the new Africa consciousness of the 1950's and 1960's took up the remainder of his piece, and he was therefore obliged to touch on the nationalist-integrationist conflict, but only lightly. This article revealed that over the decades Moore has mellowed considerably, into a pro-integrationist. Since he has always been known as a man of rather fiery and militant temperament, it might be said that his latter-day moderation is due to age (he is in his seventies), but this would be missing the point. Marxist radicalism among Negroes usually leads to integrationism (radical or reform) in the final analysis. Moore is no exception, despite the role he played in the 1920's as a member of the African Blood Brotherhood— a program so nationalistic it would neither have been tolerated by the Communists of the 1940's nor espoused by the Richard B. Moore of the 1960's. Today, Moore campaigns mainly to replace the word "Negro" with "Afroamerican," in the American vocabulary.[3] But if there is anyone close to *Freedomways'* inner circle, with sufficient background and responsibility to discuss Marxism and the Negro movement, it is Richard B. Moore. The fact that he does not assume this role seems to bear out Theodore Draper's statement that the Communists cannot tell their own history.

When the West Indian is Africa-conscious, as in the case of Moore, his ideology is the curious, Caribbean pro-British kind of West Indian-African "commonwealth-federationism," noted in

---

[3] Richard B. Moore, *The Name Negro—Its Origins and Evil Uses* (New York: Afroamerican Publishers, 1960).

Garvey's Jamaican reform politics. Seen in another context, the identification with Africa, like the West Indian's militant stand on racial discrimination, is motivated more by a psychology of non-identification with the American Negro status and accommodation to American white bourgeois values, than with other essentials of the American Negro struggle. This accounts for the fact that certain West Indian groups and associations in New York have balked at going on record in support of the civil rights movement.[4] Caught between the whites and the vast Negro minority in America, the West Indian is often cast into what is essentially a hypocritical, double standard. He exhibits, therefore, an opportunistic identification regarding himself as a West Indian dealing with whites, and regarding his relationship to American Negroes and their dealings with whites. In any case, whatever the West Indian's stance in racial politics, it can never be *his* fault in the face of failures of strategy but the fault of American Negroes for not being militant enough, or for not having the right strategy in the first place. This same motivational conflict between West Indians and American Negroes can be seen behind Moore's present semantic campaign. Whatever the validity of his argument for the use of the word *Afro-American* instead of *Negro,* it is by no means a new question. It has recurred frequently since the late nineteenth century as an issue in racial designation.* Today, the term *Afro-American* suggests and designates the Negro's African background; but it is also another way of expressing non-identification with the American Negro qua American Negro and his social status in America.

To further complicate the matter, for many years there was another trend that favored *Colored-American* over *Negro* but who would object to being "Africanized" as an *Afro-American.* There is now a faction in Harlem who want to dispense with *Afro-American* as too "moderate"—in favor of *African-American.* Then there

---

[4] Lennox Raphael, "West Indians and Afro-Americans," *Freedomways,* Summer, 1964, pp. 438-445.
* For example, see James Weldon Johnson's autobiography *Along This Way.* He says that Afro-American "is on all points a good word, but in its use in this country it quickly acquired a slightly derisive sense, a sense due mainly, perhaps, to the stamp put upon it by H.L. Mencken. Mr. Mencken and George S. Schuyler, the Negro satirist, are the only American writers who continue to make frequent use of it." (New York: Viking Press, 1933), p. 375.

is the ultimate integrationist trend that prefers simply *American,* without hyphenated qualifications (not to speak of those extreme nationalists who maintain that they have never ceased to be Africans despite centuries of separation from that continent). The problem with these various schools of semantic nationalism is that they merely create more conflict while solving absolutely nothing concrete in the way of political, economic or cultural advances for the Negro in America. Their word battles are the results of accumulated frustrations and social blind alleys that have trapped and immobilized the black radical nationalists and the "Africa-Conscious" Marxist-integrationists.

As a result, Richard B. Moore finds himself, after five decades, in the highly awkward position of criticizing the Black Nationalists—who were among the very first activists in Harlem to condemn the word *Negro,* long before Moore made an issue of it. However, the semantic gap between Moore and the Nationalists is that the latter prefer "Black people" or "Black"—a distinction that Moore refrains from using due to his own color sensitivities. The roots of Moore's intellectual and theoretical disabilities are found in his inability to deal with the new nationalism:

> It should be stated, however, that these "nationalist" groups are as yet unable to unite among themselves, due largely, it appears, to self-centered power drives and competition for leadership. The tendency persists among them, unfortunately, to oppose other organizations which have the largest following of Afroamerican people and to condemn these leaders caustically and constantly. Obviously, this hinders rather than helps to achieve united action either in support of the African liberation movements or to further the struggle for civil liberties and human rights here in the U.S.A.[5]

In his article Moore did not point out that in the 1920's, his own young African Blood Brotherhood also saw fit *not* to support the organizations that had the "largest following of Afroamerican people"—namely the Garvey movement and the NAACP—the latter, then avidly seeking "civil liberties and human rights." Moreover, the ABB itself succumbed to the same "power drives and competition for leadership," by breaking up into several different

[5] *Freedomways,* Summer, 1963, pp. 315-334.

groups, each with its own publication. In addition they supported the Communist Party against all other "Afroamerican" trends. Nonetheless, Moore is incapable of explaining to the young Nationalists why they should act any different than he did at their age. He is unable (or unwilling) to clarify for them why five decades of Marxism, Black Nationalism, and NAACP-ism have solved neither the problem of civil liberties and human rights, nor the inability of nationalist groups to unite among themselves, nor the nationalist tendency to be always caustically criticizing NAACP-ism. Moore cannot clear up this fifty-year-old mystery because, like all Negro Marxists who have toed the line, he has finally wound up in the integrationist camp, upholding abstractions. Moore and his "Africanist" blood brothers might just as well have taken this position in the 1920's and saved themselves all the agonies of the subsequent sellouts of the Communist Party between the Lovestoneite purge of 1929 and the switch in 1959 to the NAACP's integration bandwagon.

The responsibility of Richard B. Moore and his *Freedomways* colleagues should have been to essay an explanation of the persistent differences between nationalists and integrationists, and the conflict between these factions. Moreover, why did Moore put the burden of unity on the dissident nationalists, and not the other way around? Finally, if nationalists and integrationists should put aside all differences in the interests of united action as Moore demanded, the question would arise—United action for what? There was massive united action for the March on Washington, and what was achieved? Yes, the Civil Rights Act came later, but so, on its heels, did the ghetto uprisings: Hence—*what now?* Either the integrationists are a variegated collection of utopian dreamers in pursuit of sociological impossibilities, or else the nationalists are simply hopeless dissidents whose only function is to disagree with the integrationists because neither trend, at best, has any future. But there is much more to it than that.

Quite evidently, neither the integrationists nor the nationalists have truly come to grips with either themselves or the American social system. Each faction blames the other for the faults of both. Old radicals like Moore realize the seriousness of this dilemma, more than they care to admit. They know that the aggravated

problems of the Negro today in economic, political and cultural
spheres are the accumulation of unsolved issues that arose fifteen,
twenty, thirty, fifty years ago and were never honestly tackled at
the outset, when they demanded immediate, on-the-spot attention.
Negro life today is like that of a very sick man who doesn't suffer
merely from one ailment but from several at the same time, so that
no one really knows which ailment to treat first. Accumulated
social complications! All through the years, the Negro was taught
either *nothing* by his leadership, *or all the wrong things.* From the
end of World War One to the present day—the most crucial decades wherein the historical problem of the American nationality
question was posed for solution in all its manifold variables—the
white intellectuals utterly failed and the Negro intellectuals utterly defaulted. The former failed because they were afraid of the
race problem; while the latter was afraid to define it, in a period
already fraught with war, nationalism, internationalism, revolution, cultural revival, economic bust, labor radicalism, New
Dealism and more war. On the one hand, the civil rights agitators
were saying that "rights," "human dignity," "freedom," etc. (all
vague abstractions), would solve everything. On the other hand,
the Marxists revolutionaries told the Negro, "Wait for the great
social revolution like the one they had in Russia—that will solve
everything." Yes, even the Garvey nationalists, despite positive
ideals, went off the romantic deep end—"Back to Africa" was
their solution. But what this spectrum of leadership opinion did
not teach the Negro masses was how to survive in America even if
none of these great deliverances arrived as anticipated. All the
leadership factions had one fault in common—they misread and
misinterpreted the Negro's functional reality within American
capitalism. They did not teach the Negro masses the techniques of
ethnic group survival under capitalism—group economics, group
cultural self-education—in short, cooperative self-help on every
level of human experience and need in industrial society. The
Negro mass was left to the uncertain derelictions of social drift and
aimless survival without specified goals. Each generation comes of
age in a sick black world whose inner agonies are numbed by the
narcotic fantasies of the Great American Dream. And when each
generation reaches twenty-one, what do they hear the big-time
Negro leadership saying? "Let us integrate—that will solve everything!" The legacy of Negro leadership is its misreading of

America, for it mistakes the illusion of America's idealized assimilation for its power-group realities.

But the younger generation very correctly sees through the social fallacies of these illusions and puts down the integrationists and their white liberal allies as phonies. They then turn to such new nationalist variations as the Muslims, whose leaders tell them —"Let us build a separate state!" But then still other new-wave integrationists and Marxist radicals and nationalist separatists crowd the public platforms, agitating for their respective ideas on the "grand deliverance." The ghetto riots explode as suppressed energies are wasted in the pathetic and fruitless exhaustion of fighting the police. The new-wave integrationists and the radical activists support the uprisings in the ghettoes, but the conservative integrationists oppose these grassroots demonstrations. The conservatives want orderly, planned integration (*i.e.*, gradualism), while the radical activists want an integration that is rapid, immediate, if not instantaneous. For the older, now worn-out integrationists, or ex-revolutionaries like Richard B. Moore, the message becomes: unity for civil liberties and human rights— all vague, inedible, unwearable, uninhabitable abstractions. But essentially these demands all boil down to racial integration which, under American conditions, cannot be anything but very, very gradual even at best. For even should all the counterbalancing forces at play in American society remain static, this struggle can drag on for the next hundred years and the Negro will still be going through the same paces in 2067.

But these forces will *not* remain static, and herein lie both the dilemma of the integrationists and the potential promise of the nationalist opposition. The key to the eventual resolution of the integrationist-nationalist conflict is the black intelligentsia, a class which must more and more shift its allegiances to the nationalist cause if these forces are not to be defeated. The cult of integrationism and civil-rightism has run its natural course, has reached the saturation point of diminishing returns, and has met an impasse—its dynamism spent. Since the majority of the black intelligentsia is in the integrationist camp (even those who would like to think that they are not) the intellectuals, because of the civil rights impasse, find themselves with no serious role to play in real life.

The new magazines, *Freedomways, Liberator,* etc., now reveal that even those intellectuals who attempt to be *engagé* are lacking in creative and functional ideas. They are unable to reach back into the past and gather in all the threads of the American Negro's lost sense of social direction. The Negro intellectuals of today are the victims of the intellectual default of yesterday. The intellectual, theoretical, and cultural methods of self-orientation and self-leadership have been taken out of their hands. The Negro intellectual has been bereft of the means of solving his own problems because his class has traditionally been maneuvered into the position where his problems are solved by others. Instead of being able to essay his own solutions, the Negro intellectual has been transformed into a problem by the white liberal, who prefers to keep him in that position. The white liberal problem-solver has been institutionalized as an organic part of the entire civil rights movement, and is the emasculator of the creative and intellectual potential of the Negro intelligentsia. Negro intellectuals cannot effectively interpret themselves in the arts, in social criticism, in the social sciences, in research fields, etc.; nor can they make objective interpretations of their own relation to the American scene that have any impact on American affairs. The *interpretation* of the Negro is predominantly a white liberal affair, an alliance between white Christian and Jewish reformism. Within the scope of this alliance, the resulting ideology is preeminently of Jewish intellectual origin. In fact, the main job of researching and interpreting the American Negro has been taken over by the Jewish intelligentsia to the extent where it is practically impossible for the Negro to deal with the Anglo-Saxon majority in this country unless he first comes to the Jews to get his "instructions." The time has come for the Negro intellectuals to reassess seriously the implications of the American Negro's position in American society in terms of his group relations with white Anglo-Saxon Protestants and white Jews. It has come to this! At its roots this American nationality problem is a group power problem, an interethnic group power play; only when the American Negro creates an ethnic group social and cultural philosophy will he be able to deal effectively with this dilemma in real terms.

Since America is a nation of nationalities, it is a nation of nationalisms—a fact that, if squarely faced by the liberal democratic idealists, should cease to disturb their romantic preoccupations with America's unromantic past. Once it is ascertained just *whose* nationalism, among all, has been the longest suppressed and denied by others, then the implications of Black Nationalism, as a social phenomenon to be positively dealt with, become clearer to all concerned. In failing to achieve this point of view, the radical leftwing has defeated itself since the 1920's. Instead it ranted about a united labor movement comprising all races, creeds and colors and nationality groups—lined up neatly in a class-struggle front against American capitalism. As a result, the inner dynamics of American capitalism simply rolled along, unheedful of radicalism, through periods of upswing, downswing, prosperity, boom and bust, Depression, New Deal Keynesism, recession, war, the welfare state, and ultimately, the welfare-warfare state. As a result of this twentieth-century capitalistic evolution-revolution, every white nationality group (including Jews and the Catholic multiple-groupings) has been gathered up from the lower-class regions of the society and given an incorporated stake in the profit-sharing capitalistic club, if not in the private white Anglo-Saxon social club. In short, every group nationalism has been paid off, provided it is white—and in dollars and cents. Additional small payoffs are added in every important election year when the politicians become acutely aware of the ethnic vote and the Ideal American becomes a mysterious being often talked about but never seen, unless he is wearing the WASP mask concealing some other identity.

Thus, in retreating headlong from any critical association with Black Nationalism, *Freedomways* not only denied itself inductive social reasoning based on an investigation of Black Nationalism as compared to white Anglo-Saxon nationalism, Jewish (Zionism) nationalism, etc., but also refused to discuss the implications of racial integration in terms of the broad concept of American nationality. What national group, in fact, were Negro integrationists going to "integrate" into—WASPS, Jews, Catholics, Chinese, Indians, Puerto Ricans, or "others"? The true American nationality is up for grabs—everybody is claiming it without naming it. Deductive social reasoning about this American nationality could have introduced a whole discussion about the inner workings of American national group pluralism. It would reveal that racial democracy cannot be achieved unless political, economic, cultural and administrative equality among national or ethnic groups is achieved within American society. Then, and only then, could the major step be taken towards the solution of the American nationality question. Without it, racial integration as a programmatic slogan is a sociological fraud. On the other hand, nothing radical or revolutionary can take place in America until the politics of nationality becomes the main point on the social agenda. Then, and again only then, can it be decided what will happen to the Negro in America—whether he will integrate, separate, emigrate, or achieve pluralistic group equality on all levels.

This has always been the hidden but highly persuasive social imperative operating behind the dynamic of American capitalism. Ruthlessly, it rolled over and plowed under all the radical and liberal ideologies in its path toward its "manifest destiny" in the world. As such, American capitalism does not require, or even deserve, forcible overthrow, but rather a reorganization from the top down and from the bottom up. This in itself is, of course, a revolutionary idea, especially when it emanates from *without* the power elite itself. The point is, however, that the main impetus for this reorganization of the capitalistic structure in America can, and must, come from that social group whose nationalism has never been allowed its share of the capitalistic pie. It has always been claimed that capitalism is synonymous with political democracy for all, regardless of race, creed, or color; yet if this cannot prove true at home, then capitalism should be replaced by a different system in America, as well as in Africa, Asia and Latin America.

It is on this score that the American Marxists have, for over forty years, misled, disoriented, and retarded Negro intellectuals. They have never understood—have in fact refused to understand— the native American social dynamic. They have misinterpreted America and the American Negro's social role in America, and misinterpreted the Negro to himself (an explanation he has either believed, or been thwarted in his efforts to disbelieve). Marxism as a method of social inquiry is not native to America but to Europe —it was transplanted to America by Europeans who never ceased being Europeans. But there has never been a nation that developed like the United States, or a system that developed like capitalism within the United States. The history of the American

Negro is immutably entwined with this American capitalistic development. Thus, with all due credit to the original social insights of Marx, the American Negro tradition in this country must be separated from Marxian conclusions in order to be seen in the light of its own native American dynamic.

The great dichotomy, the underlying ideological schism that dominates the Negro social outlook in America, is that of integrationism vs. *all* trends that reflect nationalism, separatism or ethnic group identity. Negro integrationists become pro-Marxist Communist, and Negro Marxist-Communists become pro-integrationist because for Negro Integrationists, Marxism lends a radical flavor to integrationism which in itself is *not* revolutionary in essence. On the other hand, Marxist-Communism becomes pro-integrationist because of its essentially opportunistic pro-Negro policies. Pro-nationalist Negro trends must reject Marxist-Communism, and vice versa, because the latter, being theoretically opposed to independent black political power on internationalist premises, must seek to control nationalist trends by directing them into integrationist channels. This has been historically demonstrated.

As a result of these historical findings it has become mandatory today that every pro-nationalist tendency within the Negro movement take stringent steps to ban all Marxist-Communist influences from controlling positions within the movement. These white leftwing influences inevitably divert leadership energies, distort policies, disorient Negroes in terms of specified goals, discourage independent Negro creative thinking. If measures are not taken by Negro leaders, the implicit sociological outcome of racial or ethnic relations between Negro and white groups cannot be rationally pursued either by social revolution or social reform. What is to be the outcome—racial assimilation? Ethnic or (cultural) pluralism? Rigid separatism or emigration? These are the unspoken, critical considerations that loom behind the civil rights slogans of the various ideologies within the Negro movement as a whole. Such vital issues take precedence over, and are little affected by most minds, whether America remains capitalistic, or goes socialistic or even fascist (although the Goldwater-radical rightwing threat has caused many Negro leaders to think seriously of the latter possibility).

As matters stand, no matter how controversial integrationist aims remain for the conservatives, or the radical rightwing, or the white racist opposition, the integrationist has little to say that is *new*. He has run out of meaningful ideas on American society and contributes nothing but hackneyed, time-serving moral preachments which are irrelevant to the dynamic requirements of modern society. All he can ask now is: "How can we implement the Civil Rights Act now that we have it? What practical measures can be used?" But he has already run afoul of the very practical (and sadly, very effective) measures of white opposition. Still, his campaign for the ultimate in integration must go on. This is dangerous, and it is also a peculiar new form of social "know-nothingness." The integrationist must attack whatever becomes a threat to his plan for orderly integration—whether it comes from white conservatives, white racists, lukewarm white liberals or the rioting, cop-fighting, looting black mobs of the Harlem ghetto and beyond. The integrationist is so driven toward his mirage, he cannot afford to stop and indulge in debates with his critics from the nationalist, group-oriented camp. For these ideas he fears like some plague. Debate—simple, probing debate—panics him lest he become contaminated by ideology which might render him unfit or unacceptable for integration.

The *Freedomways* writers, by evading the great debate that thus goes voiceless within the integrationist vs. nationalist conflict, cannot avoid being pulled into one of two polarities. They do not have the intellectual and creative resourcefulness to stand fast on a commanding middle ground and arbitrate a resolution of the conflict. *Freedomways* thus becomes no more than a capsule extension of the Negro press, which Baldwin described in one of his essays as "a black man's newspaper straining for recognition in the white man's world."[6] E. Franklin Frazier's characterization is even more apt: "The Negro press is not only one of the most successful business enterprises owned and controlled by Negroes; it is the chief medium of communication which creates and perpetuates the world of make-believe of the black bourgeoisie."[7]

Of course *Freedomways* is not a successful business and many of

[6] Baldwin, "The Harlem Ghetto," *Notes of a Native Son* (Boston: Beacon Press, 1955), p. 64.
[7] Frazier, *Black Bourgeoisie* (Glencoe, Illinois: The Free Press, 1957), p. 174.

its writers consider themselves very much in advance of the current views of the Negro press. It would also be untrue to claim
that *Freedomways* has not made a halfhearted, soft-treading attempt to "provide a public forum for the review, examination and
debate of all problems confronting Negroes in the United States."
One major obstacle to this goal, however, is the fact that although
Freedomways has been forced, by the nature of recent developments, to examine the past, for too many individuals reviewing
the past is too much like reviewing their own role in that past.
Thus any analysis of past events by a writer such as Richard B.
Moore merely scratches the surface, and as *Freedomways* has more
and more come to represent the views of the official leadership, its
analysis of the present has become equally superficial. Although
the *Freedomways* writers do express more awareness than their less
"political" journalistic brethren on *Ebony,* etc., the following
point that Frazier makes is all too relevant for them, as well:

> The lack of interest of the black bourgeoisie and its mouth-
> piece, the Negro press, in the broader issues facing the modern
> world is due to the fact that the Negro has developed no eco-
> nomic or social philosophy except the opportunistic philosophy
> that the black intelligentsia has evolved to justify its anomalous
> and insecure position.[8]

Freedomways, although it pretends to transcend the intellectual
and political limitations of the conventional mouthpieces of the
black bourgeoisie, has also clung to an "anomalous and insecure
position" peculiarly its own. It *does* have an interest in the
"broader issues facing the modern world," for it discusses Africa,
China, Latin America (*i.e.* the socialist or third world) very
often. But this studied interest in foreign affairs is an old Left
trademark and the Left Negroes have, of course, imitated this custom without bringing to it a single distinctive element of political
originality. The result is that *Freedomways'* interest in foreign
affairs only serves to cover up the magazine's habitual evasions of
its responsibilities for open debate on domestic Negro-white issues.
Hence, on the domestic front it fits Frazier's description of the
Negro press. For the magazine "has developed no economic or
social philosophy" except the opportunistic philosophy that the

[8] *Ibid.,* p. 191.

old Left has imposed on it, and which the black Left intelligentsia has cultivated to justify its own privileged but insecure position in the leftwing that they dare not give up.

In other parts of the world of oppressed colored nations, it is the intellectuals who come to the fore as the molders and shapers of what is new, vital and relevant in terms of social, cultural and political opinion. It is the intellectuals who give form and content to mass liberation movements that change society. It is the intellectuals who, because of their déclassé position, can see objectively and clearly which way class forces are actually moving or aspiring to move, and which classes are advancing or retarding that advance. They make mistakes in their assessments of social trends within their societies, but they are never immobilized by any self-engendered dilemmas as has been the case of the American Negro intellectuals in our time.

Lorraine Hansberry

Richard Wright was the last important writer in the Communist leftwing who came up the hard, self-tutored way from humble beginnings "on the road." He was a child of Mississippi and a young man whose mature visions were nurtured in the years of the Great Depression. It is interesting to note that since the end of World War Two not a single Negro writer or dramatist sponsored and promoted by the leftwing has followed the difficult route traveled by Wright.

None of the creative intellectuals who emerged from the inner circle of CNA-*Freedom* newspaper could have written a book resembling George Orwell's *Down and Out in Paris and London.* For it is a disturbing fact that in the American radical movement a Negro writer-intellectual who writes and washes dishes (as Orwell did when he was on the bum in Paris) is déclassé and thoroughly looked down on by his craft colleagues. This is but one indication of how far the American Communist movement is removed from being proletarian. This leftwing accommodation to middle-class ideology was reflected in the type of literary talents that rose to prominence in the CNA-*Freedom* newspaper inner circle. These writers definitely represented a middle-class literary and cultural ethos.

The late Lorraine Hansberry was a significant example of this trend. Before the appearance of the *Freedom* newspaper group, which Miss Hansberry joined in 1951, it was rather common to see the Negro working-class intellectual, through a little education and leftwing political conditioning, evolve into an imitation middle-class individual seeking middle-class status. A brief radical flareup might intervene, but was promptly extinguished at just the right time for the politics of accommodation. In fact, the old, established Negro Communist leadership, many of whom came out of the 1930's and even the 1920's, made this policy of accommodation almost mandatory, inasmuch as they were predominantly middle class themselves. Many of them feared the young working-class militants who came on the scene after World War Two, especially if they were gifted. Once inside the social confines of the radical leftwing, this new young breed was expected not to lead, but to follow and conform. And they could only hope to enter the leadership ranks by toeing the line better than anyone else. A working-class Negro radical not only had to conform to the political line, but also to the class attributes of the ruling elite. In such an atmosphere he did not remain a part of the black proletariat very long once he began to be groomed for the ruling elite. This elite was composed of a well-entrenched bureaucracy, a socially compact and privileged group of Negroes who held various important jobs in Communist-controlled trade unions, party echelons, front organizations, cultural media, etc., and whose way of life offered all the middle-class comforts one could afford this side of ostentation. Most of the young intellectuals who functioned in what was allegedly a worker's movement did not want a worker's job category. For them it was "something" in publishing, public relations, the City, advertising, journalism, social work, or the like.

Lorraine Hansberry was neither from the Negro working-class, nor from a genteelly impoverished middle-class background that had seen better days before the Great Depression. She was the daughter of a prosperous, upper middle-class family who owned thirteen slum properties in Chicago's Negro district. In fact, the City of Chicago listed Miss Hansberry's name as one of the owners of these properties. This background afforded Miss Hansberry an extensive education at the University of Wisconsin, Roosevelt College in Chicago, and the University of Guadalajara in Mexico.

In 1959, the newspaper article[1] that revealed Miss Hansberry's ownership of slum properties reported that she was embarrassed by certain revelations stating that one of the principal targets of Chicago's "fight against slum landlords is the Hansberry family." But there was nothing intrinsically embarrassing, because it is in the economic nature of things that slums exist and must have an owner. However, what *was* embarrassing about Miss Hansberry's subsequent radical role on *Freedom* newspaper, in Greenwich Vil-

[1] *The New York Post*, July 1, 1959, p. 3.

lage and on Broadway, was the assumption that she knew all about the Negro working class, of which she was not even remotely a member. Even at the beginning of her career, Miss Hansberry was in fact better conditioned than anyone out of CNA to carry the leftwing literary trend to its ultimate conclusions—the "integrationizing" of the Negro literary image to resemble the ethos of middle-class conformity. It is significant that radical leftwing sponsorship (rather than her own class) paved the way for Miss Hansberry's literary development, demonstrating the leftwing's role as the political surrogate for the social *aims* of the Negro middle class over the social *necessities* of the Negro working class. It is also significant that none of the Negro writers cherished by the radical Left have turned their social-protest searchlight on the inner life of their own middle class. (Recall now that the defunct American Negro Theater scored its most successful hit with Abram Hill's *On Striver's Row,* a satire on the Negro middle class.)

On *Freedom* newspaper, one of Lorraine Hansberry's first journalistic tasks was to deliver a review on Richard Wright's novel, *The Outsider.* With this review Miss Hansberry joined John O. Killens in obeisance to the leftwing line, by leveling political attacks on the literary works of two ex-Communists—Ellison and Wright. This was an elite function of the literary in-group and it revealed the utter bankruptcy of the radical leftwing in the area of critical originality. One could indeed criticize *The Outsider,* but what could this young woman from upper-class colored Chicago ever know about what led Richard Wright to write such a book? What could she possibly have known about the "misery, humiliation, violence and resentment of Wright's early life in the South," described in his autobiographical *Black Boy?* Nonetheless she took off on *The Outsider* with the assertion that:

> The Outsider is a story of sheer violence, death and disgusting spectacle, written by a man who has seemingly come to despise humanity. . . .
> Cross Damon . . . is the symbol of Wright's new philosophy—nothingness. . . .
> But nowhere in his four hundred pages can he bring himself to describe—say, the beauty or strength in the eyes of the working people of the Southside [Chicago]. It seems that he has forgotten.
> Wright has lost his own dignity and destroyed his talents. He

exalts brutality and nothingness. He negates the reality of *our struggle* for freedom and yet works energetically in behalf of our oppressors [italics added].[2]

For good measure, Miss Hansberry added all the old leftwing clichéd jibes that Wright's book was "a propaganda piece for the enemies of the Negro people, of working people, and of peace," to show how well she had learned the jargon.

Now, inasmuch as Wright's latest book was just about the first Negro literary exploration of the existentialist theme, it was understandable that the political Left would disagree with it on philosophical grounds. But that was not why Miss Hansberry, *herself*, criticized it. Wright was attacked because he was a renegade from Communism who dared to explore the regions of literary expression denied to the literature of Negro radicalism. *Freedom* newspaper, however, could not criticize the book on its own terms, as an exploration of existentialism, because it is highly doubtful if anyone on *Freedom* was capable of such an exercise.

What did this Miss Hansberry mean by "our struggle for freedom"? Whose struggle, in fact? What struggle in Harlem did *Freedom* newspaper ever initiate? Did Miss Hansberry mean the Negro struggle? If so, which one—the Negro working-class struggle or the Negro middle-class struggle? The facts were that the real struggle implicit in Harlem's deprived situation had already been aborted and negated by outer-directed integrationist forces, both left radical and NAACP-ite. Hence the precise struggle Miss Hansberry was referring to was merely the struggle of the Harlem literary and cultural inner circle, the radical leftwing elite, whose political line was empty "radical" language, meaningless to anyone but themselves in the defense of their privileged status. So obsequious were these *Freedom* newspaper intellectuals in their mimicry of the critical standards of white Communists, they could not even give Wright's book the kind of original criticism it deserved. Miss Hansberry's newly acquired radical pose was further displayed when she had to quote a paragraph out of *Jet* magazine's review of Wright to make her point: "His [Wright's] almost psychopathic lust for violence gets the better of him in this second novel and his story becomes as completely phony and un-

[2] *Freedom*, April, 1953, p. 5.

real as a cheap drugstore whodunit. . . . Wright is an outsider—an outcast from his own people."[3]

As if to say that violence is nonexistent in ghetto life, or that a literary artist can never be an "outcast"; as if to say that Richard Wright was *not,* from the date of his birth, an "outsider" to Negro middle-class values. That Johnson Publications' *Jet* magazine and Miss Hansberry agreed on Wright's book was not accidental. Six years later Miss Hansberry would be welcomed by her true "class" colleagues on Johnson's *Ebony* magazine for her theater achievements and for her noble protest against the film version of *Porgy and Bess.* She was quoted as saying: "We do not like to hear our intelligent stars speak in dialect, see them reduced to the level of Catfish Row when they have already risen to the heights of La Scala." The *Ebony* writer added, parenthetically, that "Porgy has the highest percent of [actors with] college degrees ever recorded by a movie."[4] This would show that despite her radical phase in Harlem, Miss Hansberry had never really deserted her peers.

Lorraine Hansberry felt that Wright's character, Cross Damon, was an individual one would never meet on the Southside of Chicago or in Harlem. He was "a symbol of Wright's new philosophy —nothingness." Here was one more outcropping of the leftwing middle-class literary and cultural ethos. That ethos prefers its Negro types to be psychologically uncomplicated, beautifully upright, good, honest folk, *i.e.,* "real" people, who might sin occasionally but who are socially salvageable—if not in church, then in leftwing trade-union politics, Communist front groups, Negro-white cultural groups—or who are for integration à la *A Raisin in the Sun.* Note the reference to the "beauty [and] strength in the eyes of the working people" that Miss Hansberry alleges exists in the ghetto. In her view, ghettoes do not produce bitterness, viciousness, hate, hopelessness, alienation, crime and warped personalities.

But there *are* Cross Damons in every large Northern city. In real life they would not necessarily act out their roles in the same way as Wright's character. But given the very prevalent psychological state of alienation plus the physiological effects of narcotics (not to

[3] *Jet,* March 26, 1953, p. 42.
[4] "Why Negroes Don't Like 'Porgy and Bess,'" *Ebony,* October, 1959, p. 50.

mention the economic determinants of the drug trade), there follow more possibilities for violence, brutality and strange behavior than even Wright presented in his novel. The black ghettoes are the spawning ground for every psychological manifestation of spiritual alienation, and the literary mind that tries to ignore or suppress this terrible fact is simply not facing social realities.

In the Harlem ghetto during the 1930's Depression, personal exigencies and life motivations were far more simple than they are now; so much so that people were able to survive economic ravages and recover. Not so, today. Today there exists in the ghetto an entirely new subterranean world of total rejection of the values and vanities of the white world which first practiced rejection. The pimps, perverts, whores, panderers, addicts, racketeers—all the human dregs (*i.e.*, the very types abhorrent to Killens and Hansberry)—know this world and thrive on it. It is truly a world of violence and brutality and hopelessness. It *is* a frightening social region for the aesthetically squeamish to contemplate, but that attitude does not help. Moreover, those heroically upright, decent-living Negroes who are acceptable types for working-class literature are forced to live in the midst of this human degradation—they cannot all become Younger families à la *Raisin*. These "good folk" will have to cope with this demoralizing situation until told, and directed about, how to "clean house." In the meantime they must fight to keep from being dragged down into the lower depths. All of this comes about in Harlem, as well as other places, because of long years of political and social irresponsibility that border on the criminal. Who was the most responsible—that is to say—who was the most *ir*responsible, in the long history of benighted Harlem's social degradation? Whose politics were the most shortsighted, opportunistic, and irresponsible? Was it the civil rights groups? Or was it the conventional two-party practitioners? Or was it the radical Left? What about the nationalists? Separately, none of these factions are responsible; together, they all are. None of them has ever taken a total view of Harlem as a distinct ethnic community and dealt with it in such terms. Taken together, they have all committed the mortal sin of fragmenting and dividing up the torturous efforts of the people, thus making any kind of unity impossible. In place of trying to achieve a comprehensive view of Harlem's place within the social context of

America, or of Harlem's status as the cultural capitol of black America, these factions have muffled Harlem's social disintegration in the noisy din of fighting and recrimination. But all of this factional uproar does nothing but blind the man on the street to the fundamental fact that nothing less than complete economic, political and cultural autonomy can change Harlem one whit for the better. The implications of this are so tremendous that everybody evades them. Then, into this muddled and noisy confusion marches the radical Left—with its middle-class orientation, opportunistic politics that attempt to capitalize on the confusion, and squeamishly purblind writers who want to record life only as they care to see it. Only their careful cultivation of the middle-class literary ethos assures these writers any participation at all in the integrated middle-class world of the cultural arts in America. So let us not write about the decadence of the human dregs—like those traitors to "our struggle for freedom"—Ellison and Wright. And when the Muslims appear on the scene with their program for rehabilitating the human dregs (addicts, criminals, jailbirds, and such), this Muslim influence with the workers becomes a very frightening threat to the radical Left politicians and their obedient literati. Those Muslims are "anti-white, reactionary separatists" who are subverting our integration movement, said Lorraine Hansberry to *The Village Voice* about a mass meeting in Harlem: "The Muslims, and there weren't many, started chanting, 'We want Malcolm, we want Malcolm,' and dominating the rally. I left soon after and heard that evening in the news that there was violence then."[5]

Lorraine Hansberry moved to Greenwich Village around the time *Freedom* newspaper collapsed. Since the end of World War II there had been several incidents of violence inflicted on Negroes by Village whites, especially Italians, a fact that *The Village Voice* was very much afraid to bring up. Historically, it was anti-Negro violence in Greenwich Village that caused the bulk of its former Negro population to move further uptown, and finally to Harlem. During the early 1950's there was still violence and threats of violence to Negroes in the Village, due to the large influx of Negroes newly on the scene. Most white Villagers consid-

[5] *The Village Voice*, June 6, 1963, p. 9.

ered Greenwich Village *their* neighborhood and Negroes are still, today, considered tourists, commuters—or else interlopers who are merely tolerated. In the 1950's many white Villagers were uneasy whenever they saw Negroes bunching up in and about the coffee shops and in certain bars where the Beats congregated. This habit gave whites the feeling that Negroes were "up to something" threatening; although on the other hand, many liberals would have liked to see more middle-class Negroes come into the Village, especially into those new luxury, middle-class apartments going up a few blocks from Washington Square. Again it was apparent that the potential for the Negro-white intellectual class alliance cut across all political lines, and was middle-class-oriented. What many white Villagers were apprehensive about was the social behavior of the déclassé Negro, the Beat, the uninhibited, free-wheeling escapee from the ghetto whose psychological mood found its counterparts across the color line among the alienated whites.* There these ghetto-wrought Negroes found soul communion in another subterranean world: the world of marijuana fumes and esoteric jazz-buffing to the formalistic tune of "new jazz sounds" for the connoisseurs of the hip and the beat; the world of interracial sex of all modes of expression; the world where the trend of the Beat Generation made the old style Village Bohemian a "square." *The Village Voice,* a white liberal newspaper, looked down its editorial nose at this Village sub-world, and for this reason, even many of the white Subterraneans were cool to the *Voice*'s "hip" liberalism.

Lorraine Hansberry represented the class type *The Village Voice* was happy to welcome there, even though she did not immediately move into a middle-class luxury apartment. But she certainly did not move into the subterranean world either. This is the world in which LeRoi Jones was then beginning to make his way, reading original beat poetry as one of the Kerouac protégés. Jones, unlike Hansberry and others of the Artists for Freedom, did not sprout his literary wings in Harlem, but in the Village. His revolutionary zeal found its release later in Havana, Cuba (not in Russia, by way of Robeson). Jones was also destined to have his Harlem period of political conditioning before he arrived with the others at Town Hall. In his first brief stay in Harlem, however, he

---

* N.B. I have heard established Negro residents of the Village say the same thing.

knew very little about leftwing politics there; he couldn't be warned to be cautious, and thereby mishandled yet another promising black organization, as its chairman. But Lorraine Hansberry, who did not learn much about Harlem that stuck, managed to learn much more about Greenwich Village (which came out in *The Sign in Sidney Brustein's Window*). Naturally, Miss Hansberry looked askance at the subterranean world of the Beats and was heard expressing this conventional point of view much in the liberal tone of *The Village Voice*. The literary middle-class ethos of the Left functions the same in every social milieu. If the pimps, whores, perverts, panderers, racketeers, and Cross Damons of Ellison and Wright are found politically and aesthetically unwholesome for literature about the ghetto, the same applies in Greenwich Village. From the point of view of *The Village Voice* (and most of the solid, but liberal, middle-class Village citizenry) much of what Negroes were doing in the subterranean Beat world was very unwholesome. Therefore it was to be expected that beat types would not appear in *Brustein's Window*, which, after all, was not a "Negro play" and in which the one Negro was reportedly very clean-cut. However, between her Harlem days and *Brustein's Window*, Hansberry had obviously learned a lot of things she had not understood when she attacked Wright's *The Outsider* (also, only *incidentally* a book about a Negro). As *The New York Times* reviewer said of it: "The leading character is, to be sure, a Negro, but his principal problems have nothing to do with his race. They are pre-eminently the problems of the human being as such, for this is, so far as I can recall, one of the first consciously existentialist novels to be written by an American."[6]

It is interesting to examine the following remarks Miss Hansberry made in 1964:

> Few things are more natural than that the tortures of the engagé should attract me thematically. Being 34 years old at this writing means that I am of the generation that grew up in the swirl and dash of the Sartre-Camus debate of the postwar years. The silhouette of the Western intellectual poised in hesitation before the flames of involvement was an accurate symbolism of some of my closest friends, some of whom crossed each other

[6] *The New York Times*, March 22, 1953, Section VII, p. 1.

leaping in and out, for instance, of the Communist party. Others searched, as agonizingly, for some ultimate justification of their lives in the abstractions flowing out of London and Paris. . . . Mine is, after all, the generation that came to maturity drinking in the forebodings of the Silonos, Koestlers and Richard Wrights. It had left us ill-prepared for decisions that had to be made in our own time about Algeria, Birmingham or the Bay of Pigs.[7]

All of which is just so much intellectual subterfuge. Miss Hansberry's talk about "us" being "ill-prepared" has the same empty ring as her condemnation of Wright for negating "our struggle for freedom" in writing *The Outsider*. Note how in 1964, what had been "our struggle for freedom" in 1953 becomes the muddled and comfortably distanced age of "our" political innocence which left "us" ill-prepared for momentous decisions. In 1953, however, Miss Hansberry had not been so politically innocent that she did not know exactly what went into a socialist-realist book review.

In giving the thumbnail sketch of her intellectual development, Miss Hansberry consciously blotted out her *Freedom* newspaper period. She was attempting to explain why she wrote *Brustein's Window,* and what she wrote revealed a lot more about the matter than she intended. She would have had one believe that she grew up in the "swirl and dash" of the Camus-Sartre debate on existentialism (but not on Marxism and art, socialist realism, etc.). The fact is, however, that there was no such debate "swirling" on the radical Left in or out of the Harlem leftwing cultural elite. The official Left line on Sartre and Camus was laid down in 1948 by the French Communist, Roger Garaudy, in a pamphlet in which the work and ideas of these two writers as well as of Mauriac, Malraux and Koestler, were condemned as "Literature of the Graveyard." This pamphlet was immediately translated into English and distributed by the American Communist movement in all leftwing intellectual circles. Its contents remained the official Communist attitude in America until the leftwing collapsed in the middle and late 1950's. In fact, in 1951, the very same year Hansberry joined the *Freedom* staff, Lloyd Brown, the official Negro Communist-line man on Negro literature, did a series of articles for *Masses and Mainstream*—"Which Way for the Negro Writer?"

[7] *The New York Times*, October 11, 1964, Section II, p. 1.

—in which he said: "But with whom shall the Negro writer unite? With the literature of the graveyard—Koestler, Orwell, Gide, Sartre, Eliot, the rancid cults of Kafka and Pound? Or with the writers of socialism, national liberation and peace—the Soviet sons of the immortal Gorky. . . ?"[8]

The *Freedom* newspaper line on Negro literature coincided precisely with what Lloyd Brown said it ought to be. The provincially sectarian, middle-class literary ethos that prevailed permitted no debate on the cultural arts at all. It was this narrow, suppressive approach to literature that nipped a burgeoning Harlem writers' movement in the bud and channeled it along a single track, the ultimate outcome of which was *A Raisin in the Sun*.

If Miss Hansberry had been really involved in the Camus-Sartre controversy she would have observed that the closest approximation of the existentialist man was to be found in the Village subterranean world; and that the most unique personification to the existentialist mood would be the alienated Negro intellectual or artist. But since socialist realism and the middle-class literary ethos are aesthetically related, Miss Hansberry could not glorify such types on stage. Today, what Miss Hansberry called the "Western intellectual poised in hesitation before the flames of involvement" would be more relevantly portrayed by the figure of the Negro intellectual than the white intellectual hero, Sidney Brustein. Moreover, the existentialist man would hardly go in for reform politics or other such middle-class conventions. Thus Miss Hansberry, in transferring from Harlem to Greenwich Village, was simply following the developmental route that all leftwing Negro intellectuals eventually take—she became a full, unadulterated integrationist. In her case, she "became" what she had been from the start—but on another level—the playwright of social significance, a new role for someone from the Negro upper-middle class in this era of full integration.

The phenomenal success of *A Rasin in the Sun* has to be seen against the background of the temper of the racial situation in America and its cultural implications for American artforms. Broadway and the rest of the American theater has not been at all

[8] *Masses and Mainstream*, March, 1951, p. 53.

kind to the Negro playwright or performer. Miss Hansberry's play provided the perfect opportunity to make it all up, or at least assuage the commercial theater's liberal guilt. Of course, when *Raisin* burst on the scene with a Negro star, a Negro director plus a young Negro woman playwright everybody on Broadway was startled and very apprehensive about what this play might *say*. What obviously elated the drama critics was the very relieving discovery that, what the publicity buildup actually heralded was not the arrival of belligerent forces from across the color line to settle some long-standing racial accounts on stage, but a good old-fashioned, home-spun saga of some good working-class folk in pursuit of the American Dream . . . in their fashion. And what could possibly be thematically objectionable about that? And very well written also. We shall give it an award (A for effort), and so they did, amidst a patronizing critical exuberance I would have thought impossible in the crassly commercial institution of Broadway. Not a dissenting critical note was to be heard from Broadway critics, and thus the Negro made theater history with the most cleverly written piece of glorified soap opera I, personally, have ever seen on a stage. Only because it was about *Negroes* was this play acceptable, and this is the sobering fact that the aspiring Negro playwright *must* live with. If this play—which is so "American" that many whites did *not* consider it a "Negro play"—had ever been staged by *white actors* it would be judged second-rate—which was what the British called it, and what the French said of the film version. Why was it that *Raisin*, although it was hailed on Broadway, impressed no one in Europe, which has always been more appreciative and receptive to Negro art than American whites?

Here, the general attitude inspired by the success of *Raisin* was that the Negro in the theater had come of age, so to speak, and that the path was now clear for more resounding achievements. Lorraine Hansberry emerged like a Saint Joan of black cultural revival, sounding off in journalistic and television debates like a prophetess who had suddenly appeared carrying messages from the soul of the "people." The truth is that *A Raisin in the Sun,* far from being the *beginning* of anything, was the end of a trend that had been in process for a long time and had not been critically examined. *Raisin* was the artistic, aesthetic and class-inspired culmination of the efforts of the Harlem leftwing literary and cultural in-group to achieve integration of the Negro in the arts as first postulated by the Committee for the Negro in the Arts in the late 1940's. But this culmination was achieved in a very unique way. CNA had fought for the integration of the Negro in the theater without making the necessary distinction between Negro actor and Negro playwright, both of which roles represent different functions in terms of integration. Thus *Raisin* was not an integrated play of the type Negro actors strive for, but an all-Negro play supposedly passé—but with a difference: *It was an "all-Negro" play about a family in the throes of integrating into a white community.* In terms of American social and racial realities, this was a very good theme and exceedingly timely; but what all the so-called perceptive critics missed was that, from the very real standpoint of Negro urban class sociology, the author deliberately chose the wrong family for the theme.

As a poor Chicago Southside working-class Negro family, the Youngers were most atypical of poor families from the South. True to the socialist-realist tradition, the Younger family was carefully tidied up for its on-stage presentation as good, hardworking, upright, decent, moral, phsychologically uncomplicated ghetto folk; poor but honorable, they had kept their heads above water and had not sunk down into the human dregs. There were no numbers-runners in sight, no bumptiously slick, young "cats" from downstairs sniffing after Mama Younger's pretty daughter on the corner, no shyster preachers hustling Mama into the fold, no fallen women, etc. (All these were sedulously avoided, still banished to the dreary world of Ralph Ellison.)

Miss Hansberry had certainly come a long way from Robeson's "Freedom Family." This Younger family was, in 1959, not of a mind for Negro labor unity in the trade-union struggle for working class liberation; or for socialism in Robeson's world of all the oppressed peoples in the "age-long struggle of the Negro and Jewish people with the same heroes," etc. Lorraine Hansberry had definitely outgrown that poppycock to the extent of knowing that Broadway would not accept it. She was embarking on her phase of the "swirl and dash of the Camus-Sartre debate," but saving it for *Brustein's Window.* However, in the meantime, the Younger family had to be readied for something more immediately crucial and important—integration. Thus, the only working-class Negroes who are fit for integration are those who can be made to mouth middle-class values, sentiments and strivings: platitudes that are acceptable to whites of the middle classes. No wonder the Broadway audience responded to the buildup and embraced *Raisin*. "We really didn't think of it as a Negro play at all." "Why, after all, that Younger family was just like us." "Why *anybody* could have played those characters," etc. "Bravo! How wonderful for letting us know. Now here is your prize!" But nobody asked out loud some pertinent questions such as: "How could a poor ghetto family of Southern origins come by a $10,000 insurance policy and what Southern Negro insurance company would have covered it for this type of family?" "Since when does this type of Negro family have daughters in college studying medicine and where did the money come from to pay for it?" "How did the married son, a taxi driver, come by the connections and the inside political pull and the granting of credit necessary to purchase a liquor store?" All three of these circumstances in Negro life derive not from a working class status, but a lower-middle or middle-class family background. They represent the class advantages that are economic keys, guarding the very limited world of social privilege and advancement of the Negro petite bourgeoisie and bourgeoisie, a world jealously closed against black working-class penetration.[9]

Taken historically, if all things social in Negro-white relations had been equal over the past twenty-five years, all the material in *A Raisin in the Sun* would have long ago been done on the radio, with several variations during the heyday of soap opera series. It was only the racial integration theme that added timeliness to an old-fashioned genre. But *Raisin* arrived on Broadway in the midst of something unheard of when soap opera was fashionable—the Negro middle-class social revolution. Consequently, the Negro working-class characters had to mouth middle-class ideology—

---

[9] Later critical comment on *Raisin* still misses the point. Alan Lewis writes: "Lorraine Hansberry's *A Raisin in the Sun* is an Odets play with Negro replacements." "Today the working class has risen to middle class comfort, and Odets' former Bronx characters now live more comfortably in the suburbs. Audiences no longer have the same identification, save for the underprivileged and the oppressed minorities." But Harlem and Chicago ghettoes persist precisely because the Negro working class *does not* rise to middle-class comfort like Odets' Bronx Jews or the mythical Younger family. See *American Plays and Playwrights of the Contemporary Theatre* (New York: Crown Publishers, 1965), p. 112.

witness the line about Mama Younger with her wide-brimmed hat: "She looks just like Mrs. Miniver." When the Younger family moved out of the slums at the play's end and walked out of their house, out went the "Negro" theme in serious theater; and also, as far as the playwright was concerned, out went even the integration of the Negro in the theater because Miss Hansberry as a writer had departed from the Negro scene long before her Younger family put their last piece of furniture in the moving van. It could easily have been forecast that her next play would be about white folks *and would not even be integrated, as Negro actors had hoped.*

Thus the pathetic illusions about the integration of the Negro in the theater were shown up as leading to a hopeless dead end. The profound differences between playwright and actor—one the *creator* and the other *interpreter*—had never been considered. If the creator integrates herself, as Lorraine Hansberry did, it implies the end of the Negro as a creative Negro being, for the Negro playwright has nowhere to go if *A Raisin in the Sun* is considered as the ultimate in the theater. He (or she) must either be left high and dry as a creative nonentity, or follow Miss Hansberry's lead and write about white people. But can the Negro playwright attempt to do this and survive? Does American culture really need him for that? As one Negro playwright said, the Negro writer must live with *A Raisin in the Sun*, for its arrival signalizes a profound cultural dilemma for the Negro in the theater. This dilemma was further highlighted by the financial and artistic failure of Ossie Davis's *Purlie Victorious*, as measured by the standards of *Raisin's* success on Broadway.

A Raisin in the Sun demonstrated that the Negro playwright has lost the intellectual and, therefore technical and creative, ability to deal with his own special ethnic group materials in dramatic form. The most glaring manifestation of this conceptual weakness is the constant slurring over, the blurring, and evasion of the internal facts of Negro ethnic life in terms of class and social caste divisions, institutional and psychological variations, political divisions, acculturation variables, clique variations, religious divisions, and so forth. Negro playwrights have never gone past their own subjectivity to explore the severe stress and strain of class conflict within the Negro group. Such class and clique rivalries and prejudices can be just as damaging, demoralizing and retarding as white prejudice. Negro playwrights have sedulously avoided dealing with the Negro middle class in all its varieties of social expression, basically because the Negro playwright has adopted the Negro middle-class morality. Therefore, art itself, especially the art of playwriting, has become a stepping stone to middle-class social status. As long as the morality of the Negro middle class must be upheld, defended, and emulated in social life *outside* the theater it can never be portrayed or criticized *inside* the theater à la Ibsen, or satirized à la Shaw. In this regard it becomes the better part of social and creative valor to do what Hansberry did—"Let us portray only the good, simple ordinary folk because this is what the audiences want, especially the white audiences; but let us give the whites the Negro middle-class ball to carry towards the goal of integration. Beyond that very functional use of the Negro in the theater, of what other value is this thing, the so-called Negro play? None at all, so let us banish it along with that other parochial idea 'The Negro Theater.' We don't like this 'Negro play' category in the American theater anyhow, and we don't like to be told that we must write it, but we'll *use* it (as a starter) and then we'll go on to better things; that is, we'll become what they call human and universal, which in the white folks' lexicon and cultural philosophy means 'universally white.' "

But Miss Hansberry even went that theatrical strategy one better. Although in 1959-1960, she did not deny that *Raisin* was a play about a Negro family,* in 1964 when *Brustein's Window* opened, Miss Hansberry denied that *Raisin* was ever a "Negro play":

> Some persons ask how it is that I have "left the Negro question" in the writing of this latest play. I hardly know how to answer as it seems to me that I have never written about "the

---

* In 1959 Lorraine Hansberry defended *A Raisin in the Sun* against the play's unsympathetic critics as follows, in part: "We have grown accustomed to the dynamics of 'Negro' personality as expressed by white authors. Thus, de Emperor [Jones], de Lawd, and, of course, Porgy still haunt our frame of reference when a new character emerges. . . . If we ever destroy the image of the black people who supposedly do find [oppression and/or poverty tolerable] in America, then that much-touted guilt which allegedly haunts most middle-class white Americans with regard to the Negro question would really become unendurable. . . ." "Willy Loman, Walter Younger, and He Who Must Live," *The Village Voice*, August 12, 1959, p. 8.

Negro question." *A Raisin in the Sun,* for instance, was a play about an American family's conflict with certain of the mercenary values of its society, and its characters were Negroes. . . . I write plays about various matters which have both Negro and White characters in them, and there is really nothing else that I can think of to say about the matter.[10]

Miss Hansberry was essentially right about many aspects of *Raisin* and its impact on white audiences but was also adroitly evasive about what her intentions were. She intended to write a Negro play because she could not make her stage debut with anything else. But what crept into *Raisin* was the author's own essentially quasi-white orientation through which she visualizes the Negro world. This was a matter of having one's "cultural" cake and refusing to eat it. However, one indication of Hansberry's intentions about *Raisin* was her choice of the play's title, which was a line taken from a poem by Langston Hughes called "A Montage of a Dream Deferred." Langston Hughes, however, would never have said that this poem was *not* about Harlem Negroes but about a vague species of American. *A Raisin in the Sun* expressed through the medium of theatrical art that current, forced symbiosis in American interracial affairs wherein the Negro working class has been roped in and tied to the chariot of racial integration driven by the Negro middle class. In this drive for integration the Negro working class is being told in a thousand ways that it must give up its ethnicity and become human, universal, full-fledged American. Within the context of this forced alliance of class aims there is no room for Negro art (except when it pays off) or Negro art institutions (We middle-class Negroes ain't about to pay for that!), because all of this is self-segregation which hangs up "our" drive for integration. From all of this it can be seen how right E. Franklin Frazier was when he observed: "The new Negro middle class that has none of the spirit of service . . . attempts to dissociate itself as much as possible from identification with the Negro masses. . . . The lip service which they give to solidarity with the masses very often disguises their exploitation of the masses."[11]

This being the case, it is a foregone conclusion that Negro writ-

[10] *The New York Times,* October 11, 1964, Section II, p. 3.
[11] E. Franklin Frazier, "Negro Middle Class and Desegregation," *Crosscurrents,* Summer, 1957, pp. 213-224.

ers who are middle-class from birth will pass from Negro plays
(which are not Negro plays) to writing plays which are universally human, before they will ever write a play that would have to
portray some unpleasant truths about their own class. But when
can one expect a Negro writer to take up such a challenge when
James Baldwin, who is certainly not even remotely middle-class,
continues to write about The Negro just as if there is no such
thing as a distinct middle class that is setting the tone and pace of
the Negro movement? These writers are not getting down to the
facts of class factors in our struggle for freedom because they are
not telling the truth about whose freedom we are fighting for and
who is going to do what with whose freedom once "we" get it. Further, they are not attempting, in what is called their social criticism, to speculate on what "we" might have to confront just in
case "our freedom" does not materialize quite soon. These writers
have therefore achieved nothing more in print than an agitated
beating of their literary breasts. They are lost sheep bleating to
the God of Freedom for their deliverance. Sometimes they manage
to get angry, and bleat all the louder—while snapping righteously
at the white liberals. Meanwhile they analyze nothing and clarify
less and heap confusion on top of confusion. Their literary or "cultural products" (Miss Hansberry's phrase) are, for the most part,
second-rate because they reflect their creators' oversimplified and
over-emotionalized views about their own ethnic group reality.

Paul Robeson

Freedomways reached its zenith with its special Harlem issue and slid rapidly downhill, settling into a groove of integrationist reportage and conformity. By the summer of 1965, it had come full circle back to the heroic ineffectuality of the *Freedom* newspaper days in Harlem. Ironically and symbolically, the Summer, 1965, issue presented a "Salute to Paul Robeson" based on an affair that April, staged by *Freedomways* honoring the hero's return from exile, and attended, it was said, by people "who hadn't seen each other in years." One got the picture—the old leftwing clan, bereft of the glorious camaraderie of former days, gathered together in a mock-rally around the Robeson leadership symbol, as if to recapture an era that was gone forever. *Freedomways* went on to say:

> Together with these "old-timers" were young people from the Southern battle-front and Northern campus movements of today, a new generation of freedom fighters, many of whom were seeing Paul Robeson for the first time in person. Many from the Harlem and Bedford-Stuyvesant communities of New York came out because (and several expressed it) they felt "our freedom movement has now caught up with many of the things Paul Robeson fought for all these years; it's time we openly acknowledge his contribution."

At last, after almost five years, amongst a reunion of old Left friends, *Freedomways* had caught up with the movement—if only in fancy. Even John Lewis, national chairman of SNCC, was beguiled into making statements in a speech printed in the magazine that rewrote the history of Robeson's role with the Communist Left. Robeson "began to speak for Negro rights—for human rights. He talked and listened to the representatives of the Communist Party. He called for direct action to solve our problems at a time when it was not popular, even extremely 'unfashionable.'"

Where and when did Robeson ever call for "direct action" of the type carried out by SNCC and CORE? Certainly not in *Freedom* newspaper or in his book, *Here I Stand*. Direct action only arrived with the appearance of new leadership, which Robeson never called for, since all of his calls for action were addressed to established leaders. John Lewis could not have been more off beam. For example, what does he know about the role of the Communist Party during World War II (a period when Robeson was supposedly so influential) on the question of direct action by the Negro movement? The first March on Washington Movement was *not* Communist-inspired, but was led by A. Philip Randolph in June, 1941. "Randolph . . . had become increasingly aware of the need for Negro mass organization free of Communist Party influence."[1] This action resulted in President Roosevelt's Executive Order 8802, prohibiting discrimination in defense production industries, and the establishment of the President's Committee on Fair Employment Practice to enforce this policy.

Randolph's direct action was, at first, opposed by none other than the Communist Party. Later, the Communists tried to take over the MOWM because it was successful, but failed because the movement was solidly in the hands of Randolph, supported by the NAACP and the Urban League. The first direct action by CORE actually took place in Chicago in 1942. What precise role was Paul Robeson playing during all of this—besides listening to representatives of the Communist Party? Nonetheless, John Lewis of SNCC is rather innocent about certain facts of history, and the *Freedomways* inner circle would much prefer he remained that way.

The case of Paul Robeson is not just an individual tragedy involving one outstanding Negro; symbolized here is also the tragedy of all Negroes in America, which is, in essence, cultural. Robeson's active career embraced the 1920's, 1930's and the 1940's before he arrived at his *Freedom* newspaper period; something transpired during those three decades that has to explain why Robeson failed during the crucial 1950's and was, therefore, unable to personify a real link with the new Negro movement of the 1960's. It is not enough to say that Robeson

[1] Wilson Record, *op. cit.*, p. 202.

failed only because of the demise of the Communist leftwing, for he could have succeeded *despite* the Communists. There were other factors in the Robeson equation, and all of these had strongly influenced Robeson's career and his thinking in one way or another. There were the NAACP civil rights movement, the Garvey movement, and the Negro cultural renaissance of the 1920's. There were also the economic depression of the 1930's and Roosevelt's New Deal, and finally Robeson's own role as inter-pretive artist. For a Robeson, the question of what the unique role of the Negro creative intellectual in America should be, was cru-cial. It was so critical and implicit that Robeson was instinctively compelled as an artist to transcend himself and assume the role of leadership in the politics of civil rights, even though no individual or movement explicitly suggested this as a definitive program or policy for Negro intellectuals. Inasmuch as the Negro cultural renaissance of the 1920's had not evolved any philosophical guide-lines on the role of the Negro creative intellectual, Robeson con-veniently hitched his rising star to the politics of the Communist Left, then in the ascendancy in radical politics. Here, in the Communist-dominated leftwing, was the *force majeure,* offering an almost irresistible attraction for a star out of its (racial) orbit and seeking a new level of involvement in the affairs of the uni-verse.

Paul Robeson was the most controversial Negro figure in Amer-ica and the most widely known in all the world. He was the Negro's great internationalist, representing himself, in the words of a writer in Atlanta University's *Phylon* magazine, as a man who

> renounced a socially safe, financially profitable career on the concert stage for a program of agitation and action in behalf of "oppressed peoples of the world". . . . Today, Robeson, symbol of the racial system under which he was born and has lived, bears the brunt of the attack on the world race movement, not so much because of the merits of his argument on race, discrimination and segregation, as because of the political ideology of communism within which many American people seem prone to interpret it.[2]

Thus the writer, in describing very succinctly who and what Robeson was, also suggested that Robeson had compromised his

[2] Ira De A. Reid, *op. cit.,* p. 368.

own stand against discrimination and segregation, thereby impugning his undeniably moral case against American racial practices by joining it with the ideology of Communism. Usually white opponents of Robeson made Communism the issue—but was that issue the real one? Or was it something else about the Negro in America that Communism, as an issue, only obscured? The trouble was that Robeson *himself,* as well as his friends and foes, did everything possible to make Communism the issue. He was a staunch defender of the Russian social system, confusing Russian values and motivations with those of the American milieu.

At a time when Russia was not internationalistic but decidedly *nationalistic* (contrary to every dogma of the international Communist movement), Robeson was the great internationalist in the service of Soviet-oriented world politics. This transcendent but misapplied internationalism was in fact nothing but Robeson's essential integrationist thinking as an American Negro—writ large —by his own convenient adoption of an ideology that transformed him from a well-known actor-singer into a citizen of the world. The transference is easy to see: If one cannot become a universally accepted "citizen" of America—well then, one *can* become a citizen of the world, and tell America what it can do with what! For Paul Robeson, the actor-performer *par excellence,* the grand international movement of the Left became the audience—and the show must go on even if one is constrained to renounce "a socially safe, financially profitable career on the concert stage" for the politics of revolution.

There was involved in Robeson's career a unique problem in the dualism of illusion and reality. The reality was that Robeson was fundamentally an integrationist for whom the ideology of the political leftwing became a rationale for racial integration. This integration had to be both national and international, at home and abroad, among Negro and white labor or among all the oppressed people (black, white, brown and red), Negroes and Jews and Gentiles, the American minorities—essentially all those leftwing ingredients of the American melting pot gambit carried over onto the international scene. Here was the political apotheosization of a human, a social ideal in a manner that evaded and denied a social fact—the fact that racial integration on the American national scene is a sociological fraud in life and but a romantic fixture in the Negro integrationist's imagination.

In order to see Robeson for what he was, one must strip his personality of all its fervid devotion to the Russian enchantment and examine him as a Negro cultural symbol purely within the context of American race relations. Thus once the Communist issue is relegated to its proper place within that context, Robeson can be analyzed in terms of his own, native American dilemma: the great and fundamental conflict that goes on within the Negro world behind the civil rights front between integrationist and nationalist tendencies. All·Negro leaders express the point of view of either of these trends (or some suitable and comfortable middle-ground between the two). Robeson was no different, except that he was a manifestation of this conflict on the cultural front as a Cultural Personality.

In joining the leftwing in the 1930's, Robeson, as artist, encountered the old, unsolved problem of art versus politics. This problem had not even been solved in the 1920's for the white creative intellectuals such as John Dos Passos who broke with Communism in refusing to subordinate their art.* The 1930's, however, were more amenable to the wedding of the creative arts with Communist politics. Moreover, the fact that Robeson was not a creative artist but an interpretive one qualified his personal role in the leftwing as a Negro and facilitated his adoption of Left politics, inasmuch as there was no creative or aesthetic clash of values actually involved. The actor, singer, performer, offers no essential threat to the canons of Communist aesthetics, but the creative artist—the writer, poet, painter and composer—*can* and most often does. Thus Robeson, fortified with Left ideology, became the interpretive artist turned spokesman-leader. But the politics of cultural leadership within the Negro movement is the politics not of the interpretive artist but of the creative artist. Robeson therefore

---

* The first issue of *New Masses* (May, 1926), the literary and cultural magazine of the Communist movement, listed fifty-eight artists and writers as editors and contributors. This list included such well-known writers as: Robinson Jeffers, Scott Nearing, Whittaker Chambers, Joseph Freeman, William Carlos Williams, Sherwood Anderson, Carlton Beals, Van Wyck Brooks, Stuart Chase, Floyd Dell, Max Eastman, Waldo Frank, Claude McKay, Lewis Mumford, Eugene O'Neill, Elmer Rice, Carl Sandburg, Upton Sinclair, Jean Toomer, Louis Untermeyer, Walter White, and Edmund Wilson. In the debate during the 1920's over the relationship of art and leftwing politics, most of these leading writers moved away and severed their relations with the Communist-influenced political Left.

was never able to come to grips with the essential problems of the Negro creative intellectual in American culture and deal with them as a leader.

We have already seen how in the case of the American Negro Theater the motivations of Negro playwrights and Negro actor-performers were essentially at variance over the question of ethnic theater. In a broader context of American culture as a whole the same role-values apply. From the American Negro point of view, the predominance in American cultural arts of the aesthetic values and standards of white Anglo-Saxon Protestants can neither be challenged nor competed against unless the Negro creative intellectuals assume that role. When Negro actor-performers are left to decide the issue, they will usually seek integration and tend towards the adoption of the aesthetic values of the dominant group.

Two years before *Freedom* newspaper was started, the August, 1949,* issue of *Masses and Mainstream* carried a striking photograph of Paul Robeson on its cover; it also carried the article "Negro Culture—Heritage and Weapon" by Doxey Wilkerson, which was to be a rallying issue of the Harlem Writers Club. Wilkerson stated:

> Denials of the concept of Negro culture cannot be validated on the grounds that the Negro's art creations have a definite inter-relation with the whole body of American culture.
>
> The validity of the concept of Negro culture here advanced is attested by the work of Negro artists in all fields.
>
> There is, indeed, a Negro culture. It is a phenomenon qualitatively different from mere "American culture."
>
> As is true of all culture, Negro cultural creations are a form of persuasion. The artist tries to get his audience to accept his interpretation of reality.

However:

> The Negro artist . . . must address himself largely to an "alien" audience; and this fact is not without considerable influence on the genuineness of what he tries to say.[3]

---

* August, 1949, was also the month of the disastrous anti-Communist riots at Peekskill, New York, where Paul Robeson held open-air concerts. For an account of the two nights of terror during the week of August 28 to September 4, 1949, see Howard Fast, *Peekskill, USA*, New York, Civil Rights Congress, 1951.

[3] *Masses and Mainstream*, August, 1949, pp. 3-24, *passim*.

Wilkerson, of course, did not say whether or not he included white Communists and sympathizers as part of this "alien" audience, or whether the Communist Party's aesthetic or socialist realism influenced the genuineness of certain Negro artists. However, his article revealed that certain Negro Communist intellects were concerned over the challenges of this cultural problem to the extent of posing them in print. Wilkerson was asking, in effect—"Which way do we leftwing cultural workers go—toward integration or toward ethnic group identity? Are these two trends really contradictory?" But no one on the Left dared to discuss publicly a single idea expressed by Wilkerson because his article was poised to tread into cultural areas the Harlem leftwing cultural elite did not care to investigate. Wilkerson's article concluded with an evaluation of Robeson: "Paul Robeson continues to demonstrate to the world the potential power of Negro culture as a social force."[4]

Robeson was indeed a "social force," in the most limited meaning of the term, insofar as Communist Left political propaganda was concerned. However, as for delineating the unique imperatives for the future role of the Negro creative intellectual in American culture and the innate potential of this class, Robeson was a force only as long as the leftwing was a force to be reckoned with. When the Communist Left began to wane, Robeson could not free himself from being its intellectual prisoner. In the end he became a broken symbol. There were, to repeat, several unresolved native factors in Robeson's background (as in that of his artistic contemporaries) that had not been synthesized into a cultural philosophy for the Negro native to America. Wilkerson's important article vaguely hinted at the outlines of such a philosophy, but he was not prepared to develop his premises.

Wilkerson himself demonstrated that unique class-motivated oscillation between the opposite poles of integrationism and nationalism. In writing the above article he was then taking a black position, the implications of which, if logically pursued, would lead to nationalism, a banned position in the leftwing movement. However, it took Wilkerson eight more years to decide exactly where he *did* stand. In 1957 he quit the Communist Party, citing the Supreme Court Decision of 1954 on integration as his *raison*

[4] *Ibid.*, p. 24.

d'être for any political commitment to leftwing politics.[5] He had reverted back to being what he was essentially, all the time—what Ernest Kaiser called a "near-Marxist"—who had used Communist political doctrine for none other than integrationist aims.

With Robeson, as with most all Negro intellectuals today, one of the first means in gauging the source and roots of his political troubles is to ascertain exactly where he stood on the question of political nationalism. As he was a product of the Negro renaissance of the 1920's, a key to Robeson's cultural nationalism is his attitude towards the Garvey movement. In his book *Here I Stand* (1958), Robeson reveals that he, like many of his contemporaries, was unsympathetic to the Negroes' last great nationalistic resurgence. In fact in 1958, thirty-odd years later, he was still forced to find ways of discrediting this movement. Through a perverse kind of. social logic Robeson tried to prove that Garvey believed that "white power was decisive" by quoting from Garvey's essay: "The Negro's Place in World Reorganization": "The white man of America has become the natural leader of the world. He, because of his exalted position, is called upon to help in all human efforts . . . so, naturally, there can be no great mass movement or change without first acquainting the leader on whose sympathy and advice the world moves."[6]

Robeson went on to comment:

> Much has changed since those words were written, and I have no doubt that if Garvey were alive today he would recognize that the "white man of America" is no longer all-powerful and that the colored peoples of the world are moving quite independently of that "sympathy and advice."
>
> In Booker T. Washington's day it was the ruling white man of the South whose sympathy was considered indispensable; today it is the liberal section of the dominant group in the North whose goodwill is said to be the hope for Negro progress. It is clear that many Negro leaders act or desist from acting because they base themselves on this idea. . . . To the extent that this idea is prevalent in its midst, Negro leadership lacks the quality of independence without which it cannot be effective.[7]

[5] *The New York Times*, December 14, 1957, p. 8.
[6] Robeson, *Here I Stand* (New York: Othello Associates, 1958), p. 111.
[7] *Ibid.*, p. 112.

Note that, like the Artists for Freedom at Town Hall six years later, Robeson criticizes the liberal influence but does not mention Communist leftwing whites or the fact that Negro radical leaders must also win independence from white radicals in order to be effective. All through this book Robeson felt obliged to apologize for the Communists, as if it had never occurred to him that it was possible for them to be grievously wrong and destructive in their tactics towards Negroes. Not even the 20th Congress Moscow revelations nor the Hungarian revolt of 1956 could shake his almost childlike reverence for the Soviet Union. Said he: "I have never hesitated to associate with people who hold nonconformist or radical views. . . ."[8]

Hence, he had many Communist associates who, in his view, were absolutely above criticism in public. But why was it necessary for Robeson to go all the way back to the 1920's to criticize Marcus Garvey in a book written on the Negro movement in 1958? Because a man of Robeson's background *had* to be bothered and inwardly uneasy over the question of nationalism. Paul Robeson's theatrical career began at a time when the biggest stumbling block to Communist penetration into Negro life was the Garvey movement's nationalist crusade—a fact that the Communists never forgot. All the Negro creative intellectuals of the 1920's had to be impressed with Garvey whether they joined him or not—which few did. But since the Communist leftwing made it impossible to reconcile Garvey nationalism with Communist Marxism, Garveyism had to be rejected by Negroes who allied themselves with the Communist leftwing. But Communism itself was *not* the only reason most of the Negro intellectuals rejected Garveyism; many of them also stayed clear of Communism. A retrospective analysis will reveal that as far as the Negro intellectuals as a class were concerned, both Communism and Garveyism were lacking on the cultural plane insofar as native American peculiarities related to the Negro cultural movement. Garveyism was not a native American movement but a West Indian movement, transplanted to the United States for political and economic reasons. As such, it never became, on the cultural plane, an Afro-American nationalist movement but remained what it was from its Jamaican inspiration—a West In-

[8] *Ibid.*, p. 48.

dian or Afro-British nationalist movement. The Harlem Renaissance, on the other hand, *was* predicated on Afro-American cultural ingredients. There was no such comparable cultural revival in the West Indies and the West Indian influence in the Harlem Renaissance came from individuals such as McKay who had emigrated to the United States.

The Garvey movement had posed a particular challenge to the Negro creative intellectual in the 1920's, but only in the limited terms of the economics and politics of Africa within the context of postwar international politics. Insofar as its propaganda was concerned, the inspirational qualities of the Garvey movement were predicated on African revival. But in its *Realpolitik* practice, the aim of the movement was the federation of Africa and the West Indies within the British Commonwealth on a capitalistic partnership basis. As such, the Garvey movement had no real, functional cultural program. Like most politicians, Garvey considered that economics and politics take precedence over culture and art.

Thus the creative intellectuals, much as they might have been impressed with Garvey, had to deal with culture and art within the American context and in their own way, but *apart* from the Garvey movement.* Although during the 1920's Negro creative artists celebrated a rediscovery of their African heritage, through poetry, essay, graphic arts, etc., they would not join the Back-to-Africa trend. Garvey nationalism failed on the cultural plane in terms of program and methodology. It was a flaw that has persisted to this very day in nationalist trends. Intellectuals such as Robeson have been haunted by his cultural flaw ever since. The Robesons cannot explain this flaw, but they are forced to attempt to explain Garveyism away.

Yet Paul Robeson, who rejected outright nationalism for his own reasons (as well as Communist leftwing influence), nevertheless exhibited definite traces of residual cultural nationalism himself. Running all through *Here I Stand* are allusions to "Africa," "African Culture," "cultural projects," "the role of the Negro artist," "racial identification and common sentiments," "people's culture," and the like. At one point Robeson even reacts to his discovery that he was really an "African":

* One of the best examples of this approach is *The New Negro—An Interpretation*, by Alain Locke (New York: Albert and Charles Boni, 1925).

As an artist it was natural that my first interest in Africa was cultural. Culture? The foreign rulers of that continent insisted that there was no culture worthy of the name in Africa.

I came to see the roots of my own people's culture especially in our music which is still the richest and most healthy in America.

Lovers of African sculpture can be quite indifferent to the people whose hands have wrought those masterpieces, and here in America there have been many who have appreciated—and appropriated—Negro music while showing an utter disregard for its creators.

The artist must elect to fight for Freedom or for Slavery. I have made my choice.

With or without his leftwing political prop, however, Robeson was unable to create a specific cultural program—for his Afro-Americanism. He was lost in an idealistic maze, an actor trying to play a grand role he had not fully studied, but a role with some apparent design: "Now, there was a logic to this cultural struggle I was making, and the powers that be recognized it before I did."[9]

Here Robeson was referring to his activities in England where he had deep discussions with men like H.G. Wells, Harold Laski, and Jawaharlal Nehru over the "real but unknown glories of African culture." Shades of Marcus Garvey! Certainly there were many British imperialists who believed that Africans had no culture, but Robeson's real struggle for cultural identity belonged in the United States—not with British intellectuals in London's exclusive salons.

The battle that Robeson waged on his home ground was not really a "cultural struggle" but a political one; or better, a civil rights struggle with a leftwing orientation. The only cultural wars he ever waged were, first, as an individual artist-singer fighting the System, and then later, with himself, for having subordinated what should have been his specific role as a Negro artist to the role of civil rights leader in a field already overcrowded—as if to say that he, Robeson, had a better civil rights strategy than the NAACP, *et al.*:

To all groups in Negro life I would say that the key to set into motion our power of organization is the concept of coordinated

[9] *Ibid.*, pp. 42-60, *passim.*

action. . . . A unified leadership of a unified movement means that people of all political views—conservatives, liberals, radicals —must be represented therein. . . . There is a need—an urgent need—for a national conference of Negro leadership . . . to work out a common program of action for Negro Americans, etc., etc.[10]

As indicated by the above, Robeson's autobiography was a weak, muddled, sentimental book, suffused with innocent idealism and lacking a single paragraph of original thought on Negro problems. While Robeson certainly had the noblest of intentions, it took a naïve and pitiful kind of leftwing vanity even to contemplate the gathering under one roof of "unified leadership"—the conservative, liberal and radical Negroes of the 1930's, 1940's, and 1950's. It took nothing less than the SNCC and CORE direct actionists and the new nationalist wave to shake up that crowd—a fact that Robeson did not foresee.

Robeson was a unique leader who forthwith negated his own uniqueness. He had within his grasp the elements of a new brand of politics, the politics of culture, the leadership of which he only saw vaguely, if at all, as his natural role. A Negro radical leader must comprehend that when the Negro creative artist turns his back on the imperatives of the ethnic culture *he is also turning his back on ethnic politics, ethnic economics, in fact, on practically the entire range of problems inherent in the inner-group reality of Negro existence.* Once this happens, once this integrationist trend becomes the dominant theme, as it did during the postwar period and into the 1950's and 1960's, then no amount of agitational civil rightism can achieve very much. Leftwing politics restricted Robeson to the role of a mere civil rights agitator; yet if he had only been able to maintain his cultural status, and join with Negro creative artists as a class in the cultivation of an Afro-American cultural philosophy, it would have added an important intellectual, creative and political reinforcement to the civil rights struggle. A new politics of culture has long been needed in the American cultural desert, and its inspirational impetus can come only from the Negro. Robeson, however, merely gave sanction to the CNA's self-disintegration (via integration in the arts) by his own apparent lack of a cultural philosophy.

[10] *Ibid.,* pp. 106-107, *passim.*

The only possible sounding board for the pros and cons of the cultural integration issue was *Freedom* newspaper. But *Freedom*'s function was essentially political, and once the political line is established as pro-Communist leftwing, then politics and economics (*i.e.,* trade union economics) take agitational precedence over culture and art. If toeing this line, artists and intellectuals must subordinate their artistic conceptions to its programmatic demands. Of course, the ultimate logic of this political philosophy is that these artists also subordinate themselves and stop creating; but things seldom go that far because artists will eventually rebel against the restrictions of political philosophy long before they submit to becoming pure politicians. It was not Robeson's *art* that he subordinated to leftwing politics, so much as his personal career. Thus he remained, in essence, an actor-singer who, ethnically speaking, became a poor politician—a great potential spokesman with a misdirected and ineffective political line. In Robeson's personal revolt—a revolt of the black artist against capitalistic culture —he thought it necessary to use political weapons of an unconventional kind. But the situation demanded that the cultural values of the American white majority be challenged and fought with other cultural values—and that is quite another brand of politics.

American conditions have permitted many Negro actor-performers to achieve prominence, but have produced only a scattering of Negro writers, none of whom ever approached the pinnacle of spokesmanship until the advent of James Baldwin, whose own limitations as spokesman are the inevitable result of the lack of an ethnic cultural philosophy. As I have pointed out, the Negro actor-performer-singer has always developed an ambivalent communion (or none at all) with the Negro creative artist—upon whom the interpreters seldom depend for their artistic accomplishments or financial status. (Paul Robeson, for example, was an interpreter of Shakespeare, European opera, the plays of Eugene O'Neill, etc.) It is unavoidable that this interracial collaboration in the performing arts influences the ethnic outlook of the Negro actor-performer. As a result, he is in many ways the most ethnically unstable, or the most aracial of all Negro artists.

This was demonstrated quite clearly in 1959 when Negro actors set themselves to prove that they could play white roles "with no noticeable distortion of artistic values." Actors Equity at that time set up a Committee on Integration of the Negro in the Theater. It staged an experimental showcase to which leading Broadway producers were invited, in the hope that they would be induced to hire Negro actors to play roles written by white playwrights for white actors.[11] Prominent in this integrated "charade" was actor-playwright Ossie Davis, from the Harlem leftwing literary and cultural in-group. No doubt Davis would have balked if it were suggested that a white actor play the lead in his own play—"with no noticeable distortion . . . etc." to Reverend Purlie Victorious. Needless to say, the producers were not impressed. What the Negro actors could not prove was what *functional* value this would have in terms of the aesthetic illusion the American mind seeks in the theater.

The Negro actor-performer totally lacks a functional cultural philosophy. He exists in a world of illusion and there is little dividing line between his relationships with the world behind the footlights and the world of living reality. As an actor-performer, it was remarkable that Paul Robeson essayed an actual leadership role. But he never was able to escape, fully, the magic web of make-believe. He was an impassioned agitator for ideas that never touched the rock-bottom facts of life. He remained an unoriginal thinker and social critic who could do no more than expound elaborately muddled variations on the interracial politics themes already laid down for him by the Communist leftwing. As a typical example of the noble, remote idealism of his message, he wrote in his *Freedom* column: "I saw the youth and witnessed the friendship of black and white, of native and foreign born. I felt again the closeness of the age-long struggle of the Negro and Jewish people, peoples with the same heroes—Moses, Joshua, David."[12] He might have seen something resembling this idyllic state of affairs at some of those leftwing rallies he was always attending, but certainly not in real everyday American life. Thus, like other Negro leftwing idealists, Robeson sapped Negro group militancy by misdirecting it.

[11] *The New York Times*, April 21, 1959, p. 37.
[12] *Freedom*, January, 1951, p. 1.

A political or cultural line of approach that refused to recognize the principles of ethnic group autonomy could never be expected to grasp intellectually the essential nature, motivations, aspirations and necessities of a community like Harlem. It could never bring itself to an open frontal assault upon the economic entrenchments of the whites *inside* the ghettoes, who, by their privileged arrangements, were able to suck the community dry of its hard-won income. Liberation for the people in the ghetto was always some place else far off—outside the community, in the class-collaborationist dealings of trade unions, in that mythical social region of Robeson's dreams where black and white, native and foreign-born, Gentile and Jew all joined together in heavenly discourse without ethnic frictions—a world that the average Harlemite never heard of and certainly never experienced. Inside Harlem, Robeson only became super-militant when he was berating other middle-class leaders in the NAACP, the Urban League and the world of A. Phillip Randolph or Adam Clayton Powell. But the clique around *Freedom* newspaper was essentially no different in class ideology from the very people Robeson was attacking. Only the political veneer of their stodgy leftism made it possible for them to pretend that they were anything else but the leftwing of the NAACP parading under another name.

The ultimate outcome of the incompetence of the radical wing in politics was the failure of the *only* basic and meaningful protest movement to emerge out of Harlem since the end of World War II; the only one organized and directed at a tangible aspect of material living conditions. As far back as the January, 1953, issue of *Freedom*, there was a detailed article on Harlem housing problems, calling for the "merger of all tenants' groups fighting the common battle for decent housing." The article stressed rent control, actions against evictions and a "program of forcing the city administration to assume its responsibilities of forcing landlords to correct violations." Jesse Gray was first mentioned at that time as one of the guiding spirits behind the organization of tenants. But Gray's Tenants Revolt—when it finally did arrive in 1964—was *only* a tenants' movement without allied movements of an economic, political or cultural nature acting in consonance with it. It was inevitable that this movement would run up against the hard

economic barrier of outside white real estate and banking ownership of Harlem housing. Inevitably, it became bogged down in the
legal maze of administrative red tape and anti-rent-strike maneu-
vering by those in the power structure. A tenants' movement
alone is doomed to collapse.

The more the Communist leftwing supports integration the
more it becomes superfluous to the integration movement, since
racial integration accepts all the values, standards, vanities and
commitments of the capitalist establishment. From the start, the
Communist Party line on Negro liberation has been almost totally awry or irrelevant. If there, in fact, exists a revolutionary
method implicit in the interplay of class or group relations within
the American social complex, the Communist Party's theoreticians
have been unable to locate it. Thus, once the social compulsion
toward racial integration took firm hold on the Negro intelligentsia, as it had long before 1954, the American liberal-
democratic commitment proceeded from its idealistic state to its
social role as the champion of the integration cause. All the white
liberals and the high courts of the land became vocally committed
to upholding, as far as was feasibly prudent and wise, the Negro
integrationists' demand for human rights. In addition, the pro-
integration forces among the whites both outnumbered the Communist Left adherents and outranked them in social prestige—
coming, as they did, from all walks of life, from business to boards
of education, from religion to the arts.

In other words, Robeson did not really need the Communist
Left for what he was saying or doing in the Harlem community—
he only *thought* he did. His cultural status had already been won
by him and established outside the Communist leftwing; however,
his Harlem faction still needed the Communist leftwing for as long
as it took them to integrate and establish themselves in the higher
echelons of the cultural world outside Harlem. After achieving
this goal, they too would not need the Communist Party any
longer.

Paul Robeson, contrary to what Doxey Wilkerson wrote about
him, ceased being any kind of a cultural force the moment he
started functioning in Harlem with *Freedom* newspaper. After
that, he never said or did anything that would magnify or enhance

his role within the Harlem community. He simply presided over a disintegrating cultural situation until it collapsed, and then he went into exile.

Some years later, James Baldwin was to say in one of his essays:

> It is personally painful to me to realize that so gifted a man as Robeson should have been tricked by his own bitterness and by a total inability to understand the nature of political power in general, or Communist aims in particular, into missing the point of his own critique, which is worth a great deal of thought. . . .[13]

But it is highly doubtful that the Association of Artists for Freedom, most of whom are Robeson's heirs, would stop to debate with Baldwin, once their most illustrious member, what indeed "is worth a great deal of thought" in the tragedy of Robeson.

·IV·

VI

Freedomways, Summer 1963:
Black Economy—Self-Made Myth

It was never the intention of the editors of *Freedomways* to do justice to the Harlem reality historically, politically, culturally or economically. There are too many skeletons hidden in Harlem's closets, and none of the knowledgeable writers dared to probe too deeply. Among the twenty-two writer-specialists there was not one political, economic or cultural theorist who attempted to plot the course of where Harlem was going in transition. Not one dared to be so bold as to debate the imperatives of two positions: Should Harlem be broken up or should Harlem citizens band together and direct all efforts toward maintaining Harlem's separate existence? Not one was willing to undertake to corral community opinions in order to lead or direct the fortunes of Harlem in either direction. The social motivations of these writers are not inner-directed but outer-controlled; thus the writers exist in a neutral stasis subject to the outside decisions—political, economic and cultural—of the white economic and political power structure. From this initial position of subservient compromise, those who wrote the *Freedomways* special Harlem issue could not even know where to *begin* a thorough analysis of Harlem. Such an analysis, of course, had to be historical, but the historical essays were in fact the weakest.

The least instructive of all the historical articles were those of Langston Hughes and Glenn Carrington, both of whom wrote on the Harlem Renaissance: "My Early Days in Harlem"[1] and "The Harlem Renaissance—A Personal Memoir."[2] These two historical articles should have complemented two of the other, more contemporary, articles in the issue—on the Harlem theater move-

[1] *Freedomways*, Summer, 1963, Vol. 3, No. 3, pp. 312-314. Used by permission.
[2] *Ibid.*, pp. 307-311.

ments: Loften Mitchell's "The Negro Theater and the Harlem Community" and Jim Williams' "The Need for a Harlem Theater." But both Hughes and Carrington were simply descriptive and anecdotal, presenting no analysis of trends or guides to cultural conclusion. As a result, there was no broad, overall cultural theme established in *Freedomways* in which a discussion of the Negro in the theater would make any sense. The Negro creative intellectual still does not comprehend that the situation of the Negro in the theater is merely one aspect of a larger cultural question. Involved are all the other arts in America, in turn intertwined with larger political, economic and racial aspects of American society. A Langston Hughes can intuitively sense this question of cultural revolution, but he cannot express it except in poetic terms:

> Harlem, like a Picasso painting in his cubistic period. Harlem —Southern Harlem—the Carolinas, Georgia, Florida—looking for the Promised Land—dressed in rhythmic words, painted in bright pictures, dancing to jazz—and ending up in the subway at morning rush time—headed downtown. West Indian Harlem— warm rambunctious sassy remembering Marcus Garvey, Haitian Harlem, Cuban Harlem, little pockets of tropical dreams in alien tongues. Magnet Harlem, pulling an Arthur Schomburg from Puerto Rico, pulling an Arna Bontemps all the way from California, a Nora Holt from way out West, an E. Simms Campbell from St. Louis, likewise a Josephine Baker, a Charles S. Johnson from Virginia, an A. Philip Randolph from Florida, a Roy Wilkins from Minnesota, an Alta Douglas from Kansas. Melting pot Harlem—Harlem of honey and chocolate and caramel and rum and vinegar and lemon and lime and gall. Dusky dream Harlem rumbling into a nightmare tunnel where the subway from the Bronx keeps right on downtown, where the jazz is drained to Broadway whence Josephine [Baker] goes to Paris, Robeson to London, Jean Toomer to a Quaker Meeting House, Garvey to Atlanta Federal Penitentiary, and Wallace Thurman to his grave; but Duke Ellington to fame and fortune, Lena Horne to Broadway, and Buck Clayton to China.[3]

If only Hughes had had the ability to express the essence of this Harlem sketch in political, economic and cultural concepts and to

[3] *Ibid.*, p. 314.

outline them in the framework of a Harlem social reorganization program, then it could be said that the 1920's Harlem Renaissance was not in vain. But Langston Hughes unfortunately had never developed much in scope beyond the artistic, aesthetic and intellectual limits of the 1920's. He was one of the aborted renaissance men—as incomplete an intellectual and artist as the cultural transformation that nurtured him—a man of culture without a cultural philosophy.

Lacking a cultural philosophy that could have been an adjunct to a political philosophy, the *Freedomways* writers could discuss the state of Harlem politics only in the most timid reformist terms. In his article "Parties and Politics in Harlem," the civil rights attorney Paul B. Zuber wrote: "There are political clubs in Harlem and political leaders in Harlem, but I feel that this is where the similarity with any political organization ends. In other words, we have a political frosting but no political cake."[4]

Pointing out that politics in Harlem is controlled by "political bosses" from downtown, Zuber said, however:

> If the political boss wanted something done, he would contact the minister(s) who in turn would deliver the message to his congregation. There are many who will refute these observations, particularly the ministers, but I submit that this system is as strong as ever and also that the most powerful political figures in Harlem are not J. Raymond Jones and the district leaders but a group of ministers whom the white political power structure honestly believe control the thinking and actions of the Negroes in Harlem.[5]

But with all his criticism of the Harlem community politics of our two-party system, Zuber, like most Negro leaders, does not have the imagination to see anything beyond reforms within that same system of two dominant parties. These leaders boast of how the Negro vote in America holds the balance of power, but they are afraid to think in terms of making that balance an independent power through the creation of—for example—*an all-Negro political party*. That would be "nationalistic," you see, or perhaps another brand of separatism. Of course these spokesmen cry the

[4] *Ibid.*, p. 369.
[5] *Ibid.*, pp. 369-370.

integration blues when they find themselves barred from equal opportunities in the political prizes of the two-party system, yet they are so completely wedded to this political arrangement that they have what amounts to a morbid and pathological fear of even contemplating a break with Democrats or Republicans. One could even accuse Negro leadership of all persuasions of actually fearing independent political action outside the limits of the two parties. Zuber continued: "The division of the political complex in Harlem has been further complicated by another interesting fact which warrants consideration. Harlem and other Negro communities in New York City suffer politically because of the presence of the national offices of our civil rights organizations in the City of New York."[6]

In other words, there is much feuding in local politics among politicians, ministers and civil rights leaders over power and prestige priorities, appointments and patronage. The Democratic Party structure is limited, he says, and the Republican Party structure in Harlem "is a mirage." However, Zuber does not feel that "all is lost." He suggests the following: "I believe that the present political organization has to be completely overhauled. . . . The political clubs must build their program around the community and its needs rather than jobs for the party faithful."[7]

That this is tantamount to breaking with the traditional two-party system, Zuber clearly does not see at all. For if it is true, as Zuber said, that "the Negro in Harlem must learn to pay his own way," then he must learn, at the same time, to create the special kind of political organization he pays for. Zuber explained that "as long as candidates go downtown to get money for their campaigns, as long as the bills are paid by someone else, our elected officials may pay homage to two masters. The man who passed out the money will always win."[8]

But this is the traditional way of two-party politics in America and it cannot be reformed into something else more politically ethical.

Paul B. Zuber's article on Harlem politics was not the first time

6 *Ibid.,* p. 370.
7 *Ibid.,* p. 373.
8 *Ibid.,* pp. 372-373.

he had written for *Freedomways.* A year before he had written an article on economics, "The Economic Plight of the Northern Negro,"[9] which also had a Harlem orientation. What was interesting about Zuber's article was that he considered the Negro's economic position in the North more of a "plight" than his position in the South, despite the fact that the Northern Negro is economically better off. But once again the lack of clearly-defined integrationist goals inexorably drives the Northern integrationist back to the pressing reality of economic fundamentals. In the North this crisis lies precisely *inside* the Negro ghettoes—not in integrated housing projects or integrated classrooms or any other of the multitude of integrated externals over which Negroes rend the atmosphere with racial discord. Such externals are, in effect, the main social province of professional civil righters and civil writers: the province of Negro individualism as opposed to the social province of the group. When the Negro individualist-integrationist runs into trouble over the externals he reverts back to the group— sometimes. Thus, Paul B. Zuber in his article on economics returns to group considerations.

The integrationists have always said that a separate Negro economy in the United States is a myth. But is it really? The reason that the debate on the black economy has gone on back and forth for years, with no conclusions reached, is because the idea is closely linked with nationalism, and the integrationists would rather be tarred and feathered than suspected of the nationalist taint. This was the great weakness of W.E.B. DuBois—the only real flaw in the man's intellectual equipment. DuBois upheld the idea of a separate black economy as "not so easily dismissed" because "in the first place we have already got a partially separate economy in the United States."[10] Yet he remarked in 1940 that his economic program for Negro advance "can easily be mistaken for a program of complete racial segregation and even nationalism among Negroes . . . this is a misapprehension."[11] It seems not to have occurred to DuBois that any thorough economic reorganization of Negro existence imposed from above, will not be supported by the popular masses unless an appeal is made to their nationalism. In our times

[9] *Freedomways,* Summer, 1962, pp. 245-252.
[10] *Dusk of Dawn, op. cit.,* p. 97.
[11] *Ibid.*

Malcolm X had the nationalist appeal but *not* the program; Du-Bois had the program but *not* the nationalist appeal. This explains, in part, the tragedy of the Negro and his luckless leadership in the twentieth century. For notice how long it took for an avowed integrationist like Paul B. Zuber to admit, even by implication, either the reality or the potential of the black economy. The black economy is a myth only because a *truly viable* black economy does not exist. It does not exist simply because Negroes as a group never came together to create one, which does not mean that it would be a simple matter to create a black economy. But it could be done—with the aid of attributes the Negro has never developed, i.e., discipline, self-denial, cooperative organization and knowledge of economic science. But let us examine how Zuber approaches the question: "The Black economy in this country suffers for the same reasons that other phases of social action are lost to the Black American. We are sold out before we have an opportunity to shift into high gear."[12]

But how does this happen? Zuber continued: "We must look deeply into the motives of the industrialists who preach equality of opportunity in one of our organizations but who are reluctant to make the same pronouncement at the annual convention of the National Association of Manufacturers of the Chamber of Commerce."[13]

No doubt Zuber refers here to certain white industrialists high up in the inner councils of the NAACP or the Urban League, the only civil rights organizations congenial to such people. But white industrialists do not sell out Negroes; they merely exploit them just as they exploit other whites. White industrialists never joined any Negro civil rights organization that promised to help build the black economy because, in the first place, the middle-class Negro leaders never had the building of a black economy on their civil rights program. All the white industrialists are doing is making certain the Negro leaders do not get carried away with a civil rights program that goes too far too fast. Moderation! But after all, when there are some Negro leaders who actually concur, what can one expect from whites? ("We got ours the hard way, by fair

12 *Freedomways, op. cit.,* p. 251.
13 *Ibid.*

means or foul. Now you get yours the best way you can, colored folks, because we are not in the habit of giving anything away!")

Zuber knows what he means but he is inarticulate. He is saying that the big white capitalists are not giving the deserving members of the upper black bourgeoisie a fair share of the corporate pie in the forms of jobs, managerial positions, directorships, etc. But even if they did, it would merely amount to more tokenism on another level, which taken by itself, would have nothing to do with the black economy. This is upper-level class aspiration, and Zuber ought to know by now that capitalist economics in that league is truly a white Protestant or a white Jewish affair—not conducted for altruistic purposes or the betterment of outsiders. Zuber writes that "we are sold out . . ." but he does not specify exactly who he means by "we." There are the "We" who run civil rights organizations and there are other "We" who don't even belong to civil rights organizations and who are neither remotely qualified for, or interested in, high positions in the corporate world. These latter comprise the overwhelming majority of black Americans and it is they who must be considered when one talks seriously about the black economy.

Zuber wants the economic power of the Negro to be felt in the corporate structure of the United States through a massive all-Negro boycott of key corporate products, advertised on the television sets that further brainwash Negroes in their living rooms day in and day out. In other words, "we" not only do not get our fair share of the pie on the corporate-entrepreneur-managerial-executive level (because of "the motives of the industrialists"), but "we" are also not making our consumer buying power felt to offset these "motives" militating against us. Now we are getting closer—but not close enough. Further back, you will recall, I pointed out that, among Negroes, "the intellectual stratum often has the illusion that in speaking for itself it is also speaking for the masses." This is the confusion Zuber expressed in his use of "we."

In July, 1964, the world's largest privately-owned bank, the Bank of America, made E. Fred Morrow its first Negro Assistant Vice-President. At the same time, *The New York Times* reported that major corporations and Negro colleges had set up a job parley involving representatives of certain big companies and Negro college officials to discuss "wider employment horizons for Negro col-

lege graduates."[14] (The choice of the word "horizon" is interesting. One dictionary definition of this word is: "the line or circle
which forms the apparent boundary between earth and sky"—
which is another way of describing something you can see and
strive for and never, never reach.) But even if this project were
honestly and assiduously pursued, what would that have to do
with the Negro masses? If "we"—the great unskilled, uneducated, un-middle-class, unintegrated, and uninvited masses—staged
an all-black-American superboycott merely to get a scattering of
handpicked Negroes jobs in big corporations, it just would not be
worth the bother. Such are *class* aims, integrationist class aims;
they are not *group* economic aims. No matter which way you view
it, the integration movement is a movement run by the middle
class who, even when they are militant and sometimes radical,
twist the meaning of racial integration to suit their own aspirations. This is why Whitney Young, Jr. of the Urban League (who
has also contributed to *Freedomways*), could write in *The New
York World-Telegram:*

> The best answer to the fable that "Negroes don't do anything
> to help themselves" is the story of the significant rise of the Negro
> middle class.
> The riots in Harlem, Rochester and New Jersey cities have
> tended to obscure the fact that only a fraction of Negro citizens
> had anything to do with them. The first bulwark against such
> disorders is equal opportunities, the chance for Negro families to
> earn a place in the sun for themselves and their children.
> Millions have already done so. . . .
> But others must have the chance, which, in today's world,
> means a crack at a good education, a decent house, a good street
> and the opportunity to train and find work. People who live in
> $20,000 houses don't throw stones.[15]

Whitney Young, Jr. is far from being a romantic when it concerns the crying economic needs of black ghettoes such as Harlem.
However the romantic integrationists would second Young's thesis
about "people who live in $20,000 houses"—and people who don't
—by demanding: "Yes, break up the Harlem ghetto and let's

[14] *The New York Times,* July 16, 1964, p. 43.
[15] "Negro Middleclass on the Rise," *The New York World-Telegram,* September 10,
1964, p. 22.

everybody have a $20,000 home in an integrated neighborhood."
With this kind of class aspiration and utter social nonsense emanating from the mouths of the official Negro leaders one can well
understand why black Americans, in ghettoes, whose chances of
integrating out of those ghettoes in their lifetimes are practically
nil, suddenly go berserk over any provocation and start throwing
not only stones but Molotov cocktails.

The problem with Paul B. Zuber is that he knows less about
economics than Hope Stevens (who professed to know very little
but who understands more than he admits, about capitalism and
other "forms"). Philosophically, Zuber and Stevens hold similar
economic views. Zuber is too young to have come up through the
leftwing of Stevens' early years. But since Negro leftwingism and
Negro integrationism are, in the final analysis, exchangeable social
values, both Stevens and Zuber had to wind up eventually in the
pages of *Freedomways,* with integrationist-Africanists Clarke and
Moore; bourgeois African-nationalists Essien-Udom; Renaissance
men Hughes and Carrington; plus a host of other "black positions" too varied to sort out with any clarity.

But the one striking difference between the analyses of Stevens
and Zuber is that, while the former resorts to pure, practical, capitalistic time-serving, the latter's economic philosophy is simply
downright naïve. One can only be amazed that a leading civil
rights spokesman can actually believe that highly competitive
white capitalists can be persuaded to practice altruistic economic
relations on behalf of the Negro group's black economy. Obviously
Zuber does not quite believe that private enterprise (even when
black-owned) is run for private profits. No matter how many token
Negroes are absorbed into large corporations, these corporations
will still be run for private profits or stockholders' dividends.
What Zuber did was to distort the original definition of black
economy, and somehow tack the expression on to the civil rights
movement—a feat which other, perhaps wise, official civil rights
leaders have never attempted. They have always known that the
constitutional guarantees of civil liberties also complement guarantees for private corporations to make profits, hire and fire, and
exploit people and natural resources. Unfortunately, the Constitution also permits private enterprise to exclude Negroes from its
administration when it so desires. These are the economic facts of

life and for Negroes to assail these practices is tantamount to denying the "freedom" of free enterprise. Thus Negro leadership cannot expect to integrate into free enterprises—thereby inducing the capitalistic system to create Zuber's concept of a black economy.

Stevens is not as gullible as Zuber. For him, "we" must first accumulate adequate amounts of risk capital before "we" can talk the real language of economic progress. But, Essien-Udom, our cousin from the new African elite in Nigeria, is less sanguine that enough risk capital will accrue to create the "significant Negro capitalist class" needed to foster the black economy. And Zuber concludes that any effort "we" expend toward building our black economy is sold out before we begin. But none of these three gentlemen has discussed a single fundamental approach toward the black economy.

At the very outset, to create the proper basis for a black economy, one must go back to the writings of Booker T. Washington and W.E.B. DuBois and update their economic thoughts. In pursuing the black economy the integrationists are caught in the coils of the American economic status quo. Instinctively they know that upholding the idea of the black economy means confronting and challenging white economic exploitation and rule *inside* the Harlem community. It does not mean smuggling a handful of handpicked Negroes into Wall Street offices or opening up bank branches in downtown Manhattan or in Brooklyn, for capitalistic economics *alone* is not the answer to the black economy. It involves much more than sheer economics; it requires a point of view that the Stevenses and the Zubers do not possess. It takes a certain community point of view, a conditioned climate, in order to exert impact (political, economic and cultural) on the white economy. It means the studied creation of new economic forms—a new *institutionalism*—one that can intelligently blend privately-owned, collectively-owned, cooperatively-owned, as well as state-sponsored, economic organizations. It means mobilizing the ghetto populations and organizing them through education and persuasion (if not through authoritarian measures from above). In Harlem one cannot seriously talk about the black economy until the main business artery of 125th Street is turned over to Negro business administration and economic control. One cannot have a black economy until the day comes when the bulk of profits accrued from commerical enterprises in Harlem are poured back into the community for further development. When the day comes that Harlem Negroes are willing to sacrifice and discipline their buying and saving habits to the extent of a total boycott of white business control and exploitation, by buying elsewhere, *then* one can talk seriously of creating the black economy. If the Birmingham Negroes could use their feet to win dignity on the buses, Harlem Negroes should be able to use their feet and the subways and self-organized buying pools to break up economic exploitation in Harlem.

The black economy idea is neither myth nor concrete reality. The ingredients exist and merely await skillful organizational use and application. America is a nation that abounds in many myths and many realities. The greatest myth is that of democratic capitalism, which has never existed for *all* groups in America. Minorities could not have won their way into different levels of economic status if it were not through some form of group economics—either capitalistic or cooperative. Some added group politics (the Irish), and others even used group crime (the Mafia) and its rewards as the key to economic respectability. The American Jews could not have won their way into the economic power they now possess if not through various forms of group solidarity. For many reasons too numerous to explain here, the American Negro, especially in New York, has failed to learn and practice his economic group responsibilities in the Promised Land of the North. Because of inadequate, selfish and imperceptive leadership, the American Negro has been forced to play the impoverished foil for the white liberal conscience, while being blinded to the fundamental realities of political, economic and cultural survival in America. As a result, the real tragedy of the economics of the ghetto is avoided by integrationists because they are hoodwinked into playing the game of American capitalism by the rules established by those in control of the economic exchange processes of the ghetto status quo. Thus they cannot possibly win much beyond one degree of tokenism or another. But even job tokenism means very little to the Negro ghettoes today. The job market is just about saturated outside the ghettoes and the future is endangered by automation. Consequently, the economic problems of Negro ghettoes can be tackled only by dealing with the bedrock realities of the whole premise of private property. This must be challenged wherever it is found to be in conflict with the democratic group needs and aspirations of Negroes inside the ghettoes. It comes down to the basic question of who owns the ghetto and profits from it. Wherever this *ownership* and profiteering become the stumbling blocks to the economic rehabilitation and social and cultural revitalization of Negro ghetto life, these encumbrances must be removed. Toward this end, every means, every organizational, political and economic approach, every institutional and group resource, must be coordinated and intelligently applied. And it goes without saying that such a radical and thoroughgoing changeover in the racial composition of property ownership presupposes the assumption of independent political power on the part of Negroes in ghettoes. In this regard, Harlem becomes the pilot ghetto wherein this radical overturn of property relations must occur. Harlem, once called the cultural capital of the Negro in America, has become, if not the most economically depressed and retarded of all Northern black enclaves, the most politically backward and the most racially irresponsible.

Determining where to put the blame for this state of affairs is one of the purposes of this book, and the special Harlem issue of *Freedomways* becomes a prime exhibit in our investigation. There, in black and white, is a panoramic view of this all-important community, as interpreted by a broad segment of Negro intellectual opinion. Since all of the issue's articles could not be transcribed and criticized here, I have chosen those on nationalism and economics because they deal with the bread-and-butter aspects of Negro ghetto life, and the ideological questions surrounding the issue of integration. They furnish a key to understanding what is positive, negative, effective, profound, superficial, enlightening or simply clichéd about Negro integrationist leadership and Negro intellectual opinion.

There are many who will disagree with the critical conclusions presented here, on the problems of economics—or *the race factor of economics*—in the exploitation of Harlem by whites. If what I deem must be done about Harlem's condition seems radically impossible (within the context of our accepted morality about private property rights, etc.), let me stress that my outline is merely schematic and requires elaboration before being considered a comprehensive economic plan for ghetto rehabilitation. However, as I see it, given the impasse that race relations have reached in America, especially in the Northern cities, anything *less* than this offers not the slightest hope for eventual ethnic democratization.

There comes a time in the relentless war of poverty vs. profit when many ideas about economic reform become nothing but empty platitudes. The old rules of the game must be thrown overboard, and new ones adopted and enforced by every means possible within the range of the social intelligence and the economic resources of this nation. Capitalism (particularly the American brand) is highly touted as the best economic framework for political democracy, individual rights, and personal freedom. If true, it must, itself, uphold the rights of ethnic groups to participate democratically in the economic processes wherever it is patently shown that ethnic groups, economically insolvent and non-white, are subject to economic exploitation by solvent white Protestants, white Catholics or white Jews. America, to repeat, is a collective of ethnic groups. *There is more disequilibrium in the economic, cultural, and political status of ethnic groups than there is class warfare in America.* The race question or the civil rights movement or racial integration or racial equality, etc., merely reflect this longstanding social condition. It has been brought to the fore by the Negro movement simply because of the Negroes' unique position vis-à-vis the American white world. In reality, Indians, Mexicans, and other non-white hyphenated-Americans at the bottom of the ethnic totem pole are also involved.

The Negro (or any other ethnic minority) cannot simply drift aimlessly, or hope by seeking Constitutional redress of grievances to integrate into a secure status of ethnic group democracy, because the Constitution, as it now stands, does not recognize the legal validity or the rights of groups *but only of individuals.* Hence, not only must the American Constitution be brought up to date in terms of mirroring the basic group reality of America, but it is the American Negro who must press the fight for this amending. For the Negro to continue to be trapped in the unstable no-man's-land of more protest, more ghetto riots, more subsequent drift, will lead to social and racial chaos in America of such degree that the nation as a whole may not survive on a racially democratic basis. Hence, of all the ethnic groups in American society, that of the Negro becomes, of necessity, the *pivotal American ethnic group among all others.* It will depend to what degree the articulate Negro leadership comprehends its group's innate potential for enforcing democratization of ethnic group status through Federal-sponsored measures, whether the Negro will hope to survive the complicated and difficult future that lies ahead in American race relations.

Overall, the 1963 Harlem issue of *Freedomways*—a magazine which in 1961 asked "which way will we go?"—revealed but a scant awareness of the social complexities implied in the answer to that question.

Freedomways, Summer 1963:
Capitalism Revisited

Freedomways' special Harlem issue of the summer of 1963 turned out to be the best issue of that magazine to date. Neither accidental nor surprising, it reflected Harlem's crucial position in Negro affairs in terms of politics, economics, culture and—of course—leadership. Even the superficial treatment of Harlem presented by *Freedomways* could not help but reflect the profound sociological content of Harlem reality.

That issue of *Freedomways* called Harlem a "Community in Transition" without attempting to specify where this "transition" was leading. Taken as a whole, the articles on Harlem were more descriptive than interpretive. Even the Marxists who contributed, did not essay a vulgar Marxist analysis. Overall, the approach was very existential. As a result, a true analysis in depth was impossible.

Freedomways' description of Harlem as being in a state of "transition" was open to many interpretations. Is Harlem really disintegrating in order to integrate all of its hundreds of thousands of citizens into the white communities? No, it is not. Neither is Brooklyn's Bedford-Stuyvesant, nor Chicago's Southside, nor Los Angeles' Watts. There will be black ethnic conclaves in the United States well into the next millennium, but you will never induce a rampant Negro integrationist to accept that reality (and proceed from there).

Practically every Negro integrationist, no matter where he goes, whether to the suburbs, Paris, Istanbul, Moscow, Peking or Greenwich Village, is haunted by a ghetto past or a ghetto presence. The "good life" abroad or beyond is never completely free from dark ghetto adumbrations that bore into the socially enlightened consciousness of the Negro seeker of unrestricted freedom and universality. The ghettoes of color, which exist all over the United States and the non-Western world, have today become the endemic wellsprings of revolutionary ideologies that will change the social relationships of races for decades to come. Not until these relationships are completely altered will the black individual be able to walk this earth as a free and universal man. None of the Harlems of the world will ever totally disintegrate, no matter how many individual ex-colonials and ex-semicolonials make their escape. Yet the persistence of these ghettoes of color (and the meaning of ghetto reality) is not even accepted or comprehended by those who choose to remain within them. Within Harlem itself one hears the voices of these individuals, some of whom would see themselves as realists, projecting superficial analyses of Harlem in "transition."

In an article on the "Economic Structure of the Harlem Community"[1] in *Freedomways'* special issue, Hope R. Stevens, a Negro attorney and banker (president of the Carver Savings and Loan Association), outlined no future disintegration of Harlem à la James Baldwin, because such an eventuality would no doubt "integrate" his own bank out of its existence (at least as a "Negro" institution). Whatever Stevens's views on integration, his realism demanded that he discuss Harlem in purely economic, capitalistic terms, with the objective of raising Harlem's economic status as a community. His vague and optimistic conclusions were:

> There are many hopeful signs that suggest that the Harlem community can leap forward economically; not the least important of these is that the controllers of business in Harlem are anxious to find ways of changing old images and creating new ones, fresher and more realistic, and there are also those in the ranks of the blacks who feel that this is good and are working to see what can be done about it, quickly.

Before this, however, Stevens had made the point that "the gap in family income between whites and blacks is the primary determinant of the social distance that exists and will continue to exist between the two ethnic groups until the gap is narrowed."[2]

Stevens also pointed out that "Harlem lives on credit. Its fu-

[1] *Freedomways*, Summer, 1963, Vol. 3, No. 3, pp. 343-354.
[2] *Ibid.*, p. 354.

ture wages are to a great extent pledged for the consumer goods purchased in the present," and the economically enforced "mortgaging of future income" has "operated to prevent any considerable capital from being formed." Therefore, "there is little or no risk capital available in the colored community." Harlem then, as a result of its historical and economic formation, is a black community whose businesses, real estate, and credit avenues are "outer-controlled." In addition to a host of other economic disadvantages, high rentals in Harlem, coupled with constant deterioration of real estate properties, are "bringing to the tenant less value for his rental dollar than ever before." All in all, these oppressive economic conditions reap an increasing harvest of crime, poor schools, psychological demoralization and cultural deprivation.

Stevens prefaced his remarks by claiming to be only a layman. A layman, said Stevens, "should not play with charts, tables and statistics, the tools of the scientist." But the individual has "the right to think, each in his own way, interpreting one's observations or impressions."

The Harlem uprising of 1964 showed, among other things, that Hope Stevens' analysis was worse than inadequate. This analysis harked back to the early days of the 1930's Depression: then, Herbert Hoover's droll promise that prosperity was just around the corner became one of the well-known laissez-faire economic platitudes. Stevens showed just as much faith in capitalism as Hoover, and concluded in his article that "it would therefore seem to be logical and factual to conclude that there is no special economic theory applicable to the Harlem community. . . ."

Because of Stevens' political leftwing background, that statement was necessary, if for no other reason than to anticipate arguments from certain of his socialistic friends who knew him back when he was president of the New York Council of the National Negro Congress. He then slid very smoothly into what has become the "know-nothing" economics rationale of civil righters:

> Removal of educational inequality in the public school system, whatever the reason for its existence, will work a major change in the income potential of the black family. With improved participation in remunerative employment, some significant capital accumulation may be anticipated. This will lead more rapidly to

integration of non-white persons into business, trade and financial operations. Penetration of the power structure will mean inclusion in broad policy-making. It will be simpler then for black representatives in business and finance to drive home the truths, now mere postulates, to the majority, that it is costly and unprofitable to support a segregated industrial society and that non-discriminatory patterns of living avoid waste, improve business and increase profits.[3]

Stevens really knows better than this, but, like the proverbial new arrival in Rome, now that he has become a capitalist he must act and talk like one. Back in 1936, Roosevelt's New Deal policies literally saved countless Negroes from starvation, gave a measure of hope to millions of others, and created new careers for many in the cultural fields through the Works Progress Administration. Notwithstanding, such measures were not enough to satisfy the grand designs of Hope Stevens *et al.* of the NNC simply because the New Deal saved the capitalist system. Then, the NNC leadership allowed the Communist-manipulated united front to condemn Negro business aspirations (and also the Negro church) as reactionary influences. This leadership was so afraid of being called nationalistic by their white allies that they wouldn't dare muster up enough group spirit to implement the very consumer and producer economic program they themselves projected. All of this coincided with the ascendancy of Jewish nationalism in the Communist Party, forcing it to refrain from impugning business and synagogue life as reactionary influences in the Jewish community. Twenty-five years later, with the emergence of Dr. Martin Luther King, the Negro church ceased to be a reactionary institution, as the Communists jumped on King's bandwagon. But now Hope Stevens, the banker, upbraids the Negro churches for their failure in community economics: "Some churches have instituted thrift programs by forming and operating Credit Unions. . . . But the potential of the churches through their ministers for influencing the economic life of the Harlem community is far from being organized or released."[4]

Many Negro ministers preach pie-in-the-sky doctrines, said Stevens. Hence, many questions are being raised as to what such minis-

[3] *Ibid.,* p. 354.
[4] *Ibid.,* p. 350.

ters are giving in return for the money they collect from their flocks. A valid point, but today Hope Stevens cannot blame the preachers for their other-worldly economics when the more worldly social philosophers like himself failed to give leadership when it counted.

But even the Carver Savings and Loan Association was not established under conditions of pre-Hoover laissez-faire, unregulated market capitalism. Ever since the Banking Act of 1933, Federal control, supervision and capitalization assistance have made it possible for many communities to have banking facilities previously denied them. For Stevens, in 1963, the economic problems of Harlem lie in the fact that there is very little risk capital:

> Whatever the background or history of the individual may be, investment money, which is risk capital, is not in sight among colored persons of substance. There have been a few instances in which the public has been aroused to invest money, and lost— such as in the case of Marcus Garvey's Black Star Line—and the period of recovery from such disappointing experiences is understandably long. . . .
>
> The blacks have not yet been permitted to peer over the edge of the plateau on which the financial resources of the nation are constantly rearranged. *They do not know what goes on there* (italics added). They do not participate positively in influencing the economic shape of things to come. Nor is there any evidence that there will be more than token representation in this area for a long time yet.[5]

All of which is very true, but note the interesting reference to Garvey—to which we shall return later. It is amazing that when leftwingers become ex-leftwingers, they become more capitalistic in their intellectual reflexes than the men in Washington who run the Federal anti-poverty programs. Stevens seems unaware that free, unregulated market capitalism does not even exist today. While he cogitates about the absence of risk capital in Harlem, the anti-poverty braintrusters already know that the question of risk capital is irrelevant. Things have gone too far for that. To wait on the slow accumulation of risk capital is to invite a revolutionary upheaval.

[5] *Ibid.,* p. 345.

The advent of the Carver Federal Savings and Loan Bank was symptomatic of a new class development in post-World War II Negro life—the rise of a new Negro middle class. At the time of the Carver bank's inauguration, George S. Schuyler, the well-known Negro newspaper columnist (like Stevens, a former member of the NNC), reported that there were already twenty-two of the Carver-type loan associations in existence in large cities as far south as Atlanta and as far west as Los Angeles. In 1947, wrote Schuyler, the total assets of these Negro loan associations were $8,864,342; the total first mortgage loans $7,392,963; cash on hand $832,589; and government obligations $366,191.[6] In 1963 Hope Stevens boasted that "today, with continuing community support, Carver has attracted savings accounts almost exclusively from non-whites totaling in excess of $21 millions." Among other things, this notable rise in Carver's assets reflects the high level of affluence of the New York area middle class. But there is an increasing contrast between the living conditions of the higher-income strata and the impoverished Harlem masses without savings accounts. This widening gap between classes presages of potential class conflict.

The emergence of these banks in the late 1940's told a lot about the coming era of the new civil rights crusades of the 1950's and 1960's. New middle-class economic affluence signalized a new era of rising expectations. It meant a rise in Negro college attendance, which carried with it new vistas in social aspiration, mostly bourgeois in flavor. Thus rising middle-class status, the growth of banks, civil rights, integration, and similar concepts are all aided and abetted, if not partly inspired, by the political leftwing nurtured by Roosevelt's New Deal benevolence. This background sheds very important light on what was later called the Negro revolution. What were the real aims of this revolution? Which Negro class was leading it? Which Negro class did it really aim to benefit? How far do the answers to these questions go to explain why a Hope Stevens, formerly a leftist, can now see none but capitalistic theories applicable to Harlem in 1963?

George S. Schuyler gives a few answers to this intriguing problem. Schuyler is one of the old Harlem Renaissance men associated

<hr>

[6] George S. Schuyler, "Views and Reviews," *The Pittsburgh Courier*, January 8, 1949, p. 17.

with A. Philip Randolph on the *Messenger* in the 1920's. Long
known for his cynicism, his satirical and acid comment on Negro
affairs, Schuyler earned the title among the literary as the Negro
Mencken. Later he was called the Negro Westbrook Pegler. He
never went overboard for socialistic ideas and has grown more
archly conservative as the decades pass. When the Carver Federal
and Loan Association opened up in Harlem, Schuyler wrote glow-
ingly of the new loan associations, saying that they "are going to
be the salvation of the Negro Homeseeker, and don't forget it."[7]
What made the loan association banks loom so important was the
Supreme Court's outlawing of residential restrictive covenants
in 1947, which the established white banks countered by making it
more difficult than ever for Negroes to get mortgage loans. As a
result, the establishment of these Negro-operated federal loan
banks was truly for the "advancement" of colored people, especially middle-class colored people and those aspiring to that status.
Schuyler, in an article published in the *Pittsburgh Courier,* went
on to elaborate the economic philosophy of racial salvation that
Hope Stevens was to emphasize fourteen years later in *Freedomways:* "Negroes everywhere have . . . plenty of 'sleeping money' in
banks and post offices which should be brought out and put to
work for this and the next generation. There is no law stopping
this anywhere in the country. *Those who perform such services are
our real leaders not the mere mouthmaticians (sic.)* (Italics
added)."[8]

Like Hope Stevens, Schuyler sought after the elusive Negro risk
capital. He further explained: "No denunciation of American
prejudice or unfairness of the white man is going to produce for
Negroes the number of jobs, the degree of wealth, or the quality of
comfort, which every man seeks as his birthright."[9]

Although Schuyler would not be caught dead writing for *Freedomways* (inasmuch as anything that smells remotely of the leftwing is anathema to him), after all is said and done Stevens and
Schuyler are essentially class brothers, with a common economic
philosophy. They both want all Negroes, high and low, to put
their risk capital to work for racial salvation. But you will never

---

[7] See Schuyler's article, "Journalism," *American Opinion,* January, 1966, pp. 15-21
[the Birchite publication edited by Robert Welch].
[8] Schuyler, *op. cit.,* p. 17.
[9] *Ibid.*

get from these experts a survey that might reveal what percentage of ordinary Harlem Negroes actually have this "sleeping money" and how many do not. Such a survey might be the introduction to some serious ghetto economic policy. The last thing these men really want, however, is a serious ghetto economic policy for which *they* would have to be responsible. What they apparently believe, deep down, is that we shall always have the poor with us, so let those of us who have an out make the best of those few financial opportunities that come our way. Hence, it goes without saying that the economic philosophy they adopt is the one that best serves their own interests. They live in a fast changing world dominated by the politics of poverty the world over, but it never occurs to them that their economic philosophy is really very old hat. They cannot transcend their conviction that the economics of private property and private gain alone are adequate approaches to the poverty of ghettoes. Their mentality is *nouveau riche,* their *Welt-anschauung* provincial and imitative, and their suburban homes, their automobiles, their creature comforts and their new banks and establishments contradict the pre-New Deal origins of their social outlook.

This is a class that dons the mantle of leadership in a crusade for freedom but has no adequate philosophy for freedom in this age. This is a class that speaks of racial progress, racial salvation, civil rights, etc., but has not yet learned to think logically, honestly and positively on economics and politics. Take George S. Schuyler's economics: Here is a man who calls himself a conservative thinker, yet one week prior to his *Pittsburgh Courier* column on the opening of Hope Stevens' Carver bank, Schuyler had this to say about certain Negro intellectuals:

> They accepted gullibly every reactionary, totalitarian proposal of the Red New Dealers as "liberal" and "progressive," and cor-rupted a whole generation into regarding it as progress and re-form. It is difficult to think of a single Red New Deal proposal which these people have ballyhooed to their followers and readers in the past 15 years which was not in essence destructive of free-dom and thus inimical to the interests of all Americans, black or white.[10]

[10] Schuyler, *op. cit.,* January 1, 1949, p. 17.

In his column the following week, Schuyler neglected to mention that it was precisely Roosevelt's New Deal legislation that made it possible for Negroes to open and operate loan and savings banks. Without the Banking Acts of 1933 and 1935 and the Federal Savings and Loan Insurance Corporation of 1934, none of these new Negro banks would have emerged. These were New Deal measures that were definitely *not* "inimical to the interests of all Americans, black or white." There is very little risk involved in the Carver-type, Federally administered, controlled and insured mortgage banking. As an example of leadership in the economic process, it is institutionalized New Dealism and most unglamorous. Moreover, these home loan banks cannot make small business loans—an economic and financial type of bank transaction obviously more relevant to the Harlem situation than home building (since who builds new homes in Harlem?).

Schuyler's brand of ersatz Conservatism does not really educate the Negro reading public on the real economic facts of life. But the *Pittsburgh Courier,* like the bulk of the Negro press generally, does not play the role of educating the Negro masses to think beyond certain limits. These limits are set according to the goals established by the official civil rights movement; what is wanted is immediate, if not instant civil rights, more instant jobs and non-discriminatory employment.

The gradualistic economic philosophy of a Stevens, a Zuber, a Schuyler, sums up the total economic philosophy of the black bourgeoisie. Politically, it is the economics of imitation and intellectual sterility. It is the economics of time-serving opportunism and theoretical incompetence. It is a philosophy that, under tutelage, will play at socialism and then turn and uphold capitalism with a straight face. It will adopt the partisan politics of black conservatism against the traditions of the New Deal era while avidly accepting all the benefits of the same New Deal traditions. Taken as a whole, the black bourgeoisie in the United States is the most politically backward of all the colored bourgeois classes in the non-Western world. It is a class that accepts the philosophy of whites whether radical, liberal, progressive or conservative, without alteration or dissent and calls it leadership. It is a class that absorbs very little from the few thinkers it has produced—Martin R. Delany, W.E.B. DuBois, Booker T. Washington, E. Franklin Frazier and

Carter G. Woodson—men who left something behind them. It is the one non-white bourgeois class in this world that fears to express its own legitimate nationalism, waiting on the benevolent nod from the power structure before it moves to achieve its limited social aims. Eschewing its own nationalistic birthright the Negro bourgeoisie compromises itself and undercuts its own political potential in advance. Hence, this class is sold out by none other than itself, not by white industrialists in civil rights organizations. Because it refuses to be assertive about its Afro-American heritage, this class fails to be revolutionary on any social front in the United States, not even in civil rights. It is a class whose social policies are so inept it seeks civil rights without seeking group political power, and then demands economic equality in the integrated world without having striven to create any kind of ethnic economic base in the black world. It is a class that could not have the motivations to achieve these things because it fears to be nationalistic. Because of its refusal to break with the American two-party system, this class lacks independent political power, and cannot even exert a commanding role in the Federal anti-poverty programs beamed into the Negro ghettoes. Here in the rundown ghettoes are the accumulated results of years of black middle-class social irresponsibility. But Federal intervention should *not* come only through the benevolence of enforced social necessity from without, but should also be forthcoming under the pressure of political power applied from within the ghettoes themselves. That this kind of power was never cultivated is a Negro leadership default stretching back over several decades. It has robbed the Negro movement today of the powerful kind of cutting edge it ought to have. The historically true, native American radicalism is black radicalism, but the history of this radicalism's bourgeois conformism is also the history of its emasculation. Therefore it becomes understandable why a Hope Stevens (a "real leader" of the Negroes in Schuyler's book) could not speak his piece about the economics of Harlem without mentioning Garvey; no more than could Stevens' great personal friend, Paul Robeson, offer up *Here I Stand* without arguing with Garvey's ghost. Is it not remarkable that these Negro capitalists, conservatives, leftwingers and ex-radicals have so much in common?

The previously quoted allusion by Stevens to Garvey's economics is very interesting because it is highly doubtful that the NNC, during its heyday in the 1930's, had anything at all to do with the remnants of the Garveyite movement. In fact, there was no reference at all to this unique nationalistic trend in the first batch of NNC resolutions. Of course the NNC could not visualize its responsibilities in reconsidering Garvey's implications because the Communists had already relegated Garvey to political Hades back in the 1920's. Moreover, A. Philip Randolph, the president of the NNC, like many other black intellectuals of that period, was leery of overt nationalism. This fear of nationalism is rooted in that manifestation of the Negro psychology that inhibits many Negroes from *telling all white people exactly what they think of them as oppressors*. This breaks down in various ways: There is the fear of losing the support of white liberals through criticizing them; there is the concomitant fear—an ingrained conditioning of black America—of criticizing American Jews because they are an important segment of the liberal establishment and themselves oppressed by European history and Hitlerism; more than that, the fear of nationalism on the part of many Negroes is also a reflection of the fear of being forced to be *self-critical of their own incompetent and shoddy intellectual role in American society;* lastly, there is the fear of having a real confrontation with the dominant Anglo-Saxon Protestant in terms of his native, institutionalized nationalism that is today willing to sacrifice positive national purpose in subjecting the entire nation to international disgrace—in order to maintain group supremacy. These fears of nationalism are what give the lie to the claims of the integrationists that they are confronting the realities of racial discimination. Racial integrationism that evades a confrontation of nationalism confronts nothing at all, because it deals with neither black nationalism, white Anglo-Saxon nationalism, nor Jewish nationalism and their various implications. Hence Hope Stevens dealt with Garvey's capitalistic economics but not Garvey's nationalism, which is another way of saying that Stevens was merely indulging in economic platitudes.

Was the Garvey movement organized only to get Negroes to invest money? If so, then it was Stevens' business to give his views on why such an appeal to capitalistic "economics" could not have been made without the added ingredients of nationalism and Back-to-Africa dreams. Why was Garvey's attempt to get investment money not successful in the British West Indies? What was the connection between Garvey's coming to the United States and Booker T. Washington, who was Garvey's American inspiration? It is a matter of record that Garvey came to the United States in 1916 for the express purpose of linking up his movement with Washington's movement in Tuskegee, Alabama, but that Washington died before Garvey arrived. Garvey himself admitted that "it is from America that I get most of the money for my work."[11] Garvey got the money, the risk capital, as Stevens calls it, but people invested it and lost. E. Franklin Frazier maintained that Negroes fail in business because of lack of business experience plus "a predatory view of economic activity." Was this the reason Garvey's investment ventures in his Black Star Line failed? W.E.B. DuBois says it was because of business incompetence: "I begged his friends not to allow him foolishly to overwhelm with bankruptcy and disaster 'one of the most interesting spiritual movements of the modern world.' "[12]

It was estimated that over a million dollars of Negroes' money was lost investing in Garvey's schemes, of which some eight hundred thousand dollars went for the purchase of four rundown ships, plus seventy thousand dollars to eighty thousand dollars for repairs to make them seaworthy. What were the implications of all this? What was wrong was that Garvey's nationalism was more bourgeois than it was revolutionary; thus he fell into the error of trying to fight capitalistic imperialism solely with capitalistic methods of economic organization. Hope Stevens is repeating the same error (from another standpoint) in visualizing Harlem's economic resurrection through the accumulation of risk capital. Curiously enough, neither the old Garveyites, nor the new-wave Black Nationalists, nor the Negro leftwingers (old or new) have made a single new contribution to the American Negro situation in terms of economic theories. The Garveyites are still, in 1967, discussing Africa in terms of capitalistic enterprises (black banks, black private enterprises, black private entrepreneurs) when African nations are wrestling with problems of the socialist economies along African lines. The socialism of the Amer-

---

[11] *Garvey and Garveyism, op. cit.,* p. 185.
[12] DuBois, *Dusk of Dawn, op. cit.,* p. 278.

ican black leftwing, however, is strictly utopian talk, while the young, new wave Black Nationalists have no economic theories, and do not even study economic thought with any seriousness, if at all. Hope Stevens himself declares that there is no special economic theory that even applies to the Harlem ghetto. This economic "know-nothingness" is the fundamental curse of the Negro movement's ideology today. Thus the connection between the state of affairs in the 1960's and the 1920's era of Garvey is much closer than Hope Stevens suggests. Not since Garveyism collapsed through Garvey's own personal economic ineptitude has a single Negro leader, with the exception of W.E.B. DuBois, presented a creative economic idea—good, bad or indifferent.

In his autobiography, *Dusk of Dawn*, DuBois outlined a whole new concept of what he called the "cooperative commonwealth" for the American Negro. Yet this very important aspect of DuBois's thinking is never even mentioned today by the various black intellectual worshippers of the DuBois tradition. In the W.E.B. DuBois Memorial Issue put out by *Freedomways* in the winter of 1965, thirty-four black (and not so black) intellectuals were brought together to pay homage to the memory of DuBois's achievements. This lineup presented a united front of Communists, pro-Communists, anti-Communists, ex-Communists, white liberals, an African nationalist and an African anti-nationalist. They discussed practically everything about W.E.B. DuBois except the *real essentials* of the man's thinking in politics, economics and culture that might conceivably relate to Negro masses in American ghettoes. This list of writers, from Herbert Aptheker through Roy Wilkins, all skirted the essentials of the DuBois-Washington-Garvey triangular dispute over politics, nationalism, economics and culture and how it applies to the ghetto explosions today. They even refused to reexamine what DuBois himself had to say about his own mistakes in dealing with Washington and Garvey. The *Freedomways* DuBois issue recalled nothing about DuBois's economic theories. Yet from all of this history Stevens's mind can conjure up no "theory." When the assertion was made earlier in this book that the influence of the Communist leftwing on the thinking of the Negro intellectual has been disastrous, it was no extravagant charge. Men like Stevens have been conditioned (directly or indirectly) by American Marxism to think only on either of two economic levels—pure capitalism or European socialism. When they depart from the Left they revert to conformist capitalistic free-market thinking, while socialism remains only a dream, something that is supposed to exist in the Soviet Union. Negro intellectuals produce, therefore, no original economic theorists who can cope realistically with either capitalism or socialism from a Negro point of view. This is the failing not only of ex-leftwingers such as Stevens and the whole integrationist-civil rights school (Left or reform), but is grievously evident among both the old and new nationalists as well.

Not for forty-odd years have Garveyites understood that Garvey, even at the start of his movement, began with economic ideas that, for him, had been rendered obsolete by World War I. Garvey properly belongs to the early-twentieth-century, bourgeois nationalist leaders that arose in the colonized world. One of the greatest of these was China's Dr. Sun Yat Sen. But Sun Yat Sen understood in 1911 what Marcus Garvey did not, and *never* grasped, about nationalist movements and their concomitant economic platforms. Sun Yat Sen understood that the Kuomintang of China could not utilize *only* capitalistic-free enterprise economic forms in the Chinese revolutionary movement. For Sun Yat Sen, nationalism in China had to be based on three essential principles: (1) Nationalism meant racial equality with the rest of the world. Nationalism in China required the end of imperialism. (2) Nationalism in China meant socialism but not Western forms of socialism as propagated in the ideas of European Marxists. It meant that Chinese economic theorists had to create economic forms that would apply to Chinese problems of poverty in the cities and the countryside. (3) Nationalism in China meant new forms of democratic political rights applicable to the Chinese situation.

As a bourgeois nationalist of the Sun Yat Sen era, Garvey's nationalism was, by comparison, handicapped by numerous theoretical and conceptual flaws. Thus it was doomed to failure in the United States not only because its West Indian motivation was too pro-British for American race realities, but also because it did not meet the demands of twentieth-century developments. But the chief flaw of Garveyism was its capitalistic economics. The American black bourgeoisie had made its initial bid for capitalistic class power—and failed—long before Garvey arrived. Booker T. Washington had established the National Negro Business League in 1900. By the time Garvey arrived with his program, the entire colonial world was passing from anti-imperialism to anti-capitalism as a way of economic organization. Yet Garvey's program remained pro-capitalistic during its 1920's era, and the Garveyites have remained unbendingly, inflexibly pro-capitalistic ever since. Their nationalist speeches on Harlem street-corners, in favor of creating black capitalistic enterprises here and in Africa, have never been changed one iota in any aspect of economic theory.*

In 1940, W.E.B. DuBois advanced far enough in economic theory to deal differently with what he called the inner economy of the American Negro Community—and here is *the* important phase of his thought that his most vociferous supporters never discuss. DuBois admitted the partial existence and the possible development of the black economy in America. Certain of Du-Bois's detractors, such as Abram L. Harris, called the idea of the black economy a manifestation of self-segregation. But DuBois attempted to deal with this reality in a theorectical way: "There faces the American Negro, therefore, an intricate and subtle problem of combining into one object two difficult sets of facts—his present racial segregation which will persist . . . for many decades, and his attempts by carefully planned and intelligent action to fit himself into the new economic organization which the world faces."[13]

DuBois then outlined a vast program which covered the whole gamut of planned cooperative consumer and producer enterprises that were to be initiated and engineered by Negroes themselves. This economic program was never carried out because of many factors, not the least of which was the advent of World War II. What is important, however, is that DuBois demonstrated, contrary to Stevens' thinking, that there are other economic theories applicable to Harlem besides the accumulation of risk capital. What is really lacking are Negro intellectuals who are economic theorists, or who are social theorists about anything else but racial integration.

W.E.B. DuBois outlived both of his antagonists—Booker T.

---

* See Abram L. Harris, *The Negro As Capitalist* (Philadelphia: The American Academy of Political and Social Science, 1936).

[13] *Dusk of Dawn, op. cit.*, p. 199.

Washington and Marcus Garvey. Out of this amazing historic, triangular feud came everything of intellectual, spiritual, cultural, and political value to the American Negro. Even today, the views of Washington vs. DuBois vs. Garvey are still being debated; but no one attempts to systematize the essential ideas of these pioneering leaders, for the Negro generations who came after these men can not hold a candle to their predecessors in intellect. The generation of Negro intellectuals born between the two World Wars are, on the whole, an empty and unoriginal group. Their creative pretensions are mere grandstand polemics that conceal the most thorough brainwashing that Western civilization has ever perpetrated on the non-white colonized mentality. For all of DuBois's shifts, changes and intellectual permutations, he clearly saw what the end product of his life's work amounted to and wrote of his great efforts:

> I formulated a thesis of socialism for the American Negro in my *Dusk of Dawn.*
> The Second World War sent all my formulations a-whirl. . . .

Before this, he said:

> We must admit that the majority of the American Negro intelligentsia, together with much of the West Indian and West African leadership, shows symptoms of following in the footsteps of western acquisitive society, with its exploitation of labor, monopoly of land and its resources, and with private profit for the smart and unscrupulous in a world of poverty, disease and ignorance, as the natural end of human culture. I have long noted and fought this all too evident tendency, and built my faith in its ultimate change on an inner Negro cultural ideal. I thought this ideal would be built on ancient African communism, supported and developed by memory of slavery and experience of caste, which would drive the Negro group into a spiritual unity precluding the development of economic classes and inner class struggle. This was once possible, but it is now improbable. . . . The very loosening of outer racial discriminatory pressures has not, as I had once believed, left Negroes free to become a group cemented into a new cultural unity, capable of absorbing a socialism, tolerance and democracy, and helping to lead America into a new heaven and new earth. But rather, partial emancipation is freeing some of them to ape the worst of American and Anglo-Saxon

chauvinism, luxury, showing-off, and "social climbing." . . . I have discovered that a large and powerful portion of the educated and well-to-do Negroes are refusing to forge forward in social leadership of anyone, even their own people, but are eager to fight social medicine for sick whites and sicker Negroes; are opposing trade unionism not only for white labor but for the far more helpless black worker; are willing to get "rich quick" not simply by shady business enterprise, but even by organized gambling and the "dope" racket.[14]

When DuBois wrote these words in 1952, however, he had finally linked up with the Communist leftwing, even though many of the young, postwar generation in Harlem were leaving the Communist Left in utter disillusionment. DuBois said at that time:

Without the help of the trade unionists, white and black, without the Progressives and radicals, without Socialists and Communists and lovers of peace all over the world, my voice would now be stilled forever.[15]

It must be clearly understood here that, whatever were DuBois' motivations for his belated joining of the Communist Party, his status in the Party was, among other things, not that of a Negro rank-and-filer. There is a great distinction to be considered here. Regrettably, the winning over of W.E.B. DuBois was a grand feather-in-the-caps of the incompetent Communist Party leadership. Yet as an individual, DuBois' intellectual reputation stands above and beyond the influences of Marxist Communism—a philosophy which added nothing to *his* historical stature—but abused and disoriented the thinking of countless other Negroes whose potential for positive achievements in society were negated by the intrusion of Communist machinations.

It is against the background of all this that one must judge the economic philosophy of a Hope Stevens. His unqualified pro-capitalism is typical of most Negro integrationist thinking, once one cuts through their civil rights verbiage to the core of their social philosophy. When the integrationists go Left, they thought-

[14] W.E.B. DuBois, "In Battle for Peace," *Masses and Mainstream*, 1952, pp. 154-155.
[15] *Ibid.*, p. 155.

lessly swallow the European economic theories of Marxist-Communism whole, and second-hand, without the least qualification. Then when they abandon the Left, they revert to their essential integrationism, and just as thoughtlessly reclaim pragmatic capitalism. And in both these guises they claim to speak for the downtrodden Negro masses—for whom Marxist Communism never meant a positive thing of any duration, and for whom American capitalism never fulfilled its promise of democratic abundance. As P.J.D. Wiles points out in a rather important book on modern economic thought:

> The social sciences are full of unspoken, because unperceived, premises. . . .
> This book is informed by the belief that there is no such thing as the logic of institutions: that an economic model will function in the way it does, and have the political effects it has, partly for internal, purely economic reasons inaccessible to the sociologist or historian. It is claimed, therefore, that a new institutionalism is possible, neither purely descriptive nor purely bogus like the old, so justly discredited among the economists, and independent up to a certain point of other disciplines, yet drawing upon them and flowing back into them, and in its own right vigorous and respectable. . . .
> It is in countries of any type which show no capacity for institutional change that there are revolutions.[16]

What America needs at this perilous juncture in its history are new economic institutional forms, lest its unsolved racial problems explode on a grander scale than heretofore and rend the society into a disorganized chaos. However, the initial ideas on the nature, content and forms of these new institutions must emanate from the minds of an advanced type of Negro intelligentsia, or they will not emerge.

[16] P.J.D. Wiles, *The Political Economy of Communism* (Cambridge, Mass.: Harvard University Press, 1962), pp. 1, 18.

Freedomways, Summer 1963:
Nationalism Made Respectable

The next important article in *Freedomways* special Harlem issue was "The Nationalist Movements of Harlem,"[1] a very good descriptive analysis of the various blends of nationalist organizations in Harlem and their histories. This task, as one might have expected, was undertaken by the Nigerian, E.U. Essien-Udom. An Afro-American integrationist could not have been objective enough about Negro nationalism to do it justice! To do so, he would have run the risk of being labled a nationalist, which is considered worse than being called a gradualist or even an Uncle Tom (which is what some nationalists are calling some integrationists; it is harder to be a Negro in America than some imagine).

At any rate, having an African dissect black nationalism in America in *Freedomways* gives such an essay the aura of pure scholarship applied to an American ideological phenomenon from the detached objectivity of a foreigner (even if a black foreigner). Hence, no one would be able to say that *Freedomways* had permitted a real, native home-grown nationalist to penetrate its inner family under false colors. Moreover, African nationalism had already become a respectable mystique among all the black and white Africanists, even on *Freedomways;* its chief editor, Shirley Graham DuBois, sometimes prefers the other more poetic description, the "African Personality." But there is always a leftwing-nurtured, integrationist doubt, lingering unspoken in the *Freedomways* family, that this ideology really adds anything healthy to the Afro-American "Personality."

John Henrik Clarke, an associate editor of *Freedomways*, had

[1] *Freedomways, op. cit.,* pp. 335-342.

written an article in the Fall, 1961, issue on "The New Afro-American Nationalism"[2] that helped to set the tone for Essien-Udom's article nearly two years later. Clarke's article, with its open discussion of nationalism, came at a time when the magazine was committed to free inquiry on certain taboo subjects; it did not mean that *Freedomways* was seriously considering adopting any nationalist views as part of editorial policy. Clarke is an Africanist of long standing, one of the few devoted American Negro specialists in African history outside university cloisters. This distinction, plus his long-standing Harlem residence and his close working knowledge of Harlem organizational life, has earned him the title of a recognized prophet of African and Afro-American redemption. In the late 1940's, the heyday of the organized Communist leftwing in Harlem, Clarke was vocally anti-Communist. Also implicitly anti-integrationist, he was known to look askance at Negroes, especially certain writers, who lived and functioned outside the Harlem community. At that time Clarke's Harlem-bound point of view caused him to sneer at such Negroes, myself included, as "marginal Negroes." But with the advent of John O. Killens' Harlem Writers Guild, Clarke turned "Left" and entered the *Freedom*-Harlem Writers Guild inner circles, where he learned the Left language and viewpoint rather promptly. So much so, that his essay on Harlem nationalism did not appear until some six years after *Freedom* had collapsed. By then, Clarke had graduated to broader horizons downtown—to *Freedomways* offices—a stone's throw from the hangout of the integrated Negro writers in Greenwich Village.

Clarke's belated metamorphosis into his peculiar brand of leftwing-Africanist-integrationism was further encouraged by the new radical Left era of 1960 ushered in by the Cuban Revolution. Involvement with these events had broadened Clarke's interracial contacts to the point where he was unabashedly verbalizing integrationist views much like those of the "marginal Negroes" he had criticized earlier.

In writing about Afro-American nationalism in 1961, Clarke could no longer view that ideology as his own personal, political and organizational articles of belief. He now wrote "objectively,"

[2] *Ibid.*, No. 3, 285-295.

in the manner of a social analyst giving all sides of a social question their just due. For Clarke, nationalism is now a reflection of an earlier social dream of his Harlem past, never realized in life because nationalism in Harlem was too narrow in scope to contain the creative intellectual. By 1961, the new Afro-American nationalism, as Clarke described it, had developed from a mood too militant and explosive for the old guard creative intellects to mold and guide. Moreover, in casting his lot with the *Freedom-Freedomways* continuum, Clarke naturally cut all effective ties with nationalistic trends. (The Communist leftwing, remember, had established that precedent back in the 1920's when it and Garveyism became implacable antagonists.) Between the white-controlled leftwing under whose tolerant patronage *Freedomways* exists in quasi-independence, and the black nationalist world of the Harlem ghetto, there is no real meeting ground. Thus Clarke's article was merely an academic exercise in reportage that committed him neither one way nor the other.

Briefly, neither Clarke nor Essien-Udom differed very much in their ideas on the meaning of nationalism among Afro-Americans. Both were historical in their approach, and both analyzed the different variants of nationalism—the political, cultural, separatist, economic—and the various brands of religio-nationalism, such as the Muslims. Essien-Udom wrote:

> A count of contemporary Afro-American "nationalist" organizations in Harlem discloses more than two dozen and a combined membership of about 5000—considerably smaller than 30,000 membership scored forty years ago by the New York City division of the Garvey movement. They vary in size from crackpot-type sects with a handful of members, to the more serious, well-organized, and highly disciplined Muhammad's Mosque No. 7, led by Minister Malcolm X. Shabazz.[3]

Clarke had said that "presently this nationalism [in Harlem] is being hampered by too many organizations and too many leaders with conflicting programs," however "Afro-American Nationalists have moved far ahead of the articulate beggars of crumbs now being called leaders."[4]

---

[3] *Freedomways*, Summer, 1963, p. 335.
[4] *Freedomways*, Fall, 1961, pp. 286, 295.

By these "beggars of crumbs" Clarke obviously meant the official NAACP type of leadership. However, later on in the career of *Freedomways*, it was these same "beggars" whose articles on the Negro freedom movement became the mainstay of this magazine's editorial policies. No article critical of Martin Luther King's passive resistance was acceptable and all the articles and poetry from the young generation black nationalists with conflicting programs, were banned.

Clarke observed in 1961 that Afro-American nationalism differed from African nationalism in one notable respect: In Africa, nationalism had for its spokesmen the African intellectuals—not presently so in the United States, nor with the Garvey movement years ago. Naturally, Clarke could not explain (even had he wanted to) in *Freedomways* why it was that his intellectual friends (Robeson, Killens, Hansberry, Ossie Davis and Ruby Dee, Julian Mayfield, Shirley Graham DuBois, Esther Jackson, Alphaeus Hunton, *et al.*) supported not Afro-American nationalism but faraway African nationalism—*i.e.*, the "African Personality." Yet such a confrontation might have indicated a real intent on the part of *Freedomways* to become a serious magazine.

In Harlem, said Clarke, Afro-American nationalism is predominantly a proletarian movement (neither middle-class nor intellectual). He made no attempt, naturally, to explain why but hastened to add: "By proletarians I do not mean communists." Clarke had gone Left but not Communist Left, and he wanted the world to know it. But about four years later Clarke stood on the same platform with Herbert Aptheker, the leading white Communist theoretician (on black and white folks alike), while they assisted each other in condemning Ralph Ellison, the Negro novelist-essayist, for avoiding the struggle. By struggle, they meant the Killens-Harlem Writers Guild-Negro Writers Conference held at the New School for Social Research during the summer of 1965 which Ellison refused to attend. By this time Clarke had watered down his pretensions of being a protagonist of Afro-American nationalism, but had become so well ensconced among the "marginal Negroes" that he could afford to take up the cudgels of the Communist Left feud against Ellison. In response to being admitted into the *Freedom-Freedomways* inner clique, Clarke had learned his factional loyalties well enough to toady to the very Communist cabal his early Harlem Africanist background had rejected intuitively (and which Ellison had rejected from personal experience). The tragedy is that neither Clarke, Killens, nor any of the leading lights on the *Freedomways* staff have the intellectual probity to debate the Ellison issue so as to benefit the younger generation. Thus they have been kept in the dark about the entire history of destructive Communist duplicity, opportunism, negligence and ignorance on questions of Afro-American Nationalism, the role of Negro writers, etc. Clarke and company may write that African nationalism has the support of African intellectuals, but the very fact that they had to get an African intellectual from Nigeria to write about Afro-American nationalism in "depth" reveals their own inadequacy in coping with home-grown problems.

For our purposes, then, the differing conclusions by Clarke and Essien-Udom about Afro-American nationalism are much more interesting than their analyses. The Nigerian was in the favorable position of not being hampered by the ghosts in the American Negro's family closets where guilty secrets have been accumulating ever since Frederick Douglass and Martin R. Delany disagreed over Back to Africa vs. abolitionist-integration. Back in Nigeria, Essien-Udom does not have to live with his conclusions about black nationalism in America as does John Henrik Clarke in the "marginal" world of *Freedomways*. In order for Afro-American nationalism to be effective, said Clarke, "it will have to be a spiritual, political, and an economic force."[5]

Essien-Udom concluded:

> The nationalists constitute that wing of Negro protest which is most insistent on self-assertion and self-help by the Negro as a group. . . .
> A variant of this theme of self-sufficiency stresses the economic position of Negroes in the United States. This, we call, "economic nationalism." It is advocated by nearly all Harlem nationalists and stridently voiced by the Muslims. The weaknesses of Negro economic nationalism have often been stressed. It is said that a separate Negro economy is a myth; that whatever capital exists within the Negro community is insignificant in the total economy of the United States. In any case, it is said that Negroes lack both capital and experience for effective participation with the giant

[5] *Ibid.*, p. 288.

corporations of America in large scale industrial and financial undertakings. There is no doubt that the improbability of the emergence of economically significant Negro capitalist class far outweighs its probability. I am convinced that the liberation of Afro-Americans in Harlem and elsewhere in America ultimately lies in an understanding, appreciation, and assertion of his Afro-American cultural heritage. It is the exploitation and assertion of cultural and spiritual heritage that will help to usher him into freedomland during the second century of emancipation. In this, he will be engaging in tasks comparable to those of his African brother. Herein lies the foundation of our freedom and liberation; and such is the meaning of the "voices from within the veil" represented, though inadequately, by the nationalist movements of Harlem.[6]

Essien-Udom has a positive attitude toward Harlem nationalists, but with certain reservations. The "self-assertion" of the nationalists, he said, tends "to undermine important contributions of Negro effort, energy, resources, and talent to this three-century-old struggle."

Coming from Africa, Essien-Udom could straddle the fence on nationalism vs. integrationism, while upholding nationalism more strongly than Clarke because, as noted, Nigeria is not America. But note that his critical conclusions about what the nationalists "undermine," in the way of contributions of other Negro trends, actually agrees with the NAACP mentality concerning the nationalists: "Those irresponsible black nationalist extremists undermine all of our good efforts on behalf of the Negro." The problem is that few Africans and Afro-Americans really understand each other's revolution; they only think they do. The two revolutions are so related, and yet so uniquely different, that much confusion about the nature of each reigns on both sides. Thus one of the chief ideological faults of the Harlem nationalists is their naïve idealization of everything African. But at the same time, the social forces that have created both the Afro-American and the modern African are so similar, that they share ideological faults which each can see in the other but not in themselves.

Notice how similar are Essien-Udom's economic views to those of Hope Stevens, an American by way of the West Indies. The

Nigerian discusses nothing but capitalistic economics and differs from Stevens only to the extent that he speaks boldly of economic nationalism. However, although their vocabularies differ, the Harlem banker and the Nigerian intellectual share the same economic philosophy. Such economic Americanism from a colored bourgeois American is understandable, but from an African it is questionable. It reveals that Essien-Udom was sufficiently disinterested to be superficial rather than simply objective. It also reveals, unmistakably, the bourgeois aspirations of many of the new African elite for whom economic nationalism is synonymous with bourgeois achievement. This is, of course, acceptable and respectable in the money markets of the British Commonwealth; but if it is true, as John Henrik Clarke says, that Afro-American nationalism is proletarian, it is a fact that Essien-Udom did not see as rather irrelevant today, considering the economic imperatives associated with the Negro capitalist class. Essien-Udom's superficiality in economic thought is betrayed when he sees the ideas of a separate Negro economy and a flourishing Negro capitalist class as one and the same thing. In the same way that Hope Stevens forgets that he once played around with socialistic economics in the National Negro Congress, Essien-Udom does not even give lip service to African socialism in discussing the economic plight of his Afro-American "brothers." Hence the Nigerian is most inconclusive about Afro-American economic nationalism, but consider how convinced he is about the cultural heritage factor. We have already seen the importance of the cultural factor ourselves, for it is this that has confounded the Negro intellectual more than any other. But it is doubtful that Essien-Udom really grasps the profundity of this cultural factor—from the Afro-American point of view.

The African heritage is an ingredient in an historical-conceptual sense, but the assertion of the Afro-American's cultural heritage in America cannot be based solely on an African cultural fundamentalism of the traditional kind. Even Africa herself is emerging out of such traditionalism toward something newer and more modern. The weakness of Essien-Udom's views on cultural heritage is that he failed to see that culture cannot be separated from the economic and political factors; that politics, economics and culture must function together in a new and dynamic synthesis, *i.e., a new institutionalism.* W.E.B. DuBois came closest to expressing this idea, but only when this new synthesis is able to project actual cultural revolution in America will the Afro-American's assertion of cultural and spiritual heritage have any real social meaning.

Neither Essien-Udom nor Clarke grasped the fact that no existing school or trend of black nationalism in America today has been able to effect this synthesis. In the very first place, such a new nationalist synthesis cannot be achieved until the Negro intellectuals as a class are prepared to lead the way, dispensing with much of Garveyism as outmoded, escapist, unrealistic, or inadequate for this age. Much of W.E.B. DuBois's intellectual achievement will have to be re-examined and brought up to date. In addition, much West Indian and African tribalistic ideology will have to be excluded as irrelevant and superfluous to the American situation. The problem of Afro-American nationalism is as American as are its historical roots. Its origins are to be found in the nationalist vs. integrationist Frederick Douglass-Martin R. Delany-Booker T. Washington-W.E.B. DuBois conflicts down through the 1920's. Other nationalist trends, including Garveyism and the religio-nationalist movements, do *not* seek to solve the Afro-American social problem within the context of the United States. As such, most of the post-Garvey religio-nationalist creeds have developed an impractical Back-to-Africa, separatist other-worldliness which is romantic escapism; for if the Afro-American does not find his salvation in the United States he will find it nowhere. Escapist nationalism also divides and immobilizes valuable intellectual forces within the Negro movement because it perpetuates destructive and useless conflict over aims, methods and tactics. So far, *Freedomways* magazine has achieved nothing more than a mere surface exploration of the deep complexities within the Afro-American nationalist world of Harlem.

V

The Intellectuals and Force and Violence

The American social system is unlike any other in world history. America is a nation that has been pragmatically created, a nation that has emerged from the old into something new and original, never seen before. The inner-dynamics of American social change were, from the very outset, self-contained. Thus in relation to foreign ideologies the world over, America is almost a closed system. It grows, develops, and even reacts to outside social currents, according to the persuasions of its own self-contained, inner dynamic. Not only has America absorbed wave after wave of immigrants, she also absorbs all the radical ideologies of immigrants and Americanizes them by negation. Considering what has happened to revolutionary Marxism, introduced into America by German immigrants back in the 1840's, Roosevelt's New Deal of the 1930's inveigled the Communist revolutionaries into a united front, emasculated them, stole their programs, and patronized them with semi-official recognition. But after brainpicking and tolerating these radicals in order to neutralize them, the Federal power then turned on them with a vengeance, cast them out into the cold, and then prosecuted them for the sin of political prostitution.

All of this would seem to suggest that the American social system is immune to the trials of social revolution. But this is far from true, as any modern economist knows; for social revolution as such does not necessarily correspond to any preconceived formulas extracted from some foreign revolution of decades past. Each new social revolution is unique. There have been a variety of social revolutions but there will be still *others*.

The modern world emerged painfully out of a series of such revolutions, all of them rather protracted and all of them characterized by much force and violence. The United States emerged as an independent nation through the force and violence of the American Revolution. And even before 1775 this revolution was

347

being prepared by the force and violence the British, French and Indians inflicted on each other. Afterwards, the American nation grew and expanded through many decades of forceful and violent conquest. The entire nineteenth-century history of the United States is a violent one: Indian wars, slave uprisings, Civil War, more Indian wars, race violence and labor violence. After the forcible pacification of the Indians, both labor and racial violence continued into the twentieth century.

The traditionally violent nature of American society has its roots in several factors: its expansive frontier ideology, its racial composition, and its labor-capital relationships. Writing about American labor of the late nineteenth and early twentieth centuries, Theodore Draper says: "The relations between labor and capital were largely undefined and uncontrollable except by sheer force on both sides. Employers fought labor organization by every possible means. Strikes were ruthlessly crushed by armed guards, police, sheriffs, militia, and federal troops."[1] The violence that attended early American labor relations was due much more to the indigenous qualities of America than to the importation of the foreign revolutionary doctrine of anarchism. In fact, the use of force and violence did not become a controversial issue even for the professional revolutionaries themselves until the period around 1906, when three labor leaders, one of whom was William D. (Big Bill) Haywood of the IWW, were arrested for complicity in the bombing-murder of the governor of Idaho. Of this arrest and the labor unrest leading up to it, Draper says: "They were finally released, but the entire labor movement had to come to their defense, since the overshadowing issue of the case was the responsibility of the labor movement for the violence which had characterized the great American strikes for two decades."[2]

From this point on until 1912, the question of force and violence so agitated all revolutionary and reform socialists, that the Socialist party of America was forced to resolve the matter. "Long a matter of dispute as a theoretical issue," writes Draper, force and violence "now had to be settled as a matter of practical politics."[3] During the Socialist party's convention in the spring of 1912,

[1] *The Roots of American Communism, op. cit.,* p. 13.
[2] *Ibid.,* p. 21.
[3] *Ibid.,* p. 45.

"Article II, Section 6, of the party's constitution was changed to expel anyone 'who opposes political action or advocates crime, sabotage, or other methods of violence as a weapon of the working class.' "[4] This amendment was upheld by a referendum vote of thirteen thousand to four thousand. Haywood was expelled from the Socialist party's National Executive Committee for holding to the view that the capitalist system should be overthrown "by forcible means if necessary." From 1912 to 1913 about fifteen per cent of the membership left the Socialist party along with Haywood—whose real home was in the IWW, the most extreme revolutionary faction of the labor movement. Many of those who sympathized with Haywood's position on force and violence belonged to the developing radical leftwing which formed the nucleus of what later became the American Communist Party in 1919. But it was not long before the newly-formed Communists themselves began to play down all overt references to the use of force and violence in their political activities.

So, for about forty years, the question of revolutionary force and violence became mostly an academic issue in American radical politics. The indictment of the Communist Party of America in 1948 was not for overt acts of force and violence, but, among other things, for conspiring and organizing to "teach and advocate the overthrow and destruction of the Government of the United States by force and violence."[5] In 1952, William Z. Foster stated the official position of his Party: "The Communist Party, although it does not advocate violence in the worker's struggles, cannot, however, declare that there will be no violence in the establishment of socialism in this country."[6] In the struggle for socialism, the Communists believe that "a peaceful path of development is quite possible for certain capitalist countries." According to Foster, this was Joseph Stalin's view as far back as 1928.

Today, the Trotskyist Socialist Workers Party considers itself the only true revolutionary Marxist party (at least in theory) which hews strictly to the line of class-struggle politics. However, a closer examination will reveal that Trotskyists differ from Communists only in the matter of form. Their theoretical positions

[4] *Ibid.*, p. 46.
[5] *History of the Communist Party, USA, op. cit.*, p. 509.
[6] *Ibid.*, p. 552.

differ only in an academic degree, inasmuch as both Marxist factions suffer the same limitations imposed on them by the peculiarities of American capitalism which has, for all intents and purposes, negated class struggle on the part of the workers against the capitalists. The same can be said for all radical factions in American society today who claim allegiance to the Marxist tradition.

Force and violence has become a principal question within the Negro movement proper (as distinct from Negro groups allied with other white-oriented trends). Like the early pre-Communist white labor movements, the American Negro movement has experienced a long series of violent eras on the racial front, going all the way back to the slave rebellions of Nat Turner and Denmark Vesey. These historical episodes of force and violence in Negro history have become hallowed as prototypal examples of the revolutionary potential in the Negro presence in America. Everyone from Communist whites to nationalist blacks sees in these slave uprisings anything they want to see. Although Turner and Vesey never heard of Marx and Engels (and would not have known either one from a slavemaster), there are certain Communist historians who try to see a direct line from the slave revolts in Virginia to the projected socialist revolution wherein Negroes in the twentieth century will storm the capitalist stronghold. On the other hand, certain Black Nationalists of today see in these same revolts the beginnings of the Black Nationalist movement. But mere rebellions are not revolutions in themselves—especially in America. So far in America, rebellions both black and white have been piecemeal and sporadic social reactions in response to, or in reaction against, the American capitalistic revolution as it progresses. The African, by being enslaved, was drawn into the exchange machinery of the capitalistic (industrial) revolution as a human commodity. His revolt under slavery was simply a revolt against being brutally enslaved, inasmuch as all slaves in all historical eras have been known to revolt.

When seen in historical perspective, all American rebellions and uprisings have come in waves under changing capitalistic conditions and have different objectives from previous waves. Although the Negro in the South of today is still seeking the freedom that the ex-slave expected, this modern rebellion is taking place under different capitalistic conditions and is in great degree a profound response to those very conditions. Add to these regional conditions in the South proper, the penetrating influences of the larger world-embracing political conditions, and you have what some have called the revolution of rising expectations. Yet, the Negro movement is not yet a revolutionary movement, no matter what the radical idealists say about it. This movement cannot become revolutionary until it articulates objectives which transcend its present aims—racial integration. The very fact that many radicals and revolutionaries attempt to connect the present-day Negro rebellion with the slave rebellions only serves to reveal its limitations. At least the slaves knew exactly what they wanted—the abolition of the slave system. Today every Negro in or out of the freedom movement knows he wants "freedom," but actually not one knows what he *really* wants out of present-day America. Therefore, to hark romantically back to the slave rebellions for the purpose of bolstering present-day revolutionary morale is rather pointless. Moreover, it only shows just how far the modern Negro in America has retrogressed in revolutionary virtue when his leadership can talk him into accepting non-violence as a means of achieving his aims. Today, the Negro movement's most radical wing (which calls itself a non-violent committee) has recently worked hand in hand with another segment that upholds the virtues of passive resistance.

For fifty-odd years the NAACP has nurtured a race of people on policies of constitutionalism and legal redress. But, during the late 1950's, in a civil rights episode in Monroe, North Carolina, these legalistic traditions served to reintroduce the old, historical problem of force and violence in a curious and interesting way.*

Robert F. Williams had taken over a defunct NAACP branch in Monroe, reorganized it, and put the branch on a functioning basis with a program of desegregating certain public facilities. Williams' actions brought on the bitter resistance of the Ku Klux Klan, who resorted to traditional terror tactics in an attempt to frighten Williams into submission. But Williams, an ex-Marine, retaliated by

* For a more detailed account of the Monroe, North Carolina, case, see: Truman Nelson, *People With Strength—The Story of Monroe, North Carolina*, published by the author. Also: Robert F. Williams, *Negroes With Guns* (New York: Marzani and Munsell, 1962).

organizing his followers into a rifle club and drilling them into an effective armed corps against the attacks of the Klan. Without going into all the details of the Monroe affair, it is enough to say that the town became an armed camp of high tensions between black and white. There was a long reign of terror, jailings and beatings. In the course of these happenings, Williams was moved to make a public statement to the effect that Negroes might have to stop lynching with lynching. This marked the first time that a local NAACP branch leader in the South had openly espoused meeting violence with violence, and it brought Williams into a policy conflict with the NAACP. The organization censured Williams for expressing views contrary to Association policy which could "be used by segregationists to spread the false impression that the NAACP supported lynching and violence."[7] One month after his statement Williams was suspended from the NAACP for six months by the board of directors. Later, Williams publicly altered his original statement to mean that *"Negroes should have the right of armed self-defense against attack."*[8] Whichever way Robert Williams meant to use violence, that is, offensively or defensively, his armed self-defense tactic became the ideological spark that ignited a hidden potential within the newly emerging phase of the Negro movement. But this potential did not really begin to show itself until about five years later. Other ingredients had to be added.

In analyzing the Williams-Monroe affair it is interesting to note that Williams' conflict with the NAACP's official policy in 1959 resembles somewhat the old Socialist party's conflict with the left-wing labor radicals over force and violence back in 1912. There is a resemblance but there is also an important difference. The old IWW leader, William Haywood, actually espoused *offensive* direct action with the aim of overthrowing the capitalist system "by forcible means if necessary." Williams did not, and could not, espouse offensive direct action by any means possible for any tangible objective. He merely espoused self-defense—a retaliatory action. This approach grew out of the objective nature of race relations because Williams was not contemplating overthrowing

[7] *The New York Times,* May 7, 1959, p. 22.
[8] *Ibid.,* May 8, 1959, p. 16; June 9, 1959, p. 31; July 18, 1959, p. 5.

anything, much less the capitalist system. The Negro movement is fundamentally a *protest* movement, not a revolutionary movement. Furthermore, the adoption of armed self-defense does not, in itself, transform what was a protest movement into a revolutionary movement. This is true despite the fact that many of Williams's most ardent supporters in the North consider his adoption of self-defense a revolutionary accomplishment. If Williams had, at the same time, changed his *social* objective, he might have fulfilled this definition. His objective remained exactly what it was before—desegregation. And desegregation of public facilities was also the aim of the official NAACP leadership. Thus Williams differed not in aims but in tactics when he opted for armed self-defense. But this raised an important question for the entire Negro movement—one that has not yet been answered: Could armed self-defense really lead to desegregation?

The Northern-based revolutionaries who supported Williams were so eager to see Monroe, North Carolina, as the take-off location for a new revolutionary wave, that they forgot that Monroe was merely one isolated spot on the civil rights map. Because Williams defied the conservative, legalistic, and non-violent traditions of the NAACP, his supporters began to act as if armed self-defense was the latest thing in revolutionary effectiveness and also the final answer to all tactical questions for the future. Few asked themselves why it was necessary for the issue to be raised so as to suggest that the right to self-defense was a privilege that Negroes could not assume without asking the sanction of the NAACP, the public authorities and the President, or without publicizing beforehand that self-defense is a God-given right of every living man. Once more it was demonstrated how deeply ingrained is the protest tradition in Negro thinking. Even Williams' plea for the right of self-defense was, in itself, another form of protest.

It is difficult to believe that Williams had any illusions that he was going to change the policies of the NAACP, but he acted as if he did. Otherwise he would have seen clearly that the NAACP was an inhospitable place for himself and his views. He might have realized that what he had in mind had much broader implications than the immediate situation in Monroe, a small community that could not stand alone. He might have seen that his aims required a larger scope of organization, broader planning and a longer-range strategical vision. The Monroe episode actually raised important questions: How does armed self-defense relate to the civil rights movement as a whole? How would armed self-defense apply in the North, South, East or West? How would armed self-defense relate to the non-violent or the passive resistance forces? How does armed self-defense apply in certain Northern locations where desegregation of swimming pools or public libraries (as in Monroe) is not a force-and-violence issue? Or how would armed self-defense relate to Northern cities where police brutality *is* a force-and-violence issue—because it is a form of violence inflicted by an arm of the state against Negroes in particular? Lastly, but not least, how does armed self-defense relate to the various blends of Black Nationalism flourishing today?

However, as long as the Negro movement, in all its various tendencies and segments, remains essentially a protest movement seeking civil rights, its objectives will remain more moral and ethical than tangible. One can objectively shoot a Klansman "defensively" or "offensively," but to succeed in shooting one's way into voting rights, jobs, and "desegregated" public facilities calls for much deeper thought than certain revolutionaries seem to imagine.

The issue of armed self-defense, as projected by Williams in 1959, presaged the emergence of other factors deeply hidden within the Negro movement. It was not until after 1959 that these factors began to reveal themselves. Part of this fateful evolution was the rise of what John Henrik Clarke of *Freedomways* called "The New Afro-American Nationalism." As distinct from the more publicized Nation of Islam movement, this new nationalism was represented in the ideas of a new, young generation born in the late 1930's and early 1940's. This generation grew up in time to be deeply impressed by the emergence of the African states, the Cuban Revolution, Malcolm X and Robert Williams himself. They were witnessing a revolutionary age of the liberation of oppressed peoples. Thus, they were led to connect their American situation with those foreign revolutionary situations. They did not know, of course, that to attempt to apply foreign ideologies to the United States was more easily imagined than accomplished. They did not know that the revolutionary Marxists had attempted this and had come to grief. In fact, they did not even know what a Marxist was, even though they were destined to have to contend with them in their own little movements. They did not realize how little they actually understood about what they saw happening, nor did they have the slightest idea of how much they had to learn about the past forty-odd years before they could even begin to understand the revolutionary age in which they lived. They also were unaware that many of the older generation did not understand *them* or what they implied as a new, young generation. Before long, they would even be misinterpreted on *Freedomways* magazine by John Henrik Clarke, who would describe the "new Afro-America nationalism" as proletarian, when, in fact, it was crowded with young intellectuals, artists, writers, poets, and musicians. These young people were actually coming of age into a great intellectual, political, creative and theoretical vacuum. They would enter the arena of activity in search of leadership and find little but confusion, since leaders were few and destined to be evanescent. But despite all this, they would learn. One of the most outstanding of them, LeRoi Jones, learned in such a personal way as to epitomize within himself all the other things his generation learned either empirically or vicariously.

Several years before anyone had heard of Robert Williams or Monroe, LeRoi Jones had moved into Greenwich Village from his hometown of Newark in New Jersey. This was during the middle 1950's. At the time, Jones appeared very quiet, unassuming, reticent, even meek—although curious about everything. But thinking back, one wonders if perhaps his inner personality had not been grossly misinterpreted. I, for example, met Jones from time to time, here and there, without expending too much attention on him. A person of my background would have been incomprehensible to Jones anyway; and, as for Jones—he was then just another addition to the black intellectual scene of Greenwich Village—and rather late at that. From that point on, Jones made the "beat generation" scene. His name became linked with that of Jack Kerouac, and he soon began to make his name as a Beat Poet of talent. But at the same time there were others of Jones's generation emerging in Harlem—the "natives" of the black ghetto. Later, Jones would meet up with these, but not before he went through more conditioning. But his conditioning was to be for certain social objectives that others of his generation could not clearly see. They were acting intuitively and the outlines of the future were vague and undefinable, as this generation had the impossible inheritance of three decades of conflicting ideologies not their own. But the late 1950's and the present 1960's became what can be called the new era of black ideological transformation, especially among the newest wave of intellectuals.

The great transformation in LeRoi Jones was brought on by the Cuban Revolution. In July, 1960, I accompanied Jones to Cuba to "see for ourselves" what it was all about. It was the first time since Jones came to the Village scene that I had had the opportunity to observe him intimately and he had by then become rather contemptuous of individuals not of his generation. In his article about his trip, "Cuba Libre," he wrote mockingly of certain individuals in the writers' contingent as being "nineteen-fortyish" and "nineteen-thirtyish" (as if to say that the really "in" thing was to be "nineteen-fiftyish"). Jones was also disappointed by the fact that many of the "name" writers he was eager to meet did not accept the invitation to Cuba with him. At that time, though Jones considered himself a Beat and a nonconformist he was still very impressed with "name" writers. The only people on this contingent to Cuba who had any kind of reputation for being *engagé*—either literarily and/or politically—were Robert Williams, Julian Mayfield, John Henrik Clarke and myself. At any rate, his actual experiences in Cuba amply compensated Jones for the lack of representative Negro writers in his delegation.*

In Havana it was noted that Jones made a very favorable impression on the revolutionary intelligentsia of the Castro regime. Although they were all white Cubans, it was remarkable to see how much they and Jones had in common—they actually talked the same "language." As I was "nineteen-fortyish," I noticeably held back all outward exuberance for the Cuban situation. I was admittedly pro-Castro, but there were too many Communists around acting imperious and important. Moreover, there was the obvious and unclarified position of the Cuban Negro to consider. Yet we were all treated with such overwhelming deference, consideration and privilege, it was difficult to be critical. The crowning

* See "Cuba Libre," *Evergreen Review*, November-December, 1960, pp. 139-159.

event of this trip was the long journey from Havana to Sierra Maestre. Riding with us in a string of modern air-conditioned coaches was a large corps from the international press of Europe, Latin America, United States (*Look* magazine), and the Far East.

In this instance, the ideology of a new revolutionary wave in the world at large, had lifted us out of the anonymity of lonely struggle in the United States to the glorified rank of visiting dignitaries. For Jones's impressionable generation this revolutionary indoctrination, this ideological enchantment, was almost irresistible. And here, vicariously, a crucial question was engendered: *What did it all mean and how did it relate to the Negro in America?* It did demonstrate incontrovertibly the relevance of force and violence to successful revolutions, especially abroad. Beyond that, neither Robert Williams who tried mightily, nor Jones's generation, have adequately explained it in Afro-American terms.

But we hardly thought about that on the morning of July 26, 1960, at the foot of the Sierra Maestre mountains. We were caught up in a revolutionary outpouring of thousands upon thousands of people making their way up the mountain roads to the shrine of the Revolution, under the hottest sun-drenching any of us Americans had probably ever experienced. Jones and I stood shoulder-to-shoulder in a Cuban rebel army truck, packed to its side-ribbings with liberated Castroites whose euphoria we could feel profoundly, but not experience. Nothing in our American experience had ever been as arduous and exhausting as this journey. Our reward was the prize of revolutionary protocol that favored those victims of capitalism away from home. We were escorted by a guard of armed rebels to the official platform and presented to Fidel Castro. There we were seated in the company of the rebel elite as Castro tuned up and spoke for four hours to the Sierra Maestre hills covered with people as far as the eye could see. Robert Williams was the nominal leader of our contingent, but Jones was the most interesting personality. During the whole time I watched him closely and wondered what he was thinking. I wondered how this Greenwich Village Beat poet would relate politically, artistically, ideologically to this foreign revolution.

These questions were soon to be answered back in the United States, beginning with certain events of 1961 when Jones ventured from the Village to the Harlem scene. In the meantime, however,

Jones had formed personal associations with the John O. Killens literary faction through Julian Mayfield and John Henrik Clarke, via Havana. It probably did not occur to Jones either there, or back in New York, that he could never thrive literarily or ideologically with this leftwing faction. Artistically, they and Jones were poles apart. What held them together in a temporary and functional alliance was their attachment to Robert Williams and his Monroe affair, and the Cuban Revolution. But not a single one of them succeeded in analyzing the implications of their new alliance, just as none of them seriously analyzed the meaning of Williams's armed self-defense tactic. What did Negro creative intellectuals have to do with Williams and armed self-defense? Was the Negro writers' role simply to support Robert Williams verbally or organizationally? If so, this was no more than was expected from everybody else. Since for the most part, all Negro writers functioned out of New York, what did the situation there (Harlem, that is) have to do with Monroe, North Carolina—where desegregation, despite armed self-defense, was simply trying to catch up with Northern desegregation won by law? Whose movement was more important overall—Monroe's or Harlem's—or did they complement each other? Since no one seriously attempted to explore these matters, it was not at all surprising that Robert Williams and a couple of his intellectual supporters got badly botched-up in their communications between Harlem and Monroe; as a result, they were forced into exile, leaving behind them one Harlem woman who became the hostage for the authorities.

There were several factors involved in the Monroe, North Carolina, fiasco. In the first place, all kinds of factions descended on Williams and his self-defense cohorts. There were leftwing Trotskyists, Freedom Riders and representatives of other civil rights groups—all pro-integrationist forces. On the other hand, there were also nationalist-oriented individuals from Harlem, not to speak of certain writers with muddled views on integrationism and nationalism. They all saw something in Monroe that did not actually exist—an immediate revolutionary situation.

But the Monroe defeat highlighted certain Northern dilemmas—among them, the question of the new Afro-American nationalism. In the North, the bulk of Williams's supporters in the young generation were nationalists. Neither Clarke nor Mayfield, however, belonged to this group, and even Jones had not yet fully arrived. Robert Williams himself was never a nationalist, but an avowed integrationist, a fact that later created much propaganda confusion. For the young nationalists celebrated Williams as their leader, since his self-defense stand coincided with their rising interests in the adoption of force and violence tactics in the North. But in the North, armed self-defense would not be against an unofficial force such as the Klan, but would arise in opposition to the police, the Army and the National Guard—official arms of the State power.

It should be noted in passing that Williams would have welcomed the intervention of the Federal National Guard in Monroe, but that same intervention was not welcomed in Watts, Los Angeles, for obvious reasons. Watts was not Monroe and the force and violence occurring there was on a far different level. Although force and violence could be a revolutionary ingredient, self-defense as Williams projected it, is *not* revolutionary, even with arms. It is exactly what it says it is—defensive—at best, a holding action. Misconceptions about this have led to other fiascos and failures. For example, in Harlem, uprisings are ignited spontaneously over one issue (such as police brutality), but are actually deeply rooted in the general social conditions. Yet the slogan of armed self-defense was militantly raised so as to provoke the police into more severe repressive actions by giving them a ready-made excuse to shoot to kill. Needless to say, not a single one of the basic economic, political, or cultural aspects of the Harlem social conditions that feed the riotous proclivities of the population are ever touched on by the revolutionaries, who misapply the slogan of armed self-defense. The failure of the intellectuals is that they do not attempt to clarify these issues.

Another reason why the tactic of armed self-defense, in the North, is so inappropriate is that historically Black Nationalism has never upheld the use of force and violence. This is another compelling reason why Garveyism, to which many of the young nationalists hark back, is today passé. Garvey was not a revolutionary but a reformist. Garvey's scheme for a "peaceful return to Africa" creates both practical and theoretical problems for today's new Afro-American nationalists who study Garveyism historically, but are less and less inclined to peaceful methods. But the emergence of free African states with political autonomy has done Garvey's work for him; even so, most of the West Indians from Garvey's homeland in Jamaica leave home not to return to Africa, but to emigrate to the British Isles. This is a fact that the Garveyites do not like to discuss, but that must force the new, young nationalists to realize that ultimately, *their* situation must have an American, not an African, solution. This means that Afro-American nationalism must be geared organically to the native American revolutionary dynamic toward social change. Today, Afro-American nationalism is *the* main force behind that social dynamic, and as such, the last social link to the unsolved American nationality dilemma.

However, this social dynamic comprises many factors—practical, organizational, institutional, and theoretical—and each one is essential to the whole. Force and violence enters the picture only to the degree that American (white) institutions resist the pressures towards social change exerted by the Afro-American social dynamic. Strong resistance there has been and will be; yet, ironically, much of this resistance, though less overt and demonstrative than methods of force and violence, *is just as effective*. But in terms of the peculiarities of the American social system, there must evolve a more profound understanding of the real meaning of this resistance. It is much more than mere reluctance to grant racial democracy and equal rights, as the civil righters would have it. Overall, it is the natural resistance a malfunctioning social organism throws up against being rehabilitated, reconstructed, and made functional—*i.e.,* to perfect its "democratic" potential. Sick social systems, like sick bodies, tend to resist curative treatment. Historically, however, it has been amply demonstrated that America, as well as the Afro-American to whom she is wedded, are both condemned to be free: The American social system is fated to evolve according to its own innate and internal social dynamic, despite all the internal resistance exerted to the contrary. In this process, then, force and violence is part but not the whole of the strategy. The quality of resistance exerted against social change determines the quality of self-defense tactics. But the *main* front tactics must always be organizational and institutional. As the economist P.J.D. Wiles points out, revolutions occur only in those societies that resist new institutionalisms.

One of the keys to understanding the effectiveness of any tactic, idea, strategy or trend in the Negro movement, is to determine how well the American system can absorb it and, thus, negate its force. To repeat, the American social system quite easily absorbs all foreign, and even native, radical doctrines and neutralizes them. The same applies to the doctrines of the Negro movement. In fact, it applies all the more, simply because this movement is more native than others and therefore more intimately connected to the inner American social dynamic. We have seen that most of the tactics of the civil rights trends are so easily absorbed by the system as to lose their original motivational impetus; their objectives become more and more diffuse and intangible. When the issue of armed self-defense was first raised, the young Afro-American nationalists enthusiastically embraced this revolutionary innovation. But not long after Robert Williams departed into exile, a new armed self-defense organization—The Deacons of Defense—emerged in Louisiana. However it was not long before the Deacons were absorbed by the civil rights movement, both North and South. The Deacons did not, and could not, espouse any revolutionary aims beyond defending themselves and the rights of civil rights workers to pursue their aims of orderly integration. This new self-defense development did not venture beyond the original position of Williams in Monroe, but there was a difference: In Monroe the integrationist civil righters came to the rescue of Williams; in Bogalusa, Louisiana, the Deacons came to the rescue of harried civil rights workers. In effect, the Deacons became the broad organizational development that Williams should have pursued in the first place, instead of getting trapped into premature actions in isolated Monroe. Even so, the Deacons' objective remained the same—desegregation. Except for the use of armed self-defense, the NAACP could not disagree. The Northern Afro-American nationalists hailed the Deacons for their stand, but the Deacons are no more nationalistic than Robert Williams. Nationalism is, essentially, a Northern urban phenomenon which today attempts to form links with the South through the adoption of new Southern tactics. But since these naturally are most applicable in the South, tactics like self-defense become the property of the interracial integrationist trend, and are thus absorbed. As a result, when the civil rights movement gets bogged down in the South so does the concept of armed self-defense. In this way, the entire Negro movement as a whole becomes the tactical prisoner of its inherent pragmatism. This strategical defect will not be overcome until the new Afro-American nationalism of the North develops a theoretical grasp of its own leadership function within the Afro-American social dynamic. But sadly, LeRoi Jones and those of his generation did not fully understand this.

The fact that Jones and his active contemporaries were, to a great degree, creative, artistic intellectuals did not alleviate their problem. They were not the proletarians who went into the Nation of Islam to be rehabilitated. They represented a new breed of Afro-American nationalist. With its commitment to force and violence, and its support by the young creative intellectuals, the new Afro-American nationalism has historically unique facets. This does not mean, of course, that the participants fully understand all the ramifications of their movement—far from it. These young intellectuals are the victims of historical discontinuity. Marxist Communism (aided by the Great Depression), the Jewish Left and liberal seduction of the 1930's, the Jewish-Christian liberal paternalism of the 1940's and 1950's, have all combined to eradicate the living threads between the young Negro generations of the late 1950's and the 1960's, and their predecessors in the 1920's.

As a result, this new generation is called upon to make up for lost time—about forty-five years of it. They must achieve an historical perspective on what happened since about 1920, in order to transcend politically, economically and culturally every social objective projected by the Negro movement since that time. In other words, their social objectives in terms of program must be adequate to the potential of their own social dynamic *at this moment* in American history.

The first indication that LeRoi Jones and his generation were willing but not ready, came in Harlem in 1961. It became obvious that Jones and his young Harlem group did not understand their own social dynamic. They were interested, after a fashion, in politics, economics and culture, but not at all interested in political, economic, and cultural organizations *per se*. The Jones who could set up the Black Arts Theater and School in 1965 was not the Jones of 1961. Although Jones and his trend considered themselves the new wave, once they had set up their organizations they proceeded to do the exact same thing every other civil rights trend was doing—they went out on protest demonstrations. They felt they were different not only because they were young, but for other largely intuitive, ill-defined reasons. Jones once threatened to picket the NAACP, for no other apparent reason than that it represented the old guard, of which Jones was contemptuous.

From the very outset, in 1961, Jones's generation had to go through a process that revealed their ambivalence toward two concerns—their relation to whites, and to Black Nationalism of the traditional kind. As forerunners of the new Afro-American nationalism, they were in trouble over these two questions. Jones, for example, was dubious at first about what he called the Harlem Black Nats (nationalists). His first Harlem organization, the "On Guard for Freedom Committee," was an interracial group. This committee was the creation of Jones and one of his close Negro colleagues, Calvin Hicks; part of its membership came out of Jones's original group, the "Organization of Young Men" (OYM), a "downtown" movement. However, when some of the young nationalists of his Harlem committee objected to the presence of whites at their membership meetings, Jones disagreed. He said at one meeting that he could not see why it was necessary to restrict whites from participation. More than that, he said he could not understand why Harlem Negroes should hate whites. Jones was still a long way from his militant anti-white stand of 1965. He was wrestling with the unsolved problems of his intellectual antecedents which, for him, has to be posed in terms that equated pro-blackness with a hatred of whiteness. Long before Jones came on the scene this had been one of the Negro intellectual's most severe "hang-ups."

Negro intellectuals have been sold a bill of goods on interracialism by white Communists and white liberals. As a result of this, a peculiar form of what might be called the psychology of political interracialism (for want of a better term) has been inculcated in the Negro's mind. Even before the average Negro attempts to undertake any action himself, he assumes, almost involuntarily, that he must not, cannot, dare not exclude whites, because he cannot succeed without them. He has been so conditioned that he cannot separate personal and individual associations with individual whites in the everyday business of striving and existing, from that interior business that is the specific concern of his group's existence. Every other ethnic group in America, a "nation of nations," has accepted the fact of its separateness and used it to its own social advantage. But the Negro's conditioning has steered him into that perpetual state of suspended tension wherein ninety-five per cent of his time and energy is expended on fighting prejudice in whites. As a result, he has neither the time nor the inclination to realize that all of the effort spent fighting prejudice will not obviate those fundamental things an ethnic group must do for itself. This situation results from a psychology that is rooted in the Negro's symbiotic "blood-ties" to the white Anglo-Saxon. It is the culmination of that racial drama of love and hate between slave and master, bound together in the purgatory of plantations. Today the African foster-child in the American racial equation must grow to manhood, break the psychological umbilical ties to intellectual paternalism. The American Negro has never yet been able to break entirely free of the ministrations of his white masters to the extent that he is willing to exile himself, in search of wisdom, into the wastelands of the American desert. That is what must be done, if he is to deal with the Anglo-Saxon as the independent political power that he, the Negro, potentially is.

What has further complicated this emergence of Afro-American ethnic consciousness is the Jewish involvement in this interracial process over the last fifty-odd years. The role of American Jews as political mediator between Negro and Anglo-Saxon must be terminated by Negroes themselves. This inter-group arrangement is fraught with serious dangers to all concerned. The status of Jews in America is a white Christian-Jewish affair, and the ultimate status of the Negro in America is a white Christian-Negro affair since Negroes and Christians are the more populous groups.

But with LeRoi Jones and his young Afro-American nationalists, anti-interracialism was equated not only with anti-whiteness, but with *hatred* of whiteness. In other words, Negroes had become so deeply mired in an institutionalized form of political interracialism that they could not break with it unless sufficient hatred were mustered to avoid the necessity of apologizing to whites for excluding them. That this was a paranoia-producing rationalization was not understood. If Negroes were actually thinking and functioning on a mature political level, then the exclusion of whites—organizationally and politically—should be based not on hatred but on strategy. It would be much like the tradition that no one outside one's immediate family is ever admitted into a discussion of intimate family problems. It is, therefore, an unfortunate development in Negro life that political interracialism has become so doctrinaire that certain nationalistic Negroes have been forced to resort to race hate in order to block out the negative effect of interracialism on ethnic consciousness. All race hate is self-defeating in the long run because it distorts the critical faculties. Thus it happened that when LeRoi Jones finally came to the point of rejecting interracialism in Harlem in 1965, his erstwhile white friends and associates called him anti-white and a fosterer of race hate and black extremism. But a few of Jones's young collaborators had swung much further toward such extremes than Jones, and in fact rejected Jones as too moderate and pro-white.

This extremist faction represented a concept of force and violence that went far beyond the mere armed self-defense of Robert Williams in 1959. It represented a tendency toward violence that is bred out of the desperation and alienation of the Harlem ghetto; a poisonous brew of hate, hopelessness, racial envy and class inferiority complexes. It has passed even the stage of blind hate to become a form of ghetto paranoia, directed not only toward whites, but at a more immediate target—the middle-class Negro, the "bourgies." More than that, some of the young nationalists have evinced a new black form of anti-intellectualism. The Negro intellectual, too, is suspect, because he is either middle class in origins, accepted by the middle class, or has middle-class leanings. Much of this anti-intellectualism crops up in those whose desire to resort to force and violence takes on such "terroristic" designs as destruction of symbolic objects for mere propaganda effect. Hence, the new Afro-American nationalism has emerged with both a positive rational wing and an anarchistic wing with nihilistic overtones. Revolutionary nationalism in black America has developed a form of black Bakuninism.

Unavoidably, Jones' On Guard for Freedom group collapsed, for neither Jones nor his collaborators were prepared to deal with the political, economic, and cultural imperatives of their movement.

Because they were unable to start off on an all-black basis, their organizational interracialism got them ensnared, as always happens in such instances, by the white Marxist Left—both Communists and Trotskyists. This was fatal for the simple reason that neither Communists nor Trotskyists could offer either program or direction to Afro-American nationalism. This had to come from the young intellectuals themselves or it would never come. But without knowledge of the Marxist factional background in America, and without seeing the necessity of breaking with institutionalized interracialism, Jones and company were wide open for infiltration. Like all new generations in all endeavors, they had to learn by themselves; they could not be told anything by those who knew better, for having learned many bitter lessons during the past two decades. It also demonstrated that because Negro intellectuals establish no institutions which can be sustained from one generation to the next, they cannot even hand down to succeeding generations the lessons of their failures. Thus the Harlem political organization that Jones tried to establish had a certain precedence but no continuity. Since the new wave believed they owed little or nothing to the past— or more precisely, to the older generation—they made light of the fact that any new group starting in Harlem is bequeathed a raft of acute social problems, which must be reevaluated.

At the very outset, three years before the Harlem uprising of 1964, Jones' group was warned that Harlem was due for another outbreak of violence. Therefore, unless a fundamental survey of the economic problems of Harlem rehabilitation was pursued, no amount of protest demonstrations, petitions, and militant speeches would mean a thing. Needless to say, this proposal was ignored and not even discussed—because its meaning was not understood. Here was the spectacle of a group of young men, some of them college graduates, who dared to aspire to black revolution without even a glimmer of knowledge about the economics of social change. More important, they lacked the curiosity, interest or willingness to learn and study all the factors of the community situation at hand from a political, economic and cultural point of view. How could anyone talk seriously about social change without a thorough investigation of these social factors? But the blind aplomb with which Jones and his group ignored any suggestions and proceeded to outline a series of protest actions, revealed the disturbing depth and scope of technical unpreparedness of Negroes in highly organized society.

In the Negro community there is no tradition of intellectual skill in the social sciences beyond social work. As a prime victim of laissez-faire capitalism and its social imperatives, the Negro intellectual is pro-capitalistic in his every reflex. He does not see that the concepts of social equality for the entire Negro group, and unqualified capitalism, are contradictory and incompatible. The ideology of the Negro movement, in all its trends, protests against the *ill-effects* of capitalist society but *not* against the society itself. This undermines the rational and organizational viability of the Negro movement and encourages the irrationality of nationalist anarchism and nihilism. It brings the Negro movement and all of its factions face to face with the hard social dynamics of American capitalism. This inner capitalistic dynamic, if left to its own momentum, subordinates and absorbs everything, including the Negro movement and its pro-capitalistic ideology. It can be no other way. As such, without an anti-capitalistic ideology, the Negro movement is doomed to be rolled back into submission. Nothing but welfare state politics and economics will be administered from above, in response to the lingering and sporadic Negro protests from below.

It took Jones and his young Afro-American nationalists four more years to arrive at the realization that it had to establish institutions inside the Harlem ghetto in order to implement a positive program. The institution established was not economic or political, but cultural—the Black Arts Repertory Theater and School. However, no sooner was this institution established than it had to appeal to a federally sponsored economic program for survival—the HARYOU Anti-Poverty Program. Thus, the Jones group was forced to enter an uneven struggle with a federal agency over the dispensation of funds, without having prepared for such an eventuality with a grassroots economic institution of its own in the community. If such a Harlem-based economics planning group had been established, Jones would have been able to wage a more effective *political* struggle with the HARYOU administration and the Federal government over the funding of anti-poverty programs.

The most important conclusion about the Jones movement is that these young intellectuals have been unable to clarify for themselves what the specific role is of the Negro intellectuals as a class in this era. From 1960 to 1965, Jones himself went through a very unique creative development as poet, novelist, and dramatist. But this represented an individual rather than a class development; the latter is more important. For unless the Negro intellectual's role as a class is defined (or redefined), the entire Negro movement—all the way from integrationists to nationalists—is doomed to be bogged down and wasted, through confusion and lack of direction. Even when Jones and his group finally established the Black Arts Theater and School, it was merely a faltering step in the right direction. No real Harlem cultural objectives for this school were defined; nor was the peculiar role of the young intellectuals in this school analyzed, clarified and planned. True to form, it was a pragmatic step without substantial theoretical inspiration. For sadly, Negro intellectuals as a class have no cultural philosophy on which to base such a theory.

One of the main reasons Jones's On Guard group was prevented from analyzing their own role as new wave intellectuals, was their preoccupation with the Robert Williams self-defense mystique in the South. Amidst all the other domestic and international influences, such as Africa and Cuba, Williams stood out as the great American symbol of black resistance. More than that, Williams was also personally identified with the Cuban experience—making him all the more magnetic a figure. However, Monroe represented a Southern trend, while Jones's movement was definitely Northern —with no specific "Northern" program beyond civil rights integration. Thus, the attempted liaison between North and South was in fact highly impractical and adventuristic. What was presented was the spectacle of a collection of Northern romantics playing at revolution, to the extent of shipping arms to Monroe and *publishing the fact in a Northern leftwing newspaper;* for even before the Jones group could establish itself, the Northern liaison with Monroe was already under the control of white leftwingers in New York, as Williams himself had come North and bypassed Harlem in favor of leftwing support in downtown Manhattan.

The upshot of the entire Monroe affair was a series of uncontrollable events, which led to the kidnapping charge levied against Williams and his supporters. From this point on, the white left-wing in New York took over the Williams defense case for propaganda purposes, and was immediately split into two factions—dominated by Trotskyists on the one hand, and pro-Communists on the other. Considering their irreconcilable tenets, one can imagine the divisive and disorienting effects these two political factions would exert on a Negro movement. The young chairman of one of these defense groups—the Monroe Defense Committee—was Jones's friend Calvin Hicks, of the On Guard group.* After the formation of the Monroe Defense Committee, headed by Hicks, another white radical splinter faction ran a story about the Monroe affair under the heading "Afro-American Leadership is the Issue! Why Two Defense Committees?"[9] In this article, Calvin Hicks was quoted as follows:

> We are more than willing to accept the support of our white progressive friends, as our own list of supporters should prove. But right now these particular friends want to dominate us rather than just support us.
>
> They even offered us considerable financial assistance—and later withdrew it when we insisted upon our own leadership.
>
> We were shocked at this, and pretty angry at the time. But I still do not entirely blame them for their actions because it is extremely hard for them to understand why we feel the way we do.

The article said further that "some of these [white] progressives actually stated that they would not support a committee with only a [Negro] leadership." But Hicks concluded, that "considering that various white progressives helped Williams with funds and in other ways, it also seems logical that they should continue to support the defense committee without demanding leadership of it."

Note that Calvin Hicks has never departed any further from political interracialism than to demand that it be black-led. The

---

* The rival group, the Committee to Aid the Monroe Defenders (CAMD), was the Trotskyist group.

[9] The *Workers World*, September 29, 1961, p. 3. N.B. Organ of a splinter group from the Socialist Workers Party (Trotskyist); the *Workers World* group stood between the Trotskyist and Stalinist (Communist) parties.

On Guard group itself never went beyond this demand. It did not occur to Hicks that what he wanted was impossible—white participation and financial support without white leadership. The lesson that the young Afro-American nationalists had to learn was that they had to pay their own way, still another aspect of the economics question they managed to evade.

The story of the On Guard group and the two Monroe Defense Committees is a graphic lesson in the frustrating politics of interracialism. It was compounded and confounded by the mélange of incipient nationalism in the North, armed self-defense in the South, and integrationism plus leftwing political and propagandistic intervention. As a practical and expedient way out of the confusion, Calvin Hicks was able to substitute Williams's movement for the Harlem program his On Guard group was able to create for itself. But all it amounted to in the end was just another Northern protest that swiftly petered out. Not only did the original On Guard group pass out of existence, so did the two rival committees on Monroe defense. The new Afro-American nationalists had a long way to go before they could master the tactical and strategical problems of working out of Harlem. Rather than analyze the Monroe situation, they oversimplified it. However, once the white leftwing gets its hands on a Negro propaganda issue, oversimplification is unavoidable.

Without an ideology relevant to America, white leftwingers are forced to attempt to take over the control of any incipient Negro trend that appears revolutionary. Thus the Marxist factions took over the Monroe armed self-defense movement. The fact that these arms were to be used by Negroes to protect themselves against whites who were also workers (the alleged allies of the Negro) did not at all disturb the zeal of the Marxists. They were going to bake their own revolutionary cake and entice Negroes to eat it with them, without stopping to debate certain fine points of revolutionary theory out of Marx, Engels, Lenin, Stalin or Trotsky.

The American propaganda apparatus has created the great social myth that the Negro protest movement is, in fact, the Black Revolution in progress. This is stretching the word revolution to include anything from "pray ins" to the March on Washington. It is true that, to many whites, the very fact that so many Negroes are protesting all at one time in so many different places, is unsettling enough to induce certain opinion-molders to believe their own alarmist propaganda. Ghetto uprisings like Harlem and Watts lend credence to the spectre of revolution even more. But as long as these uprisings are sporadic, the American capitalistsic welfare state will absorb them and, more than that, pay for the damage in the same way the government pays for the destruction caused by hurricanes and floods. Uprisings are merely another form of extreme protest action soon to be included under the heading of Natural Calamities.

People who call the Negro protest movement a black revolution do not really understand their own system, for a real social revolution in their country would involve a social dynamic of many correlated parts. Such a revolution would have very little in common with the foreign revolutions they have read about. It would amount to a massive social transformation of a kind unheard of before, and the elements for it already exist within the society either actively or latently.

The Negro movement acts out its many-sided role under the influence of, and as a part of, the structural imperatives of the American system. This movement cannot function in any other way as it progresses from one stage to another. Its future failures or successes will depend on to what degree the movement succeeds (or fails) in mastering the imperatives of its own social dynamic. The more the Negro movement falls prey to the myths created by the system—that it is revolutionary when it is not—the longer will it take for this movement to create an advanced leadership. The more the movement absorbs the American myths, the more the American system will absorb the impetus and elements of the movement, and the more internal leadership disorientation will result.

Negro leadership generally functions, even during protest, with one foot out and the other foot inside the Establishment. Being neither "in," nor without hope of getting "in," Negro leadership encounters the difficulty of fighting and protesting against the very social system it wants to join. This means, in effect, that Negro leadership is not really fighting *against* the system, but against being *left out of it*. Therefore, what really worries the Establishment is not so much the cacophony of protest, but the problem of how to absorb the movement without too much stress and strain. The general staff of the capitalistic welfare state understands this situation much better than the muddled minds that run the civil rights movement. The administrative "brains" at the top of the American system may be pragmatically shallow, but not too shallow to understand that the Negro protest movement is not really a revolutionary movement, but rather a response to another kind of American revolution, the capitalistic revolution that threatens to alter social relations in the Southern states. Industrialization has driven Negroes off the farms and plantations into the urban centers; it has mechanized farms, built industries and increased trade. The Negro response to this process has been inspired both by rising expectations and the instability of being uprooted. If Negro leadership fails to understand both the complexities of this capitalistic dynamic and the potential power of the Afro-American social dynamic as an entity, then the entire movement is wide open to being absorbed and controlled by welfare state anti-poverty programs and their ilk.

If Negro leadership, especially the new young generation, also understood the history of the white Marxist Left, then they would better understand American capitalism and the Marxist Left's real position within it. They would see how the myth of the Negro revolution is used by both capitalism and the white Left. However, the inner dynamic of American capitalism has nullified any possibility of the Marxist Left leading a revolution according to its theories. Consequently, out of sheer political insolvency and desperation, the white Left swallows the myth of the Black Revolution and reads revolution into every actual or potential Negro uprising. The joke is that the leftwing buys its way into a pro-capitalistic movement on the hope that what the establishment calls a revolution, will in fact become one later on. But the white Left does not possess a single idea, tactic or strategy in its theoretical arsenal that can make the Negro protest movement a revolutionary one. All it can achieve is to intervene and foster such tactics as will get some persevering Negro activist leader jailed, framed, or exiled for utterly romantic reasons. As of now, the same capitalistic dynamic that absorbed and negated the white Left of the 1930's, has blunted the forward thrust of broad segments of the civil rights movement (including self-defense uprisings).

Association with white Marxists warps the social perception of leftwing Negro intellectuals to the extent that they also fail to see the factors of their own dynamic. Over the past forty-five years many of the best Negro minds have passed in, through, and out of the Marxist Left. Their creative and social perceptions have been considerably dulled in the process, and their collective, cumulative failures over the decades have contributed to the contemporary poverty and insolvency of Negro intellectuals as a class. When the intellectual output, the level of social insight, and the lackluster quality and scarcity of the Negro intellectuals' creative enterprises are stacked against the potentialities of the Negro ethnic group in America, the Negro intellectual class is seen as a colossal fraud. The Negro intellectual may have been sold out in America, but he has participated all too readily in the grand design of his own deception.

Julian Mayfield, who was to become deeply and disastrously involved in the Monroe movement, once wrote in defense of James Baldwin: "Would that the artist could be a scholar and vice versa, but he rarely is."[10] He did not advise that artists in this complex world who are not scholars should not become spokesmen in matters where scholarship is required. As a ranking member of the Harlem leftwing literary and cultural elite (although a late arrival), Mayfield never had to deal with the question of force and violence from a Left point of view until the Monroe affair. As a literary artist who would prefer that scholarship be left to others, Mayfield perhaps was not aware of how his Communist peers had reacted to the first Harlem uprising of 1935. Like the Watts outbursts of thirty years later, this Harlem demonstration of force and violence was directed mainly against the presence of white-owned business establishments. The difference was that no arms were used. Because of the fact that the bulk of businesses in Harlem were Jewish-owned, at least one leading white Communist of 1935 called the uprising an anti-Semitic pogrom. All of the Communists (black and white) were against this outbreak and it is said that a few were actively involved in efforts to put it down. Here, in a

---

[10] Mayfield, "And Then Came Baldwin," *Harlem, U.S.A.*, ed. John Henrik Clarke (East Berlin: Seven Seas Publishers, 1960), p. 160.

decade of economic desperation, was a bitter irony: Communist revolutionaries—who claimed to be against exploitation in all forms—were in fact opposing an uprising against exploitation. In view of the fact that in 1936 the Communist-laden National Negro Congress was formed with an economic program it did not pursue, the Harlem uprising of 1935 clearly demonstrated why Marxist politics cannot deal with the economic "roots" of black revolution.*

The emergence of Robert Williams in 1959 brought Mayfield into contact with the new Afro-American nationalist trend. The Cuban experience, of course, was an overwhelming factor in the metamorphosis of this trend, and Williams personified the sympathetic link between the Castroites and the Negro struggle. Williams and his followers—Jones, Mayfield, Clarke, *et al.*—were all deeply moved by these sentiments of solidarity, despite the fact that not a single Cuban leader, from Castro on down, had the slightest grasp of the complexity of the Negro struggle in the United States. Conversely, neither did Williams, Jones, and company seriously examine the real position of the Cuban Negro in the Cuban Revolution.

Back in New York, the white Marxists made propaganda for their respective factions from the Cuban Revolution (not, incidentally, a revolution made by Cuban Marxists). The Trotskyists published a pamphlet entitled "How Cuba Uprooted Race Discrimination," which Williams' followers upheld without question. Mayfield wrote an article on the same topic in a Negro newspaper.† However in 1964, a young Cuban Negro patriot, Carlos More, published a lengthy, detailed document entitled "Have

---

* In 1935 the Communists explained the Harlem riots as "resentment against hunger, relief cuts sweep Harlem" but refused to admit that the real focus of the outbreak was against white businesses and outside economic control of the ghetto. The *Daily Worker* ran a front page appeal—"Negro and White Workers! United Against Race Riot Provocation," on March 19, 1935. It took the Communist Party thirty years, plus the Watts uprising, to admit that ghetto uprisings are not provoked by outside agitation but by internal black-white relations. See Herbert Aptheker on "The Watts Ghetto Uprising," *Political Affairs*, October and November, 1965. See also, "Communications—The Meaning of Watts," Ben Dobbs and Herbert Aptheker discussion, *Political Affairs*, January, 1966, pp. 53-57.

† In 1961, Julian Mayfield wrote: "I can say without hesitation that the new government, in the brief time it has been in power, has substantially eliminated racial discrimination on the island." See his "The Cuban Challenge," *Freedomways*, Summer, 1961, p. 187.

Black People [Cubans] a Place in the Cuban Revolution?"* In this critique More took the Cuban Marxists to task on their attitudes towards Cuban Negroes who fought in a revolution that Cuban Communists did not make. None of Robert Williams' Negro Left supporters has pursued this question any further, because none would dare to criticize the American Communists the way Carlos More criticized the Cuban Communists.

In 1961 Mayfield had published an article called "Challenge to Negro Leadership—The Case of Robert Williams." The importance of this article lies in the fact that it was the first attempt on the part of any member of John O. Killens' Harlem literary and cultural group to extend their creativity into the field of social analysis. Significantly, it took the new issue of force and violence, with a self-defense theme, to prod a member of this group off the protest platform. In this effort Mayfield extended his inquiry to include the Negro movement as a whole: "For some time now it has been apparent that the traditional leadership of the American Negro community—a leadership which has been largely middle-class in origin and orientation—is in danger of losing its claim to speak for the masses of Negroes."[11]

Thus at the very outset Mayfield establishes the theoretical premise of his analysis by repeating what had for years been used and overused as a class truism. Negro civil rights leadership is middle class, the Negro masses are working class; hence the leadership has forfeited its right to speak for the masses because it is middle class. What makes this class reference important for Mayfield is that it is Marxist in tone even though *Commentary* is not a Left publication. This would mean also that all of the Killens group's leftwing friends would read the article with interest, if not with full approbation. However, the author's political upbringing left his thinking full of holes.

By "middle class," Mayfield actually meant the NAACP leader-

---

* In this article, More charges: "Thus far Cuba, contrary to all claims, *there has not been a revolution*—which explains the total absence of proletarians and Afro-Cubans in the affairs of the 'dictatorship of the proletariat' and of the 'government of the people'—What has, in fact, happened has been the displacement of a fictional national bourgeoisie in favor of a *real one.*" See Carlos More, "Le Peuple Noir a-t-il sa Place dans la Révolution Cubaine?" *Presence Africaine*, Fourth Quarter, 1964, p. 228.

[11] Julian Mayfield, "Challenge to Negro Leadership—The Case of Robert Williams," New York, *Commentary*, April, 1961, p. 297. Used by permission.

ship—the section of the black bourgeoisie with whom Williams came into conflict over "meeting lynching with lynching," "self-defense," etc. But he neglected to mention that the Communist Party had officially switched its position in 1959 to that of full support of this same NAACP line of unqualified racial integration. He also failed to mention that neither Williams nor he was the least bit opposed to the NAACP's middle-class-oriented integration. Hence, the Williams case, for Mayfield, represented not an issue of aims, but of methods (as it had also for Williams, in 1961). Thus the main conclusion Mayfield drew in his article was that the methods of middle-class Negro leadership (the NAACP) were losing their relevance to the needs of the masses because they were not revolutionary. After reviewing and forecasting events in the Southern situation he ended on a note of prophecy: "Then to the fore may come Robert Williams and other young men and women like him, who have concluded that the only way to win a revolution is to be a revolutionary."[12]

Despite Mayfield's insouciance it is not a simple matter for an avowed integrationist leader, even of Williams's fiber, to become a revolutionary and tear himself completely out of the context of the protest movement. Integration, in itself, is not a revolutionary idea. If it were, one would have to say that the Supreme Court of the United States is a revolutionary tribunal. But Mayfield was able to bypass all of these conceptual difficulties because he saw in the Southern movement a new revolutionary trend already in motion. In light of his own recent inspiration by the Cuban Revolution, it is easy to imagine what cataclysmic visions were conjured up in his mind about the situation in the United States. Whereabouts in our troubled Southland would our "Sierra Maestre" be found? Perhaps in Monroe, North Carolina. In his article, Mayfield simply transferred the old Left prophecies about the proletarian awakening to the Southern movement (with suitable variations). For example, he wrote: "But sooner than anyone now supposes, three factors may create a social climate in the South in which a Robert Williams will play a leading role. They are the growing militancy of Negro students; the intransigence of the Southern White oligarchy; and the depressed Negro workingclass and peasantry."[13]

[12] *Ibid.,* p. 305.
[13] *Ibid.*

This analysis must have greatly warmed the hearts of all of Mayfield's Marxist mentors in the tired old Communist ranks—from Herbert Aptheker to Shirley Graham DuBois. Word for word, the above would not have been out of place in *Political Affairs,* the Party's official organ (that is, with the exception of the classification "peasantry," which Mayfield borrowed from the Cuban experience). The American Communists were not in the habit of calling Negro farmers and sharecroppers "peasants," but Mayfield was bent on imagining class affinities between Cuban and American Negroes in the light of the new revolutionary wave. But not to appear to be overly carried away, Mayfield admonished:

> Predictions are risky at best, but it seems safe to say that as these forces come into sharper conflict in what is essentially an attempt to overthrow an entrenched political and economic power, the Negro leadership class will be faced with a crisis, for its purely legalistic (or passive-resistance) approach will clearly not be able to control the dynamics of the Negro struggle. Then to the fore may come [a] Robert Williams.[14]

Mayfield's article had the Trotskyists in the "Fair Play for Cuba Committee" all in a revolutionary dither, which made up for the fact that Mayfield's Communist friends were not officially pro-Williams, but were supporting the NAACP. Since Mayfield was supporting the Cuba Committee but not the Trotskyists in it, they in turn tried to woo Mayfield into their camp by giving him great play in their press. In all this factional intrigue over who would represent Cuba in the United States, the Communists came out second best; so Julian Mayfield was left in the interesting position of trying to ride different horses going in opposite directions— Robert Williams and the Communist Left. As one venerable, die-hard Communist argued when questioned about his Party's latest switch on the Negro—"Well, we have to go where the *people* are. And the people are following the NAACP's integration line." These people were obviously not the same ones Mayfield was talking about in his article, or else the conflict had not sharpened to the point of overthrowing "an entrenched political and economic power." But the people whom a Robert Williams might eventually lead, Mayfield felt would "have nothing to barter in the labor market but their willingness to work. . . . It is not [for their]

14 *Ibid.*

children that all the school desegregation furore is about."[15]

True . . . and then not quite true . . . because Negro children of all classes in the South are affected by school desegregation more or less depending on their locality. But in Monroe, Robert Williams was an integrationist just like any other NAACP-er he disagreed with over self-defense; and whatever effects school desegregation had on his followers, they were certainly behind Williams in his efforts to desegregate a Monroe swimming pool. Everything that happened in Monroe stemmed from the integration question, and many flaws in Mayfield's analysis are rooted in his inability to explore contradictory factors.

Reading old Left ideas into a new racial situation, Mayfield utterly failed to perceive the larger implications of what indeed was new. He saw the new Negro movement as a challenge to traditional middle-class leadership without understanding that it too was, with few exceptions, also strongly middle-class-oriented. In Montgomery, Alabama, the bus strike movement that started out as a grassroots affair was taken over by Martin L. King and his middle-class orientation. The first phases of the Birmingham uprising were very orderly processions led by King for essentially middle-class objectives. King's followers did not welcome the working-class uprising that followed, in riotous disorder. Williams' Monroe events were merely a notable exception to the general rule which started out within the framework of the NAACP's program.

The Negro movement has been historically propelled by a succession of new waves of middle-class origins or motivations, each wave professing to be more militant than the last—or, as Mayfield put it—the last "traditional" leadership. (What is radical today is traditional tomorrow.) Hence, what is really crucial about Negro leadership is not its class origins but its program. So far the only programs (good, bad, or indifferent) have come from bourgeois Negroes or those with bourgeois aspirations. The real problem, then, is that even when more militant and effective leadership does arrive from other than bourgeois class origins, it must have bourgeois support or else it can get nowhere. This is because effective social movements require educated people with knowledge

15 *Ibid.*

and technical skills which the proletariat, or the masses, do not possess. It is only the educated, trained, and technically-qualified who can deal directly with the state apparatus. In America, when members of the masses acquire education and skills, they cease, forthwith, to be proletarians. Even if the Marxists would rather evade these facts about class differences, they are crucial truths in the Negro struggle.

When Marxist leftwingers speak of the coming proletarian revolution (even in fancy), they know that according to the script, this projects something apocalyptic in scope, a fundamental mass assault on capitalistic property relations, the abolition of the capitalist class in toto. But do they really believe this, now? If so, it is pointless to debate such irrational beliefs. Yet, one must insist on asking—How can a social movement that is demanding more and better jobs, homes, education and other privileges—all of which are benefits that lie within the social grasp of the lower- and the upper-middle-class frame of reference—be characterized as a movement that is consciously seeking the abolition of capitalistic property relations at the same time? Such a movement is not aimed at overthrowing anything; although Negroes want jobs, they want them *within the existing economic framework,* for the simple reason that Negroes actually know no other kind of economic system, real or imaginary.

Essentially, the Negro's outlook is determined by the material conditions of the American capitalistic dynamic. The Marxists would have to agree with this assertion inasmuch as it corresponds to one of their prime postulates. However, it is also true that no foreign revolutionary ideology can really penetrate the Negro psychology, especially if it is anti-capitalistic to the point of interfering with the desire to "make good" in the world. Moreover, American capitalism is also able to offer the masses (and even members of the intelligentsia) large doses of spoon-fed socialism. These fringe benefits of American capitalism—welfare relief, health insurance, old-age benefits, anti-poverty programs, etc.—are much higher in dollar value than the wages of many productive workers in the underdeveloped world whose countries are building anti-capitalistic socialism. Thus it is the height of romantic folly to believe that the American masses, of any color, could be motivated to revolutionary actions to achieve something they already have in one degree or another. Whatever the American Negro has achieved economically, whether capitalistic or socialistic, he has won under capitalistic conditions. He will struggle for more only within that framework—unless he is induced otherwise through experience. So far, despite all the talk about the Black Revolution, he has not been educated for anything else. He is a child of the era of New Deal capitalism and all that that economic philosophy implies. It will take much more than the tactics of a Robert Williams or the social analysis of a Julian Mayfield to goad any future Negro protest wave to attempt to "overthrow an entrenched political and economic power" of American capitalism, either North or South.

The black revolutionaries of the 1960's forget that it was the Supreme Court Decision of the 1950's that gave initial sanction and set the stage for the new-wave civil rights movement that later became the Black Revolution. This surely exposes the Negro's heritage insofar as it is rooted in the patronage of New Deal capitalism. Although that decision hardly made the Court a revolutionary body (for it would never hand down a juridical decision that might turn wheels of social change the legislative and executive branches could not control), it did demonstrate the power of the Federal government. And it is in the Federal government that the integrationists—from the NAACP to King to Williams—place their ultimate faith. Even after his condemnation of the Federal government and the courts for failure to bring a "halt to lynching in the South," Williams, according to Mayfield, was "convinced that the Federal government offers the only real hope the Negro has of winning any large measure of his civil rights."[16] This means, of course, that a Robert Williams who feels this way will hardly ever come to the point of the revolutionary overthrow of that very institution in which he places ultimate hope for salvation. Moreover, that "entrenched political and economic power" which Mayfield foresees being overthrown in the future is, in reality, the power of the base of a structure at whose pinnacle towers the very same Federal power. The integrationists seek the intervention of this Federal power on behalf of all civil rights issues, and it is precisely on this possibility of Federal intervention that

[16] *Ibid.*, p. 300.

the whole revolutionary prognosis of a Mayfield falters. The Federal government is able to move in on an armed self-defense clash between Negroes and Whites just as effectively as it moved in on Little Rock, Arkansas, to uphold school integration. No vision of the proletarian revolution, whether in Mayfield's black tones or in white Leftist white tones, can seriously project overthrowing the Federal structure. It is so powerfully "big" that even the conservative rightwing is worried to the point of extremist apoplexy—and they are certainly more highly organized in every department than either the Negro movement or the white Left. The Marxists cannot admit this reality about the American Federal structure and, at the same time, hold fast to the Marxian schema about proletarian overthrow, so they do not admit it. But no more can they admit the possibility of another native American inner dynamic for social change *unrelated* to the Marxian schema. Hence, they fall victims to the American dynamic and are absorbed just as is the Negro movement. This is the price the white Marxists pay for their doctrinaire intolerance, exclusiveness and the provincialism of their nineteenth-century creed. It is the price the Negro movement pays for not being intolerant and exclusive *enough,* and for not having a social creed to be doctrinaire *about*—unless, of course, it is racial integration. This makes the American Negro intellectual the first great prototype of the American universalist: He has no social philosophy of his own, but accepts everybody else's philosophies without question. Beneath the Marxist veneer of a Julian Mayfield lies a tradition of intellectual retrogression from an age of renaissance to an age of mid-century crisis. It is only because the slogans, the appeals, the protests and declarations are dressed up with contemporary allusions to civil rights headlines and international events, that the poverty in ideas is not exposed beneath the hollow phrases.

From Monroe to Watts

In 1961, both Julian Mayfield and Robert Williams were forced into exile as a result of the fiasco in Monroe, North Carolina. Williams went to Cuba where it took *real* revolutionary force and violence to "overthrow an entrenched political an economic power." Mayfield went to Ghana where, at least until February, 1966, it could be said that political independence had been won without any force and violence at all.*

After Williams left the United States he was forced to qualify his original views on self-defense. He began to see that self-defense was not really revolutionary, even with arms. What Williams finally advocated (what he called his "new concept of revolution"), indicated what direction the young generation of Afro-American nationalists would take along the road of force and violence. The tactics of this new group would transcend self-defense to a version of anarchism, combined with some "direct action" techniques reminiscent of old IWW tactics. Since Williams himself never really ceased from being an avowed integrationist, it is ironic that only the young nationalists would dare put any of his ideas into practice. But as has been shown, the social philosophy of Robert Williams is curiously at odds with his tactical ideas. Indeed, if Williams had not been forced into exile, his original tactic of armed self-defense would probably have led him no further than the current position of the Deacons of Defense—defending the efforts of civil rights workers toward peaceful integration.†

A close examination of force-and-violence developments shows

* When Nkrumah was deposed by force and violence in 1966, Julian Mayfield went into exile from Ghana.
† For a full account of Williams's views see *The Crusader* (monthly newsletter, Robert F. Williams, Publisher-in-exile, February, 1964). See also "The Colonial War at Home," *Monthly Review*, May, 1964, pp. 1-13.

that it is only within the young Afro-American nationalist ranks that violent trends of an anarchistic nature take root. There has even been a strong nihilistic outlook cropping up among many of these groups, including the nihilism of young anti-intellectual intellectuals, such as those implicated in the Statue of Liberty bombing plot.

It is not at all strange that the ghetto has produced its Bakuninists and its Nechaievists, as well as its Marxists and anti-Marxists. The degradation that the American system heaps on the Negro lower classes, both urban and rural—the disfranchisement, the caste exclusion, the alienation of the uprooted and disinherited young intelligentsia, more educated but penurious—all of this could not help but recreate the climate known to late-nineteenth-century and pre-Soviet radical classes.*

The Watts, Los Angeles, uprising of the summer of 1965 explained much more about armed self-defense and force and violence in practice, than intellectuals, such as Mayfield, have been able to explain in theory. More than that, the non-Southern locale of this uprising indicates that the final solution of the race question in the United States will be in the North not the South. True revolutions are never settled in the hinterlands, or more precisely, the more backward regions of any nation. They may, and often do, start in the rural areas but they reach their ultimate conclusion in the capital cities.

The Watts uprising carried the concept of armed self-defense to its logical and ultimate extreme. It summed up in one devastating preview-of-coming-attractions the correlation of force and violence with the concepts of self-defense, civil rights, economics, politics, class conflict, race war, integration, revolution, even nationalism, and also the role of the Federal and state power. What was missing in Watts was the larger social strategy that might have encompassed much more than Watts. Without this strategy, the full enactment of what Watts represents—a process with a beginning, middle, denouement and end—will never take place in this society.

* For comparisons, see Albert Camus' *The Rebel* (New York: Vintage Books, 1956), pp. 149-176.

Armed self-defense is part of the Afro-American dynamic within a larger dynamic, *i.e.,* the peculiar American "dialectic." The final outcome depends on the nature of the internal interactions of multiple social forces acting and reacting within the larger American dynamic. But social forces require the conscious guidance of men who understand the different forces at work in all their essential qualities and differentiations. Otherwise the dominant forces will win out over the weaker ones, absorb them or bend them to their will. The Watts uprising brought the Negro social dynamic, spontaneous and unprepared, into full confrontation with the will and resources of the dominant social dynamic. Only the romantic and the naïve could have expected anything other than what resulted. Watts clashed with the entire organized white world as a collective organism. And behind this social organism stands the Federal and state power—the same power Robert Williams saw as offering the "only real hope the Negro has of winning any large measure of his civil rights." Both Williams and the integrationists agree on state power as the last resort.

In Watts, Los Angeles, after crushing the uprising, the Federal and state power moved in both to assay and correct the damage, and to rehabilitate the victims from either side of the barricades. The middle-class Negro leadership for whom such uprisings were an effective challenge, also repaired to the scene of destruction. Since this middle-class leadership is the only segment of the Negro population with whom the Federal power will deal in such emergencies, how can it be maintained that this leadership was really that challenged? It is not necessary to go into all the gory, hair-raising and destructive details of the Watts rebellion to prove that Negro middle-class leadership was far from being replaced by any Robert Williams-type of leadership, as forecast by Julian Mayfield. What Watts does demonstrate for the Negro movement, in any of its future developments, is that it must, in the final analysis, deal with the Federal power for better or worse, and that it must also include the Negro middle-class strata in its strategy.

In 1962, when asked about the possibility of a nation-wide race war in the United States, Robert Williams replied: "No, but I see skirmishes in many different places. Not a race war, no. There's a possibility. . . . But I don't believe that the government and the army could afford to stand idly by and allow this thing to develop into a national conflict. Because, you see, this would be certain death to the United States."[1]

In the case of the Watts rebellion, Williams was correct—the government and the army did not "stand idly by." But this does not settle the question of the relationships between force and violence and race war. Williams' self-defense was called a revolutionary idea, and the Watts affair a revolutionary uprising, but the latter also had many of the attributes of a race war. This is not just a question of semantics; despite Williams' own misgivings about race war, many of his spiritual followers among the young warrior types in the ghetto make absolutely no distinction between race war and revolution. But in reality, a race war is possible in the United States *without its being a revolution*. Absolute frankness is demanded on this question, because none of the young warrior types who were prominent in the ghetto uprisings, or who were egged on in other actions by the romantic adventurists who infest the black movement, have the least conception of a real social revolution—in political, economic, institutional, military and organizational terms. This is the new anarchism, nothing more. Its only results can be death, waste, destruction, and more compounded frustrations. The acknowledged presence of racism in the hearts of many white Americans does *not* justify the attitude adopted by many so-called black revolutionaries: that a movement must predicate itself on the inevitability of race war as the final solution while, at the time, insisting that the final solution should be for positive ends. A conflict of mutual annihilation is not a positive end. What is the logic, therefore, in basing a movement's strategy on such an end?

Williams, however, presents another side to this question of racial annihilation three years after he had quit Monroe for Cuba. By 1964, he no longer viewed armed self-defense in "local" terms (wherein the Monroe racists sought to keep the Negro in his place) but saw an aggregation of racist organizations throughout the United States aiming to exterminate the Negro in toto: "All over the U.S.A., the John Birchers, the Minutemen, the States Righters, the Nazis and Ku Klux Klanners are arming and train-

[1] John Schultz, "An interview with Robert Williams," *Studies on the Left*, II, No. 3 (1962), p. 59.

ing for total warfare against our people. . . . The Afroamerican hasn't got a chance in the U.S.A. unless he organizes to defend himself."[2]

If that be true, then Negroes *should* organize to defend themselves, but *would* Negroes be able to defend themselves against total annihilation, if that *were* the intent of the rightwingers? Whether or not such a defense were successful, the mere attempt at annihilation *would* constitute a race war. Would the Federal government and the army "stand idly by" and permit this? In 1962, Williams did not believe so, but by 1964 he had lost faith in the intervention of the Federal government: "There is no doubt as to what side the racist police, F.B.I., National Guard and the Federal Government will be on. The U.S. Justice Department has already shown its true colors by tracking down law-abiding Freedom fighters and indicting them for seeking the enforcement of the U.S. Constitution."[3]

Williams implies that if Negroes are annihilated, the Federal government will not intervene; but if the Negroes succeed in defending themselves (which he concedes can happen), they will still have to contend with a government that refused to intervene on their behalf. And after this hypothetical race war (that we hope becomes a stalemate), what then? The problem here is that Williams knows very well that the Federal Government *would have* to intervene in such a situation—of this there is absolutely no question. Why then, does he project ideas he evidently does not truly believe? Because Williams obliquely is laying the groundwork for his new concept of revolution*—one that has very little to do with armed self-defense:

> The new concept of revolution defies military science and tactics. The new concept is lightning campaigns conducted in highly sensitive urban communities with the paralysis reaching the small communities and spreading to the farm areas. The old method of guerrilla warfare, as carried out from the hills and countryside

---

[2] *The Crusader, op. cit.,* p. 5.
[3] *Ibid.,* p. 5.
* It is only because of the sobering lessons of the Watts rebellion that it is now permissible to quote Williams on this new concept. Moreover, his ideas are no longer secret as they have already been published and distributed for the edification of both the interested public and the authorities.

would be ineffective in a powerful country like the U.S.A. Any such force would be wiped out in an hour.[4]

Armed self-defense in Monroe was not even "guerrilla warfare" of the "old method." Guerrilla warfare is, however, says Williams, more revolutionary than self-defense; but, if a force using guerrilla warfare tactics would be "wiped out in an hour," then it is clear that mere armed self-defense is doomed to even quicker defeat. Even Robert Williams himself now admits that if the Deacons went over into offensive guerrilla warfare they would be doomed. When I pointed out this obvious fact back in 1962, I was accused by Left radicals and liberals of dismissing Williams' "third trend." I wrote:

> Some leftwingers see in Williams' use of arms a symbol of revolt similar to that in revolutionary colonial movements elsewhere. But this is mostly illusory not only because there is considerable difference between armed defense and armed offense, but also because armed revolt (which implies armed offense) is incompatible with Williams' avowed integrationist aim. Armed integration is very unlikely to occur.[5]

Although my views on the question of force and violence were not, by any means, completely thought through in 1962, Williams himself corroborates the fact that these views were not too far from the truth of the matter. He admits that "a powerful country like the U.S.A." is not to be compared with colonial countries elsewhere. As a result, Williams has had to alter his tactics. But do even such new tactics approach a broad social strategy for Williams' aim of complete liberation? We shall examine this a bit later. Right now, it is pertinent to go back a bit and see whether or not Williams' new tactics bear any resemblance to what his friend Julian Mayfield forecast, regarding the new Southern trend that a Robert Williams might lead. We see no resemblance at all, because Williams has devised a revolutionary concept that not a single Marxist theorist in America would swallow. Not only is it doubtful that Mayfield himself would stomach this method, it is also extremely doubtful that any organized force would go so far as to

---

[4] *Ibid.,* p. 4.
[5] Harold W. Cruse, "In Defense of Robert Williams" [reply to Clark H. Foreman], *Studies on the Left,* III, No. 1. (1962), p. 67.

adopt it. The reasons are quite simple—Negroes are given to spontaneous and emotional activist outbursts. Due to their American conditioning, they are neither theoretical nor analytical; their civil rights practices reveal that they are pragmatists par excellence.

Robert Williams' statements reveal that he is no different. His deeply ingrained protest pragmatism is revealed in his attitudes toward the Marxists. Although some of his best friends in America were the Marxists, Williams never lost an opportunity to show his contempt for them.

> I've seen communists, progressive white people, and socialists, and I've been surprised and sometimes shocked to find that they would never listen to me when I tried to tell them about this new militant trend. They would always tell me what Marx said, and that this is the symbol of certain things that are supposed to take place. But they never listen. They never want to learn. But they're always ready to dictate to us.[6]

Marxists are not only ready to "dictate to us," they are also very prone to take every "new militant trend" of the Negro and to cast it into their own Marxist image. This is what Julian Mayfield did in *Commentary* magazine. But Williams, despite his deeply-felt disdain for the Marxist point of view, was rather innocent about how to deal with Negro Marxists who are also, incidentally, his friends. He never missed the opportunity to run to them for assistance. His dependence upon Marxist support hastened the doom of his movement. As a pragmatist, Williams did not stop to examine the necessary correlations between one's *means* and one's *ends*. When one opposes the means, or better the methods, of someone else, it is logically assumed that one's ends are also of a different nature. But with all of Williams' criticisms of the NAACP, or the Marxists, on method, his objectives were always justice, liberation and integration. Any NAACP-er would heartily agree with these, as would the Marxists (although the latter would have additional objectives up their sleeves).

It is the ends Williams seeks that completely defeat the notion that his methods are, in truth, revolutionary. He made this clear when he wrote: "We prefer peaceful negotiations, but our oppressors have proved to us that they are not susceptible to such mild

[6] Williams' Interview, *op. cit.,* p. 60.

pressures for reform and that they will utilize massive violence to attempt to contain our struggle. . . ."[7] And what, in his opinion, are Negroes struggling for—*i.e.*, what are their aims and their ends?

> The demands of our people are now shifting to essential things like the right to be equally employed, educated and legally protected. These are the benefits that will raise the level of our people.
>
> These things are basic to our right to enjoy desegregated restaurants, hotels and places of amusement. These are the things that will give our people an equal chance to overcome an inferior status, etc.[8]

It does not occur to a Robert Williams that American capitalism's dynamic, plus the Federal and state power, can take every one of what he calls the essential demands of "our people" and use them to buy off and absorb every militant wave of the entire Negro movement, as fast as they emerge. It is a sad fact that with all the criticism and sniping leveled at the middle-class leadership of the NAACP by Williams, Mayfield, and the Marxists, the NAACP is the only movement (aside from the Muslims) that has a program it can live with and survive. Between the two extremes of the NAACP and the Muslims, everything else is temporary and unstable. Right in the midst of killings, lynchings, jailings and ghetto uprisings—the capitalistic dynamic does its work—*now*. While this dynamic absorption goes on, leaders and militant protestors, movements, trends, and spokesmen come and go. None of this absorption, of course, obviates the final showdown; *but*—who will be on hand to direct that final showdown after American capitalism has swallowed and digested the cream of the opposition? What will be the ultimate aims of this final showdown? Clearly, whatever these aims, it is inconceivable that they will be as passé as Williams' are doomed to be in another five to ten years. Let us note a paragraph of documentary evidence, taken from the daily press:

> There is no disputing that we are making big strides toward closing the Negro-white economic gap. Just since the Civil Rights

[7] *The Crusader, op. cit.,* p. 4.
[8] *Ibid.,* p. 3.

Act of 1964 was passed, more than 300 U.S. corporations have launched new programs to recruit and train Negro workers for more and better jobs. Negro incomes and employment rates are now rising faster than whites. The proportion of Negro families living below the poverty line is dwindling faster than the proportion of whites.[9]

This statement, of course, will not satisfy people who do not understand the meaning of median wage levels and comparisons, etc., but it does indicate how American capitalism handles "the Negro economic gap." These statistical estimates also point up how effectively the capitalistic dynamic accommodates itself to the aims of revolutionary leaders and absorbs them.

Robert Williams qualified his original views on the method of self-defense not because he had changed his aims but because self-defense as a method was not really revolutionary enough. It had no offensive dynamic inherent within its ideas. But in his development from self-defense to his "new concept of revolution," Williams ran up against the conceptual barriers inherent in the peculiarities of the unique American social system. Williams, however, knows Cuba is not North America, no matter how much political hay the Marxists and the Mayfields make over the elimination of Cuban race discrimination. Like everybody else, Williams would much prefer peaceful negotiation but sees the necessity of much militant, even revolutionary action. He knows that open, total race war in the United States would probably mean the end of any hope for the Negroes' democratic inclusion in the American scheme of things. Those Negroes who survived would either have to make peace or accept resettlement; for them, no amount of self-defense could thwart the imposition of an American apartheid. While such a grim prognostication might come to pass, it is not this possibility that confounds Williams: he wants the democratic inclusion of the Negro in American society because this is a *positive aim.* Since a total race war is *not* a positive end under American conditions, social revolution cannot countenance race war, or tactics leading to it. Thus Williams tries to solve the problem of making revolutionary methods lead to positive social ends, while

[9] Sylvia Porter, "The Negro Economic Gap," *The New York Post*, March 1, 1966, p. 26.

facing, realistically, the grim by-product of revolution—force and violence. Since his new concept of revolution cannot avoid force and violence, Negroes must be prepared to die for liberation:

> Of course, there would be great losses on the part of our people. How can we expect liberation without losses? Our people are already being admonished by the nonviolent forces to die for Freedom. . . . If we must die, let us die in the only way that the oppressor will feel the weight of our death. Let us die in the tried and proven way of liberation. If we are going to talk about revolution, let us know what revolution means.[10]

But *who* is the "oppressor" who must feel "the weight of our death"? If Negroes are to "die in the tried and proven way of liberation" for freedom, precisely *whom* must we take along with us to oblivion? Is it white people—without distinction? Or is it a certain class of white people located in the power structure? Would it be the army of the National Guard or the police? Or would it be the organized aggression of the radical rightwing? Perhaps it would be the Federal or state power? Williams has not made clear whatever or whoever constitutes the oppressor in his view. Moreover, "If we are going to talk about revolution," what kind of revolution is there that will not, cannot, challenge the power of the Federal or state governments? Standing between the Federal and state power and the whole population are the armed forces, deployable for whatever purposes the state power decides. These forces were used *against* the Negroes of Watts, Los Angeles, but *for* Negroes (and *against* whites) in Little Rock, Arkansas. Who among the population can stand up against the armed forces? Therefore, it is inescapable that the logic of Williams's concept of revolution leads simply to race war, the very thing he does not want. This is because there is no oppressor whom Williams can point to, for Negroes to die fighting against, other than white people in general. This is the logical conclusion of his argument no matter how he tries to avoid it. Yet, a race war is *not* a social revolution.

In the development of his ideas Robert Williams has solved only one side of the problem of force and violence. By eschewing non-violence as unrealistic, he accepts the full realization that the more

---

[10] *The Crusader, op. cit.,* p. 5.

militant the protest actions the more violent will be the opposition. Therefore, we must be prepared to die for freedom. But one can die for freedom in a social revolution only when one dies for social ends that are revolutionary. But Williams has not listed one *aim* among his objectives that *is* revolutionary in terms of American realities; he has only projected a *tactic* which he thinks is revolutionary. One cannot separate ends from means. "Yes," he wrote, "we should all advocate peaceful and nonviolent demonstrations in order to mobilize the masses of our people . . . but let us not be so naïve as to believe that we can conduct a revolution without violence."[11]

But the "masses of our people" have not yet said they want a revolution. They want equal rights. How can anyone seriously maintain that more and better jobs, and the temporal marginality of integrated status in education and public places, are revolutionary aims? If this were so, the NAACP would have gone out of business years ago for lack of white liberal support. The non-violent, passive-resisters will demonstrate, protest, march and sit in for such objectives, but it has been amply shown they will *not* willingly die for them. Why should they? Granted, the day may come when these non-violent resisters may find themselves with their backs against the wall and be forced to come out fighting violently in self-defense. But that would be a case of simply fighting for sheer survival because jobs, integration, etc., would not then be of much immediate importance as ends.

The real problem with Robert Williams is that while he undoubtedly understands what a revolution *means* in general terms, he does not know what a social revolution *is* in terms of the American capitalistic dynamic. He paints an imaginary picture of what the United States landscape might conceivably look like in the eventuality of a widespread racial uprising—"the day massive violence comes." He speaks of a "bedlam of confusion and chaos," "violence and terror" and other horrors. Of the aftermath to this lightning siege of violence, Williams says: "Such a campaign will bring about an end to oppression and social injustice in the U.S.A. in less than 90 days and create the basis for the implementation of the U.S. Constitution with justice and equality for all people.[12]

[11] *Ibid.*, p. 4.
[12] *Ibid.*, p. 5.

Note the typically American, expedient oversimplification implied here—the American "quickie" pattern, the "90-day wonder" concept of the package deal applied to social revolution. In defense of this fantastic idea, Williams cites American history—the righteous violence of Concord, Lexington and Valley Forge, completely overlooking the fact that that American Revolution was no 90-day wonder, but lasted for several years. Moreover, the revolution that paved the way for the American Constitution was not finished until that Constitution was *amended.* Even then, the amending process was not over, for it took another "revolution" (the Civil War) to add more amendments, with still others to follow in the twentieth century. The fallacies in Robert Williams' new concept of revolution are rooted in the fact that his *ends* do not at all warrant such catastrophic means, even could they be realized. If the aims of Williams' lightning campaign of revolution is the "implementation of the U.S. Constitution with justice and equality for all," could anyone blame a passive-resister for reasoning: "Well, if that is all Robert Williams' new concept of revolution is aiming for, why should I tread through fire and brimstone to achieve it, when I'm promised the same thing by praying up a steep hill with King, or by marching and sitting in to the tune of freedom songs?" To sing, march, protest and pray is easier than dying, particularly when the more you protest, the more handouts are dispensed by the Federal and state power. This is the bitter reality.

Williams may criticize the non-violent resisters but both he and they are the inheritors of the selfsame protest tradition implanted by the NAACP since 1909, and they are boxed in and compromised by the limitations of that tradition. They cannot easily extricate themselves from this tradition in terms of the methodology of social change. Acutely aware of this, Williams tried to break out of the protest bind, only to conceive an approach that essentially is merely an exaggerated form of protest demonstration: It outdoes the non-violent resisters only because it *is* violent. Yet it promises to change nothing in the structural makeup of the United States in terms of politics, economics, culture and administration—or what a real social revolution must achieve. The so-called Black Revolution is a gross misnomer because there is nothing in the overall strategy of this movement that aims at the reorganization of anything, including itself.

To show how limited is Williams' outlook on social strategy, it is only necessary to examine his view of the American Constitution: It is so near perfect its only flaw is merely a question of implementation. He erroneously concludes that the Constitution, as written, substantially guarantees the Negro's political, economic and cultural equality. But no social movement in the United States of America can approach being revolutionary unless it realizes the limitations of the Constitution and seeks to amend it in order to legitimize those aims which the Constitution, as written, cannot guarantee. The content of such amendments must, of course, be Negro-inspired, and must, in turn, enhance the Negro's democratic status. Such amendments should be basically *cultural,* or ethnic-oriented. The fundamental motivations behind such amendments should be to make the Constitution reflect the social reality of America as a nation of nations, or a nation of ethnic groups. In the politics of social change, Negro leadership must begin to think politically on this level if it expects to be taken seriously. Robert Williams writes, however, "As an individual, I'm not inclined toward 'politics.' The only thing I care about is justice and liberation."[13] But to be a revolutionary one *has* to be a politician, distasteful as it may be.

The American Constitution can guarantee very little to the Negro because it recognizes only the rights of the individuals, not groups. As Milton M. Gordon, quoted earlier, points out, the nature of "group life" is "legally invisible" as far as the American Constitution is concerned. Hence, the Constitution has nothing to suggest or mandate on the question of the social destiny of ethnic groups in America. Yet the American Constitution was written, conceived, defended and glorified for the implied social benefits of a group—the white Protestant, Anglo-Saxon, North European American. Thus the Constitutional celebration of the sanctity of the Individual really means that some individuals are more equal than others.

If you, as an individual, derive from the WASP-North European ethnic heritage, you have more Constitutional rights than other lesser breeds. You have more economic, political, cultural and educational privileges. You have more property rights. In fact,

---

[13] *Negroes With Guns, op. cit.,* p. 124.

you practically have an ethnic title to the lion's share of the nation's industrial and natural resources and it is all upheld, defended and ratified. Under this American Constitution the most profligate economic exploitation, squandering of natural resources, crypto-legal crime and extortion, widespread poverty and illiteracy, waste of human material, misuse of the taxpayers' money, etc., are permitted. Read down the roster of Congress in both houses, examine the types of men in America who man the intricate network of offices, agencies and departments, who make up the governing class in Washington, D.C.—the power elite—and note the white Anglo-Saxon Protestant predominance. And it is all Constitutionally legal because it is the *assumed* right of some individuals to rake and scrape as much economic and political privilege out of the system as the system will bear. It all depends on which ethnic group holds ruling power in the American hierarchy.

Naturally, Negroes, Indians, and some other "coloreds" are the very lowest on the totem pole. There will be a selected sprinkling of Negro individuals who will "make it" by Integration, inasmuch as the Constitution upholds the rights, privileges, and pursuits of some individuals in addition to certain others, all in due time. But Negroes do not have to make a revolution to achieve this. What is required is merely the threat—the clamorous, tumultuous, militant, but phantom Black Revolution. Yet, when all is said and done, when the summertime civil rights headlines have had their space quotas and are replaced by news of assassinations, space conquests, elections and new alarums over our Cubas and Vietnams, the Negro, as a mass ethnic group, will still be hanging on for dear life to the bottom of the totem pole.

If the American Constitution itself does not reflect the fact that the United States is a nation of nations, an aggregation of ethnic and religious groups having or seeking power, the racial integrationists themselves confound the situation by professing to see America divided into two worlds—black and white. They then seek the integration of the black into the white in order to erase the separation. But this is a gross oversimplification of reality, because this white world is *not* homogeneous or all of a piece. It is just this division within the white world that defeats the integrationists beyond token levels. "Total integration means assimilation," wrote Robert Williams in his *Crusader* article, "Revolution without Violence?" But assimilation with whom—white Anglo-Saxon Protestants, Jews, Catholic ethnic groupings, Indians, Mexicans, Puerto Ricans, Japanese, Chinese or others? The American Constitution allows an *individual* Negro to integrate or assimilate with an *individual* from one of the above ethnic groupings (*i.e.,* in some states) but the Constitution does not recognize the existence of these groups, and moreover, cannot force any of these groups to integrate or assimilate with the Negro *as groups.* A Robert Williams does not grasp this, hence cannot, with any precision, point out who is the real oppressor against whom Negroes must be prepared to fight and die, or where the oppressor is located. Negroes can arm themselves and shoot every Klansman in sight, but the real power of the Federal and state apparatus and the *sources* of this power will not be touched, because the ultimate source of this power is not vested in such organizations as the Ku Klux Klan. The integrationist NAACP would agree with the integrationist Robert Williams on assimilation, as well as on fighting the Ku Klux Klan (short of violence) and on the flawed implementation of the American Constitution. But this leaves Williams out on a limb with a revolutionary method whose ultimate ends (total integration or assimilation) are not only unrealizable, but whose *immediate* goals (jobs, education, desegregated public places, etc.) become prizes which the non-violent programs will get credit for achieving, *not* Williams. The dynamic of American capitalism, backed up by the Federal and state power, absorbs and legitimizes whatever it wills and subdues what it does not sanction. It is only when a social movement is able to either utilize or enlist the Federal and state power that such a movement can legitimize its aims. The fallacies in Williams' social logic (regarding the problem of force and violence) is that his *methods* would not exert a dominant force within the American context if other existent forces are mobilized against the Negro. In the American system, the dominant forces in any situation must always represent at least a tacit alliance with Federal and state power. The Negro movement can become a dominant force only if its overall social strategy is able to enlist on its side part, if not all of, the Federal and state power.

Americans do not think, act or exist *because* of what the Constitution says but *despite* what it says, even when implementing what it implies. What Williams fails to see is that organized chaos within capitalistic property arrangements would not change property relations within those arrangements. And it is capitalistic property relations that function as the economic determinants behind discrimination, exploitation and exclusion. However, Robert Williams misses the point that it is precisely such property relations that the American Constitution in fact implements. If Williams had been to war in Europe, he would have seen that nothing sabotages capitalistic property more thoroughly than the war machine of the enemy. But that did not matter, for the capitalist owners simply rebuilt their property and proceeded to exploit as before, under the same system.

What Williams has not learned about constitutions and revolutions—beginning with the American Revolution—is that revolutions write new constitutions, throw out old ones, or amend them to conform to new human aspirations. This is a world process that is still going on. But in America the peculiar features of our unique social structure have defeated Williams, just as they have defeated all social revolutionaries who came before him—from the anarchist and radical trade-unionists to every form of radical socialist that has appeared to date. They have all been subdued into seeking to reform the social system from the inside, much as our non-violent tacticians of the Negro movement are forced to do today. In order to circumvent the limitations of this groove, Williams had to visualize a path of action that would put him, in effect, outside the frame of reformist *methods*. However, he failed to get beyond even reformist *doctrine, i.e.,* the implementation of the constitution. This is the root of his "90-day" illusion about social change. Because the Negro movement is so American, it is heir to all the persuasions of the American myth of racial democracy. Integration and assimilation have all to do with individuals, but very little to do with ethnic groups. Therefore the very logic of self-defense necessitates the group consolidation of the Negro for that very purpose. But ethnic group unification for self-defense must also carry with it the logical commitment to economic, political, and cultural unification which is the very opposite of individual tendencies toward integration and assimilation.

The curious thing about Robert Williams, as is the case with many others of the new breed of the 1960's, is that he is not even aware of the contradictory elements of his position. So obsessed is he with the pragmatic pursuit of his method, he is not much concerned with the politics of his aims or justice and liberation. In his *Negroes With Guns,* he wrote:

> The label Black Nationalist is as meaningless as the Communist label. The Afro-American resents being set aside and oppressed, resents not being allowed to enter the mainstream of American society. . . . I am an Afro-American and I've been denied the right to enter the mainstream of society in the United States. . . . As for being a "Black Nationalist," this is a word that's hard to define. . . .[14]

Coming out of the Southern movement, Williams could not define Nationalism because it is essentially an ideology of the Northern ghettoes with which he never felt at home. He tried to imagine revolutionary connections between the Cuban and the Negro experience, but failed to see that Cuban nationalism played a decisive role in the bourgeois phases of the Cuban Revolution. Completely unschooled in the politics of twentieth-century revolutions, Williams never grasped the essence of the very revolution he upheld as a model.* This is because he was not interested in politics. Yet, the young Northern nationalists hailed him as one of their leaders despite the fact that he clearly avowed integration, assimilation (and also intermarriage)—the very aims the Northern nationalists say they are against. Williams added to the confusion by writing:

> No, I'm not a "Black Nationalist" to the point that I would exclude whites or that I would discriminate against whites or that I would be prejudiced toward whites. I would prefer to think of myself as an inter-Nationalist. That is I'm interested in the problems of all mankind. That is, I'm interested in the problems of Africa, of Asia, and of Latin America. I believe that we all have the same struggle, a struggle for liberation.[15]

---

[14] *Ibid.,* p. 120.

* In 1966 Williams quit Cuba for asylum in China, claiming that Cuban leaders were hindering his efforts in trying to lead the freedom struggles for American Negroes. See *The New York Times,* November 14, 1966, p. 27.

[15] *Negroes With Guns, op. cit.,* p. 120.

But what does Williams really mean? If, in the consideration of nationalism, he means he *might* be a nationalist if he could include whites in a coalition, let it be said here that the young nationalists of the Northern ghettoes have other ideas about the role of whites. Williams and his followers need to get together, quite obviously.

In particular, the issue of force and violence has served to bring out into the open what has been, for decades, a submerged problem within the Negro movement. Thus, the conflict over method that crops out between the Kings, the non-violent and passive-resisters, the NAACP, CORE, the nationalist trends, and a man like Robert Williams, is again merely a manifestation of an older, unsolved conflict over methods of achieving social change. Viewing the problem from the other side of the racial fence, we have seen that there has been a history of American radical controversies and propositions over program and method, which in terms of the broad labor movement were submerged by the advent of the New Deal and never really solved. Behind this radical sell-out stood, of course, the muted presence of the Negro, haunting the guilty consciences of white radical defectors. But the American Negro is so much a part of the American fabric he cannot be torn a\ ay from his role as a factor within the broader American dynam.'c. He has, in fact, a peculiar dynamic all his own. Hence the Negro movement inherits three decades of unsolved radical propositions over program and method, and projects them in another way, simply because it is no longer subordinate to the labor movement or to white radical parties. The Negro movement is essentially dynamically independent, although the leadership as a whole has not learned how to make the most of this.

Negro leadership of *all* persuasions, acts from the urge of immediacy and expediency. And this urgency is both a source of strength and of limitation. It can easily be seen that the pressure for justice and liberation brings to the fore trends and individuals ready to push their methods to the full extremes of revolutionary conceptions. In the place of a matured social vision there will always be those who will gladly substitute the catastrophic and glorious act of martyrdom and self-immolation for a cause. It is true that many causes are fated to require such self-sacrificing individuals, and some individuals are seemingly born to die early for them. One can think of the frightful sacrifice of untold numbers of young men of the 1930's generation of idealists who were blasted into oblivion in the Spanish Civil War. These sacrificial lambs died for ideals that were betrayed even before they took up arms. Yet whether a cause is sold out by politically corrupt leaders, or defeated by actions ill-conceived in the first place, makes very little difference to those fated to die for it—however glorious their gestures of self-sacrifice. They all die and Mother Earth cares little, why or how. Thus, it is not enough to say "Of course, there would be great losses on the part of our people. How can we expect liberation without losses?" It must also be added that life is not so cheap that great losses should be bought and paid for by exhorbitant illusory objectives. If people must die because force and violence is an inseparable factor of the methods for social change, then one must be more than certain that the ends justify the means. Up to now, the revolutionary advocates of force and violence have not met the test demanded by the realities of the American social dynamic.

So far there have been so many conceptual flaws in the thinking on force and violence that many of the young generation have become disoriented on the problem of social goals. The faulty analysis of the meaning of armed self-defense has encouraged an extreme form of one-sided activism that leads to blind alleys and dead ends. It has also nurtured anti-intellectualism to the status of a cult, with the result that a peculiar type of American nihilism has appeared. These anti-intellectual, antitheoretical trends have divided the new Afro-American nationalists into competing and warring factions, opening fertile avenues to the *agent provocateur.*

Faulty analysis of self-defense as a tactic has served to block a serious consideration of the necessity to cultivate strategies on the political, economic and cultural fronts. It has inspired such premature organizations as revolutionary action movements and black liberation fronts, which come into being with naïvely one-sided, limited programs, all proving to be abortive and short-lived. It has severely limited the potential of certain new magazines as instructive organs of social analysis and criticism. As the original social objective of the civil rights movement—racial integration—recedes more and more into the intangibles of absorption, force-and-violence tactics have emerged to compensate for the frustrations generated by the great void. The fruits of all this has been either the letdown of a confused immobilization of forces, or else the tendency toward the grand act of anarchistic and directionless defiance of the power structure.

From Southern Activism
to Northern Impasse

The purpose of this study so far has been to explore the origins of the many factors leading to the impasse the Negro movement has reached as of this moment, 1967. To repeat, the Negro movement, in all its ideologies from integrationism to the various blends of nationalism, is in crisis. Concentrically, it lies within the larger American crisis, and that in turn, within the international crisis of war and poverty, race and culture and the politics of national survival.

In order to get down to the roots of this racial crisis in America one must excavate every established factional creed and conformism, whether black or white, that has blocked the analysis and reevaluation of the American mythology. In this pursuit all intellectual superficiality on the American race question, coming from either side of the racial fence, must be shattered with the most rigorous critical assault the collective intelligence can muster. The phony intellectualism emanating from the Negro establishment and the parasitic whites who both cater to it and feed on it, must be exposed. The psychological bonds of sentimentality and immobilizing emotionalism that blind Negroes to practical realities and keep them shackled to their protest mentality, must be broken. Only then can the entire Negro movement be purged of a certain breed—the civil rights opportunists, freedom demagogues, leadership hustlers, the liberation panderers-to-downtrodden-egos, and those obscurantists who confuse semantics of Black Nationalism with its social substance. None of this can be achieved unless every hallowed interracial shibboleth is shattered.

The present-day impasse of the Negro movement cannot be understood unless as much light as possible is shed on the historical evolution of all its contributive factors—political, economic, and cultural. Broadly speaking, this is merely another way of saying that America as a nation cannot be understood without understanding the Negro, and vice versa.

The Supreme Court Decision of 1954 can be said to have reopened the pages of the history of American racial practices for review, reevaluation and correction. Following this, all through the late 1950's into the 1960's were released all the locked-up energies of the race potential that had lain, for decades, stored up in the American social dynamic. Pent up for generations, the Negro dynamic emerged as a catalyst, provoking actions and reactions from both sides of the racial fence. New movements, trends, and countertrends emerged in rapid succession. New leaders and philosophies arose and vied for the center of the civil rights' stage. But after an entire decade, it is apparent that this new leadership group, taken together, was not really prepared to solve the tasks for which they so eagerly assumed responsibility. For the most part it has been an existentialist leadership, acting out its assumed role on the basis of the here-and-now demands of justice and liberation. It has accepted the American value systems on its own implicit terms, not bothering to define the specific quality of the freedom pursued. Very obviously it was to be a kind of freedom that other Americans had never before witnessed nor vouchsafed. But this new Negro leadership never attempted to anatomize this new freedom, these new equal rights. They distinguished freedom from unfreedom, but they did not spell it out: freedom—to do what? Freedom to assume what responsibilities? In fact, this leadership acted as if the only responsibility it had was to fight for freedom leaving the aftermath to chance. Without seriously considering the problems of freedom and social necessity, they led a rather expedient and makeshift assortment of pilgrimages, haphazardly aligned into a broad movement guided by intuition. This movement had no clearly defined goals aimed to fit, in some fashion, within the American social structure; it also had little or no historical perspective on its own origins. A movement without a causative past cannot have much of an effective future.

Thus, it was absolutely predictable that the new Negro movement would encounter innumerable barriers, blocks, and dead ends—and finally, the grand impasse. One cannot have a movement in America, rooted in the protest tradition, but also rife with integrationism, separatism, interracialism, nationalism, Marxist and anti-Marxist radicalism, Communist and anti-Communist radicalism, liberalism (Jewish and Christian), anarchism, nihilism and religionism (the Muslim gambit)—and expect such a movement not to be a failure. For example, each of the following organizational debacles can be traced directly to the clash of conflicting theories within the Negro movement: the rise and fall of Malcolm X; the Monroe, North Carolina, debacle involving Williams; the failure of the Freedom-Now party movement to organize a political party in 1964; the failure of Malcolm X's Organization of Afro-American Unity (OAAU) to develop after his death; and the general collapse of the Northern-based civil rights movement.

There has been a parallel failure on the propaganda and information fronts. The Negro movement is notoriously backwards in propaganda, education, and public relations. Aside from the NAACP and the Nation of Islam (Muslims), none of the other segments of the Negro movement publish and disseminate educational material about themselves through either newspapers or journals on a regular basis. This is not just from a lack of financing, since all civil rights groups are great fund-raisers. Rather, it is because the basic aims of these groups are more moral than tangible, more for principles than for the structural goals related to the practicalities of human relations within human institutions.

Intra-factional immobilization is the state of affairs in the movement today, especially in the Northern cities. Muslim separatism has captured much of the nationalistic sentiment in the North, while non-violent integrationism has run out of objectives. Thus, all factions lying between the Muslims' extremism and the integrationists' extremism have been balanced out. The American Negro is caught in the tangled net of his own historical antecedents, and his leadership cannot even sort out the elements of his predicament and rationally discuss them for its own edification. Even the handful of literary and critical journals that the new generation of intellectuals have founded are not equipped to debate and analyze thoroughly the current situation.

We have already examined the incompetencies of the most literate of these journals—*Freedomways*—but the critique does not end there. There was another outstanding journalistic failure that also emerged in 1961—the *Liberator*. The "voice of the Afro-

American protest movement in the United States and the liberation movement in Africa" is what the masthead said in the beginning. Today, the *Liberator* is called the "voice of the African-American," published by the "Afro-American Research Institute, Inc." Although these titles mean very little, their changes tell something about the evolution, and also the rise and decline of this journal. The *Liberator,* as a journal, became heir to the same unresolved historical conflicts and past mistakes that weighed down the activist branches of the Negro movement. But the editors and writers of the *Liberator* were no more aware of this than were the activist leaders. The result was that the *Liberator* started off under the incubus of having editorial elements in its directorship that were politically and ideologically incompatible—in short, a built-in handicap that the *Liberator* was never able to overcome.

In the first place, the ownership and editorial directorship was interracial. This meant that the journal was in trouble even before it began, because it immediately attempted a pro-nationalistic editorial policy. More than that, the white members of the magazine's elite represented both white liberalism (Christian) and the white pro-Marxist leftwing (also Christian, in this instance). Allegedly, Jewish liberalism too was involved in the corporate ownership, but this influence was never exerted editorially. But to further complicate this incipient editorial conflict, the editorial board of the *Liberator* was composed of both American and West Indian Negroes (or Afro-Americans and Afro-West Indians—second-generation American-born, as Richard B. Moore would have it). Within this Negro element warred the nationalist and integrationist factions, with the dominant editorial voice Afro-West Indian. With all these seeds of editorial discontent bred into its structure, it is actually miraculous that this magazine has managed to hit the newsstands consistently since it began in 1961.

The basic prop for this publication's tenacity is its surface pro-nationalism. The *Liberator* always managed to keep its fingers on the pulse of deep Negro problems, but the writers were never able to probe far enough to strike vital chords consistently. As a result, the *Liberator* always hovered on the outskirts of the problems to which it addressed itself. It limped along precariously from month to month under the most inept, naïve, and politically unimaginative editorial leadership with which a journal of this type was ever cursed. It was a most painful process to watch because the *Liberator* had the potential of becoming the most widely-read and influential literary and critical journal on Negro affairs in the entire country.

From 1961 to the summer of 1963, the *Liberator* magazine limped along on a very meager circulation, with a Harlem distribution, allegedly, of something like two hundred. However, beginning in October, 1963, the circulation of the *Liberator* shot upward until by the winter months of 1963-1964, it was claimed that the monthly circulation had reached the phenomenal figure of twelve hundred, for Harlem and other Negro communities in greater New York. These figures are unofficial but they indicate something of the rapid growth of *Liberator* influence.

But this increase in *Liberator* influence was to exact a high price from the staff writers in time, effort, and journalistic concentration. It was the staff writers who made this magazine what it became, *not* the ruling editorial body of would-be civil rights politicians (who almost totally lacked an analytical grasp of the complexities of the civil rights situation). As a result of the gulf between the writers and the ruling body, the six best staff writers quit the magazine at the height of its influence. From that point on, the *Liberator* went downhill in quality and scope, failing to achieve an influence that even approached its potential.

The *Liberator* writers were all new and, unlike the *Freedomways* clique, had no political skeletons hidden in their career closets. Thus the *Liberator* had the unrestricted option to play a pioneering role that *Freedomways* could not (without embarrassing its closest friends). Yet, the *Liberator* writers never realized the scope of their specific role as social critics, or where to direct the criticism, or how to ferret out the issues that called for open debate. They did not even know where all their real opponents were located. They considered that the enemy, the chief antagonist was white; in fact, the real opposition was, for the most part, black—in all classes, ranks, and trends. As a result, the *Liberator* spent too much magazine space seeking a dialogue with whites.

The only Negro leader the *Liberator* ever attacked consistently was Martin Luther King—and in a most unconstructive way—for the editorial attacks on King were based on the editor's bias against passive resistance. But this journalistic militancy only showed that the magazine was in a dilemma over the problem of force and violence, just like everybody else.

The *Liberator* could never achieve its potential as a critical magazine of social opinion until three basic issues pertaining to the Negro movement were tackled and cleared up: (1) What is integration? (2) What is nationalism? (3) What is Marxist Communism, and how does it relate to the first two ideas? These crucial questions had to be thoroughly explored from the standpoint of the past, present, and future, before the *Liberator* writers could deal with the Negro movement in depth on political, economic and cultural planes. The *Liberator* writers were neither prepared to do this, nor even aware that it had to be done. In any event they would have been overruled by editorial policy.

For example, had the writers attempted to deal with the role of the Communist Party in Negro affairs, either historically or currently, they would most certainly have been stopped by one of the owners—a white pro-Communist Marxist. More than that, the *Liberator* carried what was called an advisory board: twelve leading lights, among whom were James Baldwin, Ossie Davis, Richard B. Moore, and George B. Murphy, Jr. The exact function of this advisory board was never revealed to the staff writers, but at least five of its members were either Communist or pro-Communist. George B. Murphy went all the way back to the old National Negro Congress and the *Freedom* newspaper days. One of the staff writers saw through the implications of this "advisory" board; he sought, unsuccessfully, to have it removed in order to free the *Liberator* to deal as an *independent publication* with the Communist issue.*

So shackled was the *Liberator* on the Communist issue that in the summer of 1963, when James E. Jackson, the leading Negro Communist, attacked both Robert Williams and the *Liberator* in the *Daily Worker*, the editors refrained from answering him. They also refused to print a rebuttal on Jackson and the Communist

---

* It was not until March, 1967, that the editor of *Liberator* eliminated this advisory board. Although he had been warned in 1963, it took the controversy over "anti-Semitism" among Negroes between Ossie Davis, James Baldwin and the editor to force the latter to drop the board.

Party written by one of the staff writers. The article was conveniently "lost" and never returned to the writer.

Since the crucial issue of Marxist Communism could never be openly discussed, the (superficially) anti-integrationist *Liberator* was prevented from dealing with its rival pro-Marxist-integrationist *Freedomways*—which was wide open for a critical lambasting on Negro affairs. In fact, since 1961, *Freedomways* and the *Liberator* have not debated each other on a single issue. After six years, the *Liberator* is still unable to establish an editorial policy the least bit logical or cogent on economics, politics, culture, organization or interracial ethics. Although it has editorialized against the passive-resistance philosophy time and time again, it called the Watts, Los Angeles, uprising (surely the most militantly violent demonstration yet) a "rebellion without ideology."[1] The *Liberator,* however, has been unable to explain what that missing ideology should or might be. Yet, it will continue to print articles on the theme that "violence is necessary."[2] It has characterized the late Malcolm X as "the unfulfilled promise,"[3] but without insights as to why. Although the program of Malcolm X's Organization of Afro-American Unity (OAAU) was published, the *Liberator* could not discuss the merits or demerits of such a program in its pages. What did Malcolm X want? What was his position on nationalism? On integrationism? On whites? On interracialism? On economics? On political parties? On violence? On revolution? On reformism? The following statement was made by Malcolm X in an interview on his return from Africa early in 1965, but was not published until after his death:

> I used to define black nationalism as the idea that the black man should control the economy of his community, the politics of his community, and so forth.
>
> But, when I was in Africa in May, in Ghana, I was speaking with the Algerian ambassador who is extremely militant and is a revolutionary in the true sense of the word. . . . He was an African, but he was Algerian, and to all appearances, he was a white man. And he said if I define my objective as the victory of black nationalism, where does that leave him?

[1] *Liberator,* September, 1965, p. 4.
[2] *Ibid.,* March, 1966, p. 6.
[3] *Ibid.,* March, 1965, p. 3.

Where does that leave revolutionaries in Morocco, Egypt, Iraq, Mauritania? So he showed me where I was alienating people who were true revolutionaries. . . .

So, I had to do a lot of thinking and reappraising of my definition of black nationalism. Can we sum up the solution to the problems confronting our people as black nationalism? And if you notice, I haven't been using the expression for several months. . . .[4]

Here was a statement that demanded some looking into by all the militant black publications who had been getting circulation mileage from Malcolm's reputation. It pointed up what has been long known among the more acute observers of the Negro movement—even the most ardent young nationalists have not yet defined Afro-American nationalism. As a result, a score or more of nationalistic factions are at loggerheads with each other. There is a purification process going on constantly within nationalist ranks, each faction vying with each other over standards of purity, blackness, and anti-whiteness or pro-Africaness traditionalism. Magazines such as the *Liberator* become only the journalistic reflection of these confusions, attempting to bring order and rationality to none of these warring trends.

By 1965, the *Liberator* had advanced far enough to carry an article on the white leftwing—"Black People vs. White Left"—in which it was pointed out that leftwing influence puts whites "in a strategic position to divert, convert, subvert the [Negro] movement if they so choose." This was truly a critical achievement, but the same issue carried on its cover the photograph of Paul Robeson. Inside was an unsigned encomium welcoming Robeson back home from exile; no one, apparently, on the *Liberator* staff could see the gist of this irony. The article even went so far as to say that Robeson is "sorely needed today" as a leader of "rare stature and insight," and added, "Do we not have the right and duty to ask if Paul Robeson is able and willing to once more join us in battle?"[5]

It took the occasion of the death of Lorraine Hansberry to fully expose both the pro-leftwing pull on the *Liberator* and, at the same time, the magazine's inconsistent and opportunistic approach

[4] "Interview with Malcolm X," *Young Socialist Review*, March-April, 1965, pp. 2-5.
[5] *Liberator*, June, 1965, p. 10.

to integrationism-assimilationism. There were two articles on the late playwright—"Lorraine Hansberry's World," and a review of her play *The Sign in Sidney Brustein's Window*.[6] As in the Paul Robeson article, the piece on Hansberry's "World" was unsigned. Its inspiration doubtless stemmed from the pro-Communist Left influence in the *Liberator*'s ownership. However, for possibly the first time, the pro-Communist Left discussed the implications of Miss Hansberry's class origins in connection with her writing:

> At a recent conference of Negro writers in California a pleading question came from the floor—"What should the Negro write about who is the product of neither a Southern plantation nor a Northern Ghetto?" The question might well have had Miss Hansberry in mind, for she was brought up in a socially prominent, property owning family from Chicago. . . .
>
> Considering her background and training, it is a measure of Lorraine Hansberry's remarkable strength and dedication that she did not become one of those awful people that Franklin Frazier wrote about in "Black Bourgeoisie."

The writer did not see that he had misread Frazier, and that by the 1950's when his book was published, Frazier had also misread the Communist Left and its real relation to the black bourgeoisie. The swing of the leftwing to support the NAACP demonstrated that there was very little to choose between the black bourgeoisie of the Left or of the reform wing.

The writer continued to make his case for Miss Hansberry by relating how she

> came to New York to start her writing career as an overworked and underpaid member of the staff of Paul Robeson's monthly newspaper, "Freedom." There she learned the craft and passion of crusading journalism. . . .
>
> When the paper folded in 1955, she began to direct her talents to the commercial market where, let's face it, given the present state of affairs in this country any artist has to make it if he wants to be heard and not starve.

Why has the leftwing gone to such extremely tedious lengths to explain and extol this Joan of Arc of People's Integration? Lorraine Hansberry had never starved and was not about to, whether

[6] *Ibid.*, December, 1964, p. 9, drama review, p. 25.

she made it in the commercial market or not. The leftwing felt it had to explain the commercial success of *Raisin* in the *Liberator* because the radical Left line had always been to frown on Negro writers seeking Broadway success. Ostensibly, this was because the leftwing preferred its Negro writers to write *for* the workers *about* the workers. But the real reason was that the radical leftists were against commercial success *they* could not control. The article ended by saying that Miss Hansberry "never sought the limelight or tried to pose as a 'leader' or 'spokesman.' *We only wish that other artists would adopt her style* [italics added]." This showed again that the leftwing is a pastmaster at the art of rewriting history—"even the most recent history," as Albert Camus once said. How can anyone maintain that a writer who took part in the Killens-led Town Hall debate with white liberals, and the celebrated summit meeting with Attorney-General Robert Kennedy was not trying to pose as a spokesman? The implications behind all this are so deep and disturbing for the Negro writer that the Hansberry image had to be quickly fitted with a hagiology. Inasmuch as the leftwing integrationist policies on Negro affairs were always politically opportunistic, the Left had no choice but to accept the logical consequences of its position when extended into thematic expressions in the creative arts. This also forced Miss Hansberry's following to accept *The Sign in Sidney Brustein's Window,* a play that was not acceptable as "Negro Literature" and also could not be criticized because its content was not about Negro life. After all, the end result was precisely what the integrationists (both Left and reform) had been seeking all along—the complete integration of the Negro writer personally and thematically. But is this really a creative advance for the Negro? When the *Liberator* writer said—

> Black actors were mad at Miss Hansberry because her latest play did nothing to alleviate their unemployment. Black Nationalists are mad because she did not write about the folks. These are serious and justified charges. It may be time, however, to start evaluating our artists on the basis of what they are, rather than what they are not

—he was absolutely right, but he himself failed to provide an evaluation. The real reason Miss Hansberry did not write about "the

folks" was because ideologically and psychologically she was unable to. The Negro writer has progressively lost his ability to deal
with Negro reality. He has been hemmed in by the protest tradition and inhibited against writing objectively because he is afraid
of his own truths; tongue-tied about the social implications of
middle-class values in Negro life and his own relation to such
values. But the root of the problem here is that the Negro dramatist has no theater institutions that he is bound to defend, and no
cultured middle class to defend them. These are the bitter fruits of
racial integration on the cultural plane. Consequently, one would
think that the pro-nationalist *Liberator* magazine would be the
first to take a critical stand against the leftwing on the Hansberry
image. Not so. It was on the crucial cultural plane of critical inquiry that the *Liberator* fell down, accepting *The Sign in Sidney
Brustein's Window* unquestioningly. The reviewer said: "This is
not a play that the aggressively nationalistic would like, but it is
an engaging play, probably closer to the general philosophy of
black people involved in the struggle for liberation than most
literary works which overtly have the 'cause' as its theme."

The review was written by a young and ardent Afro-American
nationalist who does not like white liberalism, white Marxism, or
white do-gooders within the Negro movement. He does not like
such people even though they claim to be the same type of idealistic crusader as Hansberry's hero, Sidney Brustein: "The play is
concerned with the necessity of making an active decision about
what one's duty will be in the face of evil and corruption. Miss
Hansberry chose an idealistic Jewish bohemian as the character
who must make this decision."

Here is another problem in pro-nationalist inconsistency. As a
leftwing integrationist, Miss Hansberry's choice of symbols of
commitment is neither strange nor accidental. Her pro-Jewishness
was always well known and her choice of this white group for
assimilative status was neither unique nor without certain political
and artistic implications about the world of American culture. But
it is the nationalists who today make much argument over the
necessity of Negroes to create and cultivate a new set of symbols
for themselves. They have become supercritical about what they
term the Negro intellectual's lack of racial identity, his white-
oriented thinking, his brainwashed education gleaned from white

folk's universities, etc. It is the nationalists who demand that Negro intellectuals stop thinking White and start thinking Black. Even when the Negro intellectuals cease their errant ways and start thinking Black like LeRoi Jones, they hardly ever think Black enough to suit certain brands of nationalism. But because neither the *Liberator* nor the Afro-American nationalists have yet developed their own cultural critique on literature, art or drama within the context of American culture, the *Liberator* accepted the white symbolism of the Hansberry play.

That reviewer might just as well give up the nationalist struggle on the political and economic fronts since he has already capitulated to the white aesthetic standard on the cultural front. The Afro-American Nationalist movement must have a program (which it hasn't) predicated on political, economic and cultural concepts. Although the young nationalists, for the most part, do not know it, the cultural front is the most crucial of the three. Without a critique on the cultural plane there can be no nationalist program in America. Acceptance of the Negro artist's thematic assimilation in American culture should logically lead to acceptance of assimilationist processes on the integration fronts in both economics and politics. This means, ultimately, full acceptance of the NAACP's objective of total integration. If so, then what is the conflict between nationalist and integrationist ideology all about?

The Hansberry play was a perfect opportunity to clear the muddled air on the question of the Negro's status in the theater. The entire theatrical structure in New York is, for the most part, a Jewish-dominated and -controlled institution. Therefore the American Jewish image on the American stage has had an ample share of dramatic exposure and aesthetic rendition. On the other hand, the American Negro has had the most marginal status of any ethnic group that has made an aesthetic contribution to American theatrical tradition. The economics of the American theater, plus its racial ideology, have combined over the decades to squeeze the theatrical Negro into the position of being used more as a gimmick and a prop for dramatists and producers, than as an American character worthy of serious thematic treatment. In any event, to see today a Negro stage writer bending over backwards to glorify the Jewish image in the face of the rising tide of color, seeking new social status and new identification in world culture, is to witness a cultural phenomenon nothing short of a political sellout. The play itself was not that important as a creative event; however, the philosophy (or lack of one) behind the writing of this play points up the brainwashed, self-repudiation complex of the Negro intellectual class. The last thing the Jewish image needs in America is glorification by the Negro—whose own American image has been so maligned and distorted he literally does not even know who or what he is. The last thing the Negro needs is an apology from a publication such as the *Liberator* for the cultural defacement American society has inflicted on the Negro personality. But the defacement process itself instills into the victim's mind the idea of his own unworthiness to such an extent he is bedeviled into a collaboration with his exploiter.

The *Liberator* magazine also horribly bungled its role in the affair of the ill-fated Freedom Now Party movement of 1963-1964, while obstinately refusing the constructive role it could have played. This movement was strictly a Northern affair, and its entire New York leadership was in hock to the white leftwing. The original idea behind the FNP was, allegedly, to organize an all-black political party. This immediately suggested the nationalist "group" concept but not a single one of the New York leaders had any real sympathy for nationalism. The main spokesmen of the new party were William Worthy, a journalist, and Conrad Lynn, an experienced civil rights defense lawyer of elite standing.* Both individuals were avowed integrationists with open ties to the white Left. Thus, for the first time since the 1920's, nationalism, integrationism, and Marxism clashed head-on within the context of an organizing committee for a so-called black political party. The results were comic, tragic and catastrophic.

The Freedom Now debacle showed up the Negro civil rights mentality for what it was—all emotion and passion but absolutely without direction in the Northern cities. It pointed up the fact that

---

* Conrad Lynn's civil rights record includes such cases as the defense of Pedro Albizu Campos, Puerto Rican nationalist in Puerto Rico, and certain phases of the Monroe, North Carolina, affair culminating in the case of Robert Williams. William Worthy, a Nieman fellow in journalism for 1956, was involved in the much-publicized conflict with the State Department in the late 1950's over his unauthorized trip to China in 1955.

the Black Revolution was nothing but an alarmist slogan—a rebellion without ideology. It revealed shockingly the approaching impasse of the Negro movement as a whole. It demonstrated that the leadership of the Negro movement is incapable of devising new tactics and strategies for new situations. If an army on the battlefield were conducted the way the Negro movement is in America, its general staff would be beset with mutinies among its troops, sacked by higher authority for incompetence, investigated for suspected sabotage and quite probably shot for treason. The only difference here is that the Negro movement has inherited so many internal troubles from the past, it has no one to replace its incompetent leaders.

Organizationally, the Freedom Now Party movement presented a new opportunity for the entire Negro movement to have a thoroughly independent rallying point. But it had to be a truly all-black movement in order to safeguard its independent quality. Yet this movement started off with an *interracial* organizing committee. Here in capsule form is once again the endemic duality of Negro social aspiration—the unresolved conflict between separatist and interracialist tendencies. So subconsciously active in the Negro personality is this contradiction that not a single participant in the Freedom Now Party's organizing committee asked: How is it possible to organize an *All-Black* political party with an *interracial* committee creating its policy? The apparent conflict was simply resolved: Not a single one of the leaders of the Freedom Now movement sincerely believed in an all-black political party.

William Worthy announced the formation of an all-black party and straightaway went to liberal and leftwing socialist whites to get advice (and money). Conrad Lynn, leftwing and thoroughly integrationist in outlook, accepted the Acting Chairmanship of the Party. To understand why this was done is, in certain ways, as impossible as understanding (as we attempted to, early in this book) why the members of the old American Negro Theater in Harlem started an all-Negro theater, an institution that only a few members really believed in. At any rate, this internal conflict actually doomed the Freedom Now Party in New York from the very outset. The tragedy was that no one seemed to realize that the party could not be organized.

Here was an "organizing" committee, meeting weekly in a

Harlem apartment, composed of Negroes belonging to the follow-ing factions: Trotskyists, Communists (pro-Peking, pro-Moscow sympathizers), CORE, nationalists, integrationists, pro-Malcolm unaffiliates, and anti-Malcolm leftists, West Indian and American Negro antagonists and competitors. Added to this Afro-American witch's brew of political stupidity, divided loyalties, outside manipulation, and leadership incompetence was the confusion of white liberals, socialists and other leftist trends. The organizing committee of the Freedom Now Party in New York represented a criminal assault on every standard of social intelligence, and an insult to the collective needs of people in ghettoes. If anyone won-ders why the ghetto has inspired such terrorist trends as are now prevalent, he should have been a quiet, unseen spectator at the Freedom Now Party meetings in Harlem. These meetings incon-testably showed that all white socialist and leftist trends should be banned from the ghettoes, using any means possible to enforce their exclusion. Black leftists are disoriented prisoners of white leftists: No matter how militant they sound, they are no more than hacks mouthing empty phrases of a bankrupt tradition.

The downfall of the Freedom Now Party movement was its inability to create a program that the organizers were prepared to fight for and to implement. This committee did not understand, or even care to grasp, the differences between a *political party* and a movement. The idea of a political party meant only one thing to most—a chance to run for political office in the manner of any ordinary office seeker in conventional district politics. The grand designs of the political, economic and cultural imperatives of such a party were not even understood. The entire proceedings dis-played an indecent and shameful spectacle of Negro adults of ten, fifteen, twenty and thirty years of political experience being told off by youths whose only claim to wisdom was participation in CORE demonstrations (whose effectiveness was already running out). On the one hand, the adults were bankrupt of new ideas on which to establish their senior authority and on the other, the youth had energy and drive but neither direction nor background.

To make matters worse, the *Liberator* magazine editorial board, with the exception of one writer, refused to support the Conrad Lynn-William Worthy leadership of the Freedom Now Party on the basis of childish and petty, power-seeking jealousies. One of the

Liberator writers was called into the Freedom Now Party committee by William Worthy to assist in drafting a party platform. The
writer was criticized and attacked on the staff for supporting the
party. The *Liberator* Editor-in-Chief then attempted to start a
rival Freedom Now Party—using the demagogic slogan that it
would be *truly* an "all black" party. The editor did this with a
straight face, despite the fact that his own publication, the *Liberator*, was being criticized in Harlem because its editorial staff was
not all black but interracial! True to form, this Editor-in-Chief
defended his own interracialism but was against everybody else's!
During all this factional strife about and within the Freedom Now
Party, that same *Liberator* editor claimed to be in favor not of the
Lynn-Worthy leadership in New York, but of the Detroit wing of
the Freedom Now Party, under the leadership of the Reverend
Albert B. Cleage, Jr. However, when the New York Freedom Now
Party leadership invited the Reverend Cleage to speak at a Har-
lem rally during May, 1964, the *Liberator* refused to print an
advertisement announcing the rally.

The *Liberator* writer who temporarily supported the Lynn-
Worthy leadership in New York, managed, after much bitter
wrangling to get the draft of the Freedom Now Party platform
published in the *Liberator*. This platform, an attempt to chart a
course along political, economic and cultural lines, was opposed by
the *Liberator* editors in the following terms:

> We disagree with some of the points raised in this draft plat-
> form, we intend to discuss our areas of disagreement in future
> issues. As we go to press the Socialist Workers Party has an-
> nounced their Presidential slate of candidates in *The New York
> Times* of January 14, 1964. For the record we wish to state that
> the Freedom Now Party has no connections with the Socialist
> Workers Party or any other political parties.[7]

Needless to say, the *Liberator* never did discuss any "areas of
disagreement" in subsequent issues and never intended to. The
real reason behind this alleged disagreement was the *Liberator*'s
opposition to Worthy and Lynn because it was the *Liberator*'s
"opposition" Freedom Now Party that had no connections with
the Socialist Workers Party. It was precisely on this issue of Social-

---

[7] *Liberator*, February, 1964, p. 4.

ist Workers Party ties that the *Liberator* was attacking Worthy
and Lynn. However, the *Liberator's* opposition to the Socialist
Workers Party was not at all based on any question of political or
theoretical principles, since this magazine's leadership had no understanding of such principles.

Indirectly, the *Liberator's* anti-Trotskyism was nothing but a
reflection of the pro-Communist Left influence. Thus the *Liberator* could express anti-Trotskyism in a way it could not express
anti-Communist Party criticisms. Therefore, when an opportunity
arose wherein the Marxist philosophy could be discussed in its
relationships to the Negro in America, it had to criticize the
Socialist Workers Party's Marxism but *not* the Communist Party's
Marxism. The political logic behind this was quite clear; for a
criticism of the pro-Communist Left also involved a criticism
of the records of Paul Robeson, Lorraine Hansberry, Ossie Davis,
Richard B. Moore and all others who had been played up and
lauded in the *Liberator's* pages. This criticism would also have
involved at least five members of its advisory board. But since
the question of Marxism *had* to be taken up in one way or another, in order for the *Liberator* to live up to its pretensions of
being a serious critical journal, the *Liberator* writer who grabbed
at the chance of knocking Marxism did so with full knowledge
that it was extremely unfair to use the Trotskyists as the whipping
boys when the real historical culprits since the 1920's have been
the Communists. This is not to say that the Trotskyists are the
innocents of the white Left, but rather that they have never been
influential enough to do any extensive political damage.

The draft platform of the Freedom Now Party printed in the
Liberator was a tentative start on a concept of social planning
from the Negro point of view. *Limited as it was, it was also the
very first of its kind to be sketched out within the framework of a
political party.* However, while the draft platform was attacked in
the *Liberator* for factional reasons, it was attacked from the Detroit wing for ideological reasons. James Boggs*, an ex-member of
the old Marxist Left, opposed the draft program in a letter cir-
culated from Detroit, saying that it was "no program at all." The

---

* Author of *The American Revolution—Pages from a Negro Worker's Notebook*
(New York: Monthly Review Press, 1963).

content of this letter cannot be dissected here but it revealed that Negro thinkers had reached a dead end—and were not even aware of it. The movement was out of hand, running pell mell without guidance, and destined to come to a standstill in a blind alley.

James Boggs' letter showed the limiting effect Marxist training has on the Negro's social imagination, within the context of American conditions. Marxist conceptions become mechanically rooted in the thinking patterns much as do religious dogmas—so much so that if the Negro Marxist does not free his mind from these dogmatic categories he remains forever unable to deal with new American realities. He will oppose every set of political, economic or cultural conceptions that do not square with his ingrained dogmas. The influence of European Marxism on the thinking of the American Negro has been disastrous. It took the *Liberator* magazine staff until 1965 to see this, and it was not until 1966 that the source of white leftwing influence was eliminated from the publication. But by then it was too late. Having lost all of its best writers and most experienced analysts the magazine had to begin all over again with younger writers who would have to learn for themselves how to resolve the conflicting and incompatible elements in nationalism, integrationism and the factions of the white leftwing.

Yet, the rise and decline of the *Liberator* is not to be compared with the rise and fall of A. Philip Randolph's *Messenger* during the fateful 1920's. In the 1960's there are additional critical forces emerging around such journals as *Black America, Soulbook, Black Dialogue* and *Umbra*. Despite many shortcomings in style, analysis and range, these magazines represent an important potential for reaching whatever new levels of orientation the Negro movement is capable of achieving in the future.

Ideology in Black: African,
Afro-American, Afro-West Indian
and the Nationalist Mood

It should not be construed from what has been said thus far that this study is so pro-nationalist it finds only the integrationist wing deserving of criticism. For the nationalist wing is by no means so solvent, nor is it an aggregation of groupings so well-oriented that its criticisms of the integrationists make it a viable factor in the world of reality. On the contrary, the nationalist wing might know what it wants generally but does not know how to achieve it specifically. In short, the nationalist wing today does not know where it is going. On the other hand, the integrationist wing, which is dominant, knows exactly what it wants and where it wants to go, even if it is blocked in these aspirations by the stubborn facts of interracial realities. And while the nationalist wing may criticize the integrationist aims in life, the integrationists at least have a program which (the impact of a Malcolm X notwithstanding) the nationalists do not.

In using the term nationalist wing, I am making an arbitrary distinction between the members of the Nation of Islam (Muslims) and others who take various anti-integrationist, pro-African, pro-black, pro-nationalist positions. This distinction must be made because the Muslims do have a working program that is effective. But the religio-separatist nature of the Muslims is unacceptable to many nationalist elements in the North who remain free-roving, unaffiliated groupings. Since these unaffiliated nationalist trends are composed mostly of young people, the remnants of the old Garveyites cannot be included in the same category. Yet this last faction, gravitating around what could be called in nationalist terms, the vital center, has, at this moment, the most dynamic potential; it is, at the same time, the most disorganized, disoriented, and planless. When the passing of Malcolm X left this faction without an effective spokesman, the Muslims made certain inroads by capitalizing on that void.

Like the Negro movement as a whole, Afro-American Nationalism has inherited a raft of problems accumulated from the past. It is almost impossible today to codify nationalist thought so as to make much practical and programmatic sense in political, economic and cultural terms. Afro-American Nationalism is so fragmented into sects, factions, and cliques that it is a morass of self-inflicted immobility and frustration. But, though the decriers of black nationalism may not realize it, a very extensive bloc of the American Negro population of all classes could be influenced by this group, should it ever organize itself into a unified force with a clear "line." But the Afro-American Nationalists cannot come to terms with themselves as American products, created out of American conditions and ingredients, requiring, in the final analysis, an American solution. Having rejected Americanization out of hand as a past, present or future commitment, they function from day to day, variously isolated from American social realities. Many Afro-American Nationalists cultivate an existence that reduces any contact with whites to the barest minimum. Many others live in an intellectual world of the teachings of Islam or the history of the glories of Africa past and present, or the projection of a future return to Africa.

The old Garveyite Back-to-Africa dream still exists for many of the new Afro-American Nationalists, but not in the strict terms of the old Garvey program. Today it is merely a spiritual return, another side of the anti-American mood and its modern form of alienation. This Back-to-Africa mood is a romance of the mind and a balm for the psyche which has a bolstering effect on black self-esteem. It is the impact of the birth of free African states with presidents, premiers, protocol and international prestige—all lending vivid substance to Back-to-Africa voyages of the imagination. This is borne out by American Negroes who wear native African costumes at parties, balls, and local poetry readings. But you will not, to be sure, see any mass emigration stampede back to the homeland. Of course, even should one million blacks return to Africa, there would still remain a race problem to be solved in the

United States. There are many Afro-American Nationalists who talk as if they do not realize this. And ironically, when the African diplomats, intellectuals, bureaucrats and other spokesmen come to America, they associate not with the Afro-American Nationalists but with the prestigious integrationists of the NAACP, the American Society of African Culture, the African-American Institute, and so forth.

Today, Garveyism is a dream deferred, because the realities of African independence and the relationships of American Negroes to the African scene do not fulfill what Garveyism promised. Things have turned out differently, and both Africans and Afro-Americans have to face up to domestic and international realities not prophesied in the 1920's. The truth of the matter is that many Afro-American Nationalists do not understand the essentials of the African Revolution any better than the so-called Black Revolution in the United States. Yet they cannot escape the facts of history, a history that created that far-flung triangular relationship between Africa, the West Indies and the United States, based on the slave trade. These historical antecedents still hang heavy over the fortunes of black destiny today, and in many imponderable ways color the outlook of the Afro-American Nationalists.

The African (whether he speaks French, English or Swahili), the West Indian, and the American Negro are so similar and yet so different, that Afro-American Nationalists are all the more pressed to program a clear-cut attack on the problems they face. For no matter how much he tries, the Afro-American Nationalist cannot tear himself away as cleanly as he thinks from the ideals, values, strivings, liabilities, achievements—the sins and virtues of the entire American Negro world. He might decry the values of the integrationists and the failings of the black bourgeoisie, but he knows that in doing so, he is criticizing a recognizable reflection of himself.

But what are the dreams of the African, and that other branch of African progeny in the Western Hemisphere, the so-called Afro-West Indian? How related really are their dreams in relation to their common ancestry? How well do these people—who are as variegated as a black-hued rainbow—really understand each other? Let us examine the things some of them have been heard to say.

Back in the middle 1950's, at an interracial party, a minor African official listened to American Negroes having a discussion on the possibilities of returning to Africa; he replied most indignantly that Africa did not want any of "you Negroes" over there, and proceeded to derogate the American Negro's attitudes, habits, and general condition.

In 1962, a very well-known woman jazz singer said, "The hell with Africans! They have their own thing going over there and they have little in common with us, and care less."

Another woman, majoring in sociology and born in the United States, identifies with Africa so strongly that she is almost tribalistic in outlook. For her, the American Negro can achieve nothing in America unless his movement is predicated on a reverent identification with Africa. But her outlook is conditioned by the fact that her parents are from the West Indies; she was therefore disturbed that, when in Ghana, she was classified as an American Negro. This young woman, of course, while belonging in the Afro-American Nationalist category admits to a dual identification.

Another woman jazz singer, now retired, with a background of travel in Europe and the Far East, wants to meet Africans but feels that there is not much rapport between them and American Negroes. She feels also that American Negroes are divided along regional lines—North, South, East and West—thus in her view seriously weakening the civil rights movement. This woman is also highly antagonistic to West Indians, who she feels do not identify with American Negroes. West Indians play a "two-faced, underhanded role with white people in undercutting American Negroes," she remarked, that having been her experience in working with West Indians professionally.

A composer-pianist of West Indian parentage has strong ambivalences on the African-American Negro identification question. He has the physical characteristics of a "mixed-blood," and constantly seeks to explain that he is not of pure African descent. Yet, his real link with his heritage is through music, and he is deeply immersed in the Afro-American musical tradition. Aware that the origins of African music are in Uganda, he derides a certain African composer who is known to favor Western forms—accusing this composer of denying his own cultural roots in music. His own roots are in the American Negro folk music tradition and he admits that his own musical development was influenced by Sissle and Blake, Ellington and others. Yet on American Negro experiences on the social, political, economic, and civil rights fronts, he often refuses to commit himself.

A West Indian couple who were friends of an American Negro couple from Virginia had to be coaxed before they would agree to visit the South. They were afraid of Southern whites. In New York, it has been noted that even the grandchildren born in the United States of West Indian immigrants are taught to make distinctions among their parents' friends. They often embarrass their parents by referring to certain visitors as either "West Indian" or "American." This is true even in the case of former Virgin Islanders: They identify with the British West Indies proper, even though all Virgin Islanders have been American citizens since 1927. The stereotype of American Negro inferiority is so strong among many West Indians that to them, an extra-intelligent American Negro either has distant West Indian antecedents, or else the ability to "think like a West Indian." This has led to another West Indian myth—that the British West Indies were peopled by a different breed of African slaves (when indeed West Indians will admit to slavery) than those who landed at American ports.

During the 1950's in the Greenwich Village interracial scene, it was noted that certain West Indian males formed themselves into a semi-exclusive social club from which camp they competed with American Negro males for the favors of white women (mostly Jewish). The West Indian women on the scene were hardly ever seen at this club's functions, for they usually consorted with white men, as did most of the American Negro women. Most of the West Indian men were ever alert to emphasize that they were "not American Negroes." The West Indian women, though fewer in number, reacted similarly, and one remarked, "You Negroes have contributed nothing to the United States but jazz music." When asked what the West Indians had contributed to the British Empire aside from calypso and labor—both slave and cheap—she replied, "Oh, that's different."

The Village interracial scene offered the best of all social laboratories for a study of race and ethnic group contacts and attitudes, involving American and West Indian Negroes, Jews, Anglo-

Saxons, Italians, Latins and even Indians. On the Harlem scene, the West Indian attitude has to be gauged by class, as does the American Negro attitude in reverse. One West Indian of long residence in Harlem constantly used to remark during race discussions, "What I want to know is, what is this Negro going to do?" Even after the civil rights upsurge he was unimpressed—and asked the same question. And so it goes . . . the West Indian psychology is a thing apart . . . distinguishing itself through myriad ways, but principally by not accepting the American Negro social status as it has been fashioned by the American way of life. Even when the West Indian finds a way of accommodating to this status, it is usually with certain reservations. Perceptive whites have noted this attitude and used it on all levels of black and white relations, including the Communist leftwing. Yet despite this subcultural antagonism between the two groups, one West Indian woman was heard to scoff: "What are they bickering about, they are all the same!"

Claude McKay was the perfect example of the difficulty the West Indian creative artist and intellectual, even when born in the United States, has in identifying with the American Negro. For one thing, because of the contrasts in the cultural and political developments in black America and the black West Indies, there is a clash of cultural backgrounds. Moreover, the black West Indies never experienced the kind of cultural renaissance that took place among American Negroes from the 1890's, to the 1920's, culminating in the advent of mass media. In fact, West Indians living through this renaissance understood it even less than the American Negroes—and they failed to conceptualize what they felt intuitively. McKay, for example, never grasped the cultural side of the American revolution.

The Trinidadian scholar and historian, Eric Williams, gives some answers to the background of this cultural differentiation: "The racial situation in the Caribbean is radically different from the racial situation in the United States and is thus rather incomprehensible to the native of the United States, black or white."[1]

---

[1] *The Negro in the Caribbean* (Washington, D.C.: Associates in Negro Folk Education, 1942), p. 62.

In the United States, the West Indian complains that the American Negro lacks cohesiveness; thus to make an even more incomprehensible comparison, Williams said: "The racial consciousness which permeates the American Negro is also not found in the islands. This is a constant source of surprise and even exasperation to the American Negro visitor or student, who goes to the islands with his clichés and his prejudices, seeking for any violations of his own code of racial solidarity."[2]

Race militancy, then, is one thing in the West Indies and something else in the United States. This clash of cultural traditions creates other confusions of values. Booker T. Washington, for example, has been symbolized as the antithesis of race militancy, by the DuBois tradition in the United States. But in Williams' criticism of the backward educational systems in the Caribbean, the worst of which was the British system, he wrote: "The education provided is furthermore woefully unsuited to local conditions. Along liberal lines, little attention is paid to vocational education, and the Caribbean has produced no Booker T. Washington."[3]

For that very reason, Marcus Garvey admired Booker T. Washington, and tried to link his movement with Washington's Tuskegee institution. Yet you will never get a young nationalist militant to admit that today, especially if he is West Indian. He will invariably uphold Garvey, put down Washington, and be confused about DuBois. This, despite the fact that Mrs. A. Jacques Garvey, herself, wrote: "While in Alabama [in 1923] we went to Tuskegee Normal and Industrial Institute. Primarily to pay homage to the late Booker T. Washington. . . ." Garvey and his wife were of the opinion that: "Since the death of Booker T. Washington there was no one with a positive and practical programme for the masses —North or South."[4]

Contrary to Eric Williams, this conflict of cultural values prompts the West Indian militant to claim more racial solidarity for his kind than for the American Negro. This ideological gambit cropped out again during the summer of 1966 when CORE and SNCC went over to the Black Power position. Prominent among the new Black Power supporters were three West Indians: Stokely

[2] *Ibid.,* p. 63.
[3] *Ibid.,* p. 75.
[4] *Garvey and Garveyism, op. cit.,* p. 26.

Carmichael, Trinidad; Lincoln Lynch, Jamaica; and Roy Inniss, Virgin Islands. To back up their rationalizations for their new position of Black Power, all three cited the political and racial status of the black West Indies. As a result, the New York press was moved to cite "the strong Caribbean and West Indian influence in the black power philosophy."[5] Overlooked was the fact that the term Black Power was copied from Adam Clayton Powell who first gave it currency in his commencement speech at Howard University on May 29, 1966 (he had also mentioned it in Chicago at a rally during May, 1965), where he said: "To demand these God-given human rights is to seek black power." But what *is* Black Power—in either West Indian or American Negro terms?

Carmichael, Lynch, and Inniss cited their West Indian background, and Lincoln Lynch was quoted as saying: "I was shocked when I came here and found that the word 'black' was almost a cuss word with the American Negroes. . . . It must have something to do with the adjustment [we West Indians] make when we come here."

The three West Indians seekers of Black Power said that their "stance of black consciousness was alienating middle-class Negroes [Americans, that is] and white supporters in Congress and in the public in general." Further, "They were tired of unenforced laws and felt that many middle-class Negroes [Americans] were trying to escape their race." What is needed, the West Indians say, is "for Negroes to reject integration as their major aim and to band themselves together into a racially oriented mass movement. . . ." If this fails, the Black Power advocates say "armed revolt" is the answer against whites. Lynch and Carmichael emphasized the fact that in Jamaica and Trinidad there "is a lot of poverty but we felt proud in being black."[6] Moreover the West Indians have political power (*i.e.,* black policemen, civil servants, public officials, etc.). Naturally these West Indians cited the Marcus Garvey nationalist precedent.

Eric Williams shows, however, that the Black Power concept, predicated on a West Indian social rationale, is deceptive, especially with regard to the actual political and class situation in the

---

[5] *The New York Times,* July 24, 1966, p. 51.
[6] *Idem.*

Caribbean. That the West Indian Black Power supporters are following in the footsteps of Garvey does not prove what they want it
to prove. Garvey did not establish any Black Power in the West
Indies because of the opposition of the West Indian black bourgeoisie: "The West Indian middleclasses were, almost without exception, viciously hostile."[7]

This West Indian middle class also has the deepest of skin-color
phobias; to them, the word "black" is even more opprobrious than
Lincoln Lynch found in the United States. Even though the West
Indian middle classes had their social power whittled down during
the West Indian working-class unrest of the 1930's, it was the labor
movement that was responsible for this progress, not the Garveyites. As Williams points out, the Garveyite success was in the
United States, but Garveyism left "not much to be seen in the
islands in the way of concrete organization." Thus, today we have
West Indian nationalists in the United States but no nationalist
movement in the black West Indies. Hence, in West Indian terms,
"political independence" is "integrationism"; what Stokely Carmichael calls Black Power in Trinidad is not nationalist separation
from the British Crown, but gradualistic, integrated Common-
wealth-partnership within the Empire. Moreover, in Trinidad, as
in former colonial days, the two major economic activities—oil and
sugar—are still in foreign (white) hands. There is fourteen per
cent unemployment (in 1966) and the job market is shrinking.
This is typical of the entire black West Indies, where Black Power
has not changed the economic situation at all; where in Trinidad
the per capita income is $520 per annum. It is these conditions
that force all the West Indian nationalists out of the West Indies
to other places, such as New York, where the wages are infinitely
higher, even *without* American Negro Black Power. But, they say,
if Black Power is not achieved by the American Negro he should
resort to armed revolt to get it. Why then, the question arises, *was
there no armed revolt in the black West Indies where the blacks
are in the majority?* For one thing, Black Power in the Caribbean
has not created and brought to the fore a black Fidel Castro—
which explains a lot about the black West Indies today.

The West Indian Black Power sponsors want the American

[7] Eric Williams, *op. cit.,* p. 93.

Negro, as a minority, to win economic power in the United States, yet they suggest no program to achieve this. Roy Inniss of CORE, for example, reveals considerable misunderstanding of Negro leadership trends. He tells the press that *he* is in favor of lionizing certain Negro leaders over others, such as Frederick Douglass, Nat Turner, Denmark Vesey, Garvey, and Malcolm X . . . people like that, because they are historic exemplars of race militancy. (The American Negro needs the *right* sort of heroes.) As Inniss could not fit Washington and DuBois into this militant trend, he left them out—without explaining how, historically, he can separate Washington from Garvey. He also claimed that the CORE members who favored interracialism and intermarriage as a solution to the race problem were trying to bring about *his* "genetic destruction." (Presumably Inniss momentarily forgot that Frederick Douglass, the great militant Abolitionist, had married a white.)

Because of the West Indian's peculiar cultural history, the alienation of the West Indian creative intellectual in the United States has come to take on unique forms. He, or she, is often faced with the problem of relating artistically to two different cultural personalities—the West Indian or the American Negro. Some solve the problem by going completely aracial and Universal; others reach back for the West Indian novel, the West Indian play. One novelist is known to have failed to publish a first West Indian novel but succeeded with a second American Negro novel. Claude McKay achieved both. One of the most outstanding West Indian novelists is known to be aracial and an acculturated black Englishman who hardly ever speaks loudly about racial differences. But he functions in England for the most part.

The American Negro actor's fight against stereotyped Negro roles in films and theater is complicated by the fact that actors of West Indian background do not object to these roles for the same reasons of image that American Negro actors do. Since the West Indian actor has problems of identification with the American idiom, "in life," stage and film artistry presents merely another level of interpretive discord. This conflict has often been observed in drama groups, especially if it concerns characters written by a Negro playwright.

A composer of Trinidadian parentage inwardly blames the American Negro situation for *his* failures in winning recognition in America. He has threatened many times to move to England. But he always fends off the rejoinder he invites from American Negroes, by declaring, "I can't go to Trinidad because there's nothing happening there [musically]." Hence he deteriorates in New York. The peculiar nationalism of the West Indian on the identity question crops out in the case of a West Indian professor of literature. Coming out of the black majority racial status of the Caribbean, this professor identifies quite strongly with the new African literary flowering—also emerging from a black majority racial and cultural background. In his lectures it was noted that the professor attempted to link the West Indian and African literary trends in terms of the anti-colonialist imperative, although the West Indian literary output was never very extensive. However he made a slight distinction concerning the South African black (or colored) writers. In South Africa the black population is subject to the most industrially advanced white population on the African continent, and also the most numerous. This implicit psychological parallel apparently prompted the professor to link the South African writers with the American Negro writers.

The cultural, political, and class background of the Afro-West Indies makes many West Indians, in America, claim they are British or French or Spanish, or Cuban, or even Puerto Rican. This is to avoid saying, "I am an American (Negro)." If they are truly anti-colonialist (which many are not), they will claim to be Jamaican or Trinidadian, or Martiniquan, Nevisian, Barbadian, etc. All of these national groups names, such as Jamaican, were created and given to them, you will note, by white people who "discovered" these islands and called them the West Indies. Thus the name "West Indian" is acceptable to African descendants who are, racially, far removed from people who are called Indians. Yet, there are West Indians, such as Richard B. Moore, who argue about the word "Negro" on the basis that this name was given to African descendants by white men. Although the word comes from the Portuguese and Spanish, meaning "black," it has come to connote the branding of slave status in the black psychology. But the white Englishmen also call Africans in the Caribbean "Negroes"; if black West Indians refuse to use it, it means merely that they prefer another name, also given by white men and just as indicative of a strong identification with those white men. This curious semantic transference of identity values explains a lot about West Indian nationalism, which, as Eric Williams* points out, is incomprehensible in American terms. Williams wrote: "In the United States there were Negroes who were nationalists, in the Caribbean there were nationalists who were Negroes."[8]

This explains why nationalists who were black in the Caribbean became, not *black nationalists,* but national spokesmen for their island nations: for instance, Antonio Maceo and Juan Gualberto Gomez, who were *Cuban* nationalists, not *black* nationalists; or Jose Celso Barbosa of Puerto Rico, a leader of "color" who spoke for his people of all races, rather than for *his* race. It almost could be said that Frederick Douglass fitted this category—it was the black slave's minority status in America that made Douglass's role that of a special pro-Negro spokesman over and above that of the nationalist Martin R. Delany. On the other hand, it does explain why American Negro Crispus Attucks, reputedly the first American to die fighting against the British in the Revolutionary War, is not today a hero to the young Afro-American Nationalists as Maceo is a hero to black Cubans for his leadership in the struggle against Spain. This peculiar historical development of nationalism in the West Indies, as opposed to that among American Negroes, helps to explain why Garveyism could take root in the United States but not in the West Indies. Garvey, unlike Maceo in Cuba, did not fight for complete independence from Great Britain, but merely commonwealth status (which Britain only recently granted).

Inherited, then, is a very muddled, distorted nationalist tradition, wherein West Indian nationalists have become adept at using the Garvey tradition demagogically, inasmuch as the 1920's nationalist wave was largely West Indian.† Opposition to Garveyism by American Negro middle-class leaders such as DuBois and Randolph is singled out as proof of the American Negro's lack of militancy. However, the latter-day Garveyites never mention the fact that the bulk of opposition to Garveyism also came from West Indians both in New York and in Jamaica.

---

* Eric Williams is now Prime Minister of Trinidad.
[8] *Ibid.,* p. 87.
† A few years ago the Jamaican authorities in Kingston started hearings for a treason trial against Garvey's latter-day followers, the Rastafari cult, for preaching Back to Africa.

A good deal of the internal dissension today among the younger trend of Afro-American Nationalists stems from this undercurrent of West Indian vs. American Negro rivalry. This competition was a strong factor in the collapse of the Freedom Now Party's Organizing Committee, mentioned before. During this effort, the most vocal dissenters and no-confidence voters were all of West Indian origin. At a conference of young Afro-American nationalists held in Harlem in April, 1965, any positive clarification was negated and disrupted by Garveyites, one of whom charged that any Negro who preferred to remain in the United States and fight for equality is a "house nigger." This slash, of course, was aimed at American Negroes—not at West Indian nationals who were emigrating to the British Isles and the United States (instead of Africa).

West Indian conservatism takes other overt forms, especially in connection with the identification dilemma. The majority of West Indians today do not identify with Garveyism in America but with a conservative kind of group identity of their own. The younger ones, who are not essentially middle class and who break away from the West Indian group to join the white Left or some trend of the civil rights movement, usually strive to maintain their separate identity. In these cases they generally become the staunchest allies of the whites. If they tend toward "Afro-American Nationalism" they are apt to accentuate their identification with everything African (another way of not identifying with the American Negro). Much of the West Indian's attitude toward the American Negro is based on the latter's lack of a cohesive ideology—which the West Indian can retain in America because his group is much smaller. The American Negro who dislikes the West Indian bases it on the latter's "pushiness." The West Indian, who usually refuses to abide by the American Negro's accepted status of social inferiority, blames the American for his lack of militancy concerning the very issue on the West Indians themselves never forced until the 1920's. However, after the Watts, Los Angeles, uprising of 1965, one of the loudest denouncers of this militant action was a well-known West Indian who said he felt ashamed that he was an American Negro—a classification that he had quite probably been denying since he arrived.

It is a fact that most Africans seem to agree with the West Indians in their general attitude toward the American Negro, citing his lack of racial cohesiveness. This point of view, of course, stems from the African and West Indian social backgrounds in which, colonialism aside, Africans and West Indians are the racial majority. The fact that the North American Negro has existed as a decided minority within a European-derived majority has given him his native psychology, however one cares to evaluate it. Hence, in certain specific terms, Africans, Afro-Americans and Afro-West Indians (not born in America) do not share the same psychology toward whites—yet in general terms, they do. On closer examination, differences are more of degree than of kind.

If an American Negro becomes more American than the Americans, the West Indian becomes more British than the Britisher; the same is true of British and French Africans. One of the politico-ideological factors behind this is that Africans and West Indians were never allowed to forget that they were colonial subjects. But the fact that the American Negro was also a subject, of a special kind of North American domestic colonialism, was never fully accepted either by the Negro himself nor by Africans or West Indians. Back in the 1920's, during the Haywood-Huiswoud-Briggs controversy within the Communist Party, the West Indians did not want to classify American Negroes as colonials. It was not until 1962 that even the new Afro-American Nationalists began to see the domestic colonialist nature of the Negro's position in the United States. It is only when such factors are grasped that it is possible to get to the bottom of the many misconceptions the African, Afro-American, and West Indian share about each other. One begins to see that these three do not really understand each other's black revolutions. And the least understood of all is the American variety. In the meantime, however, many facts are revealed and many myths are exploded.

The dynamics of the colonial revolution reveal that neither the African nor the West Indian possesses the kind of cohesiveness hitherto claimed—as the "Federation" and "African Unity" fiascos have revealed in the West Indies and in Africa. Despite the fact that Africans and West Indians are the overwhelming racial majorities in their respective regions, their accession to political independence has not broken the chains of economic bondage to the European powers. Economic neo-colonialism is the African reality. In the West Indies, the economic control is still in the hands of whites, Chinese, Indians, Syrians and other non-blacks. In Africa, overwhelming black majorities in several "new nations" are unable to oust white minorities from political control, not to mention economic entrenchment. Yet criticisms are heard from both Africans and West Indians that the American Negro has not achieved what he might have both before and since the Supreme Court action of 1954. The bulk of these African and West Indian critics, of course, do not participate very demonstrably in the Black Revolution. Principally, they are as sideline observers with an eagle eye open for every opportunity to lap up whatever crumbs the power structure tosses to the civil righters, or to profit from whatever barriers are breached to enhance middle-class status. We see this all over New York City in the social, political, cultural and entertainment world.

"These American Negroes," say most Africans, "have no cohesion; they have no race consciousness; they don't identify with us Africans." But do not ask these Africans to facilitate or abet cohesion with the Negro by, perhaps, living too closely with him or by socializing more intimately than State Department protocol would allow. That would be an affront to their "new nation" status within United Nations society. "We are Africans, not 'American Negroes.' They are ex-slaves, we are ex-colonial slaves (but in our own country)—that makes a big difference." Yet ironically deep down in the soul of many American Negroes, is ingrained the conviction that the African has just barely emerged out of his primitive-tribal past!

But even those American Negroes who go to Africa with a certain show of brotherhood idealism, to help "build," often fail the test. One African Hausa student who was working with some American Negroes in Ghana came to America embittered by the privileges the Americans received and gladly accepted. He described how a certain New York commercial artist was given a six-room apartment with three baths, one shower, an extra servant's room, on the fourteenth story of a hotel, which afforded the artist an expansive view of all Accra. This hotel, which was described as of "all-glass" construction, had two special guards from the Mussi Tribe of Upper Volta stationed there at all times. The African student claimed that the New York artist was paid about three hundred dollars a month for a job in Ghana's state-sponsored equivalent of a Madison Avenue advertising company. Out of this salary, the artist's rent for the spacious lodging, the student said, was about seven pounds, roughly twenty dollars at the present rate of exchange. The African student claimed that groups and individuals who allege to be helping Africa develop cannot demand such privileges and, at the same time, insist that they are "one with the people." However, he did not question the political sincerity of the governmental caste who alloted such privileges to the Americans. More than that, he did not know that these American Negroes had the background of membership in the privileged elite colored section of the political leftwing in New York. Hence, as a matter of course, they demanded and got what they had been accustomed to before.

There are naturally many living exceptions to generalized attitudes. Many Africans and West Indians have transcended group differences and collaborated with American Negroes, and vice versa. In 1960, Leopold Senghor, who later became President of Senegal, came to the United States and had much trenchant advice for American Negroes on cultural matters. Although Senghor speaks no English, he had a deeper understanding about this aspect of Afro-Americana than many of the English-speaking Nigerians and Ghanaians. Many African students work closely with American Negro students. Many West Indians work closely with American Negroes. Yet this collaboration does not proceed without complaint and friction. In the case of the African and the American Negro, it is more often the latter who causes the African to complain. On the other hand, with the American Negro and the West Indian, it is usually the latter who becomes the source of conflict and irritation. Under all circumstances the West Indian will let it be known, one way or the other, that he considers himself "different." The Negro is more tolerant than the West Indian —perhaps too tolerant for his own good. But this is also a reason why the American Negro is less conservative. Of all three, the African has the most liberated personality, which is not to be thought synonymous with revolutionary. As far as the Caribbean area is concerned, when one compares the English-speaking West Indians with the Cubans, Santo Domingans, and Puerto Ricans— black West Indians are the most conformist and accommodative people in the Caribbean. Moreover, it is difficult to determine who is leaving home at a faster rate—white Cubans escaping Castroism or black West Indians escaping "Federated" political independence. Yet to observe all three groups in America is to see that Africans and West Indians are much more concerned about their "image" than the American Negro usually is. In expressing this concern both the African and the West Indian reveal to what extent they have accepted the American stereotype of the Negro, a stereotype from which they try mightily to except themselves. Even their attempt to escape that myth merely creates others.

The superior attitude of the West Indians has long irked many American Negroes. One method of bolstering this superiority complex is the West Indians' old saw that there was never any slavery in the British West Indies. It is also known that in certain parts of Africa, for example in Ethiopia, American Negroes have been openly ridiculed as ex-slaves. Considering Ethiopia's history and distance from the slavery of the New World, this attitude is more understandable. But the British West Indies was the main bastion of the African slave trade long before the invention of the cotton gin transformed the United States South into the most lucrative dumping ground for human commodities. If the American Negro sharecropper remained the slave of cotton well after Emancipation, our Caribbean historian could say, as late as 1942, of the black laborer in the West Indies: "The black man, emancipated from above by legislation or from below by revolution, remains today the slave of sugar."[9] The slavery trauma of the West Indian manifests itself in many ways, even today.

In the *Freedomways* issue for the winter of 1963, a West Indian-American* wrote a communication protesting a David Brinkley television broadcast depicting life on the West Indian island of Nevis. According to the writer (a woman), Brinkley's broadcast had racist overtones because his choice of topic and panelists tended to put Nevis conditions in a bad light. Ninety-eight per cent of the people on the island are of African descent, but a colored Nevisan told Brinkley that most of them "were lazy and didn't want to work." The writer, whose family comes from Nevis,

[9] Eric Williams, *op. cit.*, p. 16.
* Louise Jeffers, Nevis, West Indies, pp. 99-102.

objected to scenes on the television screen showing black servant women laying out meals while a white woman spoke of the servants in the most degrading manner. The white woman "called them lazy and stupid," saying also, "they were even too stupid to make a cup of tea." The writer said of the white woman—"Her hatred of the Nevisans in particular and of colored people in general came across the TV screen sharp and vicious." The writer protested that Brinkley could have obtained better information from Nevisans and their United States descendants (one of whom is Hope Stevens) from the Nevis Benevolent Society in New Haven, Connecticut, and in Harlem. She went on to say:

> The Nevisans do not have the facilities for cultivating the land nor do they have people experienced in agricultural methods and animal husbandry. Most of the young people leave the island as soon as possible.
> Today there are only two doctors on the island, one hospital and clinic.
> In all the years Britain had occupied the island, there was no road built.

Federation of the West Indies islands failed, the writer pointed out, but:

> Survival of the people of Nevis and other islands depend on their uniting their forces and resources to mutually aid each other economically, politically and socially.
> Much of Nevis is still unexplored bush country which if cleared and cultivated could make a big difference in the economy of the country.

After explaining further that the economy of Nevis was depressed because of failure of the sugar industry, the writer added this last defense on behalf of the Nevisan image: *"Britain was never able to subjugate the people of the West Indies to accept slavery."* True to form, the writer had to use the occasion to defend the West Indian image against what is by now a dead issue— slavery. The West Indians did not "accept" slavery, implying thereby two things:

(1) *There was never any slavery in the West Indies.*

(2) There were other people who were subjugated and who *did* accept slavery. (Who? American Negroes.)

When the average West Indian looks askance at the American Negro's social status—his low economic level and other social disabilities—it is always the Negro's fault. "He is not militant enough. He does not stand up to *his* white folks. Unlike the black Nevisan servants depicted on David Brinkley's program, these American Negroes *are* really lazy and also a little stupid, and don't want to work," says the West Indian. "Of course, in Nevis things are backwards because *our* white folks didn't do anything for *us*. But the trouble with these American Negroes is that they are always begging *their* white folks for things they could do for themselves (as we do after we leave Nevis to come to the U.S.A. seeking a better life)." However, if we are to accept the facts of Nevis as they are today, it is to be seen that things have not changed much since the last Nevisan slave was liberated.

Why so? Because no Nevisan leaves Nevis to train in medicine in order to return to increase the number of doctors or to plan for those missing hospitals and clinics. Because none of the young people who leave, return bearing their American or British training in agriculture and animal husbandry or road building. That "unexplored bush country" of Nevis might be quite lush and could be "cleared and cultivated" to help the economy of the island. However, Metropolitan New York, London, and other Western cities far from Nevis are much lusher and the white folks who did nothing to build up the island economy are not forcing Nevisans and others in the Caribbean to build anything with their political independence one way or the other. Black West Indians are the majority and they are free to determine their own fate. But they cannot determine their own unity even under the most favorable conditions.

People who cannot achieve political cohesion in their own countries cannot afford to be supercilious and supercritical about the political failings of others. All their claims to the contrary, there is considerable doubt as to how much West Indians really love their island homelands. For it appears that West Indians are never so much in love with Caribbean heritage, or never so vehement in defending the West Indian image, as when they are indulging these sentiments from afar in England or North America. From these vantage points, such nostalgia and identification are food to the ego, but after political independence, the time has

come to show just how ready people are to enter the mainstream
of world history through the mastery of political, economic and
social organization *in one's own homeland.*

In the American context, and on other levels, this same tenor of
criticism applies to the new Afro-American Nationalists, whose
minds too are enmeshed in their own social myths. Afro-American
Nationalists are faced with a whole raft of very practical political,
economic and cultural problems that they must solve for themselves. No one else can or will solve these problems for them. Certainly the integrationist Negroes cannot and will not, but it is a
tactical error for nationalists to waste their time, energies and
propaganda fighting and criticizing integrationists. The fallacies
and weaknesses of integrationist programs can be exposed only to
the degree that the nationalists initiate counter programs along
political, economic and cultural lines. But, at the same time, this
does not mean that separatism is the perfect antidote for integrationism. An Afro-American Nationalist program that is politically,
economically, and culturally effective must be a dynamic program.
It cannot be a program that retreats from social realities of the
white power structure under the guise of separatist nationalistic
moods. It is perfectly understandable why many new Afro-American Nationalists in the cities of the North must experience a
separatist mood of withdrawal from any or all contacts with the
white world. The historical character of black and white social
relations in America makes such a mood a prerequisite for positive
reexamination and reevaluation of the black personality. For
groups as well as for individuals it is often necessary to retreat into
isolation in order to determine who one is. But in the world of realities such isolation cannot be maintained for too long, and there
comes a time when one must emerge from it and deal with the
hard facts of life. People, no matter how diverse, are interrelated
and diverse peoples must, of necessity, deal with the practical facts
of their inter-relationships.

So far, the Afro-American Nationalists have not distinguished
the difference between having a nationalistic mood and having
nationalist objectives in politics, economics, and culture that relate to how Negroes as a people exist in America. The mere fact of
self-identification, of the ideology of pro-blackness, the glorifica-

tion of the black skin, the idealization of everything African, the return to the natural quality of African hairstyles, the rediscovery of black female beauty, or the adoption of African tribal dress—all of these phases and moods signify a return to the root origins of self which can also be transformed into protective mystiques. If these black mystiques are suffused with a contempt for, a hatred and a rejection of, everything white, instead of being channeled into positive trends of action, such mystiques are capable of veering off into dangerous nihilistic fantasies of black supremacy that have little to do with the actualities of the real world. In this world of fantasy there will be a pecking order of blackness—"I am more black and more pure than thou"—in which case the enemy ceases to be whiteness but other less black breeds. This has already been manifested by the hate fringe of black nihilism—more threatening to blacks than to whites. Long predicted, this nihilistic black fringe was bound to develop when the Afro-American Nationalists failed to transcend their mystical and romantic phase.

It is the easiest thing in the world to shift the blame for the murder of Malcolm X to the CIA or their alleged black agents in the Negro community, but this murder signifies something more sinister than the followers of Malcolm X care to admit. It signifies that the nationalist wing of the black movement is capable of terrorism—aiming to obstruct, defeat, subvert and destroy every effort on the part of other Negro militants to develop positive programs of any kind. This nihilistic trend in Harlem, it must be remembered, accused Malcolm X of selling out simply because the man broke with the Nation of Islam and proceeded to modify his original attitude toward whites and his definition of nationalism.

The collapse of the Black Arts Repertory Theater and School is another case in point. Here was one of the most positive institutions established in Harlem during the last twenty-five years, with the support of a very broad representation from the Harlem youth. But this school was destroyed from the inside, and taken over by the terrorists who forced out everyone else who would not agree with their mystique. The Black Arts episode ended in a shooting which might easily have been fatal.

The Organization for Afro-American Unity has not been able to deal at all with the internal confusions and disabilities of the Afro-American Nationalist trends, become even more pronounced since the passing of Malcolm X. Taken as a whole, the various factions

do not really know what they want. They do not know whether
they want to see the United States reformed or revolutionized,
destroyed or democratized, abandoned, overthrown, or obliterated. The Afro-American Nationalists cannot make up their
minds whether they want to emigrate, separate, migrate, or simply
sit still in the ghettoes admiring each other during the quiet lulls
between uprisings. The Afro-American Nationalists are faced with
so many ghetto problems of such monumental proportions, which
they are neither prepared nor equipped to tackle, that it is small
wonder so much frustration reigns in their ranks. The black ghettoes are in dire need of new organizations or parties of a political
nature, yet it is a fact that most of the leading young nationalist
spokesmen are apolitical. It might not be entirely true, but
talk in Harlem had it that even Malcolm X was cool to the
idea of a political party. The black ghettoes are in even more dire
need of every possible kind of economic and self-help organization,
and a buyers and consumers council, but the most militant young
nationalists openly ridicule such efforts as reformist and a waste of
time. For them politics and economics are most unrevolutionary.
What they do consider revolutionary are Watts-type uprisings—
which lead nowhere. Listen to this editorial:

> Bourgeois Nationalism, or militant "Booker T-ism" (self-
> improvement) states that black people should strive to control the
> areas of the black ghettoes and communities, substituting black-
> owned businesses and establishments for the white-owned busi-
> nesses. The "radical" wing of "Bourgeois Nationalism" seeks to
> separate the black people from White America by either acquir-
> ing separate states within this nation, or being allowed to estab-
> lish a repatriation program back to Africa, to help develop it into
> an economic power. The more moderate wing seeks to develop
> black political power by forming an independent political party
> within the current structure; thereby electing congressmen, as-
> semblymen, and other officials, to office—responsible to said
> party. . . . As time goes by, "Bourgeois Nationalism" becomes
> increasingly conservative—losing its militant stance and potential
> initiative; emphasizing "culture" and "economics" instead of
> politics.[10]

These are the thoughts of some of the leading exponents of the
new Afro-American Nationalism. But note that in one paragraph

[10] "A New Philosophy for a New Age," *Black America*, Summer-Fall, 1965, p. 8.

this trend clearly reveals the depths of its own disorientation. They attempt to demonstrate how revolutionarily modernistic they are, by downgrading "Booker T-ism," the real historical meaning of which they have not yet understood. After that they dispose of Garveyism for the wrong reasons, and then the Nation of Islam's Muslims (probably because they do not like religion and the Muslims would demand too much discipline for free-wheeling young souls). They then scoff contemptuously at such efforts as the Freedom Now Party as a useless pastime for "moderates." But, interestingly enough, these young super-nationalists go even further than that—they cut the ground from under Malcolm X's OAAU because it had to be built upon the very political, economic, and cultural premises that many young nationalists reject as reflecting a childish attitude toward white America. In fact, the tentative outline of the OAAU's program, as drafted, was predicated on such political, economic and cultural ideas; and even before, these same ideas had been projected in the draft program of the Freedom Now Party published in the *Liberator* magazine of February, 1964. Recall that the Freedom Now Party platform was attacked from Detroit by James Boggs for being meaningless. Correspondingly, the young nationalists rejected the basis of the OAAU's program even before it was written. Yet in the very same issue of their publication these young nationalists refer to Malcolm X as a "real revolutionary," and take issue with those who were trying to "assert that brother Malcolm was moving closer to the mainstream of the civil rights movement."

There are serious contradictions in all of this, because although Malcolm X made revolutionary statements, his OAAU program was definitely written as a reformist document. So, also, in tone, was the draft platform of the Freedom Now Party—but merely because any political platform in America must be reformist in premise before it can be revolutionary. Otherwise such a party will never get off the ground even with strong and perceptive leadership (which the FNP did *not* have). On the other hand, even when a reformist organization such as the OAAU is established by a strongman leader like Malcolm X, it collapses if the leader is removed. This reveals an almost incurable Messiah complex, characteristic of Negro emotionalism. There must always be the great Individual Leader—the Messiah, the Grand Deliverer, the cult of the Irreproachable Personality who, even if he does not really have all the answers to the problem, can never be wrong. Negroes, including the nationalists, are led by their emotions rather than by reason or the guideposts of social analysis. This political immaturity is sustained by two factors: Negroes are not really sure what they want out of life; and, they do not understand that American society is much too complex today for the human limitations of one individual leader to encompass. What the Afro-American Nationalists need is a collective leadership, a guiding committee of political, economic and cultural experts to tackle an agreed-upon set of social goals. But who, out of the morass of nationalist confusion, can establish any goals?

In Harlem today, the American capitalistic-welfare state dynamic rules supreme, with the aid of the police department. What was once truly the cultural capital of the Negro world has become a social disaster area, a dehumanized desert of mass society in black. As a community, Harlem is beyond the purview of the integrationist program, hence it falls, by default, within the purview of the nationalist wing. If the nationalist wing fails in the task of rehabilitation, then Harlem is a lost world. What stands between the nationalist wing and the capitalistic-welfare state power apparatus are various groupings of Negro middle-class integrationist forces, emanating from civil rights organizations, newspaper groups, political machines, churches, social agencies and business groups. From these circles come the decision makers of Harlem, and since these rulers are now powerless to rehabilitate and improve the community, their permanent function is to control it. Manifested in this situation is Harlem's class problem. The nationalist wing calls it the problem of the black bourgeoisie or the middle-class Negro, and it is this that trips them up. The term Black Bourgeoisie was first popularized by E. Franklin Frazier, in his study of the same title. Previously, the common term was middle-class Negroes, its archetype the class of Negroes who ran the NAACP. However, it is clear that many Negroes who glibly use the term black bourgeoisie have not read Frazier's book at all, or if they have, need to reread it. They will note that Frazier's subtitle for his book is "The Rise of a *New* Middleclass." This meant that insofar as civil rights organizations like the NAACP and the Urban League are middle class, they are, in the main, pre-

World War-Two middle class, or older-generation bourgeois. But Frazier's "new middle class" comprises a younger generation that was certainly not a part of the older middle-class entrenchment within the NAACP. The social status of this new wave middle-class Negro was based on new developments in the American economy. Frazier wrote:

> The relative size of the black bourgeoisie in the Negro population has increased during the past decade largely because the proportion of Negro workers in clerical and kindred occupations has more than doubled and the proportion of female clerical workers quadrupled since 1940. . . . During and especially since World War II, Negro men and women in the North have been entering clerical occupations, both in public and private employment, as the result of political pressure and the Fair Employment Practices Laws enacted in eleven states and twenty-five cities.[11]

Hence the greater proportion of the Negro middle class today claims a status that is based more on occupational achievements than on family background or inherited economic and social status. And it so happens that a very large number of Afro-American Nationalists are young people who fall within this occupational range. They are clerical and professional workers, teachers, students, social welfare employees, struggling writers and journalists, etc. Many who are unemployed, aspire only to these kinds of occupations, or are aspirants for a college degree, looking forward to better jobs. Despite their nationalistic ideology they are people "on the make," and they are also some of the loudest denunciators and critics of the black bourgeoisie. Everyone who is not a factory worker, service industry employee, domestic or porter is bourgeois-tainted (with the exception of themselves), but they would be scandalized if they were offered a job in a factory or service industry. In this fashion, the Afro-American Nationalists labor under the unconscious but self-engendered liability of reflecting the values of the very class they attack. Unaware that this is but the American capitalistic dynamic at work the nationalists are sufficiently muddled, confused and blinded that they mishandle and distort the question of the black bourgeoisie.

[11] Frazier, *op. cit.,* pp. 49-50.

The nationalist movement cannot succeed unless it establishes firm alliances with certain sections of the black bourgeoisie wherever possible. However, the Afro-American Nationalists have shown a strong tendency to reject certain of the sons and daughters of the black bourgeoisie in their early twenties on a class, skin-color, and hair-texture basis. Here, the black skin and the *au naturel* hairdo becomes the nationalist standard of ideological purity. But lurking behind the façade of many of an Afro-American Nationalist dressed like a native Nigerian, is an incipient black bourgeois, American-Negro style.

One can see such people at the African parties, consular fêtes, and the Africanized cultural events where the outward symbols of the African identification also become credentials to new social status: the personal alliance with new-nation power, the job in the African-American hierarchy, or even the sinecure in Africa, if one learns the politics of cliques. In this way, the problem of the black bourgeoisie has been internationalized, from New York to Accra, Lagos, Dakar, Conakry—"back where our history began."

Moreover, the middle-class muddle within the Afro-American Nationalists undermines a positive approach to the role of the black intelligentsia, inasmuch as the nationalists are without a skilled and well-oriented group of intellectuals. Lurking behind the anti-bourgeois sentiment is the more dangerous prejudice of anti-intellectualism. But the Afro-American Nationalists cannot afford the luxury of indulging in this typical white American prejudice against intellectualism. It is true that intellectuals are a part of what is called the educated class. But a race of people who clamor for the rights to higher education as much as Negroes do cannot contradict themselves by rejecting the class results of this higher education, without due appraisal. It so happens that there are intellectuals who seek bourgeois status and the fulfillment of the American Dream, and there are those who do not. The same applies to those nationalists who disdain intellectualism, but who consider themselves much too knowledgeable to accept the economic and social status of the masses. America is a difficult society to live in without succumbing to the blandishments of bourgeois values. The real question is which bourgeois values are *positive* and which are *detrimental* to social progress. At any rate, the Afro-American Nationalists find they must depend on their intellectuals to arbitrate class conflict within the Negro group. To a great degree in America, the Negro intellectual is actually *declassé*, or at least he must steer clear of class association in order to play any kind of role. To the degree that the Negro intellectual fails to understand this is the measure of his deep crisis in America. But if the majority of the Afro-American Nationalists fail to understand this, they will but repeat a black sectarianism that resembles the early sectarianism of the fledging Communist Party of the 1920's. The Communists, too, went through a phase where class purity, style of dress, ideological exclusiveness, and anti-intellectualism took precedence over political maturity and awareness of American realities.

In Harlem today, among the Afro-American Nationalists, there is little awareness of practical political realities. Behind the pretext of rejecting everything white, lies the easy path to political escapism and irresponsibility. The Afro-American Nationalists have created for themselves a detached world of their own, full of confused and contradictory motivations. It is an inbred, exclusive, and often a make-believe world that exists only for itself, without specified goals. It is a world that awaits the arrival of an Armageddon, a day of racial reckoning, but that rationalizes away every possible positive action on the political, economic and cultural fronts. Lacking any program, the Afro-American Nationalists allow the capitalistic-welfare state power apparatus to move in and take over, by co-option, every issue on which a program could be based. On the one hand, the Afro-American Nationalists will say that you cannot trust the white man's Federal power to aid and abet the Negro's struggle. On the other, they leap on the bandwagon of every anti-poverty handout from the Federal power, and then complain that the Federal power is not doing enough. But the Afro-American Nationalists refuse to launch an independent political party of their own in order to deal more effectively with the Federal power. Their excuse is, that politics is moderation, yet they refuse to see the contradiction here that leads them deeper into immobility.

The Afro-American Nationalists fail to see the politically strategic nature of the Harlem community. Instead, they allow integrationist political leaders elected from the community to launch a widely advertised program aimed at breaking up, through planned integration, the present ethnic composition of Harlem. Such a plan, if carried out, would have very profound political and economic ramifications. It would critically undermine the Negro's already precarious political situation in New York, and rule out any possible future economic rehabilitation of Harlem *in the Negro's favor*. It is not understood by the Afro-American Nationalists that if Negroes lose the racial majority in Harlem, they are lost. Harlem is the Negro's main urban bastion in the entire country and he must fight to keep control of it. This fundamental truth could have been the rallying point for popular opinion in the Harlem Nationalists' confrontation of integrationist policies. If one talks of Afro-American unity, Harlem is the place where all of its theories and practice must be tested and proven. As a black principality within the leading metropolis in the western world, Harlem is a black city in economic bondage, lacking adequate political representation. It is presided over like a racial reserve by the armed police power of the state. It has no local press that speaks with the sentiments of the grass roots. It has no cultural institutions that cultivate the personalities of its people. There is not a single publication coming out of Harlem reflecting the deep imperatives of its blighted existence, playing the role of opinion-molder in the interests of social progress.

The Afro-American Nationalists are boxed in by these paradoxes and the pressures of reforms. Indulging in talk about revolution, they meanwhile gather in every possible crumb from the reformers. But they do not publish a single, inexpensive newspaper. The Organization of Afro-American Unity has not yet taken what should be the first step of any movement that aims to influence public opinion—to issue a regular periodical expressing the organization's views. The activist leadership tradition of oratory is too strongly adhered to by Negroes. They do not realize that the base of a new kind of movement with new ideas can be cemented only with the help of a publication. As long as the Afro-American Nationalists leave the information and propaganda field open, to be monopolized by the integrationist-reformers, they will be unable to mount a counter program.

The large cities, especially in the North, are where the decisive struggles of the Negro movement will be waged. It will be a difficult and complex struggle, but the Negro movement must win political and economic power within these urban communities, while seeking cultural freedom and equality there and beyond, in the broad cultural context. Even the land question can be solved only from an urban base of political power. In an advanced society such as the United States, the agrarian problem ceases to be a countryside "conquest" issue. The politics of land ownership and distribution stems from the political power invested in groups or state agencies located in capital cities. More than that, the land question—unsettled ever since post-Civil War Reconstruction failed to expropriate the land of the ex-slaveholders—is now an international issue involving Africa. Black Africa, the ancestral home of the Negro, is an underpopulated continent. There may well come a time when the race question in Africa will have to be solved by admitting specified numbers of white Rhodesians, Angolans, and South African Afrikaners into the United States, in exchange for an equal number of Afro-Americans to take their places in Africa. The political side of the international land question is certainly beyond the ken of the Afro-American Nationalists. Indeed, they are far from a definitive understanding of how Afro-American Nationalism relates to domestic and international situations in any organizational, political or theoretical fashion.

· VI ·

Role of the Negro Intellectual—
Survey of the Dialogue Deferred

The peculiarities of the American social structure, and the position of the intellectual class within it, make the functional role of the Negro intellectual a special one. The Negro intellectual must deal intimately with the white power structure and cultural apparatus, and the inner realities of the black world at one and the same time. But in order to function successfully in this role, he has to be acutely aware of the nature of the American social dynamic and how it monitors the ingredients of class stratifications in American society. The American people, aside from the handful of power wielders in the upper levels, have very little social control over the economic, class, and political forces of the American capitalistic dynamic. They are, in fact, manipulated by them. Therefore the Negro intellectual must learn how one might control and channel such forces.

Since the dynamics of American society create only one integrated class stratum, "the social world or worlds of 'the intellectual' and the creative and performing artist, whether literary, musical, theatrical, or visual,"[1] the Negro intellectual has the option of gravitating toward this world, under the persuasions of the American social dynamic, and resting there on his laurels. However, although this world exists rather independently of the main ethnic worlds, it manages to reflect the social aspirations of the WASP, Catholic and Jewish groups above all others. Among these three there is intense competition for recognition and group status, which, for political and propaganda reasons, is called fighting discriminatory practices. As long as the WASPS rule the roost, charges of discrimination will never cease until Catholics or Jews

[1] Milton M. Gordon, *op. cit.*, p. 58.

achieve more power and privileges than any "minority" could ever hope for in Rome or Israel.

The Negro intellectual must not be allowed to forget that the integrated intellectual world is not representative of ethnic group aspirations with regard to the world of American Negro or Indian. The Indian world of the reservation exemplifies the fate awaiting the American Negro, who is left stranded and impoverished in the ghettoes, beyond the fringe of absorption. He will be pushed there through the compulsions of the American capitalistic dynamic if, as the most populous ethnic "out" group, the American Negro fails to galvanize his potential as a countervailing force. But the Negro group cannot act out this role by assuming the stance of separatism. The program of Afro-American Nationalism must activate a dynamism on all social fronts under the guidance and direction of the Negro intelligentsia. This already implies that Afro-American Nationalism be broken down into three parts: political nationalism; economic nationalism; and cultural nationalism; in other words, organizational specialization. Therefore the functional role of the Negro intellectual demands that he *cannot* be absolutely separated from either the black or white world.

Today, Afro-American Nationalism is not Garveyism; it poses an American problem growing out of a specific American historical condition—involving three racial stocks—the white, the black and the red. The problem will be solved under specifically American conditions or it will never be solved, for Afro-American Nationalism is basically a black reflection of the unsolved American nationality question. American culture is sick not just because it is discriminatory, but because it reflects a psychological malaise that grows out of the American identity problem. As long as the Negro intellectual is beset with his own cultural identity problem, his attacks on American culture, as discriminatory, become hollow: *Two cultural negatives cannot possibly add up to a cultural positive in society at large.* Every single American political, social and cultural trend has contributed its bit of illusion to the total Americanization fantasy. Insofar as the Negro intellectual has accommodated this grand myth, his acquiescence must be examined critically before one can dispel the myth. Then, one is on clear ground, the better to deal with the *realities* of America.

In the effort to clear this ground it has been necessary to review a whole gamut of thinking on various topics: ethnic community; multi-group America; the political leftwing; nationalism vs. integrationism; Negro creative artists as thinkers and spokesmen; aesthetics; Negroes and the theater; individual vs. group roles in society; white liberalism and Negro intellectuals; culture and integrationism; culture and nationalism; literary, dramatic and social criticism; the Negro writer as revolutionary, and so on.

Under the impetus of Negro activism, agitation has been reflected in different areas of the cultural front. The Rockefeller Report on the Performing Arts, and the White House conferences on cultural matters, are two examples. In New York, jazz magazines and critics' panel discussions are taking up such topics as "Jazz and Revolutionary Nationalism." Yet the cultural front and its relation to the Negro movement, while intuitively sensed in many critical quarters, is neither broadly understood nor admitted in any definitive way. It is the vaguest of all fronts, yet in many ways the most crucial. It is so little understood, even by Negro creative intellectuals, that its implications are absent in most of the dialogues Negroes carry on with white liberals and the intellectual establishment.

The tentative acceptance the Negro intellectual finds in the predominantly white intellectual world, allows him the illusion that integration is real—a functional reality for himself, and a possibility for *all* Negroes. Even if a Negro intellectual does not wholly believe this, he must give lip service to the aims of racial integration, if only to rationalize his own status in society.

This integrated status is not threatened or challenged; it is even championed, just so long as the black world is on the move in the struggle for integration. But when voices from the black world begin to raise doubts about the meaning, the aims, and the real possibilities of integration, the Negro intellectual is forced to question his own hard-won status. At the same time, those black Doubting Thomases begin to question the status of the Negro intellectual—"What is he doing out there?" "What is *his* function in relation to *us?*"

Such questions as these arise only because the social role of the Negro intellectual has never really been defined at all. For the most part, the Negro intellectual has been a rather free agent in the black and white scheme of things. Inasmuch as the support, patronage and prestige of the Negro intellectual come from the white world and its cultural apparatus, his creative and cultural achievements have been seen by the black world as *Ebony* magazine and *Jet* see them. That is to say, such Negroes have achieved something, they have "made it." They have scored in the white world and are now recognized. It is not necessary to consider *how* they managed to score, the important thing is that they *did*. In this way, the Negro creative intellectual has never really been held accountable to the black world for his social role. If he scores, well and good. If he doesn't, that's unfortunate, but it will pass unnoticed and no one will care. This tacit agreement between the Negro intellectual and the black world has prevailed because it is understood that the black world cannot and does not, support the Negro creative intellectual. The black bourgeoisie does not publish books, does not own and operate theaters or music halls. It plays no role to speak of in Negro music, and is remote from the living realities of the jazz musician who plays out his nights in the effete and soulless commercial jungles of American white middle-class café culture.

Add to the Negro intelligentsia who have no firm cultural base in the reality of either the black world or the white (even when they *have* achieved recognition), a large fluctuating contingent who make up the bulk of new aspirants to integrated cultural achievement. The result: a rootless class of displaced persons who are refugees from the social poverty of the black world. At one time, the black world was rich in the pristine artistic essentials for new forms in music, dance, song, theater and even language; then, the black ethnic identity was seen as a unique advantage. But today the style has become a negation of that identity, in pursuit of cultural integration or assimilation. Today the failure of the black bourgeoisie as a class, to play any social role as patron or sponsor of the arts, is all the more glaring. For now the new Negro cultural aspirants are making vocal and specified demands for integration in cultural fields where the black bourgeoisie has never paid the piper, and therefore can call no tunes.

As long as the civil rights issue remained on the non-activist level of the NAACP's gradualist legalism, this state of cultural affairs remained static. But in the years right after World War II, the outlines of new factors were already clearly, visibly, coming on the scene. All at once—in a manner of speaking—a new level of protest activity, a new nationalism and a new Africa consciousness converged to transform the content and quality of black and white relations into something never before seen. Today there are questions in the air that demand new solutions. The old stock answers that were once carted in to describe the meaning of old-time Americanism no longer suffice to satisfy the new mood. African emergence now begins to raise anew the question of black identity in America. New nationalists begin to call into question the whole concept of racial integration. On the other hand, the drive for racial integration begins to encounter serious resistance and hidden barriers, located deep in the living fabric of the social structure. There is violence and rumors of more violence to come. Sure enough, this situation brings to the fore the timorous voices of the Negro creative intellectual stratum—the Baldwins, *et al.* Never before held so accountable to the black world, they are now sorely frightened by the temper of the times. Their hard-won integrated status in America (and even abroad) seems shaky and precarious. They now become interpreters for the black world to the white—a new role for them. But this new dialogue between the black and white intelligentsia somehow sounds flat and unconvincing to the ear. While Negro intellectuals are busy trying to interpret the nature of the black world and its aspirations to the whites, they should, in fact, be defining their own roles as intellectuals within *both* worlds.

The special function of the Negro intellectual is a cultural one. He should take to the rostrum and assail the stultifying blight of the commercially depraved white middle-class who has poisoned the structural roots of the American ethos and transformed the American people into a nation of intellectual dolts. He should explain the economic and institutional causes of this American cultural depravity. He should tell black America how and why Negroes are trapped in this cultural degeneracy, and how it has dehumanized their essential identity, squeezed the lifeblood of their inherited cultural ingredients out of them, and then relegated them to the cultural slums. They should tell this brainwashed white America, this "nation of sheep," this overfed, over-developed, overprivileged (but culturally pauperized) federation of unassimilated European remnants that their days of grace are numbered. This motley, supercilious collection of refugees from "Fatherland" poverty worships daily, and only, at the altar of white Anglo-Saxon Protestant superiority. Notwithstanding their alleged vows to contribute to the fashioning of an American nation worthy of the high esteem of the rest of the world, so far they have reneged. The job has hardly been begun. America is an unfinished nation—the product of a badly-bungled process of inter-group cultural fusion. America is a nation that lies to itself about who and what it is. It is a nation of minorities ruled by a minority of one—it thinks and acts as if it were a nation of white Anglo-Saxon Protestants. This white Anglo-Saxon ideal, this lofty dream of a minority at the summit of its economic and political power and the height of its historical self-delusions, has led this nation to the brink of self-destruction. And on its way, it has effectively dissuaded, crippled and smothered the cultivation of a democratic cultural pluralism in America.

The cultural mainstream of the nation is an empty street, full of bright lights that try to glamorize the cultural wreckage and flotsam of our times. Over this deranged, tormented cultural wasteland reigns a social stratum—a white cultural elite of America, the soured cream of our creative and aesthetic intelligentsia, that dominates nevertheless to the roar of prestigious acclaim. This elite has become intellectually bloated, dull, unoriginal, critically tongue-tied, smug (or downright scared), time-serving and societally dishonest. It came into existence during the 1920's, and by constantly renewing its ranks, has established and maintained its position as the supreme arbiter of American cultural styles. It has dominated the cultural arts, in all of their native trends, in every conceivable field. Even during its years of highest achievements, this elite was always, by outside standards, very second-rate and it has been steadily declining in creative virtuosity over the decades. And during all these years of gradual descent from its own Parnassus, it worshipped at the altar of the white Anglo-Saxon ideal. Thereby, it collaborated spiritually in spreading the pall of debased and unprocreative white middle-class cultural values that shroud America today.

In other words, the prognoses and prophecies about American cultural trends, written by Randolph Bourne in his critical essays of 1920, have been borne out in the forty-seven years since. Bourne warned against the stultifying and retarding effects that the idealization of the Anglo-Saxon tradition would have on the reality of American pluralism if that tradition became the main source of the "cultural makers of opinion." He argued truthfully and convincingly about the failures of the American melting-pot ideology and the presence in America of "diverse nationalistic feelings," of "vigorous nationalistic and cultural movements." He called English-American conservatism "our chief obstacle to social advance," and argued for the cultivation of a kind of culturally "federated ideal" as the main social hope of America.[2] But this cultural ideal has never taken form or even been approached in this country, making it necessary for sociologists such as Milton Gordon to survey the problem again with the advent of the Negro integration movement.

For American society, the most crucial requirement at this point is a complete democratization of the national cultural ethos. This requires a thorough, democratic overhauling of the social functions of the entire American cultural apparatus. First of all: For whom, and in whose interest, does the cultural apparatus exist in America? Does it exist for the social needs, the social edification, the spiritual uplift, the cultural development, solvency and morale of all the diverse minority groups in America? Or does it exist solely, and disproportionately, for the social supremacy, the group narcissism, and the idealization of the white Anglo-Saxon Protestant minority? Up to now, the latter has been true, just as it was in 1920 when Bourne, himself an Anglo-Saxon, decried the supremacy of the "Anglo-Saxon tradition which [they] unquestioningly label 'American.'"[3] However, the total schematic value of this Anglo-Saxon tradition is deeply entwined with the roots of the political, economic, and societal foundations of the American national structure; it, in turn, inspires ideologies of racial and ethnic exclusion, discrimination and exploitation. On this social level the Negro integration movement conducts its legal and activist struggles. Hence, through this strategy of struggle, the Negro move-

[2] See Randolph Bourne's *History of a Literary Radical and Other Essays* (New York: B.W. Huebsch, 1920); especially the essay, "Trans-National America," pp. 266-299.

[3] *Ibid.,* p. 266.

ment challenges Anglo-Saxon Protestant social supremacy in economics, politics and social life, but only indirectly and in the name of true democratic Americanism between the races—an unconscious, ignorant tactical error.

American group reality demands a struggle for democracy among ethnic groups, rather than between two races. What is called a racial struggle over civil rights is, in reality, the contention in America among several different ethnic groups, of which Anglo-Saxon Protestants and American Negroes are only two. However, among all the groups in contention these two are the most crucial: The fate of all the others depends on how they resolve the undemocratic differences in American society. Moreover, since no other ethnic minority in America is so thoroughly committed to racial democratization, the Negro group's civil rights engagement is, plainly, the most active force for social change. However, it is evident that if the Negro leadership is hampered by deficient conceptualizing of American group reality, then the Negro movement will defeat itself in the long run. It will defeat itself by encouraging other unassimilated ethnic groups to turn against the Negro minority, in a pro-Anglo-Saxon Protestant "racial" coalition. It will defeat itself by utilizing mechanical, narrow-minded agitational tactics that will discourage other unassimilated ethnic groups from assuming a pro-Negro attitude in the furtherance of their own group cultural rights. The Congress of Racial Equality (CORE) has been most guilty of such tactics in the North, for example, where it indiscriminately carries demonstrations into ethnic neighborhoods without giving due consideration to local neighborhood sentiments. This approach, however, stems out of the dominant NAACP ideology which does not sanction the reality of neighborhood group sentiments. This is yet another reason why the tactics of civil righters cannot be the same in the North as in the South. For the South is, specifically, the main bastion of the efficacy of the dominant Anglo-Saxon ideal. There, its dominance, *vis-à-vis* the Negro, is most naked and persuasive. All of these factors, and more, demand that the Negro movement adjust its strategy to fit reality, which means deepening its understanding and broadening its scope at the same time. But such an eventuality requires much educational groundwork, for here, where the role of the Negro creative intellectual is most crucial, it is most conspicuous by its functional absence.

Around 1960, a significant debate sprang up among the white intellectuals of the non-Communist Left, concerning the current relevancy of practically every dogma the Communist-oriented Left had preached since the 1930's. This debate was high-level and thoroughgoing, and nothing comparable to it has yet taken place within Negro intellectual circles. The leading inspiration of this debate was the late C. Wright Mills, professor of sociology at Columbia University, who initiated a critical review of the entire Marxist revolutionary tradition of this century, especially in Europe and the United States. The grassroots impetus behind this rather spontaneous review of the Marxist tradition was, of course, the upsurge of student sit-ins in the new Negro movement, but only a few of the critics said so. The curious thing about this debate was that not a single Negro sociologist, historian, writer, spokesman, leader (ex-Communist, pro-Communist or anti-Communist), took part in it. This, despite the fact that the only movement active at that moment on the American scene with any pretensions of radical potential, was the Negro movement. Nothing could point up more graphically the fact that the Negro intellectual does not rate as a serious thinker in the intellectual establishment. As things turned out, this debate brought out two main antagonists among the whites—Mills and Professor Daniel Bell, also of Columbia. Mills outdid all of his colleagues in critical dissent because he not only assailed the liberal establishment, but also called into question many of the sacred shibboleths of the established radical Left. Mills did not attack the Marxist philosophy as such, but left the door open for modern Marxism to render itself relevant to our contemporary issues. In fact, he went even further than that—he attempted to lay the foundations, with a new method, for a new radical criticism of American society.

As theoretical rationalizer for the decline and irrelevancy of the radical Left, Daniel Bell laid out his thinking in a lengthy tome entitled *The End of Ideology—Or the Exhaustion of Political Ideas in the Fifties.* He summed up his critique in his last chapter with the following observations:

> Today, [these] ideologies are exhausted. The events behind this important sociological change are complex and varied . . . such social changes as the modification of capitalism, the rise of the Welfare States [are causes]. This is not to say that such ideologies as communism in France and Italy do not have a polit-

ical weight, or a driving momentum from other sources. But out of all this history one simple fact emerges for the radical intelligentsia, the old ideologies have lost their "truth" and their power to persuade.

Few serious minds believe any longer that one can set down "blueprints" and through "social engineering" bring about a new utopia of social harmony. . . . In the Western world, therefore, there is today a rough consensus among intellectuals on political issues: the acceptance of a Welfare State, the desirability of decentralized power; a system of mixed economy and of political pluralism. In that sense, too, the ideological age has ended.[4]

Given the premises—historical, sociological,·and theoretical—on which he bases his conclusions, Bell is right. However, Bell's premises are invalidated because he does not base them on the complete objective picture. His book, including text and notes, amounts to 397 pages: There is not a single page devoted to any phase of the Negro movement, past or present. Negroes are mentioned four times, in very brief references to Negro voting habits, the class nature of race prejudice, Negro society, and crime waves. It seems almost incredible that in the face of a social movement of such dimensions that some people even call it a revolution, a sociologist could write such a book and not even mention the existence of this movement or its impact. What does one conclude from this? Evidently, Bell does not consider Negroes as an integral sociological quantity within Western society. Hence, being outside the Western pale, Negroes could not possibly have anything to do with the "exhaustion of political ideas in the fifties"—which just happened to be the very decade when Negroes became most insistent on being integrated within Western society.

If at this stressful moment in American history, Professor Bell could write off the 1950's as the decade of "the end of ideology," the question naturally follows: Whose ideology? Bell was talking about his own, a radical ideology that came out of the Western tradition. Since for Bell there is not the slightest possibility that anything could replace this "exhausted" ideology, the black social movement is not even worth mentioning inasmuch as the welfare

[4] Bell, *The End of Ideology* . . . (Free Press of Glencoe, Illinois, 1960), p. 373. Used by permission of The Macmillan Company and Princeton University Press (for Dr. Bell's quote from *Socialism and American Life,* D.D. Egbert and S. Persons, eds., Princeton University Press, 1952).

state will ultimately subdue it. Or could it be that Bell was frightened and nonplussed by the implications of a movement whose
ends *his* ideology cannot accommodate?

However, C. Wright Mills took serious issue with Daniel Bell
and others of the "end-of-ideology" school of thought, which Mills
discovered through his travels to exist not only in Columbia University, U.S.A., but in the NATO nations (as well as in the Soviet
Union, which is not officially a NATO nation). Mills wrote:

> I neither want nor need to overstress the parallel, yet in a
> recent series of interviews in the Soviet Union concerning socialist
> realism [*N.B.*] I was very much struck by it. In Uzbekistan and
> Georgia as well as in Russia, I kept writing notes to myself, at the
> end of recorded interviews: "This man talks in a style just like
> Arthur Schlesinger, Jr." "Surely this fellow's the counterpart of
> Daniel Bell, except not so—what shall I say?—so gossipy. . . . The
> would-be enders of ideology, I kept thinking, "Are they not the
> self-coordinated, or better the fashion-coordinated, socialist real-
> ists of the NATO world?" And: "Check this carefully with the files
> of *Encounter* and *The Reporter.*" I have now done so; it's the
> same kind of . . . thing.

Mills further observes:

> The end-of-ideology is very largely a mechanical reaction—not
> a creative response—to the ideology of Stalinism. As such it takes
> from its opponent something of its inner quality. What does it all
> mean? That these people have become aware of the uselessness of
> Vulgar Marxism, but not yet aware of the uselessness of the
> liberal rhetoric.

Hence:

> The end-of-ideology is on the way out because it stands for the
> refusal to work out an explicit political philosophy.[5]

In this article, from which the above are salient quotations,
Mills was addressing what was then called "the New Left." He
continued:

> But enough. Where do *we* stand on . . . these . . . aspects of
> political philosophy? . . . As for the articulation of ideals: there I

[5] "The New Left," *Power, Politics and People: The Collected Essays of C. Wright Mills*, edited by Irving L. Horowitz (New York: Ballantine Books, 1963), pp. 247-259.
(Published simultaneously in hardcovers by Oxford University Press, New York.
Used by permission of Oxford University Press.)

think your magazines [*New Left Review,* etc.] have done their best work so far. That is *your* meaning—is it not?—*of the empha-sis on cultural affairs. As for ideological analysis, and the rhetoric with which to carry it out: I don't think any of us are nearly good enough but that will come with further advance on the two fronts where we are weakest: theories of society, history, human nature; and the major problem—ideas about the historical agencies of structural change* [italics added].

Here Mills effectively destroys the conceptual premises of Daniel Bell's end-of-ideology school, but with the social awareness that such a challenge presents formidable problems of new social methods. In pursuit of the creation and formulation of such methods, Mills emphasizes that to be Left (wherever Left stands, ideologically, to the "left" of Right) means: "To connect up cultural with political criticism, and both with demands and programmes."

Note Mills' specific emphasis here on "cultural." The term culture has always been held in very vague and ambiguous disesteem in America. In Germany, one of Hitler's gauleiters once made himself famous by stating: "When I hear the word 'culture,' I reach for my gun." In America, however, when people hear the word culture, many of them respond with blank faces or wry grimaces, while the more practical revolutionists fail to see culture as a bread-and-butter, class-warfare issue. Hence, Mills had to advise:

Absence of public issues there may well be, but this is not due to any absence of problems or of contradictions, antagonistic and otherwise. Impersonal and structural changes have not elimi-nated problems or issues. Their absence from many discussions— that *is* an ideological condition, regulated in the first place by whether or not intellectuals detect and state problems as poten-tial *issues* for probable publics, and as *troubles* for a variety of individuals. One indispensable means of such work on these cen-tral tasks is what can only be described as ideological analysis.

From here Mills proceeded to the results of his own "analysis":

It is with this problem of agency in mind that I have been studying, for several years now, the *cultural apparatus,* the intel-lectuals—as a possible, immediate, radical agency of change. For a long time, I was not much happier with this idea than were many of you; but it turns out now, in the spring of 1960, that *it may be a very relevant idea indeed* [italics added].

He cautioned, however:

The problem of the intelligentsia is an extremely complicated set of problems on which rather little factual work has been done. In doing this work, we must—above all—not confuse the problems of the intellectuals of West Europe and North America with those of the Soviet Bloc or with those of the underdeveloped worlds. In each of the three major components of the world's social structure today, *the character and the role of the intelligentsia is distinct and historically specific* [italics added].

Then Mills sums up:

That's why we've got to study these new generations of intellectuals around the world as real live agencies of historic change. Forget Victorian Marxism except whenever you need it. . . .
"But it's just some kind of moral upsurge, isn't it?" Correct. But under it: no apathy. Much of it is direct non-violent action, and it seems to be working, here and there. Now we must learn from their practice and work out with them new forms of action.
"But it's all so ambiguous. Turkey, for instance. Cuba, for instance." Of course it is; *history-making is always ambiguous;* wait a bit; in the meantime, *help* them to focus their moral upsurge in less ambiguous political ways; work out with them the ideologies, the strategies, the theories that will help them consolidate their efforts: new theories of structural changes of and by human societies in our epoch [italics added].[6]

Now, from the analyses of C. Wright Mills, the hidden roots of the American radical phenomenon come into clearer focus. In disposing of Daniel Bell's end-of-ideology thesis as *an ideological problem in itself,* Mills abstracts a new class theory that pinpoints the locus of the American crisis in the intellectual stratum. But here we must say that Mills' analysis did not and could not go far enough, because, like Bell, he was speaking only from the white side of the American crisis. (Charles Silberman correctly termed it a *Crisis in Black and White.*) Mills' class analysis must be extended to include the role and the plight of the Negro intellectual stratum within the larger intellectual subsociety. It is a special class with its own group problems, *i.e.,* a class with its own "potential issues for probable publics, and as troubles for a variety of individuals," as Mills put it. However, the Negro intellectuals have never really exerted themselves and gotten fully involved in the ideological fracas—they only think they have. To the Negro intellectual elite, cultural issues represent no political problems for the black masses and have little connection, if any, with their troubles.

It was precisely the issue of cultural radicalism in the Mills-Bell controversy with which Negro creative intellectuals should have been involved. For in America, cultural radicalism is not so much a question of the controversial *content* expressed in art forms, as it is a question of what methods of social change are necessary to achieve freedom of expression within a national culture whose aesthetic has been cultivated by a single, dominant, ethnic group. This problem, however, was passed over by Daniel Bell and others in an extremely superficial fashion:

> The pages of *Dissent* and *Universities* and *New Left Review* are full of attacks against advertising, the debaucheries of mass culture, and the like. And, often, phrasing these criticisms in the language of the early Marx, particularly in terms of alienation, gives these attacks a seeming political content. But the point is that these problems are essentially cultural and not political.
>
> . . . and the problem of radical thought today is to reconsider the relationship of culture to society. Certainly few persons will assume the relationships of culture to politics to be as direct as Marxist critics assumed them to be twenty-five years ago. And when, with the lesson of totalitarianism and bureaucracy in mind, one comes to accept—in the mixed economy and political pluralism—moderation in social politics, *specifying the content of "cultural radicalism" becomes even more difficult* [italics added].[7]

Mills was clearly on the way toward "specifying this content" in his preoccupation with the intellectuals and the cultural apparatus. But Daniel Bell's sociological insights had not even an objective glimmer of such an attempt. In fact, Bell does not want the question answered at all. Never have I read a sociologist whose mind grasped so much data but whose eyes could look past so much objective reality—*e.g.*, the Negro movement. One is forced to suspect that there is a method to Bell's blindness.

[7] Bell, *op. cit.*, p. 299.

Bell writes that if certain radicals had a "single unifying idea," it is the "conceptualization of America as a *mass society,* and its attack on the grotesque elements of such a society." But immediately he demurs: "The concept of the *mass society,* however, has a peculiar amorphousness. Those who used the older vocabulary of radicalism could attack the capitalists or even the bourgeoisie, but in the *mass society* one simply flails out against the culture, and it is hard to discover who, or what, is the enemy."

However, he understands quite well that some decades past, another school of writers, including Karl Jaspers, T.S. Eliot, and José Ortega y Gasset, had other attitudes on mass culture: "They have had an aristocratic, or Catholic, or elite conception of culture, and for them the standards of taste and excellence, once set by the educated and the cultivated, have been torn down by the mass. They stood against equalitarianism and industrial society. In effect, they did not want to give the masses cultural voting rights."[8]

All of this is true, but T.S. Eliot, for example, did not exile himself to England because his cultural views were really challenged by true mass cultural democratization; he left because his aristocratic group culture was manifestly empty, moribund, non-regenerative—thriving only by virtue of its past accomplishments in Western society. When the branches and the leaves of the plant shrivel up and die, one's only hope is to try to save the roots—hence, Eliot went to England. What really bothered Eliot in America was that the cultural status of his ethnic group was wide open for invasion by other culturally impure ethnic groups, such as niggers, Jews, wops, Polacks and bohunks. The threat was not mass cultural democracy, but intergroup cultural competition and ideological warfare on the cultural front, disguised under the cloak of a variety of taxing issues: literary and art criticism; literary cliques; art vs. politics; the struggle between Negro and white jazz music for cultural supremacy; the patronization of newly-discovered Negro exoticism in music, dance, and theater; the simultaneous plunder of Negro music; the expatriate movement; plus other cultural vices, vanities and vicissitudes too numerous to recount here. T.S. Eliot was too much the aristocratic gentleman to be involved in much of what went on in America during the

[8] *Ibid.,* p. 298.

1920's, but his cultural compeers stayed behind to carry out their rule-or-ruin cultural policies with a premeditated vengeance. Today, in America, we are suffering from the consequences of these developments. Hence, Daniel Bell is right when he points out that the young radical cannot adopt the stance of an Eliot on cultural problems today. However, they encounter another problem:

> The parodox is that whatever is deemed radical in culture is quickly accepted, and whatever calls itself avant-garde, be it abstract expressionism or Beatnik poetry, is quickly acclaimed. When the products of high culture, from Schoenberg to Matisse . . . become best-selling cultural items, the problem of locating the source of the "corruption" of standards becomes a difficult one. The acceptance of the avant-garde has become so vexing that Hilton Kramer [an editor of *Arts*] . . . was moved to say, "The fact of the matter is that since 1945, bourgeois society has tightened its grip on all the arts by allowing them a freer rein."[9]

A "freer rein?" But how true is this? In the face of this free rein all that is grotesque, sick and corrupting in American culture persists. This is because what is called cultural radicalism is not truly radical, while what is called avant-garde, has only to do with *content* in art. "Bourgeois society" (or what I prefer to call the white cultural elite) can absorb any avant-garde content expression in art because the bourgeoisie themselves are not creating anything original. Hence, even a LeRoi Jones can be absorbed and tolerated, for the sake of being abused as a threat. The cultural status quo, then, is not challenged by any new trend in art that is termed radical or avant-garde solely on the basis of content alone. No literary or cultural movement today can be truly and effectively radical unless it presents a definitive critique of the entire cultural apparatus of America. More, it must analyze the functions of art and artists, creators and audiences, sellers and consumers, critics and group standards—or better yet—the politics of culture as expressed within the context of American intergroup status and relations in the cultural arts.

For me, the emergence of C. Wright Mills, with his critique of the policies, dogmas and vanities of the old Marxist leftwing, was a

[9] *Ibid.*, p. 298.

landmark in American social theory. That Mills was a white man did not at all negate my own personal thesis that the American Negro was destined to become the vanguard social force in the revolutionizing of American society. On the contrary, the views of Mills served to corroborate a long-range strategic issue in the Negro movement, one that becomes more and more urgent as time passes. This issue involves the necessity of the Negro movement having white allies, as well as the aims, ideology and quality of such allies. It is to be noted, again, that when Mills ruled out the white laboring classes as having no radical potential, he theoretically eliminated the sole class basis on which Marxist Communism of all brands could maintain any effective links with the Negro movement. This was the chief reason why the Marxist theorists could not agree with Mills' findings. But Mills was trying to deal with American social peculiarities as they really are, and although they cannot admit this to themselves, the Marxists' historical model is European society.

These American peculiarities pose acute problems for the Negro movement, particularly for the Afro-American Nationalists, whose strong anti-white stance tends to rule out any functional alliance with whites. Although this aversion to any white alliance is perfectly understandable, in view of the long-standing disabilities and disorientation imposed on Negroes by the institution of political interracialism, the Afro-American Nationalists cannot, in the long run, continue to oppose white alliances. The question will be—the specific type and quality of the alliances. The quality will depend on the quality of the goals, but it is the Negro movement itself that must select these goals. Without specified goals plotted on the political, economic, and cultural fronts, the nationalist wing will wither away in isolation to be swamped by the aggressive American capitalistic dynamic. But these goals must be stated unequivocally by the nationalist wing and controlled by it on its own behalf, inasmuch as no other faction—black or white—can do it for them. This is the imperative of the Negro social dynamic.

The C. Wright Mills thesis contained the seeds of a Negro-White alliance of a new type, to be anchored first around the structural question of the American cultural apparatus. But not a single one of the leading Negro intellectual spokesmen saw this implication. In view of the deeply-rooted American tradition of

Anglo-Saxon anti-theoretical, anti-cultural, anti-aesthetic pragmatism and instrumentalism, C. Wright Mills was decidedly revolutionary, although isolated by the very conservative tradition that
produced him. (He himself was Anglo-Saxon and a Southerner at
that.) The problem here is that the nature of the American ethnic
group composition—the white, black and red racial heritage—
demands that each group produce for itself a *native* radical-
intellectual trend, which trends should complement one another,
so to speak. At least, the black and white groups must do this.
Since the whites are divided into ethnic and religious subdivisions,
with the Anglo-Saxons as the dominant and representative group,
the Anglo-Saxon group must produce its representative radical-
intellectual trend; or else social progress in American will be ethnically retarded, if not checkmated.

But the Anglo-Saxons and their Protestant ethic have failed in
their creative and intellectual responsibilities to the internal
American commonweal. Interested purely in materialistic pursuits
—exploiting resources, the politics of profit and loss, ruling the
world, waging war, and protecting a rather threadbare cultural
heritage—the Anglo-Saxons have retrogressed in the cultural fields
and the humanities. Into this intellectual vacuum have stepped
the Jews, to dominate scholarship, history, social research, etc.[10]
But Negro intellectuals function oblivious to the impact of these
developments while protesting loudly about civil rights and freedom. In the face of new trends, new voices, new issues, the content
of Negro intellectual opinion never varies, never changes. Negro
intellectuals are moved by the world, but they hardly move *with*
the world.

If the Negro intellectuals of the 1920's missed out on the debate
between V. F. Calverton and the Communist Left on cultural
compulsives, their spiritual progeny of the 1950's were also deaf
to the debate between Mills, Bell and various leftwing diehards,
on cultural radicalism. These two debates, although thirty years
apart, are of course related historically, if only one would see it.
And in the same way that Langston Hughes and company stood by

[10] See "Zionist Influence on American Higher Education," *Issues*, Autumn, 1965,
pp. 1-9.

during the Negro renaissance while the white Communist theoreticians beat down Calverton, the Negro creative intellectuals of the 1950's committed a breach of critical awareness.

No sooner had C. Wright Mills begun to emerge as a creative and original radical spokesman for the New Left, than the two main theoretical spokesmen of the official Marxist movement—Herbert Aptheker of the Communist Party and William F. Warde of the Socialist Workers' Party—took to the rostrum. Aptheker criticized Mills's findings in *The World of C. Wright Mills*[11] and Warde followed suit in an article entitled "A Marxist Analysis of C. Wright Mills."[12]

Herbert Aptheker, the Marxist-Communist historian, has played a very influential and specific role in the fashioning of the Communist Party's Negro intellectual and creative elite. The entire postwar generation of Communists of the 1940's and 1950's was educated on Negro history chiefly through his writings. He became *the* authority on what it meant to be Negro in America, both historically and contemporaneously. This situation raised some very serious and delicate questions concerning the problems of racial and ethnic identity and the historical ingredients that go into the formation of the Black American personality.

For no sooner was Aptheker elevated to the rank of official Marxist spokesman on Negro history, than practically the entire corps of Negro Marxist bureaucrats and intellectuals were dutybound to pay political and theoretical homage to a man, a leader in radical thought, who, besides being white and a member of another minority, was also the possessor of distinctly second-rate theoretical equipment. Around Herbert Aptheker was built up a cult of worship as supinely uncritical as it was politically and theoretically deadening. It was the essential force of Communist dogma and organizational experience, applied to a dormant field, that wafted Aptheker to political stardom. If it were not for the fact that Negro historiography has always languished in the attics (or in the basements) of scholarship, for want of financial backing or institutional support, a man of his limited talents would not have had such a rich, untended field from which to reap such an undeserved harvest.

[11] *Aptheker* (New York: Marzani and Munsell, 1960).
[12] Warde, *International Socialist Review*, Summer, 1962, pp. 67-75, 95.

Aptheker's *Marxist* Negro historiography was supposed to be something special—unlike the more *Negro* historiography of Carter G. Woodson, W.E.B. DuBois, E. Frankiln Frazier, or John Hope Franklin. Aptheker is simply a hard-working, plodding historian and researcher whose Marxism is purely incidental; what he has achieved with Negro historical materials could just as well have been achieved by anyone else without the Marxist veneer—given the mótivation and the resources. Nonetheless, by virtue of being a trained scholar, he widened the path that had already been prepared by James S. Allen to possible Communist Party dominance in the field of Negro historiography. More than that, his ascendancy placed theoretical leftwing control, of both the historical research and the interpretation of the Negro question, completely in Jewish hands. Here was another side of the process of the "Judaizing of Communism" (mentioned by Melech Epstein and cited earlier in this study). In fact it reflected the aggressiveness of Jewish scholarship in history and research to an extent that prompted a rabbi at a meeting of the Theodore Herzl Institute to remark that American Jews no longer represent a "problem" but are now the leading "problem solvers" of everybody else's minority problems on the American scene. But here, as well, is a result of the default of the Negro intellectual. For we live in an age where many of those who speak loudest about how deeply they wish to see the Negro emancipated from capitalist bondage, can also conspire to keep the Negro eating out of their hands—simply by maintaining the grip of intellectual subservience and tutelage indefinitely.

For over twenty-five years Aptheker thought he had all the answers about Negroes past and present, and turned out nine pamphlets and books on Negro history. But in 1965, he said to an Associated Press correspondent, concerning the Communist Party: "We are less naïve than in the past. We tended to minimize the difficulties of building socialism, of the problems of power and the approach to religion and nationalism . . . we have had to learn the perils of dogma, of not growing."[13]

Nationalism! How ironic . . . for here is a historian who simply

[13] From a Saul Pett by-line, Associated Press correspondent. *Progress-Index*, Petersburg, Virginia, December 24, 1965, p. 10.

refused to accept history at its face value, who rewrote it to suit his own preconceptions. This violates every methodological tenet of the historian—Marxist or otherwise. Thus, the scholar-on-high minimized what everyone among the rank and file knew. Yet he rushed to the fore to answer C. Wright Mills, on everything from politics, culture, economics to, of course, "The Negro."

Although hardly any of the Negroes in the creative fields were aware that Mills had said anything of any import Aptheker was sufficiently impressed to answer Mills by writing one of his longest pamphlets. *The World of C. Wright Mills* reveals Aptheker's appalling ignorance of the cultural facts of life in America, the very area in which Mills excels. Aptheker could not deal with Mills' ideas about the intellectuals and the cultural apparatus. Instead, he accused Mills of turning to what he, Aptheker, calls "unreal and utopian political devices—such as appeals confined to the intelligentsia." Trotskyist William F. Warde agreed with Aptheker that Mills was wrong on the intelligentsia: "He founds his hopes for peace, freedom and progress, not on the victory of the working masses over the plutocracy, but rather on the benign influences to be exerted by scholars, ministers, scientists and writers, the peripheral and not the central forces of our society."[14]

Both Aptheker and Warde were also critical of Mills' attitude toward the Negro struggle. Says Aptheker: "His blindspot concerning the whole matter of the Negro, which impairs his analysis generally, is especially glaring." Says Warde: "Mills seemed to look upon the Negro movement as something essentially separate from the general labor struggle."[15]

These two Marxists, although both political and tactical opponents, approach Mills from *a priori* premises laid down in classical Marxism. These premises become their crutches, their sanctums of established creed. Although they both use the Negro question, in order to find weak spots in Mill's argument, it is their Marxist creed they are defending, not the Negro movement, for Mills had very aptly ridiculed the Marxist dogma about the workingclass as a "labor metaphysic." Aptheker, true to his Communist training and Jewish middle-class background, has been conditioned to a

[14] Warde, *International Socialist Review, op. cit.,* p. 73.
[15] *Ibid.,* p. 74.

peculiar type of catechism about the workers, a class he knows very little about. Thus his talk about workers is theoretical rote. The Trotskyists, however, are much more astute and resilient than the Communists. Hence, in Warde, they have a Marxist mind of far more depth and penetration than that of Aptheker.

Warde is a master of Marxist exegesis—probably the best in America. He sticks to the pithy essentials of theoretical problems. Thus, in his short debate with Mills, he more thoroughly illuminates Marxist tenets, but reveals, at the same time, why a Mills could not accept many of these tenets for American conditions. Mills would not discuss the implications of the Negro movement to any great degree, possibly because he was not prepared to. Warde criticizes this failure by claiming that the Negro movement "is an integral part of the conflict of American labor against the established order,"[16] a statement that is patently untrue. A Marxist has to say this, in order to square his class-struggle theories with the facts of life; but it blinds him to other realities, especially realities about the very Negro movement over which Warde and Mills are at odds.

Neither Warde nor Aptheker understand that, in criticizing Mills's proccupation with the intellectuals, they are ignoring the one great weakness of the Negro movement. The Negro movement is at an impasse precisely because it lacks a real functional corps of intellectuals able to confront and deal perceptively with American realities on a level that social conditions demand. But here the Marxists are simply bunching Negro intellectuals with white intellectuals, in general and as a class. Warde reveals the class narrowness of the Marxian creed in America when he relegates intellectuals to the periphery of society. But who was Karl Marx in his day but a free-floating intellectual and a member of the periphery of his times? What types of personalities were those associates of the young Marx who called themselves "Young Hegelians"? Who were they but young writers, students, philosophers, critics, rebels and assorted non-conformists? "We've got to study these new generations of intellectuals around the world . . ." said Mills, and "work out with them the ideologies . . . the theories . . . of structural changes." Warde and Aptheker would object because

[16] *Ibid.*, p. 74.

such are not central forces. Aptheker, and Marxists of his type, should in fact be the last ones to uphold this class dogma. They do not derive from the central working class themselves, but have risen to the position of high potentates of revolutionary class virtue. Therefore, we must assume that either such leaders are dishonest about crediting class factors, or that the working class is destined to make revolutions which, as a class, it is incapable of running from seats of power. What can one say of a Marxist creed that refuses to acknowledge the true authorship of active movements? William F. Warde went even further, willfully distorting living fact: "Radicalized intellectuals are particularly prone to swing faster and further to the left or to the right. . . . The initiatives of *radical intellectuals,* militant students, *oppressed minorities* [italics added] and insurrectionary peasants often serve to stimulate action by the proletariat.[17]

Here we have open, unadulterated class bias. It is the American proletariat who is more amenable to turning "right" today. Ask any Negro how much sympathy white workers have with his cause. But in addition, Warde betrays his real attitude toward the Negro as an oppressed minority: To him, the Negro movement, even though active rather than "peripheral," like "radicalized intellectuals," is merely secondary to the "action by the proletariat" which must be stimulated in due time. Here, explicitly, is the theoretical dead end of American Marxism which prevents the creed from adjusting to realities. Confounded by three problems—the Negro movement, the intellectuals, and the proletariat—Marxists cannot reconcile them without drastic alterations in their theoretical schema, which they are loath to make.

C. Wright Mills was well on the road to solving the dilemma for them—but from the white side of the intellectual class divide. He pretended not to see Negro intellectuals (which was not difficult since they were saying and doing little beside repeating civil rights slogans after the civil rights politicians). But they represented the missing elements in the class role that C. Wright Mills tried to project for the intellectuals in his aim "to connect up cultural with political criticism, and both with demands and programmes."

[17] "Who Will Change the World?" *International Socialist Review,* Summer, 1961, p. 72.

He was not sure how he would achieve this and admitted as much. But historically, the tasks of the intellectuals in America today resemble those of the young Marx's generation in Europe of the 1840's that had to fashion a new political philosophy for the European scene of their time. C. Wright Mills was simply saying that the young intellectuals of America have to do the same thing for their own country, and that *we* must help them do it. But the Marxists of today cannot admit that they are of nineteenth-century vintage and therefore, "old hat."

When C. Wright Mills delved into the problem of the cultural apparatus he knew whereof he spoke. The nineteenth-century revolutionaries dealt with nineteenth-century capitalism, but a capitalism without the cultural apparatus that has grown up as an integral part of American capitalism today. Nineteenth-century capitalists might have controlled the press, but they did not have radio, television, film industries, advertising combines, electronic recording and computer industries, highly developed telecommunications networks, and so forth. Nineteenth-century capitalism was an industrial system without the twentieth-century trappings of the new industry—mass cultural communications, a new and unprecedented capitalistic refinement of unheard-of social ramifications. Marx never had to deal with this monster of capitalist accumulation. Mass cultural communications is a basic industry, as basic as oil, steel, and transportation, in its own way. Developing along with it, supporting it, and subservient to it, is an organized network of functions that are creative, administrative, propagandistic, educational, recreational, political, artistic, economic and cultural. Taken as a whole this enterprise involves what Mills called the *cultural apparatus.* Only the blind cannot see that whoever controls the cultural apparatus—whatever class, power group, faction or political combine—also controls the destiny of the United States and everything in it.

The arguments of C. Wright Mills on the cultural apparatus were incomplete and irresolute because the Negro creative intellectuals were not involved in the debate. They did not participate because they were not prepared to debate cultural issues on this level. It is a reflection of the general intellectual backwardness of Negro thought that the Negro movement has failed, so far, to deal with structural problems pertaining to American society.

Even at this advanced stage in Negro history, the Negro intellectual is a retarded child whose thinking processes are still geared to piddling intellectual civil writism and racial integrationism. This is all he knows. In the meantime, he plays second and third fiddle to white intellectuals in all the establishments—Left, Center, and Right. The white intellectuals in these establishments do not recognize the Negro intellectual as a man who can speak both for himself and for the best interests of the nation, but only as someone who must be spoken for and on behalf of. But the present impasse of the Negro movement demands that the black and white dialogue must transcend this level of mere evasive debate if the Negro movement is to avoid defeat and racial stalemate in the United States. For the Negro creative intellectual, the watchword is this: There can be no real black revolution in the United States without cultural revolution as a corollary to the scheme of "agencies for social change." If, as Gilbert Seldes said, "the cultural institutions of a country belong to its inhabitants," the only inhabitants who will return those institutions to the people are those with the greatest conviction that this has to be done for the good of the nation and, therefore, have the most potential for carrying it out.

Negroes and Jews—
The Two Nationalisms
and the Bloc(ked) Plurality

Throughout this critique we have referred repeatedly to Jews and Negro-Jewish relations. If this shocks or offends certain readers, they might note that the Jewish press deals with these inter-minority group imperatives much more often than the diffident Negro press would ever dare to. For example, *Commentary*, the leading organ of Jewish intellectualism, hardly skips an issue in which Negroes and/or Negro-Jewish relations are not analyzed at length. This magazine is a true reflection of what the inner Jewish world really thinks about the Negro problem. Like the pre-Hitler German Jews who were "more German than the Germans," some assimilated American Jews become more American than the WASPs in their response to Negro uprisings, and more conservative than the editorial board of *The National Review*.

For many years, certain Negro intellectuals have been unable to face the Jews realistically. Among the many myths life and history have imposed on Negroes (such as that of Lincoln's "freeing" the slaves) is the myth that the Negro's best friend is the Jew. Far more accurately, certain Jews have been the best friends of certain Negroes—which, in any case, is nothing very unusual. This idea of Jewish friendship seems to have been born and given currency in the twentieth century. There is little evidence that the Jewish group was much interested in the Negro's plight for "social uplift" reasons prior to the age of Booker T. Washington and the NAACP era that followed. But this is not to say that Jews were not acutely aware of the Negro's existence. How aware certain Jews were, is revealed in a very unlikely source—the autobiographical notes of the great Russian writer, Feodor M. Dostoevski. Writing about the Jewish question in Russia, in the year 1877, he said:

> But let them be morally purer than all the peoples of the world, nevertheless I have just read in the March issue of the *Messenger of Europe* a news item to the effect that in America, in the Southern States, they have already leaped *en masse* upon the millions of liberated Negroes, and have already taken a grip upon them in their, the Jews' own way, by means of their sempiternal "gold pursuit" and by taking advantage of the inexperience and vices of the exploited tribe. Imagine, when I read this, I immediately recalled that the same thing came to my mind five years ago, specifically, that the Negroes have now been liberated from the slave owners, but that they will not last because the Jews, of whom there are so many in the world, will jump at this new little victim.[1]

It is known that during the last phases of the Civil War, Union Army generals in the South had serious difficulties suppressing the business activities of Jewish traders from the North who followed closely in the wake of the invading Union troops. The American frontier, both South and West, of course presented an open market readily available for any enterprising tradesman seeking a new stake in the world. But it was from the Jewish shopkeeper and trader that the Southern Negro got his latent anti-Semitism. Down through the years, Negroes learned to differentiate between whites and Jewish whites in trade, by the designation "Jew Store," as opposed to other kinds of stores. In one of his superb stories, Richard Wright told of certain taboo subjects that a Negro was not allowed to discuss with a Southern white man. One of these was the presence of the Jew who prospered in the South, despite anti-Semitism. W.J. Cash wrote: "The South had relatively few Jews—certainly not enough to constitute a Jewish Problem. . . . But fears and hates often clothe themselves in old forms. . . . And in addition there was the consideration I have already suggested: the Jew, with his universal refusal to be assimilated is everywhere the eternal Alien."[2]

An "alien" yes, but one who knew how to manage, prosper and

---

[1] *The Diary of a Writer* (New York: George Braziller, 1954), p. 642.

[2] *The Mind of the South* (New York: Doubleday, reprint 1941), p. 334.

be self-sufficient. American Jews had long learned how to get along with American white Christians and the latter's "Negro problem"; they learned what they as a *group* must, and must not, do about this situation. Considering the hazards involved, one cannot blame the Jews for their nineteenth-century neutrality on the race question. Thus it was that the oldest Jewish fraternal organization in America, the Germanic B'nai B'rith, established in 1843, never involved itself even in the moral crusade of the Abolitionists. As a body, American Jewry took no action, either pro or con, on the slavery issue, even while the Christian churches were rent by warring factions over the issue.

As regards the slavery issue, American Jews *as individuals* were no different from other individual American whites: They were pro-slavery, anti-slavery, slave-owners, slave-traders, pro-Union, pro-Confederate, war profiteers, army officers, soldiers, spies, statesmen, opportunistic politicians or indifferent victims of inter-sectional strife of the Civil War. There were Abolitionists such as Rabbi David Einhorn of Baltimore, and pro-slavery Confederate statesmen such as the scholarly and brilliant Judah P. Benjamin, the Secretary of State from Louisiana: "It was not, however, as Jews, but only as individuals, that the men who have been referred to espoused the pro-slavery cause; the Jewish community, as such, took no stand."[3]

But it was the Civil War itself that inspired the first notable anti-Semitic manifestation from the North, and it came from the high command of the Union Army. The collapse of its armies in the Tennessee-Mississippi districts had opened a breach in the Confederacy's economic fortress, paving the way for widespread speculation and thievery in cotton and other Southern products badly needed in the North. "Bribery and corruption in every branch of the [Union] service" was rampant, and "in the midst of this nightmare of profiteering . . . the most sweeping anti-Jewish regulation in all American history was issued. It was wired from General Grant's headquarters in Holly Springs, Mississippi, on December 17, 1862."

The order read: "General Order Number 11—'The Jews, as a

---

[3] Max J. Kohler, "The Jews and the American Anti-Slavery Movement," *Publication of the American Jewish Historical Society*, New York (1896), No. 5, p. 145.

class violating every regulation of trade established by the Treasury Department and also departmental orders, are hereby expelled from the department within twenty-four hours from the receipt of this order.' "[4]

This order, signed by U.S. Grant, created a major scandal for the War Department in Washington. Jews protested, bringing the American Jewish question into focus in such a way as to give American anti-Semitism the political tone it was to assume into the twentieth century. In 1877, anti-Semitic social discrimination created another cause célèbre when Joseph Seligman, the immigrant German-Jewish banker, was denied accommodations at a certain fashionable Northern WASP hotel. This incident, among others of less notoriety, alerted such Jewish groups as B'nai B'rith to the fact that the status of American Jewry was then less than secure. It was said that Seligman arrived penniless in the United States, yet he made such a name for himself as a financial wizard in the field of international banking that the same General Grant who issued General Order Number 11, offered Seligman the post of Secretary of the Treasury during Grant's tenure as President. The American national group problem was a long way from being cogently defined and American jimcrowism, as opposed to anti-Semitism, was even farther away from any compensatory amends from the power structure.

But the deepening anti-Semitic trends of those years were to culminate tragically before subsiding into the American mood of what is called "tolerance," when Leo M. Frank was lynched in Georgia in 1915 (the only recorded lynching of a Jew). On the basis of racist passions, Frank was judged guilty of the 1913 murder of a young white girl long before he was brought to trial. Legally, his guilt was never proven, and he is the only Southern white man ever prosecuted and judged guilty on the testimony of a Negro (who was also circumstantially implicated in the crime). Frank was a young married college graduate, the manager of a manufacturing establishment in Georgia, and incidentally the president of his local branch of B'nai B'rith. His death was instrumental in the creation of the Anti-Defamation League in 1913.

[4] Bertram W. Korn, *American Jewry and the Civil War* (Philadelphia: Jewish Publication Society of America, 1951), p. 122.

This is some of the historical background, indefinite as it is, that led many Negro intellectuals to believe there was something of a special quality about Jewish friendship for the Negro, that Jewish liberalism was different from white liberalism proper. Thus it must have been quite a shock to certain Negroes when Norman Podhoretz, the editor of *Commentary,* made public his considerable phobias toward the Negro, in his article "My Negro Problem and Ours."[5] Lorraine Hansberry, one of the most convinced exponents of Negro-Jewish unity, retorted indignantly that Podhoretz had to "hold his nose" when contemplating Negroes at close range. But after all, Podhoretz only expressed honestly what many other Jews who had intimate dealings with Negroes, had intimated in random conversations.

What lay behind Podhoretz's avowals, however, was the fact that the Jewish community was in the process of reevaluating the position of Jews in American society. A new Jewish image was in the throes of formation, calling for a studied shift from the former stock appraisals of Negro-Jewish relations. For example, on the evening of November 17, 1965, an influential rabbi—Arthur Hertzberg of Englewood, New Jersey—speaking at the Zionist Theodore Herzl Institute, stated that American Jews were no longer among the "have-nots" but associated with the "haves." He stated that this required the Jewish community to reassess its entire relationship with American society, and also with the Negro civil rights movement. He declared that he was happy to be in the presence of such "postitive Jews" as those associated with the Theodore Herzl Institute, who were unlike certain other kinds of Jews who go "crawling on their bellies to Rome." In other words, the rabbi was saying that today American Jews are a power in this land and should act accordingly. Behind this power, of course, is the State of Israel, which immeasurably enhances the new status of American Jewry as a "have" group.

To solve Hertzberg's equation the American Negro must seriously reassess *his* relationships with American Jews. Such reassessment should have taken place immediately after the establishment of Israel in 1948. For the emergence of Israel as a world-power-in-minuscule meant that the Jewish question in America was no

---

[5] *Commentary,* February, 1963, pp. 93-101.

longer purely a domestic minority problem growing out of the old immigrant status tradition. A great proportion of American Jews began to function in America as an organic part of a distant nation-state. This power, in fact, was exerted beforehand, in the very formation of this state. During the 1948 presidential election, Senator McGrath, chairman of the Democratic National Committee, had to warn his party colleagues "that our failure to go along with the Zionists [on Palestine] might lose the states of New York, Pennsylvania and California. . . ."[6] It was established that "the United States was primarily responsible for the creation of a Jewish State in the heart of the Arab world, but Soviet support made it possible."[7] This fact attests to Zionist power in the United States. But the United Nations partition of Palestine did violence to the Charter's promise of "respect for the principle of equal rights and self-determination of peoples," and made the charter "look like unblushing hypocrisy."[8]

Neither the Negro movement as a whole, nor the Negro creative intellectuals as a class stratum, has ever taken a forthright position on either the international implications of Israel vis-à-vis black Africa or the domestic implication of Jews vis-à-vis the Negro movement. Negroes have either been uncritically pro-Jewish or critically tongue-tied on both matters. Such ambivalence toward Jews stems partly from the fact that Negro intellectuals and critics allow them to deal with the Negro issue on *their own* terms from *their* position of social power. That is why the *Commentary* magazine round-table discussion in the winter of 1964, featuring James Baldwin, was such a disastrous failure in terms of clarification of issues. When Norman Podhoretz put the following question to Baldwin, the latter could not answer it, as he had neither the insight nor the knowledge to do so: "Mr. Baldwin, is it conceivable to you that the Negroes will within the next five or ten or twenty years take their rightful place as one of the *competing groups in the American pluralistic pattern* [italics added]? Or is something more radical—or perhaps less radical—more likely to happen the way things are going now?"

Nothing that Baldwin has ever written indicates that he could

---

[6] Chesly Manly, *The UN Record* (Chicago: Henry Regnery Co., 1955), p. 51.
[7] *Ibid.*, p. 50.
[8] *Ibid.*

deal, even superficially, with the implications of that question. Yet it was the most important question asked during the whole discussion, and Baldwin (along with Kenneth Clark) had to sidestep it, either from lack of knowledge or conviction. Podhoretz, of course, was merely voicing *Commentary*'s contemporary understanding of an old question. For years American Jewry has been much concerned with the implications of cultural pluralism. Jewish intellectuals have written extensively about it,[9] inasmuch as official Zionist policy has always been that of anti-assimilationist, pro-Jewish group solidarity.

The problem here is that Baldwin, strictly speaking, is not a pluralist. In fact, Baldwin does not know what he stands for, sociologically. Thus it was unfair to the public, as well as ludicrous and embarrassing, to see Baldwin floundering and frantic under the pointed questioning of Jewish experts. They, at least, even if uncertain as to where they are headed in Negro-Jewish affairs, *do know exactly what they want in America.*

It would not be correct to call Baldwin a Jew-lover, inasmuch as Baldwin simply loves everybody, even those he feels are against him. More exactly, he fits the category of apologist for the Jews, true to the tradition of Negro expreachers well-versed in Hebrew biblical lore and all that deep-river-waters-of-Jordan history. But the most critical problem for the Negro today in Negro-Jewish affairs is posed not by the apologist, but by the professional pro-Semite. Political Negro-Jewish interracialism has cropped out in all its peculiar preciousness on the American cultural front. Many of our creative intellectuals have been caught up in the rather exclusive, and often intolerant, interethnic social orbit, especially in the civil rights movement.

American Negroes (as distinct from West Indians) do not come out of the European tradition, know very little about it, and care less. I am speaking of the masses here, not the colored elite of various "sets." Hence, what European Jews suffered in Europe has very little bearing on the American experience (excepting that many of the Jewish intellectuals here tend to adopt as their own, the martyr's mantle of those who were nailed to the German Iron Cross). One cannot deny the horror of the European Jewish holo-

⁹ See bibliography of Milton M. Gordon's *Assimilation in American Life, op. cit.*

caust, but for all practical purposes (political, economic and cultural) as far as Negroes are concerned, *Jews have not suffered in the United States.* They have, in fact, done exceptionally well on every level of endeavor, from a nationalist premise or on an assimilated status. They have mastered the fine art of playing both ends against the "middle" of group status. But the fact remains that the European experience shows that when it comes to playing the role of the Chosen People in history, the danger is that *two* can play this game as well as one. When that happens, woe be to the side that is short on numbers. The European experience also shows that European imperialism was not exclusively a Christian affair: Witness the international machinations that brought about the State of Israel.

Thus no matter how many organizations are at work today, watching the ideological weathervanes for traces of anti-Semitism, the average Negro is not going to buy the propaganda that Negroes and Jews are "brother-sufferers" in the same boat. As a matter of fact, most Negroes and Jews in America are quite justifiably either embarrassed or resentful over this kind of talk. However, merely to point this out is not enough, and the whole question of Negro-Jewish relations needs to be seriously examined. The misinterpretations and misinformation involved give off very ominous overtones, and presage some very nasty group clashes when and if the racial question really explodes in America. The truth is—and has always been—that if anyone in America wants to find Anti-Negroism, Anti-Semitism, Anti-Catholicism or Anti-foreignism, one need go no farther than precisely these same Negroes, Jews, Catholics and foreigners; there, you will find black against black, Jew against Jew, Catholic against Catholic, foreigner against foreigner—plus all four ethnic categories against each other—and the WASPs against the whole lot. These are the ingredients that never blended within the American melting pot. And it is time for intelligent American opinion to recognize that the country is *not* homogenous, and that consequently, the group question has been misinterpreted and mishandled for many decades. Hence, today, a fateful triangular tension among national groups is coming to the fore, packed with the high explosives of ethnic, racial and religious conflicts. This triangle, comprising Anglo-Saxons, Negroes and Jews, cuts across class lines and has deep ramifications on the economic, political and cultural fronts. For deep within the social consciousnesses of these groups lie three nationalist ideologies—Anglo-Saxon nationalism,* black nationalism and Jewish nationalism (Zionism). The first is both overt and covert, especially in the South; the second is openly avowed and vocal, but poorly organized and even more poorly directed; the third is the most highly organized of all—the most sophisticated, scholarly and intellectual, with the most highly refined propaganda techniques—and hence the most successful of the three. A study of Jewish Zionist organizational and propaganda techniques reveals that influential Zionist thought sees Anglo-Saxon nationalism in the United States as its main potential political threat. Zionist thought also correctly sees the Negro civil rights drive for social equality and racial integration as a possible indirect threat to Jewish status, in the event that Negroes drive Anglo-Saxon nationalists into the radical rightist political camp. Hence, Jewish trends that are pro-Zionist and anti-Jewish-integration-assimilation, are forced to take a pro-Negro integration position and an anti-black nationalist position. *Thus, pro-Zionist influences within Negro civil rights organizations are strategically aiding and abetting Negro integration (assimilation), albeit Zionists, themselves, do not believe in integration (assimilation) for Jews.* This nationalist triangle is further complicated by the fact that not all Anglo-Saxons (especially the Northern liberal variety), nor all Negroes, nor all Jews, are nationalists or Zionists. Some Jews, however, are assimilationists, as are some Negroes: Witness the jesting "ethnic" idea behind the bit of dialogue in *Brustein's Window* to the effect that Brustein was an "assimilationist Jew." But this line had serious "folksy" intent, as far as the playwright's ethnic sentiments went. Lorraine Hansberry had not simply married a man who "just happened to be of Jewish antecedents" as the liberal-humanist-moralists would have it; she had "assimilated" into white Jewish cultural life.

Other Negro intellectuals who reflect this white-Negro-Jewish ideological muddle are LeRoi Jones and James Baldwin. The latter, of course, has given us his allegedly "angry" view on whites and white Jews in his essays. LeRoi Jones, however, is a rather special type. He is a writer who cannot so easily be categorized as

---

* Often called Christian nationalism.

a Negro intellectual, completely lacking a critique. This is because Jones is of a younger trend and therefore more amenable to
new styles of thought on cultural problems. As I have pointed out,
when Jones was involved in the On Guard for Freedom Committee in 1961, he had a hard time understanding why the mass of
Harlem Negroes should be anti-white. His close friend, musician
Archie Shepp, took the same position. At an On Guard meeting
Shepp took the floor and argued against the economics and the
politics of nationalism, in connection with a proposal that On
Guard set up a movement in Harlem to foster self-help economic
cooperatives among ghetto Negroes. Shepp proposed instead that
On Guard stage a black demonstration on a corner of the richest
section of New York's Park Avenue (note the protest mentality).
Yet note the direction that Jones and Shepp shortly took.

By 1964-65, both Jones and Shepp were staging bitter anti-
white diatribes downtown, in places like the Village Vanguard.
Why? What did it prove? Why did Jones and Shepp object to anti-
white nationalism *in* Harlem, only to assume it in Greenwich
Village as *individuals?* It was because Jones and Shepp are artists
who function in cultural and artistic spheres without being motivated by a serious, well-thought-out literary and cultural critique
on the white society they are attacking. They would be hard put to
explain their contradictory behavior on this score; but what they
were in fact expressing in the Village was a *cultural nationalism*
which has not been analyzed in terms of its political, communal
and cultural categories. In other words, because Jones and Shepp
wanted nothing to do with political or communal nationalism in
Harlem, they rejected it, despite the fact that their own *cultural*
nationalism had not yet matured ideologically. Harlem nationalists, themselves, have had no program for the political and communal realities of the Harlem ghetto, hence, they had no understanding of the cultural nationalism that would later emerge from
Jones and Shepp. Organizationally and ideologically, there could
be no meeting of the minds on these levels, hence Jones and Shepp
had to reject a nationalism to which they could not relate. Yet
when they began to express their own anti-whiteness—their cultural nationalism—in 1965, they were not only anti-white, but
specifically critical of *Jewish* whites. But their attitude toward
Jews was like the reverse side of James Baldwin's superficialities

on Negro-Jewish relations. Baldwin refuses to "hate" Jews on ethical grounds; both Jones and Shepp refused to "love" Jews on some other ethical grounds, which were never explored. Hence neither position is predicated on any meaningful inquiry into the real social status of Jews as compared to that of Negroes, in order to determine the very real inequality therein.

At the Village Vanguard, when Jones and Shepp were reminded of the six million Jews exterminated by Hitler, Jones replied to Larry Rivers, "You're like the others [whites], except for the cover story." Shepp added: "I'm sick of you cats talking about the six million Jews. I'm talking about the five to eight million Africans killed in the Congo. King Leopold is his name."

When a white woman expressed the view that Jones and Shepp should be thankful for the aid and assistance given by whites (and Jews) to the civil rights causes in the South, Shepp replied: "I give no civil service charity for going to Mississippi to 'assuage their consciences.' "[10]

In discussing the Mississippi murder and martyrdom of Andrew Goodman and Michael H. Schwerner, both Jews, Shepp observed that the first victim, James E. Chaney, a Negro, had been beaten into an unrecognizable state, while even in death the white lynchers had "embraced" their fellow whites by treating them "less harshly." There are profound moral and ethical problems involved here, but the question is—How far into the historical roots of these moral issues are Jones and Shepp willing to go? How far afield from New York City, where free speech is permitted all factions from Freedom Riders to Fascists, will Negro intellectuals go to search out the economic, cultural, political and imperialistic strands and bind them together into a meaningful critique? If they reject Schwerner and Goodman today, they must reject John Brown(*ism*) of yesterday and expunge his name from Negro history, along with the Abolitionists as the precursors of paternalistic freedom assistance for blacks. But the Robesons, the Apt.hekers, the Shirley Graham DuBoises, *et al.,* would not like that. To tie in the slaughter of Jews in Germany and the slaughter of Africans in the Congo, one must look into the question of Zionism and the

[10] *The New York Times,* February 10, 1965, p. 47.

role it has played in Europe, especially in Germany and Russia, but also in the Israel of today.*

The truth is that Jones and Shepp are confused on the Jews. Jones called the slain Goodman and Schwerner "artifacts" and "paintings on the wall." But Shepp said, relentingly, to Larry Rivers, "I consider you a friend, an enemy." There was laughter from the audience, but, Shepp insisted: "I spoke the truth. I mean *both* things." Of course he did, because he is mixed up emotionally about Jews (and all whites), but about Jews, especially.

Can one accept and reject Jews at one and the same time? In terms of Africa today, can an Afro-American accept American Jews and the fact of Israel together, when to most Jews in America a refusal to accept Israel's reality is an affront to all Jews? Can one fight neo-colonialism in Africa today without fighting Israel? These are tough questions because the headquarters of some big trusts who are still extracting millions upon millions in profit from African copper, gold and diamonds, have connections in Israel.† Such questions as these can be raised and lightly touched on in Greenwich Village jazz salons, but they cannot be explored or settled there. They are much too big and supercharged with political dynamite.

It has become almost axiomatic that one can determine just which political, economic, cultural, or civil rights "bag" any Negro intellectual is in, by whether or not he is willing to criticize American Jews publicly. If he is wary, he is either ignorant of the facts of life in multi-group America, or else organizationally involved with a Jewish and/or Zionist influence, as is prevalent in certain civil rights groups.

When James Baldwin writes about Jews *in* Harlem he does not

---

* Edmond de Rothschild, the early founding father of Zionist colonization, was one of the big financial backers of Cecil J. Rhodes' African explorations in the 1870's and 1880's, when the British capitalist and explorer founded the DeBeer's Mining Company and established monopoly over the Kimberley diamond production enterprises.
† Today, Israel ranks second to Belgium in the export of finished diamonds, although Israel mines no diamonds in the Negev. Her diamond exports increased from five million dollars in 1950 to one hundred and thirty million in 1965. This raises the question of Israel's relationships with the great mining interests in South Africa involving the Oppenheimer empire—the DeBeer's Mining Syndicate, the Anglo-American Copper trust, etc.

know with whom and what he is dealing. He thinks that he is dealing with Negro-Jewish relations on a strictly moralistic level. In recognizing the fact that there is much overt and covert anti-Semitism among Negroes, he lumps all of this into an international-moral equation concerning Jewish martyrdom on the European scene. Hence, he concludes that "both the Negro and the Jew are helpless; the pressure of living is too immediate and incessant to allow time for understanding." Baldwin pinpoints the essential, historical bias:

> The Negro's outlets are desperately constricted. . . . Here the Jew is caught in the American crossfire. The Negro facing a Jew, hates, at bottom, not his Jewishness but the color of his skin. It is not the Jewish tradition by which he has been betrayed but the tradition of his native land. But just as a society must have a scapegoat, so hatred must have a symbol. Georgia has the Negro and Harlem has the Jew."[11]

Just before this, Baldwin talks about his "Jewish friends in high school" who were not like those "other Jews" that other Negroes hated, or pretended to hate "because the nation does." These Jewish friends, said Baldwin, "had no intention of exploiting me, we did not hate each other." However, Baldwin points out that those Jews in Harlem who *are* exploiting are small tradesmen, rent collectors, real estate agents, and pawnbrokers, who "operate in accordance with the American business tradition. . . ." In other words, Jews don't exploit because of hate; it is rather that Negroes *hate* to be exploited. This disturbs Baldwin who feels that it is wrong and pointless for Negroes to react this way, for such criticism of Jews on this score is to Baldwin, the rebel, equivalent to anti-Semitism. Even if Harlem Negroes simply said they hated to be exploited by whites and never mentioned the word "Jew," Baldwin would still consider that anti-Semitism by implication. Presumably, Baldwin is suggesting that Negroes in Harlem should simply accept exploitation and say nothing at all, because, after all, exploitation is "in accordance with the American business tradition." What all this really means, again, is that Baldwin wants to

[11] "The Harlem Ghetto," *Notes of a Native Son* (Boston: Beacon Press, 1957), pp. 71-72.

avoid dealing with the facts of Harlem as they *exist*.

This essay on "The Harlem Ghetto" was really a chic piece of magazine journalism that rehashed all the time-worn superficialities of Harlem "local color" and decrepitude. It has been done before, and it was merely the added flavor of Baldwin's personal reminiscences that made an essay out of glorified journalese. However, the great flaw in Baldwin's approach to Harlem (and its Jews and its business traditions) is that he wants this blight totally obliterated. Yet he overlooks the fact that the same "American business tradition" from which exploitation flows will not let Harlem be erased so easily from the American scene. No one ever willingly allowed a gold mine to be blown up, so Harlem is going to remain with its Negroes, its Jews and its businesses. Somewhere along the line Negroes and Jews in Harlem are fated to confront the issues of economic and social imbalance between them.

James Baldwin looks at the Jewish question with the eyes of a rather innocent and provincial intellectual. Bending over backward to avoid criticism of Jews while pretending to be angry with whites, he overlooks the fact that if *American* Jews are "caught in the American crossfire" they are also very much in control of the situation and have their enemies well "cased" from all directions. Baldwin's unfortunate mismatch with Jewish intellectuals on *Commentary* magazine showed that Jews also have Baldwin well "cased"—only he does not know it. Baldwin has not learned that Jews themselves are divided on many issues and that some Jews are more "crossfired" than others—especially those who are neither Zionists nor pro-Zionists. But among American Jews, who is who?*

To probe this important dichotomy one must first have some understanding of the relationship of American Jews to Israel. It has been described in the following way: "They [Jews] are not one and the same, in fact, they are bewilderingly different. I mean the Jews of the world and the Jewish leaders of Israel. But a sort of

* The American Council for Judaism, an anti-Zionist organization, reported in a newsletter, "Education in Judaism," dated April 4, 1965: "The Zionist movement, subservient to Israeli national interests, plays an important ideological role in American Jewish religious education; and most parents are unaware and uninterested."

courtship goes on between them, a half sincere courtship, because both parties are married to somebody else. Yet they woo each other, the Jews, Israel; and Israel, the Jews.[12]

Since 1948, the relationship of American Jews to Israel has taken on a very special significance in terms of Negro-Jewish relations. As said before, these relations now become colored by the incipient clash of two ideologies—Black Nationalism and Zionism. These nationalisms, totally dissimilar in most respects, share one essential motivation: a yearning for national redemption through regaining a "homeland" that was lost. Both Zionism and Black Nationalism have undergone historical conditionings peculiar to themselves, and have never, to my knowledge, confronted each other on any domestic or international issue. *But today things are different, and Black Nationalism, Zionism, African affairs, and Negro civil rights organizations are intimately interlocked on the political, cultural, economic and international fronts, whether Negro intellectuals care to acknowledge it or not.* Today it is no longer possible for Negro intellectuals to deal with the Jewish question in America purely on a basis of brotherhood, compassion, morality, and other subjective responses which rule out objective criticism and positive appraisals. Taking a critical approach to the Jewish question does not preface a call to arms against Jews, so much as ensure a critical reexamination of how the national group question is handled in the United States.

Basically, all groups strive for survival and identity but certain groups cannot be allowed to survive at the expense of other groups. Hence, when American Negroes talk about survival, Negro intellectuals had better begin to study some of the necessary survival techniques, both organizational and propagandistic. Much more important than developing a critique on Jews, is the challenge of learning the methods and techniques that the Zionists have developed in the art of survival against all kinds of odds. Despite the fact, as Baldwin says, that "Jews are helpless," their helplessness has the enduring quality of a "lost battalion," which despite losses and desertions, manages to live off the land and

---

[12] Ben Hecht, *Perfidy* (An account of the birth of Israel), [New York: Julian Messner, 1961], p. 7. Reprinted with permission of Julian Messner, Division of Simon & Schuster, Inc., from *Perfidy* by Ben Hecht. Copyright © 1961 by Ben Hecht.

survive. One of the key contributions to this art of survival has been the Jewish intellectuals' open support, in large numbers, of the Jewish nationalist-Zionist cause. Very few of the Negro intellectuals, from the 1920's down to James Baldwin, have supported any such movement among Negroes.

The movement among modern European Jews to regain Palestine as the base of a Jewish nation, was founded not by a politician or a religious leader, but a Hungarian Jewish playwright named Theodore Herzl (1860-1904), a "cultural nationalist." It is this that really lent the Zionist movement its inner strength—it had intellectuals as its propagandists.* Unfortunately, Negro nationalist movements have *never* understood the significance of this. At the time Malcolm X was murdered, the young nationalists were still caught up in a highly unsophisticated and debilitating wrangle directed against writers and intellectuals, as such. The Zionists, conversely, during a period when the European Jews were really and truly helpless against the German genocidal assault, were able to launch a uniquely successful movement in America for the aid of those European Jews, garnering the support of: thirty-three United States Senators; one hundred and nine House Representatives; fourteen reigning State Governors; the same number of outstanding Ambassadors and members of Roosevelt's Cabinet; fifty-five justices and judges of various Supreme and District Courts; sixty mayors of leading American cities; four hundred rabbis in all the centers of American Jewry and almost twice as many Catholic and Protestant priests and ministers; a score of American Army generals, colonels and Navy admirals; scores of national leaders in high government posts; five hundred university professors and presidents, and an equal number of playwrights, poets, editors, novelists, star actors, singers, dancers and showmen.

These estimates, taken from Ben Hecht's book, are cited here to show that the ability to corral such broad support for Jewish

---

* Interestingly enough, Martin R. Delany, one of the first nineteenth-century Negro leaders to express the idea of Africa-for-the-Africans, was a social critic and novelist as well as a physician. His novel, *Blake—Or the Huts of America*, was published in several installments in the 1859 *Anglo-African Magazine*.

Theodore Herzl's Zionism represents the political phase which comes after the original economic colonization of the Jewish capitalists-founders of Zionism, such as Edmond de Rothschild.

causes does not exactly corroborate the "helplessness" in America
to which Baldwin refers.

Ben Hecht was no mere respectable Zionist, but a functioning
propagandist for the most extreme group—the Irgun Zvai Leumi—
the young fighters who scandalized the Weizmann-Ben Gurion
Zionists by taking up arms against the British. Hecht was a successful Hollywood writer, well known in both the early Chicago and
Greenwich Village bohemian circles of the 1920's. He was a close
friend of Maxwell Bodenheim, *et al.*, but his cultural background
did not prevent Hecht and others like him from siding with a
dissident-extremist faction within respectable Zionism when that
movement was struck by the crisis of world war and Jewish exter-
mination. Hecht revealed the fateful nature of this Zionist split
when he wrote:

> I list the number of our notables [listed above] not to show
> how powerful we were, *but how powerful was the opposition of
> Jewish Agency and Zionist organizations.* For the opposition of
> Jewish Authority won the day. Although we could break the
> conspiracy of silence in large meeting halls and in coast-to-coast
> newspapers and magazines, we could not grab the ear of govern-
> ment. *The slick and respectable Jewish organizations of the
> United States kept this ear plugged* [all italics added].[13]

The Irgun Zvai Leumi faction had accused the ruling Weizmann-Ben Gurion groups of pursuing policies that were tantamount to abandoning European Jews to their fate. Thus Hecht
involved himself in campaign committees "for a Jewish Army in
Palestine to help fight the Germans, for a Free Palestine, for the
smuggling of German-doomed Jews into British-closed Palestine,
etc. . . ." Prominent in these committees were such notables as
Kurt Weill, Arthur Szyk the artist, Billy Rose the producer and
Leonard Lyons, *The New York Post* columnist. Involved also was
S.N. Behrman, a prominent Broadway playwright on the one
hand, and a political admirer of Chaim Weizmann. (Behrman
later wrote a biography, *Chaim Weizmann—the Builder of Zion.*)
The fate of European Jews and Zionist ideology bound the Jewish
intelligentsia together—at home and abroad. Hecht wrote of
Ferenc Molnar, the prominent Hungarian-Jewish playwright who

[13] *Perfidy, op. cit.,* p. 189.

was rescued from Hungary along with other Jewish artists and intellectuals, largely through the efforts of Hecht's anti-respectable Zionist faction: "I was in especial public disfavor at the time for some anti-British, anti-Roosevelt and anti-Jewish Agency outcries I had helped loose in the press." During this time Hecht dropped by the home of Leonard Lyons where a party was in progress:

> Some sixty literary, theatrical, and financial luminaries sat dining at a dozen tables. . . .
> The guests were mostly Jews and Jewesses, with a few British— all Top Drawer.
> One figure stood up at the end of the room and walked slowly and a little dramatically toward me. It was Molnar.
> He took my hand, bowed over it, kissed it as if I were a dowager, and said, "Thank you."
> Thus Ferenc Molnar, who found it difficult to be a Jew; but having to be one, he ran up his colors under the enemy's nose— and saluted a comrade.[14]

What was demonstrated here was not mere "helplessness," Mr. Baldwin: This was also *power*—power refractorily subverted in the factionalism of partisan politics, as is often the case—but power nevertheless. The affair of the seventy thousand Rumanian Jews was another enlightening case in point in Zionist power politics. During the war, the Rumanian government had made an offer to the American and British governments to allow seventy thousand Jews to leave Rumania at the cost of fifty dollars a head for transportation. The American State Department had received the offer and pigeonholed it. Hecht and the Irgun went to work to expose the story—against the wishes of the official Zionists in New York. Hecht ran an advertisement in the New York papers announcing: "For sale, 70,000 Jews at $50 Apiece—Guaranteed Human Beings." Hecht wrote:

> On the appearance of this news advertising copy, Rabbi Stephen Wise, Zionist chieftain in New York and guiding light for the city's Jewish respectables, issued the following statement. The date was February 23, 1943. "The American Jewish Congress, dealing with the matter in conjunction with recognized Jewish organizations, wishes to state that no confirmation has been re-

[14] *Ibid.,* pp. 86-87.

ceived regarding this alleged offer of the Rumanian Government to allow seventy thousand Jews to leave Rumania. Therefore no collection of funds would seem justified.

Hecht continued:

> The Jewish Agency in London also denied the Rumanian offer. This denial was cabled to American newspapers, and carried by them. And reading it, American Jews felt grateful to the Jewish Agency for removing the ugly Rumanian problem from their consciences.

Hecht explained that this Zionist policy derived from the fact that Jewish leaders such as Weizmann, Ben Gurion and Sharett "had limited their dream of Zion to a British-Jewish suburb" in the Middle East. Thus there was really no place in their Zionist scheme for very many poor Jews from the ghettoes of Europe. Hecht condemned these leading Zionists:

> These organizations, these philanthropists, these timorous Jewish lodge members in Zion, London and America—these Zionist leaders who let their six million kinsmen burn, choke, hang, without protest, with indifference, and even with a glint of anti-Semitic cunning in their political plannings—I sum up against them. These factotums, these policy-makers . . . who hung onto their jobs, who lorded it over their real estate holdings in Palestine, who obeyed the British demand that no ruckus be raised about Europe's Jews being murdered . . . I haul into the prisoner's dock of this book.[15]

The above is intended to elucidate certain truths about American Jews and Negro-Jewish relations for Negro intellectuals such as James Baldwin. The relationships between groups in America, and on the international plane, are actuated by the power principle, not by morality and compassion for the underdog classes. However, when Baldwin discussed Negro problems with the Jewish intellectuals on *Commentary* magazine in the winter of 1964, he did not, and could not, ask a more pertinent question: Where do you Jewish intellectuals of *Commentary* stand on the question of international Zionism? For without prefatory clarification on this issue, no Negro or Jew is prepared to discuss, in any

[15] *Ibid.*, pp. 191-193.

serious way, any alleged approaches to better Negro-Jewish relations at home or abroad. In the April 30, 1954, issue of the *Jewish
Press,* an article on the Black Muslims compares them with American Nazis like Lincoln Rockwell.[16] For Jews of this newspaper's
persuasion, Muslims are racists and extremists. They conveniently
forget, of course, that the Irgun Zvai Leumi and the Stern Gang
(the Lehi) in pre-1948 Israel were called the same things—"Jewish racists and extremists." Yet it was these very people who truly
forged Israel by forcing the British Army to vacate the territory.
When Winston Churchill came to the United States after the war
and met secretly with producer Billy Rose and Bernard Baruch, an
American elder statesman and an obvious pro-Zionist,* Churchill
admitted to both of them:

> If you were interested in the establishment of an Israeli Na-
> tion, you were involved with the right people. It was the Irgun
> that made the English quit Palestine. They did it by raising so
> much hell that we had to put eighty thousand soldiers into Pales-
> tine to cope with the situation. The military costs were too high
> for our economy. And it was the Irgun that ran them up.[17]

The Irgun, of course, was cast in a position where the use of
arms was feasible, and as Palestine was an occupied war zone,
armed terror was the order of the day. Peoples and nations have a
habit of thoroughly hating everyone's nationalism but their own,
and Jewish nationalists are no exception. Eventually, terroristic
tactics will be used in Harlem against white-owned businesses by a
nationalist faction, and the Jews will certainly call it anti-Semitism. Naturally Baldwin will not like to see this, but the Jewish
writers on the newspaper *Jewish Press* do not even agree with
Baldwin that Jewish exploitation in Harlem is a natural result—
"in accordance with the American business tradition." They rationalize this exploitation by claiming that if it were not for the
Jews there would be no businesses at all in Harlem to provide jobs
for Negroes. Notice the arrogance here, boldly printed in the *Jew-*

---

[16] David Gilbert and Jack Brown, "The Black Muslims," *Jewish Press,* April 23,
30; May 7, 1965.
* Said Hecht, "Another Zionist Pied Piper was Louis Brandies, to become Supreme
Court Justice in Washington." (See *Perfidy,* p. 11.) Felix Frankfurter, Supreme Court
Jurist, has Zionist connections. (N.B.)
[17] Hecht, *op. cit.,* p. 40.

ish Press. Even if this were true, it is a good thing that Negroes do not read Jewish magazines and newspapers regularly, because such a statement would have certainly worsened already inflamed Negro-Jewish relations. What the *Jewish Press* said, however, does not tell the whole story of white-owned businesses in Harlem. There was a time, not too many years ago, when these Jewish-owned businesses *would not hire Negro help at all.* They did not do so, in fact, until forced to—*not* by the NAACP or the Urban League—but by the Black Nationalist organizations during the 1930's and early 1940's. Baldwin, however, in his Harlem ghetto essay does not even touch on such crucial and fundamental truths of Harlem history. If the Baldwins had historical perspective they would be better writers. If they knew and searched for facts, they would be better spokesmen. If they were more like Jewish intellectuals and creative artists, they would not be as afraid of becoming propagandists for their own kind in politics and culture as they are about writing "Everybody's Protest Novel"—only to wind up writing bad protest plays. If Negro intellectuals could become more objective and less subjective about the Negro-Jewish "thing," they might become more perceptive about the prevalent Jewish intellectual and literary mystique that has developed in America.[18]

What was the meaning of Nathan Glazer's article, "Negroes and Jews: The New Challenge to Pluralism"?[19] Glazer quoted Baldwin's observations on Jewish business in Harlem. Is the Negro—*i.e.*, are the Negro masses—really a challenge to pluralism, when real, truly democratic pluralism has never been achieved? Is Nathan Glazer simply confusing the needs of the Negro masses with the aims of its spokesmen? In effect, Glazer admits that these leadership aims do not square with the facts of group life in America. Yet he upholds these aims as being not unrealizable. Whether or not Nathan Glazer is Zionist, pro-Zionist or anti-Zionist, the fact remains that pro-Zionist policies in civil rights organizations are pro-integrationist for Negroes and anti-assimilationist for Jews. Frankly, Jews can take integration, or leave it. Accordingly, Glazer recognizes that "the Negro now demands entry into a world, a

[18] See Irving Malin, "Jews and Americans," *Crosscurrents*, 1965.
[19] *Commentary*, December, 1964, pp. 29-34.

society that does not exist, except in ideology. In that world there is only one American community, and in that world, heritage, ethnicity, religion, race are only incidental and accidental personal characteristics."

Glazer admits that such a world is mere illusion, yet against all manifest obstacles, he provides for its birth: "There may be many reasons for such a world to come into existence—among them the fact that it may be necessary in order to provide full equality for the Negroes. But if we do move in this direction, we will have to create communities very different from the kinds in which most of us who have already arrived—Protestants, Catholics, Jews—now live."

As a Jew, Nathan Glazer could be said to be most magnanimously free with other people's ethnicity. On the other hand, if things do not work out just right, Negro integrationists will be driven (as they already are) into a desperate blind alley with such an approach. So it remains to be asked: Just what is behind Nathan Glazer's fervent insistence that Negroes be integrated as fast as possible, and by any means? There is much evidence that today Negroes truly have a Jewish problem, and the Jew is not just a hatred symbol. There are far too many Jews from Jewish organizations into whose privy councils Negroes are not admitted, who nevertheless are involved in every civil rights and American-African organization, creating policy and otherwise analyzing the Negro from all possible angles. No matter what motivates such activity, the Negro in America will never achieve any kind of equality until more Negro intellectuals are equipped with the latest research and propaganda techniques to move into control and guidance of every branch of the Negro movement. Knowledge is power. The path to more knowledge for the Negro intellectual is through cultural nationalism—an ideology that has made Jewish intellectuals into a social force to be reckoned with in America.

Negro Writers' Conferences—
The Dialogue Distorted

During the first half of the 1960's there were no events that mirrored the utter impoverishment of Negro creative intellectuals so much as those publicized glamorous meetings that go under the imposing title of "Negro Writers' Conferences." These literary "conventions-in-black-and-tan" are, without a doubt, the nearest thing imaginable to those Congressional talkfests in Washington, D.C., where every elected representative knows it is his bounden duty to be present—for the record. But *only* for the record, because *no one* has any intention of passing one bit of positive pending legislation. This is another way of saying that Negro Writers' Conferences settle nothing, solve nothing, pose nothing, analyze nothing, plan nothing, create nothing—not even a decent new literary review—which is the least any bunch of serious, self-respecting writers with a gripe ought to do.

These conferences are comic parodies on the serious substance and reality of Negro life which Negro literature is alleged to reflect. They are engineered by leading writers who, when they are not sweating over the manuscripts of second-rate protest novels, are chafing at the bit for a "dialogue" in public with white liberals and the metropolitan press. But the iconoclastic non-participating observer at these conferences has to wonder—Why? These writers who have the unmitigated gall to pursue a dialogue with whites cannot monitor even a positive, self-critical dialogue.

In 1965, Killens and the Harlem Writers Guild staged such a conference under the auspices, this time, of the New School for Social Research in New York. In 1965, there were two writers' conferences: one in April, staged by Killens and his literary group, and one in February, by the American Festival of Negro

Arts at Fairleigh Dickinson University. The latter represented a radically dissident "out-group." Neither of these conferences can be fully understood unless one is explained in terms of the other . . . and both have to be interpreted in terms of another organization —the American Society of African Culture. This background also takes in the controversy of several years' standing in American Negro-African relations, over the philosophical and aesthetic concept of *Negritude* (the cultural mystique considered applicable to all peoples of African descent). The American Festival of Negro Arts (AFNA) conference was the direct result of a split from the American Society of African Culture (AMSAC). This split came about when AMSAC hedged on carrying out, satisfactorily, the parent body's* implied cultural program among American Negroes. Relations in AMSAC had been festering since about 1961 and finally a rival movement of international prestige splintered off.† The Killens group remained inside AMSAC, and AFNA came on the scene in conjunction with the emergence of the new young Negro creative wave in New York. Many of these young Negroes who attended the AFNA conference were not invited to the Killens conference.

The uniqueness of AFNA, its readiness to deal with Negro-white cultural fundamentals, both ideologically and institutionally, was indicated by the fact that the AFNA affair was not just a "Negro writers' conference." It attempted to deal also with painting, music, the philosophy of Negritude, literary criticism, and enlisted the participation of Africans interested in the Negro cul-

---

* The parent body is the Society of African Culture (SAC), located in Paris, of which Leopold Sedar Senghor, President of Senegal, is a ranking member.

† It was pianist-composer Dr. Robert S. Pritchard who was responsible for the planning of the World Festival of Negro Art held in Dakar this past April, 1966. (See *Life* magazine, April 22, 1966.) But the plans had been completed when Senegal was still closely tied to the French economic community. But when both Senegal and AMSAC came under the American State Department's ministrations, SAC dropped Pritchard and AFNA. It then took over Pritchard's festival plans, allowing AMSAC to run the Dakar show although AMSAC's ruling group had had nothing to do with the planning. Needless to say, these factional quarrels had ramifications that extended into Paris SAC, Dakar, other African states, and the State Department itself. It seriously affected the outcome of the Dakar festival which, according to reports, fell below expectations in terms of participation by American Negro artists.

tural image.* The conference was administered and projected by the cultural independents and the young generation. It was not well-attended, yet was a public-relations and institutional success, representing a solid and substantial new direction. Its discussions and deliberations were orderly, mature (most of the time), intelligent, critical and probing, and educational. It foreshadowed the cultivation of a new literary and cultural critique among the younger Negro creative intelligentsia.

By contrast, the much more crowded sessions at the New School in April saw the Killens literary and cultural entourage approaching the end of its fifteen-year-old reign. This conference was painfully frenetic and pitifully rhetorical, attempting to analyze the Negro writer's cultural precariousness in American society, and the fate of the American Negro in American culture, as a people. Here, the crisis of the Negro intellectual was acted out in vivid detail, with true-to-life players mouthing lines and speeches they had rehearsed for twenty years. All the in-group members were there, with representatives dating back to the heyday of Harlem's Committee for the Negro in the Arts. At the New School was represented the whole Left tradition—*Freedom* newspaper, Harlem Writers Guild, Association of Artists for Freedom, Inc., *Freedomways* magazine, *American Dialog* with its echoes of *Masses and Mainstream,* and, for good measure—shades of *Political Affairs*—the Communist Party's official theoretical organ. The leftwing literary elite was in full control, in a desperate bid to reestablish its status within the stream of the new cultural and literary trends.

The New School conference was staged in memory of the departed Lorraine Hansberry. With the exception of the poetry panel, every other panel was policed by one member (or two) of the Harlem cultural in-group. Thus the literary, cultural (and other) opinions of Killens, John Henrik Clarke, Sylvester Leaks, Alice Childress, Sara Wright, William Branch, Ossie Davis and Ruby Dee (in absentia) and Lorraine Hansberry (through her ex-husband Robert Nemiroff) dominated this writers' conference.

---

* A few of Killens' in-group attended, while others backed off. William Branch participated, as did Ossie Davis (who for the duration of AFNA reclaimed his "black position" in the arts). Loften Mitchell, the independent who constantly flirted with the Killens group but was never quite "in," also showed up. John Henrik Clarke, who seldom strayed from Killens' side, refused to participate.

James Baldwin, not originally a charter member of the group, was, nevertheless, the literary lion of the performance (but not in the eyes of the ranking members of the ex-Harlem leftwing elite).

Next in order of importance on the panels came certain whites of leftwing literary and critical fame, like Herbert Aptheker and Walter Lowenfels.* We shall see in this writers' conference how the radical Left continues to wield its influence over Negro writers.

The New York Times said of the New School conference:

> They hissed and hollered and debated one another for about seven hours yesterday [Sunday, April 25] and when it was all over—70,000 words later—they could not agree on much of anything.
>
> But that is the way it was supposed to be, free and flailing. . . .
>
> In the course of yesterday's program, James Baldwin was called a "literary prostitute." *The New York Times* was condemned for covering Harlem like a "police beat," and the National Broadcasting Company was chided for offering a talented Negro playwright a job as a janitor.
>
> The conference might still be going on now if the moderator, Allan Morrison, of *Ebony* magazine, had not simply stopped the show. But not before he himself had been criticized by the audience—both white and Negro—for suggesting that perhaps some Negroes are not now sufficiently qualified to take advantage of all the opportunities open to them in the creative and communications fields of movies, theaters, television and journalism.
>
> . . . A young woman named Myrna Baines called Mr. Baldwin "an extremely talented literary prostitute."

The truth is, however, that the total conference was not all chaos and confusion. There were many papers read—some historically informative, eloquent and pointed—some anecdotal, trite, rhetorical and superficial. But the discussions around these various papers became emotional and intellectual bedlams. Several of

---

* Lowenfels is an associate editor of the leftwing cultural magazine, *American Dialog*. The continuation of the defunct *Masses and Mainstream* (once called *Mainstream* and previously *New Masses*), it grew out of the old *Masses* established in 1912, the same year Mabel Dodge's literary salon opened in Greenwich Village. For over fifty years—from *Masses* to *American Dialog*—this magazine in its various guises has been the literary and cultural standard-bearer of the American radical leftwing.

these papers posed problems and conceptions, raised questions and suggested directions which the panelists could neither debate nor pursue to any definitive conclusions. The conference led the participants into unknown and unsurveyed regions of black and white cultural reality. *But once there, Killens and his faction were able to give not one modicum of intellectual or programmatic leadership.*

The problems of Negro writers in terms of craft, content and opportunities (integrated jobs) in the cultural media have been taken up over and over again, but these are *individual* problems, when the real substance of what Negro writers are dealing with, but can't pursue, is the *group cultural status* of the American Negro ethnic group. The future individual status of the Negro writer is predicated on this group cultural status. If the two sides of this question are separated, the Negro writer continues to be what he always was—a craftsman taking his chances as an individual, running after whatever support and patronage he can get, wherever he can find it, even in the Communist Party—and often selling out what principles he has, if any, to maintain himself. The Harlem leftwing literary and cultural elite did precisely this. They were all launched as writers by the political leftwing, which gave them patronage and support in Harlem and beyond, through leftwing connections in publishing, theater, and the broadcasting media. Some of them actually got more support than their individual talents really merited. They were awarded prizes and jobs, profitable marriages and social contacts which furthered their careers. Now they come before the public in writers' conferences, pretending to be leaders in intellectual-creative thought who are going to advance the Negro movement—purely on the strength of the dubious example of their own self-advancement. The emptiness of these pretensions was soon revealed when conference panelists demanded to know: "Where do you go from here?" "What is your plan?" "Do you have a *new* program?" Killens' literary faction had no answers. When a conferee demanded: "I want to know, how are you going to get this [cultural message] to enough people to make it effective, when most of the people don't read novels. What other forms are you planning on using?" Killens answered, "I would like to redirect the question and ask the whole audience, what are you doing, because when we write, you know it is going to be up to you to help us get to you. It is quite a bit to ask the Negro writer to write this thing and figure out how it is going to get to you, I think."

This little exchange between Negro writer and "audience" shows clearly why writers' conferences are worthless. Another participant asserted:

> I would like to suggest that the novel is a useless form of art for the urgency of the problem confronting the Negro Americans specifically and, in my own particular case, the problems confronting me. Most important is my urgent desire for freedom.
>
> First of all, end the novel. All these people on the panel were talking about the directness that a person should have. This young lady novelist said she was not interested in writing a novel about the bourgeoisie in her society, she was interested in writing a novel about the poor man. Unfortunately, you are not a poor man. But there are some Negro writers in America whom this conference has entirely overlooked, one of whom spoke in this auditorium at ten o'clock this morning saying that, "I came here to destroy Western civilization, in effect, not to let a Ford be a car that I build new parts on to make a jet plane, but to offer a jet plane that is different than the thing itself." I am talking about poetry and the directness of the people who are in the streets of Selma or all over the South and the young people who—I don't know what—but it is certainly more complicated than sitting for two years at the typewriter and knowing something about a family unit.

John O. Killens had no response to this, and Sylvester Leaks, the chairman of this panel, said: "All right. We accept your statement. Ladies and gentlemen, thank you for coming. We must adjourn now."

Roughly thirty-five Negroes in the literary arts, the media and the press (including the leftwing elite members) took part in the conference. Added to these were several white writers and critics. Of the Negroes, interestingly enough, there were only seven at the New School conference who had participated in the AFNA conference in February, 1965. They were writer and critic, Wilmer Lucas, poets Samuel Allen, Calvin Hernton and Gloria Oden, and playwrights William Branch, Loften Mitchell, and Ossie Davis. Of these seven, only Samuel Allen had figured personally in the AMSAC-AFNA split (as one of the leading founders of AMSAC, and as the only ranking AMSAC spokesman who did not boycott the AFNA conference). Various other writers who had participated in the AFNA conference either were not invited or did not appear as panelists at the New School conference. What is happening here in all this tentative crossing of lines, sorting, eliminating, and jockeying, is that the decline of AMSAC and the emergence of AFNA has left Killens' faction without the influential base it once had within AMSAC. These conferences actually reflect an incipient cultural power struggle within the New York representatives of the Negro creative intelligentsia. Involved in this burgeoning struggle are several factions: the literary and cultural Left, the literary and cultural nationalists, the "old-guard" and the "new," the unaffiliated Negro literary establishment in the universities, and certain Negro publications. Behind these lie the crucial issues of Africa and the Afro-American "image" in the arts. At the very root of the problem are philosophic and cultural implications of Negritude, as propounded by the Society of African Culture in Paris and Africa. Interestingly enough, while the AFNA conference had a panel discussion on Negritude, the New School conference did not.

At the final session of this latter conference, Dr. John Everett, President of the New School, said of the affair:

> In some ways I have been dismayed by it, and in some ways greatly heartened. I am dismayed by the fact that the white intellectual community obviously does not know of, nor does it have any real comprehension of, the vitality and the true strength of the Negro intellectual community. This has been, for me, consequently a dismaying experience. The dialogue that should be going on between the white intellectual community and the Negro intellectual community obviously has not been going on. It is one of the functions of the New School to see that this dialogue proceeds and continues.

The good president had ample reason to be dismayed, but he is, no doubt, a liberal and was being quite kind and maybe even sanguine. Yet most of what happened at the New School was not a dialogue but a frustrated diatribe. A dialogue demands a cultural methodology that these Negro writers do not have, and that the whites cannot give them. A cultural methodology must be predicated on a broad grasp of the totality of cultural factors in life, which these writers have never possessed. For Dr. Everett to suggest a continued dialogue between Negro and white intellectuals means that such a dialogue must proceed on one and the same level with both whites and the Negro community. However, Killens' group was already blocked from this kind of dialogue by the very presence of the Aptheker-Left and the ideology it represents.*

The New School conference could not separate literary art as content, theme, and form, from the material basis of cultural expression (*i.e.,* the organizational and administrative nature of the cultural apparatus), which has to be treated separately. To indulge in analogy: These conference writers behave like a bunch of defenders of morality protesting a certain residence being used as a whorehouse instead of a Sunday school, when the residence is owned, operated and built by a professional madam. Such a situation would suggest a two-sided strategy—hold the Sunday school elsewhere, and in the meantime, wage a fight (by any means possible) to oust the madam from ownership of the residence. But these conference writers want to hold their "Sunday school" in the madam's house while the girls are working on other days besides Sunday. A whorehouse, by any other name, is still a whorehouse—even if it is "integrated." Thus these conference writers want to join the prevailing cultural superstructure of America while protesting its standards and values, under the misapprehension that the injection of *their* values (whatever they are alleged to be) can change that superstructure. This is ridiculous. No one can hope to change America's cultural standards and values unless the proprietorship, the administration, and the uses to which the cultural apparatus are put, are changed to allow for more democratic social control. It is only on this basis that there can be any dialogue between the Negro and the white intellectual, and it is only along this methodical route that the white intellectual can be prodded and challenged into taking a stand on social change. The white intellectual will never take this position on his own, because there will always be some "establishment" posture

* At the New School, Aptheker reserved the right to clarify to Herbert Hill exactly what John Henrik Clarke meant when the latter pressed his attack on Ralph Ellison. In response to this typical bit of Apthekerian paternalism, Clarke responded: "I think Dr. Aptheker put it correctly."

and privilege he will want to defend, be it Anglo-Saxon supremacy, the Jewish intellectual mystique, or the assimilationist worship of the WASP ideal in the cultural arts. (That there are some blacks participating in this latter category can certainly be deemed a source of ideological confusion for all concerned.)

This very schizoid ambivalence is what befogs the clique consciousness of the writers who staged the New School conference. Most aptly, this conference was "dedicated to the memory of the late Lorraine Hansberry," for indeed, ideologically, she was the group's inspiration, and her literary and aesthetic ideals are theirs. Consequently, not a mumbling word that smacks of criticism of Hansberry's work will ever come from this group, for that would be tantamount to criticizing themselves. They could never admit that they have been accepted by different establishments mostly on the basis of inferior work, or that they are talking out of both sides of the mouth: projecting the Afro-American image in literature as Negro writers today, and tomorrow, switching images (à la Hansberry's *Brustein*), yet swearing that they are still projecting the "black" image, just as if everybody were truly color-blind.

Sylvester Leaks opened his panel discussion with a paper titled "The Failure of the Black Writer." A most brave and intrepid declaration, considering who was listening and watching, he then proceeded to criticize not a single Negro writer by name—present or absent. The topic of the panel was: "What Negro Novelists are Saying." However, the first person to speak on this panel was Lorraine Hansberry's husband, Robert Nemiroff, not previously listed on the panel of six. Nemiroff's only reference to the subject at hand—Negro novelists—was that his late wife had started a novel that would not be published. This panel, opening up the dam of confusion, seemed to establish an approach designed to forestall any threat of serious criticism of any literary in-group member. Hence, with the exception of the blasts at Ellison and Baldwin, nothing emerged but bland critical platitudes and impersonal generalizations. At one point Killens delivered his prepared assault on Ellison:

> Herbert Hill, newly blossoming literary expert on Negro affairs . . . acclaimed Ralph Ellison for all the wrong reasons because Ellison's work, according to Mr. Hill, transcends the traditional occupation of the Negro writer. . . .

Well, now Mr. Hill, aside from the insufferable, paternalistic arrogance of this statement, let us take up this question of the mainstream and face the fact that it contains some rather sickly fish from top to bottom.

Killens obviously thinks the literary mainstream rather polluted unless one, of course, enters either from the Left or from the *Urbanite*. At the time of *Freedom* newspaper, however, the word mainstream had not come into vogue; rather it was "Negro-white" unity plus "socialist realism."

John Henrik Clarke also got in his blows at Ellison:

I particularly wanted to take up with Mr. Hill this continued love affair with Ralph Ellison who is standing outside of his people's struggle, making olympian remarks about how that struggle should be conducted.

Hill, who is the NAACP's Labor Secretary, replied:

I would categorically deny that, by the way. I am sorry that we don't have a chance to discuss Mr. Ellison's work. I would simply challenge that point of view.

Clarke:

I hope Mr. Hill can be brief with this exaggeration of the role of Ralph Ellison who has spent so much time in the last ten years in flight from his own people and has not even answered most mail addressed to him by his fellow black writers and has said positively that art and literature are not racial. He won't come into any Afro-American writer's conference. I think Ellison wrote one very interesting thing. From the point of view of craftsmanship it was a very good and powerful work. Whether Ralph Ellison will follow up, whether Ralph Ellison has grown up is open to question in many quarters starting with me.

Hill:

Let me say that I do not see how any intelligent person not committed to a previous bias can read *Invisible Man* and affirm that Mr. Ellison stands aside from the struggle for racial justice in the United States. . . . I am not authorized to speak for Mr. Ellison. He speaks very well for himself.

Enter Herbert Aptheker:

I just wanted to say that I assume Mr. Clarke has read Ralph Ellison's book and probably many in the audience have; and I have also. The *Invisible Man* was done about ten years ago. . . .

Clarke:

1952.

Aptheker:

It is unfortunate that Mr. Ellison is not here. . . . I would say that his work, since the *Invisible Man,* even though he is not here and I prefer not to talk that way in his absence, but in terms of what he has published and also his published assertions, he has made himself rather not particularly visible in the struggles of the Negro people.

Clarke:

I want to take the qualification further than that. I think Dr. Aptheker put it correctly. I was referring to the last ten years. And the last ten years when Baldwin took flight and went to Paris hating himself and his people, literally, but did come back and enter the mainstream of the struggle. Whether he is psychologically back home completely opens maybe a question. But at least he knows the road that leads to home. But Mr. Ralph Ellison seems to have been going further away from home in that sense.

We can see now that the Killens' group, in a precarious situation these days, cannot attack Ellison on craftsmanship, or even content any more (as Killens did on *Freedom* newspaper), because none of them has written anything even remotely comparable to Ellison's achievements. Hence they must assail him on the question of participation in the "struggle," and the fact that Ellison once stated that art and literature are not "racial." But Clarke forgets that Lorraine Hansberry, their great mentor, said precisely the same thing—*Raisin* was not "racial," it was not a "Negro play," it was about "Americans." At the 1959 writers' conference sponsored by Killens' group and AMSAC, Lorraine Hansberry's paper was not about "Negro writers' problems" but about the "decadence" of such white writers as Tennessee Williams and others.* Nobody protested that her remarks were not racial. Nothing was said until after this conference when Hansberry scandalized the leading lights of the Harlem Writers Guild by declaring that "Negro writers are retarded!" *That* raised some ire.

However, even if Ellison did express the view that literature and art are not racial, as Clarke insists, the evidence remains that all of Ellison's work as exemplified in *Invisible Man* and *Shadow and Act* is definitely racial. I would rather believe that Ellison expressed this view in 1959, when he refused to attend the AMSAC conference, in order to avoid being involved with Killens whose *Freedom* newspaper review of *Invisible Man* Ellison had every right to resent on more than political grounds. Moreover, Ellison never went as far as Miss Hansberry did to show all concerned that she truly believed literature and art were not racial. The literary leftwing has always functioned on the principle that *some* Negro writers are more privileged than others.

But there is much more behind this Clarke-Killens attack on Ellison than comes out. Killens has a personal literary stake in all this, which Clarke does not. Moreover, Killens' leftwing background precedes that of Clarke by several years. The truth is that the radical leftwing will never forgive Ellison for writing *Invisible Man,* no matter what Ellison does or does not do about the "struggle." Thus for Clarke to chide Ellison for refusing to attend any Afro-American writers' conference is naïve in the extreme—especially conferences run by all the leftwing's favored Negro writers with political axes to grind in the presence of the leading white Communist Party theoretician and historian on the Negro.

Moreover, there would be little value in Ellison's attending a Killens-led conference, unless permitted to discuss socialist realism and Negro writing on the Left. But there are no Pasternaks among these leftwing-sponsored Negro writers. Thus in 1959, both Killens and Mayfield refused to allow a debate at the AMSAC conference on the influence of socialist realism on the freedom of Negro writers. Since Ellison's writing career on the Left precedes that of

* This paper was so inappropriate that it had to be omitted from the "Selected Papers from the First Conference of Negro Writers—The American Negro Writer and his Roots" published by AMSAC, March 1959, despite the fact that Lorraine Hansberry was the star writer at the conference.

Killens, Ellison knows much better than Clarke what happens to Negro writers on the Left who refuse to submit themselves to the standards of socialist realism. Clarke, who is not really a *creative* writer, never had to cope with this question.

Ralph Ellison does not owe the Left anything, since the Left did not make him as a writer. Hence Ellison is not morally obligated to support any struggle or any Negro writers' conferences initiated by the Left. Let the leftwing writers' clique in the Harlem Writers Guild get *their* own house in order and beamed in on reality. They have no right to demand that other writers fall in line behind *them* because the struggle is larger and broader than they are, with more ramifications and complexities than their limited imaginations can encompass. Let them remember that there are still writers functioning today who long ago assumed their writer's prerogative to tell the radical Left: *You people do not understand the black people's dilemma in the United States.* What has happened to those writers?

But note how obediently John Henrik Clarke, the Africanist-Afro-American Nationalist, mouths every twisted, hypocritical ambivalence of the leftwing integrationists in Killens' group. Hill was right when he intimated Clarke was critically moved by a "previous bias."

In 1959, the same Killens crew decided that Frank Yerby was no longer to be considered a "Negro writer," having joined Wright, Baldwin, etc., in Paris to rewrite new versions of *The Foxes of Harrow* that got whiter and whiter. Would Clarke put Ellison in Yerby's category? He would. But Clarke ought to go back to the May, 1961, issue of *Urbanite* and read the last paragraph of Lorraine Hansberry's article. There he will see that in *her* mind, Frank Yerby was in the same category with Charles White, Leontyne Price, Lena Horne, Harry Belafonte, James Baldwin, John Killens, Nina Simone, Paul Robeson, Langston Hughes, Julian Mayfield, Odetta, P.J. Sydney, Eartha Kitt and Pearl Bailey. They were, in her words, "a band of angels hurling forth the art of twenty millions."* Well, this was Miss Hansberry's opinion, and Clarke should take note of the multicolored witches' brew

---

* Probably remembering her previous attack on *The Outsider*, Miss Hansberry did not include Richard Wright.

of ethnic imagery comprising *this* list of candidates for high honors in the field of racial identity.

John Henrik Clarke is to be respected for one thing—he has never equivocated on his pride in being black and Africanesque. Today, however, it seems Clarke has been placed in a most awkward and degrading ideological position. He has to defend and play second-fiddle to certain Johnny-come-latelys whose "black pride," in literature and art, is turned at will according to its cultural marketability.

Instead of attacking Ralph Ellison, Clarke should have been asking for some clarification from Herbert Aptheker as to what Aptheker meant by this statement:

> Thus, the components of what Veblen saw in the intellectual pre-eminence of European Jews, and what Ashley Montague saw in the natural superiority of women, and what Karl Marx saw as the saving quality of those who labor all are present in the American Negro, men and women.
>
> One does not have to move from these opinions to perverse distortions leading off into insidious nationalism, but one should see in these opinions additional suggestions towards understanding the centrality of the Negro question.

Notice that Aptheker did not ascribe natural superiority to the working class, but only a "saving quality" (no longer even a revolutionary quality!). However, Aptheker's paper propounded what he calls "The Superiority of the American Negro." In the abstract mass concept, Aptheker used to view the Negro people across historical vistas, as a beautiful, untarnished and noble folk struggling for equality. These were the ingredients of that peculiar genre of leftwing romanticism in Negro history writing. That historical stream continued, unbroken, from Nat Turner and Denmark Vesey to Sojourner Truth, from John Brown and Frederick Douglass to W.E.B. DuBois and Herbert Aptheker and ultimately to the Communist Party. But this abstract mass concept was applicable only to Aptheker's brand of writing—so easily translated into dogma; to most Negroes, in the flesh, he was quite arrogant. Today, this peculiarly inverted racial attitude holds the Negro "superior," a patronization carried to its ultimate dogmatic degree for political purposes. For a Black Muslim to say this, doubtless would bring from Aptheker the charge of "reactionary race chauvinism," similar to his own attitudes to the Garvey movement.

Questions about Negro-Jewish relationships on the cultural front were raised during the New School conference, but the Killens group was absolutely tongue-tied on that score. The Anglo-Saxon cultural question, too, was injected—not by a Negro writer, however—but by David Boroff, a Jewish critic. Aptheker, in the course of his paean to Negro superiority, had made one of his rare references to the Jewish question, indirectly and historically, by his mention of Veblen. But Boroff put his "ethnic" cards on the table and—to quote Killens' favorite preachment—"told it like it was": "I think it can be accurately and soberly said that Jews represent the single most creative segment of the artistic community today. I don't say this with the faintest amount of chauvinism. It seems to be a sign of the times." And then to drive the nail squarely into the palpitant heart of the diseased, dying and wasted body of the American cultural establishment, Boroff added: *"White Anglo-Saxon creativity is at a kind of low ebb."*

He then agreed with Kristin Hunter, one of the new Negro novelists, on upholding "the creative individuality of the Negro writer," implying that there are as many black images as there are Negro writers so why attempt to fuse thematic multiplicity into one literary and cultural image. And consciously or unconsciously, to preclude and negate the necessity or possibility of such a literary, cultural and thematic fusion, Boroff declared: "We are here to discuss literary values, not political values."

No one discerned more quickly than Boroff that this impecunious crew of literary conferees were getting into very deep critical waters. Thus he hustled back to safer shores by declaring that he did not want to get into a hassle over this "Jewish thing." He acted shrewdly, however, because not a living soul in Killens' literary camp was prepared to go into that question, even had there been ample time for it. Yet ironically, he had verged on permitting the great bedrock facts of American cultural existence to spill forth onto the agenda for open, honest discussion.

Aptheker claimed that today Negroes are superior—by which he possibly meant morally superior. But the New School conference was not debating morals, as such, but literary values. Aptheker, deep in his leftwing patrician soul, knew very well that Negroes might claim a superior moral stance because of civil rights, but, in terms of literary values it "jus' ain't so." However Boroff made it clear who in his estimate were superior in literary values. Aptheker most likely agreed with Boroff's sentiments on the preeminence of American Jews, although Aptheker seldom spouts his Jewishness, no doubt for fear of being taken for a pro-Zionist parading under Communist colors. But Boroff stepped again into the breach, demanding that literary and political values be separated, as if to say that art, literature and culture should not be confused with politics. Although possibly Boroff had no overt political axe to grind in Jewish affairs, one can never be sure on this question. However Aptheker as a leading Marxist could never agree that literary values and political values are separate, because the aesthetics of socialist realism dictate otherwise. Nevertheless, in his criticism of C. Wright Mills, Aptheker had gotten around the issue of culture vs. politics by charging Mills with seeking "unreal and Utopian political devices," for indulging in "appeals confined to intelligentsia."[1] Yet Aptheker had actually understated Mills' position on the intelligentsia by failing to spell out just what *were* Mills' appeals. On this same page in Aptheker's critique he mentions the "intensifying cultural and ethical degeneration, the reality of persistent racism" in American society. Yet Aptheker could not, or would not, see that Mills had clearly said to the intellectuals—This cultural and ethical degeneration *must become a political issue,* and we must get to the root of the matter by the formulation of new demands and programs for these issues. To Aptheker, this is utopian! Perhaps this is a natural conclusion for a man who has tried for more than twenty-five years to apply his European Marxist dialectic to American realities. But in terms of the American dialectic, it is *his* Marxism that is utopian and irrelevant. With all of Aptheker's stodgy Marxian platitudes about the "centrality of the Negro question" and the "reality of persistent racism," he cannot see this racism other than as a manifestation of class struggle, when in fact it is an ethnic group struggle. Despite the mounting sociological evidence that the working class of America has no labor party nor wants one, and in fact supports

[1] "The World of C. Wright Mills," *op. cit.,* p. 83.

capitalistic ideology with every fiber of its class being, both Aptheker and William F. Warde remain victims of their own myopia.

In *The Sociological Imagination*,[2] C. Wright Mills pointed out that many political policies "are based on inadequate and misleading definitions of reality." Mills explained: "If we take the dogmatic view that what is to men's interests, whether they are interested in it or not, is all that need concern us morally . . . we may become manipulators or coercers, or both, rather than persuaders within a society." Mills avoided this trap, by exercising great intellectual integrity, and added: "What I am suggesting is that by addressing ourselves to issues and to troubles, and formulating them as problems of social science, we stand the best chance, I believe the only chance to make reason democratically relevant to human affairs in a free society, and so realize the classic values that underlie the promise of our studies."[3]

Thus what is at the bottom of the clash between Marxian and Millsian ideology is purely a question of social methodology. The Marxian methodology has not worked, but the Marxists did not want to allow Mills the social scientist's right and responsibility to seek other refinements of method to cure the present crisis in social science practice. Aptheker argued that "a singular failure on Mills' part to show some 'sociological imagination' . . ." was his refusal to see that the social cures he pursued are "part of a generalized political and social attack upon the ruling class which maintains and benefits from such crisis [in social science]."[4] In other words, Aptheker's only cogent reply to Mills was: Become a Marxist and that will solve everything. And so conflict and argument over social method circle indefinitely in search of a theoretical resolution within a new synthesis.

The basic elements of such synthesis were present, in the disordered debates that raged at the New School writers' conference, but such a task is complex, and none of the Negro panelists were sufficiently conversant with other related controversies that had raged beforehand over the role of the intellectuals. Since Aptheker had downgraded C. Wright Mills' appeal to the inteliigentsia as

---

[2] Mills, *The Sociological Imagination* (New York: Oxford University Press, 1959), p. 194.
[3] *Ibid.*, p. 194.
[4] "The World of C. Wright Mills," *op. cit.*, p. 111.

utopian, Aptheker should have been forced to state his views on the special role of the Negro intelligentsia (beyond that of tail-gaters on the civil rights bandwagon). If intellectuals as a *stratum* have no special role to play, neither do *Negro* creative intellectuals. Patently that is not true; therefore Marxists like Aptheker and William F. Warde of the Trotskyists, who intervene at every opportunity into the affairs of the Negro movement, must be sharply criticized and debated on their views. Warde, for example, cannot be permitted to get away with the attitude that scholars, ministers, scientists and writers are "peripheral and not the central forces in our society." This is a serious point, for if the *Negro writer* is peripheral, then what intrinsic value lies in the much-heralded dialogue between Negro and white intellectuals? Of what value are Negro writers' conferences?

The New School conference was valuable in that it demonstrated clearly the limitations of a conference composed only of writers, rather than practitioners of all the arts. This conference revealed that Negro writers are struggling under severe illusions, intellectual handicaps, and many societal and cultural misapprehensions about reality. As David Boroff pointed out (whether intentionally or inadvertently) the Negro writer is up against the real ascendancy of the Jewish writer and artist in a country of white Anglo-Saxon Protestant dominance in every field but the creative and cultural. For David Boroff to admit that the white Anglo-Saxon creative impulse is just about dead might be news to some of Killens' group, but in truth, it has been on the wane ever since its last spurt in the 1920's. Since that time, Jewish writers and artists have not only filled that particular creative void, they have also preempted a considerable portion of Negro thematic material both in literature and in the field of social science studies.

During the 1920's, when the Anglo-Saxon creative artist was still fecund and original, there was much Anglo-Saxon-Jewish collaboration, especially in the theater. The late Lorraine Hansberry condemned the stereotypes of a *Porgy and Bess;* far more significant is the fact that this great symbol of the Negro's second-class status in the cultural arts was a product of Jewish and Anglo-Saxon collaboration.* Civil-writers, however, like Lorraine Hansberry,

* George and Ira Gershwin, and DuBose Heyward.

will be very careful to limit their charges of literary paternalism to writers like the Frenchman Jean Genet, far removed from the home ground where native WASPs and Jews have been battening off the "folk" for decades, both in literature and music. As a play, *The Blacks* does not touch the heart of the American cultural problem. Moreover, it is in a class by itself as theatrical literature in terms of its newer quality and form. It shows up writers of the level of the Killens' group as rather pedestrian, parochial, uninspired, unimaginative latecomers to the 1930's tradition of protest and pure realism. Now, when Baldwin, Killens, Hansberry and others have finally caught up with the 1930's, the Jewish writers are doing something else. Hence, the Killens group stands helpless (albeit vocal) before a situation in American culture whose historical derivatives they do not comprehend. Yet they themselves unwittingly played certain purblind roles in the recent history of this cultural development.

No one can much blame Negro writers for drifting leftward in culture and politics at some point in their individual careers. But once they do, too many either become captives for the balance of their intellectual lives, or else are ultimately disillusioned (if not expelled) and drift into a negative kind of isolation or exile. Few of them ever seem to learn anything positive about reality from this experience. The radical Left of the 1940's and 1950's was *not* a movement of Anglo-Saxons or their ideology. It was an ethnic movement dominated by Negroes and Jews, and it was the Jews who ideologically influenced the Negroes. Thus the radical Left in America has developed in such a way that the Jewish ethnic group, one of the smallest in the country, had more political prestige, wielded more theoretical and organizational power, than the Negro who in fact represented the largest ethnic minority. Consequently, all political and cultural standards on the radical Left were in the main established and enforced *by* Jews *for,* and *on,* Negroes. This Negro-Jewish state of affairs was paralleled outside the radical Left as well, in the civil rights organizations.

One can explain this development, rationalize it, excuse it, condemn it or uphold it, call it negative or positive, but the fact remains that it was ethnically undemocratic. More important, it has retarded and smothered the Negro's intellectual and political development. On the cultural front, it has prevented Negro writers and artists from grappling in a creative fashion with the underdeveloped cultural status of the Negro within a multicultural and multiethnic society. The Negro has been boxed in, politically, economically and culturally. He has been unable to improvise on another group's standards and rules of playing the game. On the other hand, many Negroes have developed their own brand of laissez-faire acquiescence to the status quo. These writers did not realize they were limiting the range and the scope of their own talents, so bent were they on "making it." Nor did they see through the cultural ruse being perpetrated on them, and the cultural paternalism and control exercised behind that ruse. Herbert Aptheker's tumultuous praise for William Branch's play *In Splendid Error,* in *Masses and Mainstream,*[5] went unchallenged; no one would admit that it was actually a bad play that happened to be about John Brown and Frederick Douglass, thus praiseworthy as an historical "civil rights-protest play." Leftwing Jewish writers, however, were *not* writing this kind of a play. One of the big theatrical hits of the time was *The World of Sholem Aleichem,* a dramatization of the Jewish folkwriter's stories, and certainly *no* protest play. The Killens group were very impressed with this example of creative Jewish theater art—mainly because Ruby Dee was given a white role to play as an "integrated" casting gift—*this* was the great achievement!

John O. Killens' summing up of the New School conference was an exercise in literary and cultural double-talk. He took no stand on a single question of literary principle, simply paying lip service to all points of view on that intangible called "universality."

While Killens did not *openly* say he favored the "black-outside-white-inside" literary school, or the "I am just a writer who happens to be a Negro" stance of James Baldwin and others, he did make the following revealing comments:

But most of the writers that were here this weekend seemed to be asking—does art have any nobler purpose—has art ever had any nobler purpose? The question kept being raised on the platform and from the audience, and it reminded me of Sidney Brustein and *The Sign in Sidney Brustein's Window,* the ques-

[5] November, 1954.

tion how? The how is important. I should say the how is damned important. How do we reach the ears of the Negro people of our country?

Note the flicker of the twin-image, the Negro-Jewish identity-exchange motif of the Hansberry dramatic saga, referred to by one who has always maintained that *he* was never in doubt as to *who* he is and *what* he is as a writer. I am a Negro writer, said Killens, and my materials are basically the Negro people. But, after all is said and done, Killens must still peer from the outside into "Sidney Brustein's Window" to find out how to "reach the ears of the Negro people." The New School writers' conference demonstrated, without a doubt, that the former Harlem leftwing literary and cultural elite are possessed of an intellectual, literary and creative ethnic duality they refuse to admit. Taken as a whole, they are neither white, black nor Jewish, but an amalgam of all three.

Unless the Negro creative intellectuals, as a stratum, can evolve creative and artistic policies that will govern cultural programs, organizations and self-sustained and -administered research institutions, they cannot achieve cultural democracy against the competition of white and/or Jewish intelligentsia.

America today is a cultural desert strewn with the corpses of commercialized commodity-art where sweet voices sing lullabies of cultural degeneration; its aesthetics are anti-life, its images those of lunacy and the propaganda of destruction. In America the political power and economic status of the white Anglo-Saxon are considered ample compensation for the nation's lack of cultural prestige imposed on it by WASP rule. In this void, the Jew has played a many-sided role as the ethnic middleman of culture, whereas the Negro has been a mere commodity on the cultural market to be bought out, sold short, sold out, or else frozen out. This situation cannot long endure if this nation is to haul itself out of its own internal mire and rehabilitate its image in the eyes of the world. The Negro creative intellectual has a potentially powerful role to play in this process, if he can master a literary and cultural critique of his own. But this will require a vast intellectual and critical reorientation which it is doubtful the old-guard Negro writers of the New School writers' conference can achieve. New, younger, more willing and imaginative creative forces are needed.

Back in 1932, Wallace Thurman wrote a novel in which he satirized the Negro artists and writers of the 1920's Negro renaissance. One of the characters complained that "the average Negro intellectual and artist has no goal, no standards, no elasticity, no pregnant germ plasm." After praising only one Negro artist of that time who had "the elements of greatness," the character observed again: "The rest of us are mere journeymen, planting seed for someone else to harvest. We all get sidetracked sooner or later. The older ones become warped by propaganda. We younger ones are mired in decadence. None of us seem to be able to rise above our environment."[6]

Wallace Thurman called his novel *Infants of the Spring.* Yet, in over forty years, the Negro writers of the New School conference, the former Harlem leftwing literary and cultural elite, have not really advanced much further than the Negro renaissance writers in terms of ideas. If the 1920's Negro writers were "infants of the spring" the present 1967 elite are "adolescents of the long hot summer." They are intellectuals in a crisis, but a crisis occasioned not merely by an inherited backlog of unresolved history, but by the fact that they are not truly *intellectuals,* by any historical and cultural definition.

[6] Thurman, *Infants of the Spring* (New York: Macauley Company, 1932), p. 221.

Intellectuals and the Theater of the 1960's—
As Medium and Dialogue

The American Negro has been an integral ingredient in the development of native American theater since the days of the old plantation minstrel form which he originated. His innovations in musical theater merged with elements of British operetta imported from abroad, to form the typical American stage musical. Since the 1920's the American Negro has been floundering about on the fringes of the legitimate theater, sometimes in, mostly out, through ups and downs, good times and bad. He has contributed many outstanding performers and performances, a few playwrights, and a nostalgic tradition for theater lovers with a penchant for Negro theatrical exoticism. Yet, at this very moment, the Negro does not own, operate or sustain a single theater institution of any critical importance anywhere in the United States.

The reader can rightly comment—Well, it was shown much earlier in this critique that the events which led to the collapse of the American Negro Theater of the 1940's demonstrated that Negroes do not want a separate Negro theatrical institution. Hence why dwell on the question? It must be dealt with again, because Negroes in the theater persist in carrying on a witless dialogue on the issue, a most evasive, double-talking, illogical dialogue.

Accordingly, the theater—a collective art—is the cultural form that most signally reflects *all* the collective and critical liabilities of Negro creative intellectuals as a class. The plea for integration of Negroes in a sick theater parallels the extreme absurdity of the civil rights plea for an integrated open society to be contrived out of the social reality of group pluralism. Let us review some of the dialogue on theatrical integration during the 1960's.

James Baldwin, whose protest play *Blues for Mr. Charlie* was a

prize example of literary civilwritism, would have achieved more
had he talked less about the Negro in the theater and devoted
more time to constructing his drama, molding his characters and
making a closer study of Mississippi society, both black and white,
which his play revealed he was not very well acquainted with.
Instead, Baldwin botched up a potentially great play, which need
not have been the mere protest tour de force he made it.

Contrary to what some of Baldwin's writings reflect, this writer
lives in a world of his own—a world often removed from the realities of the present as well as from much pertinent history of his
own Harlem. He has become too glib about facts and trends. In a
Herald Tribune interview,[1] Baldwin confessed to the reporter that
he did not think much of the American theater as an institution—
"the theater fails when it ceases to experiment and discover"—but
then went on to say that he did not believe "there is a Negro
theater in the United States, or that such a development would be
especially worthwhile." "What is crucial," Baldwin said, "is that
the country must be willing to hear the black man's own version
of himself and of white people." He then fell back on what, by
1964, had already become canard—integration of the Negro in the
American theater. (Integration in the theater had been given its
hearing in the Actor's Equity Integrated Showcase for top producers in 1959.)

Baldwin, in his *Herald Tribune* interview, garbled Harlem's
theatrical history by projecting events of the 1920's into the decade when he grew up—the 1930's. He confused the Lafayette Players (a Negro repertory company organized well before World War
I) with the Lafayette Theater which, during the 1930's, was
strictly a vaudeville house and later the site for Federal WPA
Theater productions. He had stars like Bill Robinson and Louis
Armstrong being discovered in the 1930's. "Looking back to the
1930's, when he was growing up in Harlem," the *Herald Tribune*
said, "Mr. Baldwin spoke of a communion between the whites and
the Negroes that does not exist today." "It was a Negro renaissance, and had a real importance for the people of Harlem," said
Baldwin. This was the same Harlem Baldwin had described in his
essay "The Harlem Ghetto," but there was no mention *there* of

[1] *The New York Herald Tribune*, April 19, 1964, Magazine Section, p. 22.

any "communion between the whites and the Negroes." In that essay, Harlem was a dire dungeon for its humanity, where nothing happened of "real importance for the people of Harlem." And what Negro renaissance took place in Harlem in the 1930's? Harlem history has it that the Negro renaissance of Hughes, Robeson, *et al.*, blossomed in the 1920's and was killed by the Depression of the 1930's. Just what Harlem is Baldwin talking about?

James Baldwin has no real historical insight into the Negro in the theater as a particular cultural development. That is why he garbles his arguments over integration and compounds an already confused situation. As a playwright he shows no awareness that the Negro in the theater cannot be discussed as an entity separate from the development of the Negro playwright within the theater as a whole.

The Negro, as a professional writer of dramatic theater material, did not appear until after World War I. Before then, Negroes who did any writing at all for the theater contributed sketches and librettos for Negro musicals and revues. Some of these people were quite good, it is recorded, but they were not *playwrights.**

As one theatrical historian points out about the early decades of the twentieth century: "The Negro was eager to play serious drama, but there was almost no effort on his part to write it."[2] Thus, the developments in the theater having to do with integration, or the lack of it, begin in the 1920's, when Negro playwrights began to emerge. (Among the most notable were Frank Wilson in 1920, Willis Richardson in 1925, and Eulalie Spence in 1927.) Since it so happens that the Negro actor and performer, for most of his history, has not depended on the Negro playwright for theatrical roles, *there has never been any real rapport and collaboration between Negro dramatist and Negro performer.*

---

* Historian John Hope Franklin records that William Wells Brown, anti-slavery leader and author, "was the first Negro to write a play—*The Escape; or a Leap to Freedom,* which appeared in 1858." See Franklin's *From Slavery to Freedom,* New York, Alfred A. Knopf, 1948, p. 230. As theatrical history, however, this fact falls within the same category as the career of Ira Aldridge, the Negro tragedian who died in Lodz, Poland, in 1867, after becoming famous in Europe. His career was "in no degree a direct factor in the Negro's theatrical development." See James Weldon Johnson, *op. cit.,* p. 87.

[2] *The Negro Caravan,* ed. Sterling A. Brown, Arthur P. Davis, and Ulysses Lee (New York: Citadel Press, 1941), p. 499.

In *The Village Voice* during 1959, Lorraine Hansberry compared Walter Younger (of *Raisin*) and Willy Loman (of *Death of a Salesman*) on certain levels as characters of similar dramatic intensity.[3] In comparing Willy Loman to Hamlet, later on in the article, she thereby created a new triumvirate of high-intensity *dramatis personae*. *The Village Voice* had the patronizing gall to print this nonsense, no doubt in the interest of furthering middle-class Village-Negro radicalism. Yet in 1964, *The Village Voice* critic hardly went overboard on *Brustein's Window*—a "Village" play—despite the fact that many of Miss Hansberry's admirers considered it better than *Raisin*. Critic Michael Smith commented that "the play takes itself seriously, therefore it is serious. It has an air of importance, therefore it is important." He then neatly punctured the balloon—*"But the play is dreadful* [italics added]."

Lorraine Hansberry always tried to say important things, and she also took herself very seriously. The pity of it all was that she took herself *too* seriously, in light of what relatively little she had to say. She probably truly believed that *A Raisin in the Sun* was great. Yet the very fact that this specimen of Negro dramatic writing was so highly-graded by the critics attests to the low esteem in which Negro creators are held in this world. This "A-for-effort" criticism is meant to keep the Negro creator at just that level of aesthetic achievement. The strange thing about the critical reaction to the plays of Baldwin and Hansberry was that *Mr. Charlie*, on which the critics were divided, was chockful of all the elements anyone needed for a first-rate, high-voltage dramatic shocker, although Baldwin wasted the play's potential. *Raisin,* on the other hand, which won unanimous approval, was essentially nothing but souped-up soap opera. Of course no positive criticism was forthcoming on craft, or on how these plays related to the Negro world in terms of realism, or better, naturalism. This indicates other crucial reasons why the Negro creative intellectual must cultivate his *own* literary and cultural critique.

When Negro playwrights attempt to discuss integration in the theater, they are just as far removed from reality as they are in their plays, thematically. They will not discuss openly the fact that

3 "Willy Loman, Walter Younger, and He Who Must Live," *The Village Voice*, April 12, 1959, p. 7.

Negro-written plays are not produced with Negro money, but with white money, a fact that has as much to do with integration as anything else. Yet I recall that somewhere in *The Village Voice* Lorraine Hansberry attacked Jean Genet's play, *The Blacks*, as another example of white paternalism practiced on the Negro in the theater. She no doubt had her reasons, but I do not recall hearing any of the Negro actors who played in *The Blacks* complaining about paternalism. Moreover, Miss Hansberry never mentioned that certain of the people responsible for producing *The Blacks* were some of her old paternalistic friends from the uptown-downdown cultural leftwing axis. She probably did not know it, but there are and were, leftwing theatrical producers who would produce a play written by whites *about* Negroes, but who would never produce such a play *by* a Negro—their record proves it. But the existence of this kind of paternalism was never admitted by the literary and cultural elite on the Negro Left. Today's Negro creative intellectual is so confused, tortured and bedeviled that he does not know what he wants, where he is going, or how to get there—or if he really wants to go there at all. If he is not backtracking along the route from the leftwing era of *Freedom* newspaper to the *Urbanite* era of sophisticated affluence, he is shifting his position from one pole to the other—from nationalism to integration.

Ossie Davis is a case in point. Recall his great outpouring of the profound rediscovery of his "blackness" in *Freedomways'* Spring, 1962, issue. There he recounted how *Purlie* taught him how to take a black position in the cultural arts, *i.e.,* in the theater. We must learn to "create for our own people," Davis avowed. We must think, act, live and write from a black position. That was surely strong nationalistic brew for *Freedomways,* so someone must have gotten to Davis subsequently and advised him that he could not say such things out loud and remain within the family as there were too many "black sheep" out there who had to be disowned. Hence two years later Ossie Davis changed his tune, on the theater page of *The New York Times,* where he switched to a new theme of universality in the theater. He did not specify that this universality had to be black (like Purlie), but by now, Ossie Davis was dedicating himself to saving the theater as an institution by attempting to use it for reforming the "common morality and to elevate public taste." This can be done "only by a profound alteration of what the audience has come to buy from us. We must revolutionize the nature of pleasure in the American theater." And how did Ossie Davis see himself, as a playwright, pursuing this new thematic vista of reformed taste? He said:

> Once I feel the truth, the internal *is*-ness of, say, a Negro, a Jew, a Gentile, a Catholic, a Communist, a homosexual or a Nazi, I can no longer pretend that he is a stranger, or a foreigner, or an outcast. What is more, I will be so pleasured in my new knowledge that I would not want to so pretend. I will myself have become, at one and the same time, all of these things.[4]

This could be called, for lack of a more apt term, the de-blacking of Ossie Davis as he progressed from the specific to the general. For Davis, the proverb "Know thyself" was a theme that lasted only as long as it took an issue of *Freedomways* to be printed, read, and forgotten. Baldwin must have cheered at the proof, at last, that *Giovanni's Room* had not been written in vain. The aesthetes of Broadway must have sighed with happy relief that with this new promise of no more Negro protest plays they could now welcome the Negro author into the universal fraternity, without the least thought about his color. On June 15, 1964, there was a big spread in *The New York Times'* theater section under the headline: "New Role of Negroes in Theater Reflects Ferment of Integration." Featured prominently were all the original members of the Harlem in-group from former days, who had "made it." The article quoted the following people on the state of the Negro in the theater: LeRoi Jones, Baldwin, Lorraine Hansberry, Ossie Davis, Alice Childress, Gloria Foster, Diana Sands, Louis Peterson, Lonnie Elder, Frances Foster, among others. The total philosophy of these celebrities can be summed up as pro-integration; but their individual statements contradicted this concept when stacked against the prevailing condition of the theater both on and off Broadway. The inner logic of what they all said as an elite body, a select group, is that for them, integration means they are going to integrate *themselves.* In other words—*We Negroes don't want to destroy the illusion that whites are really white; we want you*

---

[4] *The New York Times*, August 23, 1964, Section II, p. 1.

whites to destroy the illusion that black is really black. In discussing integration in the theater in *The New York Times,* no one was honest enough to admit that the question of skin color has a great deal to do with which Negro gets integrated first and where. Thus, the following prize statement on integration: "Diana Sands said recently, 'Why can't you have an interracial couple in the comedy *Mary, Mary?* For an interracial couple to play *Mary, Mary* is preposterous. I don't think interracial couples should play anything but interracial couples. Would you cast a white actor in *The Blacks?* It's a terribly complex problem.' "

That must have stopped them all, but no one, reportedly, replied to Diana Sands. The ironic humor in this honest remark is that Miss Sands, a very fair-skinned Negro, was playing a white woman in the lead role in the comedy, *The Owl and the Pussycat.*

As we have seen, the theme of integration in the theater is primarily an actor's and performer's plea. It is a bread-and-butter issue of work, and has little to do with anything institutional. Due to the persuasions of the civil rights demands of the 1960's, integrated opportunities for performers rose to a high then fell off, due to the unstable and highly speculative nature of theatrical production in New York City. Here are Actor's Equity figures for Negro actors working from 1960 to 1965:

Jobs Available

	1964-65	1963-64	1962-63	1961-62	1960-61
On Broadway	74	168	51	123	126
Off Broadway	32	116	26	50	29

These figures, it must be noted, only partially explain integrated casting. During the high season of 1963-64, three *all-Negro* shows accounted for 99 of the total of 168 Negroes employed during that season on Broadway. Of the 24 shows employing Negroes that season, 16 had integrated casts. And of course many more shows hired no Negroes at all. In the 1964-65 season, on-Broadway jobs for Negro actors dropped to 74. The percentage figures for off-Broadway told pretty much the same story.

These above figures were quoted in an article[5] written by Fred-

[5] "The Negro in Today's Theatre—Problems and Prospects," *Negro Digest,* April, 1966, pp. 4-12.

erick O'Neal, a Negro actor who is also President of Actor's Equity Association. It so happens that Mr. O'Neal was the co-director of the old American Negro Theater back in the 1940's. O'Neal merely reiterated all of the timeworn clichés about the Negro's plight in the American theater—"The Negro actor feels that he is grossly discriminated against in the casting of shows in all of the entertainment media. Surely his talents could have been used in many parts in a manner that would not have distorted the artistic concept of the production." Then O'Neal goes on to say that the headway made in integrated casting had to do with Negro actors hired for parts where race was "not thematically necessary to the story and not so directed as to imply racial identification." This integrated casting is hardly an artistic or thematic problem in the theater, where a play's theme is central to its stage fate. It comes down to being a problem for a predominantly white-oriented theater to find crevices in a play's structure where a few Negroes can be stuck in; where they can be seen, but where their presence will not interfere with the real theme of the play which is not about Negroes at all. If the play was about, say, a week in the life of a modern President of the United States involved in a foreign policy crisis, where could Negro actors appear? If the playwright limited his characters to only the President's intimate advisers from governmental departments, this would be a difficult play to integrate because our colored folks have not penetrated these circles. Negro actors would have to wait for a play about a President involved in a civil rights crisis (they'll wait a long time) for the Negro presence to be thematically valid. However much O'Neal tries, he cannot see the theater through the eyes of the Negro playwright. He is critical of the trend of protest drama. "For a number of years," he writes, "the Negro writer seemed to approach his work out of a peculiar psychological or doctrinal fixation. . . . The result is that literary work suffers." He agreed with the late Negro scholar Dr. Alain Locke, that "propaganda, pro-Negro and anti-Negro, has scotched the dramatic potentialities of the subject [Negro drama]." O'Neal wants the Negro playwright to transcend these limitations, but he avoids the issue of what kind of a theater institution will permit this. Having participated in one separate Negro theater institution which collapsed, O'Neal appears to be unfavorable to the building of another. He remains impaled on the horns of the integration dilemma. He admits that, for the Negro, "it is very difficult to establish oneself in the theater. There are many heartaches, disappointments and frustrations. In some cases, this has led to mental instability." But despite all the odds, despite the realities of a seriously sick theater system, O'Neal is committed "to pursue on a continuing basis the ultimate objective of complete desegregation of the performing arts." What O'Neal means by desegregation is a completely de-ethnicized theater in America, but there is not, and can never be in our times, any such cultural animal.

O'Neal's article was in contribution to a symposium on Negroes in theater, which included articles by Ossie Davis, Ruby Dee, James Baldwin and LeRoi Jones. This time, Davis espoused "Back to the 'Harlems'—The Flight from Broadway." Unlike Frederick O'Neal, Davis could not, with a straight face, avoid bringing up the ghosts of the old American Negro Theater that haunt all the personalities of his generation. After twenty years, Davis is for the creation of a community theater in all the "Harlems." He wrote: "Harlem has had no significant community theater since ANT closed up shop in 1949-1950. Why? I think the decisive answer is that Broadway discovered ANT's production of *Anna Lucasta* in 1944 and gobbled it up. That, I believe, was the beginning of the end. For suddenly, there was a place 'downtown' on Broadway, for the Negro actor."[6]

ANT, of course, had collapsed long before 1949-1950, at which time there were efforts to revive a lost cause. But Davis cannot tell the whole truth about *Anna Lucasta,* because the scandalous outcome of this play reflected the end result of an internal deterioration that had taken place within ANT before the play was produced. *Anna Lucasta* was first produced in the spring of 1944. It was *not* an original play by an ANT playwright member. Neither was the play orginally about Negro life, but about a Polish family which Abram Hill, ANT's director, *adapted* to Negro life. This was the first basic defection from thematic integrity—the curse of racial imitation. There was something wrong with ANT's playwrights and their intrinsic point of view on

[6] *Ibid.,* p. 16.

Negro life. It took George Freedley, a white drama critic from downtown, to put his finger on the internal problems of ANT, in a review of a revival of ANT's first important and original play-writing achievement—Abram Hill's *On Striver's Row*—first produced in the fall of 1941. The revival of this play indicated that by 1946 the creative resources of ANT had run dry.

In *The Morning Telegraph* of March 2, 1946, Freedley wrote: "When the ANT returns to the kind of experimental work which won it fame, then this reviewer can be expected back but not before."

The American Negro Theater had ceased to experiment, which is the main thing any off-Broadway theater institution must do in order to survive. A Negro theater institution must experiment in order to live, and conversely, must come into being in order to experiment—and never cease to experiment. This is the only way the Negro dramatist can be developed and maintained on any high level of creativity, and the Negro in the theater has no sure future in the theater until then. It will not be achieved in any lasting way in the white-oriented theaters either on or off Broadway, but only in Negro community experimental theaters. Whatever Negroes achieve in the theater elsewhere is secondary, no matter how successful momentarily. *Anna Lucasta* was a great theatrical and financial success, but not for ANT, which created the vehicle. The white producers made the profits and the white playwright of the original script won the fame, which sent him on to a rewarding Hollywood writing career. The production made a star out of Hilda Simms, and rewarded several Negro actors with long-term work contracts, travel and experience. But not a single member of that cast was ever to have such success in the theater again; moreover, it was a success for which ANT paid a terribly high price, for it had over borrowed against the future. The failure of ANT cut the ground from under the Harlem theater movement and prematurely scotched the futures of several potentially good dramatists. Yet Ossie Davis, now seeing little hope for the Negro on Broadway, looks merely for a "decentralization of the theater" to bring more racial democracy within it: "Broadway's loss is bound to be Harlem's gain. At least I hope so. And I want to be there when it happens!"

Ruby Dee, interestingly enough, follows suit by de-emphasizing integration, her main ploy ever since she envisioned a great future for the Negro in the theater downtown, back in her *Freedom* newspaper days. Her contribution to the symposium was an article on Negro actresses, "The Tattered Queens," which though valuable, does not begin to attack the roots of the problem. But she *is* more "ethnic," now: "But are we not, basically, of African descent? In better times to come, there will be equal place on our stage and screens for all shades, all types, all colors. We must see to it that this is so."

James Baldwin's piece was lifted out of the *Urbanite* magazine of 1961 and is too discursive and dated to be of value here. That brings us to the provocative LeRoi Jones and his theme, "In Search of the Revolutionary Theater." For a long while now, Mr. Jones has been plying the thesis of the revolutionary theater, but his analysis of such theater is roughly as effective as describing on paper what an atomic machine can accomplish, without telling how the machine is to be manufactured, mounted, and activated. This approach may fire the social imagination, to be sure, but what are the elements of revolutionary theater that distinguish it from other theater? "The Revolutionary Theater should force change, it should change. . . . The Revolutionary Theater must EXPOSE! Show up the insides of these humans, look into black skulls. . . ." It must "teach [white men] their deaths . . . must Accuse and Attack anything that can be accused and attacked." It "must take dreams and give them reality." The revolutionary theater "should be a theater of World Spirit." And what is that? "Force. Spirit. Feeling," says Jones. "We will talk about the world, and the preciseness with which we are able to summon the world will be our art. Art is method."

"Wittgenstein said ethics and aesthetics are one," says Jones, and "I believe this. . . . So the Broadway theater is a theater of reaction whose ethics like its aesthetics, reflect the spiritual values of this unholy society." Revolutionary theater is a "social theater, but all theater is social theater. But we will change the drawing rooms into places where real things can be said about the real world, or into smoky rooms where the destruction of Washington can be plotted." Jones concluded:

Americans will hate the revolutionary theater because it will be out to destroy them and whatever they believe is real. American cops will try to close the theaters where such nakedness of the human spirit is paraded. . . . We must make an art that will function as to call down the actual wrath of world spirit. We are witch-doctors, and assassins, but we will open a place for the true scientists to expand our consciousness.

Now we see where LeRoi Jones stands, but his kind of theater is just as improbable and impossible as that completely desegregated theater fiction of Frederick O'Neal and the integrationists. Jones has turned the problem on its head. He is confusing an art method with a social method—a method of social change. It is *not* the content of plays (Jones' or anybody else's) that changes the world. On the contrary, it is a world changed (or in the process thereof) by a social method that also changes the contents of plays. Mr. Jones, when he discusses the content of revolutionary theater, thinks this content alone has the power to change society. But nothing is further from the truth. The content of plays determines *their* form but not *social* forms, although social forms are influential in shaping both the form and content of plays. In our society, however, there is no such thing as revolutionary theater. The Marxists tried something like that, decades ago, which failed. However, there can be a cultural method of revolutionizing the society in which the theater functions as an institution. The problems of a sick theater institution are the problems of the entire malfunctioning cultural apparatus as a whole, and the former will not be cured until the latter is. This is *cultural revolution*. If ethics and aesthetics are one, then the ethics of property relations are related to aesthetic values. And one cannot talk about revolutionizing anything unless one discusses changing property-relations ethics between contending classes and ethnic groups in America. LeRoi Jones has not understood this at all, and thus shares the basic conceptual flaws of most of the younger generation of social revolutionaries. They are long on intense ideology, but very short on structural conceptions of what constitutes revolutionary or reformist social change under capitalistic conditions.

With these articles in the *Negro Digest* by O'Neal, Davis, Dee and Jones, the question of the Negro in the theater goes through a twenty-five-year cycle from Harlem to integrationism and back toward Harlem—*but not all the way.* Today it will take much more overturning of the community soil to plant a theater institution than it took in 1941. For one thing, the soil has been left very much untended and unfertilized. Too much has transpired in Harlem since 1941 that requires explaining. For another thing, neither Ossie Davis nor Ruby Dee will talk about the Harlem leftwing or the white leftwing from downtown whose long shadow lies behind the history of Harlem theater after ANT's collapse. Ossie Davis may write with a touch of nostalgic regret that the "functioning cadre of ANT joined the march into the theatrical mainstream," because "the suction, the sweeping undercurrent, flowing toward Broadway, only a subway ride away, was irresistible," but he refrains from revealing the role the white Marxist cultural left played in this development. When the critics of this trend spoke up in Harlem around 1950, Ossie Davis was not even listening. It can be said here with certainty, however, that if there is any theatrical return to the Harlem community base today, it will not involve the white radical Left.

The Harlem Black Arts Theater—New
Dialogue with the Lost Black Generation

Thus ends my critique, yet this long analysis does not end the inquiry, nor does the inquiry treat every possible aspect of the problem. It is my conviction, though, that enough has been revealed of the antecedents to indicate the "clear and present" danger, in several of its many facets. Although I began by saying that this unraveling of ideas would relate to eighteen years of my own personal experiences and observations, it was not to deny that these, too, were not historically determined, but rather that when I began to have such experiences I did not realize that they were determined by what had happened before.

It seems that every generation has the illusion that what they discover in life as personal problems had never previously existed. Often there are grounds for this attitude inasmuch as old problems simply recur in new forms, with new qualities. The catch is that, with old problems in new guises further and further removed from their origins, the new generation often fails to see the historical connections. And if the new generation happens to be uninterested in history—and this is characteristic of the American existential mood—we have on our hands yet another Lost Generation who, unlike the Hemingways, find the contemporary world offering fewer and fewer paradises for exile that are not either swamped, or threatened by, revolutions. However, the first Lost Generation was white—notwithstanding those Negro intellectual emigrés to Europe who were the black parallel to that 1920's phenomenon.

But today we do have a Lost Black Generation—very young and very historically conditioned. They are lost within the deep canyons of the Northern urban cities, aliens to white western culture of the American style, whose exile is within themselves. Their alienation is reflected in many ways—in delinquency, crime, sex, drugs, hatred of whites, hatred of the United States, sometimes in hatred of themselves, and sometimes even in poetry and other art forms. These outlets become *their* manner of self-exile within a social system from which there is no longer any easy escape. Yet, if earlier Lost Generations escaped to Europe for inspiration, many of the contemporary black generation, without exiling themselves bodily, find their inspiration not in Europe, but in Africa. In this sense I find today's mercurial young black generation quite unprecedented, radically surprising, and beyond the conventional scope of politics. Although I find them exasperatingly anti-historical, many are extremely mature in their thinking—especially in a situation that many say offers no future for black people (or for anyone else, for that matter). These are the qualities that distinguish this young black generation from the one that was emerging when I first ventured into that Harlem YMCA amateur drama group just prior to America's entry into World War II. As I said at the outset of this study, "One of my first acts in the pursuit of becoming a more 'social being' was joining that theater group."

I and my generation thought that we were the "greatest," the most "hep," with our garrulous, undigested knowledge of pseudo-radical-Left social wisdom. We were planning and plotting to do great things as we dissected Marx, Shaw, Ibsen, O'Neill, DuBois (and Hitler). Little did we know that we were being groomed to be "wasted" in the Pacific, Africa, Asia and Europe despite the fact that the moving finger was visibly writing its message on the wall. And even afterwards, when we emerged as the "war generation," we still considered ourselves the chosen people of contemporary history. We, the Veterans, were the most important, the most pampered of any segment of the population. However, the *Negro* veteran, a misplaced, outlandish product of the second international world war among the imperialists, was ironically, a man of history who was being pushed further and further adrift from the consciousness of his own particular history in America, not to speak of his African beginnings. I have felt for a long time that World War II severed the American Negro not only from his prewar American provincialism, but from whatever tenuous moorings he might have had with his own historical past. Practically every able-bodied Negro either had made more money than he ever had in his life, or else had gone through the psychological trauma of being purged by the American military machine. Most of us Negro soldiers who survived this ordeal were, like myself, never quite the same again, *inside*. Those, especially, who had served in the European, Mediterranean theaters and who had known Ireland, Scotland, England, North Africa, Italy, France, Belgium, etc., became very "internationalist" in outlook after the war. This mood served to enhance the feeling that we were still the Chosen Generation, the generation of accomplishments, of experiences, whose demands would and must be met. But time has shown that we were in fact the Wasted Generation, destined to be used up in the war years as a means of dealing with that sole historical emergency. I say this in order to account for a personal sense of rootlessness that has never left me since the end of the war. In retrospect, I can see now that this rootlessness was my own personal form of alienation, but the word was not then in vogue. I also see, from a distance, that this rootlessness was related to that qualitative difference between "purpose" in war and "purpose" in peace. The war was forced on many of us, whether we liked it or not. The Negroes in the army swore, cursed, bitched and "snafued"—but they carried out army orders. Yet none of us realized that the war would banish forever our prewar way of life and obliterate our former social frame of reference so completely as to make it seem the vicarious experience derived from a book describing America of 1940. Hence, the period from 1946 to the 1950's was a new era, a new frame of reference, but what new purpose had we found? Were we actually as crucial a generation as we thought? The fact is, we had no purpose. We did not know that our "purpose" had already been served. As a result, quite a number of us were led into the radical leftwing, where we were "wasted" again. Through all those years of rather blind, intuitive and frenetic searching, many of us did not realize that another generation would have to emerge on the scene before a purpose could be divined in all its many ramifications. That new generation was being born into the world as we boarded the troop ships.

As it turned out, it was in the new Harlem Black Arts Repertory Theater and School in May, 1965, that I realized the full potential of the new young black generation. There, at a round-table discussion on Negro playwrights and the black theater, a young man, in his early twenties, discussed his views on the theater. He said, in effect, that *a black theater should be about black people, with black people, for black people, and only black people.* Immediately, there are startled objections to this radical idea, from both the panelists and the audience: "This is impossible, impractical and anti-humanistic EXTREMISM!" . . . "Black people cannot close themselves off in a compartment separate from whites" . . . "Art is universal" . . . "Art is for everybody" . . . and so on. Then came the question: *"Suppose the Black Arts Theater wanted to put on a play with Negro and white characters?"* "You see," said the opponent with a smug smile, "you would have to eliminate such a play. You would limit the repertory of the Black Arts Theater. You would limit the range of your playwrights to writing only about black people." But the young man, the ranting extremist, said: "Oh no, it won't be that way—you dig? We have black actors who can play white roles—you dig? *They can be made up to play white people.*" In other words, this young man was intent on having a truly *black* theater, come what may. And the whole historical truth is, that this young man was absolutely right. Even *I*, who have been castigated and refuted for eighteen years by the theatrical integrationists for my views on the need for a purely ethnic Negro theater, could not have put the question so clearly. *I* would have made room for the mixed-cast play in a black theater repertory by having white people play white roles, whenever demanded. Beyond that, my own standards for a black theater would be one where Negroes themselves would finance the institution and man all the technical and administrative posts.

But Negro theatrical history has demonstrated time and time again the inexorability of that unique Negro-white aesthetic, that culturally false symbiosis that undermines and negates the black theater idea. First off, the Negro creative intellectual, as writer, artist and critic has no cultural philosophy, no cultural methodology, no literary and cultural critique on himself, his people, or on America. Hence he cannot create, establish, and maintain a code of cultural ethics, an artistic standard, a critical yardstick or any kind of cogent and meaningful critique on society that might enable him to fashion viable and lasting institutions in the cultural spheres that motivate progressive movements.

If any group of Negroes were to start a black theater in a black community without a well-thought-out rule of thumb on administration, Negro playwrights, white playwrights, Negro actors, white actors, Negro technicians, white technicians, Negro directors, white directors, Negro audience, white audience, Negro plays, mixed-cast plays, etc.—such a theater venture would soon collapse. Even if this theater group started with the hopes of becoming "for, or, about, and by" black people, *without a code,* it would soon be integrated out of existence. Somewhere down the line the first white integration breach would be made, probably the first breach would be the drama about Negroes by a white playwright *negating the Negro writer,* but accepted by the Negro actors, eager for roles. Next would come the drama about whites with a Negro cast (for instance Shakespeare, Shaw, Ibsen, Williams or Miller). The Negro actors would suggest this gambit in the interest of perpetuating the classics, further ignoring the Negro writer. In the meantime, there would be a "name" Negro writer off somewhere peeping at the "signs" in white people's "windows" in search of themes; all the Negroes in the theater, from avowed integrationists to vocal but pseudo-nationalists, would stop and applaud his achievement. Next would come the white "name" directors and the Negro group would forget about the necessity of training a corps of black ones. Then would come the white technicians who, downtown, had gained the invaluable experience backstage in several off-Broadway groups where they often grant token administrative and technical posts to favored fair-haired Negroes in the interests of integration. Last would come the exhilarated white liberal or Communist leftwinger with the final message: "How wonderful! Let us all broaden this great theatrical beginning by integrating it into an institution of humanistic universality for the whole wide world to see and enjoy!" The Negroes would agree, and that would be the beginning of the end of the group. It has happened time and time again in the annals of the Negro in the theater.

For these reasons, and more, the young extremist at the Black Arts Repertory Theater was historically accurate. For at the *outset* it will require precisely such uncompromising hard-line cultural philosophy to maintain and sustain the kind of black ethnic theater he wants to see. Give the Negro integrationists one foot in the door of that theater and it is dead. It does not matter whether or not, in the long run, this young extremist will relent on white casting, in the interests of stage realism. Maybe he will, maybe he won't, but no damage will be done because by then, he will have *established a theater*. After that, local public opinion will head this theater group in its proper direction. For, after all, if such a black theater seeks to educate a black audience, it will be the audience who has the final say about the intrinsic value of a Black Arts Repertory Theater in the black community. When this young extremist said "We will have black people, made up as white people to play white roles," the symbolic cycle in the history of the American theater had made, in my view, a complete revolution. Back in the nineteenth century, in the years following the Civil War, white theatrical companies did not even allow Negro performers to play Negro roles in their productions. They used white actors in blackface, and it was considered standard procedure in the American theater. James Weldon Johnson tells the story of what a startling revelation it was to the theatrical producers of 1876 when it was decided to permit a real Negro performer to play the lead in the stage version of *Uncle Tom's Cabin*. "Why not have a real Negro play Uncle Tom?" someone said.[1]

The Black Arts Repertory Theater and School was started by LeRoi Jones and others, and hence my reticence in this book in discussing much of Jones' work. Jones has come so far and so fast since 1961, and in the meantime been so contradictory, that it is difficult to place him. In 1961, after my own personal ideological tussle with the Jones-Shepp-Hicks contingent in Harlem, no one could have made me believe that in 1965 LeRoi Jones would start a Black Arts Repertory Theater and School in Harlem. But he did—in itself amazing, because Jones is not a ghetto product. Any of my personal early misgivings about Jones grew out of my critical responses to his different poses and postures. As it turns out these Jonesian posturings have not been all upstage antics, but rather the ambivalence of the supreme actor brazenly in search of just the right "role" that would best suit the purposes in life of the real man inside Jones. Nevertheless, it is my belief that his play, *The Slave*, stamps Jones as the most original dramatist Negroes

[1] *Black Manhattan, op. cit.,* p. 91.

have produced since Oliver Pitcher (who still remains unheard of by the general public). Nonetheless, the Black Arts Theater and School, after an auspicious beginning, lasted about seven months and collapsed. It had a very short, stormy, creative career that has left an indelible impression on the minds of both its supporters and detractors. The causes of this collapse deserve examination because they relate graphically to the general theme of this critique—the social role of the Negro creative intellectual. The Black Arts was not a failure in achievement, so much as a failure in its inability to deal with what had been achieved. When Jones, the radical, avant-garde, literary integrationist, turned nationalist, he did not go far enough in his understanding of nationalism. Moreover, he had too much to overcome—forty-five years of leadership mismanagement on this question. As a result, the Black Arts Theater began without the foundation of a tradition of cultural nationalism. Lacking this tradition, the role of the Negro creative intellectual as nationalist is not understood even by the nationalists themselves. Even Garveyism, for example, was not cultural nationalism in Afro-American terms. Note this description of a Garvey meeting in New York during the 1920's.

> Garvey held a mass meeting at Carnegie Hall, in downtown New York City. It was packed to overflowing; white people attended too, as it was well advertised in white newspapers. . . . Items on the musical part of the programme were: Ethel Clarke, Soprano, singing Eckert's Swiss song, and Cavello's Chanson Mimi; The Black Star Line Band, in smart uniforms, rendering Overtures from "Rigoletto" and "Mirello"; New York Local Choir, fully robed, singing The Bridal Chorus from "The Rose Maiden" and "Gloria" from Mozart's 12th Mass; the "Perfect Harmony Four" in Sextette from "Lucia"; Basso Packer Ramsay sang Handel's "Hear me ye Winds and Waves." The second half of the programme were speeches by the Officers and [Garvey]. Subjects were: "The future of the black and white races, and the building of the Negro nation."[2]

It is very likely that all these singers were West Indians, which accounts for their Anglicized or Europeanized musical tastes. Not a note of the American Negro musical heritage was sounded on

[2] *Garvey and Garveyism, op. cit.,* p. 103.

this occasion (and this was typical), not even a spiritual, not to mention jazz or a classical melody by an Africanized composer such as J. Rosamond Johnson or Samuel Coleridge Taylor. This nationalist blindspot on cultural affairs is .characteristic, and the general lack of rapport between nationalistic trends and the creative intellectuals no one-sided affair.

However, when the creative intellectual moves toward the nationalist wing, he must understand the implications of what he is tackling—a trend without a cultural school of thought. The Negro writer must be firm in his role because the nationalist trend will not respect it, and will attempt to force the writer into the mold of being a political, rather than a cultural, leader. The Negro writer will be negated as creator if his cultural role is not paramount. On a larger scope, and in a different way, that is what happened to Paul Robeson.

LeRoi Jones, after establishing the Black Arts Theater, tried then to play the role of political spokesman on nationhood, in the absence of any official organization established to back up his political pronouncements about "destroying the system." Although again Jones was advised that these steps would have to be taken if the Black Arts was to be sustained, he failed to pay adequate attention. He made no attempt to link up a cultural institution with political and economic organization; without it, the Black Arts could not win the broader community support it needed to survive. Instead Jones attempted the triple-threat role of writer, cultural leader, and political spokesman, and consequently, all three roles were inadequately filled.

LeRoi Jones considered that to have established the Black Arts Theater was enough, but even so he did not pursue this cultural trend to its full potential. For example, his successful book, *Blues People,* suggested that much greater effort be mounted in the jazz field. Indeed, as jazz is his specialty, Jones' next step should have been to found a critical Negro jazz publication. Beyond that, Harlem could well use a jazz institute, a type of foundation that has never existed, to further the creative, economic, research and educational interests of the jazz musician. The problem here is that despite *Blues People,* the white jazz critics are still deciding the status and fortunes of Negro jazzmen. Cultural nationalism must be expressed by all possible organizational and educational means that might further and equalize the status of the Negro artist as creator, interpreter, or critic. Such an aim is certainly in consonance with the cultural development of the Negro community.

It is not the role of the Negro creative intellectual or writer to play the Big Leader Spokesman. His role as spokesman is to see what has to be done, point to it, and then explain why. He must be able to instruct others in what he cannot (or should not) do himself. Jones' failure to implement this kind of leadership in the Black Arts inevitably forced him into the position of being told by his "opposition" what to do—within the very institution he had founded. These oppositional elements in the Black Arts were dangerously irrational, misguided, negative, and disoriented. They represented the terrorist fringe of the nationalist wing—an alienated and psychotic separatism that has developed as a result of the long-standing cultural neglect and leadership default endemic to Harlem. This nihilistic fringe has its counterparts, no doubt, in all the great urban ghettoes, especially in the North. This trend is anti-middle class, anti-intellectual, anti- anything that resembles the establishment—from a college education to pressed-suit manners, whether Negro or white. Mainly it is anti-bourgeois—covering a rather broad spectrum of class "sins." This trend carries its separatism and black irrationality to such extremes that it bans Negro spokesmen from television, radio, and panel programs involving whites, among other things. In the absence of their own viable and positive program, the Afro-American Nationalists will have severe difficulties with this trend. Unless many more representatives of the Negro middle classes and the intelligentsia become increasingly committed to basic political, economic and cultural issues in the ghettoes, aggravated class conflict is in store for the Negro movement as a whole.

The experiences of LeRoi Jones in the Black Arts Theater reveal several hard truths about the nationalist wing. In dealing with Afro-American Nationalist trends, Negro writers and other creative elements must maintain their own autonomy absolutely; they must not permit themselves to come under the domination of activists and politicians who do not favor cultural front activities. The political activists will attempt to either suppress or control the creative elements, and especially the writers. This is, of course, a problem of long standing for all radical or revolutionary movements, especially those of the Marxist Left. The Negro writer, who is nationalistically oriented, must, at all times, fight within movements to maintain his creative and critical independence within a reasonable context of the general aims of the movement. The American system, unlike the Soviet, Chinese or African, has had its full flowering of the industrial revolution on the economic front; thus the Negro movement as a whole has no need for the politics of suppression and control of criticism and creativity. As a matter of fact, the precise cultural aim of the Negro movement *has* to be for the enhancement of criticism and creativity, not the other way around.

In this regard, Jones' defeat in the Black Arts Theater is attributable to the fact that the Afro-American Nationalists do not understand the functions of criticism on the cultural front. For example, *Liberator* magazine carried Jones on its masthead as a contributor to this publication. It also hailed the establishment of the Black Arts and ran a two-part series interpreting LeRoi Jones as creative artist and spokesman.[3] Yet not a single problem relating to the internal conflicts within the Black Arts Theater program was ever aired, debated, or criticized in the pages of this magazine. What was the validity of the experimental plays performed in the Black Arts? What value was there in the plays that expressed Jones' revolutionary theater concept? What was the value of the courses taught at the Black Arts? Where did the Black Arts get its money? Was it or was it not "politically" appropriate for the Black Arts to obtain funds from Federal sources? Why was it not possible to get financial assistance for the Black Arts from Negro middle-class sources? Why did so many Harlem nationalist groupings of the separatist variety, who had been condemning every Negro reform leader for begging for Federal assistance, rush in to obtain a share of the Black Arts program's Federal assistance funds? What were the limitations of the Black Arts cultural program? Why was the "opposition" within the Black Arts permitted license to drive young representatives of the middle class out of the institution? Why did not Jones himself prevent this, since he is from the Negro lower-middle class? These are a sample of issues that should have been aired in *Liberator*. But this magazine, like its predecessors, was unable to achieve any organic or functional journalistic rela-

[3] L.P. Neal, "Development of LeRoi Jones," *Liberator*, January, February, 1966.

tionship to any Harlem community issue or institutional movement.

The history of the Negro intelligentsia indicates that the role of the Negro creative intellectual is an interim role at best, insofar as leadership is concerned. This role is necessary, in the absence of other willing, or able, spokesmen, in order to bring the cultural front (as differentiated from the political and economic fronts) into its proper focus. Negro creative intellectuals must not become political leaders or mere civil rights spokesmen in the traditional sense. To do so, means that intellectuals who are creative will be forced to subordinate their potential to the narrow demands of the politics of nationalism and civil rights. The only real politics for the creative intellectual should be the politics of culture. The activists of race, nationalism, and civil rights will never understand this, hence this dilemma becomes another ramification of the manifold crisis of the Negro intellectual.

Postscript on Black Power—The Dialogue
Between Shadow and Substance

The old proverb, "Necessity is the mother of invention," was given a unique civil rights configuration when the slogan of Black Power was popularized during the summer of 1966. The necessity lay in the fact that the SNCC-CORE united front, in its direct-action-protest phase, had bogged down. Like an army that had outdistanced its supply units, it had finally been stopped by the enemy counter-attack—the backlash.

The slogan Black Power was conjured up and used in the manner of a rallying victory cry. In effect it covers up a defeat without having to explain either the basic reasons for it or the flaws in the original strategy; it suggests the dimensions of a future victory in the attainment of goals while, at the same time, dispelling the fears of more defeats in the pursuit of such goals. Yet, each and every goal was already implicit in the direct-action movements even before the slogan was projected. Black Power, then, was raised when social reality forced so-called revolutionaries to put action aside and start thinking. A movement that up to then had placed its highest premiums on practical activism now turned over a new leaf and began to get theoretical about the real *substance* of its civil rights objectives. The old slogans about "justice," "liberation," "Freedom Now," etc., were now mere shadow terms. If direct action-protest had been defeated by certain structural barriers of society, the new slogan became a commitment to deal with the real substance of those barriers that block the attainment of civil rights. Thus fears, opposition, and startled cries of alarm were immediately raised. A new threat fell across the land like an ominous shadow, even though the exact concept of Black Power has not yet been clearly defined. At this writing, as a concept it remains as vague as the former abstractions—Justice and Liberation. Although the Black Power concept is a more specific and provocative abstraction than Freedom, it is open to just as many diverse and conflicting interpretations. While it tries to give more clarity to what forms Freedom will assume in America as the end-product of a new program, the Black Power dialogue does not close the conceptual gap between shadow and substance, any more than it plots a course for the program dynamic. Whatever Black Power is supposed to mean to its adherents and its foes, its implications cannot be clearly understood unless one examines the slogan's aims and origin. Who originated the slogan? Are its aims revolutionary or reformist?

It was originated by a leading member of the radical wing of the black bourgeoisie, Adam Clayton Powell: He first mentioned it at a Chicago rally in May, 1965, and elaborated upon it in his Howard University Commencement speech of May 29, 1966. It was picked up and popularized by a leading member of the radical wing of the civil rights movement, Stokely Carmichael, from the lower-middle-class students' front. Carmichael was then joined by certain nationalist elements from integration-minded CORE, the radical wing of the civil rights movement in the North. Thus, the slogan of Black Power appeared to signal a concerted shift from SNCC-CORE radical-protest integrationism—not to nationalist separatism—but to some intermediate position between separatism and racial integration.

Since all of these diverse protest elements, separatists, nationalists, and direct actionists, had made up the sum total of what was called the Black Revolution, formal logic would conclude that this tumultuous shift to Black Power denoted a turn to a more revolutionary posture than formerly held by SNCC and CORE when their direct-action battering rams were at full strength North and South. But a closer examination of every analysis by each Black Power exponent from SNCC and CORE reveals that while the slogan cast a revolutionary *sounding* theme and a threat of more intense revolt across the land, the *substance* was, in fact, a methodological retreat to black social reforms. In pragmatic America the slogans catch the imagination while the implicit substances are glossed over and ignored. The Negro thinks and acts like the American he is; thus the leaders of the Black Revolution who seized so readily upon Black Power had never made the distinction between social revolution and social evolution, or social reform.

As this entire critique has tried to show, there can be no such thing in America as a *purely* economic, or political or civil rights revolution. There *can* be economic or political or civil rights reforms, but these are all *evolutionary* social changes that are part and parcel of the very gradualism of the NAACP. Never mind the fact that Roy Wilkins and his "class-brothers" are frightened by Black Power—that proves nothing. What a Wilkins is really saying is—"Please don't start throwing around power you don't really have, or power which you *might* have but which you obviously don't know how to use. All you are doing is scaring people (like me) and provoking other people to mobilize white power for a showdown which you are not ready for." What these gentlemen want most avidly are a number of civil rights, legal, economic, social, and educational reforms in America. But the radical direct-action civil righters (plus the nationalists) vociferously claim that this is inadequate. They say: "Those bourgeois NAACP Uncle Toms can't reform this white man's society. Man, you got to resort to revolutionary tactics if you want to shake up these white folks!" But what were these so-called revolutionary tactics? The Black Revolution included everything in the pot: sit-ins, freedom rides, demonstrations and marches of all kinds, ghetto uprisings, stall-ins, voter registration, self-defense, boycotts, black (third) party attempts, etc. These were the elements of the revolution, particularly in the South. But today when the main bulk of the direct actionists of SNCC and others have quit the South, what have they left behind? Scattered groups devoted to voter registration and economic programs for self-help. CORE has left a "cooperative marketing program for farm produce" in Louisiana. There were a few local election victories here and there, but the political reform movement of the Mississippi Freedom Democrat Party has closed its doors in LeFlore County. This is not to say that the achievements of the direct actionists are not valuable bases upon which other things can be structured, but they are still *reformist and gradualistic ideas with which not a single NAACP-er nor King passive resister could argue.* The question arises: Why was it necessary for all those idealistic and intrepid direct actionists to submit themselves to such a terrible physical and psychological battering in the South to establish a few struggling groups for local reforms in politics and economics, attempting in vain to breach the jimcrow barriers, which are, in effect, "separate" movements? It was because these young radicals did not understand, at the outset, the divergent natures of reforms and revolutionary movements for social change. They confused the methods without understanding them, thus imputing revolutionary interpretations to merely reformist methods. Hence, when direct-action methods failed against hardening barriers, they had to fall back on what few political and economic reform gains they had won. From this point on, the direct actionists advanced to the slogan of Black Power, as if to convince themselves that they were taking a revolutionary step forward, to wit: instead of radical integrationism the theme became *economic and political control by blacks in the black ghettoes and in geographical areas of black majority in the South.* But is this a step forward or backward . . . or perhaps a one-step-backward-two-steps-forward sort of gambit? Whatever it is, it is essentially another variation of the old Communist leftwing doctrine of "self-determination in the black belt areas of Negro majority"—but with certain innovations. The old Communist Party doctrine did not include the Northern ghettoes in this scheme as the Black Power exponents do. Moreover, the Communists did not envision any separatist black party movements as part of "self-determination," nor include any separatist economic reforms for self-help (such as cooperative consumers and producers movements). For the Communists then, and forever more, trade unionism was of paramount importance. The Northern CORE found itself in the 1960's, for instance, still forced to battle for integration in certain unions such as the building and construction trades. But when the subterranean nationalists inside the organization came to the fore in 1966 in answer to Carmichael's Black Power call, they demanded that Negroes reject integration as their major aim. Negroes were called on to band themselves into a racially-oriented mass movement, using political power and economic boycotts to win complete economic and political control of Northern ghettoes and Southern counties in which they are in the majority. Except for time, place, circumstances, plus a few innovative, ideological twists, there is very little that is new in all of this.

In essence Black Power represents nothing more than a strategic retreat for a purpose. It proposes to change, not the white world outside, but the black world inside, by reforming it into something else politically and economically. In its own way and for other purposes the Nation of Islam has already achieved this in a limited way, substituting religion for politics.

Malcolm X quitted the Nation of Islam because this type of Black Power lacked a dynamic, was static and aloof to the broad struggle. He proposed to create another movement (the Organization for Afro-American Unity, OAAU) and link up with all the direct actionists and even passive resisters, believing that one must be involved in all forms of struggle wherever they are on all fronts. But after Malcolm's passing, the most dynamic of all the direct actionists gave up their dynamism and took a position almost in the lap of the Nation of Islam. They merely substituted politics for a parochial religion to go along with economics, but they added a more secular religion of Black Power invented by a Baptist minister-politician. As the fates would have it, all of this took place at a time when Powell, in whom more black political power was invested than in anyone else at the moment, was under fire from a Congressional white backlash in Washington, D.C.

On the face of it, Black Power adds up to some profound questions: Does this strategic retreat from integrationism mean that the civil righters are settling for gradual evolutionary reforms within the black communities? Can these economic and political reforms be achieved without effect on, and interaction with, the white world? Will the achievement of certain levels of Black Power enable the exponents to deal more effectively with the white world than the dynamics of direct-action integrationism? What manner of social dynamic is to be added to Black Power to make up for the dynamic that was discarded along with direct action? The real answer at this stage is that the Black Power slogan has no other dynamic than what is implied in its emotional necessity. Taken by themselves, all purely economic and political reorganizations of any type in America can be only reformist movements, whether in black ghettoes or the white world. In order to be revolutionary in method to effect social change, such as transforming ghettoes, other dynamic elements must be added to the economic and political combination. The Black Power exponents have not understood these elements. Yet there is a unique inner dialectic at work in all this that must be examined.

For this purpose the Black Power exponents themselves have laid out their thinking for all to see. We can discount the frenetic avowals of black consciousness that made *New York Times* headlines and television panels, that frightened the bourgeois "Toms," white resisters, and lost "friends." It was but a new way of singing the same nationalist theme heard before from other quarters. But the CORE Black Power exponents came out in midwinter with a new publication called *Rights & Reviews* (Winter 1966-67), subtitled the "Black Power Issue," in which the substance of the slogan was discussed at some length. Here it was revealed that behind the brave verbalizations of Black Power, lay a muddled intellectual world of vague ideas and conceptual confusion. Sixteen articles by an interracial lineup of nationalists, Black Power integrationists, white leftwingers, Jews, Africans and others, spelled out the implicit Black Power retreat to the more leveled progression of an evolutionary black reformation. One cannot argue against this tactic since it is premature to state categorically where it will lead; but one should not, in this instance, refrain from calling reformism what it is. After all, the social realist must be aware that the New Deal heritage of the 1930's still hangs heavy over the land, and the American social dynamic has the built-in persuasion to bend all so-called revolutionary inclinations into the reformist groove. This is what Anti-Poverty is all about; it is why the Anti-Poverty program is able to buy off all the ghetto rebels with consummate ease. At a recent Anti-Poverty meeting in Harlem where an Independent Citizens' Committee* was challenging the efficiency and propriety of HARYOU-ACT's dominant role in

---

* This Independent Citizens Committee of Harlem has its roots in a rank-and-file oppositional move against the undemocratic control of HARYOU-ACT over the dispensation of Anti-Poverty funds. Active within this ICC are individuals from the Harlem Neighborhoods Association (HANA), a pioneer middleclass civic organization established in 1958. HANA grew out of the Central Harlem Coordinating Council established in 1938 for the purpose of encouraging and supporting "resident involvement and self-determination in community affairs." Harlem community politics is such that HANA was actually the creator of HARYOU and a number of other autonomous social welfare groups. The executive director of HANA, James Soler, is active in the ICC.

Anti-Poverty politics, certain CORE leaders were present—and silent. It remains to be seen just how Black Power will handle Anti-Poverty issues within CORE.

But in the maiden issue of *Rights & Reviews* on Black Power, Roy Inniss opened up with "Black Power—Phase 1: Psychological Warfare," in which he said:

> There is an impelling need to emphasize the socio-psychological aspect of Black Power. We can cry "Black Power" until doomsday, but until black children stop saying, "You're blacker than me and so is your mama"; until grown black men stop using black as a curse word; until *Ebony* stops asking such asinine questions as: "Are Negro women getting prettier?" and stops carrying bleaching cream advertisements; until black people stop saying such things as: "She's dark, but pretty"; in short, until black people accept values meaningful to themselves, there can be no completely effective organizing for the development of Black Power.[1]

Mr. Inniss, a West Indian nationalist (once removed), was not merely being rhetorical about the much maligned values of "blackness." He himself is black and Africanesque. In fact, his sensitivity to this question was shown much earlier, in a *New York Times* article where he discussed his fears of "genetic destruction" through enforced "integration." Yet, if one is to discuss the color question among Negroes one cannot be as superficial as Mr. Inniss and leave it there. Granted, the Negro in America has been conditioned in many ways to a disrespect of blackness, but this is not as universal as Inniss makes out. On the other hand, if Inniss truly believes that there can be no "effective organizing . . ." (even for Black Power) until Negroes stop derogating "blackness," then he will never see "Black Power," whatever he means by it. Ideas about skin-color and the social values attached thereto are like ideas about all things social. Take the notion, for example, that holds slavery as a human institution to be a good thing. Had the slaves waited for the slavemasters to *change* their views on slavery before fighting for freedom, they would never be free. For even *after* the slaves won their freedom there would still be ex-slave-masters and ex-slaves who thought that slavery was a good thing.

[1] *Rights & Reviews*, Winter 1966-67, p. 5.

By the same token, even after the hoped-for ascent to Black Power, there will still be Negroes who will wish they were white inasmuch as Black Power will demand more responsibility than some blacks care to assume. However, the conceptual flaws noted here in Mr. Inniss' thinking on social dynamics are typical of the social thinking of all black revolutionaries. Either they are activists without ideas or they fail to connect their ideas to the appropriate kind of social actions. If a person has a low opinion of himself and is unhappy because he lives in a filthy, dilapidated, rat-infested house, you cannot tell him to apply positive thinking—and "Be happy!" Happiness will begin to blossom only when he finds a way to get out of his physical trap into improved surroundings. In other words, what are the social dynamics of the program implicit in a Black Power kind of happiness?

It was noted that this Black Power magazine issue went to great lengths to play up the ideas, the imagery and the symbolism of the African Personality. All of the artwork, with exception of an amusing Jules Feiffer cartoon, relied on African tribal symbolism. One of the articles, written by a Black Nationalist-Africanist, Yosef Ben-Jochannan, asked—"What is Black Power?" He said:

> It is that power which black peoples had in Africa before the invasion and domination of Africa by the Europeans under the guise of "taking Christianity to the heathen Africans." . . . It is that power which caused Africans to build their many civilizations of high culture and institutions of science, law, medicine, philosophy, religion, etc., while Europeans were still asleep in their ignorance of the universe around and about them.[2]

Here, along with the historical romance of the African past, was an echo of Back-to-Africa Garveyism. For Ben-Jochannan, Black Power means that Negroes in America must take their "rightful place within the African community." "Why all the sudden fuss and fury against the call for Black Power?" he asks. Why the fear? —"Fear by those who allegedly lead those of us who remain on the colonial plantations throughout the Harlems of the United States of America." There is an element of truth in Ben-Jochannan's message, but also much propagandist rhetoric, and it is the rhetoric

[2] *Ibid.*, p. 28.

that one must watch out for. It is from a school of Harlem thought that condemns *any* effort on the part of the American Negro to seek racial equality within the American system.

Thus, within the CORE Black Power outlook reappears the old dichotomy between DuBois-NAACPism and West Indian nationalist-Garveyism, for one must remember that CORE, the first direct-action group following World War II, merely extended the NAACP philosophy on another level. Even the present transition of the CORE philosophy to Black Power reformism is not complete, for witness the interracial lineup of the magazine content. The Black Power concept is due for a possible split between African Black Power and Afro-American Black Power, two related but different propositions in terms of emphasis. The clue to all this lies in the fact that neither in Ben-Jochannan's article, nor elsewhere in the issue, is the status of the West Indies (or the West Indian) discussed. Recall that when Black Power was first projected, the white press plus Inniss, Carmichael, and Lynch, played up the alleged Caribbean influence behind the slogan. Yet, although Ben-Jochannan discusses White Power vs. Black Power all over the world wherever it involves "the undying and unquenching energy of African peoples everywhere . . . ," he makes no reference to either the black West Indies or the British Commonwealth. The implicit, typically Garveyite, assumption here is that the black West Indies already has Black Power (poor but proud), and that the Caribbean islands, unlike the "Harlems of the United States . . ." are not what Ben-Jochannan calls "colonial plantations." For the West Indian nationalists in the United States, the Caribbean "image" must be preserved and the exact nature of the "political independence" achieved is not to be examined too closely especially since the success of Black Power (at home and abroad) is predicated on both *political and economic independence.*

However, let us see what an African representative says about Black Power in the same publication. Chief S.O. Adebo is Nigeria's Permanent Representative to the United Nations. Writing on "The Black Revolution—An African View,"[3] he discusses the "parallel movements" for freedom and independence of Africans and people of African descent in the United States:

[3] *Ibid.,* p. 32.

Where the blacks constitute the majority of the country's population, as in Africa, the movement has taken the form of a struggle to take over the exercise of the governing power; where, as in the United States, the blacks are a minority, the struggle has been one for participation on level terms with everybody else. . . .

So far even the NAACP and King would concur, but Chief Adebo added "but, fundamentally, the objective is the same, an objective which can be described as securing a square deal for the black man in this world."

On the implementation of this objective, every faction from the NAACP to the Nation of Islam—clear across the spectrum, including the Black Power exponents themselves—are divided. But, as Chief Adebo said, "The wind of change has of course caused a lot of transformation on the African continent" and in the United States. "But you will no doubt agree with me that here, as in Africa, the task still to be done is more than that which is already accomplished. For both of our communities it is a long, long way to Tipperary."

"We must coordinate and work together," Adebo advised. "In order to do this, an essential prerequisite is that we should strive to remove the misunderstanding created between the African and the American Negro by centuries of lack of intelligent communication between our communities." And he concluded:

> The African must recognize the American Negro as his brother, and American Negroes must acknowledge Africa as their ancestral home, and Africans as their kith and kin. This mutual understanding already exists within the top echelons both in Africa and in the United States. But this is not enough; it must go right down to the grass roots.

Again, curiously, the African said nothing, even in passing, about the West Indies, the natural home of Garveyism abroad. And, exactly who are those "top echelon" leaders in Africa and America who have this "mutual understanding" of which Adebo speaks? Such American Negro top echelon leaders would also, presumably, support Black Power. But which top leaders besides Powell support Black Power? They are not found in the NAACP, the Urban League, or in King's top echelon (the very leadership, in fact, that Ben-Jochannan sees as fearing Black Power). No, there is much confusion here both in the outlook of Africans such as Adebo and in the Afro-American Black Power exponents over the African Revolution, the alleged Black Revolution, and their parallels. There is too much romanticizing about Africa going on in certain nationalist circles; too much rhetoric and too much Garveyite Back-to-Africa lip service by certain black redemptionists in America who haven't the least intention of going to Africa unless there is the guarantee of a good job or a money-making scheme in the offing, or the possibility of a "top echelon" marriage into the African diplomatic corps.

Africans such as Chief Adebo are just as much in the dark about the inner dynamic demands of the American Black Revolution as the Black Power exponents are about the dynamic substances of their new slogan. As a result, the readiness of most Black Nationalist trends, to lean heavily on the African past and the African image, is nothing but a convenient cover-up for an inability to come to terms with the complex demands of the American reality. A Roy Inniss, for example, will have one believe that no one in the black world but the American Negro has a complex about being black. In a black African country, inasmuch as nearly everyone is black, there is no basis for any psychological conditioning of inferiority complexes. However, pick up any popular African magazine such as *Spears* from Nigeria, *Parade* from Rhodesia, *Post* from South Africa, and also *Drum* of Ghana and Nigeria, and Lo and behold! There are skin-bleaching advertisements galore, also hair-straightening creams and black women in long-haired wigs— just like Harlem. Said one full-page, Madison Avenue-ish spread in *Drum:* "Amazing ARTA made my skin—Lighter, Smoother, Clearer . . . Because it is Pure White." "This is how I look now that I use pure white Arta." But, . . . "this was how I looked before. . . ." (She was *dark,* but pretty!)

Roy Inniss thinks *Ebony's* query "Are Negro Women Getting Prettier" rather asinine. But if he looks, he will observe that the African male in the United States has a female-beauty standard that parallels not only the prevailing standards of American Negro males and *Ebony* magazine, but also the standards of the vari-colored spectrum of the United Nations. On this question there is very little misunderstanding between the two ancestral progeny. The problem is deeper: The American Negro is wedded to America and does not want to return to his ancestral Africa except in fancy, perhaps. The African *has* Africa, but a severe psychic problem has cropped up among Africans sent to the United States on various assignments: Many of them have very little contact with American Negroes, feel alienated within themselves, *but do not want to return to Africa.* Alienated or no, they have become passionately attached to the ways of the cosmopolitan West, the high standard of living, the creature comforts of the affluent society. These sons of Africa do not care to share the enforced status of the American Negro (who can blame them?), but they exist from day to day, from year to year, in levels and areas of American society where for years our American Negro integrationist leadership sought to be accepted on a peer basis of merit and educational qualifications. Despite his blackness, the African is handed this status almost *gratis*, without a "civil rights" struggle. This is what he wants, and he likes it, and regrets to have to give it up. Compared to the American Negro, he is *persona grata*. Ironically, however, for the Black Nationalists and the Black Power exponents in Harlem, any American Negro from the black elite functioning in these privileged areas of metropolitan interracial life has sold out his birthright to the white power structure.

Despite the historical affinities, the African and the Afro-American dilemmas differ—each has its own qualities, peculiarities, and imperatives. And the Black Power controversy illuminates all too well the deep confusions about these imperatives. What *is* the program for Black Power? *That* is the fundamental, unanswered question. In *Rights & Reviews*, Julian Bond, formerly of SNCC, wrote: "Black Power must be seen as a natural extension of the work of the civil rights movement for the past few years. From the courtroom to the streets in favor of integrated public facilities; from the streets onto backwoods roads in quest of the right to vote; from the ballot box to the meat of politics, the organization of voters into self-interest units." This is the dialectic of reformism! But, Bond advised that "conflict and struggle are necessary for social change."[4]

However, another writer said: "Forget Black Power. There is more to it than that, and our life might perhaps become the truth

[4] *Ibid.*, p. 6.

of the moment we seek without the need of slogans. In times past people were content to *experience* their lives, but today one is not really living unless one has a program."[5]

Floyd McKissick, CORE's top man, wrote: "The doctrine of Black Power is this new thrust which seeks to achieve economic power and to develop political movements that would make changes that are vast and significant."[6] *But economic power for whom?* For workers? Black capitalists? Black farmers? Black middleclass? Black racketeers? Welfare clients? The crucial economic issue in the ghettoes today is Anti-Poverty, *but Anti-Poverty is not only a black issue.* How would CORE Black Power deal with this question? Or, on the question of political movements—around what particular issues would these political movements be developed? So far, the mentality of the Black Power theorists is so narrow that they see politics on merely one plane—running some black candidate for office—a hackneyed reformist tactic. No one can beat the Democrats and Republicans in the field of reform politics, especially black reform. Black radicals do not understand the art of creative politics, which is to make the superabundance of people's grievances political. But this is not all that is awry in Black Power ideology.

When one starts with the skin-color premise of a Roy Inniss on the Afro-American problem, one is, unfortunately, feeding a strong tendency within the Black Nationalist movement towards black-skin chauvinism—a policy which cannot work politically in the United States. It has never worked in the West Indies either; it can work only in Africa, it seems. But, in the United States, the American Negro group is too large and mixed with too many racial strains for the ideology of black-skin supremacy to function within the group. It can lead to the reasoning that "I'm blacker than you, and so is my mama, so I'm purer than you and your mama. Therefore, I am also more nationalistic than you, and more politically trustworthy than you and your mama, in the interests of Black Power." But inside America this is a pure fiction. The blacker skin does not always denote the deeper racial pride. In fact, some of the darkest Negroes are the most "white-minded."

[5] *Ibid.*, Lorenzo Thomas, "Spontaneous History and the Ethics of a Revolution," p. 9.
[6] *Ibid.*, p. 7.

In America, the Negro group is more an *ethnic* than a racial group
—meaning a group of mixed African, Indian, and white strains. Of
course, the American-West Indian fusion of Black African-nationalists prefer their converts to be truly "black" both in pigmentation and ideology, and look rather doubtfully at others. There
have been several trends who have tried to exclude Negroes with
non-Negroid features and straight hair, overlooking the fact that
Marcus Garvey's second wife, just such a female type, wrote of
Garvey: "My hair let down, thrilled him. It was long and naturally wavy, he asked me never to cut it. The first time he saw it
down, curiously he felt some strands and said, 'why it is soft,' as I
tossed my head, he exclaimed, 'Oh, but it is so live.' "[7] There is
little doubt that Mrs. Garvey, a racial hybrid, was just as much of a
Black Nationalist as the great redemptionist. And in our time, the
two leading exponents of Black Power and Black Nationalism
have been racial hybrids—Adam Clayton Powell and Malcolm X.
The color problem among American Negroes is more complex
than Roy Inniss admits.

Yet this problem among Negroes is of less signal importance
today than the glaring fact that the Black Power theorists have
learned very little from Afro-American history, which is of more
immediate political significance than how many black Africans
sat on the thrones of ancient Egypt. The trouble with the Black
Nationalist Africanists is that most of their intellectual capacities
are used up glorifying the most attractive aspects of Africa's pre-
slavery past, while most of the African elite today have ceased
being revolutionaries (if they ever were). In fact, most American
Negroes who have been to Africa and back have almost as low an
opinion of the African elite in Africa as some of the Africans have
of the American Negroes' lack of cohesion. Hence, it would serve a
very good purpose here in America for Negroes to cease romanticizing Africa and pre-feudal tribalism.

The radical wing of the Negro movement in America sorely
needs a social theory based on the living ingredients of Afro-American history. Without such a theory all talk of Black Power is
meaningless. One of the keys to the confusion over the meaning of
the slogan, is the ambivalence in CORE's publication over the

[7] *Garvey and Garveyism, op. cit.,* p. 186.

choice of historical leadership symbols and the interpretation given to the implications of these leadership trends. For example, the strong tendency of the Black Power theorists to associate only the names of Denmark Vesey, Harriet Tubman, Nat Turner, Marcus Garvey, Elijah Muhammed and Malcolm X with the social, political and ideological implications of Black Power is being absolutely false to history. Even the addition of Frederick Douglass to this historical leadership gallery is insufficient. For one thing, Douglass was no nationalist, and no pre-Civil War data is complete without the name of Martin R. Delany, the real proto- type of Afro-American Nationalism.

But of more relevance to the present-day Negro movement as a whole are the twentieth-century leaders and their trends—Wash- ington, DuBois, and Garvey. *These are the big three for our cen- tury.* Anyone who does not understand this cannot talk seriously about Black Power or any other slogan. But the Black Power theo- rists are romantics who do not understand this. Of course, spokes- men like Roy Inniss, Ben-Jochannan, etc., will find it difficult to accept this. In their conceptual scheme of things they would accept Marcus Garvey and reject Washington and DuBois. But this is pred- icated not on any profound theoretical or scientific examination of historical facts but on passion, emotionalism, and prejudice. They accept Garvey without Washington because they have not ex- amined the reasons Washington was Garvey's only American hero. Similarly, they accept Douglass without DuBois, although it was DuBois who upheld Douglass and carried his abolitionist-protest- civil rights trend into the twentieth century. Although in terms of economics, Elijah Muhammed carried out Booker T. Washing- ton's philosophy of economic self-sufficiency and self-help more thoroughly than any other movement, the Black Power theorists accept the Nation of Islam, yet reject Booker T-ism. They fail to see the fallacy of such reasoning because they have no understand- ing of economics as a science or the different schools of economic theory and how to apply them to the Negro movement. With such an innocence about economics, politics becomes child's play once the direct-action dynamic is taken away. Unschooled in the deep politics of the Negro movement since World War One, the leaders of CORE and SNCC are unaware that even the few economic cooperatives they initiated in the South are forty years too late.

How can people like this expect to cope with the economic policies of Anti-Poverty today?

In terms of economics, the Negro's heritage today is New Deal capitalism and Anti-Poverty, broadly speaking. His only "race" economics of any importance are those of Elijah Muhammed. Garvey's economic ideology which was tied to the African scene is useless today, since there is no Back-to-Africa momentum. The only leader of the big three who left behind, in writing, an economic program for the United States was W.E.B. DuBois, yet nationalist prejudice against him prevents Negro leaders from acknowledging this. Moreover, it was DuBois' brand of Pan-Africanism that won out in Africa, not Garvey's, *because Garvey was not a socialist but a thoroughgoing capitalist.* In terms of economics, neither Africa nor the West Indies has achieved the kind of independence and autonomy Garvey wanted. However, the unreality of Garvey's program in the 1920's meant he would have had even less chance of expunging neo-colonialism from Africa than the leaders of the African Revolution have had today. The result has been that Garveyism has failed to muster up any aid or political and economic assistance from Negroes in the Western hemisphere. The real foreign aid must come from both capitalist and socialist governments. The politics of certain African leaders are sufficiently ambivalent that they avidly seek this capitalistic and socialistic aid with one hand (for their version of Black Power), while with the other they either point the finger of criticism at the American Negro or else mouth vague platitudes about black cooperation. They simply do not understand the Afro-American's complex problem and its imperatives.

The Black Power enthusiasts practice the same dubious verbal skin-game in another way. They cannot cope with the realities of the economics of their own foreign aid, *i.e.,* Anti-Poverty, yet they talk boldly about economic independence as the basis of real power. How can such people talk seriously of cooperating with Africa when they cannot help themselves with a definitive economic program for Black Power in America? The "reluctant African" in the United States has adequate reasons for his stand-offishness. He has deep personal problems of identity to cope with, in the midst of a situation that has trapped the American Negro both physically and intellectually. The worst effect of his American conditioning is not his color-complex about blackness, but that it renders him unable to look at his own history and influence in America objectively and understand it scientifically. He is so bedazzled by the personalities of his chosen leadership symbols that he cannot peer behind the façade and examine what were the political, economic, class, and cultural trends that influenced the actions of those chosen leaders.

Another impórtant issue the Black Power theorists evade is the class problem among Negroes. When one talks bravely about developing political and economic black power one had best start clarifying which class is going to wield this power. Better yet— which class among Negroes has the most power now? And which class will benefit from Black Power when it arrives? Here is another clue to the essential reformism inherent in the Black Power slogan: The theorists, although they snipe at the black bourgeoisie, are themselves prey to bourgeois aspirations—major or minor. This is by no means a bad thing in itself. To better one's material (if not spiritual) condition in America necessarily means adopting either the petty or the garish trappings of middle-class existence. However, the Black Power theorists are thrown into a reformist muddle involving class aspirations and economic power for the simple reason that they have no recognizable basis for economic power. To be brutally frank, some do not even know what economic theory is, while others do not want to be bothered with it. Despite their vaunted anti-Americanism, they are more American than they think. Congenitally pragmatic to the core, they are anti-theoretical. Thus, the white power structure does their economic theory and practice for them. New Deal economics, in force for thirty-four years, decides how Anti-Poverty funds are allotted to black ghettoes, but people in ghettoes have no say in how much funds or how often they are to be allotted. Is *this* economic Black Power? If not, ask any Black Power theorist what kind of politics can change this arrangement. Or better—ask any Black Power theorist whether economics determine politics, or vice versa? Ask any Black Power theorist why Anti-Poverty funds pay out so much money in middle-class salaries? Is this good or bad—for Black Power economics? You will get no clear answers.

However, from one familiar source we get some very clear convictions on the question of which class attributes and Black-Power economics go together. Discussing Black Power in the *Negro Digest* of November, 1966, our literary sojourner from the old Left, John O. Killens, had this to say:

> It seems to me there need be no strong schism at this moment between the advocates of black power and the "black bourgeoisie". . . . If one of the principle [sic] tenets of Black Consciousness is economic power, the starting place is with the black middle class. May their tribe increase. Black Power advocates are no present danger to them.[8]

When Black Power was simply Black Nationalism unqualified, Killens was by no means so certain that no middle-class Negroes were endangered. But since Black Nationalism is obviously here to stay, let us reform it nearer to the heart's desire. If John O. Killens had been told during the early 1950's that the black middle class on *Freedom* newspaper, with Robeson leading, had reformed leftwing Communism into leftwing integrationism (which is not Black Power) in the interests of the black middle class, Killens would have replied something like this—"Oh no, Robeson's *Freedom* appeals to the black working class, may their tribe increase. But this is no present danger to the black middle class." In fact, it was not. But today it should be clear to all Black Power advocates that these two "tribes"—workingclass and bourgeois—cannot both increase. Somebody has to give in, or give up, or simply "give" somewhere. Moreover, when a John O. Killens declares "all power to the black bourgeoisie" instead of the black proletariat, he admonishes: "Black Power is not an advocate of violence. It advocates non-violence, but in depth. It keeps everybody non-violent. It stays the hand of the practitioners of violence."[9] Of course, it was not long ago that Mr. Killens was upholding "violence" when "necessary."

Nothing better demonstrates the reformist ideology behind Black Power than the Killens stamp of approval. Never the originator of a single new concept, style, or exposition whether in literature or politics, Killens has been the neutralizing temporizer, the non-controversial, moderating lid-sitter par excellence. He is not averse to changing his opinions or shifting his position when nec-

[8] *Negro Digest*, November, 1966, p. 34.
[9] *Ibid.*

essary; but he possesses that reform politician's knack of catching on belatedly to all advanced demands and slogans, once it is certain that the establishment must bend to popular appeal. He then becomes the propagandizing expert just as if he were *always* of that opinion. Thus, it is quite proper for Killens to say of Black Power today: "It means that all the Harlems of the U.S.A. should be in the hands of Harlemites. This is the starting point for black liberation. . . ."[10]

. . . But you will find no such declaration of this tenor in a single issue of Robeson's *Freedom* newspaper in the early 1950's. *Freedomways* tried to prove that Robeson anticipated SNCC's direct action but it cannot be proven that the *Freedom* newspaper family anticipated Black Power in Harlem even when conditions existed in the Harlem radical movement of the late 1940's and early 1950's for such a slogan. Certain members of the pioneer Harlem Writers' Club, not Killens' Harlem Writers Guild, raised the idea that the black radical movement in Harlem should be run by blacks. The Harlem Writers Club, not Killens' group, forced the first conference on Negro cultural problems, the root problem of black consciousness. The leaders of the Harlem Writers Club first challenged the Committee for the Negro in the Arts' (CNA) concept of Integration in the Arts as cart-before-the-horse cultural policy in Harlem, *not* the Killens group. And, members of the Harlem Writers Club first attempted to debate these issues in their magazine *Harlem Quarterly* in 1949 and 1950, *not* the Killens Harlem Writers Guild and *Freedom* newspaper cliques. True, these issues were not debated with the thoroughness they should have been, but they *were* raised. Hence, it was the members of the Harlem Writers Club who took the brunt of the attacks, the slander, the abuse, and the ostracism from the interracial leftwing Harlem establishment. There is nothing new under the Harlem sun, but if John O. Killens had said of the black middle class—"May their tribe increase!"—in the pages of *Freedom* newspaper, everything would have been clearer for all concerned. For the black bourgeoisie *is* important as a class within the Negro movement. One cannot analyze leadership trends unless it is done within the context of the role of the black bourgeoisie. The problem is—the Black Power theorists have not done so.

10 *Ibid.*

The last outstanding leader was Malcolm X, but did his followers really understand the man's positive side, or his limitations, or why he acted as he did? Did they see any Afro-American historical trends repeating themselves in Malcolm X's career? Unfortunately, they did not. The editors of CORE's magazine leaned heavily on quotations from Frederick Douglass' speeches and writings. But, historically, Douglass' Abolitionism and Reconstructionism are nineteenth-century achievements that became overshadowed by American twentieth-century developments. Besides, Frederick Douglass is also the chief hero of the NAACP integrationists, hence, the Black Power fellows are in strange company, sharing "heroes." Yet Malcolm X was no hero to the NAACP worshippers at Douglass' shrine, so how then, do divergent integrationist and nationalist trends wind up honoring the same hero? Because neither integrationists nor nationalists truly understand the crucial impact of the integrationist vs. nationalist conflict within the contours of American Negro history.

The Black Power exponents who uphold Malcolm X, yet cannot come to terms with either Washington or DuBois as historical leaders, understand neither the break between DuBois and Washington, nor the break between Malcolm X and Elijah Muhammed. These two breaches are historically related and stem from the same root in Afro-American history, albeit under different circumstances. Malcolm X broke with the Nation of Islam because of Muhammed's refusal to participate in the broad struggle for human rights, as Malcolm X explained it. But W.E.B. DuBois, the turn-of-the-century radical, broke with Booker T. Washington's leadership school for the same reasons (as a reading of *The Souls of Black Folk* will show). DuBois said that Washington shied away from participating in the struggle for the Negro's manhood rights. Malcolm X's break was that of a radical nationalist with the conservative nationalism of Elijah Muhammed, the latter inherited from Booker T. Washington, by way of Garvey who had "radicalized" Washington's economic philosophy.

The only way to understand this process is not to be led astray by mere slogans, but to see the fundamentals at work: the underlying conflict between integrationist and nationalist tendencies historically projected in the contrasted outlooks of Douglass and Delany. No matter how nationalistic Malcolm X remained after his break, he was forced by circumstances to swing closer to the civil rights-integrationist forces in order to participate more fully in the broad struggle.* That was why certain of Malcolm X's former followers could charge him with "selling out" by seeking an alliance with the direct-action-integrationist forces.

American Negro history is basically a history of the conflict between integrationist and nationalist forces in politics, economics, and culture, no matter what leaders are involved and what slogans are used. After Malcolm X's death, the Black Power slogan was actually a swing back to the conservative nationalism from which Malcolm X had just departed. The pendulum swings back and forth, but the men who swing with it always fail to synthesize composite trends. W.E.B. DuBois came the closest of all the big three to understanding this problem, when he wrote in *Dusk of Dawn:* "There faces the American Negro therefore an intricate and subtle problem of combining into one object two difficult sets of facts:"[11]

The "two difficult sets of facts" DuBois refers to are integrationism (civil rights, racial equality, freedom) versus nationalism (separatism, accommodationist self-segregation, economic nationalism, group solidarity and self-help). This was truly the first theoretical formulation of the historic conflict between tendencies, but DuBois never developed his basic theoretical premise. He failed to go beyond this first principle into a greater synthesis of all the historical ingredients of Afro-Americana, which he knew better than all the Washingtons and the Garveys combined. Like Karl Marx, W.E.B. DuBois was one of history's great researchers—a sifter, interpreter and recorder of historical and contemporary knowledge; but unlike Marx, he could not reinterpret his data into new conceptions of social reality. Still, he came close, albeit late in life.

It was historically unfortunate that the American Negro created no social theorists to back up his long line of activist leaders,

---

* Malcolm X's plan to take the Negro issue to the United Nations as a Human Rights question in 1964 had been first attempted in 1947 by W.E.B. DuBois in collaboration with the NAACP. See "Appeal to the World," A Statement on the Denial of Human Rights to Minorities in the Case of Citizens of Negro Descent in the United States and an Appeal to the United Nations for Redress (NAACP, pamphlet, 1947).

[11] *Dusk of Dawn, op. cit.,* p. 199.

charismatic deliverers, black redemptionists, and moral suasionists. With a few perceptive and original thinkers, the Negro movement conceivably could long ago have aided in reversing the backsliding of the United States toward the moral negation of its great promise as a new nation of nations. Instead the American Negro has, unwittingly, been forced to share in many of the corrupted values of the society—not enough, to be sure, to cancel out completely his inherent potential for social change. However, the intellectual horizons of the black intelligentsia have been so narrowed in scope and banalized by the American corrosion that Negro creativity has been diminishing since the 1920's. An examination of the pronouncements of the Black Power theorists reveal that they have not advanced one whit in their thinking, beyond the 1919 writers of A. Phillip Randolph's *Messenger* magazine. They have, in fact, retrogressed. There is not a single Negro publication in existence today that matches the depth of the old *Messenger*. CORE's new Black Power publication talks of developing "political and economic power" as if speaking for the first time. But back in the 1920's, when Randolph's writers were chastising DuBois and boasting of how they were "correctly" giving precedence to economics and politics over culture and art, they knew what they were talking about and said it with infinitely more expertise than today's Black Power exponents. In fact, the Black Power theorists do not even know how to deal with culture and art, as the CORE publication reveals. This is shocking to contemplate.

Black Power slogans reveal the depth of unpreparedness and the lack of knowledge that go along with the eagerness of the new black generation of spokesmen. The farther the Negro gets from his historical antecedents in time, the more tenuous become his conceptual ties, the emptier his social conceptions, the more superficial his visions. His one great and present hope is to know and understand his Afro-American history in the United States more profoundly. Failing that, and failing to create a new synthesis and a social theory of action, he will suffer the historical fate described by the philosopher who warned that "Those who cannot remember the past are condemned to repeat it."

Supplementary Bibliographical Sources

Anonymous, "A Negro Theatre," *Theatre Arts Monthly*, December, 1927, pp. 483-491.

Anonymous, "Negro Drama," *The Nation*, Vol. 124, No. 3217, March 2, 1927, pp. 242-243.

Anonymous, "Who Invented Jazz?," *Collier's Weekly*, January 3, 1925, p. 22.

Bell, Clive, "Plus de Jazz," *Since Cezanne*, London: Chatto and Windus, 1922, pp. 213-229.

Bond, Frederick W., *The Negro and Drama*, Washington, D.C.: Associated Publishers, 1940.

Brawley, B.J., "The Negro Literary Renaissance," *Southern Workman*, April, 1927, pp. 30-32.

Brown, Sterling, "Negro Character As Seen Through White Authors," *Journal of Negro Education*, April, 1933, pp. 42-49.

Butcher, Margaret Just, *The Negro in American Culture*, New York: Alfred A. Knopf, 1956.

Chapin, E., "Where Jazz Comes From," *Popular Mechanics*, January, 1926, p. 97.

Clime, Julia, "Rise of the American Stage Negro," *Drama Magazine*, January, 1931, pp. 56-57.

Dett, R.N., "The Emancipation of Negro Music," *Southern Workman*, April, 1918, p. 172.

DuBois, W.E.B., *The Gift of Black Folk*, Boston: Stratford Company, 1924.

————, "Shall the Negro Seek Cultural Equality?" (Debate with Lothrop Stoddard of Harvard, Chicago, March 17, 1929. Published by Chicago Forum. Property of Schomburg Collection, New York).

Edmonds, Randolph, "Some Reflections on the Negro in American Drama," *Opportunity*, October, 1930, pp. 303-305.

Gregory, Montgomery, "The Negro Actor," *The New Republic*, November 16, 1921, pp. 523-526.

Halperin, Samuel, *The Political World of American Zionism*, Detroit: Wayne State University Press, 1961.

Harrison, Hubert H., "Black Man's Burden," *International Socialist Review*, April, 1912, pp. 660-663.

Hughes, Langston, "The Negro Artist and the Racial Mountain," *The Nation*, June 23, 1926, p. 692.

Locke, Alain, "Toward a Critique of Negro Music," *Crisis*, November, 1934, p. 60.

Redding, Saunders, "Negro Writing in America," *New Leader*, May 16, 1960, pp. 8-10.

————, "The Problems of the Negro Writer," *The Massachusetts Review*, Autumn-Winter, 1964-1965, pp. 57-70.

Schuyler, George S., "The Negro Art Hokum," *The Nation*, June 16, 1926, pp. 662-663.

Smith, Morgan, "The Negro As Artist," *The Radical*, Vol. 2, 1867, pp. 27-31.

Van Vechten, Carl, "Beginning of Negro Drama," *Literary Digest*, May 1, 1914, p. 1114.

Washington, Booker T., speech (Prospectus of the New Rochelle Cooperative Business League, New Rochelle, New York, March, 1908. Property of Schomburg Collection, New York).

————, "The Negro in Business," Hertel, Jenkins Company, 1907, place not stated.

Young, Stark, "Negro Material in the Theater," *The New Republic*, May 11, 1927, p. 92.

INDEX

A Note About the Author

Harold Wright Cruse is professor of history and Afro-American studies at the University of Michigan. In addition to *The Crisis of the Negro Intellectual*, Professor Cruse is author of *Rebellion or Revolution?* and numerous articles for professional journals and periodicals in the United States and Europe.